Lavender fields. SONOMA COUNTY CVB/SUSAN & NEIL SILVERMAN

INSIDERS' GUIDE® SERIES

INSIDERS' GUIDE® TO
CALIFORNIA'S WINE COUNTRY

Including Napa, Sonoma, Mendocino, and Lake Counties

SEVENTH EDITION

JEAN SAYLOR DOPPENBERG

INSIDERS' GUIDE®

GUILFORD, CONNECTICUT
AN IMPRINT OF THE GLOBE PEQUOT PRESS

To buy books in quantity for corporate use or incentives, call **(800) 962–0973, ext. 4551,** or e-mail **premiums@GlobePequot.com.**

INSIDERS' GUIDE®

Text design by LeAnna Weller Smith
Maps by XNR Productions, Inc. © The Globe Pequot Press

ISSN 1539-9923
ISBN 0-7627-3688-7

Manufactured in the United States of America
Seventh Edition/First Printing

Wine grapes in the Russian River Valley. JEAN SAYLOR DOPPENBERG

Stags Leap appellation sign. JEAN SAYLOR DOPPENBERG

The tower at Korbel Champagne Cellars near Guerneville. JEAN SAYLOR DOPPENBERG

[Top] *Hop Kiln Winery near Healdsburg.* JEAN SAYLOR DOPPENBERG
[Bottom] *Kenwood Inn and Spa in Kenwood.* JEAN SAYLOR DOPPENBERG

[Top] *The wild Sonoma County coastline.* JAN BLANCHARD
[Bottom] *The coastline near Bodega Bay.* JEAN SAYLOR DOPPENBERG

Chateau Montelena in Calistoga. JEAN SAYLOR DOPPENBERG

[Top] *Jade Lake at Chateau Montelena Winery in Calistoga.* JEAN SAYLOR DOPPENBERG
[Bottom] *Barrels at Field Stone Winery near Healdsburg.* JEAN SAYLOR DOPPENBERG

Clos Pegase Winery in Calistoga. JEAN SAYLOR DOPPENBERG

Redwoods. SONOMA COUNTY CVB

Sonoma coast sunset. SONOMA COUNTY CVB/SUSAN & NEIL SILVERMAN

The Mendocino County coastline. JEAN SAYLOR DOPPENBERG

Winter vineyard. SONOMA COUNTY CVB/SUSAN & NEIL SILVERMAN

A country road in Sonoma Valley. JEAN SAYLOR DOPPENBERG

CONTENTS

CONTENTS

Directory of Maps

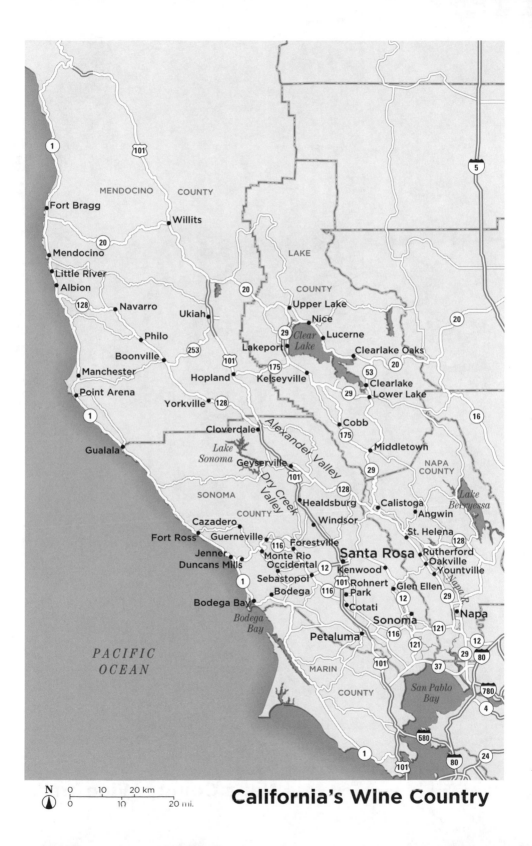

California's Wine Country

N 0   10   20 km
   0   10   20 mi.

PACIFIC
OCEAN

MENDOCINO COUNTY

Fort Bragg
Willits
Mendocino
Little River
Albion
Navarro
Ukiah
Philo
Boonville
Manchester
Point Arena
Yorkville
Hopland
Cloverdale
Gualala
Geyserville
Cazadero
Fort Ross
Guerneville
Jenner
Duncans Mills
Bodega Bay
Sebastopol
Bodega
Occidental
Monte Rio
Forestville
Windsor
Healdsburg
Santa Rosa
Kenwood
Rohnert Park
Cotati
Sonoma
Glen Ellen
Petaluma

LAKE
COUNTY
Upper Lake
Nice
Lucerne
Clear Lake
Lakeport
Kelseyville
Clearlake Oaks
Clearlake
Lower Lake
Cobb
Middletown

NAPA COUNTY
Calistoga
Angwin
St. Helena
Rutherford
Oakville
Yountville
Napa

Lake Sonoma
Alexander Valley
Dry Creek Valley
SONOMA COUNTY
MARIN COUNTY
Lake Berryessa
San Pablo Bay
Bodega Bay

1 101 20 128 253 175 53 29 16 5 37 121 12 80 780 4 580 24 116

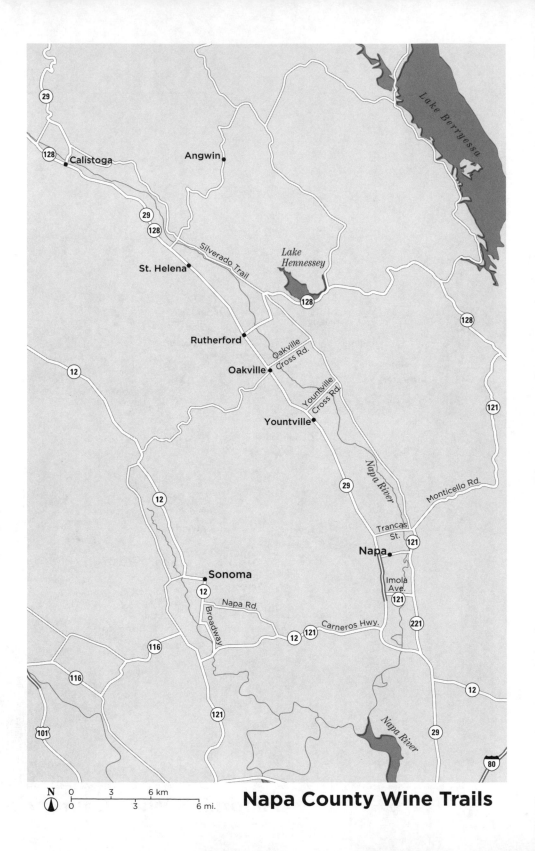

Napa County Wine Trails

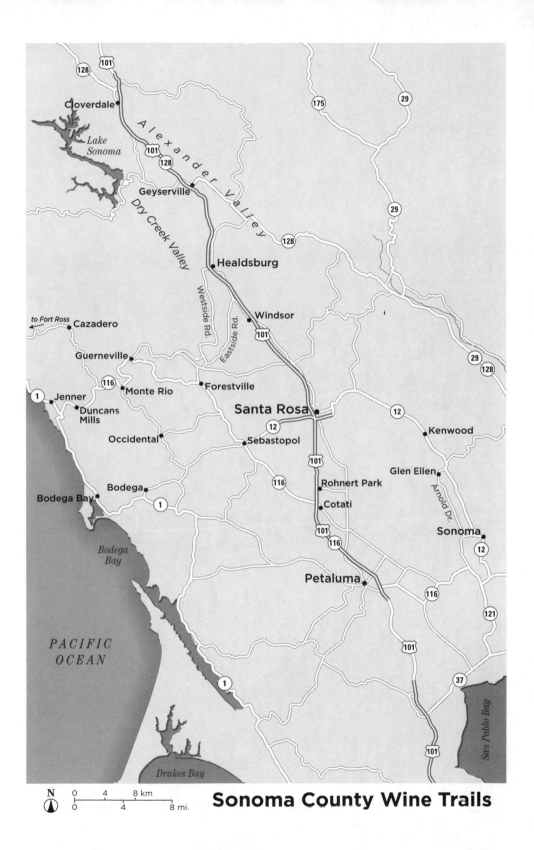

Sonoma County Wine Trails

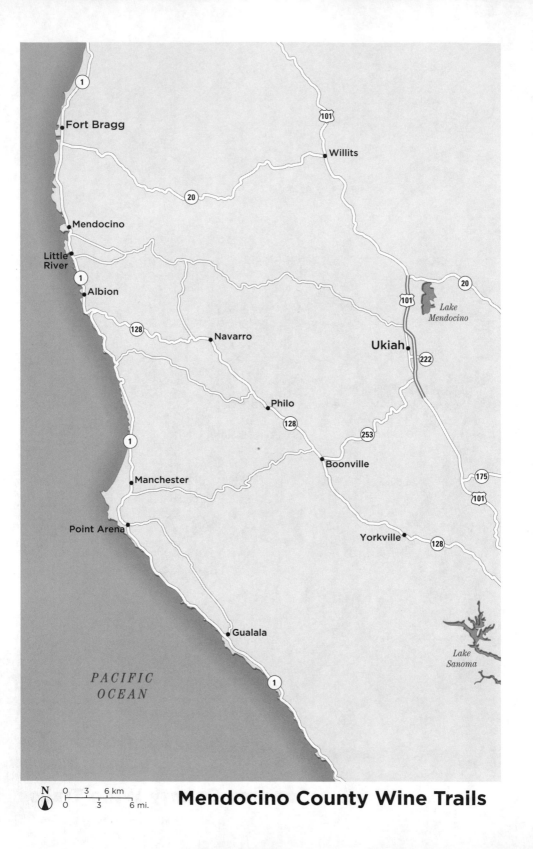

Mendocino County Wine Trails

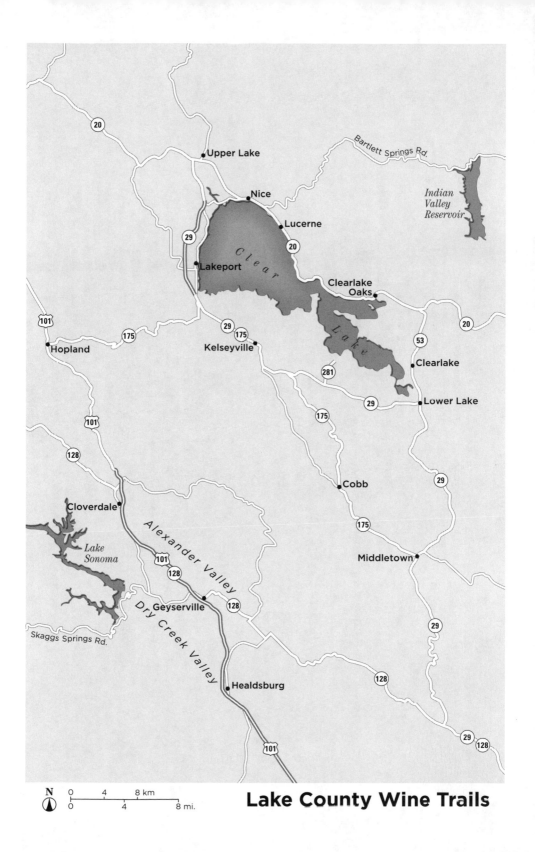

Lake County Wine Trails

PREFACE

With so many "wine country" guides on the market, there are several things that make this one special.

First, *Insiders' Guide to California's Wine Country* offers what most of the other guides do not: in-depth listings and insights into restaurants, wineries, inns, and attractions fit for all budgets. Check out the Insiders' tips, those helpful nuggets of information you won't find in other books. You'll find them flagged with the **i** symbol.

Second, other guides focus mostly on Napa and Sonoma Counties, and some exclusively on Napa Valley. Many guides do a good job of scratching the surface of these regions, but the book you hold in your hands goes several steps beyond the norm with an inside look at an additional must-visit wine region: Mendocino County.

Third, *Insiders' Guide to California's Wine Country* devotes a chapter to Lake County, a lesser-known locale for visitors to Northern California, yet a popular destination for those who love water sports and off-the-beaten-path wine tasting.

But it doesn't stop there. As you flip through these pages, you'll see detailed information on getaway destinations and attractions along the Sonoma and Mendocino coastlines—some of the most beautiful scenery you will find in all of California, if not on the planet. There's also an overview of the many attractions to be found in nearby San Francisco and ideas for day trips beyond the boundaries of Wine Country.

Finally, with the help of the Relocation chapter, you will have practical information close at hand about real estate, retirement, schools, health care—all crucial for new and prospective residents. Try finding information like that in those other guides.

It's your choice, but this guide—page for page—is superior to the others in the volume of data offered about the Northern California region known around the world as Wine Country.

Whether visiting Wine Country as a tourist or a settler, *Insiders' Guide to California's Wine Country* welcomes you with open arms. Let us know if the book worked for you. If you discover something we missed, we'd like to know about that too. We update this guide annually, and we want to be as accurate and helpful as possible.

Write to us at:

Insiders' Guide to California's
Wine Country
The Globe Pequot Press
P.O. Box 480
Guilford, CT 06437-0480

You can also visit us on the Web at www.insiders.com.

ACKNOWLEDGMENTS

Only one author's name appears on the cover of this book, but pulling together so much information is not accomplished without the help and cooperation of scores of friends, acquaintances, and even total strangers. I have nearly as many people to thank for their assistance as there are grapes in Wine Country. It's impossible to name them all, but here are several that stand out, in no particular order:

For their true insiders' insight into the wine industry, I thank Clay Gregory, former president of the board of directors of the Napa Valley Vintners Association, and Nick Frey, executive director of the Sonoma County Grape Growers Association. My gratitude also goes to Lisa Walter of Sonoma for her support of the book, and to Tom Fuller of Auction Napa Valley for his help. Many thanks to Lynnette Sands of Napa for her expertise on that city's hospitality industry, and Rocki Graziano of Lake County's Tulip Hill Winery for her assistance. My appreciation also extends to the many helpful folks at the Bureau of Land Management for their special insight into the wild places in my little corner of the planet.

Tricia Jornada, my fact-checker, was a trooper, providing valuable assistance with many of the chapters. A big thanks also to Jan Cronan, my editor at Globe Pequot Press on the previous two editions of this book, and editor Paula Brisco, who helped me bring this edition to print. My husband, Loren, was patient and understanding when piles of writing and research littered the house.

Last but not least, I can't thank my parents enough for instilling in me a lifelong curiosity about new places and new people. John and Gert's four children shared in their countless drive-all-day vacation adventures in overpacked and overheated station wagons, and I am grateful they always brought me along for the ride.

HOW TO USE THIS BOOK ?

Skimming through *Insiders' Guide to California's Wine Country* is a bit like channel surfing with your TV's remote control—you flip here and there, back and forth, looking for something to grab your attention. It might be an interesting name, a familiar place, or an intriguing topic that leaps out and demands closer investigation.

Go ahead and chapter surf to your heart's content. Land on any page that strikes your fancy, whether it's for a restaurant, winery, or lodging listing. That's OK. Data-heavy books such as this one are designed for thumbing through. But at some point you might want to find a particular "thing" by region, so it will help to understand the book's structure.

The table of contents indicates the chapter topics, but if any questions remain, a quick peek at chapter introductions should answer them. Beyond that, each chapter is organized geographically, more or less, with Napa County listings first, followed by those of Sonoma County and Mendocino County. In general, the listings for hotels, attractions, wineries, and so forth appear in order in the book as you would encounter them while driving in each region, approximately south to north and east to west. (To make the Sonoma County listings more manageable—there are scads of them—I further divided the county into Southern, Northern, Sonoma Coast, and West County/Russian River subheadings.) Refer to the list below for the general order by town and city. (Lake County has its own chapter. Please see the table of contents.)

Note: Many of Wine Country's world-class eateries are known by name and not necessarily by their location. So I've organized the Restaurants chapter using the same geographical method explained above, then listed the restaurants alphabetically within their respective towns and regions.

NAPA COUNTY

Napa, Yountville, Oakville, Rutherford, St. Helena, Angwin, Lake Berryessa, Calistoga

SONOMA COUNTY

Southern Sonoma

Sonoma, Glen Ellen, Kenwood, Petaluma, Cotati, Rohnert Park, Santa Rosa

Northern Sonoma

Windsor, Healdsburg, Geyserville, Cloverdale, Alexander Valley, Dry Creek Valley, Lake Sonoma, Westside Road

Sonoma Coast

Bodega, Bodega Bay, Jenner, Fort Ross

West County/ Russian River

Sebastopol, Occidental, Forestville, Guerneville, Monte Rio, Cazadero, Duncans Mills

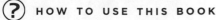

MENDOCINO COUNTY

U.S. Highway 101

Hopland, Ukiah, Willits

Highway 128

Yorkville, Boonville, Philo, Navarro

Mendocino Coast

Gualala, Point Arena, Albion, Little River, Mendocino, Fort Bragg

Be aware that several chapters cover topics that venture beyond Wine Country or otherwise defy a strict county-by-county organization. These include the Golden Gateway (San Francisco) and Day Trips chapters, which focus on more distant destinations. Likewise, the Spectator Sports chapter covers professional teams in and beyond Wine Country and is thus organized by sport. The Flora, Fauna, and Climate chapter and, to some extent, the Getting Here, Getting Around chapter, deal with phenomena that have no respect for county lines and thus have their own unique breakdowns. And the Festivals and Annual Events chapter logically follows a chronological order.

You may notice that some material teeters on the categorical fence that divides chapters, so I have cross-referenced information wherever it made sense, briefly mentioning a related event, activity, or locale where appropriate and referring you to the chapter where it is described in more detail.

For those who wish to extend their stay in Wine Country by becoming a full- or part-time resident, check out the information-packed Relocation chapter. There you will find useful details about real estate, educational opportunities, health care, retirement options, and other important information you should know before—and after—making your move.

I hope the book answers all your questions and raises a few you might not have considered. If you find anything you believe to be inaccurate or misleading, I urge you to let me know.

AREA OVERVIEW

Napa, Sonoma, and Mendocino—three words synonymous with beauty and the good life. Although I live here and gaze upon that beauty every day, I'm endlessly fascinated by its changing vistas. Trust me, visitors never go away disappointed by the scenery.

Although it is promoted as a nirvana for foodies and as "Eden to a wine grape," Wine Country has much more to offer than its famous agricultural crops. I'm happy to report that it's composed of vibrant small cities, sleepy rural communities, an expansive coastline blissfully free of commercialism, some of the tallest trees in the world, and an endless collection of colorful characters who call it home.

In this chapter, Wine Country is put under the microscope to reveal the cities and towns you'll encounter as a visitor to the region.

NAPA COUNTY

Of the Wine Country counties profiled in this book, Napa is by far the most dependent on wine and tourism and the region most associated with those two industries in the minds of visitors. Always rural in nature, Napa County has seen the rise and fall of wheat, cattle, and prunes as the dominant product. For the past three decades, it has been the ultra-premium wine grapes—and the visitors who love them—that drive the economy.

Though Napa County is the Bay Area's least populated county, the population has increased a bit over the past few years—growing to 132,339 residents, according to the California Department of Finance. The median income of these hardworking folks hovers at $35,200. But we have a good share of celebrity residents too, who earn a bit more. Property owners in Napa Valley and its environs include Francis Ford Coppola (see the Wineries chapter), Robin Williams, Robert Redford, Woody Harrelson, Joe Montana, Boz Scaggs, Danielle Steele, David Wolper, and Mario Andretti.

Even if they don't commit to buying their very own villa or vineyard, celebs flock to the area for getaway jaunts the same as you, the probably-not-world-famous visitor. Because of the number of high rollers and famous faces flitting about, filmmaker/wine baron/longtime resident Coppola once quipped to the local press that he feared Napa Valley was turning into the East Hampton of the West Coast. Yet if you should spot Redford pedaling the Silverado Trail on his bicycle or dining in a local eatery, please be discreet.

The southern gateway to Napa Valley is the city of Napa, which, at about 75,900 people, makes up more than half of the county's population. Napa has several gracious, older districts left over from the horse-and-buggy days—the lettered streets known as Old Town, the Fuller Park area south of downtown, and Alta Heights—connected by more down-to-earth neighborhoods.

Yet downtown Napa continues to undergo major renovation that was triggered by the development and construction of Copia (see the Attractions chapter) and a $238 million flood-control project along the Napa River. Where once it was seen primarily as the commercial core of the valley proper, lacking tourist-oriented amenities, the city of Napa has become a destination in itself. New hotels and B&Bs have opened, many new eateries are getting rave reviews, and the city center in general has been spiffed up and transformed.

Though Napa owes much of its prosperity to the wine industry, government is the largest employer in the city. Napa is the seat of the county government, and the Napa Valley Unified School District and Napa State Hospital account for hundreds of jobs.

To the north of the city of Napa is Yountville, named after Napa Valley pioneer George Yount (see the History chapter). It is a small community (population 3,000) that self-proclaims more fine restaurants per capita than any city in America. New subdivisions built in the late 1990s have increased the population slightly, but this is a town that caters almost exclusively, and with a lot of class, to visitors.

Oakville and Rutherford appear frequently in addresses throughout the book, but usually the reference is to nearby countryside locales. The towns themselves are hardly more than wide spots around Highway 29. This is, however, a beautiful part of the valley—a midway sector where the mountains begin to encroach upon the valley floor.

When most visitors imagine the quintessential Wine Country village, they envision St. Helena—with its gingerbread cottages painted glistening white, canopied sidewalks of a thriving-yet-nostalgic downtown, pocket gardens with not a blade of grass out of place, and only three traffic lights! Though it has its peripheral subdivisions and apartment complexes, the overall look of St. Helena (pronounced Hel-LAY-na) is defined by high-priced neatness (see the Relocation chapter). Much of the housing is pre–World War II and nearly all has been immaculately maintained, and the residential streets in the heart of town are lushly lined with mature trees. About a quarter of the town's approximately 6,000 residents are 65 or older, making it a popular spot for retirees with comfortable bank accounts. Due east of St. Helena is Deer Park, a small community with about 1,800 souls.

The hilltop hamlet of Angwin, up Deer Park Road/Howell Mountain Road off the Silverado Trail, orbits around Pacific Union College. The town's population (heavily Seventh-day Adventist) tops out at about 3,100, most of them college students—a full 61 percent of the inhabitants here are under age 30.

To the east of Angwin is man-made Lake Berryessa (see the On the Water chapter). The settlements are on the western and southern shores of the lake, especially along Berryessa–Knoxville Road. The eastern perimeter is virtually inaccessible to any vehicle. Unlike Clear Lake in Lake County, Berryessa is not encircled by hotels and restaurants. It is known more as a spot for vacation homes.

Calistoga, the northernmost town of Napa Valley, is an iconoclastic slice of California, a burg that sees itself as real and unadulterated even as it supports itself almost entirely through tourist dollars, with the corner on the spa and mud bath market. As one local wag likes to describe it, "Calistoga is to pickup trucks what St. Helena is to Range Rovers." The population hovers at around 5,200, with about 28 percent age 65 and older. Wine isn't the only refreshment bottled in Napa Valley: On the east side of Calistoga are two major suppliers of mineral water, Calistoga and Crystal Geyser, and some excellent beers are brewed and bottled at the Calistoga Inn and Silveradro Brewing Co., south a bit on Highway 29.

SONOMA COUNTY

Encompassing nearly 1,600 square miles from the Pacific coast to the Mayacmas Mountains and San Pablo Bay, Sonoma County is the most populous of the four Wine Country counties. But most of the approximately 472,700 residents live in a relatively narrow corridor along U.S. Highway 101 from Santa Rosa to Petaluma. The rest of the county—approximately 56 percent—is farmland. The farms consist of apple, peach, and plum orchards; livestock rangeland and dairy farms; and of course vineyards.

It's no surprise that grapes and wine are the most prized agricultural commodities, with a crop value of approximately $375 million. Yet agricultural employment accounts for less than 4 percent of the total workforce. The services, retail, and manufacturing sectors by far employ the most people—approximately 62 percent.

Santa Rosa is the county seat and the largest city, with a population of 154,400. In May 2002 *Forbes* magazine ranked the city No. 2 in its list of the top-10 dynamic economic regions in the nation.

Some of the largest employers include such clean industries as Agilent Technologies, St. Joseph Health System, JDS Uniphase, Medtronic, and state and county government offices. As in Napa County and the rest of California, the Hispanic population is booming in Sonoma County (currently at 15 percent). Asian peoples are the second largest minority (4 percent), followed by African Americans and Native Americans (each at 1 percent).

Santa Rosa's downtown is split in two by US 101—a planning decision that many have long since regretted. To the west of the highway are multiple antiques shops and historic Railroad Square, whose sturdy buildings were constructed of locally quarried stone. To the east, especially along Fourth Street, are restaurants, coffeehouses, music stores, and similar hangouts. The Luther Burbank Home and Gardens (see the Attractions chapter) are also nearby.

Due south of Santa Rosa are the residential communities of Cotati, Rohnert Park, and Petaluma. The latter is the third-largest town in Wine Country, with more than 55,000 people and stately homes and art deco commercial palaces (such as the McNear Building).

On the southeastern edge of the county is the town of Sonoma. This small enclave of approximately 9,300 residents is largely defined by its historic sites, especially those along the town's eight-acre central plaza. There you'll find the Mission San Francisco de Solano, the Sonoma Barracks, the Swiss Hotel, and several nearby wineries within walking distance (see the

The wine industry is serious business in California, worth about $45 billion to the state's economy. California's 1,049 wineries produced 3.12 billion bottles of wine in 2002, according to the Wine Institute, the industry's advocacy organization.

Wineries; Hotels, Motels, and Inns; and Bed-and-Breakfast Inns chapters).

North of Sonoma are the tiny hamlets of Glen Ellen and Kenwood. Tucked away from the traffic of Highway 12, Glen Ellen's Main Street is only two blocks long, so you might have to invent an excuse to spend the whole day here. One possibility is Jack London State Historic Park, just west of town (see the Attractions chapter). Kenwood is equally small, if not smaller, but no less charming.

At the north end of the county is the town of Healdsburg, with a population of 11,000. Like Sonoma, the town has a delightful core centered around a classic town square. There you can find good food, good books, and a good dose of fine old relics and shopping options.

Just a short hop north on US 101 from Healdsburg is Geyserville, named for an area northeast of the town where natural steam vents from the earth. These fumaroles, as they are called, are visible from many points in the county, particularly on cool mornings. (See the Lake County chapter for more information about the geothermal activity along the Sonoma County/Lake County border.)

Still farther north on US 101 is Cloverdale, a small, pleasant town of 7,200 souls nestled at the far end of the peaceful Alexander Valley, one of the county's prime grape-growing regions. From this point north, the coast redwoods start to take over (see the Big Trees section in the Day Trips chapter), though there are still large expanses of vineyards to be found in Sonoma's northern neighbor, Mendocino County.

Phone Numbers for Tourists

Napa County

Napa Valley Conference & Visitors Bureau
1310 Napa Town Center, Napa
(707) 226-7459
www.napavalley.com

Napa Chamber of Commerce
1556 First Street, Napa
(707) 226-7455
www.napachamber.org

Yountville Chamber of Commerce
6516 Yount Street, Yountville
(707) 944-0904
www.yountville.com

St. Helena Chamber of Commerce
1010 Main Street, St. Helena
(707) 963-4456
www.sthelena.com

Calistoga Chamber of Commerce
1458 Lincoln Avenue, Calistoga
(707) 942-6333
www.calistogafun.com

Sonoma County

Hispanic Chamber of Commerce of
Sonoma County
1111 Stony Circle, Santa Rosa
(707) 577-7129
www.hccsc.com

Sonoma Valley Visitors Bureau
453 First Street E., Sonoma
(707) 996-1090
www.sonomavalley.com

Sonoma Valley Chamber of Commerce
651 Broadway, Sonoma
(707) 996-1033
www.sonomachamber.com

Petaluma Chamber of Commerce
800 Baywood Drive, Petaluma
(707) 762-2785
www.petaluma.org

Petaluma Visitors Program
799 Baywood Drive, Petaluma
(707) 769-0429
www.petaluma.org/visitor

Cotati Chamber of Commerce
8109 La Plaza, Cotati
(707) 795-5508
www.cotati.org

Rohnert Park Chamber of Commerce
5000 Roberts Lake Road, Rohnert Park
(707) 584-1415
www.rpchamber.org

Santa Rosa Convention & Visitors Bureau
and California Welcome Center
9 Fourth Street, Santa Rosa
(707) 577-8674
www.visitsantarosa.com

Santa Rosa Chamber of Commerce
637 First Street, Santa Rosa
(707) 545-1414
www.santarosachamber.com

Sonoma County Tourism Program
520 Mendocino Avenue, Suite 210, Santa
Rosa
(707) 565-5383
www.sonomacounty.com

Mark West Area Chamber of Commerce
4795 Old Redwood Highway, Santa Rosa
(707) 578-7975
www.markwest.org

Windsor Chamber of Commerce
8499 Old Redwood Highway, Windsor
(707) 838-7285
www.windsorchamber.com

Healdsburg Chamber of Commerce
217 Healdsburg Avenue, Healdsburg
(707) 433-6935
www.healdsburg.org

Geyserville Chamber of Commerce
Information Center
21060 Geyserville Avenue, Geyserville
(707) 857-3745
www.geyservillecc.com

North Coast Wine and Visitors Center
105 North Cloverdale Boulevard,
Cloverdale
(707) 894-0818
www.cloverdale.net

Sonoma Coast Visitor Information/
Bodega Bay Area Chamber of Commerce
850 Highway 1, Bodega Bay
(707) 875-3422, (707) 875-3866
www.bodegabay.com

Jenner Visitors' Center
10451 Highway 1, Jenner
(707) 865-9433

Sebastopol Chamber of Commerce
265 South Main Street, Sebastopol
(707) 823-3032
www.sebastopol.org

Monte Rio Chamber of Commerce
(707) 865-1533
www.monterio.org

Forestville Chamber of Commerce and
Visitors Center
6652 Front Street, Forestville
(707) 887-1111

Russian River Region Visitors Bureau and
Chamber of Commerce
16209 First Street, Guerneville
(707) 869-9000, (800) 253-8800
www.russianriver.com

Occidental Chamber of Commerce
3692 Bohemian Highway, Occidental
(707) 874-3279
www.occidental.org

Mendocino County
Hopland Chamber of Commerce
www.hoplandchamber.com

Ukiah Chamber of Commerce
200 South School Street, Ukiah
(707) 462-4705
www.ukiahchamber.com

Willits Chamber of Commerce
239 South Main Street, Willits
(707) 459-7910
www.willits.org

Anderson Valley Chamber of Commerce
(707) 895-2379
www.andersonvalleychamber.com

Redwood Coast Chamber of Commerce
(707) 884-1080, (800) 778-5252
www.redwoodcoastchamber.com

Fort Bragg-Mendocino Coast Chamber of
Commerce
332 North Main Street, Fort Bragg
(707) 961-6300, (800) 726-2780
www.mendocinocoast.com

The Alexander Valley south of Cloverdale offers wine tasters a more relaxed alternative to the relative bustle of Napa and Sonoma Valleys. It may not have as many wineries, but it does have some good ones (see the Wineries chapter), and the traffic is comparatively light. In spring, when the winter rains have turned the hills a vivid green, the valley is especially charming—like a wee bit of the rolling Irish countryside.

Another smaller and similarly charming vale is the Dry Creek Valley, which lies west of Alexander Valley above Healdsburg. Here row upon row of vineyards line the rich valley floor and terraces climb up the gentle hillsides. At one time, Dry Creek Valley extended farther to the north, but much of it was submerged when Warm Springs Dam was built in 1982. The dam gave birth to Lake Sonoma, a recreational area profiled more thoroughly in the On the Water chapter.

Despite the scarcity of wineries compared with other areas, western Sonoma County offers much to see. Bodega Bay is the gateway to the Pacific, and it is where Highway 1 kisses the coast and begins its circuitous trek northward. Much of the Alfred Hitchcock thriller *The Birds* was filmed in 1963 in both Bodega Bay and the slightly inland enclave of Bodega. The movie featured Bodega's Potter School, a one-room schoolhouse built a century before Hitchcock's cameras rolled into town.

Bodega Bay is one of the largest fishing ports between San Francisco and Eureka. In September and October the locals like to celebrate what they call "secret summer," when temperatures are relatively mild and the morning fog quickly disperses. The hook-shaped peninsula that shields the harbor from the open sea is Bodega Head. You can drive out on the headland along Westshore Road, which offers brilliant views and access to beaches and cliffs.

The town of Jenner lies about 7 miles north of Bodega Bay, at the point where the Russian River meets the sea. Dozens of harbor seals congregate near the town, growing fat on steelhead and other fish that migrate upriver. North of Jenner the coastal settlements are few and far between. Once the easternmost outpost of czarist Russia, Fort Ross is now a state historic park (see the History and Attractions chapters).

Russian geographers will also recognize the name Sebastopol. The Wine Country town with a population of 7,700 that shares this name with the Crimean city is located between Santa Rosa and the coast. Sebastopol rose to prominence on the cores of a billion Gravenstein apples—the delectable fruit that got its start here. The community has honored the revered apple by naming Highway 116, which runs through the heart of town, the Gravenstein Highway, and every summer it hosts the Gravenstein Apple Fair (see the Festivals and Annual Events chapter).

West and north of Sebastopol is the town of Forestville, which serves as a way station for travelers headed to the Russian River and the Pacific coast. Nearby is the all-but-forgotten town of Occidental, perched at the top of a hill in the middle of redwood country. It's delightfully romantic, but what would you expect of a village whose main thoroughfare goes by the name Bohemian Highway?

Where the Bohemian Highway meets the Russian River just north of Occidental is the tiny town of Monte Rio, whose freestanding movie theater, the Rio, is covered in colorful murals. Farther to the east along Highway 116 is Guerneville (pronounced GURN-ville). This former lumber capital-cum-summer resort is sometimes referred to as the Gay Riviera, because of the large gay population that lives and weekends here.

While Guerneville is the largest town in the Russian River resort area, Duncans Mills is one of the smallest. Located about 4 miles before Highway 116 joins Highway 1, the town looks much as it did when it was the western terminus of the Northwest Pacific Railroad. A museum recalls the glory days of the beloved choo-choo, and a host of art and antiques shops and restaurants provide plenty of distractions.

MENDOCINO COUNTY

Mendocino County is double the land size of Sonoma County, covering nearly 3,500 square miles. The population, at approximately 89,200, is widely dispersed, with only a quarter of the residents living in urban areas. Most people find employment in the service sector, specifically tourism. The county's economy has historically been centered in the lumber and fishing industries, and both still have a foothold here. In inland areas such as the Yokayo Valley, agriculture is paramount. And because of the large holdings of public land in Mendocino County, the state parks system has become another important employer.

Hopland is a town that came by its name honestly. Awash in a field of hops in the early 1900s, it was the perfect choice as a home base for Mendocino Brewing Company, when in 1982 it became California's first brewery since Prohibition. At the south end of Hopland is the Real Goods Solar Living Center (see the Attractions chapter), a 12-acre site created by Real Goods, retailer of alternative energy products and services.

With a population of 15,900, Ukiah is Mendocino's largest town. Lumber is a major commodity here, as it has been for decades, but Ukiah also has become the financial, business, medical, and service center not only for Mendocino County but also for portions of Sonoma, Lake, and Humboldt Counties. The town is home to many descendants of the Pomo tribe, the first inhabitants of the area.

Willits, to the north, also was kick-started during the 19th-century lumber boom, and most of the larger companies in the area are involved in manufacturing wood products. Driving along US 101 6 miles south of town, look for a boulder directly across the highway from White Deer Lodge—it was a reputed hideout of

Black Bart, the stagecoach robber who roamed the area more than 100 years ago.

Highway 128 courses through the Anderson Valley, linking the tiny towns of Yorkville, Boonville, Philo, and Navarro. The valley's northern latitude and salty breezes make it appropriate for growing cool-weather grapes such as Gewürztraminer and Riesling.

Gualala, pronounced "Wah-LA-la," is the southern gateway to the Mendocino Coast. Along with Anchor Bay, 4 miles to the north, it forms what locals call the Banana Belt, a relatively warm and fog-free pocket of coastline. Gualala was a thriving lumber town until the supply of unprotected trees dwindled in the 1960s. Today the town is an arts community, with resident painters, sculptors, photographers, writers, and musicians (see the Arts and Culture chapter).

About 16 miles north of Gualala is Point Arena. With about 474 people, it's one of the smallest incorporated cities in the state. Once a lumber and fishing center, Point Arena now sticks mostly to the tourist trade. Surfers say the harbor is one of the best surfing spots in Northern California.

Moving up the coast, Albion (between Whitesboro Cove and the Albion River) and Little River (near the waterway of the same name) are further possibilities for weary Highway 1 drivers and white-knuckled passengers. Most people who stop there, other than those on their way to the Little River Inn (see the Spas and Resorts chapter), are heading for Mendocino, a village with about 1,000 residents. It was little more than an economically depressed former lumber town when the Mendocino Art Center was founded in 1959, seeding an artists' colony that revitalized the community. The art center lives on, offering more than 200 classes, workshops, and seminars each year (see the Arts and Culture chapter).

The village of Mendocino, a National Historic Preservation District, is a delightful mix of gingerbread architecture, steep gables, and white picket fences that seem straight out of an Edward Hopper painting of New England. Yet some people have been critical of Mendocino's "perfection"—one local scoffs that it is "more of a movie set than a town." A few of the more outstanding architectural structures include the Mendocino Hotel, the Ford House, and the Presbyterian Church of Mendocino, all on Main Street. The latter building is the oldest continuously operating Presbyterian church in California.

Almost as charming, and more diversified economically, is Fort Bragg. With a population of 7,000, its beaches are prized for beachcombing, surf fishing, and picnicking. Noyo Harbor, on the south end of town, is a bustle of activity when fishing boats arrive to unload their hauls and clean up. It's one of the largest ports between San Francisco and Eureka, and it is preferred by the vast majority of local seals and sea lions. You can get a map for a walking tour of the town from the Fort Bragg Chamber of Commerce at 332 North Main Street.

GETTING HERE, GETTING AROUND

First-time visitors to the region known as Wine Country are usually surprised by the large expanse of this three-county area. It may take more time than you think to get from one destination to another. For example, it's about 142 miles from Infineon Raceway at the southern tip of Sonoma County to the town of Piercy at the north end of Mendocino County. And that's as the crow flies somewhat diagonally across the map; it is considerably farther as the visitor weaves. Wine Country is not crisscrossed by fast-moving freeway systems, thank goodness. Instead, you will drink in spectacular scenery and witness a more laid-back lifestyle as you wind your way along our highways and byways.

Major Wine Country thoroughfares run north–south, generally along the principal valleys. They are occasionally linked by roads and highways that run east–west, with the latter often traversing the hills and ranges that divide the region. I cover the major highways here, starting with the four primary routes. Unless otherwise stated, all roads mentioned are two-lane highways.

In addition to the route descriptions, I've provided information on public and private transportation, including airports, shuttle services, Amtrak and Greyhound, taxis, limousines, and public buses.

One word of advice: Use your common sense when it comes to wine tasting and driving. If you plan to drive to a series of tasting rooms, designate one person to drink in moderation (or literally only "taste"—as in swirl, sniff, sip, and spit) or, preferably, rent a limo and see Wine Country safely and in style. Remember, the legal blood-alcohol threshold in California is 0.08 percent. That is lower than

some visitors are accustomed to, and it is possible to be over this limit without feeling particularly buzzed. So play it safe. If you're not sure, you probably are drunk, at least by California Highway Patrol standards. Finally, even if you are sober, others on the road might not be. As the public-service ads say, drive defensively.

BY AUTOMOBILE

The Main North–South Arteries

HIGHWAY 29

This is the main traffic corridor of Napa Valley, not to mention the perimeter route for half of Lake County's Clear Lake. The highway begins in Vallejo and, after passing through the city of Napa about 12 miles later, quickly becomes a ride in a wine-theme amusement park. It passes through some of the finest wine-grape country in America and connects the valley's towns: Napa, Yountville, Oakville, Rutherford, St. Helena, and Calistoga. Its shoulders are weighed down by châteaus, fortresses, Victorians, and renowned restaurants. Wine Country heavyweights such as Domaine Chandon are here, and so are great historic wineries like Beringer and Charles Krug (see the Wineries chapter). Highway 29, the tourism artery of Napa Valley, is commonly referred to as St. Helena Highway, and you will see it used frequently in addresses, as in this book. You will also see and hear the expression "upvalley" from time to time. This generally refers to St. Helena and points north.

Highway 29 is four lanes from Vallejo to Yountville; two thereafter. The road makes a sharp right when it gets to Calistoga and proceeds through the mostly vintage downtown. It leaves Calistoga and heads due north, climbing the flank of Mount St. Helena and dropping into the flats of Lake County. The highway then takes a serpentine path up to Lower Lake, where it veers sharply and heads northwest, skirting the southern and western shores of Clear Lake. Highway 29 hits Kelseyville and Lakeport, then heads north and dies at the town of Upper Lake.

HIGHWAY 12

Highway 12 travels east–west for most of its length, but it garners acclaim for a relatively short north–south stretch that runs through the Sonoma Valley. Soon after joining with Highway 29 just below Napa, Highway 12 breaks west, hooking up with Highway 121 and skirting the Carneros Valley before crossing the Napa-Sonoma border. It then splits north to begin its renowned tour past wineries and hot springs and through classic Wine Country towns. It veers west after Kenwood, soon widening to four lanes in east Santa Rosa and continuing through stop-and-go and freeway-style traffic before reaching Sebastopol, where it narrows again to two lanes.

U.S. HIGHWAY 101

U.S. Highway 101, also known as the Redwood Highway, doesn't have the charm of Highways 29 or 12. As the major freeway for Sonoma and Mendocino Counties, it serves commuters, truckers, farmers, and all manner of passersby, who may travel it south to Hollywood or north to Oregon.

US 101 enters Sonoma County about 5 miles south of Petaluma and continues on to Rohnert Park, Santa Rosa, Healdsburg, Cloverdale, Ukiah, Willits, Laytonville, and other, smaller towns. The southern Wine Country stretch of US 101—from Petaluma to Windsor—is rather developed and populated, and traffic tends to bog down close to rush hour, but snarls can occur any time of day. US 101 is four lanes

almost to the Marin County line; north it alternates at intervals between two lanes and six.

HIGHWAY 1

Highway 1 is a destination unto itself. Though this Sonoma–Mendocino section of the highway may not be as celebrated as the Big Sur–Carmel section to the south, it does offer approximately 135 miles of breathtaking coastal landscape, jaw-dropping vistas of the craggy coastline and the ocean to the west, and stands of coast live oak, pine, fir, or coast redwoods to the east.

The highway intersects about two dozen state parks, state beaches, state reserves, regional parks, and county parks on its ascent through Wine Country (see the Parks and Recreation chapter). It also is the main artery for such towns as Jenner, Gualala, Point Arena, Albion, Mendocino, and Fort Bragg.

Snaking its way north through Marin County, Highway 1 cuts over to the ocean at Bodega Bay, about 8 miles after it enters Sonoma County. The highway leaves the sea again north of Rockport in the upper reaches of Mendocino County. You'll notice that between Bodega Bay and Fort Bragg in Mendocino County, the road is often designated as Coast Highway 1. And one note of realism: This is not 135 miles that you can drive in two hours. The route regularly curves up, down, and around the rocky coast. Doing the entire trip in one full day will leave little time for beachcombing and otter spotting.

Other Wine Country Roadways

HIGHWAY 121

This highway joins Sonoma with the Lake Berryessa highlands, via Napa. The route is born at Sears Point, site of the famed Infineon Raceway at the southern tip of Sonoma County (see the Spectator Sports

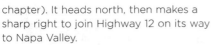

chapter). It heads north, then makes a sharp right to join Highway 12 on its way to Napa Valley.

Highway 121 travels through the Carneros grape-growing region, which has only a few wineries but some of the most coveted vineyards in the state. The road intersects Highway 29 and is lured north, but it quickly departs with three sharp turns—right, left, and right again—through the city of Napa. Highway 121 then assumes a winding northeasterly course into the hills before it enters Highway 128 not far from Lake Berryessa.

HIGHWAY 128

Highway 128, best known as the path through the Alexander Valley wine region, is a rambling roadway that periodically hitches northward rides to augment its own northwesterly journey. It enters Napa County from the east, navigating the steep hills that hug Lake Berryessa. It sneaks around the southwest fingers of the lake, then follows Sage Creek west into Napa Valley. When it gets to Rutherford, Highway 128 joins Highway 29 on a northern jaunt through the vineyards. But when Highway 29 makes a right turn into Calistoga, Highway 128 continues northwest, into rustic Knights Valley and then lovely Alexander Valley with its first-rate wineries.

Highway 128 meets US 101 just north of Geyserville and follows it to Cloverdale. It then breaks away again, heading northwest through Boonville and Philo on one of California's most unheralded scenic routes. Before it reaches Highway 1 near Navarro Point, Highway 128 cuts into Navarro River Redwoods State Park, a skinny swath that basically straddles the highway.

HIGHWAY 20

If you want a detailed lesson in California geology, drive the length of Highway 20, which begins high in the Sierra Nevada Mountains, descends through gold country, and crosses the fertile Sacramento Valley on its search for the ocean. Highway 20 enters Wine Country in eastern

Highway 1 several miles north of Jenner follows a steep serpentine route— affectionately but unofficially called Dramamine Drive. The highway climbs high up the Coast Range, offering spectacular views of the ocean below.

Lake County and bears generally west along the northern edge of Clear Lake through towns such as Clearlake Oaks and Lucerne. The highway passes north of Lake Mendocino just before it hits US 101 at the town of Calpella. The two highways then merge on a northerly course. Highway 20 breaks away from US 101 at Willits, where it embarks on a jittery, handsome west-by-northwest track to the coast. It meets Highway 1 just south of Fort Bragg.

HIGHWAY 116

Highway 116 is the paved shadow of the Russian River for a good part of its length. After connecting Sonoma and Petaluma in southern Sonoma County, it joins with US 101 up to Cotati, then splits off and heads northwest through Sebastopol and Forestville. It's a perfectly nice highway during all of that, but Highway 116 really shines just as it reaches Guerneville and follows the river to the coast. The water sparkles, the sunlight blinks through the trees, and the ocean feels just a few curves away.

HIGHWAY 253

Crooked Highway 253 connects Boonville and Ukiah in Mendocino County; in other words it connects US 101 and seaward Highway 128. If, by contrast, you want to go from Boonville to the coast, take Mountain View Road.

HIGHWAY 175

Highway 175 is an alternative to Highway 20 as a connection between Sonoma and Lake Counties. It's also a pleasing drive, one of the roads less traveled in Wine Country. Highway 175 leaves Middletown in Lake

County and proceeds north past the town of Cobb and Boggs Mountain State Forest. It joins Highway 29 and goes almost to Lakeport before it breaks west. It then wiggles through the Mayacmas Mountains and ends up in Hopland at US 101.

BY AIR

Three major airports serve Wine Country on its periphery—San Francisco, Oakland, and Sacramento—each of them as inconveniently located as the next.

Among the big three airports profiled here, the Oakland and Sacramento airports are slightly more efficient if you are entering Wine Country through Napa or the town of Sonoma. Figure on 75 to 90 minutes to drive from Oakland or Sacramento to Napa, and about the same from San Francisco to Santa Rosa. Of course San Francisco offers a longer lineup of airlines. Six major rental car companies—Hertz, Avis, Budget, Dollar, National, and Alamo— serve all three airports.

Major Airports

San Francisco International Airport
San Francisco
(650) 876–2377
www.flysfo.com

With about 40 million passengers a year, San Francisco International Airport (SFO) is the fifth-busiest airport in the United States and the world's ninth busiest. Located 14 miles south of downtown San Francisco, the airport is surrounded by more than 2,700 acres of undeveloped tidelands. The runways you see today were built on land reclaimed from San Francisco Bay.

The airport has undergone a huge renovation and expansion at a cost of approximately $3 billion. This includes a 2.5-million-square-foot international terminal that increased the number of gates from 10 to 24; two parking garages; a centralized rental car facility; a BART (Bay

Area Rapid Transit) station; and an Air-Train system to move passengers between terminals. Construction will continue for some time, as the old international terminal is converted to domestic use.

Every major airline carrier, and virtually every smaller carrier with any sort of presence in the western United States, touches down at SFO. If you're in doubt about service from a specific airline, contact the airport or your travel agent.

There are outlets for all the expected rental car companies at the airport. Here are the contact numbers you will need: National, (650) 616–3000; Budget, (650) 877-0998; Dollar, (650) 244-4131; Hertz, (650) 624-6600; Avis, (650) 877-3156; Enterprise, (650) 697-9200; Thrifty, (650) 259-1313; and Alamo, (650) 347-9911.

Parking fees are $1.00 for 12 minutes, $28.00 for the first full day, and $35.00 for the second.

Oakland International Airport
Oakland
(510) 577-4000
www.flyoakland.com,
www.oaklandairport.com

Oakland International Airport (OAK) is smaller and less ambitious than its neighbor to the west, and that is exactly what makes it more attractive to many Wine Country visitors. With only two terminals and a dozen airlines, it can be a painless experience.

South of downtown Oakland, take the Hegenberger Road exit from Interstate 880 to reach OAK. Once inside there are 14 boarding gates at Terminal One and 8 at Terminal Two, where no gate is farther than 400 feet from the curb. Terminal Two is devoted entirely to Southwest Airlines, which bases 300 of its pilots and nearly 500 flight attendants in Oakland.

Several major and regional airlines service OAK. These include Alaska, American, America West, Continental, Delta, jet-Blue, Southwest, and United. Seven major car rental companies operate at the airport. Local numbers are Hertz, (510) 639-0200; Avis, (510) 577-6370; Budget,

(510) 568–6150; Dollar, (510) 638–2750; National, (510) 639–2411; Thrifty, (510) 568–1279; Fox, (800) 225–4369; and Enterprise, (510) 638–8600.

All the parking lots charge $2.00 for the first 30 minutes, but the rates vary for a day: It's $27.00 in the hourly lot, $17.00 long-term in the daily lot, and $14.00 in economy.

Sacramento International Airport
Sacramento
(916) 929–5411
www.airports.co.sacramento.ca.us

It used to be that politicians shuttling back and forth between their constituents and the state capitol created most of the traffic at Sacramento International Airport (SMF), about 10 miles north of downtown Sacramento (and accessible from Interstate 5). But this is now the 46th-busiest airport in the nation, and a terminal that opened in 1998 effectively doubled the size of the facility.

Ten major air carriers serve the Sacramento airport—Alaska, America West, American, Continental, Delta, Frontier, Horizon, Northwest, Southwest, and United. Several of the usual rental car agencies can provide you with wheels at SMF. Local numbers are Hertz, (916) 927–3882; Avis, (916) 922–5601; Budget, (916) 922–7317; National, (916) 568–2415; and Alamo, (916) 646–6020. Parking (12,000 vehicle capacity) runs about $1.00 for the first hour, $2.00 per hour thereafter in the hourly lot, with a maximum of $24.00 a day. The daily lots charge $7.00 to $10.00 per day.

Charles M. Schulz–Sonoma
County Airport
2200 Airport Boulevard, Santa Rosa
(707) 565–7240
www.sonomacountyairport.com

This airport, one of Wine Country's best, was renamed in 2000 to honor the late Charles Schulz of "Peanuts" fame, who lived in Santa Rosa for several decades. A $3 million upgrade of this airport's runways

and main taxiways was completed in 2001. Upgrades and renovations continued in 2004, and at press time the airport was in negotiations to add a carrier large enough to offer daily flights to other airports.

Meanwhile, private planes are always welcome, and 20 hangars were built in 2001 to accommodate them. There are no landing fees, though the overnight rate is $6.00 to $17.00, and the monthly rate can range from $36.00 to $109.00 (depending on wingspan).

The airport is about 7 miles north of downtown Santa Rosa, 2.2 miles west of US 101 on Airport Boulevard. Hertz, (800) 654–3131 or (707) 528–0834, and Avis, (877) 252–6600 or (707) 571–0465, both offer rental car services at this airport. The daily rate for long-term parking is $5.00, or it's $25.00 per week.

Smaller Wine Country Airports

The region includes several smaller airports open to private planes. I start with a description of the larger of these airports, then follow with an alphabetical listing of the most accessible, with numbers you can call for details. Figure on no landing fees and inexpensive overnight charges.

Napa County Airport
2030 Airport Road, Napa
(707) 253–4300
www.co.napa.ca.us

Perhaps the most elaborate of the small airports, Napa County offers Bridgeford Flying Service and Jonesy's Famous Steakhouse. Japan Air Lines maintains a multi-million-dollar pilot training facility on the grounds. The airport is 1 mile west of the intersection of Highways 12 and 29. There is no landing fee for private planes. The overnight fee is $5.00 for a single-engine plane, $8.00 for a double-engine, and $20.00 for a commercial plane.

Angwin Airport
100 Angwin Avenue, Angwin
(707) 965-6219

Boonville Airport
Airport Road, Boonville
(707) 895-9918

Cloverdale Municipal Airport
220 Airport Road, Cloverdale
(707) 894-1895

Healdsburg Municipal Airport
1580 Lytton Springs Road, Healdsburg
(707) 433-3319

Little River Airport
43001 Airport Road, Little River
(707) 937-5129

Petaluma Municipal Airport
601 Sky Ranch Road, Petaluma
(707) 778-4404

Sonoma Sky Park
21870 Eighth Street East, Sonoma
(707) 996-2100

Sonoma Valley Airport
23980 Arnold Drive, Sonoma
(707) 938-5382

Ukiah Municipal Airport
1411 South State Street, Ukiah
(707) 467-2817

Airport Shuttles

If you enter Wine Country via San Francisco, Oakland, or Sonoma County Airport, you don't have to be stranded at the baggage carousel. The following carriers specialize in airport transportation.

Evans Airport Service
4075 Solano Avenue, Napa
(707) 255-1559, (800) 428-5612
www.evanstransportation.com
Evans Airport Service, long the prime mode of getting to SFO from Napa (or vice versa), now goes to OAK too. Evans has eight daily departures to San Francisco and five daily runs to Oakland. The buses are full-size and comfortable. The fare is $29 one-way from Evans's large, patrolled lot, but children younger than 13 ride for half price. The office is open from 5:00 A.M. to midnight, and you can leave a reservation with the answering service if no one is home. To get to Evans take Highway 29 to Trower Avenue and go west 1 miniblock to Solano Avenue, the frontage road. Turn right and look for the first building past the fire station. Parking is $4.00 per day. Charters and wine tours can also be arranged.

Sonoma County Airport Express
175 Fairgrounds Drive, Petaluma
(707) 837-8700, (800) 327-2024
www.airportexpressinc.com
The Airport Express makes 15 daily runs from the Sonoma County Airport to San Francisco International Airport and 10 runs daily to Oakland International Airport. There are three intermediate pickup/drop-off points: Days Inn at 3345 Santa Rosa Avenue, the DoubleTree Hotel at 1 DoubleTree Drive in Rohnert Park, and the Petaluma Fairgrounds at 175 Fairgrounds Drive in Petaluma. The one-way fare to either airport is $26 for adults, $24 for seniors, and free for kids under 12. Long-term parking at the Sonoma County Airport is $5.00 per day, parking is free at the DoubleTree lot, and secured parking at the Petaluma site costs $4.00 per day.

Sonoma Airporter
18346 Sonoma Highway, Sonoma
(707) 938-4246, (800) 611-4246
www.sonomaairporter.com
The Airporter makes six daily runs (five on Saturday) from Sonoma Valley to SFO, with a connection in San Rafael. The nine-passenger vans will pick you up practically anywhere in Sonoma, Boyes Hot Springs, Glen Ellen, Kenwood, or Oakmont and deposit you at your terminal about one hour and 40 minutes later. The fare is $40.00 for adults, $30.00 for children 2 to

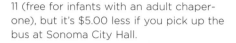

11 (free for infants with an adult chaperone), but it's $5.00 less if you pick up the bus at Sonoma City Hall.

BY BUS/TRAIN

Amtrak
1275 McKinstry Street, Napa
(800) 872-7245
www.Amtrak.com
The only viable railroad lines in Wine Country are tourist-oriented puffers described in the Attractions chapter and in this chapter's "Vintage Railroad" close-up. There are no Amtrak stations, but the company has contracted Amador Stage Lines to run buses from Napa, Petaluma, Rohnert Park, Santa Rosa, Cloverdale, Ukiah, and Willits. These buses will drop you off at an Amtrak station or deliver you from a station. The fee varies with destination but generally is reasonable. From Martinez the rail line can take you practically anywhere in the country. Call Amtrak for details.

Greyhound Bus Lines
435 Santa Rosa Avenue, Santa Rosa
(707) 545-6495, (800) 231-2222
www.greyhound.com
Greyhound's only true Wine Country station is in Santa Rosa. Other towns—Napa, Petaluma, Sonoma, Willits, and Ukiah included—are flag stops. That means they have infrequent but regular pickups at specific corners and parking lots. Call for details.

PUBLIC TRANSPORTATION

Public buses and vans might not be a viable option for a week of exploring and wine tasting, but they are handy for specific errands. And for those of you who live here or stay with friends for any significant time, they can be a blessing. The Wine Country has an extensive network of intercity and intracity public vehicles, many of which are connected by a trans-

If you find yourself in slow-moving traffic on US 101 or any other multilane highway in California, keep an eye out for motorcycles passing cars in between the lanes. Such riding is legal in the state of California.

fer system. Only basic information is provided below; please call for more details.

Napa County

The VINE (Napa Valley Transit)
1151 Pearl Street, Napa
(707) 255-7631, (800) 696-6443,
(707) 226-9722 (TDD)
www.napavalleyVINE.net
The VINE is a multiline municipal bus service within Napa Valley. Five lines are within the city of Napa and its environs; a sixth runs all the way from Vallejo to Calistoga (this was formerly known as the Napa Valley Transit, and locals might still refer to it as NVT). The basic fare in town is $1.00 for adults (more for the longer route), 75 cents for students, and 50 cents for seniors and the disabled. All the buses are accessible by wheelchairs and have bicycle racks. Seven-day-a-week service is offered, but weekend schedules are slightly more limited.

Sonoma County

Golden Gate Transit (Santa Rosa to San Francisco)
Pioneer Way and Industrial Drive
(707) 541-2000, (415) 257-4554 (TDD)
www.goldengate.org
Golden Gate Transit (GGT) is a comprehensive network that connects San Francisco with that amorphous region known as the North Bay. Most of the routes end in Marin County, but several continue north into Wine Country. There are service

points in the Valley of the Moon, Petaluma, Cotati, Rohnert Park, Santa Rosa, and Sebastopol. The basic adult fare is $5.00 or $5.75 to San Francisco, depending on where you embark. There are discounts for kids, seniors, and the disabled. Once in the city you get transfer privileges for the Bay Area Rapid Transit system (BART) and the San Francisco Municipal Railway (Muni). Call for schedule information and locations of GGT's 11 park-and-ride lots in Wine Country.

Healdsburg Municipal Transit
401 Grove Street, Healdsburg
(707) 431-3324
www.transitinfo.org/providers
This in-city bus has only one route, but it tries its damnedest to hit every corner in town, making almost 60 stops. The busier pickup points get hourly service between 8:30 A.M. and 4:30 P.M. The standard adult fare is $1.00, falling to 75 cents for students and 60 cents for seniors and the disabled.

Petaluma Transit
482 Kenilworth Drive, Petaluma
(707) 778-4460
www.transitinfo.org/providers
Three routes serve downtown Petaluma and its surroundings. Buses generally run every hour between 6:30 A.M. and 6:00 P.M. with a condensed schedule on Saturday and no service on Sunday. Adults and students ride for 90 cents, seniors and the disabled for 45 cents, and children five or younger for free. Discounted monthly and multiride passes are available.

Santa Rosa CityBus
Second and B Streets, Santa Rosa
(707) 543-3333, (707) 543-3926 (TDD)
www.transitinfo.org/providers
This network offers 13 convenient routes within the Santa Rosa city limits plus free transfers to Golden Gate Transit or Sonoma County Transit. Most CityBuses operate from 6:00 A.M. to 8:00 P.M. Monday through Friday, 8:00 A.M. to 5:30 P.M. on Saturday, and 10:00 A.M. to 5:00 P.M. on

Sunday. The fares are $1.00 for adults, 75 cents for students, 50 cents for seniors, and free for children five or younger. Monthly passes are available.

Sonoma County Transit
(Petaluma to Cloverdale)
335 West Robles Avenue, Santa Rosa
(707) 576-7433, (800) 345-7433
www.sctransit.com
Sonoma County Transit (SCT) serves an area bounded by Petaluma to the south, Sonoma to the east, Cloverdale to the north, and Occidental to the west, with most of the action in the vicinity of US 101. Basic adult fares run from 95 cents to $2.35, depending on distance. Kids get a small discount, while seniors and the disabled get a larger one. SCT offers transfers to Santa Rosa CityBus, Golden Gate Transit, and the Sonoma County municipal transit systems that lie within a designated area. Most buses run from 5:00 A.M. to 10:30 P.M. during the workweek and 7:00 A.M. to 7:00 P.M. on weekends.

Volunteer Wheels of Sonoma County
153 Stony Circle, Santa Rosa
(707) 573-3377, (800) 992-1006
www.volunteernow.org/wheels
Volunteer Wheels, a door-to-door service in Sonoma County, is part of the Americans with Disabilities Act program, administered locally as a nonprofit organization. As its name implies, all drivers work on a volunteer basis. The one-way fare is $2.00 within the Santa Rosa city limits and between $1.80 and $4.30 elsewhere in Sonoma County.

Mendocino County

Mendocino County Dial-a-Ride
241 Plant Road, Ukiah
(707) 462-1422 (Ukiah), (707)
459-9038 (Willits), (800) 696-4mta
www.4mta.org
Though the phone numbers are different, these three lines are coordinated by the same office. Service is door-to-door, with

customers sharing vans. The fare is $2.50–$3.00 within the respective city limits, and rates climb as you travel through concentric, mapped-out zones. The high end is about $15.00. Seniors and kids get discounts.

Mendocino Transit Authority (Santa Rosa to Fort Bragg)
241 Plant Road, Ukiah
(707) 462–1422, (800) 696–4682
www.4mta.org
MTA has four lines in Sonoma and Mendocino Counties. Taken as a whole, they form a long rectangle with US 101 (Santa Rosa to Willits) on the east, Highway 20 (Willits to Fort Bragg) on the north, coastal Highway 1 (Bodega Bay to Fort Bragg) on the west, and Bodega Highway (Santa Rosa to Bodega) on the south. One other route cuts across the rectangle from Ukiah to Albion, on Highway 253/128. The MTA buses run only once or twice a day, so don't miss the one you're after. Fares vary wildly according to distance. Call for specifics or check the Web site. Seniors and the disabled ride for half price; children younger than six ride for free.

BY LIMOUSINE

You see so many stretch limos in some parts of Wine Country that you'll swear the Academy Awards are at the next intersection. And it makes sense when you think about it. If no one in your group volunteers for designated-driver duties, a limousine will escort you from tasting room to tasting room, freeing you up to daydream and act silly.

Many of the limo services provide drivers who are knowledgeable about the region and its vintages. Most limo businesses prefer not to quote rates until you call, because the variables—type of car, size of party, day of the week, distance, and so on—are multiple. But in general there's usually a three- to four-hour minimum, and basic rates can start at $45 and go up. Fuel surcharges may also apply,

and your driver should be tipped generously. Here's a sampling of services offered by a few regional limo companies.

Napa County

Antique Tours
Napa
(707) 226–9227
www.antiquetours.net
This company stands out for one simply luxurious reason: its small fleet of restored 1947 Packard convertible limos (and one 1948 hardtop), which can accommodate up to seven passengers. Little did you know that postwar Packards were equipped with stereos, ice drawers, and air-conditioning.

Napa Valley Crown Limousine
Napa
(707) 226–9500, (800) 286–8228
www.napalimo.com
The proprietors of this service have plenty of experience in the tourist biz. Before getting behind the wheel, they ran a bed-and-breakfast inn and a tourist information office, so their winery knowledge is superior. Basic eight-passenger rentals are $65 an hour during the week, $75 an hour on weekends.

Royal Coach Limousine Service
Napa
(800) 995–7692
www.royalcoachlimousine.com
You have a choice of six- or eight-passenger cars and a range of itineraries. Ask for Matt if you want to customize something special.

Napa Winery Shuttle
(707) 694–4877
www.wineshuttle.com
Sip, swish, and spit all you wish, then leave the driving to these folks. Though not a traditional limo service, this shuttle service operates much like one but for fewer bucks. Providing door-to-door pickups and drop-offs at just about any Napa Val-

Vintage Railroad: All Aboard the Napa Valley Wine Train

As soon as you set foot in Napa County, the ads are everywhere. Tourist brochures, billboards, and bus benches urge you to ride it with someone you love. Napa motels promote themselves as "minutes from" it. Leaflets lie in the living rooms of practically every bed-and-breakfast inn in the land.

And if you spend any significant time driving the length of the valley, you will eventually see it: a chain of exquisite railroad cars, painted "burgundy, champagne gold, and grapeleaf green," rumbling along at a luxuriously unhurried gait. It's the Napa Valley Wine Train, the uncontested champion of Napa tourist attractions.

The train cars are beautiful, with Honduran mahogany paneling, brass bathroom fixtures, etched glass partitions, crystal chandeliers, and wool carpeting. Norman Roth, the San Francisco–based designer who oversaw the interior design, patterned the cars after early-20th-century classics such as the Venice-Simplon Orient Express and the Andalusian Express, and they aren't far off the mark. (In 1997 the Wine Train added a double-decked dome car, built for the Milwaukee Road Railroad Line in 1947.) Seated in one of the plush seats that swivel 360 degrees, you can point yourself at the window and watch the Wine Country pass by at a leisurely 15 to 20 miles per hour. It's a hypnotic sensation.

The Wine Train Depot is at 1275 McKinstry Street in Napa, near the corner of Soscol Avenue and First Street. Before you board, a Wine Train representative conducts a quickie seminar, explaining how the senses of taste, smell, and touch combine to help you enjoy that complimentary glass of wine you're holding.

All in all, you'll travel 36 miles from Napa to St. Helena, past 26 wineries and countless acres of vines. St. Helena is the midpoint, and there is no turnaround loop there. The two engines, connected back-to-back, are moved along parallel tracks to the back of the train, which then becomes the front. And then it's time for you to move too.

Unless you are in the dome car, you will either start with an hors d'oeuvres course in the parlor and move to a dining car for lunch, or eat the first two courses in a dining car, then retire to the parlor for dessert. The food is complemented by some 40 still wines and a

The Napa Valley Wine Train is popular with locals and visitors. COURTESY OF NAPA VALLEY WINE TRAIN

small selection of sparkling wines; some are big names, some small, but all are from Napa Valley.

Prices for the Wine Train vary widely, depending on whether you choose lunch, dinner, or brunch or prefer to dine on the twice-monthly Murder Mystery run. If you opt to sit in the dome car, the price is higher still. But expect to pay from $50 to more than $100 per person for this unique experience, and allow three to three-and-a-half hours to do so.

The Wine Train accepts most credit cards. Smoking is not permitted anywhere on board.

Whenever you ride the Napa Valley Wine Train, and whichever package you choose, reservations are a must. You can call (707) 253-2111 or (800) 427-4124 or visit the Web site at www.winetrain.com.

To toodle around downtown Napa, jump on the free trolley. There's a fixed route and a varied schedule, with several stops for hopping on and off, so check the latest postings at locations around downtown.

ley hotel or bed-and-breakfast inn, the cheerful drivers chauffeur you to a series of wineries, with pit stops at a couple of restaurants. Upon request, they can personalize your journey and pack picnic lunches, and they will pick up and deliver your wine purchases too. The service's fleet of white, 14-passenger, nonsmoking vans is top of the line, with plush interiors for extra comfort. The drivers, all longtime valley residents, provide interesting commentary and history as you glide worry free from one place to the next. A full-day excursion with unlimited stops runs about $38 per person.

Sonoma County

California Wine Tours
22455 Broadway, Sonoma
(707) 939-7225, (800) 294-6386
www.californiawinetours.com
These operators deserve mention for their extensive wine knowledge and detailed suggestions. It's a full-service transportation company, offering just about everything from intimate sedan and stretch limo service, to minibuses and custom vans, to deluxe motor coaches for larger events and tours.

Pure Luxury
Sonoma County
(707) 775-2920, (800) 626-LIMO
www.pureluxury.com
Pure Luxury will take you anywhere in Wine Country, for any reason: wine tours, weddings, airport transportation—you name it. Call to customize a tour.

Pacific Limousine
Rohnert Park
(707) 792-1500, (877) 333-3613
www.pacificlimo.com
Pacific has been operating since 1994. The charge is $50 per hour for a town car limo. The flat rate to either San Francisco International or Oakland International Airport is $135.

Just D-Vine Limousine Service
Santa Rosa
(707) 576-1725
www.winelimo.com
This owner-operated company (established 1985) prefers to stay within Sonoma and Napa Counties. A tour of Napa and Sonoma Counties, with wine tasting and lunch, runs about $280.

Heaven on Wheels
Windsor
(707) 838-7778
Greg Baker, the company's owner/operator, checks out all wineries before suggesting them for tours. His basic package is four hours. Rates are customized, and the cars go anywhere in Northern California.

Odyssey Limousine
Windsor
(707) 836-0672
This is another service that customizes by car and number of people. Odyssey has been gliding around Napa and Sonoma Counties since 1988.

Mendocino County

Mendocino Wine Tours and Limousine
Fort Bragg
(707) 964-8294
www.mendocinowinetours.com
This limo service operated by Stephen Seago offers a range of options for chauffeuring you around Mendocino and Lake Counties or for venturing into Sonoma County and Napa Valley—even to Bay

Area airports when the need arises. The fleet has been upgraded recently to include a 10-passenger limo that rents for $99 an hour.

BY TAXI

Your chances of flagging down a taxi on the roads of Wine Country are statistically smaller than your odds of being trampled by a cow. Here, "hailing a cab" means saluting a robust Cabernet Sauvignon. But there are several companies to get you from curb to curb. The standard rate is $2.50–$2.80 baseline and $2.50 per mile thereafter.

In Napa County, you'll find Black Tie Taxi, (707) 259-1000 or (888) 544-8294; Napa Valley Cab, Napa, (707) 257-6444; Taxi Cabernet, St. Helena, (707) 963-2620 or (707) 942-2226; and Yellow Cab of Napa, (707) 226-3731 or (866) 226-3731.

In Sonoma County, there's A-1 Taxi of Petaluma, (707) 763-3393; A-C Taxi, Santa Rosa, (707) 526-4888; Bill's Taxi Service, Guerneville, (707) 869-2177; George's Taxi/Yellow Cab, Santa Rosa, (707) 546-3322 or (707) 544-4444; and Vern's Taxi Service, Sonoma, (707) 938-8885.

Mendocino County's cab services are provided by Mendocino Limousine, (707) 964-8294. In the Ukiah area, it's Hey Taxi, Inc. at (707) 461-1200 or (707) 962-0800 in Fort Bragg.

HISTORY 🏛

The flags of Spain, England, Imperial Russia, Mexico, and the Bear Flag Republic have all flown over Wine Country at one time or another, a testament to the ambition, struggle, victories, and bitter disappointments of numerous explorers and conquerors. But before all the hubbub started, the region was home to Miwok, Pomo, Mayacoma, Yukia, and other indigenous peoples. Early descriptions of their lives evoke visions of a kind of Eden, where food was abundant and the mild climate permitted a life without the burden of clothes.

The gold rush of 1849 is perhaps the most renowned and defining event of Northern California history. The accidental discovery of one tiny nugget in 1848 by James Marshall, a moody carpenter working a sawmill in the Sierra foothills, set off one of the most frenzied mass migrations in history.

California was then newly a part of the United States, having been acquired from the Republic of Mexico—a remote, sparsely populated region cut off from the United States by 1,800 miles of broiling desert and nearly impassable mountain ranges. As news of the California Eldorado spread, hordes of gold seekers stampeded west, while others sailed from the East Coast around South America's Cape Horn. Some came from as far off as Germany, England, Wales, Ireland, and China. By the summer of 1849, more than 100 vessels floated empty in San Francisco Bay, their passengers and crew having forsaken all for a chance in the mines.

Through all of this, the various settlers of the region had experimented with growing vines north of San Francisco. However, the area's potential was not fully recognized until a man by the name of Count Agoston Haraszthy arrived on the scene (see the close-up in this chapter). Not long afterward, vineyards began to stretch in neat rows to the horizon. With time, numerous wineries sprang up and the region began to slowly gain international fame as the California Wine Country.

NAPA COUNTY

For 10,000 years or more, the Pomos were the undisputed occupants of the lands of the upper Sonoma and Napa Valleys, on up to Clear Lake and the surrounding lands. They lived an orderly life, with the men carrying on the outdoor work and often specializing in fishing or crafting arrowheads. Marriage was conducted in traditional fashion, and babies were the domain of the women—mothers, grandmothers, aunts, and cousins.

The first white settler in the Napa Valley was George Yount—frontiersman, hunter, trapper, and mountain man. He had left his wife and three children in Missouri in 1832 to drive mules with a pack train to Santa Fe. The job fizzled, but Yount saw no reason to return to Missouri. Instead, his restless feet took him to California's coast, where he trapped beaver for a while. He eventually made his way north in the summer of 1834 to the mission in Sonoma.

Yount was a resourceful man who could do almost anything. In time he became acquainted with the Mexican commandant Mariano Vallejo, who needed a new roof for his hacienda. Soon Yount was turning out 1,000 shingles a day, and his payment likely came via a 12,000-acre Napa Valley land grant he received with Vallejo's help.

In 1836 Yount set about building a Kentucky-style blockhouse for himself. Then he erected a flour mill and a sawmill, planted wheat and potatoes, and started a small vineyard. Initially he believed that grapes were for eating, not for turning into wine. But Yount's name would eventually live on in Napa Valley history—the town of Yountville was named in his honor.

Soon another settler appeared on the scene—Dr. Edward Bale, a young English surgeon. His marriage to a niece of General Vallejo made him a Mexican citizen, and as such he was given a land grant north of Yount's. Bale established a sawmill to cut timber and a gristmill (still standing and known as Bale Mill) to grind the settlers' grain. The mills became centers of great activity and supplied work for new settlers, but the best was yet to come for Bale. When gold diggers poured into the state, flour became a premium product, and Bale's mill was a gold mine in its own right.

The near-wilderness aspect of the Napa Valley changed dramatically after gold was discovered in the Sierra foothills, 100 miles east of San Francisco, in 1848. The city by the bay, which boasted a population of less than 450, was virtually abandoned in the rush to the gold fields. And although Napa was 40 miles to the north—not exactly on the direct route to the foothills—large numbers of gold seekers did wander off course and find their way into the valley, on foot or on horseback.

Miners also found the valley a popular wintering place when rains drowned the mines. Some stayed in the area. In two years Napa's population tripled to 450. A census two years later showed a jump to 2,116 (including 252 women). In just one decade, wilderness had been transformed into populace.

City on the River

The first town in the valley, founded in 1836, was Napa City—not that it amounted to much. But soon after the discovery of gold, prosperity set in. The chief places of business were saloons, and the method of payment was likely to be gold dust. In fact, the change brought about by gold was amazing.

The only route into town, the Napa River, soon opened the region to the world. The channel was deep, so before long steamboats were plying the river, transporting passengers to San Francisco and Sacramento for a $1.00 fare, lunch included. But the river's main value was for moving freight. The valley's fertile soil was producing such a profusion of fruits and vegetables that ships lined up daily at the Napa docks to load up for the San Francisco market.

In the outlying Berryessa Valley, some 30 miles inland, wheat grew so abundantly it became an international product. Ships from foreign ports arrived regularly at the Napa embarcadero to load Napa County wheat. The river brought in industry that would last until the end of the century. Lined up along its shores were potteries, iron works, tile factories, and tanneries. The term "napa leather" earned its own listing in the dictionary as "a type of leather resembling the original glove leather made in Napa by tanning sheepskins with a soap and oil mixture."

Many residents prospered beyond their wildest dreams, and by the 1880s Napa had achieved fame for both its charm and vast wealth. That reputation brought in the bankers, who were by no means above ostentation in the building of their great Victorian mansions. Some of those homes still stand today as an architectural reminder of other times.

But it came to an abrupt end. Napa's river traffic was killed by a single structure—a bridge built across the Carquinez Straits between Martinez and Vallejo. That allowed trucks to come into Napa Valley for the first time.

Those Amazing Hot Springs

During the 1860s it became fashionable all over the country to "take the waters." Soaking in hot mineral baths or mineral-rich mud was touted to cure virtually every known ailment. The first entrepreneur to capitalize on these bubbling springs was Sam Brannan, who had become a millionaire selling shovels and picks to miners.

Some of that wealth was spent acquiring 1 square mile of land in the northern valley. It was Brannan's vision to build an extravagant resort spa that would become a holiday retreat for San Francisco's shamefully rich. He called the place Calistoga—a combination of his fondness for Saratoga Springs and the word California. On the grounds there soon appeared a lavish hotel, 25 gingerbread cottages, an observatory tower, large stables with fine horses, a winery, and a distillery. The benefits of the hot springs, of course, were obvious and needed no further publicity.

In time, another hot springs resort, Napa Soda Springs, was developed 5 miles east of Napa City and took the place of Calistoga in the fickle favor of San Franciscans accustomed to lavish living. Banked against a flower-carpeted hillside, it presented an unequaled view of Napa Valley and San Pablo Bay. A good deal of faith was put in the healing powers of "a course at the springs." According to the report of a Dr. Anderson, the waters were beneficial "in the treatment of chronic metritis and ovaritis, for Bright's disease, acid blood, and dyspepsia."

The Silver Commotion

In the winter of 1858, rumors started percolating that silver had been discovered in the mountains. In no time at all, every unemployed man had turned prospector. Most of those wielding a pick knew nothing of the characteristics of silver ledges, and outcrops of barren rock of any description were equally valuable to their ignorant eyes. Miners hauled their rocks to San Francisco, where reports came back "no silver at all" or "a trace." Fortune quickly turned to folly, and tons of shiny rocks were unloaded by the disenchanted miners to make paving material for the streets of Napa.

Of more serious import were the quicksilver mines that developed in the 1860s in the Mayacmas Mountains that separate the Napa and Sonoma Valleys. Mining quicksilver, or mercury, was a hazardous process, and newspapers of the day were filled with accident stories.

In the 1870s, silver fever struck again. A vein of silver was discovered in the Calistoga hills, and a new town sprang up around the diggings—Silverado City. The hillsides soon were pocked with mining claims, and the city prospered briefly. The vein was short lived, but the town's hotel and mining office became famous, for it was here that Robert Louis Stevenson spent his honeymoon.

It was a strange entourage that straggled into the Napa Valley on a warm May day in 1880—the gaunt, ailing Stevenson; his new bride, Fanny; her 12-year-old son; and a setter-spaniel named Chuchu. They had decided to honeymoon in Calistoga, hoping to cure the Scottish author's lung problems. They arrived at the Springs Hotel, where they lived a short time in a "cottage on the green," but after a couple of weeks they located cheaper quarters. They moved into the assayer's office and the bunkhouse of an abandoned silver mine as squatters, paying no rent.

With a secondhand cookstove and a few household effects pulled up the mountain by a new neighbor who was also a squatter, they settled down for the summer, living the free life of gypsies. Here Stevenson wrote in his journal the notes that became his first literary success, *The Silverado Squatters*.

The Emergence of Fine Wine

Although Yount and Bale were the first to raise grapes in Napa Valley, it seems doubtful either had the inclination to cultivate fine wines. That distinction came to several German immigrants who arrived in the 1870s: Jacob Schram (who barbered by day and planted vines by moonlight), Charles Krug (known as the father of Napa viniculture), Jacob and Frederick Beringer (Jacob was Krug's winemaker until he built his own winery), and Gottlieb Groezinger (his winery stands as Yountville's Vintage 1870).

The 1870s marked tremendous growth in the Napa Valley wine industry. Local viticulture clubs began organizing in 1875, with Charles Krug chosen president of the largest. (A note that will come in handy: Generally speaking, we use "viticulture" when talking specifically about the science and practice of growing grapes, and "viniculture" to discuss the process of making wines.) About the same time, the Beringer brothers established their winery, complete with a cellar dug into a hillside by Chinese laborers and reinforced with stone—a feat of advanced architecture as well as masonry. Adding to the growth of the industry was an outbreak of phylloxera (a ravenous louse that eats the plant's roots) in French vineyards. Napa wineries continued to expand, with some 140 wineries producing almost five million gallons of wine.

Unfortunately, this led to overproduction. In the late 1880s growers were all feeling the pinch, and Charles Krug's vineyards and cellar went into receivership. More bad times loomed in the form of a general nationwide depression in 1890. But the blow that brought valley growers to their knees was the discovery that the dreaded, grapevine-ravaging phylloxera—for which there was no cure—had infected the vineyards of the entire area. By the turn of the 20th century, almost every vineyard had been ruined.

Plantings of resistant varieties brought fresh hope. Viticulture looked to be getting back on track. But those bright hopes were dashed by a new cataclysm called Prohibition. For the Old World grape growers, who considered wine the elixir of life, the law was inexplicable madness.

The plague of Prohibition lasted for 14 years, from 1920 to 1933. Some vintners survived it by making sacramental or pharmaceutical wines. But for others it would take years to build back their businesses. Still, one thing was clear: There would be no returning to wheat or cattle raising. Napa County was on its way to becoming America's premier wine region.

By 1966 wine was becoming fashionable, not only in California but across the nation. Between 1966 and 1972 wine consumption doubled. Visitors started pouring into the area to look, sample, and buy. By the mid-'70s there were again more than 50 wineries in operation in Napa Valley, and a new promotional technique had been developed—wine tastings. To let the public see how great the product was, vintners opened their doors and uncorked their bottles for sampling. Many offered their cellars for touring.

In the 1980s viticulture became a sort of dream occupation—a creative endeavor that could be both financially rewarding and personally satisfying. New wineries popped up almost overnight, many operated by individuals drawn into the field because they savored living close to the soil. Wineries started gaining public acceptance by offering extra attractions—Shakespearean plays and readings in the caves and Mozart played on expansive green lawns. Wine Country golf courses and croquet courts drew international competition. Cooking classes featured famous chefs. It all drew attention to the work of the winemaker.

SONOMA COUNTY

In 1823 a zealous young Spanish priest, Father Jose Altimira, arrived in California and established the Mission San Francisco de Solano, northernmost in a chain of missions spaced a day's journey apart along California's coast. This mission was the only one to be dedicated after Mexico overthrew Spanish rule earlier that year. In fact, not everyone in the mission hierarchy thought it was a good idea. But Altimira was nothing if not enthusiastic, and he convinced his colleagues it would be a

The Father of California Viticulture

Although many early settlers had started vineyards north of San Francisco, the first individual to recognize the area's potential for growing fine wine grapes was Count Agoston Haraszthy.

A flamboyant man who may or may not have been a true aristocrat, Haraszthy fled political turmoil in his native Hungary to seek his fortunes in America. His first endeavor in the New World was founding Sauk City, Wisconsin, where he built homes, mills, and stores; planted hops; and started a vineyard. The town remains to this day.

Once weary of that project, he headed to California along the Santa Fe Trail. He arrived at the gold fields on horseback, an argonaut in silken shirt, red sash, and velour hat, seeking whatever opportunities might exist. Haraszthy was working as an assayer at the San Francisco mint when General Vallejo heard of the man's interest in viticulture. Vallejo invited him to Sonoma in 1856,

whereupon Haraszthy quickly recognized the potential of Sonoma's soil. Convinced that grapes could prosper without irrigation, he sailed for Europe and returned with 300 varieties of grape cuttings, the basis for his 6,000-acre vineyards.

The winery he built was of massive stones, with cellars dug into the hillsides. For himself, he built a grand Pompeian-style villa. His fame spread quickly, and vintners from other parts of California, as well as those newly arrived from Europe, came to him for advice and for cuttings. It created something of a "grape rush" in the Sonoma and Napa Valleys.

But by 1868 the count was again restless and decided to turn his enthusiasm to raising sugar in Nicaragua. He left his two sons (who had married Vallejo daughters) to run the winery business. They never saw their father again, for he vanished mysteriously in the jungle.

better climate than San Francisco for the Native American converts.

The mission was doomed from the start. A decree was passed down from the Mexican government that all church properties would be "secularized" (that is, confiscated). In 1834 a young lieutenant, Mariano Vallejo (who later became General Vallejo), was sent from Monterey to seize all mission property and dispose of grain fields and thousands of head of cattle, sheep, and horses. It was outright

thievery carried out under the guise of eminent domain.

The mission's converts—turned loose to fend for themselves—were likely to have been grateful. They didn't much like Altimira, a cold and impersonal man, and they didn't care for the Spanish or the Mexicans, who were sometimes oppressive. In any case, the Mexican government had another, more serious reason to send an emissary into the territory—to discourage foreign invaders. Trappers were arriv-

A modern replica of Agoston Haraszthy's Sonoma home. JEAN SAYLOR DOPPENBERG

According to legend, he fell from a tree into a river and was devoured by crocodiles.

The villa he built in Sonoma was destroyed by the passage of time, but in the 1980s townsfolk built a replica next to the first vineyards he planted. Both are there to see today. Find it on Castle Road east of Sonoma, on your way to Bartholomew Park Winery.

ing in ever-increasing poaching forays over the Sierra Nevada Mountains, and some were staying on as settlers. And on the north coast Russian settlers had arrived from Alaska.

Meanwhile, young Lieutenant Vallejo brought his beautiful, cultured wife, Francisca Benicia, to this rough, untamed land and set up house in the abandoned mission. In one of its 37 rooms, their first daughter was born. In time, Vallejo set about creating the town of Sonoma. Using a pocket compass, he laid out an eight-acre plaza around which the town would rise. The plaza would serve as a promenade area for the populace as well as a parade ground where young soldiers could drill and practice their horsemanship. At the same time, Vallejo was preoccupied with developing a 66,000-acre ranch in the grasslands of Petaluma Valley, some 10 miles away. Built as a defense against intruders, the structure's walls were 3 feet thick, braced by redwood beams. It became a second home for the growing Vallejo family, which eventually numbered 15 children.

Some 2,000 American Indians (most of them transfers from the mission ranks) answered roll call daily in the courtyard before going to work making saddles and boots. These products were marketed to settlers or shipped to coastal communities as far south as San Blas, Mexico. Though it all seemed like a sustainable arrangement, trouble was brewing behind the scenes. That trouble was the Bear Flag Republic.

The Bear Flag Rebellion

"About half past five in the morning of Sunday, June 14, a group of desperados surrounded the house of General Vallejo and arrested him," wrote his sister. "Vallejo, dressed in the uniform of a general, was the prisoner of this group of rough-looking men, some wearing on their heads caps made with the skins of coyotes or wolves. . . . Shoes were to be seen on the feet of 15 or 20 among the whole lot."

The issues surrounding this drama were complex. England, France, and the United States were each vying for the California territory, which Mexico was sure to relinquish (whether by force or purchase). General Vallejo argued in favor of American rule, while his rivals, Gen. Pio Pico of Los Angeles and Gen. Jose Castro of Monterey, strongly preferred the English or French to the Americans. Adding to this tense situation was the unexpected arrival in Monterey of Lt. John Charles

Frémont of the U.S. Topographical Service, a surveyor purportedly on a mission to map a more direct route to the Pacific. Frémont rode in accompanied by a contingent of 62 armed U.S. cavalry.

Frémont did not hesitate in inciting the Mexican generals, going so far as to raise the Stars and Stripes over his camp. After some fierce posturing but no real fighting, Frémont moved north to Oregon. Following his departure, rumors began circulating that the Mexicans were about to evict all Americans from California. The story incited rage among local settlers, having been lured to California by the Mexican government's promise of land. They decided to take matters into their own hands.

Thirty-three renegade malcontents went to the Sonoma presidio to dispose of the Mexicans. Along the way they hastily fashioned a flag for the new republic, made of a woman's red flannel petticoat and a length of unbleached muslin. For their emblem they used berry juice to paint on it the picture of a bear (it looked more like a pig) and the words *California Republic*. The ever-cordial Vallejo brought up some wine for the group, and they spent some time in convivial conversation. But in the end, he was carried off to Sutter's Fort in Sacramento, where Vallejo's friend John Sutter reluctantly jailed him.

The California Republic lasted 26 days. On July 9, 1846, U.S. Navy Lt. Joseph Revere lowered the bear flag and replaced it with the American Stars and Stripes. Vallejo was released from jail August 6. He had been away no more than a month, but in that time his horses and cattle had been stolen and his fields stripped of grain.

The New State of California

The months that followed the rebellion brought mass confusion. Nobody knew who was in charge. A group of military volunteers known as Company C from New York City's Bowery arrived. But since there wasn't much for the soldiers to do (unless they wanted to stoop to manual labor), they improved their leisure by riding spirited horses, hunting waterfowl, and staging cruel bear-and-bull fights in a makeshift stadium behind their barracks.

The discovery of gold suddenly shifted everyone's attention. Settler and soldier alike left Sonoma to the womenfolk. The village sank into stagnation. Vallejo, on the other hand, wasn't too bad off. He had seen what was coming and had hedged his bets. While serving Mexico loyally (virtually without pay), he had also taken steps to ingratiate himself with the United States. In time he actually became a California senator.

But Vallejo's plans of becoming a prominent American somehow went awry. Lawsuit after lawsuit went against him, and his land empire disappeared. He slipped deeper into debt. One by one his dreams vanished. He did manage to hold on to his Sonoma home, Lachryma Montis, and here his wife—once pampered—sold dried fruit and chili peppers for the San Francisco market. In old age Vallejo became a symbol of the link between an idealized Mexican era and the Yankee-dominated present. In his unfailing dignity and hospitality, he seemed to personify all that was best about the past.

By the mid-1860s Sonoma had become almost totally neglected. There were no trees, and the plaza had degenerated. A fire in 1866 destroyed much of what the settlers had built. Some of the early pioneers responded by organizing a Pioneer Society of 340 members to revitalize the town. They planted trees, built fences, and cleaned up the plaza (appointing one member to be in charge of keeping livestock out of that area of town). Gradually the town took on a more respectable look, though the society itself fizzled out.

About 1888 many Italian immigrants came to quarry cobblestones for the streets of San Francisco. Among them was Samuele Sebastiani, who quickly recognized the possibilities for growing wine grapes. In no time at all he was supplying the demand of the growing Italian community for wine and making a name for his winery. Today the strong Italian influence remains in and around Sonoma.

One of Vallejo's mandates when he took over as commandant was to ensure that lands north of San Francisco were settled. At the time, this northern frontier was a lonesome wilderness, and Vallejo had some trouble convincing any of his fellow Californians to apply for grants. But he had plenty of relatives, so most of them fell heir to large tracts. In 1837 he convinced his widowed mother to leave her San Diego adobe and travel 700 miles to an area near Santa Rosa Creek. She packed up her nine children and seven-trunk wardrobe and built the Cabrillo adobe, the first bona fide home in the Santa Rosa Valley. In time it became the nucleus of a settlement.

Santa Rosa

In 1854 the town of Santa Rosa was little more than a trading post. A few small businesses and houses had sprung up along the creek, and the town had a representative in the state senate. That man was William Bennett, another former Missourian, and his ambition was to snatch the county seat from Sonoma. To help voters make up their minds on the issue, he hosted a big Fourth of July barbecue attended by, according to one historian, "the lame, the halt and blind if they could influence a vote." Not surprisingly the vote went in favor of Santa Rosa. At daybreak a group of Santa Rosans, fearing Sonoma wouldn't release the county records, hired a wagon and raced to Sonoma, grabbed the records, and raced back to Santa Rosa.

Reporting the hijacking, the *Sonoma Bulletin* editor wrote, "We are only sorry they did not take the adobe courthouse too . . . its removal would have embellished our plaza." Within three years, according to the newly launched *Sonoma Democrat,* Santa Rosa had grown to 100 buildings. After the arrival of the railroad in 1870, the town's population exploded to 6,000.

About this time a shy, trim New Englander named Luther Burbank opened a nursery in the town and began experimenting on flowers, fruits, and vegetables. His uncanny talent for interpreting the results of his experiments earned him the lasting title of "plant wizard."

A wizard of a different sort next appeared in town—spiritualist-sage Thomas Harris, a man of magnetic personality and piercing eyes "like revolving lights." In the outlying area called Fountain Grove, Harris established the esoteric Brotherhood of New Life, a colony of communal living that separated its members from their spouses (and their cash) to await their celestial mates in another world. Harris claimed these other worlds were revealed to him during his conversations with the angels. It was left to a woman reporter to provide the impetus to drive Harris from the gates of his Eden. She joined the group long enough to write a lurid exposé that sent the preacher packing.

The infamous 1906 earthquake that leveled San Francisco also struck Santa Rosa—nearby Petaluma, Santa Rosa's then rival, escaped virtually unscathed. The courthouse collapsed, and downtown buildings suffered devastating damage. Nearly 100 people died in the rubble, but the city's spirit survived. While some residents did head for other parts, many townsfolk simply rolled up their sleeves and began to rebuild.

ℹ *Take a brief walking tour of Petaluma's historic Victorian homes beginning on Fifth Street at A Street, and continuing on Liberty Street, switching over to Sixth Street, up D Street, and then down Fifth Street.*

Petaluma

Before the advent of the railroads in the mid-1880s, rivers were the principal means of shipping goods inland. In the Petaluma River, steamboats—introduced to California during the gold rush—operated regularly during the 1850s, hauling wool, butter, cream, eggs, and live chicks down the twisting tidal river to San Francisco Bay. By the 1890s Petaluma was the third-busiest waterway in the state.

But it was neither the river nor steamboats that gave Petaluma its enduring fame. In the 1880s, it became known as the Egg Basket of the World when the first practical chicken incubator was invented there and marketed on a mass scale. Immigrants from Europe thronged to Petaluma to set up hundreds of hatcheries and thousands of chicken-feed mills. As many as 600 million eggs per year were shipped to worldwide points. But chicken-related prosperity declined in the 1930s due to high feed costs. Leghorn hens were replaced by Holstein cows. Today the Petaluma countryside is mostly dairy land.

Jack London in Glen Ellen

Glen Ellen, 9 miles north of Sonoma, lies in an area forested with oak, madrone, redwood, and buckeye trees. Author Jack London came to this countryside in 1903 at the invitation of friends who owned the Wake Robin Lodge. There, at age 30, he met their vivacious niece, Charmian. Instantly attracted to one another, the couple spent their days riding horseback and having sprightly conversations. They were perfectly matched, adventurous individuals, and London stayed on to marry Charmian.

At first they lived at her family's lodge, but London fell in love with the land locally known as the Valley of the Moon. He started accumulating property until he had a 1,500-acre tract, and here the Londons lived in a simple white house. He called the place Beauty Ranch, and it was there he wrote most of his prodigious output of books. London's success as an author had initially been spurred by the appearance of a Yukon story in *Atlantic Monthly* magazine and confirmed by publication of *The Call of the Wild* when he was 22.

Within eight years he was America's highest-paid author. In his short lifetime he wrote 54 books, 1,300 articles, and 188 short stories, some translated into 30 languages. His house overflowed with guests—scientists, actresses, writers, and socialites. And exuberance marked just about everything London did. He took up scientific farming and designed a pigpen that gave each pig family an apartment. Later, he took a long sea voyage with Charmian on a ship he designed himself.

But London's most wondrous dream was Wolf House, his 26-room mansion, an imposing affair of redwood and huge stone blocks, with arched windows opening onto forested slopes and offering views of the entire valley. London wrote, "It will last one-thousand years, God willing." But one midnight in August 1913, billows of black smoke filled the sky as a raging fire burned out of control. The author watched silently from a nearby hill as his dream crumbled to the earth. London never quite recovered from the calamity. Three years later he died at age 40. The official cause was uremic poisoning, but rumors persisted it was suicide. The magnificent ruins of Wolf House, as well as all of Beauty Ranch, live on as a California state park.

Northern Sonoma County

The Pomo tribe lived for centuries in what is now northern Sonoma County. In 1841 Mexico granted a portion of their domain to a New England sea captain, Henry Fitch (nobody consulted the Pomos, of course), who had eloped with General Vallejo's sis-

ter. But Fitch, having received such an excellent dowry, saw no reason to live out his life in such a lonely land. He hired Cyrus Alexander to manage a ranch there with immense herds of cattle. The names of both men live on as landmarks—Fitch Mountain looms over the town of Healdsburg and to the east lies Alexander Valley, Cyrus's payment for work on the ranch.

Healdsburg itself bears the name of Harmon Heald, a disenchanted forty-niner who arrived on the scene in 1852 and claimed land for a town site. He surveyed the town and sold lots for $15 apiece around a central plaza. By the end of the decade, Healdsburg had a population of 500.

Russian River and Western Sonoma County

Called Slavyanka (Slavic girl) by Russian settlers during their tenure in California, the Russian River flows from the hilly regions above Hopland, past Cloverdale, Healdsburg, Guerneville, Duncans Mills, and finally Jenner, where it meets the Pacific. The Russians explored the length of the river basin—a territory that the Spanish had largely ignored—initially to scout out a suitable settlement site and thereafter to occasionally chase down otter. They saw the area for what it was, a rich river valley dense with towering virgin redwood stands, bounded by fertile plains, and awash with fish. But the Russians abandoned their foothold in California before ever establishing a settlement upriver, leaving the region behind for others to exploit.

When the first American loggers arrived in the Russian River valley, they could hardly believe what they saw. The trees were enormous, some measuring as wide as 23 feet in diameter and 300 feet in height. The first sawmill opened in the valley in 1861, with others springing up soon thereafter. Stumptown, renamed Guerneville in 1870 after lumberman

George Guerne, was the region's logging epicenter.

The trees offered the woodsmen a rich bounty for a time. Around the turn of the 20th century, however, many trees had been harvested, and the mills began to close. In an effort to shore up profits, the Northwest Pacific Railroad—which had been servicing the mills—began to promote the Russian River area as a tourist destination. Urban vacationers from San Francisco and other parts were soon hopping aboard trains in droves to escape to the region—with the railroad cars rolling right onto a ferryboat for the ride across the Golden Gate. Hotels and resorts sprang up, as did bevies of summer cottages. In the 1930s revelers boogied all night at the Rio Nido Inn to the sounds of Benny Goodman's clarinet and Ozzie Nelson's band.

Another popular local name also harks back to a Russian source. Settlers at Fort Ross introduced the Gravenstein apple to the county in the mid-19th century. In 1883 Nathaniel Griffin demonstrated that "Gravs" could be grown commercially, and he was dubbed "Grandfather of the Gravenstein." The apple became popular in the county because of its exceptional flavor and early ripening. The fruit was so well liked that locals inaugurated an annual celebration—the Gravenstein Apple Festival—in 1910 in its honor. The festival continues to be held today.

Other western Sonoma towns include Valley Ford, Bloomfield, Forestville, and Occidental. The latter was first settled by Bill Howard, who had survived a shipwreck off New York, malaria in Africa, and a revolution in Brazil. He and a sawmill operator lured a railroad into the territory and after that success built the whole town of Occidental in four months. Italian woodcutters from Tuscany worked the forests, and a few opened restaurants where a traditional Italian feast could be had for two bits. Today, Occidental is still the place to go for Italian dinners; it is also a hub for artists and environmental activists.

The Sonoma Coast

For almost 60 miles along the jagged coastline, Sonoma County's Highway 1 (called Coast Highway 1 in many locales) snakes through rangeland and small towns that lie between the Coast Range and the Pacific. Centuries ago Miwok and Pomo tribes fished these coastal waters. Later, Russians and the Aleut hunters they brought down from Alaska harvested otter here—to near extinction—in nimble kayaks called baidarkas. The hunters skillfully negotiated their small craft through the surf and swells of the rugged coastline, occasionally seeking refuge in one of the few protected coves hidden among the bluffs. Bodega Bay, near Sonoma County's southern border, was one of the few places where larger ships could safely drop anchor. It thus wasn't long before the bay became a shipping center, dispatching lumber and agricultural products to San Francisco and beyond.

Bodega Bay became famous as the site where Alfred Hitchcock filmed his classic thriller, *The Birds*. A wall-size photo at Bay View Restaurant at the popular Inn at the Tides (see the Hotels, Motels, and Inns chapter) commemorates Hitchcock's work.

MENDOCINO COUNTY

Rumors of gold brought the first adventuring white pioneers to Mendocino County in the 1840s. The rumors were false, but the land itself was pleasant—a good place to settle down and raise sheep, plant fruit trees, and grow hops. Sam Orr, a Kentuckian, arrived in 1857 with his wife, along with a quantity of grape cuttings to start a vineyard. Soon another American wandered in, a prospector from the gold country named Seward. He bought some of Orr's cuttings and also started a vineyard to grow around his imposing colonial-style house, which soon included a winery—he had clearly found success in his mining venture. Still, the valley's immediate future rested not with grapes but with hops.

By the 1890s, the Ukiah Valley had achieved modest fame for its vast hop fields. The town of Ukiah boasted 2 hotels, 3 livery stables, and 10 saloons. But traffic on its dirt streets kicked up clouds of dust in summer and churned up thick mud in winter. One especially wet year a two-horse wagon sank hub-deep in the middle of Main Street.

Most incoming travelers arrived by way of Fort Bragg on a stagecoach that left at 7:00 A.M. and made a loading stop at Mendocino, before rumbling over twisty, dusty, roads to Ukiah. Along the route, the stage stopped for a meal and change of horses, with passengers arriving in Ukiah about dinnertime. When the railroad finally arrived with service to and from San Francisco, it started a tourist boom. By then the hop fields had achieved notoriety, and travelers came from hundreds of miles away just to spend a weekend in the country.

Other attractions arose to bring tourists. This was the age of the curative mineral bath, and the area boasted several. Most elegant was Vichy Springs, an upscale resort featuring such niceties as croquet, horseback rides, hunting safaris, and dancing under the stars. The water in the swimming pool was allegedly "charged with electricity and gas, a real Champagne Bath." Vichy Springs had a long fallow period, but in the late 1980s it was revived, reconstructed, and rejuvenated, and it is once again an elegant resort spa (see the Spas and Resorts chapter).

Meanwhile, in the early 1900s, grape growing and winemaking started to become more serious. Dozens of small operations were producing wine in light volume; Zinfandel was the main product. Hardworking Italians planted grapes on the hillsides. For the most part, however, the wine industry in Mendocino County at this time involved growers shipping their fruit to other wine-producing regions for blending. Typical of early growers were the Mal-

one family, who sold their grapes as reds and whites, with no varietal distinction.

Today's wine industry is based not so much on quantity as on quality. And enologists around the world now recognize the premier quality of Mendocino.

The Mendocino Coast

The jagged Mendocino coast bears little resemblance to its southern relative, that stretch of beach that's lined with sunbathers from Santa Barbara to San Diego.

It's a rugged coast, dotted with dog-hole ports (big enough only for a dog to turn around in), that prospered for two decades in the rush for building materials following the 1906 San Francisco earthquake. Many of these burgs have vanished or are greatly diminished. For some years, Point Arena was the largest, most active lumber port between San Francisco and Eureka. It was also a whaling station and regular port of call for passenger steamers. Today, its most impressive feature is its classic, soaring lighthouse, 115 feet up from the tip of a narrow, bleak, eroding rockbound point. It's the closest point to Hawaii on the west coast. The light tower was built in 1870, then rebuilt after the devastating 1906 earthquake. For 36 years, it faithfully guided ships through the treacherous rocks, but today's visitors will see only seals, migrating gray whales, and cavorting sea lions.

Even before the 1906 quake, the Mendocino coast had been turned into a lumberjack's paradise by the gold rush. San Francisco burgeoned into a bustling city in urgent need of lumber to build houses.

Each year on the third Saturday in July, Fort Ross State Historic Park hosts Living History Day. The event features singing, dancing, theatrical performances, period dress, gunfire, and cannon blasts. For more information, call (707) 847-3286.

Legendary racehorse Seabiscuit, subject of a best-selling book and a blockbuster movie, lived out his retirement years at Ridgewood Ranch, south of Willits, and is buried beneath a giant oak tree on the property. For information about tours, call the Willits Chamber of Commerce at (707) 459-7910.

At the time, the only lumber available came from the Sandwich Islands (now known as Hawaii) and was very costly. When news of the great redwood forest on the North Coast trickled down, there was no holding back the tide. The history of the coast changed overnight.

Logging had been booming in Little River for 10 years when Silas Coombs selected it as one of the best-weather ports on the coast to build a mill. The mill wasn't memorable (it burned in 1910), but the mansion Coombs built lives on as Little River Inn, one of the coast's loveliest, with gabled windows and eaves festooned with wooden scrollwork.

There's another historic inn nearby. Heritage House is a Victorian farmhouse dating from the 1850s. It was an early base for smuggling both liquor and foreign laborers and once was a hideout for 1930s gangster "Baby Face" Nelson. Today, it's a luxury retreat with a commanding view of the craggy coast.

The Village of Mendocino

The picturesque town of Mendocino lies at the mouth of the Big River, on a rocky headland overlooking a small bay. In its heyday around 1870, it was a raucous, thriving port and lumbertown, often called Fury Town by locals. Nearly everything in Mendocino was and is built of wood, including the sidewalks and the water towers that stand on the skyline. The set-

tlement was initially named Meiggsville for "Honest Harry" Meiggs, a San Francisco politician and wharf owner with a weakness for speculation. The town changed its name in 1854 after Meiggs got into financial hot water and had to flee the country. He recouped his losses by building the first railroad over the Andes in South America, but his partners in Mendocino were left facing bankruptcy.

Meiggs came hotfooting to Mendocino in the first place when a Chilean bark loaded with silks and spices wrecked nearby. The captain of the ship had lost his way to San Francisco and accidentally guided his vessel straight into the rocks at Point Cabrillo. When Meiggs sent a salvage party, they found no silks but instead great forests of redwood. Meiggs, a born entrepreneur, rounded up a schooner, some mill equipment, and some partners and headed for the forested coast. Soon mills sprung up in every gulch, and mansions with leaded-glass windows rose up on hillsides filled with fine furnishings shipped around Cape Horn. Breweries, churches, and schools followed. On Steamer Day, when passengers came into port, carriages from eight hotels met ships from all over the globe.

When the forest had been cut and the mills closed down, Mendocino fell asleep and snoozed for a long while. In the 1960s, the town suddenly blossomed as a center for artists and bohemians seeking freedom of style and life on the cheap. William Zacha came up from the Bay Area to open an art gallery, then conceived the Mendocino Art Center, a rambling collection of buildings on a rise at the edge of town (see the Arts and Culture chapter).

It was this art colony that first attracted a more affluent breed of visitor, seeking escape from urban living. They came to stroll boardwalks and sniff ocean breezes. With them came a blossoming of gourmet restaurants and some uncommonly civilized inns. It is this ambience that sets Mendocino apart from other North Coast villages. The fact that Mendocino looks a lot like the coast of Maine has not escaped the notice of filmmakers. Devotees of the television series *Murder, She Wrote* will recognize some "Cabot Cove" settings.

Fort Bragg

Originally established as a military outpost in 1857 as a check on the nearby Mendocino Indian Reservations, Fort Bragg went on to become a major hub in the lumber trade and commercial fishing. The city's Noyo Harbor, a snug refuge just inland on the Noyo River, is the quintessential fishing port. In the predawn you can see the parade of boats heading down the river to the sea, their lights making an attractive scene.

The lumber mills have progressively closed in recent years, and most visitors now come to Fort Bragg to enjoy a small city that offers pleasant seaside lodgings, art galleries, fine food, a popular microbrewery, and the Skunk Train. The train's route, established in 1885, is 40 miles of track between Fort Bragg and Willits with some 30 bridges and trestles, 2 tunnels, and several switchbacks snaking through dense redwood forest. A nightmare to build, Chinese laborers did much of the work. (Read more about the Skunk Train in the Attractions chapter.)

GOLDEN GATEWAY

An icon of the American West, San Francisco (called "the City" by locals) lives up to its legends. The classic old cable cars really do climb halfway to the stars (or at least as far as Nob Hill). Luminous fog does swirl around the Golden Gate Bridge. At eventide the golden glow of the setting sun glints from the windows of Alcatraz Island, making the old prison seem almost romantic, as errant sailors tack home against the late and misty sky. And taquerias in the Mission District, dim sum eateries in Chinatown, Italian coffeehouses in North Beach, to name just a few, make up a fascinating and tasty cultural mélange. Even the frequently chilling summer weather and traffic-snarled streets fail to diminish the multicultural excitement and avant-garde aura that pervade this town. It's a city with an irrepressible spirit, a noble grande dame on a hilltop throne, proud and resilient after the terrible earthquake of 1906 and the Loma Prieta temblor of 1989.

So . . . if you had only two days in San Francisco, what places should you not miss? Everyone's tastes are different, but here are a few sites that most folks are sure to enjoy.

Nob Hill, at the top of California and Sacramento Streets, with its posh hotels, private clubs, and smart addresses, retains much of the glamour and gentility it possessed at the end of the 19th century, when men who had made fortunes in silver erected grand mansions for the world

to envy on these unobstructed, commanding heights.

Fisherman's Wharf, with its picturesque views, pungent aromas, street performers, steaming crab pots, and fine restaurants, draws many visitors—it's all hustle and bustle during the summer tourist season. Fishing boats bob alongside the wharf, while seagulls float overhead and sea lions bask and bark on large rafts moored at the wharf's edge. Local gourmets (and commoners alike) consider West Coast Dungeness crab among the best seafood in the world. Walkaway shrimp cocktails are sold from the sidewalk, along with clam chowder and sourdough bread, and it's pleasant to nibble on a little seafood while watching the fishing boats return. Parking is available in public lots along Beach and North Point Streets.

Check out the Hyde Street Pier and look at the tall 19th-century ships permanently berthed there. Ghirardelli Square, a short walk uphill on Hyde Street, is one of San Francisco's most successful attempts to hang on to the transient past. Until 1964 it was a crumbling, abandoned factory that had once turned out Civil War uniforms and later served as a chocolate factory where Domingo Ghirardelli made cocoa. Within the rambling complex are a dozen fine restaurants, snug cafes, and almost 100 shops and galleries.

Del Monte Square (formerly called the Cannery), just down the street on Leavenworth, is where Del Monte once tinned fruit. Now it's a delightful and original collection of sprightly shops, art galleries, and restaurants; a place to buy French lingerie, English antiques, primitive art, and the newest in contemporary furniture. Often there's entertainment in the courtyard—small combo bands, magicians, and jugglers.

---

i *The completely refurbished Ferry Building at the foot of Market Street is now a food lover's paradise. There are farmers' markets, a tea shop, and numerous purveyors offering everything from chocolate to oysters.*

Alcatraz Island, once the end of the line and the beginning of hopelessness for federal prisoners, is now part of a national park. It can be reached by boats that leave several times a day from Pier 41 at Fisherman's Wharf. A cell-block tour gives insight into life behind bars for men like Al Capone and Machine Gun Kelly, who lived out their days here without visitors.

An excellent audio tour narrated by former guards and inmates is full of fascinating anecdotes about some of the more notorious criminals, escape attempts, and the prison riot of 1946. Plan on staying at least a couple of hours on the island to soak in the history, and dress warmly. Same-day tickets are available at Pier 41 (you'll run into long lines in summer), or you can get them one month in advance by calling (415) 705-5555.

A $25 million renovation of Union Square, the heart of the city's shopping district, was completed in 2002. There are now more green spaces, light sculptures by R. M. Fischer, and a stage large enough to accommodate an orchestra. The underground parking garage beneath the square, the first in the world, was also significantly renovated. It was originally built during World War II to serve as a bomb shelter. Around the square or close by are Saks Fifth Avenue, Macy's, Neiman Marcus, Dior, Williams-Sonoma, the Apple Store, and a Virgin Megastore.

Chinatown is just a short walk up Grant Avenue from Union Square. This "city within a city" is home to more Chinese than any other place outside of Asia. Some 80,000 San Franciscans live, work, shop, worship, and play in Chinatown. It's packed with open-air markets, a variety of bakeries, restaurants, temples, souvenir shops, and, yes, people. Grant Avenue is touristy, but Stockton Street, a block west of Grant, offers a real taste of Chinatown. Tearooms, temples, Chinese schools, and shops lining the streets offer exotic produce and delicacies such as yellow croaker salted fish, and dried papaw, fish peel, and black fungus.

Making reservations can frequently be a challenge in San Francisco's world-famous restaurants and trattorias. But if you can't get a table, ask the concierge if you can be served at the bar. There you can often sample from the menu while partaking in San Francisco's No. 1 pastime, people watching.

For a rare treat, stop for a dim sum lunch at one of the restaurants offering this unusual fare. Servers wheel different carts around the room, each offering a unique cornucopia of delights—some of it mysterious, all of it delicious. They call out their particular specialty in Chinese, and you order whatever you like. (Some restaurants sell their more popular items, such as steamed pork buns, in to-go bakery-style cases for those who want to savor this delicacy on the run.)

Between Chinatown and Fisherman's Wharf is North Beach, the Italian district of the city. Pasta, provolone, and dark, rich espresso are in abundance here, as are a wide variety of cafes, galleries, small theaters, and nightclubs. Beat poets Jack Kerouac, Allen Ginsberg, and William Burroughs chose North Beach as their principal hangout, contributing to San Francisco's international reputation as a funky, hip literary city. In 1953 Lawrence Ferlinghetti, then a struggling poet who later became a Beat legend, opened City Lights Books at 261 Columbus Avenue. It has since become one of the city's most cherished landmarks as well as a leader among the many feisty independent booksellers that have staked their claim in the Bay Area. For the full Beat experience, wander through the little store's voluminous stacks, then take 10 steps across Jack Kerouac Alley to lift a tall, cool one at Vesuvio's Bar—a legendary watering hole that still draws the city's more colorful creative types.

If you're into museums, you'll appreciate the world-class offerings in San Fran-

Though it seems as if it's been around forever, the fortune cookie is not an ancient Asian delicacy. Local legend claims invention of the cookie in San Francisco about a century ago by Makota Hagiwara, who was a gardener at the Japanese Tea Garden in Golden Gate Park.

cisco. The Asian Art Museum reopened in 2003 in its new home at the Civic Center, filling 40,000 square feet of gallery space with $4 billion worth of Asian treasures. And the San Francisco Museum of Modern Art, at 151 Third Street, can always be counted on for spectacular shows.

Get the feel of the Pacific Ocean along the Great Highway. Start at Point Lobos Avenue and the Great Highway, then visit Cliff House, a once-famous resort that overlooks the ocean and nearby Seal Rock. From there, the long windswept strand of Ocean Beach stretches to the great sand dunes to the south. Leave your bathing suit at the hotel, and stay out of the roiling surf, where the southbound tidal currents traveling at 12 mph have a habit of swallowing swimmers and surfers alike.

Along this highway you'll discover an entrance to Golden Gate Park, the city's great green retreat, bordered by the Great Highway, Lincoln Way, Stanyan, and Fulton Streets. When the park was built in 1887, it included 730 acres of dunes and 270 acres of arable land. Today, its 1,000 acres are lush with meadows, lakes, and 5,000 varieties of shrubs, flowers, and trees. Within its borders you can visit an aquarium, a planetarium, and a plant conservatory that looks a lot like Kew Gardens in London.

When you get hungry in San Francisco, you're never too far from a restaurant. In fact, there's one on nearly every corner. It's hard to make recommendations, but keep in mind that there are some 3,200 eating and drinking establishments in the city, which breaks down to about one restaurant for every 230 residents. Wherever you decide to dine, you're not likely to be disappointed.

When the sun begins its slow descent into the ocean and the late afternoon fog snakes its tendrils over the hills and into the bay, the city takes on a more romantic feel. San Francisco may be a sightseer's paradise during the day, but it is also a great place to spend an evening. Ease into a silky-smooth night of jazz at the New Orleans room at the Fairmont Hotel, California and Mason Streets, and also inquire as to who's playing at the velvet-gloved and sedate Venetian room there. Give an amen for some soulful gospel music at Biscuits and Blues, 401 Mason Street, or enjoy an evening of comedy at Punch Line, 444 Battery Street. One of the best comedy shows in town is the long-running Beach Blanket Babylon at Club Fugazi, 678 Green Street. It's wacky, it's fun, and it's ever-changing—skewering whatever and whoever has recently shaken up our pop culture.

Of course, this listing of attractions only scratches the surface. It is said that everyone who visits San Francisco wants to come back again, and our tour leaves plenty more to see on a return trip. It would be nice, for instance, to take in the Cable Car Barn and Museum on Washington and Mason Streets to see the historic old paraphernalia and glimpse the innards of these machines in action. (Just how does that cable car work anyway?) Kids and parents alike should see the Exploratorium, Marina Boulevard and Lyon Street, which contains more than 600 interactive science exhibits.

The city's Victorian architecture is almost as famous as its cable cars. Handsome and slightly irrational, painted brightly in all combinations of colors, these structures are certainly unique. Some of the best can be seen in Pacific Heights, particularly on these streets: Vallejo, Broadway, Pacific, Jackson, Washington, Pierce, and Scott, generally in blocks between 1600 and 3000.

One thing visitors should keep in mind is that San Francisco weather is, well, unlike what you would expect. True, temperatures don't often vary outside a range of 50 to 70 degrees, summer or winter. But sometimes January and February can be the sunniest, most glorious months. On the other hand, summer can be so cold that tourists who mistakenly thought California called for tank tops and flip-flops huddle in downtown doorways to keep warm. Mark Twain reportedly once said, "The coldest winter I ever spent was a summer in San Francisco." So you may want to have that sweater or jacket handy if you're walking about. What is the best time of year to visit? Locals will tell you the most pleasant months are September and October.

Much like Manhattan and some quaint and compact European cities, San Francisco is best enjoyed by walking its many neighborhoods. Besides, driving a car in San Francisco—and then trying to park it here and there—can be an exercise in futility. But if you must drive, be prepared for the traffic idiosyncrasies you will encounter.

In negotiating the city by automobile, be aware of red-light-running fools, and expect traffic jams at any hour. On-street parking is virtually nonexistent—at best scarce—and those who overstay their legal welcome are subject to heavy fines and might even be clamped with "the boot," which immobilizes the vehicle. An impounded car is endless trouble to retrieve.

Fortunately there are a number of public parking facilities; one of the handi-

Admission to some of San Francisco's most popular attractions—including the Museum of Modern Art, Asian Art Museum, Cartoon Art Museum, Exploratorium, San Francisco Zoo, and Legion of Honor—is usually free on the first Tuesday or Wednesday of every month.

est offering underground parking is at Union Square. In hilly San Francisco, it is illegal to park a car on most hills (technically, those exceeding a grade of 3 percent) without setting your parking brake and turning the wheels into the curb. When parking uphill the wheels must be "heeled," with the inside front tire resting securely against the curb. Parking downhill, tires must be "toed"—turned in.

Complicated enough for you? We recommend letting your hotel valet park the car when you first arrive and forgetting about it until you're ready to leave town. You'll be glad you did.

So if you only have a day or, heaven forbid, even less, and you're still wondering what to do, our advice is this: Go out and simply walk. Enjoying yourself comes easily here. It costs nothing to breathe the fragrance of a vendor's flowers on Union Square, hike up Telegraph Hill (where rowhouses climb steep slopes), take in the breathtaking view from Coit Tower at the crest, stroll through Chinatown or Little Italy, or photograph the busy fleet at Fisherman's Wharf. And don't worry, you will be back.

FLORA, FAUNA, AND CLIMATE

U pon arriving in the Santa Rosa area in 1875, famed horticulturist Luther Burbank could barely contain his excitement, declaring that "this is the chosen spot of all earth as far as Nature is concerned." Many Wine Country visitors have since echoed Burbank's sentiments, inspired by the bucolic scenery and the mild Mediterranean climate. From the marshes of San Pablo Bay to the mountains of Mendocino National Forest, and from the roaring Pacific to shimmering Clear Lake, the terrain is rarely less than wondrous. Few places on the face of the planet are so blessed with natural gifts.

Every season reveals a different facet of the landscape. In spring a kaleidoscope of wildflowers lines the roadsides. In summer the grapevines practically beam with verdant life. In fall the fields are quilted with bright patches of red and orange. And in winter, always wet but not too harsh, a misty and mysteriously beautiful hush descends on the hills and valleys. But that's not all. Behind the Wine Country's ever-changing beauty lies a fascinating natural history. Though it's impossible to summarize all there is to tell, here's a sampling of salient geologic, climatic, and ecological features.

GEOLOGY

A hundred million years ago, the Wine Country area was exceptionally poor as a grape-growing region. In fact, all of it was under water. It took a lot of tectonic activity—movement of the massive plates that together form the Earth's crust—to swing Napa, Sonoma, and environs eastward onto dry land. It was all part of the succession of north–south "island arcs" that violently, if patiently, crashed into the North American continent and sent California on the way to its modern-day topography, which includes the prominent Mayacmas Mountains—which divide Sonoma and Napa and Lake and Mendocino Counties— and the steep Coast Range.

Of course, the movement hasn't exactly stopped altogether, and you can feel their effects every now and then. The renowned San Andreas system (a massive network of strike-slip faults that forms the border between the Pacific and North American tectonic plates) runs the length of Sonoma and Mendocino Counties, sometimes on the mainland and sometimes beneath the sea. Several smaller, generally north–south faults lurk beneath Wine Country, including the Rodgers Creek Fault, which caused some destruction in Santa Rosa with a 1969 quake that measured 5.7 on the Richter scale.

Things could be worse. In fact, they used to be. Much of the region was the scene of frightful volcanic activity three to four million years ago. Those eruptions, combined with unrelenting seismic activity, have given California's North Coast ranges a highly complex geologic profile. And this is of more than theoretical interest, for two of the lures that historically have drawn people to the region are direct results of geology.

The most obvious of these is geothermal activity. Sonoma and Napa Counties are pierced by fault "pipelines" that send water heated by magma 8 miles below the Earth's surface percolating upward. In the Calistoga area you can pay to gawk at a burst of hot water (at the Old Faithful Geyser) or to soak in the stuff (at the many spas). And around one section of the Sonoma–Lake County border, geothermal sites are even used to generate electricity. In fact, the Geysers steam field weighs in as the world's largest complex (19 units) of geothermal power plants, owned and operated by the Calpine Corporation.

But the peculiar North Coast geology has spawned a lot more than mud baths. The second regional drawing card with its roots in plate tectonics is the mighty grapevine.

SOIL

Soils reflect the rocks they used to be, so it makes sense that an area of convoluted geology will contain many types of soil. And because soil composition greatly affects the chemistry of a growing grape, it follows that precisely where you plant your vines has a lot to do with the quality of your wine.

The soil within a single vineyard can vary substantially. Red soil tends to produce soft wine; light, "fluffy" soils are known for hard, austere wines; and gravelly ground, which has a hard time holding water, tends to result in earthy wines. Moreover, wine made from hillside grapes usually is riskier and more robust than valley wine, because the grapes are smaller and therefore have a higher skin-to-pulp ratio. (The intense flavor is in the skin.) And some of the best vineyard soil in Napa Valley is found on the Oakville and Rutherford "benches"—broad, nutrient-rich alluvial fans that have been washed from the Mayacmas Mountains.

Of course, all of this is gross oversimplification. You'll find more information on the whole business of "appellations"— slightly varied microclimates that produce grapes and yield wines with specific, refined characteristics—in the Wineries chapter, but sorting out such details is what separates a successful vintner from the rest of us guzzlers. The point is that, in

The Chalk Hill grape-growing appellation in Sonoma County is named for its light-colored soil. It's not chalk at all, but a white volcanic ash.

a manner of speaking, the Merlot you're savoring today has been in the works for about 100 million years.

CLIMATE

Northern California is one of five regions in the world that enjoys a Mediterranean climate, characterized by warm, dry summers and mild, moist winters. While the area's geographic location helps to shape its climate—Santa Rosa is about par with Athens on the latitude scale—local environmental influences are also important. Weather varies dramatically throughout the region, and you can often find a huge difference in conditions just by driving a few miles.

To understand what causes Wine Country weather, think of the Pacific Ocean as a giant climate-control device, set on Mild. In general, the farther you stray from salt water, the hotter your summers will be and the colder your winters. Temperature variations along the coast are minuscule, and river towns such as Guerneville and Napa also are fairly mild. There's only about a 5-degree differential in the usual maximum winter high temperature on the Mendocino Coast (56 degrees) and the average summer high (the low 60s). Though coastal winter nights are cooler, they don't often see temperatures drop lower than 40. There is morning summer fog and evening sea breezes.

That is in stark contrast to places such as Ukiah, Calistoga, and Middletown, where hilly terrain serves as a barrier to ocean influences. Each of these towns can be uncomfortably still and hot in August. Inland Lake County reaches upward of 100 degrees regularly in summer, and its winters can dip well below the freezing mark. On the other hand, when it's hot, it qualifies as "dry heat." Californians tend to consider that phrase a meaningless cliché, but long-suffering midwesterners and easterners can immediately feel the difference. A 100-degree day is a test no matter how you look at it, but the night air has a chance to cool considerably when humidity is low.

Rainfall too varies across Wine Country. The Mendocino Coast gets about 39 inches, St. Helena about 34, and the Clear Lake Basin about 25. Regardless of volume, however, you can expect most of the rain between November and February, with residual storms in March and April. Summer and fall downpours are rare.

In general, spring and autumn are the best months to visit. The weather is exceptional, and there is added color from wildflowers or turning leaves. Summer temperatures in Sonoma County usually edge into the mid-80s, but the nights are still comfortable (chilly even), with the mercury falling into the 50s.

FLORA

A flora list from the Covelo Ranger District in Mendocino National Forest alone refers to 18 different coniferous trees, 13 varieties of oak, 6 types of willow, and 6 species of manzanita. So I won't try to construct any sort of comprehensive list here—it would be voluminous. I can, however, state a few generalities.

Two types of ecosystem—oak woodland and chaparral—dominate the rolling hills of Napa and Sonoma Counties. It's

Docent-led tours of the magnificent flowering rhododendrons at Mendocino Coast Botanical Gardens near Fort Bragg take place in May, the peak blooming month. Call (707) 964-4352 for details.

impossible to drive along U.S. Highway 101 or Highway 29 without noticing the stolid oak trees, but the collection includes many varieties. Coast live oaks are perhaps the most impressive, with a single tree able to spread its branches up to 130 feet. These trees prefer moist locations, such as creek bottoms and north slopes. Canyon live oaks, with their exceptionally hard wood, thrive on steep hillsides. Blue oaks like hot, dry slopes, and California black oaks pop up on mesas with deep soil and gentle slopes.

Chaparral, made up of shrubs such as manzanita, ceanothus, and toyon, is more closely associated with the hills of Southern California, but it is prevalent here too. It is an environment inhospitable to humans and designed to burn—many of its plant species have highly flammable oils in their bark, and the underbrush can be thorny and impenetrable.

While most of the grapes are grown at lower elevation, Wine Country counties include a lot of mountainous, forested topography. That's especially true in the upper half of Lake County and the northeast corner of Mendocino County, which form part of Mendocino National Forest.

The standout citizen of the damp, misty Coast Range forests is the coast redwood, the tallest tree in the world. Though Mendocino and Sonoma have several preserves devoted to redwoods (see the Parks and Recreation chapter), the biggest of all are found in Humboldt County (see the Big Trees section of the Day Trips chapter). You might also stumble on a redwood in steep, darker canyons along Wine Country streams. Other dominant trees include the ponderosa pine, with its arrow-straight trunk; the Pacific madrone, whose gnarled trunk will creep 50 feet horizontally to find sunlight; and the Douglas fir, the Western Hemisphere's premier lumber tree.

No matter which Wine Country microclimate you're in, you are likely to see wildflowers if your timing is sound. Somewhere between February and June, depending on elevation and intensity of sunlight, literally hundreds of shrubs and herbs burst into bloom. The most eye-catching include the California poppy—the bright orange state flower that pops up just about anywhere—and mustard, which lays a breathtaking yellow carpet in the early spring vineyards (and inspires all sorts of reverent celebrations—see the Festivals and Annual Events chapter). Other native wildflowers to look for include orchids, irises, monkey flowers, Indian paintbrushes, golden bushes, wild roses, lupines, violets, shooting stars, fiddlenecks, lilies, wild onions, and buttercups.

FAUNA

It isn't exactly a jungle out here, but keen observers will spy a wide range of furry, feathered, or fishy creatures in Wine Country.

Drive the scenic routes at dusk in summer and fall and you are likely to see the omnipresent black-tailed deer nibbling scrub oak or buckbrush in the meadows. You are even more likely to see skunks, raccoons, and opossums, though it might be in the form of roadkill. They are among the most common of the region's mammals, especially in semideveloped areas. The more mountainous areas are home to black bears, mountain lions, bobcats, coyotes, bats, diminutive gray foxes, porcupines, badgers, feral pigs, and even the occasional ringtailed cat or tule elk. Many of them are nocturnal and all are elusive, but they are out there, trying to stay downwind of humans. Once in a while, however, a bear or bobcat wanders into the eastern city limits of Santa Rosa, nestled along the western side of the Mayacmas Mountains, in search of some easy food and water. A mountain lion even startled commuters one afternoon when it strolled onto US 101—a jungle of a different sort—in the middle of the city. Though these sightings are rare, it serves to remind us that we are surrounded by wild and unpredictable beauty.

The Napa Registry of Significant Trees was founded in 1995 to protect special trees on private properties in perpetuity until their natural death. To be listed on the registry, the tree must have historic significance and high public visibility, be native to Napa Valley, and be extraordinarily beautiful.

The rugged coastal areas have their own communities: seals and sea lions on the rocks; river otters in the estuaries; and gray whales offshore, migrating southward from the Bering Sea to Baja California between December and April. The nutrient-rich waters of the coastal areas also teem with benthic life, including eight species of the highly desirable—and highly endangered—abalone. River otters are found in much of Wine Country's freshwater. The reptile and amphibian crowd includes alligator lizards, pond turtles, king snakes, rubber boas, skinks, and the ones you need to watch out for: western rattlesnakes.

The local waterways—primarily the Napa, Eel, and Russian Rivers—are dominated by anadromous fish, that is, species that travel from the sea to spawn in freshwater. The three big fish in Wine Country (as in most of Northern California) are chinook salmon, coho salmon, and steelhead—the latter are basically rainbow trout that have learned to migrate. Most of the good lake fishing is for bass (smallmouth and largemouth) and catfish, though none of them are native sons. (See more on fishing in the On the Water chapter.)

Audubon Society chapters are active throughout the region, and they have plenty to catalog. There are swallows and swifts, American robins, northern mockingbirds, woodpeckers and warblers, finches and flycatchers. There are at least six species of hawk and seven species of owl, including the northern spotted, that rather harmless old-growth percher despised by a generation of loggers.

Golden eagles (the nation's largest raptor, with a wingspan of up to 7 feet), ospreys, kestrels, and peregrine falcons ride the thermals along high bluffs and cliff faces. Peregrines, with a maximum flight speed of 275 mph, have been known to overtake small airplanes. Herons and egrets poke about in swampy spots, such as the Napa-Sonoma Marshes Wildlife Area, south of those two towns, and we've got a varied collection of ducks and geese. And if jet lag and ambitious wine tasting have you feeling dehydrated and fatigued, don't fret too much about those California turkey vultures circling overhead. It's nothing personal—the hefty, red-faced scavengers are quite populous in Wine Country.

HOTELS, MOTELS, AND INNS

O nce upon a time, finding an exceptional hotel in Wine Country was a challenge. Today the challenge is having to choose between the many new and upgraded hotels, motels, and inns that have opened within the past few years.

In this chapter you'll find lodging options for every budget, from the widely known chains (Best Western, Marriott, Hilton, and Days Inn, for instance) to special places that defy the standard definition of a hotel, motel, or bed-and-breakfast inn (Milliken Creek Inn, Hotel D'Amici, Duchamp Hotel, and Stanford Inn by the Sea, to name a few).

All of these lodgings are well equipped to provide you with a good night's sleep, but most go beyond with amenities that make your stay more comfortable and enjoyable. Some are full-service hotels that can be as charming as B&Bs (but with more amenities), and some are less expensive, basic motel rooms. Several could even qualify for mention in the Spas and Resorts chapter.

Unless stated otherwise, assume that hotels, motels, and inns accept major credit cards. Pets are usually not welcome, but don't be afraid to ask—a few places cater to both two- and four-legged creatures. Many facilities set aside rooms for their guests who smoke, but some are entirely smoke-free environments. In addition, high-speed Internet access is becoming commonplace at the larger hotels and motels, and even some of the elegant inns have added this service. Always inquire about these specifics when calling for information.

Hotels, motels, and inns are listed using the south-to-north geographical sequence explained in the How to Use This Book chapter. I start with Napa Valley accommodations, followed by those in Sonoma and Mendocino Counties. Afterward, I list agencies specializing in vacation rentals.

PRICE CODE

The following price ratings are based on the approximate cost of a one-night, weekend, double-occupancy stay, not including tax, gratuities, or other amenities such as room service or premium movie channels.

$	Less than $80
$$	$81 to $120
$$$	$121 to $150
$$$$	$151 to $200
$$$$$	More than $200

NAPA COUNTY

Embassy Suites Napa Valley   **$$$$$**
1075 California Boulevard, Napa
(707) 253-9540, (800) 362-2779
www.embassynapa.com
A group of three-story canary and burgundy buildings, the Embassy Suites offers a nice combination of corporate know-how and Wine Country charm. There are indoor and outdoor pools, wet and dry saunas, swans in the koi pond, and a soaring lobby with terra-cotta tiles and parlor chairs. Every guest unit is a two-room suite with extra pullout sofa, wet bar, and microwave. The tariff includes a full, cooked-to-order breakfast and an afternoon Manager's Reception with complimentary drinks.

Napa Valley Marriott $$$$
3425 Solano Avenue, Napa
(707) 253-7433, (800) 228-9290
www.marriott.com

The 232-room hotel (including several suites) is just off Highway 29, north of the Trancas Street/Redwood Road exit. Each room has individual climate control, in-room pay movies, iron and ironing board, a work desk, and voice mail. The Harvest Cafe, specializing in steaks and California vegetables, serves breakfast and dinner; Character's Sports Bar & Grill serves lunch and dinner. Amadeus spa offers massages, exfoliations, body treatments, and facials. (See the Web site at www.spame.com.) The Marriott also has a heated outdoor pool and Jacuzzi, lighted tennis courts, and a fitness center.

Milliken Creek Inn $$$$
1815 Silverado Trail, Napa
(707) 255-1197, (888) 622-5775
www.millikencreekinn.com

In its short life, this "boutique inn" set on the Napa River has become one of the valley's most luxurious and popular retreats for couples wanting to get away from it all. It's only two minutes to Copia (see the Attractions chapter) and downtown Napa's restaurants, yet you will feel far removed from city life. More than a bed-and-breakfast, but not a hotel, this inn is in a class by itself. Luxurious and inviting, it's in a tranquil setting, thanks to the natural expanse of the river wherever you look. Enhancing the grounds are gardens, fountains, Adirondack chairs, and even a waterfall and koi pond.

The innkeepers, Lisa Holt and David Shapiro, have many years of experience in the upscale hotel industry, and it shows in their attention to detail. The guest rooms are elegantly noncluttered, in what Lisa calls "British campaign" design, but these rooms have modern amenities such as DVD players (there's a lending library of 200 movie titles), well-appointed mini-bars, telephones with modem hookups, and in-room continental breakfast service. There's even a pillow menu—soft or firm, feather or foam? In early evening guests can sip wine in the lobby while listening to David tickle the ivories on the piano (he's an accomplished jazz musician). Massage and spa treatments, along with private yoga classes, are offered on-site. Needless to say, this inn is intended for the enjoyment of couples.

Napa River Inn $$$$$
500 Main Street, Napa
(707) 251-8500, (877) 251-8500
www.napariverinn.com

When the historic Napa Mill and Hatt Building were renovated along the Napa River in 2000, this hotel was the result. It offers luxury accommodations in 66 guest rooms and suites in various themes—from nautical to "California rustic" to vintage 1800s. All rooms feature large TVs, two-line data and voice ports, refrigerators, and in-room coffee. Many rooms have fireplaces, river views, and balconies. A full-service spa is nearby for use by guests, and restaurants and shops are handy right next door in the refurbished Hatt Market building. Pets are welcome here for $25 per night and treated as VIPs. Also ask about special package deals for a gondola ride with Gondola Servizio, which docks right outside the hotel (see the Attractions chapter). All rooms are nonsmoking.

Wine Valley Lodge $$
200 South Coombs Street, Napa
(707) 224-7911, (800) 696-7911
www.winevalleylodge.com

South of downtown Napa, close to Highway 121, the mission-style lodge has 53 guest rooms. There is a heated pool in the motor court and complimentary continental breakfast on summer weekends. Ask about the Elvis Presley and Marilyn Monroe suites, which run a bit higher in price and larger in size, each sleeping four adults comfortably. The stars stayed in these rooms at different times in their careers—the King was making a movie nearby, but nobody seems to remember the reason Marilyn checked in.

River Terrace Inn $$$$
1600 Soscol Avenue, Napa
(707) 320-9000, (866) NAPA-FUN
www.riverterraceinn.com
Planning a visit to Copia, the American
Center for Wine, Food and the Arts? You
might consider staying at this new hotel in
downtown Napa, along the Napa River
near Copia. Most of the 106 rooms and
suites have balconies with either Napa
River or Napa Valley views, 10-foot ceilings, king-size beds, whirlpool tubs,
DVD/CD players, rich linens, minibars, and
high-speed Internet access.

The private spa provides in-room massages, facials, hydrotherapy, and body
treatments for individuals or couples. An
outdoor pool and full fitness room complete the body-pampering extras.

A complimentary breakfast buffet is
available each morning in the River Terrace
Cafe, which offers light meals and salads
at lunchtime and nightly dinner specials.
(A Japanese restaurant, Budo, is right next
door.) There's also a wine bar, where many
local boutique wines are poured. And if
you need a place to properly store that
special bottle of Cabernet Sauvignon until
you're ready to uncork it, the hotel provides a wine storage unit upon request.

Best Western Inn at the Vines $$$
100 Soscol Avenue, Napa
(707) 257-1930, (877) 846-3729
www.innatthevines.com
Best Western offers few surprises, which
is probably why it's one of America's most
popular chains. The Napa version has 68
rooms, including 8 suites. All rooms have
cable TV and refrigerators. There is a
heated pool and spa, a meeting room for
up to 50 people, and a 24-hour Denny's
restaurant on the property. This is a non-
smoking hotel.

Hawthorn Inn & Suites $$$$
314 Soscol Avenue, Napa
(707) 226-1878, (800) 527-1133
www.napavalleyinns.com
One of Napa's newer hotels is this 60-
room, three-story structure that focuses

on comfort, with a nod to business travel-
ers. The rooms are wired with high-speed
Internet access, and there are irons, iron-
ing boards, microwaves, refrigerators, and
executive chairs with oversize desks. Busi-
ness services, a daily newspaper, a hot
breakfast buffet, and a boardroom for
meetings are also available. The deluxe
suites have in-room Jacuzzis. Vacationers
who like a little exercise will appreciate
the hotel's swimming pool and spa, as well
as the fitness center.

Napa Valley Downtown
Travelodge $$$
853 Coombs Street, Napa
(707) 226-1871, (800) 578-7878
www.travelodge.com
If location is everything, the Travelodge
has it all. The downtown Napa locale puts
you two blocks from Riverwalk, four
blocks from the Wine Train depot (see the
Getting Here, Getting Around chapter),
and a few steps away from shops and
cafes. The 45-room motel has a heated
pool. Each unit comes with a two-line
phone with a fax port, individual air-conditioning, and a big-screen TV with VCR.

Chardonnay Lodge $
2640 Jefferson Street, Napa
(707) 224-0789
The lodge offers convenient Napa central-
ity and beds of various proportions. The
20 rooms are air-conditioned, and they
have phones and cable TV.

The Chateau $$$
4195 Solano Avenue, Napa
(707) 253-9300, (800) 253-NAPA
www.napavalleychateauhotel.com
Somewhere between a budget motel and
a major corporate hotel, the Chateau offers
comfort and reliability, if not luxury. The 115
rooms are sizable, and each has a separate
vanity dressing area and individual climate
control. The two-story motel has six spa-
cious suites too, with wet bars and foldout
couches. Also on the grounds are two con-
ference centers that hold up to 500 peo-
ple, and a swimming pool and spa.

The John Muir Inn $$$
1998 Trower Avenue, Napa
(707) 257-7220, (800) 522-8999
www.johnmuirnapa.com

We can't imagine John Muir, the naturalist who wandered through the Sierra Nevada range, staying here at the intersection of Trower Avenue and Highway 29. But the inn that bears his name is a solid midprice choice with a courtyard swimming pool and whirlpool spa, conference room, a 24-hour front desk, and free continental breakfast. About one-quarter of the 60 rooms have kitchenettes, and some have wet bars or private spas. Children 13 and younger stay free. The entire property is a smoke-free environment.

Yountville Inn $$$$$
6462 Washington Street, Yountville
(707) 944-5600, (800) 972-2293
www.yountvilleinn.com

This rambling hotel has seven buildings and 51 bright and spacious rooms. Each unit boasts a fieldstone fireplace, French doors leading to a patio, a wood-beamed ceiling, and a refrigerator. All guests in this nonsmoking hotel receive free continental breakfast. The inn also has a heated pool and spa and is near the Vintners Golf Club (see the Parks and Recreation chapter). Should you be mixing business with pleasure, the elegantly comfortable Club Room facilitates groups of up to 60 people.

Vintage Inn $$$$$
6541 Washington Street, Yountville
(707) 944-1112, (800) 351-1133
www.vintageinn.com

This elegant, country-style inn is spread out on a large, landscaped lot. It has 80 units—basic rooms, minisuites, and villas—divided between the outer court and the more protected inner court. Most have

---

i *Vintage Inn in Yountville (and its sister property, Villagio Inn & Spa) made the 2004 500 Best Hotels in the World list compiled by* Travel & Leisure *magazine.*

---

patios or balconies. All of them have fireplaces and come with a complimentary continental breakfast buffet, including California champagne. Vintage Inn offers room service, a 60-foot lap pool and hot tub, tennis courts, bike rentals in the summer, and a private limousine service. The inn also has executive conference facilities that can handle 20 to 200 people.

Napa Valley Lodge $$$$$
2230 Madison Street, Yountville
(707) 944-2468, (800) 368-2468
www.napavalleylodge.com

If you've ever stayed at one of Woodside Hotels' Northern California establishments, you'll be keen to reserve a spot at this 55-room hotel at the north end of Yountville. The exterior incorporates classic Tuscan-style architecture, with arched loggias, iron railings, and limestone details. Woodside is known for its gracious service and amenities, and Napa Valley Lodge is right in step—from the 400-book lending library and hearth in the lobby to the free champagne buffet breakfast to the Spanish-tile double vanities, duvet bed coverings, and reproduced vintage tapestries in the rooms. About three-fourths of the units have fireplaces, and all feature a balcony or terrace with views of vineyard or pool and gardens.

Besides the pool, the hotel has a spa, a redwood sauna, and a small exercise room.

Rancho Caymus Inn $$$$$
1140 Rutherford Cross Road, Rutherford
(707) 963-1777, (800) 845-1777
www.ranchocaymus.com

If Father Junipero Serra had built a really fancy mission to impress the folks back home in Spain, it might have looked like this. Rancho Caymus, a couple of blocks east of Highway 29 on Rutherford Cross Road (a.k.a. Highway 128), carries off the hacienda motif flawlessly, from the adobe-looking stucco to the tile roof. The rough-hewn white oak and pine beams were salvaged from an 80-year-old barn in Ohio; the parota wood chairs, tables, and dressers are from Guadalajara; and the wool rugs and wall hangings were made by indigenous Ecuadorians. A central, tiled courtyard brims with flowers and small trees.

Most of the 26 nonsmoking units have fireplaces and a split-level layout, and 5 of them have kitchenettes. Continental breakfast is included, and the site includes fine dining at La Toque restaurant (see the Restaurants chapter).

El Bonita Motel $$$$
195 Main Street, St. Helena
(707) 963-3216, (800) 541-3284
www.elbonita.com

The old neon sign and poolside layout point to this motel's roots as a classic 1950s roadside motor hotel, but there have been upgrades galore since then. The 42 rooms are nicely furnished and painted in subdued gray-green tones. About two-thirds have microwaves and refrigerators. Some allow pets for a small fee. There is a fireplace in the recently remodeled lobby, and each guest receives a continental breakfast. Flowers and fountains proliferate in the lawn areas, while the pool is complemented by a sauna and a Jacuzzi.

Harvest Inn $$$$$
1 Main Street, St. Helena
(707) 963-WINE, (800) 950-8466
www.harvestinn.com

The inn's reception building, the Harvest Centre, is built to evoke the English countryside, with its corkscrew brick chimneys and oak-paneled great room. But rustic this place isn't. It is a sprawling, manicured complex that specializes in (but isn't limited to) corporate functions, with conference facilities accommodating as many as 60 captains of industry. Set between Sutter Home Winery and Sulphur Springs Avenue on the southern fringe of St. Helena, and bordering a sizable vineyard, Harvest Inn has 54 nonsmoking rooms. Most of them have king beds, brick fireplaces, wet bars, and dressing vanities, and some have patio balconies. There are

two heated pools and whirlpool spas on the grounds, and all guests are served continental breakfast.

The Wine Country Inn $$$$
1152 Lodi Lane, St. Helena
(707) 963-7077, (888) 465-4608
www.winecountryinn.com

This hard-to-categorize accommodation does a good job of blending the comforts of a bed-and-breakfast with the convenience of a small hotel. The Wine Country Inn offers a full buffet breakfast, afternoon appetizers and wine tasting, distinctive rooms filled with hand-picked antiques, a large pool and Jacuzzi, a well-trained staff, and easy parking. No matter how the inn is defined, Lodi Lane, about 2 miles north of St. Helena, is hard to beat for serenity. Immediately to the east is a working vineyard; almost all of the 20 rooms have private patios or balconies that practically sit on the trellises. Most units have fireplaces, and some even have private hot tubs. There are also four suites and five cottages. The hotel, popular with honeymooners, caters to adults rather than to families with children, and there are no in-room TVs here.

The Inn at Southbridge $$$$$
1020 Main Street, St. Helena
(707) 967-9400, (800) 520-6800
www.innatsouthbridge.com

This upscale St. Helena hotel looks something like a winery with its earth tones and creeping vines. The resemblance is no coincidence, as architect William Turnbull Jr. is known for his winery design. The Inn at Southbridge has 21 ample rooms (only 2 smoking units), each with a vaulted ceiling, fireplace, sisal-style carpets, and down comforter. French doors open onto a private balcony overlooking the courtyard. The rooms are set up for corporate clients, with high-speed Internet access. The inn has a lap pool and a full-service health club with steam, weights, and stationary bikes.

Hotel St. Helena $$$$
1309 Main Street, St. Helena
(707) 963-4388, (888) 478-4355
www.hotelsthelena.com

This restored hotel in the heart of downtown is quintessential St. Helena: immaculate, charming, and not cheap. It was an upscale hotel when it was built back in 1881, but it soon deteriorated into a second-floor flophouse over the local Montgomery Ward. Now it has recaptured and redefined its glory. At ground level are shops and a flowery arcade, plus a wine and coffee bar in the lobby. Upstairs are 18 antiques-filled rooms painted in combinations of subdued tones: burgundy, mauve, chocolate, dark tan, and pale gold. Fourteen of the rooms have private baths, some with old claw-foot tubs. There is a sitting room at the top of the stairs and a TV-equipped solarium overlooking the arcade. A large continental breakfast is included in the price. This is a nonsmoking property.

i

Need help locating accommodations? Call Napa Valley Reservations Unlimited at (800) 251-NAPA or, within the area, at (707) 252-1985 or (707) 944-0709, or visit www.napavalleyreservations .com. Staff will assist you in selecting a hotel, motel, resort, bed-and-breakfast inn, or condo, and they won't charge you a cent.

Calistoga Inn $
1250 Lincoln Avenue, Calistoga
(707) 942-4101
www.calistogainn.com

For a no-frills (OK, maybe a couple of frills), ambience-thick stay in Calistoga, try the Calistoga Inn, an old western-style hotel that dates from 1882. The 18 second-floor rooms, connected by a creaking wood-floored hallway, sit over a restaurant and microbrewery/bar (see the Restaurants and Nightlife chapters). Each room has a sink and a queen or king bed, but there are central, shared bathrooms and showers, and no in-room TVs.

Mount View Hotel $$$$
1457 Lincoln Avenue, Calistoga
(707) 942-6877, (800) 816-6877
www.mountviewhotel.com

This is the closest Calistoga comes to the Ritz-Carlton. The mission revival building, now a National Historic Landmark, was constructed in 1919 and served the area for years as the European Hotel, haunt of literary bigwigs and first ladies. (It is said that Mrs. Herbert Hoover planted the roses in the garden.) An elegant lobby takes you to either the hotel, Mount View Spa, or Stomp Restaurant; all three are run separately and cataloged separately in this book. The hotel has 32 rooms, suites, and cottages, the latter being detached units (with private Jacuzzis) out by the pool. The other rooms are on the second floor, and some have antique furnishings. Continental breakfast is delivered to your room. No smoking is allowed anywhere on this property.

Hotel D'Amici $$$$
1436 Lincoln Avenue, Calistoga
(707) 942-1007
www.hoteldamici.com

If Calistoga had luxury apartment suites, they'd look something like this. Hotel D'Amici is downtown, perched on the second floor of a 1936 building once known as Green Hotel. (The "secret door" is just to the right of the Flatiron Grill entrance.) The hotel has four spacious, well-appointed rooms, two of which share a balcony over Lincoln Avenue, making them coveted spaces during the Fourth of July and its Silverado Parade (see the Festivals and Annual Events chapter). All have private baths and kitchenettes. The owners also run Rutherford Grove Winery. You pick up your keys there (1673 Highway 29 in Rutherford) and get a complimentary wine tasting. You also get a bottle of Rutherford Grove wine in your fridge at the D'Amici.

Comfort Inn $$$
1865 Lincoln Avenue, Calistoga
(707) 942-9400, (800) 228-5150
www.napavalleyus.com
Only in Calistoga would the Comfort Inn have a mineral-water swimming pool and whirlpool tub. It also has a sauna and steam room. Each of the 55 rooms (including a 2-room suite) features individual temperature control, cable TV, coffeemakers, and hair dryers; most are in the functional style Comfort Inn is known for. Continental breakfast is included in the price.

Stevenson Manor Inn $$$$
1830 Lincoln Avenue, Calistoga
(707) 942-1112
www.napavalleyus.com
This motel is affiliated with Best Western. Stevenson Manor has a pool, a sauna, and a gazebo-sheltered central courtyard. The 34 rooms are done in subdued shades of green and burgundy. Four have private whirlpool baths, and seven are warmed by fireplaces; all of them are equipped with refrigerators, microwaves, and coffeemakers. Guests of the inn receive a discount at the nearby Calistoga Village Inn & Spa (see the Spas and Resorts chapter). All rooms are nonsmoking.

SONOMA COUNTY

Southern Sonoma

Ledson Hotel & Harmony Club $$$$$
480 First Street E., Sonoma
(707) 996-9779
www.ledsonhotel.com
This is quite likely Sonoma County's smallest luxury hotel. Opened in 2003 and overlooking the Sonoma Plaza, Ledson Hotel was created by the owners of Ledson Winery (see the Wineries chapter), who know a lot about constructing unique properties. The hotel's six guest rooms are on the second floor; the Harmony Club, offering food, wine, and live music most evenings, is on the first floor.

Each guest room has its own unique personality, and all have king beds, whirlpool tubs, fireplaces, and balconies. Modern amenities include surround-sound TVs and high-speed Internet access.

The Harmony Club, open to both guests and visitors, is an elegant space with marble tables, a fireplace, and a grand piano. French- and Italian-inspired cuisine is served.

El Dorado Hotel $$$$$
405 First Street W., Sonoma
(707) 996-3030, (800) 289-3031
www.hoteleldorado.com
On the northwest corner of Sonoma Plaza, the El Dorado has had a checkered history as a government office, college, winery, and hotel. Salvador Vallejo, brother of Gen. Mariano Vallejo, built the adobe between 1836 and 1846; subsequently, it was occupied by Bear Flag Party members (see the History chapter) as well as Gen. John C. Frémont during the opening days of the Mexican War. Today its 26 rooms have an aura of casual elegance. It's definitely the right choice for those who want to revel in the plaza's historical ambience. Some rooms face the plaza and have balconies that give a view of the city below. Other rooms face onto a garden courtyard and overlook flowers and trees. Continental breakfast is included in the room rate.

El Pueblo Inn $$
896 West Napa Street, Sonoma
(707) 996-3651, (800) 900-8844
www.elpuebloinn.com
Built of adobe brick, this is the classic L-shaped motel of the 1950s. With a large, heated swimming pool, a spa, and a grassy, shaded garden around the 38-room complex, it is an excellent location for either families or couples. Cribs are available, and there's a coffeemaker, hair dryer, and refrigerator in each room, plus cocoa for the kids.

Sonoma Hotel $$$$
110 West Spain Street, Sonoma
(707) 996-2996, (800) 468-6016
www.sonomahotel.com

Situated on the northwest corner of Sonoma Plaza, this fine old hotel was originally a town hall built in the 1880s. Rooms are furnished with antique furniture and one, the Vallejo Room, has a bedroom suite of carved rosewood once owned by Gen. Mariano Vallejo's family (see the History chapter). All rooms are furnished in keeping with the 19th century, and all have been given names to match their decor—Bear Flag room, Yerba Buena, and Italian Suite. In one of the rooms, author/poet/actress Maya Angelou holed up to write her third novel. All 16 rooms have private baths and air-conditioning. Breakfast is served in a quaint foyer that retains the original fireplace and stained-glass windows.

Best Western Sonoma Valley Inn $$$$$
550 Second Street W., Sonoma
(707) 938-9200, (800) 334-5784
www.sonomavalleyinn.com

This hotel was built in 1987, but it has been designed in California mission-style architecture to match the ambience of the town's early Mexican heritage. One of its great assets is its location: It's only two blocks from the city's plaza (see the Shopping chapter), yet away from city hubbub with rooms that face onto an inner courtyard. Most rooms have patios or decks for outdoor privacy. The spacious rooms feature either a fireplace or a Jacuzzi. Open the refrigerator in your room, and you'll find a complimentary bottle of wine. A laundry room is available, and continental breakfast is delivered to your room.

Sheraton Sonoma County Hotel $$$$
745 Baywood Drive, Petaluma
(707) 283-2888
www.sheratonpetaluma.com

Opened in 2002, this marina-front hotel featuring Asian architectural details has 180 guest rooms, including 3 suites. (The grand staircase is a stunner.) The setting is convenient to U.S. Highway 101, yet the hotel offers views of adjacent protected wetlands along the Petaluma River, about 300 acres' worth. The rooms are decorated in earth tones and include state-of-the-art phone systems in addition to the usual amenities you would expect from a Sheraton. Meeting spaces total nearly 10,000 feet, including a 4,300-square-foot grand ballroom. Begin your day in the fitness center, equipped with men's and women's saunas and outdoor swimming pool and spa. End your day dining at Jellyfish Grille, which leans toward a fusion of Asian and Mediterranean cuisine (see the Restaurants chapter).

Quality Inn $$
5100 Montero Way, Petaluma
(707) 664-1155, (800) 221-2222
www.qualityinnpetaluma.com

Built in 1985, the hotel features seven clustered Cape Cod–style buildings nestled amid landscaped grounds and redwood arbors planted with grapes. Its 110 guest rooms include 36 with in-room spas and 4 two-room suites with private spas. The outdoor pool is surrounded by a large sundeck with a sauna adjacent. Its location near Adobe Creek Golf & Country Club and its Robert Trent Jones Jr.–designed course makes it appealing to golfers (see the Golf section of the Parks and Recreation chapter), and shoppers will be glad to know it's the closest inn to Petaluma Village Premium Outlets. A full continental breakfast is served.

DoubleTree Hotel $$$$
1 DoubleTree Drive, Rohnert Park
(707) 584-5466, (800) 222-TREE
www.doubletree.com

Set on 22 acres between two golf courses, the hotel evokes Sonoma County's Spanish heritage with tile roofs and arched windows. For business travelers, the DoubleTree offers every convenience and amenity necessary for meetings and full conferences, including 17,000 square feet of conference space; it's also conveniently located near US 101 and offers express bus service to the San Francisco airport. But those on business will also find, as do great numbers of tourists, that it's a very enjoyable resort, with 245 luxurious guest rooms and suites, a restaurant, a pool and Jacuzzi, and live entertainment.

Hyatt Vineyard Creek Hotel, Spa & Conference Center $$$
170 Railroad Street, Santa Rosa
(707) 528-4542, (888) 920-0008
www.vineyardcreek.com
This hotel in downtown Santa Rosa opened in 2002. The $30 million property with Mediterranean-inspired architecture and courtyards has 155 plush rooms with upscale amenities and the extra touches business travelers appreciate: dual-line speaker phones with voice mail and complimentary domestic and international newspapers. Some rooms have fireplaces and whirlpools; all have deluxe minibars. The Seafood Brasserie is the hotel's fine dining establishment, focusing on French-inspired fresh seafood dishes (see the Restaurants chapter). You can get an in-room massage treatment too. Facials, massages, bodywork, and treatments of many types are offered, including a warmed river-rock massage.

The 21,000-square-foot conference center is the largest in the area, with a multitude of meeting rooms, big and small. All this, and it's a two-minute walk to Railroad Square's restaurants and antiques stores.

Courtyard Santa Rosa by Marriott $$$
175 Railroad Street, Santa Rosa
(707) 573-9000, (800) 354-7672
www.marriott.com
Right on the edge of historic Railroad Square, this Marriott hotel has close access to enough antiques shops to delight any collector looking for bargains or the unusual. All the standard amenities are available in this 138-room inn. Kids will love the swimming pool, spa, and in-room movies, and adults may wander down for

cocktails between 5:00 and 10:00 P.M. or explore any of the interesting restaurants located within walking distance. Kids younger than 12 stay free. There are wheelchair-accessible rooms.

Hotel La Rose $$$$
308 Wilson Street, Santa Rosa
(707) 579-3200, (800) 527-6738
www.hotellarose.com
A quaint and romantic hotel in Santa Rosa's historic Railroad Square, Hotel La Rose was reconstructed in 1985 and designated a National Historic Landmark. The hotel is graced with a charming English country interior decor that belies the fact that this is a very modern hotel. The four-story hotel has elevator access to its 29 nonsmoking rooms, and the carriage house, added in 1985, has 20 additional guest rooms (3 are designated for smokers) built around a lovely courtyard. One of the hotel's great assets is its proximity to the restaurants in Railroad Square, including its own, Josef's. Now under new management, the hotel planned a remodeling of the guest rooms and lobby for 2005.

Flamingo Resort Hotel & Fitness Center $$$
2777 Fourth Street, Santa Rosa
(707) 545-8530, (800) 848-8300
www.flamingoresort.com
Lush landscaping makes this resort hotel very appealing both as a vacation spot and as a business center offering conference facilities for 600 people. This property was extensively freshened up in 2004, with approximately $1 million spent on remodeling and renovations. For the harried executive or the tourist, there's plenty of physical activity available on-site, including a heated pool, Jacuzzi, tennis courts, a lighted jogging path, basketball and volleyball courts, and table tennis. Available for a modest fee is the Montecito Heights Health & Racquet Club. The 170 rooms are luxuriously appointed with elegant furnishings—some rooms also have copy machines and refrigerators. This is a favorite base camp for Hol-

lywood moviemakers when they come to town. In fact, portions of the film *Bandits* were filmed at the Flamingo.

---

i *For a room like no other, book one of the luxurious tent cabins at Safari West, an African-style wildlife preserve located between Santa Rosa and Calistoga. You'll get a king-size bed and private bath, plus the sounds of exotic animals nearby. See the Attractions chapter for more details.*

Fountain Grove Inn $$$$
101 Fountaingrove Parkway, Santa Rosa
(707) 578–6101, (800) 222–6101
www.fountaingroveinn.com
In harmony with the natural environment, the Fountain Grove Inn's design is all redwood and stone, sweeping low across historic Fountaingrove Ranch. The lobby too is far from ordinary, dominated by a large redwood sculpture of the legendary horse Equus. Utmost restraint and understated elegance mark the inn's 125 rooms, which all have separate dressing alcoves, double closets, and work spaces with dataports. The inn's pool, waterfall, and spa offer a view of the historic Round Barn, which sits atop a small nearby hill. Guests gather in the restaurant each morning for a generous buffet breakfast. The inn's restaurant, not surprisingly called Equus, carries out the theme, with the legendary horse etched in glass and redwood carvings.

Hilton Sonoma Wine Country $$$$
3555 Round Barn Boulevard, Santa Rosa
(707) 523–7555, (800) 445–8667
www.hilton.com,
www.nectarsonoma.com
Just off US 101 north of downtown Santa Rosa on 13 acres of Fountaingrove Ranch, this hotel has let stand the historic landmark known as the Round Barn to mark its entrance. New in 2004 was a $6 million makeover of much of the facility. This chalet-style hotel has 246 rooms and

suites and boasts many amenities, including a state-of-the-art in-room phone system, business center, the on-site restaurant called Nectar, an outdoor patio with a panoramic view of the Santa Rosa valley, a Junior Olympic–size swimming pool, and an on-site workout facility.

Vintners Inn $$$$$
4350 Barnes Road, Santa Rosa
(707) 575–7350, (800) 421–2584
www.vintnersinn.com
Your first vision of Vintners Inn may make you feel as if you've dropped into a charming European village. From the French country decor to the arched windows and wrought-iron railings, the hotel exudes old-world atmosphere—a group of three red-roofed buildings is arranged around a plaza and fountain, surrounded by acres of vineyards. Many of the oversize rooms in this Provence-inspired inn have fireplaces, exposed-beam ceilings, and pine furniture, some of which dates from the turn of the 20th century. Ground-floor rooms have patios; second-floor suites have balconies with vineyard or courtyard views. A conference center with a lounge was being added to this property in 2005. On the premises is John Ash & Co., a nationally acclaimed restaurant serving some of the best cuisine in Sonoma County (see the Restaurants chapter).

Northern Sonoma

Hotel Healdsburg $$$$$
25 Matheson Street, Healdsburg
(707) 431–2800, (800) 889–7188
www.hotelhealdsburg.com
The biggest thing to pop up in Healdsburg in quite some time is this three-story, 55-room, $21 million luxury hotel that overlooks the quaint plaza in central Healdsburg. It has proven extremely popular with visitors and made the list of 100 great escapes for 2002 compiled by *Travel & Leisure* magazine.

The rooms all feature oversize bathrooms with walk-in showers and soaking tubs, French doors opening to private balconies, wood floors with Tibetan rugs, bathrobes and fine linens, and the usual modern amenities for business travelers. Even more luxurious suites are available (there are six of them), if that's your pleasure. Room service is offered from the Dry Creek Kitchen (see the Restaurants chapter) and breakfast is delivered to your door. The lobby features a grappa bar, the garden has a 60-foot pool, and there's a cardio-fitness room for a quick workout. All this and a spa too! You can get pampered to your heart's content, from massages to facials to a couples room with a soaking tub for two. Thai massage and healing techniques are a specialty.

Duchamp Hotel $$$$$
421 Foss Street, Healdsburg
(707) 431-1300, (800) 431-9341
www.duchamphotel.com
This contemporary European-style hotel is made up of 10 cottage suites that are all unique, with artist Marcel Duchamp as the inspiration and the namesake. Unlike any lodgings in Wine Country, six of the rooms are poolside and creekside "villas" that are nearly spartan in their luxurious opulence. The four "artist cottages" are named Man Ray, Miró, Picasso, and Andy Warhol. The latter, once a small house, is now a tasteful salute to Warhol's genius and style. All the rooms feature modern amenities, fireplaces, down comforters on king-size beds, and fabulous bathrooms with spa showers (the Warhol room has a sunken Japanese soaking tub too). The complimentary breakfast will start your day off right, and the 50-foot pool and heated Jacuzzi beckon after wine tasting and sightseeing.

Condé Nast Traveller magazine proclaimed the Duchamp as "one of the world's top 25 new hot hotels." It's a great location, down a quiet side road off the main thoroughfare through Healdsburg, yet an easy 2-block walk to the shops and restaurants on the town's plaza. This is a nonsmoking property that is unsuitable for children. English, German, and French are spoken here.

Best Western Dry Creek Inn $$
198 Dry Creek Road, Healdsburg
(707) 433-0300, (800) 222-5784
www.drycreekinn.com
The distinguishing factor here is this motel's outstanding location for wine touring in the beautiful Dry Creek Valley. The 102 rooms (including some "executive minisuites") are pleasant, in the standard motel style. (Sixty additional guest rooms and a new conference room were planned for this property in 2005.) A continental breakfast is included. There's a pool, whirlpool, and exercise room.

Travelodge/Vineyard Valley Inn Motel $$$
178 Dry Creek Road, Healdsburg
(707) 433-0101, (800) 499-0103
www.travelodge.com
Built in 1992, this is not your ordinary Travelodge. The Vineyard Valley Inn Motel has 23 rooms and suites that blend into the Wine Country setting while providing all the modern amenities that seasoned travelers expect. Rooms are furnished with two double beds or one queen. A two-room suite is available with wet bar, refrigerator, and entertainment area.

Geyserville Inn $$$
21714 Geyserville Avenue, Geyserville
(707) 857-4343, (877) 857-4343
www.geyservilleinn.com
Situated at the north end of the town of Geyserville and surrounded by vineyards, the location of this hotel is ideal for visiting Dry Creek and Alexander Valley wineries as well as hitting the bike trails that crisscross this rural countryside. It's also close to Lake Sonoma (see the On the Water chapter). The 38 rooms have a Wine Country feel, decorated in shades of vineyard green and the russet colors of autumn. Rooms are graced with various amenities—for example, patios or balconies and fireplaces—and there is also a

swimming pool and spa. A continental breakfast is served each morning.

Sonoma Coast

Bodega Bay Lodge Resort $$$$$
103 Coast Highway 1, Bodega Bay
(707) 875-3525, (800) 368-2468
www.woodsidehotels.com
Luxurious and intimate on eight land-scaped acres, the lodge overlooks wild-flower-covered dunes, protected marshlands, the Pacific Ocean, and the gentle surf of Doran Beach. While it's close enough to enjoy the sound of the surf, the wood-shingled lodge is sheltered from coastal winds. All 84 spacious guest rooms have fireplaces, private balconies, and original artwork. Many feature vaulted ceilings, spa baths, refrigerators, wet bars, and coffeemakers. The 5,000-square-foot conference center is impressive, with high, arched ceilings supported by thick beams of polished oak. The Duck Club Restaurant can be counted on for imaginative cuisine. Complimentary wine is served in the late afternoon. An 18-hole Robert Trent Jones Jr.–designed golf course is next door at Bodega Harbour Golf Links (see the Parks and Recreation chapter).

Inn at the Tides $$$$
800 Coast Highway 1, Bodega Bay
(707) 875-2751, (800) 541-7788
www.innatthetides.com
Six coastal acres with natural landscaping surround this inn, which is actually an enclave of 12 separate lodges that appear to be part of the rumpled hills and tawny headlands. Each of the 86 guest quarters overlooks Bodega Bay, home port for one of the coast's most productive fishing fleets. Amenities include a heated indoor-outdoor pool, spacious spa, soothing sauna, and luxurious logo bathrobes. A continental breakfast is served, and gourmet cuisine is featured in the Bay View Restaurant (see the Restaurants chapter).

Fort Ross Lodge $$
20705 Coast Highway 1, Jenner
(707) 847-3333
www.fortrosslodge.com
Just north of historic Fort Ross State Historic Park (see the Attractions chapter), the lodge is situated above a sheltered cove where seals lounge on rocky outcroppings. There's plenty of space in the guest rooms to stretch out and relax, or you can unwind in the hot tub and sauna. The 22 rooms are decorated in natural tones and hues. There's a barbecue on each deck and a country store across the highway. Children younger than 12 stay free. Intimate, secluded suites are available for adults only. And the lodge now offers a private two-bedroom home.

Salt Point Lodge $
23255 Coast Highway 1, Timber Cove
(707) 847-3234, (800) 956-3437
www.saltpointlodgebarandgrill.com
This is a well-maintained, older motor lodge, with 16 rooms. Situated on a knoll overlooking the ocean, Salt Point Lodge includes a restaurant with a full bar. Lovely gardens surround the place, and it's open year-round. There are TVs and VCRs in the rooms, but no phones. Besides the nearby beaches, there are miles of hiking trails to explore.

Sea Ranch Lodge $$$$$
60 Sea Walk Drive, Sea Ranch
(707) 785-2371, (800) 732-7262
www.searanchlodge.com
On bluffs above the Pacific, this lodge features one of the best ocean vistas in Wine Country. All but one of its 20 rooms face the sea, and cozy window seats offer front-row viewing for spectacular sunsets. If you're in need of a peaceful getaway, this is the place. Rooms are walled in knotty pine, and the aura is rustic. Hiking trails along the bluffs are well marked, and you can follow them down to the beach. A challenging 18-hole golf course is available, and there's a restaurant. Some units

have fireplaces, and family units are available. All are luxuriously appointed. TVs are missing from most rooms. All rooms are nonsmoking.

West County/ Russian River

Sebastopol Inn $$$$
6751 Sebastopol Avenue, Sebastopol
(707) 829-2500, (800) 653-1083
www.sebastopolinn.com
Conveniently located near downtown Sebastopol's quaint shops and eateries, this inn features comfortable rooms equipped with coffeemakers, microwaves, and hair dryers. On-site is a full-service day spa, a pool and Jacuzzi spa, and a coffeehouse with frequent live entertainment. Fireplace and spa tub suites are also available.

Fife's Guest Ranch $$
16467 Highway 116 E., Guerneville
(707) 869-0656, (800) 734-3371
www.fifes.com
Among the most popular resorts on the Russian River, Fife's features 15 forested acres of towering coast redwood. The resort offers cabins that range from the basic one-room variety to an elegant two-bedroom, two-bath deluxe version with fireplace and hot tub. The restaurant at Fife's includes a fine selection of continental dishes with fresh local vegetables and house-made desserts. The resort is also walking distance to downtown Guerneville, where you can peruse the antiques shops, have coffee at a local cafe, or dance the night away at Club FAB (see the Nightlife chapter).

Brookside Lodge Motel $$
14100 Brookside Lane, Guerneville
(707) 869-2470, (800) 551-1881
www.brooksidelodge.net
A charming family resort located at the edge of Guerneville's Korbel vineyards and

bordered by Fife's Creek, Brookside offers 36 spacious rooms, some with their own patio and kitchen. Amenities include a pool, sauna, table tennis, and satellite TV. The lodge also offers one- and two-bedroom cottages, some of which have a private hot tub and spectacular Wine Country views.

MENDOCINO COUNTY
U.S. Highway 101

Days Inn $
950 North State Street, Ukiah
(707) 462-7584
www.daysinn.com
Yes, it's a chain, but the rooms are spacious and luxuriously decorated; the inn is comfortable and convenient, and the staff is professional. This Days Inn has 54 units, a swimming pool, and a restaurant. It offers free local calls, and pets are welcome. Breakfast is included in the nightly rate.

Discovery Inn $$
1340 North State Street, Ukiah
(707) 462-8873
This is the largest of Ukiah's motels, with 177 units, two heated pools, four indoor spas, a restaurant, and a conference room. A workout room is a recent addition, and guest laundry facilities are available. Complimentary breakfast is included.

Baechtel Creek Inn & Spa $
101 Gregory Lane, Willits
(707) 459-9063, (800) 459-9911
www.baechtelcreekinn.com
An attractive two-story hotel built in 1992, Baechtel Creek Inn has 43 rooms, a heated swimming pool, an on-site spa with a full menu of treatments, and conference rooms. Baechtel Creek runs right past the inn, providing considerable entertainment for kids and grown-ups by attracting such wild creatures as rabbits, squirrels, deer, and an occasional turtle.

Mendocino Coast

Breakers Inn $$$$$
39300 South Coast Highway 1, Gualala
(707) 884–3200, (800) BREAKER
www.breakersinn.com

The 24 oceanfront rooms at the Breakers are designed to offer spectacular panoramic views of the dramatic coast through large picture windows and spacious decks. Enjoy incredible ocean sunsets and the sound of waves crashing on the shore. In winter and spring, the deck provides a front-row seat to the migration of gray whales. Each room is individually decorated in the theme of a country or state in a seacoast region, highlighting locations such as Cape Cod, Ireland, and Japan. All rooms except the three garden rooms feature decks, fireplaces, wet bars, and ocean views, and deluxe continental breakfast is included each morning. The Luxury Spa Room is near a picture window so you can soak and enjoy the view.

Gualala Hotel $
39301 South Coast Highway 1, Gualala
(707) 884–3441, (800) GUALALA
www.thegualalahotel.com

Built in 1903, the Gualala Hotel has weathered a century of Pacific sun and storm. Yet the building's classic facade looks much the same as it did a hundred years ago, when travelers waited on its deck for the coastal stage to arrive. Five of the hotel's 19 rooms boast a beautiful ocean view and private bath—the remaining rooms share hall baths in the European style. Though some of the individual accommodations are a bit cramped, a large central sitting room, complete with sofas and a wood-burning stove, offers plenty of space to snuggle up with a good book or to enjoy a board game. A restaurant and saloon are on the premises—the latter features a mahogany bar where you can sip your favorite vintage or brew while drinking in the local color.

Greenwood Pier Inn $$$
5928 South Coast Highway 1, Elk
(707) 877–9997
www.greenwoodpierinn.com

Perched atop a high bluff overlooking the sea, the Greenwood Pier Inn is a quiet, meditative spot, resplendent in colorful flower gardens. The inn's 12 rooms are located in several architecturally interesting buildings, such as the Cliffhouse, Garden Cottage, and North and South Sea Castles. The latter pair indeed resemble castle towers, and each has a tub in the uppermost level—perfect for soaking your weary bones while scanning the horizon for whales. The Lighthouse Suite in the main house has a cupola that offers an even more lofty perspective on the mighty Pacific beyond. Other inn amenities include fireplaces, private decks, nearby hiking trails along the bluffs, and in-room therapeutic massage.

Albion River Inn $$$$
3790 North Coast Highway 1, Albion
(707) 937–1919, (800) 479–7944
www.albionriverinn.com

Six miles south of Mendocino, Albion River Inn occupies a prime oceanfront spot on 10 secluded acres of gardens and ocean bluffs. Guests are quartered in 20 cliffside, New England–style rooms for two, most in duplex arrangements and all with spectacular ocean views. All have fireplaces and private decks, and many have a spa tub or tub for two. A full breakfast is included in the adjoining restaurant, which shares the view.

Hill House Inn $$$$
10701 Palette Drive, Mendocino
(707) 937–0554, (800) 422–0554
www.hillhouseinn.com

You'd swear you were on the New England coast, because the Hill House Inn captures the essence of the coast of Maine in the spectacular and unspoiled land and sea along California's scenic Highway 1.

Forty-four guest rooms feature brass beds with comforters, lace curtains, elegant wooden furnishings, and the convenience of private baths. Hill House not only attracts vacationers but also caters to seminars and small conferences, with rooms designed to accommodate up to 80 people. A chapel is available for wedding ceremonies.

Stanford Inn by the Sea $$$$$
Coast Highway 1 and Comptche–Ukiah Road, Mendocino
(707) 937-5615, (800) 331-8884
www.stanfordinn.com

This elegantly rustic lodge has so many diversions that guests will find all they need here. A firm believer in preserving the health of our environment, owner Jeff Stanford offers guests bicycles for local transport and a fleet of canoes and kayaks for paddling up Big River. His terraced gardens are tended organically, and he also keeps grazing llamas, horses, and a few cats. Jeff serves vegetarian dishes in the Ravens restaurant, along with organic wines. Hors d'oeuvres are available in the evening, champagne with breakfast.

The site is stunning, sloping from a high meadow down to the sea. And the 33 accommodations have all the amenities expected of the finest hotels—wood-burning fireplaces, down comforters, ocean views, decks, refrigerators, VCRs, and DVD/CD players. Some have kitchens. There's a heated indoor swimming pool and group Jacuzzi/sauna.

Mendocino Hotel $$$$
45080 Main Street, Mendocino
(707) 937-0511, (800) 548-0513
www.mendocinohotel.com

Built in 1878, the venerable Mendocino Hotel is an opulent Victorian jewel named "best small hotel in Northern California" by *Focus* magazine. Guests register at a teller's cage from an old bank and congregate for drinks in a front parlor replete with antiques, leaded windows, and Oriental rugs. The historic section offers suites

with balconies overlooking the Pacific as well as rooms with shared baths in the European style. The garden suites, across the courtyard, are fully modern but still maintain the Victorian decor. Look for lots of solid wood paneling, leaded glass, brass, and walls papered in period fabrics in the 50 rooms in the main hotel and the garden suites. An elegant dining room features California cuisine and an extensive wine list. The Garden Cafe is open in the daytime, as is the Garden Bar. The Lobby Bar operates in the evening. Advance reservations are almost mandatory during the summer months.

Anchor Lodge Motel $
32260 North Harbor Drive, Fort Bragg
(707) 964-4283
www.wharf-restaurant.com

Located in the heart of Noyo Fishing Village, Anchor Lodge has been a focal point for visitors and locals for more than 40 years. You can't get much closer to the water without being in it. There are 18 rooms here, and guests have their pick of four options: economy (two persons), waterfront (two persons), or an apartment with kitchen for two or four persons. All but the economy rooms are nonsmoking.

Harbor Lite Lodge $
120 North Harbor Drive, Fort Bragg
(707) 964-0221, (800) 643-2700
www.harborlitelodge.com

This rustic redwood motel has balconies that overlook Noyo River and its fishing fleet. If you're awake in the early dawn, you can see the lights of the fleet as boats head out for the day's fishing, stretching in a colorful parade out to sea. In late afternoon, the parade reenters the harbor. The lodge has 79 comfortable rooms, some with wood-burning stoves. A meeting center for business or educational conferences has two large rooms accommodating 30 and 50 people, respectively. Complimentary coffee, tea, and cocoa are served in the lobby each morning.

North Cliff Hotel $$$$
1005 South Main Street, Fort Bragg
(707) 962-2500, (866) 962-2550
www.fortbragg.org
This is Fort Bragg's showiest hotel, perched at the entrance to Noyo Harbor. From your private balcony you can watch the fishing boats go out to sea in the morning, and then wave to them when they return at night—it's that close to the waterway. With all rooms facing the ocean, the views are mesmerizing (bring binoculars for scanning the horizon)—even as you take the waters in your private spa tub next to the window. All rooms have fireplaces, minirefrigerators stocked with juice and water, microwaves, and plush bathrobes. A continental breakfast is left at your door each morning. Not all rooms have the spa tubs, but most rooms have king-size beds.

A great place to observe seals is at the mouth of the Russian River in Jenner. If you want to climb down to the beach to get a close-up photo, you must stay at least 100 yards from the animals. Getting too close can result in a fine, so bring a good zoom lens.

Hi-Seas Inn $$
1201 North Main Street, Fort Bragg
(707) 964-5929, (800) 990-7327
www.hiseasinn.com
All 15 of the rooms here have a full ocean view. Just slide back the big glass door that leads to the deck. Between the deck and the ocean is a two-acre lawn. And right behind the inn is a 10-mile hiking trail that goes through Fort Bragg and back into the nearby hills.

Pine Beach Inn & Suites $$
16801 North Coast Highway 1, Fort Bragg
(707) 964-5603
www.pinebeachinn.com
You can walk to a beach and cove from this 50-room hotel, which is on 12 acres of landscaped grounds in a majestic setting of redwoods. The beach is secluded, the private path is paved, and you'll enjoy breathtaking views all the way down to the mighty Pacific, as it thunders in against the high rocks and cliffs. The rooms (nine are suites) are large, decorated with fine furniture, and many of the units have ocean views. If you're in the mood for tennis, championship courts await, offering the chance to lob into the clear blue skies.

Seabird Lodge $$
191 South Street, Fort Bragg
(707) 964-4731, (800) 345-0022
www.seabirdlodge.com
Seabird is an affordable option on the south edge of Fort Bragg, with the village of Mendocino just a short drive south on Highway 1. This motel's 65 rooms feature refrigerators and coffeemakers, and there's a heated pool and whirlpool. Ask about the special package deals to ride the Skunk Train (see the Attractions chapter).

Super 8 $
888 South Main Street, Fort Bragg
(707) 964-4003, (800) 206-9833
www.super8.com
This inn offers affordable accommodations, a convenient location, and old-fashioned hospitality. The 54 rooms have cable TV and private phones, and there is a full-service restaurant on the premises. Staff will be delighted to give a rundown on all the natural wonders to be explored in the vicinity—Mackerricher State Park, for instance, or Glass Beach or Pudding Creek Headlands—as well as family activities available on sea and land.

Vista Manor Lodge $$
1100 North Main Street, Fort Bragg
(707) 964-4776, (800) 821-9498
www.callodging.com
Located at the north end of Fort Bragg, about a mile from downtown, this Best Western motel features 55 units. There's an indoor heated pool, complimentary continental breakfast, and a coffeemaker

in every room. All rooms have ocean views, and a nearby tunnel dips beneath Highway 1, giving you about a five-minute walk to the beach.

VACATION RENTALS

Sonoma County

Russian River Vacation Homes
14080 Mill Street, Guerneville
(707) 869-9030, (800) 310-0804 (in
California), (800) 997-3312
www.riverhomes.com
Since 1975 this firm has provided a large selection of vacation rental homes throughout western Sonoma County at nightly rates ranging from $145 to $450; weekly rates from $550 to $1,600.

Russian River Getaways
14075 Mill Street, Guerneville
(707) 869-4560, (800) 433-6673
www.rrgetaways.com
This friendly rental company would like you to "experience getaway heaven in your very own home away from home." All the homes the company offers are first class, with many choices in size, location, and amenities. Picture yourself in a cozy hideaway for two in the redwoods or rendezvous with your family or friends in a beach house that sleeps 18. Or you might prefer an elegant lodge with a dramatic river view in the wine-tasting region. Many houses are dog-friendly, and there's only a two-night minimum. Prices range from $125 to $750 per night, $600 to $4,500 per week.

Sea Coast Hide-a-Ways
21350 North Coast Highwy 1, Jenner
(707) 847-3278, (800) 937-7546
You have a choice of oceanside vistas or seclusion among the redwoods. Hot tubs and fireplaces are featured, with boat rentals available at Sea Coast's Timber Cove boat landing.

Rams Head Rentals
1000 Annapolis Road, Sea Ranch
(707) 785-2427, (800) 785-3455
www.ramshead.com
More than 120 vacation rentals are offered, from two-night stays to multiple weeks. Sites are available in the meadows, in the forest, or on the oceanfront. The most desirable oceanfront sites offer grand vistas and the dramatic crashing of the waves.

Mendocino County

Coast Getaways
10501 Ford Street, Mendocino
(707) 937-9200, (800) 250-0049
www.coastgetaways.com
If you're looking for a romantic studio for two or a large house that will hold your whole family, this service can match you up with one of more than 30 homes along a 20-mile stretch of the Mendocino County coastline from Albion to Cleone. Choose from oceanfront studios or bungalows nestled in the redwoods, with hot tubs or without—whatever appeals to you. Like the properties themselves, the fees are all over the map.

Mendocino Coast Reservations
1000 Main Street, Mendocino
(707) 937-5033, (800) 262-7801
www.mendocinovacations.com
Here you'll find listings of the finest in weekend and vacation lodging, from cozy cottages to oceanfront estates. Some are right in the village of Mendocino, some on the coast, some in the forest. In July and August a three-day minimum is imposed. Rental fees vary due to weekly or weekend occupancy, time of year, size, and property amenities.

BED-AND-BREAKFAST INNS

There's nothing quite like entering a rambling, antiques-filled home—with a grandfather clock ticktocking in the corner and logs burning in a marble fireplace—to make you turn off the cell phone and lose yourself in a crystal goblet of tawny port. If this doesn't describe your own home life, we understand. In large part, that's probably why you're visiting Wine Country—to capture the serenity of another place and time. It's not only possible here, it's available in abundance. Scores of Wine Country lodgings fit the description above.

If you love bed-and-breakfast inns, you'll find one here to suit your taste, from grand and historic to more modest and modern. Unlike hotels and motels, B&Bs are a throwback to a time when lodgings were small and homespun, offering travelers not just a bed and a basin but a social experience as well. That basic premise still holds here, but the B&Bs themselves and the amenities they offer are nothing like what travelers of yesteryear could have imagined.

In this chapter, a wide range of B&B styles and choices are offered, from easy on the budget to top of the line. Unless you read otherwise, you can expect that the inns listed feature rooms with private bathrooms. Some have gone high-tech, complete with TVs, phones, and Internet access. Afternoon munchies of wine or port and hors d'oeuvres are usually offered. Oh, yes, they serve breakfast—in most cases, a morning meal like you've never seen before. Be aware that nearly all innkeepers prohibit smoking in the rooms and do not allow pets. Many establishments also have a two-night minimum on weekends—always inquire when booking.

What about kids? B&Bs usually do not forbid children, and current California law apparently won't let them make any such prohibition. However, innkeepers acknowledge that many of their guests are attempting to get away from children for a few days. In general, assume that bringing the little ones along is not a good idea.

PRICE CODE

The following price ratings are based on the cost of one night's lodging for double occupancy on a weekend in high season (generally May through October). Most inns offer significant discounts for off-season or midweek stays. Note that prices do not include taxes, gratuities, or services that are considered extra.

$	Less than $130
$$	$131 to $160
$$$	$161 to $200
$$$$	More than $200

NAPA COUNTY

The Blue Violet Mansion $$$$
443 Brown Street, Napa
(707) 253-2583, (800) 959-2583
www.bluevioletmansion.com
Every detail is celebrated with a flourish here, from the in-room port (complimentary) and rack full of wine (pay as you go), to the brass door frame salvaged from the Bank of Italy, to the iron front gate reproduced to match the original. The Queen Anne Victorian home was built in 1886 by Emanuel Manasse, executive at Sawyer Tannery and pioneer of patent leather production. Manasse's trade is evident in a most distinctive feature—embossed leather wainscoting that runs through much of the house.

The Blue Violet Mansion has 17 rooms on three floors. Each of them has a king-size or queen-size bed and a modem jack. Two ground-floor rooms are equipped with Murphy beds, making them ideal for upscale corporate meetings. And upstairs is the Camelot Floor, four rooms painstakingly hand painted in trompe l'oeil fashion. Book the Royal Suite and sip your wine from Arthur and Guinevere silver goblets. On the one-acre grounds you'll find a heated swimming pool, a spa, an herb garden, and roses. Afternoon tea service, by reservation, is also presented on most Sundays throughout the year.

Churchill Manor Bed & Breakfast Inn $$$$
485 Brown Street, Napa
(707) 253-7733, (800) 799-7733
www.churchillmanor.com
In the heart of the Fuller Park Historic District is a grandiose, three-story Second Empire mansion built in 1889 for local banker Edward Churchill. With close to 10,000 square feet of space (and that doesn't include the full basement or the pillar-supported, three-sided veranda), it was said to be the largest domicile in Napa Valley for decades. The interior is essentially unaltered. There are four grand parlor rooms with beveled and leaded glass and redwood moldings and fireplace frames.

Several of the inn's 10 guest rooms underwent major renovations recently, while preserving the historic charm of the property.

You get a full breakfast in the dining room, plus complimentary wine and cheese (and fresh-baked cookies) in the afternoon. Play croquet in the side garden, borrow a tandem bicycle, or just stroll around the acre of grounds and toast the fat wallet of Edward Churchill.

Cedar Gables Inn $$$$
486 Coombs Street, Napa
(707) 224-7969, (800) 309-7969
www.cedargablesinn.com
Chances are you've never seen a house like this one. Designed by British architect Ernest Coxhead in 1892, it's an immense, brown-shingled home that you might expect to find on an estate in England's Cotswolds. In fact, the feeling here is decidedly masculine, making it a logical choice for people who begin whining when they hear the expression "bed-and-breakfast." Cedar Gables' nine guest rooms are sizable and brimming with period antiques. The Churchill Chamber, originally the master bedroom used by Edward and Alice Churchill, has a walnut-encased whirlpool tub to match the fireplace. Several of the rooms have old coal-burning fireplaces, converted to gas. Breakfast is served either at the long, formal dining room table or cafe-style in the adjacent sun room.

Inn on Randolph $$$$
411 Randolph Street, Napa
(707) 257-2886, (800) 670-6886
www.innonrandolph.com
This modest, tasteful inn is on a quiet street in a neighborhood of historic homes. The main house, an 1860 Gothic revival Victorian, has five rooms with seasonal themes (the fifth is called Equinox). Spring, for example, boasts intricate flowers painted on the walls and ceiling, and Autumn features a handcrafted bent-willow canopy bed. Five more expensive rooms are in cottages dating from the 1930s. All of the cottages and some of the main-house rooms have gas fireplaces and two-person whirlpool tubs; some have private decks. Roses line the front walk, and the gardens are flanked by a common deck, a gazebo, and hammocks. The Inn on Randolph serves a full breakfast, and in-room massage can be arranged upon request.

The Beazley House $$$$
1910 First Street, Napa
(707) 257-1649, (800) 559-1649
www.beazleyhouse.com
On a row of rambling turn-of-the-20th-century mansions, this house was originally built for local surgeon and politician Adolph Kahn in 1902, but he and his wife divorced and left the area seven years

later. Subsequent owners included the Hanna Boys Center and San Francisco jet-setter Joan Hitchcock, who reputedly had an affair with JFK and for a fact had seven husbands.

The Beazley, the first B&B in the city of Napa, now has 11 rooms, 6 in the main house and 5 in the carriage house. The latter are large units, each with a fireplace and two-person spa tub. Ask for the Sun Room, a bright and nostalgic corner with a two-sided balcony and a 6-foot soaking tub. Full breakfast is served in the formal dining room. Children are permitted, and pets are assessed on a case-by-case basis.

Beazley House, the first bed-and-breakfast inn in Napa, is still considered the best in that city, based on a local survey conducted in 2004.

Candlelight Inn $$$$
1045 Easum Drive, Napa
(707) 257-3717
www.candlelightinn.com
In the tradition of all good bed-and-breakfast inns, this English Tudor–style mansion with 10 guest rooms will pamper you with four-poster beds, French doors, private balconies, and a three-course breakfast. The Garden View room has a private entrance and deck, with—you guessed it—views of the garden and 30-by-60-foot swimming pool. Other rooms look out on the surrounding hills, and several rooms have Jacuzzi tubs for two and marble fireplaces. All rooms have TVs and phones.

Hennessey House $$$$
1727 Main Street, Napa
(707) 226-3774
www.hennesseyhouse.com
Adjacent to the Jarvis Conservatory on the fringe of Napa's turn-of-the-20th-century downtown, Hennessey House is an Eastlake-style Queen Anne built for Dr. Edwin Hennessey, one-time mayor of the town, in 1889. The 10 rooms (6 in the main residence, 4 in the carriage house) are air-conditioned, and most have canopy, brass, or feather beds. Some have claw-foot or two-person whirlpool tubs in the bathroom, and the carriage-house rooms have fireplaces.

Breakfast has been known to feature delights such as blueberry-stuffed French toast or basil-cheese strata. A hand-painted, stamped-tin ceiling shelters the dining room. In the evening you can enjoy wine and cheese by the garden fountain.

Arbor Guest House $$$$
1436 G Street, Napa
(707) 252-8144, (866) 627-2262
www.arborguesthouse.com
In the Napa neighborhood appropriately known as Old Town, the Arbor Guest House is a pretty, whitewashed colonial with a porch swing in front and a shady garden in back. The house is compact, but the rooms—three units upstairs, two more in the original carriage house—manage to be ample. Two of them have spa tubs, three have fireplaces, and the main-house rooms are cooled by a reliable cross-breeze (and air-conditioning, if the temperature spikes). Breakfast is served in the dining room or the garden or, if you're staying in the carriage house, it is brought to your door with prior notice.

La Belle Epoque $$$$
1386 Calistoga Avenue, Napa
(707) 257-2161, (800) 238-8070
www.labelleepoque.com
In 1893 Napa's leading hardware dealer built this splendid Queen Anne for his infant daughter, who died shortly thereafter. Tragic origins aside, La Belle Epoque beams with class: multigabled dormers, Oriental carpets, divans, marble-topped dressers, and radiant stained glass, much of it transplanted from an old church. There are a total of nine rooms (two are deluxe suites in a property across the street from the main house), which were recently remodeled. You get your full

breakfast in the formal dining room, on the garden patio, or delivered directly to your suite.

The Old World Inn $$$$
1301 Jefferson Street, Napa
(707) 257-0112, (800) 966-6624
www.oldworldinn.com

This 1906 Victorian isn't as noisy as you might think, despite being situated on busy Jefferson Street (where it meets Calistoga Avenue). The inn is touched up in mellow pastel blue, rose, peach, and mint—colors inspired by Swedish artist Carl Larsson— and the interior walls bear hand-lettered quotations, most of which could be filed under the heading "Be Kind to Strangers."

You'll receive a complimentary carafe of local wine upon arrival, evening hors d'oeuvres such as smoked salmon or Moroccan eggplant on sourdough bread, and a late-night buffet of chocolate treats. Of course, you get a full, hot breakfast in the dining room. Some of the 10 guest rooms, all named for artists, have canopied beds; some have claw-foot tubs. Others have fireplaces and private Jacuzzis. There is also an outdoor Jacuzzi shared by all guests.

Brookside Vineyard
Bed & Breakfast $$
3194 Redwood Road, Napa
(707) 944-1661, (707) 252-6690

With seven acres of land, Brookside offers plenty of room for blending with nature. Tom and Susan Ridley's homey spot is full of images and relics true to the house's mission style. The three ground-floor guest rooms are off a long hallway, and each opens onto the garden. About half the acreage is devoted to vineyard, and visitors have been known to join the autumn crush. Elsewhere, fruit trees, California poppies, and Douglas fir trees abound, and a path descends to a creek-side clearing. (At least it's creekside when Redwood Creek is flowing.) Brookside has a swimming pool, and the largest bed-

room has a dry sauna. The Ridleys accept personal checks but no credit cards.

La Résidence $$$$
4066 Howard Lane, Napa
(707) 253-0337, (800) 253-9203
www.laresidence.com

Is La Résidence a hotel disguised as a bed-and-breakfast inn or a B&B masquerading as a hotel? Does it matter when you're sitting in the elegant, sun-infused dining room at a table for two, eating a three-course breakfast from the fixed but ever-changing menu? La Res, as it is called, is a nice surprise within shouting distance of Highway 29. The 16 rooms and 4 suites, divided between the 1870 Gothic revival mansion and the newer French Barn, are decorated in French provincial style. Most include working fireplaces and patios or verandas. The inn sits on two and a half acres of heritage oaks, pines, and fledgling vines. There is a swimming pool, a separate Jacuzzi, and a small meeting room for up to 15 people.

Oak Knoll Inn $$$$
2200 East Oak Knoll Avenue, Napa
(707) 255-2200
www.oakknollinn.com

The land around Oak Knoll Inn is part of Napa County's agricultural preserve, but businesses such as this were allowed to operate before the zoning regulations changed. It has a virtual monopoly on 360-degree vineyard views. There is a big wooden deck outside the rooms, so you can spend all day looking at the grapes and the mountains. Oak Knoll Inn has four units, each with a fireplace and private entrance. There is a heated pool and spa for common use. The place is known for its breakfasts; on a typical day the morning meal may include baked pears in cognac sauce, baked herbed eggs, and fresh muffins. But mostly the inn is renowned for the detailed itineraries that owner Barbara Passino customizes for guests. This is not a good option for couples with young children.

Maison Fleurie $$$$
6529 Yount Street, Yountville
(707) 944-2056, (800) 788-0369
www.foursisters.com
In the middle of Yountville (but a block away from most of the traffic) is this French-style country inn. The 100-year-old main building has 2-foot-thick stone walls, terra-cotta tile, and a gas fireplace in the brick parlor. Two other structures—the Old Bakery (a working bakery in the 1970s) and the carriage house—bring the total number of rooms to 13. You get a gourmet breakfast (or breakfast in bed if you'd rather) and a jar of homemade cookies in the lobby. There is a swimming pool, spa tub, and mountain bikes for guest use. Maison Fleurie is part of Four Sisters Inns, a group of nine bed-and-breakfast establishments, most of them on the California coast.

---

i

California's gold rush brought an influx of new residents to the state, and with them came a variety of eastern U.S. architectural styles. For example, many of San Francisco's new Victorian homes were constructed in the Italianate style. An exceptional example can be found in St. Helena's Ink House, built in 1884.

Bordeaux House $$$
6600 Washington Street, Yountville
(707) 944-2855, (800) 677-6370
www.bordeauxhouse.com
A mixture of new (1980) and old (1895) structures, this inn is a bit of a bargain for this neck of the woods. In the heart of Yountville, it is surrounded by lovely trees and gardens, and the world-class restaurants and shops of the whole town are within easy walking distance. (The French Laundry is just steps away, in fact.) The inn's newer, main building has five guest rooms with fireplaces and private patios or decks. Modern amenities are provided in each room; all have private exterior entrances. The Old Water Tower, overlooking the garden, is about 15 steps up and

down. The inn's reception area is where you can enjoy your morning buffet breakfast and late afternoon port and munchies.

Burgundy House Inn $$$
6711 Washington Street, Yountville
(707) 944-0889
www.burgundyhouse.com
Yountville's main drag may not be the place you'd expect to find an old-world country inn, but Burgundy House has the requisites. It's a durable cube with 22-inch-thick walls, hand-hewn posts and lintels, and lace curtains. Built as a brandy distillery in the 1890s from local fieldstone and river rock, it has also been a winery, a hotel, an antiques warehouse, and, now, a six-room inn. Buffet breakfast is served in the "distillery" or outside on the rose garden patio. Children older than 12 are welcomed.

The Ink House $$$$
1575 St. Helena Highway S., St. Helena
(707) 963-3890, (800) 553-4343
www.inkhouse.com
This remarkable house is a wedding-cake Italianate Victorian with a wraparound porch and a third-floor crow's nest. Built by Theron H. Ink in 1884, it's now a seven-room bed-and-breakfast inn where the highway meets Whitehall Lane. The Ink House has a formal parlor and dining room for guests. You get a full breakfast in the morning, appetizers and wine, usually poured by a local winery, in the afternoon.

The rooms are lovely but not huge—five have private baths; two share a bath. The observatory serves as the TV room. While taking advantage of the 360-degree panorama, you might pop in a video of *Wild in the Country,* an Elvis Presley romp filmed at the Ink House in 1960. The inn also offers 18-speed bicycles and an antique pool table in the basement. A steep staircase makes this an unsuitable choice for families with kids.

Shady Oaks Country Inn $$$$
399 Zinfandel Lane, St. Helena
(707) 963-1190
www.shadyoaksinn.com

The buildings are full of history at Shady Oaks, but it's the two acres of outdoor space that really sell the inn. On one side of the house is a working walnut orchard; on the other are grapevines. And in back, a twisted 100-year-old wisteria vine protects the patio. Shady Oaks offers two suites (each with private entrance) in a two-story, stone structure that operated as a winery from 1883 to 1887. Three more rooms are found inside the 1920s Craftsman-style home. Each unit features its own small collection of antiques; particularly lovely are the beds, such as the brass and ivory king in the Winery Retreat. Three of the rooms have fireplaces, and the Sunny Retreat has an adjoining second bedroom.

Afternoon wine is served on the patio. Champagne breakfast, meanwhile, is a splendid affair likely to entail eggs Benedict or Belgian waffles served in elegant style.

Glass Mountain Inn $$$$
3100 Silverado Trail, St. Helena
(707) 968-9400, (877) 968-9400
www.glassmountaininn.com
Glass Mountain was named for its large deposits of obsidian, or black glass. That obsidian is evident in the dining room of the Glass Mountain Inn, where guests can peer into a wine cave dug by Chinese laborers (originally for perishables, not Pinots) in the late 1800s. The house, with its wood shingles and steepled roof, isn't nearly as old as the cave. The inn has three large rooms with private baths, each room with individual strengths—the queen-size bed in the Mountain View Suite is framed by five arched windows; the Garden Suite has an oversize oval whirlpool tub; and the Treetops Suite has a claw-foot tub and a private deck. Guests are greeted with a full breakfast each morning. Bring the children; they are welcome.

The Ambrose Bierce House $$$$
1515 Main Street, St. Helena
(707) 963-3003
www.ambrosebiercehouse.com
Ambrose Bierce was a novelist, a poet, an essayist, a cartoonist, and a noted misanthrope. He wrote *The Devil's Dictionary* before disappearing in Mexico in 1913. The 1872 Victorian home he left behind in St. Helena bears his name and offers visitors three lovely rooms and a covered balcony tucked next to a grand redwood tree. The Ambrose Bierce Suite, secluded on the second floor, has a private sitting room (with a television) that can be converted into a second bedroom. All rooms have plush, raised beds; stools are provided to help you make your way up under the covers.

A full champagne breakfast is served in the morning, premium wine and cheese in the evening. Each guest room is equipped with a crystal decanter of port. Relax to classical music in the parlor, or soak in the home's hot tub. Parents, please note that children are not recommended here.

Forest Manor $$$$
415 Cold Springs Road, Angwin
(707) 965-3538, (800) 788-0364
www.forestmanorbandb.com
Six miles into the forest above St. Helena is this magnificent property with 20 acres of wooded trails and a huge 54-foot swimming pool. The six rooms are named for writers; the two honeymoon suites are the William Shakespeare and the Ernest Hemingway. All of the rooms have refrigerators and robes, and most have king-size beds, fireplaces, and Jacuzzis. A full gourmet breakfast is included in the tariff.

Scarlett's Country Inn $$$
3918 Silverado Trail, Calistoga
(707) 942-6669
www.members.aol.com/scarletts
A "country inn" can sometimes mean a suburban cul-de-sac and a large rose garden. But Scarlett's is the real thing, a bucolic acre midway between Calistoga and St. Helena, where guests share space with friendly dogs and chickens. The early-20th-century farmhouse now holds two of the three guest units—the Gamay Suite and the Camellia Suite, which actually can be opened into a full house for larger parties. Each room boasts a sepa-

rate entrance, a queen-size bed, a TV, a microwave, and a fridge. But the outdoor space is the big selling point here: a hammock, a tree swing, an aviary with finches and canaries, a lush fig tree, a pine-protected swimming pool, and a spa. Note that Scarlett's does not accept credit cards, though personal checks are all right. Full breakfast is served.

Christopher's Inn $$$$
1010 Foothill Boulevard, Calistoga
(707) 942-5755, (866) 876-5755
www.christophersinn.com
This inn was crafted by an architect who combined a house with two cottages to make one large building. It's nice enough from the outside, but that doesn't hint at the luxury held within the 22 rooms. Laura Ashley prints, exquisite antique desks, fresh flowers, and high, open ceilings—it's a tasteful experience. Some rooms have private Jacuzzis. Breakfast—yogurt, baked cobbler, etc.—is delivered to your door. For those who must conduct a bit of business while relaxing in splendor, modem ports are available in most rooms.

Christopher's also has two voluminous flats in back, facing onto Myrtle Street, that sleep as many as five people. Children are allowed at the inn.

Calistoga Wine Way Inn $$$
1019 Foothill Boulevard, Calistoga
(707) 942-0680, (800) 572-0679
www.winewayinn.com
This bed-and-breakfast inn, opened in 1979, was the first in Calistoga. It's near Calistoga's busiest intersection, and the owners want you to know up front that there is some street noise. Nonetheless, from the solid oak front door with etched glass to the patchwork quilts in each second-story room, the owners have managed to create a pleasant environment in their circa-1915 home. In addition to the five interior rooms, the Calistoga Room is a detached unit—it's out by the multi-tiered deck that backs up to a wooded hillside. The breakfasts alternate daily

between sweet and savory, with specialties such as frittata and tomato omelets.

The Elms $$$$
1300 Cedar Street, Calistoga
(707) 942-9476, (888) 399-ELMS
www.theelms.com
A. C. Palmer, the first circuit judge of Napa and Sonoma Counties, went to France for his honeymoon sometime around 1870, and he and his bride returned to Calistoga with two important items: designs for a new home and a small number of elm seedlings. The house lives as the Elms, shaded by the now-towering trees. Without a doubt, it is one of the most impressive homes in the valley. Palmer ran a lumberyard just across the Napa River, and the Elms is full of richly detailed, hand-hewn wood. It's also brimming with antiques.

The inn has four rooms in the main house. Two of them face Cedar Street, while another gazes upon pretty Pioneer Park. At the rear of the property are three rooms in the refurbished carriage house, including the Honeymoon Cottage, a large unit with a two-person shower and views to the river. Five of the rooms have fireplaces, and all seven come with a TV, plus port and chocolate. The Elms is not a good choice for those with children.

La Chaumiere $$$$
1301 Cedar Street, Calistoga
(707) 942-5139, (800) 474-6800
www.lachaumiere.com
La Chaumiere is a small, picturesque house with a pitched roof and an arched window that looks across the street to Pioneer Park. There are two well-appointed rooms in the house (one has a sitting room in addition to the bedroom), plus a detached cabin in the rear. The bathrooms are part of the attraction—one has antique lavender and black tile work, the other has a mirror framed by an old billiards cue rack.

The log cabin, built in 1932, isn't exactly the kind Abe Lincoln grew up in. The whole-timber redwood uprights and cross-beams are complemented by touches of comfort, including a woodstove, a fireplace built of petrified wood, and a large kitchen. The outdoor common areas include a flowery patio and a treehouse built around the trunk of a redwood. You get a full breakfast in the morning, plus wine and cheese in the afternoon and port in your room. La Chaumiere is just a block off Lincoln Avenue.

Chelsea Garden Inn $$$
1443 Second Street, Calistoga
(707) 942-0948, (800) 942-1515
www.chelseagardeninn.com
This small, six-suite bed-and-breakfast on the corner of Fair Way and Second Street tries for neither Victorian splendor nor designer finery. Each unit has a sitting room, bedroom, and private bath; some have kitchen facilities. Air-conditioning is provided in all rooms. There is a latticed courtyard, pool, and hot tub. A full breakfast is served.

Hideaway Cottages $$$
1412 Fair Way, Calistoga
(707) 942-4108
www.hideawaycottages.com
If you want a classic bed-and-breakfast experience without the breakfast, try this establishment on peaceful Fair Way. Look for the hedges and palm trees in front of a two-story gingerbread house. In back are 17 cottages facing onto a landscaped courtyard. Many of the rooms have full kitchens. Hideaway, an affiliate of Dr. Wilkinson's Hot Springs (see the Spas and Resorts chapter), has a large mineral pool and spa tub. No children under 18, please.

Brannan Cottage Inn $$$$
109 Wapoo Avenue, Calistoga
(707) 942-4200
www.brannancottageinn.com
About 130 years ago, this spot had row upon row of one-story white bungalows, all with five-arch fronts, intricate gingerbread gable boards, wraparound porches, and scalloped cresting. Now only one of them remains on its original site, and it's a

The last of the so-called Great Eight mansions built in Calistoga in the 1870s is now the Elms B&B, a Queen Anne Victorian Second Empire listed on the National Register of Historic Places.

six-room inn. (Two of the rooms are out back in the carriage house.) The look of the place—the 11-foot ceilings, oak floors, and ceiling fans—whisks you right back to the days of Sam Brannan (see the History chapter). Each unit has a queen bed and a refrigerator. Full buffet breakfast is served in the dining room or on the patio. Children 12 and older are accepted.

Cottage Grove Inn $$$$
1711 Lincoln Avenue, Calistoga
(707) 942-8400, (800) 799-2284
www.cottagegrove.com
This location was once the promenade area of Brannan's Hot Springs Resort, the spa that gave birth to Calistoga (see the History chapter). The grove of Siberian elms was planted by Brannan in the 1850s, and today they form an effective visual barrier to the traffic of Lincoln Avenue.

Each of Cottage Grove's 16 private cottages has a wood-burning fireplace (and a basket of wood on the porch), a CD stereo system, TV and VCR, air conditioner, private bath with two-person Jacuzzi tub, Egyptian cotton towels, and an ironing board. Each has a theme too, like the Music Cottage, the Audubon Cottage, and the Fly Fishing Cottage. Continental breakfast and evening wine and appetizers are served in the common room. The owners allow children age 12 and older. Smoking is not allowed.

Culver Mansion $$$
1805 Foothill Boulevard, Calistoga
(707) 942-4535, (877) 281-3671
www.culvermansion.com
Proprietor Jacqueline LeVesque has done a magnificent job of renovating this circa-1875 Victorian mansion to make it homey and inviting. The six guest rooms are

If you want a bed-and-breakfast experience without the legwork, here's a helpful agency to call. B&B Style covers our entire four-county area—reach it at (800) 995-8884 or (707) 942-2888.

nicely furnished with comfortable McRoskey mattresses, handmade in San Francisco, and as Jacqueline explains it, "the choice of the Queen of England for a wonderful night's sleep!" There's a private pool, spa, and sauna out back, and a full breakfast is included in the tariff. The resident feline will make you feel right at home while you enjoy the sweeping views from the old-fashioned veranda. Children 16 and older are welcome.

Calistoga Wayside Inn $$$
**1523 Foothill Boulevard, Calistoga
(707) 942-0645, (800) 845-3632
www.calistogawaysideinn.com**
This split-level, Spanish-style home, built in the 1920s, is more like something you would expect to see in an older Los Angeles neighborhood, but it seems right at home in Napa Valley. The living room has rough beams and a wood fireplace. The backyard is densely shaded by trees—a dogwood, English walnut, loquat, and at least a dozen others. The three guest rooms are comfortably furnished and cooled by ceiling fans. One of them, the Camellia Room, has sole use of the home's original master bathroom.

The Pink Mansion $$$$
**1415 Foothill Boulevard, Calistoga
(707) 942-0558, (800) 238-7465
www.pinkmansion.com**
Alma Simic was a colorful character. She was the previous owner and longest resident to live in this stately home, and she had eclectic tastes in decorating, with a mixture of Victorian and Oriental influences. Fortunately for visitors, the current owners have made certain that Alma's sense of style remains intact. The six guest rooms are elegant and tasteful, and most have views. The Master Suite and Honeymoon Suites are large—900 and 800 square feet, respectively—and feature king-size beds, two-person Jacuzzis, and private decks and sitting rooms. There's also an indoor heated pool and spa. By the way, the mansion has been pink since the 1930s.

Bear Flag Inn $$$$
**2653 Foothill Boulevard, Calistoga
(707) 942-5534, (800) 670-2860
www.bearflaginn.com**
Just northwest of the intersection of Highway 128 and Petrified Forest Road, this five-room bed-and-breakfast is a renovated farmhouse built in the 1930s. Purportedly it was on this very site that Peter Storm constructed one of the flags used for the Bear Flag Revolt in 1846. The Bear Flag Inn sits on three acres, surrounded by vineyard and meadowed hillside. Four rooms are in the two-story house; the cottage is a detached unit with a sitting room. All guest rooms have private baths, queen-size beds, robes, cable TV and VCRs, and air-conditioning. There is a swimming pool and an outdoor hot tub for guests. A full breakfast is served, with wine and appetizers in the afternoon.

Foothill House $$$$
**3037 Foothill Boulevard, Calistoga
(707) 942-6933, (800) 942-6933
www.foothillhouse.com**
One of Calistoga's most renowned B&Bs sits in a woodsy setting on the northwest outskirts of town. Fountains and cascades lend a soothing air, and views to Mount St. Helena help to keep you oriented as you sit in the arbor or Jacuzzi. Each room includes TV and VCR, CD player, refrigerator, and fireplace or woodstove. Three of the four have whirlpool tubs. Each has its strengths, but the Quails Roost, a detached cottage just up the hillside, is clearly the palatial unit. Quiet and private, the Quails Roost has a full kitchen and a washer/dryer setup; guests have been known to rent it for a week and go into

hiding. (If you are bringing children, please book the Foothill Cottage.) Doris, trained as a chef, oversees breakfast and the afternoon "wine appreciation hour."

SONOMA COUNTY
Southern Sonoma

The Cottage Inn and Spa   **$$**
302 First Street E., Sonoma
(707) 996-0719, (800) 944-1490
www.cottageinnandspa.com
Located on a quiet street a block off the plaza, the Cottage invites visitors into its courtyards, which include fountains and a seating area. A nearby six-person hot tub is available to all guests. Five of the seven rooms open onto the courtyards, five have their own private outdoor spaces, and five include fireplaces. The studio room has a cathedral ceiling.

Thistle Dew Inn   **$$$**
171 West Spain Street, Sonoma
(707) 938-2909, (800) 382-7895
www.thistledew.com
This is a prime location for Wine Country visitors. Just a half block off the Sonoma Plaza, the Thistle Dew puts guests within walking distance (or biking distance, if you want to borrow from the inn's stable) of fine restaurants, shops, wineries, and historic sites. The six guest rooms manage to provide a feeling of seclusion and privacy in spite of the fact that the inn is on a busy street on the edge of downtown. Breakfast is served in the dining room looking out on Spain Street. All rooms have private baths, and some have whirlpool baths.

Victorian Garden Inn   **$$**
316 East Napa Street, Sonoma
(707) 996-5339, (800) 543-5339
www.victoriangardeninn.com
It's a farmhouse built in 1870, but it's only blocks from the downtown plaza. The wraparound porch with wicker chairs

harks back to a simpler time. But it's the gardens that make this inn unique. Lawns and paths wind through the trees and along the creek, with occasional spots to sit and contemplate.

The four guest rooms—one in the main house and the rest in a century-old water tower—have private baths and are elegantly decorated. Woodcutter's Cottage is a private retreat with a fireplace, claw-foot tub, and garden view. Breakfast is served in the dining room, on the patio, or in your room. The inn now offers professional massage services in your room or on the patio.

Trojan Horse Inn   **$$**
19455 Highway 12, Sonoma
(707) 996-2430, (800) 899-1925
www.trojanhorseinn.com
This is a charming B&B decorated with English and French antiques. Each of its six rooms has a different theme, decorated individually. Especially popular is the room called Grape Arbor, boasting a fireplace and double Jacuzzi, but all rooms are furnished with antiques of the 1880s, when the original house was built. Children older than 12 are welcome with advance notice. A full breakfast is served along the lines of French toast or banana pancakes, lemon chicken sausage, fresh fruit, and gourmet coffee. Join other guests for complimentary wine and hors d'oeuvres between 6:00 and 7:00 P.M.

Above the Clouds   **$$$$**
3250 Trinity Road, Glen Ellen
(707) 996-7371, (800) 736-7894
www.abovethecloudsbb.com
The mountain road called Oakville Grade (up Trinity Road on the Sonoma side) straddles the Mayacmas Mountains that rise between the Sonoma and Napa Valleys. Trinity Road sprouts from Highway 12 about 8 miles north of the Sonoma Plaza and winds through thickets of manzanita and scrub oaks for 3 miles before reaching Above the Clouds bed-and-breakfast inn. When the fog rolls through the Sonoma Valley, this inn lives up to its name. It's a

secluded mountain retreat that surveys forests and catches the sunset. Three guest rooms are furnished with antique iron or brass beds, and each has a private bath, queen-size bed, down comforters, and lots of pillows. Robes are provided for those who want to take advantage of the swimming pool and Jacuzzi spa. A gourmet breakfast is served.

Beltane Ranch $$$
11775 Highway 12, Glen Ellen
(707) 996-6501
www.beltaneranch.com
The place has an exotic—even romantic—past. The land was first settled in 1882 by Mary Ann "Mammy" Pleasant, whose exploits as a madam to San Francisco's upper crust (plus suspicions of a possible homicide in her posh establishment) led to alarming headlines. It was said she conducted black magic sessions too. But Mammy had another side: She became known as the western terminus of the Underground Railroad, making frequent trips to the South to secretly help thousands of blacks escape to Canada.

Beltane Ranch's architectural style suggests Deep South, with a stylish veranda set off with an elaborate gingerbread railing. But the ranch's recent past is more mundane. In the 1920s it was the bunkhouse for a turkey ranch. Inside are six guest rooms (and one cottage), each with an individual outdoor entrance. The rooms are rustic but cozy, furnished with antiques. The 1,600 acres include a working vineyard, and the owner is happy to tour the grounds with you and explain what viticulture is all about.

This is a popular lodging place, and reservations are definitely recommended during the harvest season of August through October.

Gaige House Inn $$$$
13540 Arnold Drive, Glen Ellen
(707) 935-0237, (800) 935-0237
www.gaige.com
An elegant Italianate Victorian, restored from its original 1880s construction, Gaige

House Inn has a prime location at the edge of the village of Glen Ellen in the heart of Wine Country. It has six guest rooms and one suite in the main house and eight garden rooms with outside entrances. The signature room is the Gaige Suite, a spacious sunny room with large windows on three sides and a wraparound deck overlooking the garden.

New in 2005 are eight fabulous spa suites in contemporary Asian designs. Each of these suites has its own private garden, sliding glass walls, and a large granite soaking tub for the ultimate in relaxation.

The Kenwood Carriage House is one of four off-site cottages available for rent. It's a one-bedroom, second-floor accommodation with use of a private estate's swimming pool. Long stays are encouraged. The creekside setting includes a large swimming pool and Jacuzzi. A formal breakfast is included, as are afternoon hors d'oeuvres and beverages.

Glenelly Inn $$$
5131 Warm Springs Road, Glen Ellen
(707) 996-6720
www.glenelly.com
This is one of the few Wine Country bed-and-breakfast inns that was actually built as an inn. Visitors of the 1920s and '30s came by railroad and basked in the sun on the inn's long verandas. Each of the eight rooms has a private entrance and is furnished in a country motif, with antique furniture and down comforters. The Jack London Room has a sleigh bed and wood-burning stove, and all rooms have clawfoot tubs and antique sinks. An outdoor spa is set amid native landscaping. In the morning, a full breakfast is served by a large cobblestone fireplace in the common room. Children younger than 12 stay free.

The Gables Inn $$$
4257 Petaluma Hill Road, Santa Rosa
(707) 585-7777, (800) 422-5376
www.thegablesinn.com
Built in 1877 at the height of Victorian Gothic revival architecture, this home was

built with 15 gables rising above some unique keyhole-shaped windows. There are seven rooms in the main house, five up a mahogany staircase, and two accessible to disabled guests, some of which include fireplaces, and all of which share central air-conditioning. Each room is furnished in unique decor that displays its history and character; each has a claw-foot tub in its private bath. An adjacent cottage is furnished with a kitchenette, TV with video library, stereo, woodstove, two-person whirlpool tub, and private phone/data port. A lavish country breakfast is served.

Melitta Station Inn $
5850 Melita Road, Santa Rosa
(707) 538-7712, (800) 504-3099
www.melittastationinn.com
Once this was a busy railroad station; before that it was a general store and post office. Today it's a warm inn with six guest rooms (five if the two-room suite is occupied) furnished with antiques and folk art. The inn's former life is evident in its unique plank flooring and hand-sawed fir boards with the sawyer's strokes still well marked. The style here is American antique, with lots of collectibles to admire. The setting is part of the charm: The inn is surrounded by state parks, hiking trails, and biking opportunities. A full buffet breakfast is served by the wood-burning stove in the large sitting room on the balcony.

Pygmalion House $
331 Orange Street, Santa Rosa
(707) 526-3407
www.bedandbreakfast.com
Built in 1880 down near Railroad Square, where Santa Rosa had its beginnings, this Queen Anne home has been restored to a bed-and-breakfast inn of five rooms, all with private baths featuring showers and claw-foot tubs. It's furnished with pieces that include Gypsy Rose Lee antiques and memorabilia. Decorated in the European style, the parlor has a fireplace, TV, and telephone. There's a private garden and parking behind the inn. A hearty breakfast and afternoon treats are served.

Northern Sonoma

Belle de Jour Inn $$$$
16276 Healdsburg Avenue, Healdsburg
(707) 431-9777
www.belledejourinn.com
This inn's hilltop setting is on six acres and looks out on rolling hills. The farmhouse, a single-story Italianate built around 1873, is the residence of the innkeepers, and it is here guests enjoy a hearty breakfast. Guests are quartered in five white cottages, all with fireplaces and some with decks. Each cottage is its own country experience. The Caretaker's Suite, for instance, has a king-size canopy bed and a fireplace in the sitting room. There's a sunny studio atelier room with a high, vaulted ceiling, and the grand Carriage House has everything, including views and a tub for two.

Camellia Inn $$$
211 North Street, Healdsburg
(707) 433-8182, (800) 727-8182
www.camelliainn.com
From November to May the inn is overtaken by blooming camellias, hence the name. Built in 1869, the house served at one time as Healdsburg's first hospital, and in fact the room you rent might have been the lab. As a plus, the Camellia Inn is just two blocks from historic Healdsburg Plaza and its chic shops and restaurants. When you return to your room from your excursions, you might recuperate from the rigors of shopping in your whirlpool tub for two, light up the gas fireplace if you're chilly, and have a lovely night's sleep in your four-poster bed. The Camellia Inn includes a family suite—unusual in an industry largely geared toward couples.

Breakfast is served buffet style, with a selection of entrees and breads that will keep up your energy until noon (maybe later).

George Alexander House $$$
423 Matheson Street, Healdsburg
(707) 433-1358, (800) 310-1358
www.georgealexanderhouse.com
This historic house was built in 1905 by

George Alexander, the 10th child of Cyrus Alexander. Cyrus was the first settler in the north county, and Alexander Valley is named for him (see the History chapter). There are four rooms in this lovely inn. The Alexander room has a fireplace and bay windows, while the Back Porch has a private entrance with a deck, whirlpool tub for two, and wood-burning stove. If you're hungry for a hearty breakfast, you'll be happy to see such menu items as ricotta pancakes with sautéed apples. Two spacious parlors are available to guests, as is the sauna in the garden. Stay two nights (a minimum on weekends) and get a bottle of wine.

Grape Leaf Inn $$
539 Johnson Street, Healdsburg
(707) 433-8140
www.grapeleafinn.com

Pssst! Don't look now, but there's a secret room behind that bookcase in the corner. Yes, this inn takes the B&B experience a step further with a hidden speakeasy just for guests. A gentle push on the bookcase and it swings open to reveal a secret wine cellar and gathering spot. Here you will find many local small-production wines available for tasting, sometimes poured by the winemakers themselves. Elsewhere around the 1900 Queen Anne Victorian are 12 guest rooms ranging from masculine to feminine—there's a room for just about any taste. Some feature fireplaces and spa tubs. Expect a full gourmet breakfast that might include Grand Marnier croissant French toast with mango-papaya salsa. Another plus: The inn is just a five-minute walk from the town plaza.

---

i

The Grape Leaf Inn in Healdsburg has a special "speakeasy" hidden behind a bookcase. Each evening, guests at the inn are treated to a generous pouring of Sonoma County wines in the secret hideaway.

Haydon Street Inn $$
321 Haydon Street, Healdsburg
(707) 433-5228, (800) 528-3703
www.haydon.com

In a quiet residential area within walking distance of Healdsburg's historic plaza, this Victorian inn has nine charming guest rooms. One of the most popular is the Turret Room, tucked into the slope of the roof, with a step-down entrance to the sleeping level. Each of the other rooms is distinctively different in decor, from iron bedsteads and handmade rugs to French antique furnishings. Six of the guest rooms are in the main house, a 1912 Queen Anne structure, and three are in the adjoining two-story Victorian cottage. All rooms have private baths; those in the cottage also have double whirlpool tubs.

Healdsburg Inn on the Plaza $$$$
110 Matheson Street, Healdsburg
(707) 433-6991, (800) 431-8663
www.healdsburginn.com

The front entrance is unpretentious enough, but it opens onto a handsome art gallery. Once a Wells Fargo building, the inn now rates high on the luxury scale. A staircase leads to the 10 antiques-filled rooms—most with fireplaces, all with private baths, in-room phones, and TVs, and some with whirlpool tubs for two. A solarium in the roof garden is the common area where guests meet for breakfast and afternoon refreshments, when wine and fresh buttered popcorn, coffee, tea, and a bottomless cookie jar are offered. A carriage house—complete with a kitchenette—is available for rent.

Honor Mansion $$$
14891 Grove Street, Healdsburg
(707) 433-4277, (800) 554-4667
www.honormansion.com

The architecture, decor, and surrounding gardens give this inn a feeling of turn-of-the-20th-century grace. You can almost imagine women in ankle-length frocks carrying on polite conversation with gentlemen in tennis sweaters as they stroll along the garden path. The property includes a full-size croquet court, boccie ball courts, a swimming pool, and a koi pond. Its 11 guest rooms and suites are furnished with antiques and feather beds, and each has a private bath. Expect a breakfast of home-baked pastries and gourmet entrees. Spa services have been added to make your visit more enjoyable.

Madrona Manor $$$$
1001 Westside Road, Healdsburg
(707) 433-4231, (800) 258-4003
www.madronamanor.com
Tucked away in the lush Dry Creek Valley, Madrona Manor is an estate for which adjectives like *elegant* and *majestic* were invented. Originally built in 1880 by business tycoon John Paxton, Madrona Knoll Rancho, as it was then called, became one of the grandest showplaces in all the valley. Today it stands as a wonderful exponent of a bygone era of grandeur and refined taste. The manor's accommodations include 21 rooms in four buildings on eight acres of wooded and manicured grounds. Eighteen of the rooms have fireplaces, and eight have a balcony or deck. A buffet-style breakfast is included. Need more elegance? World-class gourmet dining can be enjoyed each evening in a romantic candlelight setting (see the Restaurants chapter). This is a no-TV environment.

Midnight Sun Inn $$
428 Haydon Street, Healdsburg
(707) 433-1718
www.midnight-sun.com
Somewhat different from many bed-and-breakfast inns, Midnight Sun is decorated in a modern country style, with almost no antique decor. The linens are top of the line, as are the beds and mattresses. There are three guest rooms in the main house: Juliet's Balcony invites a second-story stroll across the entire front of the house. Inside, there's a canopy bed to stretch out in. The other two rooms are the Enchanted Garden Room and the Provence Room.

There's also a cottage in the backyard; it has a Wine Country theme and is said to be the most romantic room of all. Both the Garden Room and Juliet's Balcony have Jacuzzis for two.

The Raford House $$$
10630 Wohler Road, Healdsburg
(707) 887-9573, (800) 887-9503
www.rafordhouse.com
Here's a Victorian inn with an expansive porch ideal for sipping wine. The Raford House sits on a knoll surrounded by vineyards and palm trees, and the view from the porch is worth the price. The structure dates from the 1880s and is listed as a Sonoma County historical landmark. The six affordable guest rooms are furnished with queen-size beds, and each has a private bath. A hearty breakfast is dished up every morning. The rooms are all non-smoking, but puffing is allowed on the porch and in the gardens.

Villa Messina $$$
316 Burgundy Road, Healdsburg
(707) 433-6655
www.villamessina.com
The setting is unbelievable, with a 360-degree view of three exquisite valleys— Alexander, Dry Creek, and Russian River. The Italian villa-style inn was built in 1986 on top of the foundation of a former water tower. The inn's five guest rooms are furnished with antiques, and the floors are carpeted with Oriental rugs. All rooms have private baths, plus TVs, VCRs, and phones. Some have Jacuzzis or fireplaces. For breakfast the chef prepares such treats as fresh-squeezed orange juice and blueberry pancakes with bacon. There is a swimming pool and hot tub.

Hope-Bosworth House $$
21238 Geyserville Avenue, Geyserville
(707) 857-3356, (800) 825-4233
www.hope-inns.com
Driving down Geyserville Avenue, you'll have no trouble recognizing the Hope-Bosworth House—it's the Queen Anne

with the picket fence covered with "roses of yesteryear" varieties that were popular when the house was built in 1904.

All four of the guest rooms are a step into the past. The original oak-grained woodwork is evident everywhere, from the sliding doors in the hallway to the upstairs bedrooms. Polished fir floors and antique light fixtures enhance the period furnishings. A country breakfast is served in the formal dining room and includes fresh fruit, egg dishes, homemade breads and pastries, and coffee or tea.

Hope-Merrill House $$$
21253 Geyserville Avenue, Geyserville
(707) 857-3356, (800) 825-4233
www.hope-inns.com
In its former life, it was a stagecoach stop of the 1870s. Now it's an enchanting inn, listed on the Sonoma County landmarks register. Anyone interested in architecture will recognize the squared-off look of Eastlake Stick style, popular between 1870 and 1885. J. P. Merrill, who was a land developer, saw to it that he had the best of everything for his house, and he built it entirely of redwood. The inn has eight rooms, all with queen-size beds and private baths. Four rooms have fireplaces, two have whirlpool baths, and one has a sitting room. There's also a swimming pool. Breakfast is superb, served in the dining room.

Old Crocker Inn $$$$
1126 Old Crocker Inn Road, Cloverdale
(707) 894-4000, (800) 716-2007
www.oldcrockerinn.com
Dripping with history, this fine old Victorian was recently converted into a comfortable B&B with rooms in the main house and several outdoor cottages. Set on five acres southeast of the town of Cloverdale, the inn was once the home of railroad tycoon Charles Crocker of the Central Pacific Railroad, who used the property as his summer hunting grounds. He occasionally brought along other railroad barons to enjoy a bit of the sport, as well as President Ulysses S. Grant. From the main house are wonderful views of the Russian River, vineyards, and

surrounding hills. Each lodge room has a door that opens onto the main deck and another that opens to reveal the atrium-covered swimming pool. The rooms are equipped with private baths, gas fireplaces, ceiling fans, DVD/VCRs, and high-speed Internet access.

Vintage Towers Inn $$
302 North Main Street, Cloverdale
(707) 894-4535, (888) 886-9377
www.vintagetowers.com
Mining executive Simon Pinchower had an unusual idea when he asked an architect to design a Queen Anne house in 1901. He wanted three towers, all built in different shapes—one round, one square, and one octagonal—so his house would be different from its neighbors.

Pinchower is long gone, but his legacy has given travelers a fine way to spot the seven-guest room Vintage Towers Inn. Each of the three tower suites has its own sitting area, sleeping quarters, and private bath. Three of the other rooms have private baths, and two share a conveniently located bath. The wide front veranda's porch swing is a pleasant place to relax after a day of touring the countryside. A hearty breakfast can be expected.

West County/ Russian River

The Inn at Occidental $$$$
3657 Church Street, Occidental
(707) 874-1047, (800) 522-6324
www.innatoccidental.com
This is the type of romantic getaway where you can be together surrounded by the forested hills of western Sonoma County. Each of the 16 rooms is decorated with meticulous care. All rooms have a private bath, one room has wheelchair access, and all but one have fireplaces and decks. Several units have double spa tubs and views of the courtyard, and a two-bedroom guesthouse is also available. For eye-popping yellow walls, ask for the

Cirque de Sonoma room. A full breakfast is included.

The Farmhouse Inn & Restaurant $$
7871 River Road, Forestville
(707) 887-3300, (800) 464-6642
www.farmhouseinn.com
In 1878 it really was a working farm, with a row of cottages off to the side for the workers. Now it's a country inn by the side of the road, and the workers' cottages have become charming private guest rooms with amenities the original occupants never dreamed could exist. All the rooms have jetted spa tubs, CD players, TV/VCRs, personal saunas, refrigerators, fireplaces, feather beds, luxurious linens, and European-style rain showerheads. Full concierge services are offered, as well as on-site massage and facials, which can be enjoyed poolside. (Farmhouse Inn was honored by *Travel & Leisure* magazine in its top-30 great inns list.)

The inn also features three-day culinary adventures for guests. These excursions provide an up close and personal look into wine making, a chance to pick your own vegetables for your evening meal, or visits to artisan cheese makers, oyster farms, and more.

In addition, there's an events center on-site, where business affairs and weddings can be held. The facility and gardens can accommodate 300 guests.

Ridenhour Inn $$
12850 River Road, Guerneville
(707) 887-1033
www.ridenhourinn.com
Louis Ridenhour came to this land in 1850 and began farming 940 acres along the Russian River. This house, however, was not built until 1906. What guests find today is a large living room overlooking redwoods, and eight guest rooms, each with a private bath. One of them, Hawthorne Cottage, has a fireplace and cozy window seat. New owners have significantly upgraded and redecorated the rooms. Korbel Champagne Cellars is within walking distance (see the Wineries

chapter), and the Russian River is five minutes away by foot. Breakfast is ample.

Applewood Inn & Restaurant $$$
13555 Highway 116, Guerneville
(707) 869-9093, (800) 555-8509
www.applewoodinn.com
Nineteen stylish rooms and suites fill three multistory Mediterranean-style villas set among apple orchards and redwood trees. Each is individually decorated, romantic, and formal, yet familiar—like the home of a wealthy great-aunt you may have visited. The newer rooms have fireplaces, sitting areas, private verandas or decks, and either couples showers or spa tubs for two. The common area is centered around a huge stone fireplace. The restaurant seats 50 (see the Restaurants chapter). The kitchen, once reserved for breakfast, now offers dinner Tuesday to Saturday. A full breakfast is served.

Fern Grove Cottages $
16650 Highway 116, Guerneville
(707) 869-8105
www.ferngrove.com
A small, quaint village of 22 romantic cottages, Fern Grove provides a stylish country atmosphere and a base for exploring the back roads of the neighborhood. Cottages range from spacious one-bedroom suites to intimate guest rooms with sitting areas. All have a refrigerator; some have fireplaces, spas, or TVs. Stroll the gardens, swim in the pool, feel romantic in general! The buffet breakfast features homemade pastries. The shops of downtown Guerneville are within walking distance.

MENDOCINO COUNTY

U.S. Highway 101 and Nearby

Hopland Inn, a California Roadhouse $$
13401 South US 101, Hopland
(707) 744-1890, (800) 266-1891
www.hoplandinn.com

In 2002 this historic 21-room hotel—like those you've seen in a hundred western movies—underwent a complete makeover, including a name change. No longer encumbered with velvet drapes and heavy furnishings, the former Thatcher Inn is now awash in sunlight, repainted and decorated with a lighter touch. Without taking away from the inn's colorful role in Mendocino County history, the new owners lovingly spruced up the old Victorian, which is listed on the National Register of Historic Places. The restaurant menu was upgraded as well, incorporating lighter California cuisine alongside traditional steak-and-potato entrees. Continental breakfast is served to hotel guests.

Valley Oaks Inn at Fetzer $$
13601 Old River Road, Hopland
(707) 744-1250, (800) 846-8637
www.fetzer.com
Located in the Fetzer Vineyards complex of tasting room and organic gardens is a charming 10-room bed-and-breakfast inn, housed in the ranch's original carriage house. Each room is beautifully appointed and features panoramic views of the surrounding vineyards (or organic gardens) from a private patio. The interiors are country casual, with overstuffed chairs pulled up to large coffee tables in the sitting rooms. All guests enjoy continental breakfast and access to a secluded pool. Two master suites have whirlpool tubs in their oversize bathrooms, separate bedrooms, large sitting rooms, and small kitchens. (For more on the Fetzer complex, see the Wineries chapter.)

Anderson Creek Inn $$
12050 Anderson Valley Way, Boonville
(707) 895-3091, (800) 552-6202
www.andersoncreekinn.com
This inn is a rambling ranch house set on 16 acres at the junction of two creeks, with views of the hills beyond. Each of its spacious and spotless five rooms offers a different view and feeling, and each has a private bath, king-size bed, and complimentary bottle of local wine. Two rooms have fireplaces, and one has a Franklin stove. The friendly family livestock includes llamas, sheep, horses, and a goat. Come in March and see the newborn lambs! Breakfast is a special event and is served in the courtyard, weather permitting.

Mendocino Coast

Whale Watch Inn $$$$
35100 North Highway 1, Anchor Bay
(707) 884-3667, (800) 942-5342
www.whale-watch.com
Whales swim by this stylish inn, perched on a cliff's edge 5 miles north of Gualala. This charming complex of five buildings is set on two acres of woods and gardens. There are 18 rooms and suites, most with whirlpool tubs and all with fireplaces, private decks, and awesome views of the rocky coast. The inn's decor slants toward contemporary rather than traditional, elegant instead of woodsy. Romance is the calling card here, so be prepared for some serious creature comforts. Breakfast is hearty: fresh seasonal fruits, freshly baked pastries, and an entree that changes daily, all delivered to your private deck.

Wharf Master's Inn $$
785 Port Road, Point Arena
(707) 882-3171, (800) 932-4031
www.wharfmasters.com
When Point Arena bustled with sailors hauling lumber and fish to supply California's gold rush, the wharf master had only to step onto his porch to make sure all was proceeding in an orderly fashion in the harbor below. The view is much more peaceful these days. The Victorian, built in 1865, and several newer buildings together form the Wharf Master's Inn, an accommodation that is hard to pigeonhole. All of the 23 rooms have feather beds, private baths, and TVs, and most have fireplaces and spa tubs. A continental breakfast is served.

Glendeven $$$
8205 North Highway 1, Little River
(707) 937-0083, (800) 822-4536
www.glendeven.com
Named for a Scottish grand estate, Glendeven consists of 10 rooms in three separate buildings, one containing an art gallery. The gallery is a showplace for 10 local artists and craftspeople. The central building was a farmhouse from 1867 until the late 1930s. The mood is of casual elegance. It's light and spacious, and all rooms have private baths and most have fireplaces. Wine and hors d'oeuvres are served by the fireplace in the sitting room, to the tinkling music of the baby grand. Breakfast is generous and will be delivered to your room should the fancy strike.

Auberge Mendocino Inn
& Cottages $$
8200 North Highway 1, Little River
(707) 937-0088, (800) 347-9252
www.aubergemendocino.com
This inn borders 2,500-acre Van Damme State Park and its wooded hills sloping toward the sea (see the Parks and Recreation chapter). The inn is surrounded by informal gardens and century-old cypress trees. Cliffs overlooking the ocean are just a stroll away. A lane behind the inn leads to the beach. Each of the nine rooms and two cottages is tastefully appointed but different from the rest. The morning meal is also unique.

Seafoam Lodge $$
6751 North Highway 1, Little River
(707) 937-1827, (800) 606-1827
www.seafoamlodge.com
The lodge has eight separate buildings offering 24 guest accommodations and a conference center. Guests can look forward to panoramic ocean views and breathtaking sunsets from every private room. Some rooms have kitchens, some have fireplaces, and all have VCRs and refrigerators. Two spas let you enjoy the outdoor space. The Crows Nest Conference Center, with its magnificent ocean view, will accommodate up to 50 guests—

perfect for business meetings, seminars, family reunions, and wedding receptions. A continental breakfast is delivered to your room each morning. Pets and children are welcome.

Stevenswood Lodge $$
8211 North Highway 1, Little River
(707) 937-2810, (800) 421-2810
www.stevenswood.com
There could scarcely be a more enchanting setting than the one this lodge enjoys, surrounded on three sides by 2,500 acres of Van Damme State Park forest. Leave your room and it's a short walk to the ocean, Fern Canyon, and the headlands. The mood here is decidedly upscale, with nine one-bedroom suites and one guest room (with wheelchair access) that overlooks the gardens. All the room options have beckoning views, cozy wood-burning fireplaces, spacious private baths, and stocked honor bars. Breakfast is a gourmet delight to remember, and there is an on-site restaurant.

Dennen's Victorian Farmhouse $$
7001 North Highway 1, Little River
(707) 937-0697, (800) 264-4723
www.victorianfarmhouse.com
How charming is this bluff-top house south of Mendocino? Your heart could definitely end up here, on a two-acre parcel bordered by a creek on the south. Dennen's Victorian Farmhouse does not have an ocean view; however, Buckhorn Cove—a public beach that feels quite private—is a five-minute walk. There are four rooms in the old structure and six more split between two separate buildings. Seven of the units have fireplaces; two have double spa tubs. A full breakfast is served in-room, and co-owner Jo Bradley will cater to your dietary needs, adding to an overall feeling of attentive comfort.

Elk Cove Inn $$$$
6300 South Highway 1, Elk
(707) 877-3321, (800) 275-2967
www.elkcoveinn.com
Secluded high atop a bluff overlooking nearly a mile of coastline, the Elk Cove Inn

captures the essence of peace and tranquillity. Built in 1883 as an executive guesthouse for a lumber company, this beachfront retreat offers the quintessential "room with a view." Massive windows bring dramatic, panoramic views and the unspoiled beauty of the outdoors to each of the 15 large accommodations (seven rooms, four cottages, and four luxury suites). A trail leads down to the beach, and an outdoor hot tub leads to tranquillity. A multicourse gourmet breakfast is served daily in the oceanfront dining room.

Harbor House Inn $$$$
5600 South Highway 1, Elk
(707) 877-3203, (800) 720-7474
www.theharborhouseinn.com

The main building of this inn was built in 1916 by the Goodyear Redwood Lumber Company as an executive residence and for the lodging and entertainment of company guests. Situated on a bluff overlooking Greenwood Landing, Harbor House is a sanctuary for relaxation and privacy that is reminiscent of a leisurely, romantic era.

The guest rooms at this intimate inn have been refurbished, some with a masculine feel. Rooms in the main building and adjacent cottages are individually heated and have private baths. A sumptuous breakfast and four-course dinner are included in the price. Products are all from local sources. In addition to home-grown vegetables, the cuisine includes naturally raised meats and cheeses from nearby farms.

Sandpiper House Inn $$$
5520 South Highway 1, Elk
(707) 877-3587, (800) 894-9016
www.sandpiperhouse.com

In 1916 when the house was built, Elk was a bustling harbor, where schooners loaded with redwood set sail for the San Francisco market. The gray, shingled inn is decidedly unpretentious, though it was then one of the finest homes in town. Coffered ceilings and raised panel walls typify the craftsmanship of the era. Its five rooms are tastefully appointed in the style of a European country inn, decorated with antiques, comfy chairs, fresh flowers, and down comforters. All have private baths. Look forward to breakfast served on a lace tablecloth that's brightened with a bouquet of fresh flowers.

Fensalden Inn $$$
33810 Navarro Ridge Road, Albion
(707) 937-4042, (800) 959-3850
www.fensalden.com

Once a Wells Fargo stagecoach way station, Fensalden rests on 20 tree-lined, pastoral acres on a majestic ridge crest. At this 400-foot elevation, the ocean and meadow views are spectacular. The inn's eight rooms are divided among the main house, the water tower house, and a separate bungalow, with three common rooms in the main building. One is a guests' office, one a parlor, and the third the Tavern Room, a namesake common for way stations in the raucous Old West lifestyle. (Check out the bullet holes that pock the original ceiling.) In the evening, wine and hors d'oeuvres are served in this room, while guests view the sunset over the Pacific. In the morning, a gourmet breakfast is served there.

Brewery Gulch Inn $$$$
9401 Coast Highway 1, Mendocino
(707) 937-4752, (800) 578-4454
www.brewerygulchinn.com

The owner of this inn, Arky Ciancutti, bought the 10-acre property in 1977, then a few years later turned the original farmhouse into a small B&B. When he learned that a huge amount of virgin-growth redwood, cut a century earlier, had been discovered deeply buried in silt nearby, he found his inspiration to build a new inn. This "guiltless" redwood, mineralized by time, encompasses the major building blocks of this structure, crafted from 100,000 board feet of the nearly petrified redwood. The property was once home to a successful dairy and a brewery—hence the name. Now the gardens dominate the scenery, with thousands of blooming flower bulbs around ponds and streams, and a two-acre woodland garden with more than 600 rhododendrons and a thousand delicate ferns.

The 10 luxurious guest rooms feature ocean views, leather club chairs, fireplaces, phones, CD players, and TVs. Some have Jacuzzi tubs for two as well as private decks. A gourmet breakfast is served (try the caramelized banana and praline pecan pancakes), and an evening wine hour is offered at the special tasting bar. There's also a library with a large selection of books and CDs and a telescope and binoculars for gazing at the stars or watching for whales. This non-smoking property is aimed at couples seeking quiet romance.

Agate Cove Inn $$$
11201 North Lansing Street, Mendocino
(707) 937-0551, (800) 527-3111
www.agatecoveinn.com
Agate Cove Inn was built as a farmhouse in 1860, and for the past few decades it was a comfortably funky inn with spectacular views. With breakfast cooked on an antique wood-burning stove, its current incarnation still feels like a farmhouse. The views are still breathtaking too. Many of the eight cottages and two farmhouse units feature oversize tubs and showers for two, fireplaces, and huge beds with down comforters. Hearty breakfasts are served with an unobstructed floor-to-ceiling view of the headlands and the waves crashing against the rocks.

Blair House Inn $$
45110 Little Lake Street, Mendocino
(707) 937-1800, (800) 699-9296
www.blairhouse.com
This is perhaps the best-known home in Mendocino, because millions of people have seen it by watching the TV show *Murder, She Wrote*. The show's producers used the exterior of Blair House as Jessica's Cabot Cove home. The house was built in 1888; the extensive use of virgin, clear-heart redwood, now prohibitively expensive, is probably what has kept the house so well preserved. Four guest

rooms are equipped with plush queen-size beds and handcrafted quilts. Angela's Suite is a two-room suite with 10-foot ceilings and bay windows that offer a view of both the village and ocean. Three other guest rooms share a large bathroom in the hall. Blair Cottage is the one-time carriage house on the property, with a kitchenette that makes it convenient for families. Pets are also allowed in this unit. Breakfast is served on-site. Two-night minimum on weekends.

Inn at Schoolhouse Creek $$
7051 North Highway 1, Mendocino
(707) 937-5525, (800) 731-5525
www.schoolhousecreek.com
The amenity guests appreciate most about this coastal inn is its eight surrounding acres of outdoor space, replete with tall cypress trees and an open meadow. The east end of the property leads to Schoolhouse Creek itself, and for beachgoers Buckhorn Cove is a short walk to the south. The inn offers 15 accommodations—nine freestanding cottages, two suites, and four units in a small lodge. Some have ocean views. In every room you will find a TV/VCR, CD player, and phone. Families are welcome, and dogs are allowed in some rooms. The inn has a hot tub on the property, situated at the top of the meadow and with a sweeping ocean view.

John Dougherty House $$$$
571 Ukiah Street, Mendocino
(707) 937-5266, (800) 486-2104
www.jdhouse.com
Historic John Dougherty House, built in 1867, is one of the oldest houses in Mendocino. The main house is furnished with country antiques of the 1860s. Two guest rooms are in the main house, six more are in the adjoining cottages or historic water tower. The Captain's Room has a private veranda. The First Mate's Room has hand-stenciled walls and antique pine furniture. Some rooms have four-poster beds and village views (two boast spectacular vistas); most have a small refrigerator and a

wood-burning stove; four feature jet tubs. Breakfast is served by a crackling fire in the New England–style keeping room.

Joshua Grindle Inn $$
44800 Little Lake Road, Mendocino
(707) 937–4143, (800) 474–6353
www.joshgrin.com
Situated on two acres, this lovely home was built in 1879 by Joshua Grindle, who came from Maine to enter the booming lumber business and stayed on to become the town banker. The house features unmistakably New England–style architecture, and the decor of the inn is a reflection of the same early-American heritage. There are five rooms in the main house, two in the cottage, and three in the water tower. Some have views of Mendocino and the ocean; others have wood-burning fireplaces. All have well-lighted, comfortably arranged sitting areas and private baths. (A two-bedroom oceanfront home is also available off-site for rental.) Breakfast is a time to enjoy a delicious morning meal as well as conversation with other guests around the circa-1830 pine harvest table. The inn has received many honors, including *Focus* magazine's Inn of the Year award.

MacCallum House Inn $$$
45020 Albion Street, Mendocino
(707) 937–0289, (800) 609–0492
www.maccallumhouse.com
Close your eyes and think of dramatic ocean views, sleigh beds, soaking tubs, and breakfasts prepared with organic ingredients. That describes the amenities at MacCallum House Inn, a two-acre property consisting of the main Victorian house (with six guest rooms) and seven cottages scattered around it. All rooms are fitted with TV/DVD players, CD stereos, telephones, and dataports. In addition, the original barn on the property has been converted to six rooms with ocean views and river-stone fireplaces. The extras here are impressive: Massage and spa services can be arranged, pets are allowed in some rooms, and children are welcome. There are concierge services, bicycles for borrowing, and a complimentary afternoon wine hour. (Nearby is a two-bedroom, two-bath vacation rental as well as a luxury home perched on a hillside overlooking the ocean, ideal for a honeymoon retreat or family reunion.) When you're ready to enjoy fine cuisine, step into the inn's restaurant (see the Restaurants chapter), or have an after-dinner drink in the Grey Whale Bar. All of Mendocino's fine shops and attractions are within strolling distance of MacCallum House Inn.

Sea Gull Inn $
44960 Albion Street, Mendocino
(707) 937–5204, (888) 937–5204
www.seagullbb.com
Built in 1878, one of Mendocino's oldest standing houses is also one of its oldest continuous inns. The Sea Gull began welcoming tourists in the 1960s. It has nine rooms, some of which offer hints of ocean blue from the windows. All have private bathrooms, though the unit known as the Shed does not have bathing facilities. Two rooms accommodate children. One of those is the Barn, a funky, self-contained structure with a private deck and a secondary sleeping loft. This is the only unit with a television. Continental breakfast might include offerings from the Mendocino Cookie Company.

Sea Rock Inn $$
11101 North Lansing Street, Mendocino
(707) 937–0926, (800) 906–0926
www.searock.com
Every guest room here has an ocean vista, on a continuum that ranges from "peek" to "spectacular." And the grounds include benches perched atop the bluffs for watching the crashing waves and barking sea lions far below. The Sea Rock comprises six private cottages, four deluxe suites, and four rooms in the refurbished Stratton House. Each unit is equipped with private bathroom, queen-size bed, cable TV, VCR, telephone, hardwood furniture, fine linens, and down

pillows. Many have feather beds and/or Franklin fireplaces. Some have whirlpool tubs, and two rooms have an ocean view from the tub. The Sea Rock Inn is about a half mile north of Mendocino.

Whitegate Inn $$$$
499 Howard Street, Mendocino
(707) 937-4892, (800) 531-7282
www.whitegateinn.com

The framework for this bed-and-breakfast inn is an elegant house dating from 1883. A cobblestone path bordered with primroses leads to a terrace and gazebo. Restored in splendid style, the house is furnished with a collection of French, Italian, and Victorian antiques. Award-winning gourmet breakfasts are served on bone china and sterling silver and include such offerings as caramel-apple French toast or eggs Florentine. Seven lovely bedrooms with private baths provide comforts from fireplaces to cable television. Guests receive a welcome basket and are invited to a wine and cheese serving at 5:00 P.M. If you need a larger place to stay, a four-bedroom, three-bath home is available for rental.

Annie's Jughandle Beach Inn $$
Gibney Lane and Highway 1, Fort Bragg
(707) 964-1415, (800) 964-9957
www.jughandle.com

This five-room Victorian-style inn built in 1883 sits midway between Mendocino and Fort Bragg. Guests enjoy private baths, spa tubs, fireplaces, and, in some rooms, ocean views. The place overlooks the Jughandle State Preserve, and footpaths lead down to the ocean. There's access to plenty of hiking trails nearby, and in the springtime visitors can watch the whales right from the inn during breakfast—and all through the day.

Country Inn at Fort Bragg $
632 North Main Street, Fort Bragg
(707) 964-3737, (800) 831-5327
www.beourguests.com

Inside this 1890s residence, innkeepers Bruce and Cynthia Knauss's intention is to transport you back to "the carefree turn-of-the-20th-century." The sloping ceilings, decorative wallpaper, and inviting fireplaces are part of the journey. Each of the eight rooms has its own theme, such as Granny's Attic, with its clothing niche, walnut wainscoting framed by redwood molding, and old-fashioned bathtub. The Country Inn is a short walk from the beach and features a full breakfast, free newspaper, and afternoon wine and cheese. Baked eggs on a bed of artichoke hearts might be one of the breakfast offerings during your stay.

The Grey Whale Inn $$
615 North Main Street, Fort Bragg
(707) 964-0640, (800) 382-7244
www.greywhaleinn.com

The first bed-and-breakfast in Fort Bragg, the Grey Whale has gathered a coterie of longtime admirers who come back time after time for the ambience and cozy comforts of its spacious guest rooms. Thirteen rooms on the first and second floors offer various amenities—some have gas log fireplaces, some have views of the coastline, some are in French country style, and one has an antique sleigh bed. Two rooms in the penthouse have private sundecks; one has a double-size Jacuzzi. All rooms have private baths. The recreation room has a pool table and VCR. Breakfast is lavish.

Lodge at Noyo River $$
500 Casa Del Noyo, Fort Bragg
(707) 964-8045, (800) 628-1126
www.noyolodge.com

The lodge overlooks Noyo Harbor, and suites are particularly spacious, with a solarium-style parlor and bedrooms with king-size or queen-size beds, window seats, and plenty of fluffy pillows scattered about. Most rooms have fireplaces. There are seven guest rooms and suites in the main lodge (one is said to be haunted!) and nine in an adjoining modern building. All rooms have private baths, down comforters, and first-class bathroom amenities. In the evening you can watch pink sunsets over the Noyo bridge, then wake up in the morning to the far-off barking of harbor seals. A sumptuous breakfast is served in the wood-paneled dining room.

Old Stewart House Inn $
511 Stewart Street, Fort Bragg
(707) 961–0775, (800) 287–8392
www.oldstewarthouseinn.com
Old Stewart House is Fort Bragg's oldest, a pre-Victorian erected in 1876. The proprietors bill it as the perfect spot for fami-

lies or honeymooners. A third-story deck overlooks the ocean. All six of Old Stewart House's rooms have a European flair. The most formal, the Queen Anne Room, has a gas fireplace and a bathroom with a big soaking tub. (There's a Jacuzzi tub room below the main house.) An outside cottage has a Greek theme. The carriage house is more of a family unit, with bunk beds for the kids, a minikitchen, and a separate room for mom and dad. A two-night minimum is required on weekends.

SPAS AND RESORTS

Enjoy playing in the mud? In addition to premium wine grapes, the region known as Wine Country has unlimited quantities of rich volcanic ash just below the surface, thanks to prehistoric eruptions of our resident inactive volcano, Mount St. Helena (pronounced Hel-LAY-nah). The ash and the hot water that naturally percolates way down in the Earth's strata constitute the main ingredients of our legendary mud baths that attract visitors by the thousands.

Some of the nation's finest and famous full-service resort spas are here—heavyweights such as Auberge du Soleil and the Fairmont Sonoma Mission Inn—and most of them revolve around mud, steam, massaging fingers, and the like. There is variety, however. Silverado Country Club & Resort pampers with world-class spa services and provides a world-class golf course; Little River Inn on the Mendocino coastline has a front-row seat to the Pacific Ocean.

Many of the facilities listed offer amenities and services above and beyond a standard lodging—places that will rub you, wrap you, soak you, feed you, and give you a bed in which to drop your newly detoxified body. Nearly all of these properties accept credit cards, welcome children but not pets, and prohibit smoking. Always ask about specifics before booking.

Don't be intimidated by all those dollar signs in these listings. You can still get exceptional spa services at the more affordable facilities in this list—or contact one of the day spas listed at the end of this chapter to arrange for a few hours of pampering.

PRICE CODE

The following price ratings are based on double occupancy on a weekend night in high season (generally May through October). Most spas and resorts offer discounts for off-season or midweek visits. The tariff usually includes use of facilities such as tennis courts and gyms, but you will pay separately for spa services. The prices do not include taxes and tips.

$	Less than $150
$$	$151 to $200
$$$	$201 to $250
$$$$	More than $250

RESORTS

Napa County

The Carneros Inn $$$$
4048 Sonoma Highway, Napa
(707) 299-4900
www.thecarnerosinn.com
What happens when you take a 27-acre former trailer park and spend $57 million toward its transformation into a world-class spa resort? You get the Carneros Inn, Napa Valley's latest—and probably last—getaway destination of its kind to be built here. The property is southwest of the city of Napa by a few miles in the Carneros grape-growing appellation and is surrounded by vineyard landscapes and sprinkled with fruit orchards and flower gardens. Many celebrities have already partaken of this inn's rural luxuries, and you can too.

Each of the 96 guest cottages has its own private patio and garden space, accessed through French doors. The cottages provide all the comforts of home—and then some: wood-burning fireplaces, cherrywood floors, spacious bathrooms with heated slate floors (and a choice between showering inside or outside), high-speed Internet access (even on your porch and patio), flat-panel TVs, DVD players, and more. The cottages range in size from 975 to 1,800 square feet of private indoor and outside living space.

Spa treatments borrow from the natural rural setting and incorporate mixtures of herbs, fruits, and flowers. Take the Huichica Creek Bath treatment overlooking the creek of the same name, where your weary muscles will be soothed by jets of warm water. There's also boccie and croquet when you're ready for some spirited competition, and full concierge services when you wish to investigate the area's many attractions.

The inn's restaurant, for guests only, is located in the Hilltop reception building. Meals can be delivered to your cottage for private dining. A more casual eatery and wine bar, Boon Fly Cafe, is open to the public.

Champagne is both fun to sip and to rub on your body: The ingredients of white wine yeast extract and the skins of the grapes (with antioxidant-rich properties) can promote skin regeneration. Several spas in Wine Country offer body treatments using these grapes.

Silverado Country Club & Resort $$$$
1600 Atlas Peak Road, Napa
(707) 257–0200, (800) 532–0500
www.silveradoresort.com
It is hard not to be impressed by this megaresort at the base of Atlas Peak. For one thing, it's big. Silverado includes 1,200 acres and more than 400 rooms—every one of them a deluxe accommodation with living room, wood-burning fireplace, full kitchen, and a private patio or terrace. Most of the hubbub is centered around the two 18-hole, Robert Trent Jones Jr.–designed golf courses. But there is a slew of additional activity, including mountain-bike rentals, 9 swimming pools, jogging trails, 17 plexi-paved tennis courts, and a 16,000-square-foot spa and gym. Check-in and concierge service are in the circa-1870s colonial mansion, originally owned by Civil War Gen. John F. Miller. There you'll also

find a conference center with 15,000 square feet of flexible meeting space (including a 5,200-square-foot grand ballroom) and a fully staffed catering and conventions department. Dining options include the Bar and Grill for breakfast and lunch and the Royal Oak for dinner.

Villagio Inn & Spa $$$$
6481 Washington Street, Yountville
(707) 944–8877, (800) 351–1133
www.villagio.com
Here's an inn inspired by the colors and architecture of Rome and Tuscany. The images of nine Roman goddesses give this property a mythical atmosphere, complete with fountains, vineyards, and gardens galore. The inn has 112 rooms in two-story clusters of buildings; 26 of these are minisuites. Each room comes equipped with fireplace, refrigerator, welcoming wine, TV, terry robes, and the usual modern amenities. Daily continental champagne breakfast is included; afternoon tea, coffee, and cookies are also served. Outside are two heated pools and two tennis courts.

The 3,500-square-foot spa features 10 treatment rooms where your epidermis will be delightfully recharged. They can do it all here: facials, massage, a Mediterranean salt scrub, and body wraps (including a grapeseed polish). Treatment packages include the Juventas (goddess of rejuvenation) at $230 and the Juterna (goddess of the healing waters) for $190.

Auberge du Soleil $$$$
180 Rutherford Hill Road, Rutherford
(707) 963–1211, (800) 348–5406
www.aubergedusoleil.com
It began as a restaurant more than 20 years ago but has blossomed into one of Wine Country's most exclusive resorts, nestled among 33 acres of olive trees and chaparral. The whole operation exudes brightness and health, with terra-cotta tile floors, fresh bouquets, natural wood and leather furnishings, and Mediterranean color schemes. The 31 guest rooms and 19 suites all have private terraces, fireplaces,

down comforters, and stereo CD systems. The sizable bathrooms have double sinks and huge tubs under skylights. All of the lodgings have recently undergone remodeling, with fresh new furnishings and fabrics.

The recreational opportunities include three tournament-surface tennis courts, a swimming pool, a whirlpool tub, and an exercise room. There is a sculpture garden and three separate facilities for meetings, receptions, or special occasions. The spa services are an attraction in their own right. You can get a facial, a body wrap, or a scalp treatment and choose from a variety of massage styles. The spa also delves into ayurvedic treatments (a holistic approach developed in India some 5,000 years ago), yoga, and somatics, based on "neuromuscular retraining principles." Auberge du Soleil is not appropriate for children younger than 16.

Meadowood Napa Valley $$$$
900 Meadowood Lane, St. Helena
(707) 963-3646, (800) 458-8080
www.meadowood.com
In the 1800s Chinese laborers harvested rice in the small valley known as Meadowood. The full-service, Relais & Châteaux estate that now graces the area would have been beyond the wildest dreams of those immigrants. There are 85 suites, lodges, and cottages spread among 250 acres and often tucked into the hillside scenery. All accommodations feature high-beamed ceilings, heated bathroom floors, private porches, and down comforters. If you're feeling active, choose among two pools, a whirlpool, saunas, seven tennis courts, two championship croquet lawns, a nine-hole golf course, and a 3-mile hiking trail. The Health Spa features a dizzying array of fitness classes, personal training, yoga, skin-care treatments, salt treatments, and body wraps. Two restaurants—a casual grill and a more formal dining room—round out the resort experience.

Meadowood's staff of resident experts includes a wine director who leads Friday night wine receptions and a croquet pro—one of only two in America. The resort also has five private conference and event rooms with a total reception capacity of 200. Accommodations start at $500 and go up to several times that: The lodges top out at more than $3,500.

White Sulphur Springs
Resort & Spa $$
3100 White Sulphur Springs Road,
St. Helena
(707) 963-8588, (800) 593-8873
www.whitesulphursprings.com
California's oldest hot-springs resort (established in 1852) retains its 19th-century charm, thanks to a laid-back management style and an idyllic setting. Take Spring Street west from downtown St. Helena; soon the town ends, but the road keeps going until you're tucked into a forest of redwood, fir, and madrone.

The 330-acre resort has 37 rooms—14 in the Carriage House (shared baths), 14 in the Inn (private baths), and nine creekside cottages. There is a warm (85 to 92 degrees) sulphur pool fed by a natural spring, and you can smell it anywhere in the main residential area. Children are OK in the cottages. The spa treatments involve massage therapy and aroma/thermotherapy, including herbal facials, mineral mud wraps, seaweed wraps, and herbal linen wraps.

Calistoga Ranch $$$$
580 Lommel Road, Calistoga
(707) 254-2800, (800) 942-4220
www.calistogaranch.com
Continuing a trend in Wine Country toward pricey, upscale lodgings that offer it all is Calistoga Ranch, a resort spa that opened in 2004 outside the town of Calistoga. This exclusive enclave of 46 guest lodges, the Bathhouse spa, and for-guests-only Lakehouse restaurant means you can disconnect from the world for a few days of quiet bliss. Of course your room comes with high-speed Internet access when it's time to plug back into reality.

The lodges—available in three sizes and tastefully furnished—are equipped with minibars; entertainment centers with

Rub-a-dub-dub . . . the Spa Experience

If you're planning a special spa visit while in Wine Country, get ready for a vacation within your vacation as you surrender to a luxurious pampering that redefines "relaxation." Here's a brief sampling of some of the many body treatments and techniques you will find at our spas.

Mud baths: This is the signature body treatment in Wine Country, and Calistoga is one of the best places to get muddy. Typically a mixture of volcanic ash, white clay, peat moss, and hot mineral water, the magical mud is warmed to a temperature of about 106 degrees. The one-hour mud bath procedure varies among spas, but in general goes something like this: You are immersed and swathed in the gooey mixture up to your neck for about 12 minutes. Attendants watch closely and supply you with cold water and cloths soaked in soothing oils. The hot mud detoxifies your system as it raises your body temperature and increases circulation. When your time is up, you pull yourself out of the ooze and thoroughly rinse off. Follow that with a mineral Jacuzzi bath or five minutes in a eucalyptus steam cabinet. After steaming, you might retreat to a private room and be covered with light sheets for a brief nap.

Wraps: Indulge your skin with this ancient Egyptian spa technique. Many

---

TV, DVD, and CD players; and down duvets. Prices range from $525 to $825 per night. The estate lodge on the property is a two-bedroom, two-bath suite with 3,000 square feet of living space. This unit includes a full kitchen, private drive-up entry, and even butler service (an indulgence at $4,500 per night).

The Calistoga Ranch provides its guests with a full-service fitness center, boccie courts, valet service, a wine cave for private events, wine seminars and classes, 24-hour concierge service, and 24-hour in-lodge dining. There's even a poolside menu, and picnic baskets may be arranged for day trips.

The spa features a natural, spring-fed mineral pool, outdoor treatment tents, and a yoga deck. Because of the resort's setting in a secluded canyon, there are also 157 acres of hiking options.

Silver Rose Inn & Spa   **$$$**
351 Rosedale Road, Calistoga
(707) 942–9581, (800) 995–9381
www.silverrosespa.com
The setting is quite pleasant—a quiet road just off the Silverado Trail, about a half mile south of Calistoga. The inn has a total of 20 rooms divided between two buildings, Inn on the Knoll and Inn on the Vineyard. Most units face onto vines; some have vines planted right outside the windows. Each room is themed, such as the gold-accented Cleopatra Room and the art deco–inspired Hello Hollywood.

Guests are free to make use of the Jacuzzi, tennis courts, putting green, and different mixtures may be used, from mineral-rich mud to seaweed to herbal concoctions. Also used in some spas are grape seeds and grapeseed oil. Rich in antioxidants, grapes make a great exfoliant. These mixtures are generously smoothed over your body to purify and tone the skin.

Salt or sugar rubs: These ingredients don't come out of a Morton's box or C&H bag. It could be ancient sea salts from Austria or native Amazon sugar, combined with scented oils and massaged over the skin for a radiant and aromatic finish. You may also find rubs of organic olive oil, used over the entire body to add moisture to skin and hair.

Massage: Swedish massage is the most common type offered in Wine Country, but some spas also provide massage methods such as Esalen, shiatsu, Thai, cranio-sacral, Jin Shin—and even underwater techniques. Facials, foot reflexology, and scalp treatments are also on the menu at most spas.

Hot rock massage: Heated stones are placed on strategic areas of your body to warm and relax muscles and joints. A light massage with lava rocks may follow.

Don't forget to keep yourself hydrated during the spa experience. Plan to drink lots of water before, during, and after your treatments to assist in flushing the toxins from your body. If you don't, you may feel worse the next day instead of feeling better.

wine-bottle–shaped swimming pool, and breakfast is served in the tiled dining hall. There is also a state-of-the-art conference room. The spa services include massage, body and facial treatments, several "champagne" treatments, hydrotherm massage, and herbal body wraps (some available in room). Prices range from $50 for a reflexology session to $249 for a three-hour-plus, all-purpose body reclamation project. No children younger than 15, please.

Dr. Wilkinson's Hot Springs $$
1507 Lincoln Avenue, Calistoga
(707) 942-4102
www.drwilkinson.com
This has been a Calistoga institution since the late John Wilkinson opened his spa in 1952, and it celebrated its 50th anniversary in a big way in 2002. More than a million people have passed through the doc's treatment rooms, and the facility has been profiled on *Good Morning America* and cable travel programs and in the *Los Angeles Times* and *GQ* magazine. A perennial favorite for five decades, "the works"—mud bath, facial mask, mineral whirlpool bath, steam room, blanket wrap, and half-hour massage—is still the most popular package. But expect to pay about $99.00 rather than the original $4.50. Individual spa services start at $49.00 for a half-hour massage. Children must be 14 or older to take a mud bath. Doc also offers an on-site salon where you can get facial and skin-care treatments or select from a wide range of related products.

Doc was a local legend who once served as the town's mayor. As often as not, the fit octogenarian could be found prowling the town's streets, serving as a walking billboard for his health treatments. His two children, Mark and Carolynne, now run the business.

Dr. Wilkinson's has 43 rooms, some with kitchens, all with refrigerators and private baths. Rooms in the adjacent five-unit Victorian are slightly more expensive.

Indian Springs $$$$
1712 Lincoln Avenue, Calistoga
(707) 942-4913
www.indianspringscalistoga.com
If this collection of teal and white buildings evokes the heyday of the recuperative spa, it's appropriate. Indian Springs is on land that was once part of Sam Brannan's inspired attempt to make this town the Saratoga of the West. The bathhouse and Olympic-size swimming pool date to 1913, and most of the bungalows were built in the 1930s. The property has a scattering of squat buildings (most units are duplexes) and open vistas. In addition to the 17 studio and one-room units, Indian Springs offers the Merchant Bungalow, a three-bedroom, two-bath suite that sleeps six and goes for $550 a night. The spa services include 100 percent volcanic-ash mud baths starting at $75, mineral baths with a full massage for $155, facial or body polish treatments, and combinations thereof.

The Olympic-size swimming pool at Indian Springs spa in Calistoga is one of the oldest and largest in California. Built in 1913, it is naturally heated by mineral water from nearby geysers.

Calistoga Spa Hot Springs $$$
1006 Washington Street, Calistoga
(707) 942-6269, (866) 8CALSPA
www.calistogaspa.com
Considering Calistoga Spa's services, excellent in both quality and quantity, this has to be considered something of a bargain. The spa is a block off Lincoln Avenue, behind the depot and other commercial buildings (on the site of the old Roman Olympic Pool). All 57 rooms come with kitchenettes (all the basics provided except an oven), air-conditioning, and cable TV; two suites have full kitchens. Guests are free to use the small but well-maintained gym (the only one in Calistoga) and four naturally heated mineral pools that range from 83 to 105 degrees. And then there is the typical lineup of spa services: mud baths, mineral baths, massage, and steam-and-blanket combos. Prices start at $16 for a basic steam-and-blanket; a mud dunk, mineral bath, blanket wrap, and one-hour massage go for $92. Calistoga Spa also has a conference room that accommodates as many as 40 people.

Roman Spa $$$
1300 Washington Street, Calistoga
(707) 942-4441, (800) 820-4461
www.romanspahotsprings.com
The Roman Spa is a straight-up motel, but you can get pampered next door at Calistoga Oasis Spa. The two establishments have the same owners, though they're run separately. Roman Spa, just a block from downtown Calistoga, has water-lily ponds; a large, heated outdoor pool; an indoor, hydro-jet therapy pool; and outdoor hydro-jet and Finnish-style saunas. The 60 rooms include everything from a single with a queen-size bed to a family suite with two full rooms. About a third of the rooms have kitchen facilities, and there are five smoking rooms. Roman Spa does not take credit card reservations over the phone; you'll need to send a check or show up in person.

Golden Haven Hot Springs $$
1713 Lake Street, Calistoga
(707) 942-6793
www.goldenhaven.com
This is a comparatively affordable spa in a quiet section of Calistoga. The exterior is nothing special, but the rooms are clean and full of conveniences, including air-

conditioning, color TV, and refrigerators. All the soothing spa treatments are there if you want them. The lineup features mud baths (including private rooms for couples), herbal mineral baths, herbal facials, and massage. Those fees range from $45 for a half-hour massage to $159 for a mud bath, hour massage, and herbal facial package. Golden Haven also promotes a European body wrap guaranteed to take off 6 inches of unsightly fat ($145). Guests use the swimming pool and hot mineral pool free.

Calistoga Village Inn & Spa $$$
1880 Lincoln Avenue, Calistoga
(707) 942-0991
www.napavalleyus.com
Another of the town's older (post–World War II) spas, the Village Inn is a long row of whitewashed bungalows along the northern end of Lincoln Avenue, just before it reaches the Silverado Trail. There are plenty of reasons to be semiclothed here: a swimming pool, a wading pool (children are welcome), a Jacuzzi, and a dry steam room. Among the numerous spa treatments are mud baths, massage, salt scrubs, facials, foot reflexology, and body wraps. The inn also offers 16 different types of mineral baths, including the aromatic seaweed bath, Dr. Singha's mustard bath, and the Moor mud baths. A package known as the Ultimate features a mud bath, salt scrub, minifacial, and one-hour massage for $185. Guests of the inn receive a 10 percent discount for all of the above. The Village Inn has two conference rooms and 42 guest suites.

Sonoma County

The Fairmont Sonoma Mission
Inn & Spa $$$$
18140 Sonoma Highway,
Boyes Hot Springs
(707) 938-9000, (800) 862-4945
www.fairmont.com
The style is Spanish-influenced early California, a sprawling pink building with red tile roof, arcade, and bell tower. Lobby decor features heavy Spanish furnishings grouped around a massive fireplace, where guests sip late-morning coffee on Sunday while reading the *San Francisco Chronicle* or the *Wall Street Journal.* It would be no surprise to see a Hollywood star or world leader—Mikhail Gorbachev and Billy Crystal have stayed here. The health and fitness program covers all bases—aerobics, aromatherapy, body sculpting, yoga, herbal wrap, seaweed sauna, and steam room. For total indulgence, ask for the 100-minute Harvest Kur ($209 for one, $418 for two). To recharge after all this activity, two great restaurants—Sante, in the main building, and the nearby Big 3 Diner—both offer low-calorie cuisine (see the Restaurants chapter). Guests at the resort also have privileges at the inn's private golf course when they feel like knocking around little white balls. It's just a few blocks away on Arnold Drive.

The inn itself has a colorful history. The first spa was built in 1860 by an eccentric doctor who burned it down after a tiff with his wife. But it was rebuilt, and by the 1890s San Francisco society was journeying north by rail and auto to "take the waters." The present inn dates to 1927, when it took shape in the style of a California mission. In 1985 a total renovation brought 70 new rooms and a conference center. The hot springs, however, lay dormant, lost in the earth until 1993, when the legendary waters were brought back to the surface from 1,100 feet below the Inn. And today this spring water is the water that fills the two pools and whirlpools.

Further expansion totaling $36 million took place, culminating in the inn's affiliation with Fairmont Hotels & Resort corporation. An additional $12 million restoration was completed in 2004.

MacArthur Place $$$$
29 East MacArthur Street, Sonoma
(707) 938-2929, (800) 722-1866
www.macarthurplace.com
One of the newer spa resorts in Wine Country, MacArthur Place began its life as a 300-acre horse and cattle ranch with

vineyards. The two-story Victorian house dominating the former Burris-Good ranch was built in the 1850s. Constructed with wooden pegs and square nails, the house was home to David Burris and his family of nine children. Burris was also a banker; he founded Sonoma Valley Bank, still in business today, in the corner library on the home's first floor.

It became a luxury destination in 1997, when it was transformed into a 64-room hotel with full-service spa and a steakhouse restaurant called Saddles (see the Restaurants chapter). Ten of the rooms are in the original stately home; the inn's 29 newest suites are luxuriously appointed with fireplaces, wet bars, flat-panel TVs with DVD players, and king beds. Borrow one of the inn's bicycles to explore the town at your own pace.

The Garden Spa lives up to its name, using the herbs, flowers, and fruits grown on the property in its treatments. Most of the massages, facials, body polishes, and mud wraps (with grapeseeds) run about $100; a Lomi Lomi massage, practiced by Hawaiians for centuries, will set you back about $200. Several signature treatments, also about $200 each, utilize rose petals, grapefruits and oranges, and essential oils.

---

i *MacArthur Place in Sonoma has lush landscaping that creates many private corners featuring benches, rusted sculptures, a giant chess set, and a checkers table.*

The Lodge at Sonoma $$$$
1325 Broadway Avenue, Sonoma
(707) 935-6600 (lodge),
(707) 931-2034 (spa)
www.thelodgeatsonoma.com,
www.raindancespa.com
Sonoma is a spa town, and this world-class facility helps keep the town's reputation for hot water and luxurious body

scrubs intact. The 182 spacious guest rooms are nicely appointed with fireplaces, balcony or patio, two-line phones, cable TV, and complimentary breakfast in the restaurant, Carneros (see the Restaurants chapter), or in room.

Hot mineral waters flow right beneath the property, so the Raindance Spa is the perfect source for therapeutic bathing treatments. There are outdoor soaking and watsu therapy pools, and underwater massage is offered. The full-service spa has a full menu of massages, skin-care treatments, body wraps, facials, and an assortment of "kurs"—a series of treatments using mineral water, algae, therapeutic mud, and essential oils and herbs to detoxify and hydrate your overstressed bod. Prices range from about $100 for facials to $295 for a kur treatment. A full-day spa indulgence, with lunch too, costs about $475; a half day is $275.

The Kenwood Inn & Spa $$$$
10400 Sonoma Highway, Kenwood
(707) 833-1293, (800) 353-6966
www.kenwoodinnandspa.com
Intimate in scale with a peaceful, old-world charm, the Kenwood Inn offers the ambience of an Italian country villa nestled in the heart of Sonoma Valley.

The inn is situated on a secluded hillside facing more than 1,000 acres of sloping estate vineyards. A recent expansion brought the number of rooms to 30, with two more courtyards. The suites contain feather beds, down comforters, European antiques and lush fabrics, private baths, and fireplaces. A complimentary bottle of wine greets guests on arrival. Breakfast is served either in the dining room or at outdoor tables in good weather. A full-service spa pampers guests and day visitors alike with different therapeutic massages, 11 special skin-care and spa body treatments—such as clay and chamomile, seaweed body wrap—and ancient ayurvedic body purification rituals. Half-day spa experiences are available, including the popular couples "togetherness massage," as well as the Faccia Bella facial. Spa treatments are priced individually.

River Village Resort & Spa $$$
14880 River Road, Guerneville
(707) 869-8139, (888) 342-2624
www.rivervillageresort.com

This recently renovated resort features 20 cottages clustered around two swimming pools, a hot tub, and two large decks in a courtyard on the edge of town. Owners Gary and Donna Klauenburch have lived in the area for more than 20 years and together have created a charming get-away that offers a wide range of rejuve-nating and relaxing therapies. Services include Swedish, deep tissue, reflexology, and aromatherapy massage as well as salt scrubs, mud wraps, full facials, and herbal body wraps. The resort also features nutri-tion and diet counseling—from an herbal-ist and certified nutritional consultant and diet counselor. The location affords rela-tively easy access to the nearby Russian River, where you can swim, canoe, kayak, or just bask in the sun.

Mendocino County

Orr Hot Springs $
13201 Orr Springs Road, Ukiah
(707) 462-6277

The hot spring waters bubble up from the earth into a redwood tub and spill over into the swimming pool below. The spa has had a checkered history and at pres-ent could only be described as rustic. The first bathhouse was built in the 1850s and is now used as a dormitory. A 14-room lodge and three cottages serve as the main buildings today. During the 1970s the 26-acre hot-springs facility became a kind of commune. Today, the situation is infor-mal (clothing is optional); and you can bring a picnic lunch and store it in the communal kitchen. Besides the basic facil-ities (some of which have half baths),

Kenwood Inn & Spa was recently named one of the best Wine Country retreats in all of California and one of the 10 best in the world by Food & Wine magazine.

camping is also an option. Day use is another option.

Vichy Springs Resort $$$
2605 Vichy Springs Road, Ukiah
(707) 462-9515
www.vichysprings.com

Named after the world-famous springs first discovered by Julius Caesar in France, the waters of Vichy Springs bubble up from deep within the Earth and are virtu-ally identical in chemistry to those of the French namesake. Available in abundance for bathing and swimming, the waters are naturally warm and effervescent (dubbed "champagne baths"), filled with minerals and energy renowned for healing and restorative qualities. Opened in 1854 and now a California Historical Landmark, the resort was a favorite retreat of Mark Twain, Jack London, and Presidents Ulysses S. Grant, Benjamin Harrison, and Teddy Roosevelt. Today, the resort is restored and renovated to tastefully com-bine its historic charm with modern com-fort and conveniences. More contemporary visitors have included Wavy Gravy and Patch Adams.

Twelve individually decorated rooms with private baths have been created from the ancient, broken-down former facilities that date from the 1860s. There are also four cottages with kitchens, bedrooms, and living rooms. Just steps away from the accommodations are the renovated indoor and outdoor bathing tubs, thera-peutic massage building, and mineral-water-filled, Olympic-size swimming pool. Offered at varying rates are therapeutic massage, Swedish massage, and herbal facial. Day visitors are also welcome to use the pool, baths, and the property.

Little River Inn $$$
7751 North Highway 1, Little River
(707) 937-5942, (888) 466-5683,
(707) 937-3099 (spa)
www.littleriverinn.com
Built in 1853 by Silas Coombs, a lumber-
man from Maine, this classic coastal resort
once was the Coombs's family home.
Eucalyptus trees, planted as a windbreak
for the Coombs's orchard, now shelter a
golf course. The wisteria-covered front
porch of the original home, where Silas
once spotted ocean freighters, now beck-
ons guests into the dining room. The inn
has a long tradition of hosting Hollywood
celebrities—Joan Fontaine and a crew of
40; Jonathan Winters, who provided
impromptu entertainment; Ronald Reagan,
who sprawled on the floor to illustrate
football plays. (All rooms are nonsmoking.)

The inn's Third Court Salon and Day
Spa offers classic European facials, aro-
matherapy wraps, and a host of other
body treatments, hydration skin treat-
ment, and massage. Reservations are
required year-round. There is no charge
for children younger than 18. Sunday
brunch and dinner are served.

Sweetwater Spa & Inn $$
955 Ukiah Street (spa), 44840 Main
Street (inn), Mendocino
(707) 937-4140, (800) 300-4140
www.sweetwaterspa.com,
www.mendocinoinn.com
The Sweetwater complex takes up most
of the two blocks between Ukiah and
Main Streets in the village of Mendocino,
and that's not all. Besides the 22 units
downtown, the company has 6 rooms in
Little River and the cozy Redwood Cottage, a popular lodging about five minutes
east of Mendocino.

For 14 years Sweetwater has maintained one of the premier massage staffs
in Northern California. They offer a full
range of massage and bodywork options.
Sweetwater also has hot tubs and sauna,
with prices that vary according to privacy
and tub size. Kids are welcome.

DAY SPAS

Along with the destination spa resorts,
you also have the option of luxuriating at
one of several day spas. Spend a few reju-
venating hours sunk neck deep in mud, or
enveloped in a stress-relieving hydro wrap,
or soothed by the skilled hands of a
masseuse, and then be on your way
(reservations recommended). Here are
just a few of the many possibilities.

Napa County

Mount View Spa
1457 Lincoln Avenue, Calistoga
(707) 942-5789, (800) 772-8838
www.mountviewspa.com
In the Mount View Hotel building (see the
Hotels, Motels, and Inns chapter), but run
separately, this spa is the ultimate in luxury. The tasteful furnishings, personalized
service, and waffle-weave cotton robes in
the dressing rooms all combine to set a
mood of elegant decadence. Mount View
offers five types of massage, from stone
therapy to reflexology; customized
whirlpool baths with additives such as
fango mud, mineral salts, powdered milk
whey, and herbal bath oils; and body
wraps. The latter include the herbal linen
wrap, the stress-relief hydro wrap (a
warm, aloe vera–based gel), and the Enzy-
matic Sea mud wrap, which is painted
over your entire body like a dusky leotard.
All of it is performed in private rooms. The
massages cost $50 (for 25 minutes) to
$110 (for 80 minutes). A bath treatment
followed by a 55-minute massage runs
$85; add an herbal wrap and a 25-minute
basic cleansing facial and pay $170.

Lincoln Avenue Spa
1339 Lincoln Avenue, Calistoga
(707) 942-5296
www.lincolnavenuespa.com
Set in an old stone building in the heart of
town, this spa is an upscale companion to
Golden Haven Hot Springs (see the listing

earlier in this chapter). Lincoln Avenue specializes in the easygoing Swedish/Esalen style of massage, with rates ranging from $45 for back, neck, and shoulder work to $109 for a full-body massage and a foot reflexology treatment. The mud treatments are longtime favorites too. Recline for an hour on a steam table while wearing a suit of herbal mineral body mud (with 34 herbs), sea mud (with kelp), or mint mud. If you're not allowed to play in the mud, try on the herbal wrap. The spa also offers facials and acupressure "facelifts." Packages are available of course, such as the Ultimate Pamper Package, a four-and-a-half-hour slice of heaven that costs $278.

Lavender Hill Spa
1015 Foothill Boulevard, Calistoga
(707) 942-4495, (800) 528-4772
www.lavenderhillspa.com
This intimate retreat bills itself as "A Garden Spa for Couples," and indeed, the verdant grounds in back of the bathhouses are a suitably romantic spot for postmassage reverie and sweet talk. Inside, Lavender Hill offers elegant trappings and a warm staff. Choose from four basic bath treatments: volcanic mud bath, seaweed bath, herbal blanket wrap, or aromatherapy mineral salt bath, all of which come with a facial mask and a foot massage. Other options include a stone massage, therapeutic massage, and foot reflexology. Prices range from $55 for a basic half-hour massage to $165 for a bath treatment with one-hour massage and minifacial.

Calistoga Massage Center
1219 Washington Street, Calistoga
(707) 942-6193
www.calistogamassage.com
The Massage Center is for connoisseurs of massage. The staff offer deep tissue and sports massage, shiatsu, Thai, and esoteric methods called cranio-sacral and Jin Shin. Select a mode and a duration—it's $45 for 30 minutes, $80 for an hour, or $125 for 90 minutes. (Swedish/Esalen–based mas-

sage is a little less expensive, running $40, $70, and $100.) The center also offers massage for two ($130 for an hour each), massage instruction for couples ($240 for three hours), foot reflexology ($80 for an hour), herbal facials ($70 an hour), and various combinations of the above. Ask about discounts for students, seniors, upvalley residents, and anyone visiting Tuesday through Thursday.

Sonoma County

Sonoma Spa on the Plaza
457 First Street W., Sonoma
(707) 939-8770
www.sonomaspaontheplaza.com
When you've worked yourself into a tizzy shopping and dining in Sonoma, slip into this conveniently located spa for a relaxing tune-up. You'll find everything from specialty massages to body treatments and herbal facials, in package form or a la carte. Deluxe packages, lasting from two to five hours, run from $138 to $298. Three types of one-hour, mud-based body treatments are offered at $65 each.

Osmosis Enzyme Bath and Massage
209 Bohemian Highway, Freestone
(707) 823-8231
www.osmosis.com
Named the best day spa in America by *Travel & Leisure* magazine, Osmosis features a Japanese enzyme bath of fragrant cedar fiber, rice bran, and more than 600 enzymes. The action of the enzymes produces a special quality of heat that improves circulation and metabolism and cleanses skin pores and beautifies the skin. Massage treatments include the Swedish/Esalen method and many others. If you like, you can have your massage outdoors under a pagoda near Salmon Creek. The enzyme bath is $75/$80, with massage $155/$170. Osmosis is located off Highway 12 in the small town of Freestone, about halfway between Sebastopol and Bodega.

A Simple Touch Spa
239 Center Street, Healdsburg
(707) 433-6856
www.asimpletouchspa.com
This lovely little spa in downtown Healdsburg offers aromatherapy baths, massage,
facials, and body treatments. One of the
specialty baths features detoxifying fango
mud made from dehydrated volcanic ash.
The body wraps range from fragrant
herbal or rose petals—the latter wrap
involves painting the body in rose whey
and then wrapping it in a heat blanket—to
the more common remineralizing seaweed
wrap. Several special packages are available that range from $70 for a bath and
half-hour massage to the deluxe package
for $210, which includes a bath, salt scrub,
one-hour massage, herbal facial, and rose-
petal wrap.

Mendocino County

Gualala Sea Spa
39151 South Highway 1, Gualala
(707) 884-9262
www.gualalaseaspa.com
In the heart of Gualala is this pleasant day
spa that offers many types of massages,
facials, and body treatments.

Visage Day Spa
45064 Ukiah Street, Mendocino
(707) 937-2602
www.visageofmendocino.com
Open daily from 10:00 A.M. to 5:00 P.M.,
Visage will improve your body from head
to toe with a detox wrap, hydroactive
mineral salt scrub, or heated stone massage. Visage also offers facials, pedicures,
and manicures. Reservations are required.

CAMPING ⊕

If you're on a budget or desire more in the way of outdoor adventure, many campgrounds in Wine Country afford ample opportunities for backpacking, hiking, and fishing. Campgrounds in northern Mendocino County are generally among the most remote and primitive, where nary a wine taster is likely to be found.

Unless I say otherwise, assume that each campground has piped, potable water, a desirable part of any outdoor experience. If it doesn't, arrange to bring or pump your own. And note that some of the listed sites are part of the region's state parks. In those cases you'll find the basic camping information here, but for a more thorough description of each park, you should turn to the Parks and Recreation chapter.

To pitch your tent or park your RV, expect to pay from $12 to $25 nightly, depending on the location and the degree of development. (State park camping fees took a leap in 2004, and most campsites now cost from $11 to $25 per night, and even higher for desirable coastal sites.) Senior rates are offered in many places, while some of the more primitive campgrounds are free.

NAPA COUNTY

Napa Town & Country Fairgrounds
575 Third Street, Napa
(707) 253-4900
www.napavalleyexpo.com
The fairgrounds are just off Third Street in Napa as it approaches the Silverado Trail. There are about 75 motor-home spaces and a group campground for 15 to 500. On-site are restrooms and showers, and close by are a laundry and a market. Pets are permitted on leashes. Note that Town & Country is closed to campers for the latter half of July and most of August.

Spanish Flat Resort
4290 Knoxville Road, off Highway 128,
Lake Berryessa
(707) 966-7700
www.spanishflatresort.com
Spanish Flat has 120 campsites for tents or motor homes, a few of them with partial hookups. Rustic lakefront cabins were recently added, as well as several yurts. Picnic tables, fire pits, flush toilets, and showers are provided. The hosts also have complete marina facilities, a boat launch, and rentals. A laundry and a restaurant are a short drive away.

Bothe–Napa Valley State Park
Highway 29, south of Calistoga
(707) 942-4575 (info),
(800) 444-PARK (reservations)
www.parks.ca.gov/default.asp?page
_id=477
While a million or so industrious tourists whiz by on Highway 29, you can lie next to your tent and look up at the boughs of oaks and pines or at the stars of the Milky Way. The park has a first-rate campground along Redwood Creek, with 9 tent-only sites and 50 for tents or RVs up to 31 feet long. You get picnic tables and fire pits, toilets, and showers. Wheelchairs can be used here, and pets are allowed (campground only). There is a spring-fed swimming pool, where you can take the plunge for $1.00 (free for children). Blackberries are for the pickin' in summer.

Napa County Fairgrounds
1435 North Oak Street, Calistoga
(707) 942-5111, (707) 942-5221
www.napacountyfairgrounds.com
If you're going to pick a municipal campground, you could do a lot worse than Calistoga's. The scenery is nice, you can walk to restaurants and spas, and next door is Mount St. Helena Golf Course (see the Parks and Recreation chapter). There

are 46 drive-through campsites with electrical hookups, plus a small grassy area for tents.

Restrooms, showers, and propane are available, but campfires are not permitted. Pets are allowed on leashes. The campground is closed from mid-June through mid-July as the grounds are prepared for and cleaned up after the Napa County Fair (see the Festivals and Annual Events chapter).

Hunting Creek Camp
Knoxville-Devilshead Road, Knoxville
(707) 468-4000
www.openspacecouncil.org/camp/
huntingcreek.html
This is one of Wine Country's least-known campgrounds and, because of its isolation in the uppermost northern tip of Napa County, that isn't likely to change anytime soon. Located about 17 miles north of Lake Berryessa near the small community of Knoxville, Hunting Creek has only five sites for tents or RVs, but it does have picnic tables, fireplaces, and vault toilets. Pets are permitted on leashes. Be forewarned that the campground is popular with off-road enthusiasts and hunters. Take Lake Berryessa Road to Devilshead Road. A map of the area is available from the Bureau of Land Management at the number listed. There is no charge for camping here.

SONOMA COUNTY

Southern Sonoma

Sugarloaf Ridge State Park
2605 Adobe Canyon Road, Kenwood
(707) 833-5712, (800) 444-PARK
(reservations)
www.parks.sonoma.net/sugarlf.html
This locale in the Mayacmas Mountains has 50 campsites for tents or motor homes up to 24 feet long. There is piped-in water and restrooms. In 1996 Sugarloaf Ridge State Park became the home of the largest observatory in the western United

States that is completely dedicated to public viewing and education. Hiking is the main recreation at this popular state park (see the Parks and Recreation chapter). Pets are OK.

Spring Lake Regional Park
5585 Newanga Avenue, Santa Rosa
(707) 539-8092
www.sonoma-county.org
A group camping area and 30 family campsites (4 for tents only) at Spring Lake Park have centrally located restrooms and shower facilities. Also available are 200 picnic sites, barbecue pits, a bikeway, a hiking trail, and equestrian trails. No electricity is available at this campground, which is open daily from the week before Memorial Day until the week after Labor Day and open weekends only during the winter. Please reserve at least 10 days in advance during high season.

Northern Sonoma

Windsorland RV Trailer Park
9290 Old Redwood Highway, Windsor
(707) 838-4882
www.gocampingamerica.com/windsor
land/index.html
There are 66 sites here, with 56 full-hookup, pull-through sites. Windsorland also features a laundry, playground, a small store, showers, and restrooms. A pool is open seasonally. The park is open all year, and night registration is available.

Cloverdale KOA
26460 River Road, Cloverdale
(707) 894-3337
www.koacampgrounds.com
This campground has 152 campsites (50 for tents), plus a swimming pool, recreation hall, store, minigolf course, stocked fishing pond, ball courts, and horseshoe pits. Located 1 mile from the Russian River on a hill overlooking the Alexander Valley, the Cloverdale KOA is open all year. There are also 14 Kamping Kabins for two (with no water or electricity).

Lake Sonoma–Liberty Glen
3333 Skaggs Springs Road, Lake Sonoma
(707) 433-9483
www.parks.sonoma.net/laktrls.html
Eleven miles northwest of Healdsburg, off Dry Creek Road, this Lake Sonoma park offers more than 17,000 land and water acres. Lake Sonoma facilities include a visitor center and fish hatchery (see the Kidstuff chapter), with 118 campsites available for tents or RVs up to 50 feet. There are two group sites for up to 50 campers (advance reservations required). In addition, there are eight boat-in/hike-in primitive campgrounds around the lake and a privately operated marina that offers boat rentals and a launch ramp. Piped water, flush toilets, solar-heated showers, and a sanitary disposal station are available in the developed area.

Sonoma Coast

Doran Regional Park and Westside Regional Park
Highway 1, south and west of Bodega Bay
(707) 875-3540
www.sonoma-county.org
Doran's facilities include 113 sites for RVs or tents, 19 first-come, first-served sites, 1 hiker/biker site, and 1 reservable group site. Westside has 47 campsites. There are tables, fire rings, and a trailer disposal site. For extra comfort, showers and flush toilets are available too. Parking is $5.00 in summer, $4.00 the rest of the year. What to do? Try fishing, beachcombing, clamming, boating, and picnicking.

A boat ramp and fish-cleaning station are available. There's an extra charge of $5.00 per vehicle and $1.00 per dog.

Stillwater Cove Regional Park
22455 Highway 1,
approx. 15 miles north of Jenner
(707) 847-3245
www.sonoma-county.org
This 210-acre park comprises open meadow and coastal forest with spectacular ocean views from Stillwater Cove.

Every summer, forest fires rage in various parts of California, many of them caused by careless smokers and campers. Please be cautious when using fire in our wilderness areas—which are tinder-dry by midsummer—and always make certain campfires are extinguished thoroughly.

There is a half-mile trail leading to the historic one-room Fort Ross Schoolhouse. Twenty-three campsites serve most campers (drivers of large RVs and trailer campers should contact the park office to ensure that their vehicle will fit) and there is a hike-in/bike-in area. Facilities include pay showers, flush restrooms, and day-use parking.

Salt Point State Park
25050 Highway 1,
approx. 20 miles north of Jenner
(707) 847-3221, (800) 444-PARK
(reservations)
www.parks.sonoma.net/coast.html
This campground offers picnic areas, hiking trails, diving, horseback trails, and the beautiful adjacent Kruse Rhododendron State Reserve (see the Parks and Recreation chapter). It's open all year, but there are no RV hookups. There are 107 campsites in summer but only 28 in winter. Piped water and flush toilets are available. In early winter this is headquarters for local abalone divers.

Gualala Point Regional Park
Highway 1, 0.5 mile south of Gualala
(707) 785-2377
www.sonoma-county.org
The 195-acre park is located near the coast, adjacent to the Gualala River. The overnight camping area is across the highway from the park's day-use facilities, and it contains tables and stoves. Water and restroom facilities are nearby. Recreation options for day-use or overnight campers include fishing, bike trails, hiking (one trail beside the bluff is especially good for bird-watching), and picnic areas. It's open

all year and offers 19 family campsites for tents and motor homes up to 28 feet, 7 hike-in/bike-in campsites, and a trailer sanitary station.

West County/ Russian River

Village Park Campground
6665 Highway 12, Sebastopol
(707) 823-6348
Village Park is open from May 1 to October 31 for overnight or weekly stays. Laundry facilities and restrooms with showers and hot water are offered, and children and pets are welcome.

River Bend Campground
11820 River Road, Forestville
(707) 887-7662, (800) 877-0816
www.openspacecouncil.org/camp/river bend.html
Eleven miles from U.S. Highway 101, off the River Road exit, this campground has 65 sites, 35 with full hookups. Canoe rentals, volleyball, barbecue pits, and basketball courts are among the amenities. Other features include flush restrooms, hot showers, groceries, tepees for rent, and a huge Paul Bunyan statue. It's open all year.

i *To reserve a campsite in one of California's state parks, you must go through the Reserve America booking service at (800) 444-PARK. Reserve America will add a one-time $7.50 surcharge to any reservation; get more details at www.reserveamerica.com.*

Faerie Ring Campground
16747 Armstrong Woods Road, Guerneville
(707) 869-2746
www.russianriver.com/campgrounds.htm
Tucked away on 14 acres near Armstrong Redwoods State Reserve (see the Parks and Recreation chapter), this gay-friendly campground features 44 campsites—33 for tents and 4 full hookups—in either a sunny or shady location. Hot showers and flush toilets are available. It's near the Russian River, 1.8 miles north of Highway 116, and it's open all year. Faerie Ring also has a popular adults-only area. Pets allowed. No credit cards.

Schoolhouse Canyon Campground
12600 River Road, Guerneville
(707) 869-2311
www.openspacecouncil.org/camp/school house.html
This camping option lies adjacent to a 200-acre wildlife sanctuary, with tent and RV sites set in the redwoods. Hot showers, fishing and swimming along the nearby Russian River, hiking, and nature trails are among the attractions. It's open April through October.

MENDOCINO COUNTY

U.S. Highway 101

Manor Oaks Overnighter Park
700 East Gobbi Street, Ukiah
(707) 462-0529, (800) 357-8772
There are 53 motor-home spaces (15 of which are drive-through) with full hookups. Picnic tables, fire grills, restrooms, showers, and a swimming pool are provided. A laundry and ice are available, and right next door are the tennis courts and barbecue facilities of Oak Manor Park. Leashed pets are allowed in the campground. Manor Oaks is open year-round.

Quail Meadows Campground
23701 North US 101, Willits
(707) 459-6006
Most of the 49 motor-home spaces here have full or partial hookups, and there is a special section for tents only. Amenities include patios, picnic tables, restrooms, showers, and a sanitary disposal station. A laundry, propane, ice, and TV hookups are available. Pets are allowed on leashes.

Willits KOA
1600 Highway 20, Willits
(707) 459-6179
www.koacampgrounds.com
There are 18 sites for tents only and 50 RV spaces (27 of which are drive-through) with full or partial hookups as well as 12 cabins. Piped water, flush toilets, showers, picnic tables, playground, swimming pool, and sanitary dump station are provided. And that's just the beginning. The Willits KOA has hiking trails, fish pond, petting zoo, minigolf, arcade, weekend barbecues, and even seasonal horseback riding. A grocery store, laundry, and RV supplies are available too. Pets are allowed on leashes.

Highway 128

Hendy Woods State Park
18599 Philo-Greenwood Road, Philo
(707) 937-5804
www.parks.ca.gov/default.asp?page_id=438
The park campground offers 92 sites for tents or RVs up to 35 feet long, including 4 wheelchair-accessible sites. Piped water, flush toilets, hot showers, a sanitary disposal station, picnic tables, and fire pits are provided. A grocery store and a propane gas station are available nearby. Pets are permitted.

Paul M. Dimmick Wayside State Camp
Highway 128, 6 miles east of Highway 1
(707) 937-5804
www.parks.ca/gov
Located about 6 miles inland from the Pacific Ocean, this campground features 30 sites for tents or RVs up to 35 feet long (no hookups). Restrooms, fireplaces, and picnic tables are provided, and pets are permitted, but there is no potable water. The nearby Navarro River is the highlight. In summer it's a spot for swimming or canoeing; in late winter the river gets a fair steelhead run. The state camp is open year-round.

Mendocino National Forest
(707) 983-6118, (530) 934-3316
www.fs.fed.us/r5/mendocino
With approximately one million acres of land, Mendocino National Forest is a great destination for serious camping enthusiasts. The choices for bedding down under the stars are numerous, ranging from developed to primitive sites. Most are pack-it-in, pack-it-out—meaning there are no garbage cans in the campgrounds. Many of the primitive sites are free; most others range from $6.00 to $20.00 per night. Group sites run about $50.00. Full details about the many campgrounds here are available on the Web site. (Read more about Mendocino National Forest in the Parks and Recreation chapter.)

Mendocino Coast

Manchester State Park
41500 Kinney Road, Manchester
(707) 937-5804,
(800) 444-PARK (reservations)
www.parks.ca.gov/default.asp?page_id=437
Bordered by large sand dunes, this popular state campground offers 46 sites for tents and motor homes up to 30 feet long. It also includes a 40-person group site and 10 environmental camps. Most sites have piped water, chemical (non-flush) toilets, picnic tables, and fireplaces. The campground has a sanitary dump station. No pets are allowed.

Van Damme State Park
Highway 1, 3 miles south of Mendocino
(707) 937-5804,
(800) 444-PARK (reservations)
www.parks.ca.gov/default.asp?page_id=443
Van Damme offers quiet rain forest groves and great ocean views, with 70 campsites for tents or motor homes up to 35 feet long. There are also 10 primitive campsites reached by a 1.7-mile hike, plus a group

Be aware that some seaside camping locations can be breezy and cold any time of the year. Come prepared with plenty of warm clothing.

camp that accommodates 50 people. Piped water, flush toilets, a sanitary disposal station, hot showers, picnic tables, and fireplaces are provided in the main campground. A grocery store, laundry, and propane are available nearby. Pets are permitted.

Russian Gulch State Park
Highway 1, 2 miles north of Mendocino
(707) 937-5804,
(800) 444-PARK (reservations)
www.parks.ca.gov/default.asp?page_id=
432
Set near some of California's most beautiful coastline, this park offers 30 campsites for tents or RVs up to 30 feet long—as well as several hike-in/bike-in sites. There is also a wheelchair-accessible site and a 40-person group site. Piped water, hot showers, flush toilets, picnic tables, and fireplaces with cooking grills are provided. Pets are permitted. The campground is open April through October.

Mackerricher State Park
24100 Mackerricher Park Road, Fort Bragg
(707) 937-5804,
(800) 444-PARK (reservations)
www.parks.ca.gov/default.asp?page_id=
436
There are 11 hike-in/bike-in campsites (for up to four people) and 143 sites for tents or motor homes up to 35 feet long—but no hookups—at this beautiful coastal park 3 miles north of Fort Bragg on Highway 1. One site is wheelchair accessible. Piped water, hot showers, flush toilets, a dump station, picnic tables, and fireplaces are provided. Pets are permitted.

Fort Bragg Leisure Time RV Park
30801 Highway 20, Fort Bragg
(707) 964-5994
www.fortbragg.com/campgrounds.html
The wooded setting is a highlight for RV campers. There are 82 sites for tents or RVs, many with full or partial hookups. Restrooms, picnic tables, satellite TV, fire rings, coin-operated hot showers, and a sanitary disposal station are provided. A laundry is available. Pets are allowed on leashes.

RESTAURANTS 🍴

In this chapter I redefine the region as "Food and Wine Country," because some visitors are here not only for the wine. They come for the experience of dining in world-class establishments, and the wine is a nice bonus.

Some of the region's restaurants consistently are named to the "top" lists published in gourmet, wine, and travel magazines. These restaurants achieve accolades by inventing some of the most delectable dishes imaginable. Just a quick read through this chapter will have your mouth watering and your fingers reaching for the phone to make reservations.

I make no attempt to include every great eatery in this huge area, but I have listed restaurants that are well established and highly regarded for their food, service, and overall reputation. Some are tried-and-true favorites. Others are newer establishments helmed by prestigious chefs who made names for themselves in places like Los Angeles, San Francisco, New York City, and Paris before deciding to ply their trade in a more laid-back environment.

Remember, menus change frequently, depending on the season and the availability of fresh, local ingredients. Wine Country chefs enjoy concocting new dishes and making the best use of the region's bounty, so they can—and do—transform menus daily or weekly to suit their fancy. Take the tasty descriptions in these listings as a guide to what you might find on a particular restaurant's menu during your visit. Also keep in mind that days and hours of operation are subject to change, and it helps to call ahead to avoid disappointment.

Note: This chapter is organized a bit differently from the rest. It still follows the geographical method of listing Napa County first, followed by Sonoma and Mendocino Counties. But to make it easier

to locate that famous greasy spoon you read about in *Bon Appetit* magazine, restaurants are listed alphabetically within their respective regions and cities.

As you read these entries, remember that unless a listing says otherwise, you can count on certain things: The restaurant serves beer and wine but does not have a full bar, it accepts major credit cards, it is wheelchair accessible, and it takes reservations. Most of the upscale restaurants do not have children's menus, but the down-home places do.

PRICE CODE

Each price code refers to the average price of two entrees only—no appetizers, no dessert, no drinks, no tax or gratuity. I don't actually expect you to eat that way—or forego the tip!—I just wanted to keep the calculations simple.

$	Less than $20
$$	$21 to $30
$$$	$31 to $40
$$$$	More than $40

NAPA COUNTY

City of Napa

Angèle $$$
540 Main Street, Napa
(707) 252-8115
www.angele.us
Adding to the revitalization of the Hatt Building complex is this restaurant serving French brasserie cuisine. The building was once a boathouse along the first bend of the Napa River. In addition to the large indoor dining area, there is also a pleasant patio that seats 80. Some examples of the entrees you can expect are roasted striped bass on bean stew; petrale sole with baby spinach, capers, and raspberry

vinegar; chicken with morels and asparagus; and duck breast with roasted finger-
ling potatoes. Dessert options include
gratin of banana with almond crust or
vanilla ice cream with candied chestnuts.
There is a full bar, and reservations are
accepted for daily lunch and dinner.

Bayleaf   **$$$$**
2025 Monticello Road, Napa
(707) 257-9720
www.bayleafnapa.com
If you need a special place for a big party
or wedding reception, Bayleaf may be the
answer. It's big, with four separate dining
rooms and a 150-seat patio. Each dining
room has its own distinct feel—huge skylights in one, a large wood bar and fireplace
in another. The food portions are generous,
and menu items might include seared scallops, garlic mint chicken breast, and several
pizza selections. For your sweet tooth
there's mango-apple cobbler. Lunch and
dinner are served daily except Tuesday.

Bistro Don Giovanni   **$$$**
4110 St. Helena Highway S., Napa
(707) 224-3300
Giovanni Scala's restaurant is romantic.
The subdued earth tones, the unpolished
wood, the tiles, the vineyard views, the
high ceilings, the fireplaces in and out—
your date will be putty in your hands. Just
make sure you can still concentrate on the
food, which favors regional Italian dishes
while tossing in a bit of Provence. The
pan-seared salmon filet with buttermilk
mashed potatoes is excellent, as is the
grilled portobello mushroom appetizer.
Side dishes not to be missed are the
sautéed spinach with garlic or the house-
marinated Mediterranean olives. The
restaurant is also noted for its risottos and
pastas. Don Giovanni is open seven days a
week for lunch and dinner. The menu
changes daily, and there is a full bar.

Celadon   **$$$**
500 Main Street, Napa
(707) 254-9690
www.celadonnapa.com

Global comfort food is the emphasis of
this pleasant eatery housed in the historic
Napa Mill and Hatt Marketplace along the
Napa River. In addition to the main dining
room, there's a spacious patio and all-day
dining in the bar. The flavors are inspired
by Asia, the Mediterranean, and the Amer-
icas. The chef might tempt you with crab-
cakes or flash-fried calamari, followed by a
truffle-and-honey-glazed pork chop or
braised Algerian-style lamb shank.
Celadon is open daily for lunch and dinner,
and reservations are accepted.

Cole's Chop House   **$$$**
1122 Main Street, Napa
(707) 224-6328
www.coleschophouse.citysearch.com
As its name implies, this is where one
goes to get red meat—in huge portions.
The menu's pricier steaks include the 21-
day Chicago dry-aged New York strip or
porterhouse, and a 2-inch-thick Black
Angus filet mignon. For noncarnivores,
there's plenty of fish and even a short
stack of portobello mushroom caps.

Housed in a restored historic building
dating from 1886, the restaurant, with din-
ing rooms on two levels, features stone
walls and a wood-beamed ceiling. The cozy
booths are set with white tablecloths and
copper-beaded lampshades over candles.
It's elegant and masculine at the same time.
Another draw here is the great old bar,
where you can belly up for a classic Man-
hattan, martini, or cosmopolitan. Not sur-
prising is the varied assortment of bold
Napa Valley Cabernets on the wine list. Din-
ner is served Tuesday through Sunday,
accompanied by live jazz on weekends.

Foothill Cafe   **$$$**
2766 Old Sonoma Road, Napa
(707) 252-6178
Foothill Cafe sits in a nondescript little
strip mall, an unlikely venue for a locally
adored restaurant. Enter the cafe and your
faith will be rewarded with food that relies
heavily on fresh local produce and a hick-
ory smoker in the kitchen. Nightly specials
accent favorites such as baby-back ribs,

seared ahi tuna with wasabi and ginger dipping sauce, or roasted free-range chicken breast with creamy polenta. Foothill Cafe is open for dinner from Tuesday through Saturday.

Julia's Kitchen $$$$
500 First Street, Napa
(707) 265-5700
www.copia.org
Named for the late Julia Child, who was one of the first diners when it opened its doors inside Copia (see the Attractions chapter), this eatery has about 20 tables and an open, active kitchen led by executive chef Victor Scargle. What was once a rackety dining room has been softened by the addition of carpeting and draperies, making conversation much easier.

The menu selections during your visit may include sand dabs on celery root puree with lemon caper brown butter, a pork chop sliced and fanned around chard, duck confit served with cherries and arugula, or petrale sole rolled into medallions. The chef might also send out small plates of interesting "tastes" between courses, such as a bit of salmon or shrimp atop vegetables.

As you would expect from a restaurant inside a center for wine and food, the wine list is ample. The service is professional, caring, and friendly without being intrusive. If you enjoy a lively, bustling atmosphere—with an international clientele all around—you'll feel right at home in Julia's Kitchen. It was named restaurant of the year by *Esquire* magazine in its 2002 listing of great new dining experiences in the United States.

You can dine at Julia's without paying admission into Copia. Needless to say, reservations are a must.

Pearl $$
1339 Pearl Street, Suite 104, Napa
(707) 224-9161
www.therestaurantpearl.com
Proprietors Nickie and Pete Zeller have created a comfortable bistro with soaring ceilings and lots of artwork to ponder as

you enjoy fresh oysters served in a multitude of ways. There are soups, pizzas, sandwiches, and chicken and beef dishes with Mexican, Italian, and even Asian influences. Try the triple-double pork chop with an apple-Dijon brine, or a New York steak with blue cheese and roasted garlic butter. The wine list includes several obscure Napa Valley labels. Open Tuesday through Saturday for lunch and dinner; closed Sunday and Monday.

Piccolino's Italian Cafe $$
1385 Napa Town Center, Napa
(707) 251-0100
www.piccolinoscafe.com
Food has always meant comfort to Joe Salerno, who grew up stirring pots and making sausage with his extended Italian family in upstate New York. Salerno now does his best to create fond memories at Piccolino's, his unpretentious, child-friendly restaurant in downtown Napa. The cafe offers fresh fish dishes, house-made sausage, and four types of pizza. The pasta entrees are highlighted by the colorful fettuccine Calabrese, with its multitude of simple ingredients; and the lasagna, a family recipe that employs a light ricotta shipped in from the East Coast. Lasagna and spaghetti are available in immense family-style portions. The wine list is primarily Napan, though it does include a small line of Italians. Piccolino's is open daily for lunch and dinner, plus brunch on weekends. See the Nightlife chapter for information on live music.

Pilar $$$$
807 Main Street, Napa
(707) 252-4474
www.pilarnapa.com
Pilar is Pilar Sanchez of the husband-and-wife chef team (Didier Lenders is her husband) who has been working in Napa Valley for many years, in places such as Meadowood and the Wine Spectator restaurant at Greystone. Now they run their own restaurant in downtown Napa, where they feature an innovative selection of cuisine. It could be king salmon with

bacon vinaigrette, grilled rabbit loin in whole-grain mustard sauce, grilled ahi tuna, sea scallops, or veal chops. The dessert menu consists of soufflés that change nightly. A wine list of pairings is offered here, with about 35 California wines matched with wines from other regions the chefs like to call "soulmates" to the California vintages. Lunch and dinner are served Monday through Saturday; the restaurant is closed Sunday.

Tuscany $$$
1005 First Street, Napa
(707) 258–1000
www.tuscanynapa.com
Guess the specialty: the cooking of northern Italy. Start with a traditional minestrone with a bevy of vegetables and pancetta. Follow that with risotto *con quaglia,* featuring walnuts and a touch of Gorgonzola cheese topped with two roasted quail. Classic cannoli is the perfect finishing touch. The menu also includes pizzas from the wood-fired oven and rotisseried rabbit, veal, pork, and chicken. There's a counter with stools where you can watch the chefs preparing such fare as a halibut steak with roasted red and golden beets on the side. Open daily for dinner; lunch is served Monday through Friday.

Yountville

Bistro Jeanty $$$
6510 Washington Street, Yountville
(707) 944–0103
www.bistrojeanty.com
Philippe Jeanty opened his comfortable, two-room bistro in 1998 and quickly occupied a niche that, Philippe explains, is part Paris, part French countryside. You won't find a single pasta on this small menu, no Caesar salad or hamburgers. Instead, be on the lookout for lamb tongue and potato salad, beef tournedos in black pepper cream sauce, cassoulet, and mussels steamed in red wine. The setting is just as authentic, with French furnishings and

paintings by Guy Buffet. And the color of the walls? Dijon, of course. Bistro Jeanty is open for lunch and dinner seven days a week. It has a full bar; the staff calls the giant rooster that sits atop it "Philippe."

Bouchon $$$
6534 Washington Street, Yountville
(707) 944–8037
www.frenchlaundry.com
If you're looking for a place to have a late-night dinner, here's one of the few gourmet delights in Napa Valley, owned by chef Thomas Keller of the French Laundry, that will serve you till the wee hours—closing time is 2:00 A.M. The fare here is classic French bistro ("bouchon" is the local term for "bistro" in Lyon, France). But it's typically not the trendy stuff; instead, it's classics like mussels marinières and leg of lamb with flageolet beans. The appetizers include an extensive raw seafood bar. The sweets run to crème caramel or tarte tatin. The wine list is terrific and the prices are down-to-earth.

The atmosphere is lively and loud, but that's part of the charm. Because it keeps late hours, Bouchon is a favorite with local winemakers and staff from other restaurants. Open for lunch and dinner daily.

Brix $$$
7377 St. Helena Highway, Yountville
(707) 944–2749
www.brix.com
Grilled rare ahi tuna with tomatillo crème fraîche, chanterelles, and purple potatoes? Grilled salmon with sesame mustard sauce, crisp salsify, red chard, and pickled shiitakes? Hoisin grilled rack of lamb with pearled barley, radicchio, and mint oil? What do you call this? "Asian fusion" if you're Brix, the restaurant just north of Yountville. Brix is surrounded by several acres of vineyard and a couple of acres of olive trees. They have a full bar, including what the *San Francisco Chronicle* called an "Academy Award–winning wine list." Brix is open for lunch and dinner seven days a week.

Compadres Mexican Bar & Grill $$
6539 Washington Street, Yountville
(707) 944-2406
Mexican fare is more than appropriate here, on a portion of the land grant deeded to Salvador Vallejo by the Mexican government in 1838. Compadres is a sprawling, 165-seat restaurant with both indoor and outdoor seating. There is depth to the margarita list, which includes what *San Francisco Focus* magazine once ordained the best margarita it had sampled. The food is wide ranging too, with traditional Jaliscan *carnitas,* seafood tacos, daily fish specials, and at least eight types of enchilada. Compadres is open seven days a week for breakfast, lunch, and dinner.

Domaine Chandon $$$$
1 California Drive, Yountville
(707) 944-2892, (800) 736-2892
www.chandon.com
Parked against the hills west of Yountville, Domaine Chandon sits amid century-old oaks and the winery's own vineyards. The atmosphere is elegant, immaculate, and très français. The menu changes weekly, but expect such dishes as smoked trout or salmon, foie blond pâté, caramelized scallops, and local lamb. Domaine Chandon is open for dinner every night except Monday and Tuesday. (Gentlemen, jackets are recommended for dinner.) It's open for lunch seven days a week. Reservations should be booked well in advance.

The French Laundry $$$$
6640 Washington Street, Yountville
(707) 944-2380
www.frenchlaundry.com
Thomas Keller's restaurant is at the corner of Washington and Creek Streets in Yountville, in a century-old fieldstone house that was once, indeed, a French steam laundry. The French Laundry has been elevated to almost mythical status among foodies, many of whom have never come close to eating here, possibly because it's so difficult to procure a reservation. If you do make it in, congratulations. But be pre-

pared for a very pricey three hours-plus experience. It's a prix fixe menu only: $115 per person for a nine-course vegetarian offering; $115 for a more robust five-course meal; or $135 for the nine-course Chef's Tasting Menu. Keller, though a devotee of traditional French principles, is also known for his whimsical takes on common meals, like "macaroni and cheese" that turns out to be butter-poached Maine lobster with creamy lobster broth and mascarpone-enriched orzo, or "coffee and doughnuts" that are in fact fresh-baked cinnamon-sugared doughnuts with cappuccino semifreddo. The French Laundry is open for dinner seven days a week and lunch from Friday through Sunday.

Hurley's $$$$
6518 Washington Street, Yountville
(707) 944-2345
www.hurleysrestaurant.com
Bob Hurley has a long history in Napa Valley as a chef at Domaine Chandon for many years before helming the kitchen at Napa Valley Grille. He opened his namesake restaurant in 2002, where he specializes in lighter preparations of California cuisine with Mediterranean influences. The food here has been designed with Merlot in mind, and the sea bass with Merlot sauce is one of the most popular dishes. You will also find grilled rib-eye steak with buttermilk mashed potatoes, roast chicken with onions and peas, and a spicy Moroccan eggplant.

Mustards Grill $$$
7399 St. Helena Highway, Yountville
(707) 944-2424
www.mustardsgrill.com
Roadhouse meets fine dining at Mustards Grill. The restaurant is situated on Highway 29, and the casual dining room looks onto a beautiful swath of the Napa countryside. But the real action here is in the kitchen.

The menu changes seasonally, but classics like Mongolian pork chops (marinated, grilled chops with braised cabbage and garlic mashers) and hanger steak are available year-round. Everything is made from scratch—don't miss the house-made ketchup served with paper-thin onion rings. The menu tends toward creatively reinvented American classics, with daily fish specials providing the haute end of the cuisine. Mustards has a full bar with a huge wine list and is open for lunch and dinner seven days a week.

Napa Valley Grille $$$
Highway 29 at Madison Street, Yountville
(707) 944-8686
www.napavalleygrille.com
Like most restaurants in Wine Country, the chefs here dish up a changing menu that uses seasonal ingredients produced locally, described as California cuisine with Italian and French influences. A past award-winning dish here was the wild mushroom and pine nut raviolini, voted recipient of the People's Choice award in the 2002 Napa Valley Mustard Festival.

There are as many as 800 wine selections to choose from, including rare and older vintages. The dining room looks out onto vineyards, and the exhibition kitchen adds interest. Lunch and dinner is served daily, with brunch on Sunday.

Père Jeanty $$$
6725 Washington Street, Yountville
(707) 945-1000
www.perejeanty.com
Master chef Philippe Jeanty recently opened this restaurant down the street from his other established eatery, Bistro Jeanty (see the entry in this section). Both restaurants serve French-inspired food; this one also features favorites such as pizza, pasta, seafood dishes, and grilled meats. Choose from thyme-roasted monkfish or mesquite-grilled salmon, or perhaps select braised rabbit or a grilled quail salad.

Piatti $$$
6480 Washington Street, Yountville
(707) 944-2070
www.piatti.com
Dwelling on the Mediterranean end of Italy, the Piatti menu is filled with fresh herbs and seafood. The restaurant offers daily pizza, pasta, and fish specials. How about carbonara with English peas and egg yolks, porcini, and rosemary; or gnocchi with red-wine braised lamb shoulder and saffron; or a Mount Shasta porcini salad with Parmesan and Tuscan olive oil? Piatti also features oven-roasted rabbit with summer squash, wood-fired quail with pancetta, and a selection of pizzas with interesting toppings. The spice-rubbed rotisserie chicken is another favorite. The restaurant has a full bar (with many Italian wines) and is open for lunch and dinner seven days a week.

Rutherford

Auberge du Soleil $$$$
180 Rutherford Hill Road, Rutherford
(707) 963-1211
www.aubergedusoleil.com
Before Auberge du Soleil the inn, there was Auberge du Soleil the restaurant. It's known as one of Napa Valley's premier eateries, not just for the food but for the remarkable vistas from the dining terrace. Following a multi-million-dollar makeover, the dining rooms and kitchen reopened in 2003. The cuisine has included marinated raw yellowfin tuna with baby beets, radish slices, and Meyer lemon oil; and slow-cooked wild salmon with calamari, cranberry beans, and arugula. The sweeter stuff runs to filo-wrapped chocolate dumplings with tarragon ice cream or vanilla bean gratin with fresh Oregon huckleberries. The prix fixe, four-course dinner without wine is $79 per person (a la carte ordering is also offered). The restaurant is open for lunch and dinner seven days a week, and it has a full bar.

La Toque $$$$
1140 Rutherford Road, Rutherford
(707) 963-9770
www.latoque.com
French-inspired with occasional Asian influences—that's one way to describe this elegant restaurant once listed among the top 20 in America by *Wine Spectator*

magazine. The decadent five-course prix fixe menu changes with the seasonal ingredients available locally, and it can include pan-roasted squab, a Niman Ranch beef or pork selection, and duck and mushroom consommé. But La Toque goes one step further in its pursuit of excellence with its annual truffle menus, offered when fresh white truffles come into season for a few months in the fall. When white truffle season slows down, out come the first black truffles. Season permitting, the black truffle menu options are available from January through Valentine's Day.

Dining at La Toque is an excuse to dress up a bit, so blue jeans should be left back at your hotel. Cocktail dresses and sport coats are more in line here, a place many diners choose for celebrating a special occasion or popping the question.

Rutherford Grill $$$
1180 Rutherford Road, Rutherford
(707) 963-1792

This restaurant is easy to spot by the large Phoenix date palm trees swaying in front. It's a casual "neighborhood" roadhouse that offers American comfort food in big portions. The mashed potatoes are legendary and make a yummy accompaniment to the rotisserie chicken, steaks, burgers, and prime rib offerings. (Start your meal with the Maytag blue cheese chips.) The decor is warm, with redwood walls made from old wine barrels. The huge outside patio is a great place to watch Wine Country visitors hurrying by on the highway. More than 100 Napa Valley wines are offered, with at least 30 available by the glass. Open daily for lunch and dinner.

St. Helena

Cindy's Backstreet Kitchen $$$
1327 Railroad Avenue, St. Helena
(707) 963-1200
www.cindysbackstreetkitchen.com
At this local favorite, Cindy Pawlcyn, renowned for her Mustards Grill farther

down Highway 29 in Napa Valley, serves the more traditional comfort food for which she is revered. The menu ranges from innovative salads (the curry chicken salad is delightful) to small plates such as shiitake mushrooms and asparagus, to the popular rabbit tostada, spice-crusted lemon chicken, or wild mushroom tamales. This is a friendly place on two floors, with an inviting and comfortable bar. The wine list is equal opportunity, not devoted entirely to Napa Valley.

Gillwoods Restaurant $$
1313 Main Street, St. Helena
(707) 963-1788

1320 Napa Town Center, Napa
(707) 253-0409
You have to get up pretty early in the morning to beat the locals to Gillwoods, St. Helena's favorite breakfast spot. (You'll recognize it by the people milling about outside for the short wait for a table.) It's casual, intimate, and filled with good cheer and caffeine. The big draw always has been the scrambles—eggs and cheese mixed with various ingredients.

The restaurant is open for breakfast and lunch seven days a week and does not take reservations. Gillwoods has a second location in Napa Town Center. The menu is the same there, except it includes dinner on Friday and Saturday nights.

Market $$$
1347 Main Street, St. Helena
(707) 963-3799
www.marketsthelena.com
Ready for some comfort food? It's hard to beat the offerings here. This restaurant bustles with locals and visitors, who come for the exceptional buttermilk fried chicken with mashed potatoes and corn bread, the chicken potpie, and the glazed meatloaf. Start your meal with the chopped Market salad with blue cheese and bacon. End the experience with home-style goodies such as a waffle cone sundae, a root beer float, or a plate of freshly baked cookies. You can even have s'mores (yes!) prepared right at your

table. Market is a homey, comfortable eatery with an interesting bar, fieldstone walls, and friendly and efficient service. It's open daily for lunch and dinner.

Most Wine Country restaurants are not picky about how you dress for dinner. Blue jeans are almost always acceptable, and "casual" is the byword, as long as you're well groomed.

Martini House $$$$
1245 Spring Street, St. Helena
(707) 963-2233
www.martinihouse.com
Housed in a vintage California Craftsman bungalow originally built by an opera singer, this restaurant has garnered fabulous reviews since opening in 2001. Famed restaurant designer Pat Kuleto teamed with chef Todd Humphries (formerly of the Wine Spectator Greystone Restaurant) to create a beautiful setting as well as a unique dining experience. Martini House excels in rare wines, with a Wine Cellar bar that includes a 600-bottle list. The menu changes with the seasons and the availability of local produce. Among the options may be seared Maine sea scallops, sautéed squab breast and leg confit, grilled prime beef tenderloin, or Atlantic striped bass. Save room for persimmon pudding with ice cream, maple cheesecake tart with pomegranate glaze, or a chocolate crepe soufflé.

Model Bakery $
1357 Main Street, St. Helena
(707) 963-8192
www.themodelbakery.com
You'd think it was a film set if those whiffs of fresh-baked bread didn't call you from the kitchen. The look is perfect for a small-town bakery, with ceiling fans and a black-and-white checkerboard floor. The Model Bakery makes scones, croissants, danishes, bagels, and at least a half-dozen types of muffins. The repertoire includes

six or so daily breads, plus regular daily specials. The bakery also sells juices, soups, and prewrapped sandwiches and, as you would guess, coffee and espresso drinks. It's open every day but Monday.

Pinot Blanc $$$
641 Main Street, St. Helena
(707) 963-6191
www.patinagroup.com
A country bistro on the south side of St. Helena, Pinot Blanc has always-creative pasta, fish, and meat dishes complemented by a plat du jour. Monday it might be Bellwether Farms spring lamb with potato, fava beans, and truffle oil; Sunday it could be braised pig with herb-mustard spaetzle and red cabbage. The fall menu features wild game, and the Liberty duck breast with celery root puree and fresh huckleberries is heavenly. This is hearty food in big proportions. Pinot Blanc is open seven days a week for lunch and dinner and features a full bar.

Taylor's Refresher $
933 Main Street, St. Helena
(707) 963-3486
www.taylorsrefresher.com
Retired traveling salesman and pharmacist Lloyd Taylor opened the Refresher for business in 1949. It's now owned by the Gott family, who spruced it up—but managed to retain the quaint atmosphere—in 1999. Taylor's cooks up lunch and early dinner seven days a week. The menu includes burgers, hot dogs, tacos, salads, and fountain treats. There are nice picnic grounds behind the eatery.

Terra $$$$
1345 Railroad Avenue, St. Helena
(707) 963-8931
www.terrarestaurant.com
Terra sits one block away from Main Street in a historic landmark, a hardy fieldstone foundry constructed in 1884. The open redwood-beamed ceilings in the two dining rooms give you the feel of a Tuscan villa. Chef Hiro Sone's one-page menu

aims for southern France and northern Italy, though he admittedly takes a few geographic twists and turns. The most popular main course might be the broiled, sake-marinated sea bass with shrimp dumplings in shiso broth. Terra is open for dinner every night except Tuesday.

Tra Vigne   **$$$**
1050 Charter Oak Avenue, St. Helena
(707) 963-4444
www.travignerestaurant.com
Chef Michael Chiarello made it to the top of the Napa Valley hall of fame on the strength of this cozy trattoria in St. Helena. The stone building is an old landmark, and Tra Vigne has become a contemporary one. The regional Italian menu encourages grazing, with a host of interesting small plates, pastas, and pizzas to complement the meats and fish. The restaurant is open for lunch and dinner seven days a week. There is a full bar and a wine cellar stocked with Italian reds and whites, plus a good selection of Californians.

Wine Spectator Greystone
Restaurant   **$$$**
2555 Main Street, St. Helena
(707) 967-1010
www.ciachef.edu
Don't worry, eating at the Culinary Institute of America's restaurant doesn't make you a guinea pig for fresh-faced chefs-in-training. This branch of the CIA is for the continuing education of chefs.

Dishes here might include mussels steamed in Fritz Winery Melon, torchon of foie gras, or oxtail roulade. Second-course selections could be wild mushroom lasagna or a grilled pork chop with sage spaetzle, apples, braised escarole, and whiskey sauce.

Try not to dribble while craning your head around the dining room, with its cement floor and stone walls lightened by blues and yellows. Greystone has a full bar. It is open seven days a week for lunch and dinner.

Calistoga

All Seasons Cafe   **$$$$**
1400 Lincoln Avenue, Calistoga
(707) 942-9111
www.allseasonscafe.com
If you read the food-and-wine magazines, you've probably been introduced to All Seasons. It has been profiled in *Gourmet* and *Wine Spectator,* among others, and its high standards haven't faltered in nearly two decades. Mixing the quaint and the luxurious, the cafe has a wine bar that makes use of a truly exceptional wine list— it ranges far beyond the valley and is especially deep in Pinots and Zinfandels. The menu changes often, but you can expect "seasonal California" dishes along the lines of grilled rib-eye steak with Cabernet glaze and creamy horseradish sauce; or English pea risotto with asparagus, spring garlic, tomato, and mushrooms. All Seasons is open for lunch and dinner daily.

Brannan's Grill   **$$$$**
1374 Lincoln Avenue, Calistoga
(707) 942-2233
www.brannansgrill.com
Brannan's is physically arresting both inside and out, with refinished trusses and ironworks (all original to the 1911 building, long used as a motor garage) and windows that open onto Lincoln in warm weather. Most notable is the bar, a mahogany Brunswick design that was shipped around Cape Horn in the late 1800s. The food is regional American, decidedly carnivore. Try the grilled hanger steak with potato-leek gratin and roasted portobello mushrooms or the blue cheese and walnut-crusted filet mignon. Brannan's has a full bar. It's open seven days a week for lunch and dinner in high season, but lunch is Friday through Sunday in the winter.

Cafe Sarafornia   **$$**
1413 Lincoln Avenue, Calistoga
(707) 942-0555
Calistoga's most popular breakfast spot playfully incorporates the other half of

Sam Brannan's legendary malapropism: "I'll make this the Calistoga of Sarafornia." The busy, sun-infused dining room has a central counter and sidewalk booths. Regulars swear by the cheese blintzes, the Brannan Benedict (two poached eggs with guacamole, bacon, and Cajun cream on toast), the chicken-apple sausage, and the Wildcat Scrambler (three eggs scrambled with mushrooms, Italian sausage, spinach, and choice of cheese). The burgers are good at lunchtime. The cafe does not take reservations, which makes it easy to spot on Sunday morning—it's the place with the line out the door.

Calistoga Inn & Restaurant $$$
1250 Lincoln Avenue, Calistoga
(707) 942-4101
www.calistogainn.com

Popular any time of year, business at this restaurant really booms in the summer, when dining moves to the delightful creekside patio. (The meat is even grilled outside, over hardwood.) Regional American cuisine is served here. The marinated Australian lamb sirloin, the Jamaican jerk half chicken, and the tri-tip sirloin finished with blue cheese butter are all winners. There are fish specials too. The inn is open for lunch and dinner every day of the year but Christmas. The restaurant has a full bar, including an extensive wine list and its own line of beers (see the close-up in the Nightlife chapter for more on that).

Calistoga Roastery $
1426 Lincoln Avenue, Calistoga
(707) 942-5757
www.calistogaroastery.com

This place must be doing something right: Half the inns and restaurants in the vicinity boast about serving Roastery coffee. The owners roast almost 20 varieties of beans—sometimes right on the spot in a preserved 1919 Probat roaster, the oldest of its kind in the nation. If the regular house coffee isn't exciting enough for you, there is a selection of espresso drinks, frappes, and ice-cream mochas, not to mention iced teas, Rocket Juices, and Ital-

ian sodas. Yes, there are fresh-made baked goods too: bagels, croissants, scones of various stripes, banana bread, granola, and more. The Roastery opens at 6:30 A.M. every day and doesn't close its doors until 6:00 P.M. It's an atmosphere designed for lounging, so bring a newspaper. A St. Helena location of the Roastery can be found at 617 St. Helena Highway, near Dean & Deluca; call (707) 967-0820.

Flatiron Grill $$
1440 Lincoln Avenue, Calistoga
(707) 942-1220
www.flatirongrill.com

Hungry for steak? Slip on in to the Flatiron Grill, which beckons with a bovine-inspired sign outside. The stylish cow theme continues inside in the artwork. You can usually count on the house specialty, the Flatiron steak (boneless shoulder steak), roast chicken, grilled salmon, pork chop, seafood pasta, and maybe stuffed roast quail and beef brisket. Open daily for lunch and dinner.

Hydro Bar & Grill $$
1403 Lincoln Avenue, Calistoga
(707) 942-9777

In a town where the sidewalks sometimes roll up at dusk, the Hydro is the restaurant that doesn't sleep. It offers dinner until 11:00 P.M. on weekdays and midnight on weekends, then greets you for breakfast the next morning. (It's closed only for lunch on Thursday.) It does daily fish specials and top-notch hamburgers, and the crispy skin boneless chicken with warm white Tuscan beans, grilled red onions, arugula salad, and herbed pan jus might be just the ticket after a relaxing mud bath. The full bar has 20 carefully selected microbrews.

Pacifico Restaurante Mexicano $$
1237 Lincoln Avenue, Calistoga
(707) 942-4400
www.pacificorestaurant.com

Calistoga isn't your typical small town, so why should Pacifico be your typical Mexican restaurant? Instead of mountain ranges of rice and beans, the kitchen cooks up traditional specialties from Jalisco, Veracruz, and Oaxaca. The restaurant is especially noted for its fish dishes, such as grilled fish tacos with avocado tomatillo salsa or *camarones a la diabla*—sautéed prawns with garlic, onion, arbol chilies, and lime.

There is a full bar, and the margaritas won't let you down. Pacifico is open seven days a week for lunch and dinner. It's also popular for Saturday and Sunday brunch. (The morning favorites are huevos Benito and huevos Pacifico, Mexican eggs Benedict with a mulato chili hollandaise.) The restaurant takes reservations for parties of seven or more.

Soo Yuan $
1354 Lincoln Avenue, Calistoga
(707) 942-9404
The Fang family opened their first restaurant in Taipei in 1974, and they have operated in Calistoga since 1985. The tried-and-true favorites include pepper-sauce spareribs, asparagus with prawns, and mu shu pancakes. If you can't reach a decision, go for the multicourse Soo Yuan Special Dinner. Soo Yuan is open daily for lunch and dinner.

Stomp $$$$
1457 Lincoln Avenue, Calistoga
(707) 942-8272
www.stomprestaurant.com
Located in the Mount View Hotel, Stomp is a delightful middle-of-town location to people watch in Calistoga (ask for a table by the window). It's also a great place to enjoy a fine dinner composed of small plates and bowls. Some choices might be English pea soup with Maine lobster, mackerel with orzo pasta, Alaskan halibut with ravioli, ahi tuna, quail with leeks, and much more. Stomp is open for dinner Tuesday through Sunday.

Wappo Bar & Bistro $$$
1226 Washington Street, Calistoga
(707) 942-4712
www.wappobar.com
One of the few Calistoga restaurants not found on Lincoln Avenue, the compact Wappo Bar is easy to miss—and that would be a big mistake. The scene is fairly informal and always gratifying, especially in the summer when the arbor-protected brick patio takes center stage. The inside features copper-topped tables and a wine bar with redwood interior; in the warmer months, ask for a table next to the fountain outside.

Signature dishes include the chili relleno with walnut pomegranate sauce; a paella of chorizo, rabbit, prawns, clams, and mussels; and the Chilean sea bass with Indian spices. The Wappo Bar is open for lunch and dinner six days a week (closed Tuesday).

SONOMA COUNTY

Sonoma

The Big 3 Diner at the
Fairmont Sonoma Mission Inn $$$
18141 Sonoma Highway, Sonoma
(707) 939-2410, (800) 862-4945
www.sonomamissioninn.com
This is a great place for breakfast—the eggs Benedict with rosemary potatoes will draw you back time after time. Since this is connected to the Fairmont Sonoma Mission Inn Spa (see the Spas and Resorts chapter), the menu also includes dishes for the calorie watcher that are equally good— especially apple oatcakes with walnuts and crème fraîche. Lunch and dinner are served each day, with a fine wine list and full bar. Service is friendly but not intrusive.

Carneros at the Lodge
at Sonoma $$$$
1325 Broadway, Sonoma
(707) 931-2042
www.carnerosrestaurant.com
This restaurant can be found within the hotel/spa complex the Lodge at Sonoma (see the Spas and Resorts chapter), but you needn't be a guest at the lodge to enjoy dining here. There are interesting

dishes that change with the seasons. Here are a few examples of what you might find: wood oven–roasted whole fish with baby artichokes, horseradish *pappardelle* with short rib ragu, rotisserie rib eye with caramelized shallots, and Sonoma lamb offered with braised fennel or slow-roasted with tomatoes and lemon thyme. The atmosphere is relaxed and casual. It's open for breakfast, lunch, and dinner daily.

Della Santina's   **$$**
133 East Napa Street, Sonoma
(707) 935-0576
www.dellasantinas.com
This intimate, no-frills Italian trattoria-pasticceria faces onto the main street, and the food is authentic Italian prepared from recipes inspired by owner Dan Santina's grandmother. All dishes are made from scratch, using a rotisserie to contain the flavors of all the herbs and spices used in such dishes as locally raised chicken, rabbit, and duck. The menu offers traditional northern Italian fare such as lasagna Bolognese, pressed squab, and all sorts of antipasti. One of the best entrees—maybe the best in all of Wine Country—is *pollo allo spiedo,* a traditional Italian roast chicken. Della Santina's serves lunch and dinner every day. Because the restaurant is small, reservations are advised.

Depot Hotel Cucina Rustica   **$$$**
241 First Street W., Sonoma
(707) 938-2980
www.depothotel.com
Located in a historic stone building a block from the plaza, this was once a hotel but it is now a delightful restaurant serving northern Italian cuisine. The chef does wonders with such dishes as ravioli *al bosco* (shiitake mushrooms and herbs sautéed with white wine and shallots) and hand-stuffed tortellini. One of the real delights of the restaurant is its garden, with Roman fountain and poolside dining. Vegetarian dishes and heart-healthy choices are also offered. The wine list is strictly from the Sonoma and Carneros Valleys and has won *Wine Spectator* mag-

azine's Award of Excellence several times. Lunch is available Wednesday through Friday and dinner is served Wednesday through Sunday.

Deuce   **$$$**
691 Broadway, Sonoma
(707) 933-3823
www.dine-at-deuce.com
A popular eatery for more than 10 years, Deuce recently changed ownership, which resulted in a new menu and refurbished dining room. The food reflects mostly French and Italian influences, and you can expect such dishes as a caramelized pork chop, skillet roasted clams, goat cheese ravioli, and roasted halibut. Deuce serves lunch and dinner daily.

The Girl & the Fig   **$$$$**
110 West Spain Street, Sonoma
(707) 938-3634
www.thegirlandthefig.com
The name conjures up a sensual experience that's slightly naughty. Perhaps it's because the food is sinful, the service attentive, and the decor awash in pastels. On the ground floor of the Sonoma Hotel on the plaza, the Girl & the Fig promises and delivers country-style Provençal-inspired cuisine. Figs figure prominently in some of the dishes, especially the signature fig salad with goat cheese, pancetta, pecans, and arugula. Several cheese cart and charcuterie selections are offered (a goat cheese sampler, for instance), spring vegetable risotto, free-range chicken, and sea scallops with bean and lobster ragout. The owner, Sondra Bernstein, emphasizes local seasonal produce, so the menu selections will vary. Also a nice touch in a town that rolls up the sidewalks early: a late dinner menu from 9:30 to 11:00 P.M. on Friday and Saturday.

La Casa Restaurant   **$$$**
121 East Spain Street, Sonoma
(707) 996-3406
www.lacasarestaurant.com
In a town dedicated to Italian cuisine, La Casa's smashing Mexican food is as wel-

come as a breeze in the heat of summer. The ambience is as close to authentic as you can get north of the border, with Mexican woven leather chairs and a tiled bar. The nachos are sensational, the salsa and chips addictive. For a view of the Sonoma Mission and Barracks (see the Attractions chapter), ask for a window seat. Or choose to eat outdoors on the patio facing onto El Paseo de Sonoma courtyard. Fiesta hour (from 4:00 to 6:00 P.M. Monday through Friday) is popular among the locals, thanks to the ambience and the great margaritas.

Saddles $$$$
29 East MacArthur Street, Sonoma
(707) 933-3191
www.macarthurplace.com
Within the classy MacArthur Place hotel and spa (see the Spas and Resorts chapter), this restaurant exudes a rustic, bunkhouse feel, because it's in the original barn on the property. It has a cowboy motif—with real saddles made into chairs in the lobby and the wait staff in denims—but don't expect beans and boiled coffee here. What you will find is plenty of red meat and fixins, primarily midwestern corn-fed, mesquite-grilled USDA prime beef. For lighter appetites, there's salmon, mahimahi, and chicken entrees. Start your meal with the cornmeal onion rings—a crunchy, tasty bit of heaven. The wine list runs about 70 labels strong and there's a martini bar that offers 14 different oversize libations. Saddles is open daily for lunch and dinner, with a weekend brunch to boot.

Sante at the Fairmont
Sonoma Mission Inn $$$$
18140 Sonoma Highway, Sonoma
(707) 938-9000, (800) 862-4945
www.fairmont.com
If you're ready to go upscale, walk to the main building of the inn for a Sunday brunch overlooking the pool, or have lunch or dinner in an ambience that has country-club class—elegant but not stuffy. This is a spa, after all (see the Spas and Resorts chapter), so the cuisine leans

toward healthful preparations using lighter sauces, lots of vegetables, and delicate fish and chicken dishes. But have no fear—you can still order a bit of decadence by topping off your meal with crème brûlée. The award-winning wine list features 300 selections from Napa and Sonoma vineyards. Reservations are recommended for dinner. Sante is open daily.

The Swiss Hotel $$$
18 West Spain Street, Sonoma
(707) 938-2884
www.swisshotelsonoma.com
It's a wonderful old building—a remarkably preserved adobe that was once the home of General Mariano Vallejo's brother, Salvador, who built it in 1850. It became "the Swiss" when a stagecoach operator bought it and changed the name. Today it is easily recognizable by the Swiss flag flying over the door.

For decades the restaurant was patronized largely by local families who came for the generous family-style Italian dinners. The barroom was a hangout for locals as well, who came to meet and greet friends.

The menu is a bit upscale from the days of the massive Italian feasts, but the pastas are still served al dente, and the pizzas are turned out of wood-burning brick ovens. It's open daily for lunch and dinner.

Glen Ellen

The Fig Cafe and Wine Bar $$
13690 Arnold Drive, Glen Ellen
(707) 938-2130
www.thefigcafe.com
Sondra Bernstein owns two restaurants in the Sonoma Valley: the one described in the Sonoma listings, and this one, which moved into the space previously occupied by that fig girl. This bright and airy restaurant serves American comfort food with French accents. Figs are featured in some dishes, but you can also expect several different pizzas and sandwiches, duck

confit, braised pot roast, chicken stew, and such satisfying desserts as a mixed nut tart with caramel sauce. Prices are reasonable, kids are welcome, and the blues can be heard on the sound system. Open for dinner only.

Garden Court Cafe & Bakery   **$**
13647 Arnold Drive, Glen Ellen
(707) 935-1565
www.gardencourtcafe.com
This popular cafe's bright green awning is easy to spot. Breakfast is the big draw, with eggs Benedict in three varieties leading the popularity list and a variety of omelets following close behind. The cafe is open for breakfast and lunch seven days a week, and dinner is served on Friday night.

Glen Ellen Inn Restaurant   **$$$$**
13670 Arnold Drive, Glen Ellen
(707) 996-6409
www.glenelleninn.com
Set inside a Cape Cod–style cottage, this tiny restaurant delivers one delight after another. You have three choices of where to eat—the indoor dining room, the sun porch, or the patio. Expect California fusion cuisine, such as grilled halibut with an orange and star anise beurre blanc atop a sticky coconut rice cake. The desserts are truly decadent. If you can manage two, go for the Bailey's Irish Cream mousse scented with chocolate and the French vanilla ice cream rolled in toasted coconut and drizzled with caramel sauce. The restaurant is open for dinner every night except winter Wednesday.

Kenwood

Kenwood Restaurant   **$$$$**
9900 Sonoma Highway, Kenwood
(707) 833-6326
www.kenwoodrestaurant.com
The parking lot is always full—which is a sure sign of the restaurant's well-deserved popularity. The chef makes an extraordinary

bouillabaisse, using seafood from Bodega Bay in a flavorful broth. The roast duck, using local fowl, is crispy on the outside, tender inside. And the prawns in succulent sauce with puff pastry are sheer inspiration. *Gourmet* magazine once voted this one of the top-20 restaurants in the entire Bay Area. One of the real pleasures of dining here is the opportunity to drink in the exquisite view as the late-afternoon sun hits the peaks of Sugarloaf Ridge. The scene is particularly rewarding from the deck. The wine list is acclaimed for featuring the best wines produced in Kenwood (bar drinks are also available). Lunch and dinner are served Wednesday through Sunday.

Petaluma

Jellyfish Grille   **$$$**
745 Baywood Drive, Petaluma
(707) 283-2900
www.sheratonpetaluma.com
Despite being named for a poisonous sea creature, the small restaurant in the Sheraton Sonoma County Hotel is remarkably appealing. Begin by perusing the list of specialty cocktails, or order from the sake menu, then take a look at the impressive wine list, which offers 30 wines by the glass and 14 half bottles. The cuisine is Asian fusion, and the *negamake* (asparagus and scallions wrapped in beef) and the Hog Island oysters are reportedly sensational. There's also ravioli, sea bass, Petaluma Liberty duck breast, lamb loin chops, and much more.

McNear's Saloon and Dining House   **$$**
23 North Petaluma Boulevard, Petaluma
(707) 765-2121
www.mcnears.com
It's friendly, funky, and great fun. Every square inch of the walls is covered with historic memorabilia and old photographs, including old sleds, skis, street signs, flags, and banners. The name McNear looms large in Petaluma history, stretching back to 1856 when John McNear came to town,

creating a business empire and becoming the first owner of the McNear Building. The goal of the present-day owners is to provide a meeting, eating, and entertainment spot for locals and fun-loving visitors (see the Nightlife chapter for more about the entertainment at McNear's Mystic Theatre next door). Barbecue is the house specialty, with an extensive menu to back that up; the saloon is well stocked. The dining room is large, but the sidewalk cafe in front is the popular place to sip espresso on Sunday morning. McNear's is open for lunch and dinner every day of the week, plus breakfast on Sunday.

Volpi's Ristorante $$$
124 Washington Street, Petaluma
(707) 765-0695

There's a lot of old-world charm in this place run by the Volpi family; it's been on the local scene since 1925—in a building that was once a speakeasy. This is family-style dining in an unhurried atmosphere. The cuisine is Italian, created by chef Glen Petrucci, who specializes in homemade pastas, veal, and seafood. The fully stocked bar serves tavern and restaurant patrons. If you're up to it, you can listen to live accordion music Friday and Saturday evenings. Lunch is served Wednesday, Thursday, and Friday; dinner Wednesday through Sunday.

Santa Rosa

John Ash & Co. $$$$
4330 Barnes Road, Santa Rosa
(707) 527-7687, (800) 421-2584
www.johnashrestaurant.com

John Ash is no longer there, but the cuisine he created carries on, with each entree made a masterpiece of taste, texture, color, and design. Nothing here is ordinary. The fare is "Wine Country cuisine," i.e., California cuisine using only the freshest produce from local farmers and local goat cheeses—a signature dish is the Dungeness crab cakes. Large, arched windows give an open airy feeling to the din-

ing room. The wine list is one of the best, with a good selection sold by the glass. John Ash & Co. is adjacent to Vintners Inn, a Provençal-style hotel arranged around a central plaza and fountain, all set in a 45-acre vineyard (see the Hotels, Motels, and Inns chapter). The restaurant and bar are open for dinner seven days a week, but John Ash & Co. does not serve lunch on Monday.

Equus $$$$
101 Fountaingrove Parkway, Santa Rosa
(707) 578-0149
www.fountaingroveinn.com

Because this is the restaurant for Fountain Grove Inn (see the Hotels, Motels, and Inns chapter), the decorating theme is horses and honors Equus, the legendary horse. The menu changes with each season, and a couple of dishes to try are the gold-dust salmon stir-fry or pan-fried Alaskan halibut with saffron risotto. The desserts have won double gold awards at the Sonoma County Harvest Fair—they are *that* yummy. You may choose to sink into a spacious booth or dine center stage under the coffered mahogany ceiling. Take time to examine the Gallery of Sonoma County Wines, a display of nearly 300 premium wines, chosen personally by each winery's own winemaker. Dinner is served daily.

La Gare French Restaurant $$$
208 Wilson Street, Santa Rosa
(707) 528-4355

La Gare has been voted "most romantic" and "best restaurant" by the *Press Democrat* newspaper. The *Bohemian* also has awarded La Gare its "best restaurant" award for the past few years. Tucked away in Santa Rosa's historic Railroad Square, it's a favorite of the locals, who come for hearty, country-style, traditional French cooking. Romantic it is, with lace curtains, soft lighting, and stained glass. It is one of the few places in Wine Country that you are offered (gasp!) French wines. La Gare ("railway station") is open for dinner Wednesday through Sunday.

Latitude $$$$
5000 Roberts Lake Road, Rohnert Park
(707) 588–1800
www.latitudegrill.com
Latitude is a large restaurant with both a dining room and a cafe area with full bar. For alfresco seating in warm weather, there is also a patio overlooking pleasant Roberts Lake. The food here is called "new American," meaning it's inspired by many different international flavors and paired with Sonoma County's freshest products. For example, you can expect dishes such as goat cheese fritters, wild mushroom risotto, and lemon oregano chicken. Meal starters might include butternut squash soup or lobster and crab salad. The cafe/bar has its own menu that is served all day, and you can also order off the regular lunch and dinner menus. Latitude is located in Rohnert Park, just outside the Santa Rosa city limits.

Mixx Enoteca Luigi $$$
135 Fourth Street, Santa Rosa
(707) 573–1344
www.mixxrestaurant.com
This popular longtime restaurant in Santa Rosa's Railroad Square got a new owner in 2005 and a new menu focusing on Tuscan-inspired cuisine. Owner Luigi Lezzi is from southern Italy and chef Rita Faglia is from Rome, so the food is authentic and reasonably priced. Expect lots of pasta, many kinds of antipasti, steak and veal dishes, and fish and lamb specialties. A tableside Caesar salad for two can be whipped up while you watch. The restaurant is open daily, except Sunday, for lunch and dinner.

Omelette Express $
112 Fourth Street, Santa Rosa
(707) 525–1690
If you happen to be walking around Santa Rosa's Railroad Square on a weekend morning, you'll see as many people on the sidewalk waiting to get into this restaurant as there are patrons inside. The menu lists more than 40 different varieties of the humble omelet—both plain and fancy, including vegetarian and seafood. The choices for lunch include two dozen "Pullman Car" sandwiches. You might want to bite into the Hot Express Special—grilled onions, mushrooms, melted jack and cheddar cheese, served open face on dark rye. The restaurant is open for breakfast and lunch seven days a week and most holidays.

The Seafood Brasserie $$$
170 Railroad Street, Santa Rosa
(707) 636–7388
www.vineyardcreek.com
Vineyard Creek is one of two major new hotels in Sonoma County. Surprisingly, both of the restaurants at these hotels are well above average. The Seafood Brasserie leans toward seafood, and lots of it. There are dishes revolving around swordfish, scallops, Sacramento Delta crayfish, Dungeness crab, Alaskan halibut, and Hawaiian opah. The wine list is heavy on Sonoma County selections, with reasonable prices. The service in particular is very good.

Willi's Wine Bar $$$$
4404 Old Redwood Highway, Santa Rosa
(707) 526–3096
www.williswinebar.net
Willi's emphasis is on small plates that are meant to be shared. The flavors and the prices for each plate vary widely, but everything is tasty. There are more than 30 plates to choose from, plus desserts, and it's fun to mix and match many different items into a complete and satisfying meal. Some plates to try are the black truffle risotto with Parmesan, caramelized parsnips and leeks, skillet-roasted shrimp, and Hog Island oysters prepared two ways. Among the dessert items are Rice Krispie treats. Another plus: Many wines are available in two-ounce and five-ounce pours, so you may try a particular wine without buying an entire bottle. The restaurant is located in a house built in 1886, and there are plenty of nice old touches to the place, including a copper ceiling above the 14-seat wine bar.

Zazu $$$
3535 Guerneville Road, Santa Rosa
(707) 523-4814
www.zazurestaurant.com
When it was the Willowside Café, loyal droves from as far away as San Francisco came to partake of the cuisine. Reincarnated in the same location, Zazu offers familiar food with a twist. There are small plates and big plates to choose from, with choices such as Hog Island oysters; butternut squash hash with quail eggs; bacon-wrapped sweetbreads; duck soup with white truffle oil; and venison, swordfish, and flatiron steak. Zazu is open for dinner Wednesday through Sunday.

Healdsburg

Bistro Ralph $$$$
109 Plaza Street, Healdsburg
(707) 433-1380
Bistro Ralph offers a somewhat formal but unstuffy atmosphere, featuring American country French cuisine. The place is plain enough, with white-linen-covered tables lined up along one wall in an arrangement reminiscent of earlier San Francisco Italian restaurants. The food is prepared with an imaginative touch and fresh ingredients. Chef-owner Ralph Tingle can be seen at the farmers' market Saturday mornings, selecting from the seasonal bounty of vegetables that will be on his menu that night. The smoked salmon starter with an unusual focaccia pastry is a good choice. Enjoy a bottle of local wine or beer with your meal or the specialty of the house: a dry martini. Bistro Ralph is open for lunch and dinner on weekdays and for dinner only on weekends.

Dry Creek General Store $
3495 Dry Creek Road, Healdsburg
(707) 433-4171
It's an old-time grocery store that looks as it it's been there forever. But if you've been cruising the Dry Creek vineyards for hours and your tummy says it's picnic time, you'll love the simple, delicious homemade sandwiches and salads, the wine selection, and the gourmet food section. Take your purchases to any one of the many wineries in the area, buy yourself a bottle of their best, and settle in for a beautiful picnic. The store is open seven days a week from 6:00 A.M. to 6:00 P.M. The bar adjacent to the store is open from 3:00 to 8:00 P.M. weekdays and 3:00 P.M. to midnight weekends.

Dry Creek Kitchen $$$$
317 Healdsburg Avenue, Healdsburg
(707) 431-0330
www.hotelhealdsburg.com,
www.drycreekkitchen.com
Maybe you've heard of Charlie Palmer. He was named New York City's best chef in 1997. His restaurant ventures include Aureole, with locations in New York and Las Vegas; Alva American Bistro in Manhattan; and Charlie Palmer Steak at the Four Seasons Hotel in Las Vegas. A few years back he brought his award-winning way with cuisine to Wine Country, in the restaurant of the Hotel Healdsburg (see the Hotels, Motels, and Inns chapter).

Charlie's approach is to present American cooking with European influences and do it spectacularly with a hearty heaping of locally grown organic produce. Expect fabulous flavors and presentations around duck, salmon, beef—to name a few—and appetizers and desserts to die for. There's also a fixed-price seven-course tasting menu. To accompany your meal, you're sure to find just the right vino among the eight-page wine list. The dining room is delightful, with soft lighting, fine art, and views of leafy Healdsburg Plaza. Lunch is served until 3:00 P.M. daily; dinner begins at 5:00 P.M. daily and lasts a bit later than most places—10:00 P.M. on weekdays and 10:30 P.M. on weekends.

Healdsburg Bar & Grill $$
245 Healdsburg Avenue, Healdsburg
(707) 433-3333
www.hbg4fun.com
Is it a restaurant, or is it a bar? It's both, and the proprietors handle the food and

drink equally well. The cuisine isn't gourmet or snooty, but it's well above the standard fare you might expect. There's an adequate wine list too, with many wines available by the glass. For dinner, choose from a blackened snapper sandwich, lamb chops, or salmon sautéed with radicchio and coarse-grain mustard sauce. Top off your meal with crème brûlée or mousse, then stick around for the live entertainment on weekends (see the Nightlife chapter) and be prepared to do some dancing. The atmosphere is friendly and upscale, and there's an outdoor patio when the weather turns warm. Hotel Healdsburg is just steps away.

Lotus Thai Restaurant $$
109-A Plaza Street, Healdsburg
(707) 433-5282
www.lotusthai.com
Here's where Bangkok meets Healdsburg. The chef has managed to strike a near-perfect balance between authentic dishes of Thailand and the tastes and desires of Californians. His is arguably the most succulent chicken satay with the best peanut sauce north of the Golden Gate. It's a neat, clean, and well-lit storefront restaurant. Service is unobtrusive and adequate. Open for lunch and dinner daily.

Madrona Manor $$$$
1001 Westside Road, Healdsburg
(707) 433-4231
www.madronamanor.com
Nestled on a wooded knoll surrounded by lush vineyards, Madrona Manor is a majestic sight, its mansard roof rising three stories into the treetops (see the Bed-and-Breakfast Inns chapter). The dining room is opulent, the atmosphere romantic. Chef Jesse Mallgren specializes in New California cuisine, using the freshest produce and ingredients available in Sonoma County. He might create an appetizer of crab with ruby red grapefruit, avocado, arugula, and pancetta vinaigrette; and an entree of roast venison loin with carrots, leek risotto, nectarine-rosemary bro-

chettes, and vanilla sauce.

A fixed-price menu and two gourmet tasting menus are offered daily. There's an extensive a la carte menu Sunday through Thursday. It's open daily for dinner, but prior to eating you might want to stroll through the delightful eight-acre gardens. Long story short: Madrona Manor is everything you love about Wine Country.

Manzanita $$$$
336 Healdsburg Avenue, Healdsburg
(707) 433-8111
Manzanita opened in 2001 with standard Wine Country menu selections such as cassoulet and roast sea bass—California cuisine with European influences. But chef Bruce Frieseke has created an outstanding example of what makes a restaurant great: food with flair, combined with terrific service in pleasant surroundings. The first-course options are exceptional—baked black mussels, a truffled beet salad, carrot soup—and the entrees might include grilled rabbit set off with polenta, sweet cooked prunes, and black chanterelle mushrooms. There's a small wine bar, and the wine list is impressive. Dinner is served Wednesday through Sunday until 10:00 P.M.

Ravenous $$$
420 Center Street, Healdsburg
(707) 431-1302
Once a tiny restaurant next to the Raven Film Center, with just a few tables and many people milling about outside waiting for those coveted tables, Ravenous has moved up in the world. It's now a full-size restaurant not far from the old place, and the food is better than ever. Chef Joyanne Pezzolo serves generous portions of amazing cuisine that defies categorizing. You can order Liberty duck legs steamed and roasted, presented atop noodles, and accompanied by grilled white and black eggplant; or choose the beef brisket braised in red wine. It comes with potato fritters and tasty vegetables too. Lunch and dinner are served Wednesday through Sunday.

Zin $$$$
344 Center Street, Healdsburg
(707) 473-0946
www.zinrestaurant.com

Why name a restaurant after a wine varietal? Because Zin delivers great food and offers lots of great Zinfandels too. Much of the cuisine is created to be enjoyed with Zinfandel and features an all-American accent. You might find St. Louis–style ribs one night and roasted chicken with polenta on another night. Chefs Jeff Mall and Scott Silva call their cuisine "New American"—updating classic American dishes with more interesting flavors and imagination. The dining room is simple, with big bouquets of flowers and soothing paintings. You can get dinner here every night but Tuesday and lunch on weekdays (except Tuesday).

Sonoma Coast

Bay View Restaurant $$$$
800 Coast Highway 1, Bodega Bay
(707) 875-2751
www.innatthetides.com

Bay View is part of Inn at the Tides, one of the most relaxing hostelries at Bodega Bay (see the Hotels, Motels, and Inns chapter). The restaurant features a menu that changes weekly and goes well beyond the local catch. Look for grilled ahi tuna on the menu, bouillabaisse, grilled wild king salmon, and rack of lamb. Cocktails are served in the lounge, a romantic setting as the sun goes down over the Pacific. The restaurant is open for dinner Wednesday through Sunday.

Lucas Wharf Restaurant & Bar $$$
595 Highway 1, Bodega Bay
(707) 875-3522
www.lucaswharf.com

This is a cozy, romantic place, with a vaulted ceiling and a fireplace to warm you when the weather cools (as it often does on this coast). Seafood will never be fresher than it is here, for this is a commercial fishery that supplies grocers and the public with fresh Pacific catch. The chef's special of the day is based on the best of the day's catch—salmon, halibut, crab, calamari, and oysters. Bask in the glow of the setting sun while you enjoy your meal or watch sea birds cavort as fishermen deliver their bounty at the pier (ask for a window table). Lucas Wharf is a great place to pick up fresh cracked crab or custom-smoked fish. The restaurant is open for lunch and dinner seven days a week. Fresh crab season is mid-November through June, and fresh salmon season is mid-May through September.

River's End Restaurant $$$$
11048 Highway 1, Jenner
(707) 865-2484
www.rivers-end.com

From its position on a bluff where the Russian River flows into the Pacific, River's End has an extraordinary view. Menu offerings have left local seafood far behind and moved on to upscale comfort foods with a European flair. Here you can have beluga caviar for an appetizer, whiskey-marinated lobster for the fish course, and roasted rack of lamb filled with oysters for the entree. The house specialties sound almost as exciting—say, beef Wellington or medallions of venison. Another might be crunchy coco shrimp. Either way, the restaurant is open for breakfast, lunch, and dinner Friday through Sunday.

The Tides Wharf & Restaurant $$$
835 Highway 1, Bodega Bay
(707) 875-3652
www.innatthetides.com

If the setting looks familiar, it's because you saw it in Alfred Hitchcock's film *The Birds*. If you didn't see the movie, you can get a taste of the action through a poster on the wall. Aside from the renown that has come from Tippi Hedren fending off birds, the restaurant has earned its own fame as the long-standing favorite of regulars who have been popping in since the place was small. There's both a snack bar and a full-service sit-down restaurant, as well as a fish market. Pick up some fresh

Dungeness crab at the market when it's in season (see the close-up in this chapter), along with wine, bread, cheese, and many other deli items. The restaurant is open every day for breakfast, lunch, and dinner, and it offers full bar service.

West County/ Russian River

Alice's Restaurant at 101 Main $$$
101 South Main Street, Sebastopol
(707) 829-3212
www.alicesrestaurant.net
This small, cozy restaurant—with comfortable upholstered chairs and fresh flowers on every table—is friendly and inviting, and the food is among the best in town. The grilled chicken Caesar salad is excellent, as is the duck confit, which includes crispy fried organic baby spinach and garlic mashed potatoes. Alice's also serves delicious crab cakes, and there's a menu for kids too. Open daily for lunch and dinner. North Coast labels predominate on the wine list, many available by the glass. Alice also serves locally produced Ace Pear Cider, and her desserts are made on the premises with Ghirardelli chocolate.

Applewood Inn & Restaurant $$$$
13555 Highway 116, Guerneville
(707) 869-9093, (800) 555-8509
www.applewoodinn.com
Snuggled among the redwoods just south of Guerneville, Applewood Inn is famed

i

Wine lists can be confusing if not intimidating at times, with many obscure labels from boutique wineries unfamiliar to the average diner. Don't hesitate to ask a restaurant's sommelier (pronounced suh-muhl-YAY) for help in making your selection. These wine experts can recommend a good, reasonably priced bottle to complement your meal.

for its sophisticated meals and comfortable lodgings (see the Bed-and-Breakfast Inns chapter). It's one of those special places you want to keep to yourself, but you can't stop talking about it. The fire-lit dining room serves 60 at individual candlelit tables with windows facing the redwoods on three sides. The restaurant does wonderful things with a crisp duck breast set off with corn and bing cherries, stuffed pork loin cured in spiced black tea and basmati rice, or roasted salmon with mushrooms and chive-caviar butter. Leave room for the blueberry and *fromage blanc* cheesecake in semolina cookie crust. Applewood is open for dinner Tuesday through Saturday.

Cape Fear Cafe $$
25191 Main Street, Duncans Mills
(707) 865-9246
If you can, try to visit this restaurant for one of its weekend brunches, when the chef's phenomenal menu of Benedicts is available. The cooking here is a mixture of California cuisine with a southern bent, so expect such dinner entrees as Carolina chicken (with bourbon and pecans) or pork tenderloin with mahogany ginger sauce. But it's those Benedicts that can make your weekend. Instead of English muffins, the poached eggs are served on peppered grits. Similar to polenta, the grits are cooked, cooled, mixed with cheese, and then grilled.

Chez Marie $$$
6675 Front Street (Highway 116), Forestville
(707) 887-7503
www.chezmarie.com
Chez Marie offers a cozy, unpretentious atmosphere, exceptional food, a glowing fireplace on cool nights, and French country-kitchen and Mardi Gras decor. Thursday through Sunday the restaurant features Cajun-Creole dishes done in an authentic New Orleans style—the chef's hometown—and French-continental cuisine. The rotating menu includes such items as escargots, cassoulet, bouilla-

baisse, lamb chops, étouffée, and gumbo. From the homemade bread served hot from the oven to the elegant desserts, all items are prepared to order. The outdoor patio, which borders the restaurant's herb and flower garden, offers a charming setting in which to enjoy a meal.

The Farmhouse Inn & Restaurant $$$
**7871 River Road, Forestville
(707) 887-3300
www.farmhouseinn.com**
The bed-and-breakfast service includes dinner, and the Farmhouse restaurant is open to visitors as well as guests. The menu changes frequently, but one dish that appears regularly is rabbit, prepared three ways. Count on braised pork shank, Merlot-and-mint–braised lamb shank, and petrale sole filet crisped with couscous. For dessert you can choose baked Alaska or chocolate soufflé. The romantic dining room seats no more than two dozen, with views through French doors onto the magnificent gardens. Open for dinner Thursday through Sunday (see the Bed-and-Breakfast Inns chapter).

Negri's $$
**3700 Bohemian Highway, Occidental
(707) 823-5301
www.negris.com**
It's a toss-up whether the hungry folks of Sonoma County head first for Union Hotel or Negri's—they're both terrific purveyors of great Italian meals. Negri's has been cooking pasta since 1940. Its fame is well established, as is the expertise of the family that has been running the place since it opened. A family-style meal starts out with a tureen of minestrone that's so popular people come in to buy it by the bucket. The pasta list is long, including vegetarian spaghetti, penne, and homemade ravioli. After that, if you choose, you can order some of their other specials, such as deep-fried calamari, grilled red snapper, and prawns—wash it down with a drink from the fully stocked bar. Open for lunch and dinner every day.

Smoking is not permitted in California restaurants and nightclubs.

Sparks $$
**16248 Main Street, Guerneville
(707) 869-8206
www.sparksrestaurant.com**
California is vegetarian heaven, and this small but hip gourmet eatery serves extraordinary fare that seems sinful, but it's not. Like San Francisco's renowned Millennium Restaurant, the menu is 100 percent vegan, meaning absolutely no animal products. Even ruthless carnivores will enjoy such dishes as the rich, smoky "sausage" and potatoes (made with protein-rich wheat gluten), the polenta torte (made with layers of spinach and tomato polenta and a garlic-tofu ricotta), or the tempeh vegetable loaf. Add a glass of local organic wine and it's the quintessential California experience. Open for breakfast, lunch, dinner, and weekend brunch; closed Tuesday.

Stella's Cafe $$$
**4550 Gravenstein Highway N.,
Sebastopol
(707) 823-6637
www.stellascafe.net**
Set in an unassuming building in outer Sebastopol, Stella's Cafe is where locals go to enjoy a revolving menu of creative delicacies, whipped up by chef-owner Greg Hallihan. Items such as the steamed half artichoke stuffed with a scoop of purple-black niçoise olive tapenade, the hearty lentil-carrot soup, the lamb kabob, or the pan-roasted chicken with truffled mashed potatoes—not to mention the mocha crème brûlée and other luscious desserts—keep this place packed on most nights. If you are too stuffed for dessert, buy a Gravenstein apple pie to go at Mom's Apple Pie Shop, a Sonoma County institution, located right next door. Open Wednesday through Monday for dinner, and lunch every day except Sunday. The restaurant is closed on Tuesday.

Underwood Bar & Bistro $$$
9113 Graton Road, Graton
(707) 823-7023

North of Sebastopol just off Highway 116 in the tiny town of Graton is Underwood Bar & Bistro, housed in a newly refurbished building that still feels old and familiar. Here's where to get tapas and small plates, such as a fresh asparagus appetizer with baguettes with tapenade. There's a cheese plate and several excellent salads and oysters to choose from. Try the fish stew made with prawns, monkfish, and mussels; roasted duck breast on a bed of lentils; or lamb with Moroccan spices.

Union Hotel Restaurant $$
3731 Main Street, Occidental
(707) 874-3555
www.unionhotel.com

It seems like the Union Hotel dining room has been there forever, housed in a building that dates from 1879. The restaurant has not been around quite that long, but the same family has run it since 1925. The great fame of the place comes from the huge portions of pasta that are served family-style—it's known far and wide for the heaping helpings. The portions are outsize, and the family really knows how to cook pasta. But there are other great items on the menu, chicken cacciatore for one. The establishment has its own bakery and makes great croissants and muffins to serve in its cafe. The restaurant is open for lunch and dinner every day, serving family-style meals and drinks from the saloon.

MENDOCINO COUNTY

U.S. Highway 101

Bluebird Cafe $$
13340 South US 101, Hopland
(707) 744-1633

Housed in a building that was once a bordello, this roadhouse serves up generous portions of familiar American classics. Kid friendly and comfortable, Bluebird presents small-town cooking at its finest. If you're in the mood for a burger, you've come to the right place: Besides beef, there's elk, wild boar, ostrich, and buffalo burgers. In addition to an assortment of sandwiches, pasta dishes and other familiar favorites are served. Open daily.

North State Cafe $$
263 North State Street, Ukiah
(707) 462-3726

The logo says it all: "A Casual Experience in Fine Dining." The atmosphere here is that of a fine restaurant, without being too dressy—somewhere between tank tops and neckties. The fare, known as "California Italian," features fresh local ingredients.

Ukiah is not a town with a heavy influx of tourists, and the cafe's clientele is mostly local—much of the patronage coming from the staff at the nearby courthouse. The cafe is open for lunch Monday through Friday from 11:00 A.M. to 2:00 P.M., and for dinner Tuesday through Saturday from 5:00 to 9:00 P.M.

Valley Oaks Deli $
Fetzer Vineyards, Highway 175 and Eastside Road, Hopland
(707) 744-1250
www.fetzer.com

This gourmet deli is in the visitor center of Fetzer Vineyards (see the Wineries chapter) and offers an extraordinary selection of fresh salads and sandwiches, all made daily with organic vegetables, fruits, and herbs grown in Fetzer's adjacent Bonterra Garden. Try a grilled vegetable sandwich on focaccia with jambalaya pasta salad. For dessert, go for a cappuccino and the "devil's triangle," if you're a chocolate lover. If you are on your way to a picnic, Valley Oaks can supply you with a special gourmet bag lunch, created to fit your needs. The deli is open daily from 9:00 A.M. to 5:00 P.M. and adjoins the tasting room. Pick up some of Fetzer's best and take it all out to a table on the patio.

Mendocino Coast

Albion River Inn Restaurant   **$$$$**
3790 North Highway 1, Albion
(707) 937-1919, (800) 479-7944
www.albionriverinn.com

A spectacular ocean view, California cuisine, and an award-winning wine list combine to make this an especially romantic dining place. There's seafood, sure, but lots of other options too, such as roast breast of duck with lentils and carmelized bacon, or pasta with rich Bavarian cambozola cream sauce.

Dinner is served nightly seven days a week: 5:30 to 9:00 P.M. Monday through Friday, and 5:00 to 9:30 P.M. Saturday and Sunday. Reservations are essential. (See the Hotels, Motels, and Inns chapter for more information on this inn.)

The Ledford House Restaurant   **$$$$**
3000 North Highway 1, Albion
(707) 937-0282
www.ledfordhouse.com

If you've ever been to Provence in southern France, you'll recognize the style and ambience of this restaurant. The expansive windows look out on the Pacific. Add candlelight and music and you've got the basis for a most romantic evening. The food is Mediterranean, and the menu changes monthly. Regulars are rack of lamb, steak, Pacific salmon, and a selection of vegetarian entrees. Be adventurous and try the tiger prawns flamed in vermouth for dipping in a smoky hot-and-sweet mustard sauce. Dinner is served Wednesday through Sunday from 5:00 P.M., and reservations are advisable.

Little River Inn   **$$$$**
7750 North Highway 1, Little River
(707) 937-5942, (888) 466-5683
www.littleriverinn.com

Unlike that of most coastal restaurants, the menu here is not partial to seafood but leans to classics like leg of lamb filet, Cornish game hen, and grilled pork chops. Salads are made from locally grown lettuces and greens. Desserts too may feature local items—don't leave without trying the ollalieberry cobbler. The restaurant at Little River Inn is open every day for breakfast and dinner and also offers Sunday brunch. (For more on the inn, see the Spas and Resorts chapter.)

If you're ready to open that special bottle of wine you purchased at the tasting room to enjoy with a special meal, corkage fees at many restaurants are waived on certain nights of the week. Always inquire when making a reservation.

Pangaea Cafe   **$$$**
39165 South Highway 1, Gualala
(707) 884-9669
www.pangaeacafe.com

Walls are lined with paintings by local artists, giving the small restaurant a feeling of serenity. The food is distinctive, based on the chef's long experience living in other parts of the world (the Middle East, Portugal, Spain), and a changing menu reflects the global influence. Breads are baked fresh daily in a brick oven. Mendocino County wines are featured, often from small, offbeat wineries that don't get much attention. When it comes to desserts, you've hit the culinary big time with the chocolate cake with brandied cherries. Pangaea is open for dinner Wednesday through Sunday.

Mendocino Village

Cafe Beaujolais   **$$$$**
961 Ukiah Street, Mendocino
(707) 937-5614
www.cafebeaujolais.com

It was once a Victorian farmhouse at the edge of town. But the town has expanded and engulfed the farm. The ambience inside is not overwhelming—two dozen well-spaced tables occupy a rather plain room. But the food! It's been praised by

Make a Meal of Dungeness Crab

Traveling in Wine Country between late autumn and early spring? Your visit won't be complete without sinking your teeth into a delicious Dungeness crab, a fine delicacy that's usually available from November through March. Fresh fish purveyors such as the Tides Wharf and Lucas Wharf in Bodega Bay—and most supermarkets—are well stocked with the crustacean during its special season. The coast markets also carry fresh bread, cheeses, bottles of wine, and many other goodies for assembling a daytime picnic or after-dark dinner in the privacy of your hotel room.

One two-pound crab feeds two nicely as an appetizer; with two crabs, a side salad, and crusty bread you have a substantial meal for two. Ask the fish market to clean the crabs (a nasty job better left to the pros) and crack the shell lightly. Stock up on napkins or paper towels (mining the crabmeat can get messy, but that's part of the fun) and have your favorite cocktail sauce or other condiment nearby for dipping. Use the hard, pointy end from one of the legs to help extract the meat from the legs, claws, and body. Pour yourself a glass of Sauvignon Blanc (tastes great with crab), then dig, dip, and devour!

restaurant critics for more than two decades and remains something of a legend in Mendocino. Borrowing from France, Italy, Asia, and Mexico, the menu features local produce and free-range poultry as much as possible. Entrees run from sturgeon with truffle sauce, for example, to boneless veal roast. During good weather, you can dine on the large deck out back, which faces onto a beautiful garden. Another option: Call and ask what the menu is for the evening, pick up the entire meal at the "call window," and dine in your hotel room. Dinner is served nightly.

MacCallum House Restaurant   **$$$$**
Grey Whale Bar & Cafe, 45020 Albion Street, Mendocino
(707) 937-5763
www.maccallumhousedining.com
Daisy MacCallum's 1882 Victorian house is one of the earliest of Mendocino's lumber era. Now a bed-and-breakfast inn, the MacCallum House has a dining room open to the public, and the Grey Whale Bar & Cafe offers cafe fare served at friendly prices on the sunporch or parlor. The dining room is more formal, warmed by a stone fireplace. The menu emphasizes fresh local seafood and organic produce from neighboring farms. You might consider grilled portobello mushrooms or pan-seared duck breast. Dinner is served nightly, and a Sunday brunch is available after 11:00 A.M. The restaurant is closed from the first of January to mid-February.

Mendocino Hotel Restaurant
& Garden Room   **$$$**
45080 Main Street, Mendocino
(707) 937-0511, (800) 548-0513
www.mendocinohotel.com
Perhaps it's the graciousness of the hostess, or maybe it's the welcoming decor of this Victorian dining room, but somehow just being here is a pleasant experience.

California cuisine is the specialty for dinner, and it is influenced considerably by local seafood. Service is warm but not intrusive. Breakfast and lunch are available in the Garden Room, a large, airy room with a skylight ceiling that really was a garden at one time. (See the Hotels, Motels, and Inns chapter.)

The Moosse Café   **$$$**
390 Kasten Street, Mendocino
(707) 937-4323
www.theblueheron.com
Take a seat on the deck, relax, and gaze at the sea, then order some delicious food—maybe an eggplant sandwich or smoked salmon pâté. If the weather is inclement, the indoor cafe is warm and casual and the service agreeable, with beer and wine available. For the most part, the menu features fresh regional ingredients. Try the velvety-smooth chicken and potato soup, for instance. The salmon sandwich and portobello mushroom sandwich on focaccia are exceptional lunch options. Open seven days a week for lunch and dinner.

955 Ukiah Street Restaurant   **$$$$**
955 Ukiah Street, Mendocino
(707) 937-1955
www.955restaurant.com
Located in what was once an artist's studio down a garden path next door to Cafe Beaujolais, this may be one of the major reasons visitors from California and the rest of the country like to come to this coast. Basing its fame less on elegance per se than on memorable meals, the restaurant offers a wide-ranging menu and uses local products whenever possible. Options include steaks, roast duck, lamb, and pasta. The restaurant is open every day but Tuesday from 6:00 P.M.

Fort Bragg

Egghead's Restaurant   **$$**
326 North Main Street, Fort Bragg
(707) 964-5005
www.eggheadsrestaurant.com

It's known as the local's favorite, and yes, the locals do brag that there are no better omelets or eggs Benedict in the entire United States. Beyond that, Egghead's features some 40 varieties of crepes, specialty pancakes, and waffles for breakfast. For lunch, there are creative salads, unusual sandwiches, and many unique vegetarian treats. The restaurant is distinguished by another feature: a yellow brick road that runs from the front door to the kitchen (here it's known as Oz). Open seven days a week.

A national model for food recycling is taking place in some Wine Country vineyards. In a program called Four Course Compost, tons of food scraps from San Francisco restaurants are processed into high-grade compost that is spread among the vines. Giving back to the earth is good for the crops, reduces trash-hauling costs, and keeps food waste out of landfills.

Mendo Bistro   **$$$**
301 North Main Street, Fort Bragg
(707) 964-4974
www.mendobistro.com
Upstairs in the Company Store complex of shops along historic Main Street is a fine dining experience in a town not generally known for its gourmet cuisine. Mendo Bistro has changed Fort Bragg's reputation by creating a delightful environment with plenty of large picture windows looking out over the town. Entrees might include seared sea scallops on avocado with citrus dressing, grilled beef tenderloin, and herb-crusted Diestel turkey with risotto. Lighter appetites and thinner wallets might appreciate having the freedom to choose a meat (or portobello mushroom or tofu), have it cooked any way they choose (roasted to fried), then have it topped with one of seven sauces.

After an early dinner in downtown Napa, enjoy something completely different: Saturday Night Opera, when vocalists from around Northern California take turns on stage at the Jarvis Conservatory, 1711 Main Street. For $15 you get two hours of stellar operatic vocal performances on the first Saturday of every month. To book your seats, call (707) 255-5445.

The Rendezvous $$$$
647 North Main Street, Fort Bragg
(707) 964-8142
www.rendezvousinn.com

California continental–style seafood, poultry, veal, and steak are served in cozy, comfortable surroundings in one of Fort Bragg's classic early homes. Chef Kim Badenhop studied under master chefs in Switzerland and France, and much of the food served at the Rendezvous reflects the labor-intensive European style of cooking. Seasonality is important to him, and his menus reflect this—in winter he works with wild game and Dungeness crab; in summer fresh vegetables and king salmon figure strongly on his menu. Dinner is served Wednesday through Sunday, and reservations are advisable.

The Restaurant $$$
418 Main Street, Fort Bragg
(707) 964-9800
www.therestaurantfortbragg.com

Like the meeting place of the friends on television's *Seinfeld*, this place is simply called the Restaurant, as it has been for the past two decades. It offers light meals such as grilled polenta with mozzarella and sautéed mushrooms, and a delightful chicken piccata cooked in fresh lemon and white wine sauce. But whatever you eat, save room for the desserts because they're memorable—especially the tiramisu. The Restaurant presents live jazz on Friday and Saturday. It's open for dinner Thursday through Tuesday and for Sunday brunch. Reservations are recommended for Sunday brunch.

Wharf Restaurant $$$
32260 North Harbor Drive, Fort Bragg
(707) 964-4283
www.wharf-restaurant.com

The Wharf is a favorite spot for both locals and travelers, as it has been for more than 40 years. Relax as you enjoy a cocktail or specialty of the house, watching the boats bring in the catch of the day or head out for some night fishing. The chef's pride is the menu of fresh seafood, with steaks as an alternate. Open for lunch and dinner seven days a week.

NIGHTLIFE 🍸

Though most towns around here start rolling up the sidewalks after sundown, there are a number of popular music venues and dance hot spots to keep your toes tapping well into the night. Napa and St. Helena have a few options, and the downtown areas of Petaluma and Santa Rosa can be relied upon for several good shows on the weekend. Guerneville too gets lively in the summer, and Lake County's Konocti Harbor Resort is always kicking up its heels in an environment dedicated to mixing music with water sports.

So if after eating gourmet meals and drinking wine all day you are still looking for more decadent fun, here are a few Wine Country music halls, bars, and clubs where you can look for after-hours entertainment. Some of the smaller establishments don't collect a cover charge, but many do. In general, expect to pay from $2.00 to $5.00 to watch local talent, more if someone of greater renown is taking the stage. Guidelines for pricier show tickets are given in the listings.

The bar and club listings are followed by movie theaters in the region. Check a local newspaper for more up-to-date information.

I don't want to nag about this, but one thing bears repeating, especially in this chapter: Please observe the same common sense about drinking and driving that applies anywhere. California's legal blood-alcohol threshold is a stringent 0.08, so taking to the road after more than one drink can be expensive and embarrassing as well as extremely dangerous. If you need a taxi, consult the Getting Here, Getting Around chapter.

BARS AND CLUBS

Napa County

Downtown Joe's
902 Main Street, Napa
(707) 258-2337
www.downtownjoes.com
This riverside microbrewery offers a variety of rock, pop, and blues bands every Thursday, Friday, and Saturday. Sunday evening is for karaoke, and Tuesday is open-mike night.

Silverado Country Club & Resort
1600 Atlas Peak Road, Napa
(707) 257-0200
www.silveradoresort.com
A classy joint indeed, Silverado features jazz piano from 5:00 to 9:00 P.M. on the patio terrace Wednesday through Saturday. On Friday and Saturday the soloist is followed by a band that plays from 9:00 P.M. to 1:00 A.M. The regular act of late has been the five-piece Paul Martin Band.

Piccolino's Italian Cafe
1385 Napa Town Center, Napa
(707) 251-0100
www.piccolinoscafe.com
On Friday and Saturday evenings, this centrally located restaurant provides jazz accompaniment, perhaps augmented by a little R&B or salsa. Hours are generally 5:00 to 9:00 P.M.

Pacific Blues Cafe
6525 Washington Street, Yountville
(707) 944-4455
This popular restaurant and watering hole sits right outside the east entrance of the

Vintage 1870 shopping complex. In addition to serving what it calls "Maverick American" cuisine, the cafe spices things up with live blues on Saturday in summer from 5:00 to 8:00 P.M.

Ana's Cantina
1205 Main Street, St. Helena
(707) 963-4921
This tropical-themed Mexican restaurant heats up from 9:30 P.M. to 1:30 A.M. most Friday and Saturday nights, with a stream of bands that run from Latin-Mediterranean to jazz to rock to reggae. Wednesday and Sunday are karaoke nights. Thursday is open-mike night.

1351 Lounge
1351 Main Street, St. Helena
(707) 963-1969
www.1351lounge.com
A small club with a capacity for packing 'em in, that's 1351. It's usually live blues or rock on weekends, and there's always a cover charge. Acoustic singer-songwriters can be found there on the occasional weeknight.

Nonsmokers, take note: Smoking has been banned in bars and nightclubs in California since 1998. Smokers are still welcome to get in on the fun inside, but they must light up outside at least 6 feet from the establishment's entrance.

Calistoga Inn & Restaurant
1250 Lincoln Avenue, Calistoga
(707) 942-4101
www.calistogainn.com
The bartender here slings Napa Valley Brewing Company beers, and every Saturday from 8:30 to 11:00 P.M. (and often on Tuesday and Friday), live music fills the small oblong bar. The material varies but tends toward intimate, singer-songwriter stuff. Wednesday is open-mike night.

Hydro Bar & Grill
1403 Lincoln Avenue, Calistoga
(707) 942-9777
Calistoga's late-night eatery is a perfect spot for everything from swing music to rock 'n' roll, generally from 9:00 P.M. to 1:30 A.M.

Sonoma County

Murphy's Irish Pub
464 First Street E., Sonoma
(707) 935-0660
This pub keeps sleepy Sonoma awake, usually every Thursday through Sunday night. The genre is hard to predict. It could be blues one night, traditional Celtic the next. Or it could be folk ballads followed by a melodious string ensemble. There is no cover, but expect a two-pint minimum.

Kodiak Jack's
256 North Petaluma Boulevard, Petaluma
(707) 765-5760
www.kodiakjacks.com
On different nights, there is West Coast swing dancing, two-step, line dancing, "beginner couples," power country, and honky-tonk. You can take lessons every night. There's a restaurant (Sundance Steakhouse) with cuisine to match the country theme. Call for cover information.

Mystic Theatre & Music Hall
23 North Petaluma Boulevard, Petaluma
(707) 765-2121
www.mcnears.com
Not as big as Konocti Harbor, not as polite as the Luther Burbank Center, the Mystic Theatre might be Wine Country's coolest venue. Built in 1911 in the historic McNear Building, it's a vaulted, double-decker palace that wouldn't be out of place on the Sunset Strip. Much of the music is classic rock of all shades and tones, from the Dave Alvin Band to Tower of Power,

Richard Thompson to Tommy Castro, Emmylou Harris to Todd Rundgren. Van Morrison even recorded one of his live albums here. Stand-up comedy passes through from time to time, featuring jokers like Will Durst. Tickets generally range from $15 to $30.

A'Roma Roasters and Coffeehouse
95 Fifth Street, Santa Rosa
(707) 576-7765

Come down to Railroad Square on a Friday or Saturday night for live music and a hot cup of chai or joe. A'Roma does a lot of folk music, plus some world beat, jazz, and blues. Shows start at 8:30 P.M.

Last Day Saloon
120 Fifth Street, Santa Rosa
(707) 545-2343
www.lastdaysaloon.com

This is the northern outpost of the venerable San Francisco nightclub that's been rocking the Bay Area for more than 30 years. On a busy corner in Railroad Square, Last Day is 8,000 square feet of music, Bloody Marys, and food too. DJ music is provided three nights a week, with weekends dedicated to live music of all kinds—you're likely to hear Motown or disco, funk or new wave. Owner David Daher draws on his three decades in the music business to bring in some terrific acts that might have previously overlooked Santa Rosa on their tour itineraries. Recent legends appearing in the main music room have included Elvin Bishop, Nils Lofgren, the Tubes, Dr. John, and members of the Grateful Dead. Sunday night is generally reserved for showcasing local rock bands. DJ nights usually carry a $5.00 cover; tickets for live shows can range from $10.00 to $20.00, depending on whether the artist is a household name. There's also a full menu of decent pub grub, and it's served until midnight—a nice bonus for late-night revelers.

Flamingo Resort Hotel
2777 Fourth Street, Santa Rosa
(707) 545-8530
www.flamingoresort.com

Sure, it's a hotel bar, but it's better than most. Count on soul and rhythm & blues bands on the weekends, and DJs spinning discs during the week. The dance floor is one of the best around, and it's always packed with hoofers of all ages.

The Cantina
500 Fourth Street, Santa Rosa
(707) 523-3663

Generation Next moves to its own beat at the Cantina, in the heart of downtown—upstairs from the restaurant of the same name. Thursday is college night during the spring and summer. Friday and Saturday you get a mix of top 40, R&B, disco, house, and Latin beats.

Ellington Hall
3535 Industrial Avenue, Santa Rosa
(707) 545-6150
www.ellingtonhall.com

If you don't know how to dance but want to learn, or if you are a rising star looking to improve your style, then this is the place for you. You can take lessons almost every night, and you get to practice afterward during the nightly open dance parties. Tuesday it's ballroom dancing, Wednesday it's West Coast swing, Thursday is salsa night, Friday brings on the big bands and the Lindy, Saturday is variety night, and Sunday is West Coast swing. Call for prices and details.

Healdsburg Bar & Grill
245 Healdsburg Avenue, Healdsburg
(707) 433-3333
www.hbg4fun.com

Nightlife improved significantly in this sleepy burg when HB&G opened its doors. Expect live bands on weekends, usually rock 'n' roll from established local groups such as the Remedies or the Pulsators.

Sip Wine by Day, Lift a Pint at Night: A Guide to Wine Country Brewpubs

You know you've wandered into serious microbrewery territory when you can sip—at the source—satisfying suds that bear such colorful names as Death and Taxes Black Beer, Twist of Fate Bitter, Hop 2 It, Damnation, Lunatic, Ugly Dog Stout, Bony Fingers Malt, Rat Bastard Pale Ale, and Workingstiff Red.

The Wine Country ferments much more than just grape-based beverages. If you prefer ambers and blacks to reds and whites and put more stock in a drink's head than its legs, you'll feel right at home. Brewpubs are plentiful, and they have coexisted comfortably for many years alongside more established emporiums devoted to vino.

Following are descriptions of several microbreweries in Wine Country that craft unforgettable ales and lagers and have found fame beyond the four-county region. Most serve better than average pub grub. After a day of sniffing, sipping, and chewing on Cabernets, these friendly establishments might be just the place to quaff a cold one. Many offer live entertainment too, especially on weekends (see individual listings in this chapter for more information).

We begin lifting our glasses in Napa Valley and wrap up the journey in Mendocino County.

Downtown Joe's
902 Main Street, Napa
(707) 258-2337
www.downtownjoes.com
Pick a pint of Ace High Pale Ale or Golden Ribbon (or the Golden Thistle Very Bitter Ale, if your palate prefers that) and enjoy the view of the Napa River outside. Joe's has the standard pub fare (fish-and-chips, burgers, and sandwiches), with fancier dinner items that range from pancetta-wrapped grilled chicken breast to a Virginia smoked pork chop.

Silverado Brewing Company
3020 St. Helena Highway N., Suite A, St. Helena
(707) 967-9876
www.silveradobrewingcompany.com
This is a full bar with six beers made on-site—and 30 wines by the bottle, if you just can't get enough of the grape. It's located about 2 miles north of St. Helena in the Freestone Abbey complex (watch for the sign—it can sneak up on you). My companion and I liked the tap handle for the Blonde Ale—a blonde in a red dress—and the warm ambience of the small bar. The extensive menu has something for everyone, including St. Louis–style ribs.

Calistoga Inn Restaurant and Brewery
1250 Lincoln Avenue, Calistoga
(707) 942-4101
www.calistogainn.com

This may be one brewery where the food gets more attention than the brews. Choose from a wheat ale, a pilsner, red ale, or a porter on most nights, with some seasonal recipes thrown in. To accompany your foamy brew, order the paella, a pork tenderloin, or pepper-crusted duck breast. Calistoga Inn can boast that it has "survived the Depression, periods of neglect, and five major wars." In other words, it's been around a few years.

Dempsey's Sonoma Brewing Company
50 East Washington Street, Petaluma
(707) 765-9694
www.dempseys.com

This brewpub has been quietly serving Petalumans for more than a decade, combining its Red Rooster Ale and Petaluma Strong Ale with hearty meals like a marinated pork chop. Much of the produce used in the cuisine is organically grown locally. When the weather is fine, take a seat on the outside patio on the Petaluma River. If you're overnighting in Petaluma, get ye to Dempsey's.

Third Street Aleworks Restaurant and Brewery
610 Third Street, Santa Rosa
(707) 523-3060
www.thirdstreetaleworks.com

There are lots of brews to choose from here, and the pub fare to go with it. Have a pint of Annadel Pale Ale or the Stonefly Oatmeal Stout, or sample one of the "occasional" ales, such as Drunken Weasel and Burgher's Kolsch. Use any of these fine brews to wash down English bangers and mash or a selection of pizzas. It's an ethnic menu here, with appetizers ranging from hummus to quesadillas. Burgers too, of course.

Russian River Brewing Company
725 Fourth Street, Santa Rosa
(707) 545-2337
www.russianriverbrewing.com

This brewery had its humble beginnings at Korbel Champagne Cellars near Guerneville, but now it's gone uptown, or more precisely, downtown in Santa Rosa. The hops are grown in Sonoma County, and the brews include an amber ale, a golden wheat ale (a gold medal winner at the 2001 Great American Beer Festival), a pale ale, and a porter. Check the chalkboard behind the bar for the current selection of suds. Live music, mostly rock, can be enjoyed here on Saturday night. Pizza rules the menu, but calzones and focaccia are included too.

Bear Republic Brewing Company
345 Healdsburg Avenue, Healdsburg
(707) 433-2337
www.bearrepublic.com

There are usually 11 beers and ales on tap for sampling, most of them award winners (try the Red Rocket or Black Raven and see why). If you like what you taste, you can usually get a one-gallon reusable box of your favorite to go. (For the kids, there's homemade root beer and cream soda.) In the shadow of Hotel Healdsburg, the patio is a relaxing spot to nosh on calamari fritti, a huge chicken sandwich called "the Press," or such specials as chicken Parmesan, lobster bisque, or chicken potpie.

Mendocino Brewing Company
13351 U.S. Highway 101, Hopland
(707) 744-1361
www.mendobrew.com
This is the oldest microbrewery in California, established in 1983. Red Tail Ale is its best-known label, but it also produces Peregrine Pale Ale, Black Hawk Stout, Blue Heron IPA, and a seasonal offering such as Yuletide Porter. A 100-year-old brick building is where you'll find the pub; the beer itself is made about 12 miles away in Ukiah. No food is served at this alehouse. Hours are daily from noon to 7:30 P.M.

Ukiah Brewing Company
102 South State Street, Ukiah
(707) 468-5898
www.ukiahbrewingco.com
In another first for California, this establishment is the only certified organic brewpub in the nation. Six brews are on tap, all made from organic grains and hops. Try the Sun House Amber, or go all out with an Emancipator (8.3 percent alcohol content). In addition, all the food is chemical free and certified organic—it's only the second restaurant in the nation to receive this distinction. There are vegan offerings as well as beef dishes, such as Flemish pot roast and shepherd's pie.

Bear Republic Brewing Company
345 Healdsburg Avenue, Healdsburg
(707) 433-2337
www.bearrepublic.com
A microbrewery that offers music, Bear Republic often has entertainment on Thursday and Friday nights. It might be blues; it might be surf music; it might sound like heaven after a couple of pints.

Jasper O'Farrell's
6957 Sebastopol Avenue, Sebastopol
(707) 823-1389
O'Farrell's keeps Sebastopol busy every night of the week—mostly blues, some rock, some soul, some original songwriting, and even the occasional Celtic group. Tuesday is open-mike night. It's eclectic and very local.

Main Street Station
16280 Main Street, Guerneville
(707) 869-0501
www.mainststation.com
When Guerneville gets a little too hot, duck into the Station for some cool, breezy jazz. The Benny Barth Jazz Trio are regulars on Tuesday. Other hipsters blow in and out on Thursday, Friday, and Saturday.

Rainbow Cattle Company
16220 Main Street, Guerneville
(707) 869-0206
Heading toward its 26th year in business, the Cattle Company hasn't slowed down a bit. It's still where the Russian River's gay clientele gather for loud, uninhibited fun. The club has a DJ on Friday and Saturday nights and holidays.

Anderson Valley Brewing Company
17700 Highway 253, Boonville
(707) 895-2337
www.avbc.com
Get your Barney Flats here. This is a brewery with a tasting bar, open daily from 11:00 A.M. to 5:00 P.M. (to 6:00 P.M. on weekends). Take a tour daily at 1:30 or 4:00 P.M. and see how the brews are made, then test several types of the foamy stuff for a $5.00 fee. Besides the Barney Flats Oatmeal Stout, this brewery produces Boont Amber Ale and Deep Enders Dark. There's no food service at the brewery other than salty snacks, but its brews can be quaffed into the evening, along with pub food, at the historic Buckhorn Saloon down the road apiece (14081 Highway 128, Boonville; 707-895-3369).

North Coast Brewing Company
444 North Main Street, Fort Bragg
(707) 964-3400
www.northcoastbrewing.com
Wow, but I do love that Scrimshaw Pilsner. The Red Seal Ale and the Blue Star are nifty too, as are the Acme Pale Ale, Acme Brown Ale, Old No. 38, and Old Rasputin Russian Imperial Stout. In 1998 this brewery was ranked by the Beverage Testing Institute as one of the world's 10 best breweries. The food is well above average, and the service friendly. The grilled salmon with dill butter is always a favorite, as are the Cuban hanger steak, Bahia escolar, and seafood étouffée. There's also a daily pasta special.

Club FAB
16135 Main Street, Guerneville
(707) 869-5708
www.fabpresents.com
Proclaiming itself as the largest gay dance club north of the Golden Gate, Club FAB is housed in an old cinema in downtown Guerneville. Since opening its doors in 1998, it's been the most happening scene along the Russian River. When there's not a name act playing, the DJ revs up dancers on Friday and Saturday nights with foot-tapping rhythms.

Mendocino County

Greenwood Pier Cafe
5926 South Highway 1, Elk
(707) 877-9997
www.greenwoodpierinn.com
If you find yourself in the village of Elk, south of Albion on the rugged Mendocino coast, you might be surprised to hear the sound of guitar chords floating on the breeze. They will lead you to Greenwood Pier Cafe, which has music every Friday and Saturday from 7:00 to 9:00 P.M.

Patterson's Pub
10485 Lansing Street, Mendocino
(707) 937-4782
www.mcn.org/a/pattersons
Beer and tall tales are paramount at Patterson's, but the pub also keeps your sports appetite satisfied with four TV sets. Live music is featured on occasion, though it is rare. Look for the old London taxi in the driveway. Patterson's is open daily.

The Caspar Inn
14957 Caspar Road, Caspar
(707) 964-5565
www.casparinn.com
It's a long way from San Francisco, but Caspar Inn has the same type of colorful

rock 'n' roll history as the Fillmore. This old (1906) roadhouse-style inn has been in business since Caspar was a booming logging town, and many a big name has stepped through its doors and onto the stage (Mose Allison, B. B. King). Today you can expect karaoke on Wednesdays and such diverse musical concoctions as Afro-Cuban salsa and cowpunk on weekends. Bonnie Raitt reportedly comes in now and then and just hangs out, singing along with the jukebox. Cover charges range from $5.00 to $10.00.

Headlands Coffeehouse
120 East Laurel Street, Fort Bragg
(707) 964-1987
www.headlandscoffeehouse.com
This is the epicenter of local culture in Fort Bragg, a hipster java joint where there's almost always something interesting to listen to as you stay wired. Sunday is classical music night: maybe a string trio, maybe a guitar-and-flute combination. On Friday there is usually a jazz piano trio. Beyond that you're most likely to encounter jazz or acoustic singer-songwriter stuff.

MOVIE THEATERS

Napa County

Napa CineDome 8
825 Pearl Street, Napa
(707) 257-7700

Cameo Cinema
(occasional art movies)
1340 Main Street, St. Helena
(707) 963-9779

Sonoma County

Sebastiani Theatre
(historic building; occasional art movies)
476 First Street E., Sonoma
(707) 996-2020
www.sebastianitheatre.com

Sonoma Cinemas
200 Siesta Way, Sonoma
(707) 935-1234
www.cinemawest.com

Boulevard Cinema
Corner of Petaluma Boulevard S. and C Street, Petaluma
(707) 762-SHOW
www.cinemawest.com

Rohnert Park 16
555 Rohnert Park Expressway W., Rohnert Park
(707) 586-0555

Sonoma Film Institute
Sonoma State University, Darwin Theater, 1801 East Cotati Avenue, Rohnert Park
(707) 664-2606
www.sonoma.edu

Airport Cinema 12
409 Aviation Way, Santa Rosa
(707) 522-0330

Rialto Cinemas Lakeside
551 Summerfield Road, Santa Rosa
(707) 525-4840
www.rialtocinemas.com

Roxy on the Square
620 Third Street, Santa Rosa
(707) 522-0330

Roxy Stadium 14
85 Santa Rosa Avenue, Santa Rosa
(707) 522-0330

The Raven Film Center
415 Center Street, Healdsburg
(707) 433-5448
www.raventheater.com

Clover Cinemas
121 East First Street, Cloverdale
(707) 894-7920
www.cinemawest.com

Sebastopol Cinemas
6868 McKinley Street, Sebastopol
(707) 829-3456
www.cinemawest.com

Rio Theater
20396 Bohemian Highway (Highway 116),
Monte Rio
(707) 865-0913

Mendocino County

Noyo Theater
57 East Commercial Street, Willits
(707) 459-0280

Ukiah 6 Theatre
612 South State Street, Ukiah
(707) 462-6788

Arena Theatre
214 Main Street, Point Arena
(707) 882-3020

Coast Cinemas
167 South Franklin Street, Fort Bragg
(707) 964-2019

WINERIES

This is the chapter that was the excuse to create this book in the first place. In the Wine Country galaxy, the wineries are the sun around which all of our other attractions orbit. And just as the grape varietals that grow here are dramatically different from one another, so too are the wineries that produce them. If you take time to drop in at more than a few, you'll discover that each place has its own special story to tell.

So when you visit Wine Country, set aside at least a day or two for a sampling of the region's wineries. On the outside they can range from rustic barns to grand estates resembling castles. Once inside you are warmly welcomed by genial guides and tasting-room hosts who gladly explain the mysteries of the craft.

Whatever you do, please refrain from rushing through Wine Country. There's nothing to be gained from sprinting between tasting rooms. Take the time to learn about the winery, the wine-making process, and especially its people. Usually they are as mellow and unhurried as the wines themselves.

A TASTE OF EACH REGION

So...with hundreds of wineries within the region, how do you get started? First, I'll give you a taste of what separates this coverage area from the rest of the wine-making areas of California and the world—qualities that have given this region the undisputed title of California's Wine Country. Next, I'll provide a brief overview of the wine and wineries of each of the counties in our coverage area. Then comes the part where you get to pick and choose: detailed listings for more than 120 individual producers throughout Wine Country.

Despite the number of wineries here and the number of acres under viticulture,

Wine Country's grape harvest represents only a relatively small contribution to California's total wine production. The annual grape harvest of Sonoma County adds up to a minuscule 4 percent of the state's total volume, about the same as neighboring Napa County. This deceptively small percentage stands in stark contrast with the lofty reputation Wine Country's vintages have deservedly attained.

There are scores of wineries here, but they are not the oil-refinery-scale tank farms of the jug wine, bulk business. With a few exceptions, nearly all our wineries are small- to medium-size operations, often family owned. This is as good a reason as any to visit—you will nearly always find a tasty vintage to call your own personal discovery. Pour another glass of your favorite red, and read on about the climatology of fine wines.

Understanding Appellations

Understanding appellations is this simple: The quality of the grapes is the key to the quality of the wine. Where grapes are grown makes up almost 80 percent of the characteristics of a specific wine. The mellow in your Merlot? The zest in that Zinfandel? The panache of a particular Pinot Noir? It all can be traced back to the grapes, the climate that fostered their growth, and the soil from which they emerged.

Areas with hot days, warm nights, and deep, peat-rich soils might be good for growing corn and other vegetables (and even table grapes), but they produce wine grapes that are too high in sugar content and, therefore, not good for creating fine wines. A cooler, dryer climate and the volcanic soils so common in Napa, Sonoma,

Mendocino, and Lake Counties lead to the production of ultrapremium wines.

Within this four-county area, there are many microclimates. Each of these areas has specific characteristics that affect the wine grapes grown there. In the wine industry, these special growing regions are called American viticultural areas (AVAs). Around here we refer to them as "appellations," a French word you will run into frequently in this guide, but which is not used officially by the Alcohol and Tobacco Tax and Trade Bureau (formerly called the Bureau of Alcohol, Tobacco, and Firearms), the agency of the federal government that monitors these things.

How important is the term *appellation?* Some grapes grow better in one appellation than in another. Also, the same grape varietal grown in one appellation may produce a wine that is distinctly different from one made with the same grade of grapes grown in another appellation.

At first, it may sound to the novice as if the wine snobs are splitting hairs. But the differences in the wines from different appellations (and different winemakers within the same appellation), when tasted side by side, are distinct and remarkable.

Appellations also are important economically. A wine labeled with a certain appellation name must be produced using a minimum of 75 to 85 percent of grapes from that region. For example, a Sonoma Valley Zinfandel must take at least 85 percent of its Zinfandel grapes from the Sonoma Valley AVA. Such distinctions add value to the wine and raise the shelf price. By comparison, a Zinfandel with the appellation "California" on the label means that the grapes could have come from anywhere in California. These wines often are produced with grapes from less-prestigious growing areas such as the San Joaquin Valley, where the long, hot summers allow production of massive quantities of grapes that are used primarily for jug wines and the so-called "fighting varietals" (wine industry jargon for lower-priced varietals).

The generally dryer and cooler microclimates of Napa, Sonoma, Mendocino, and Lake Counties produce fewer grapes, but they are of a much higher quality for making fine wine. Grapes from these regions are more expensive (often as much as four to five times higher per ton), and they are in high demand.

Here's another French word worth remembering: *terroir* (pronounced ter-war). Roughly translated, it refers to all the factors involved in growing the grape, such as soil, climate, water, topography, and sunlight.

Of course, grapes are not the only element that goes into making a fine wine. The object of the winemaker's craft—a blend of skill, experience, science, art, taste, and inspiration—is to take the special qualities of certain grapes and maximize their potential. Without getting too highfalutin about it, a tour of Wine Country can include the dimension of a search for the perfect blend of the region's finest grapes and the winemaker's skill.

Napa County

When people hear the words "California Wine Country," they may first think of Napa, where the wines have been established as the yardstick by which other American vintages are measured. Even the French have taken notice of this world-famous source. Compared to Europe, however, where vineyards have flourished for centuries, Napa Valley is still in its infancy. Yet it has grown quickly, and with approximately 250 wineries, it is believed to be the world's most densely concentrated winery region. Because of this, there is some concern that traffic and crowds will destroy the bucolic landscape, particularly in summer when the tourist count is high.

Motorists who know the region well are inclined at such busy times to abandon the main highway through the valley, Highway 29, and turn onto the Silverado

Trail, which runs parallel to the east. From there, they can cross over, using any of several connecting lanes that bind the two north–south roads. Silverado Trail is a delight in itself, winding between meadows and wooded slopes to the east and vineyards to the west. Its slight elevation produces some striking vineyard panoramas, eminently suited to photography. (For more on negotiating the byways of Wine Country, see the Getting Here, Getting Around chapter.)

Napa Valley boasts so many tasting rooms it is almost impossible to classify them as a group. They range in style from quaint to elegant, sparse to cluttered, disarmingly casual to alarmingly commercial. But beyond atmosphere and physical trappings, the valley's tasting rooms provide the makings of a truly unique wine experience. In these pockets of hospitality, you will find an abundance of wines rivaling any in the world.

At its widest, Napa Valley is no more than 3 miles across. It is 27 miles from north end to south end, framed on both sides by hulking mountains. Most of the valley's two million annual visitors come to see its 35,000 acres of groomed vineyards—some newly replanted, some ancient, with gnarled vines that stand like regiments of old soldiers.

Food-and-wine pairings are staged in several wineries, and many have picnic grounds that give new meaning to the great outdoors. Artesa has a charming museum with some 17th-century winemaking casks and paraphernalia from its home country of Spain. And many wineries have elegant and eerie caves open for exploring.

Sonoma County

The Napa and Sonoma Valleys are separated by the Mayacmas Mountains, but much more distinguishes these two prime grape-growing regions. Napa, which enjoyed early prestige as a wine-growing region, is often considered the glitzier cousin of the more down-home Sonoma. Yet beneath Sonoma's rural charm is an elegance and sophistication that you can sample in both the wine and local culture.

Saying that a wine comes from Sonoma doesn't say enough to those who know their wines. There are differences—sometimes subtle, sometimes dramatic—among the same types of wine produced by different Sonoma County vintners in different appellations.

With the exception of the bluffs overlooking the Pacific and the cool redwood forests, grapes grow in almost every corner of Sonoma County. Major grape-growing areas include the Russian River, where ocean fog makes the climate ideal for Pinot Noir and Chardonnay and for an exceptional Sauvignon Blanc; Los Carneros, where wind and fog from San Pablo Bay create conditions that produce intensely flavored Pinot Noir and Chardonnay; Sonoma Valley, whose many microclimates are suited to many grape varieties; Alexander Valley, known for its Cabernet Sauvignon and Sauvignon Blanc; and Dry Creek Valley, where the wines have been earning much publicity and numerous gold medals of late.

Wineries here range from small, family-operated enterprises, where bottle labels still are applied by hand, to huge corporations where ageless wine-making skills are blended with computerized technology.

If you are eager for some serious wine tasting, there are more than a half dozen small- to medium-size wineries within a short drive of Sonoma Plaza. These include Ravenswood, known for its excellent Zinfandels; Buena Vista, which also has a tasting room on the plaza; Gundlach Bundschu; and Bartholomew Park Winery (all are listed in this chapter). If you are headed south to San Francisco from the town of Sonoma, you will travel through the Carneros region with its many wineries. Stop in at Viansa (which also has an outstanding deli) and Cline Cellars.

If you are able to visit and taste the wines of even half the places mentioned, you will have had a full and enjoyable day. The big-name producers in the county include Sebastiani, Glen Ellen, Clos du Bois, and Korbel, but don't neglect the smaller wineries: Benziger, Kenwood, Foppiano, Hop Kiln, Martinelli, and so on.

Besides the wine itself, touring Sonoma County offers the sheer pleasure of driving along winding roads with views of vineyards and farms that alternate between the dramatic and the sweetly rural. From some mountaintops and parts of the Carneros district at the southern border, the skyline of San Francisco is visible on clear days (and nights).

Mendocino County

While not as well known as Sonoma or Napa, Mendocino County is gradually getting the word out about the Anderson Valley's extraordinary wines. Originally an area of orchards and sheep and cattle ranches, it was discovered during the 1970s as a fine growing area for wine grapes. This rolling land, drained by the Navarro River, has quickly become braided in long rows of Pinot Noir, Chardonnay, Gewürztraminer, and Zinfandel grapes.

If anyone deserved to be called the grandfather of Mendocino wine success, it would be Adolph Parducci. From Prohibition times until the end of the 1960s, Parducci Wine Cellars in Ukiah was one of the few—and at times the only—wine producer in the county. Parducci launched his operation in 1918, when fear of Prohibition was driving everyone else out of the business. He bought some casks, a crusher, and some elementary equipment and began making wine in an old barn in Cloverdale. He survived the Prohibition years in part because the law allowed home winemakers to have 200 gallons of "juice" for their own use.

By 1927 Parducci had pulled together enough money to buy some land in Ukiah Valley (now fondly called the Home Ranch) and plant 100 acres of grapes. From that time on, he and his four sons

tended the vineyards, harvested the grapes, and built a winery. With the repeal of Prohibition in 1933, they opened a small tasting cellar in the basement of their home. Soon the charming family winery became a favorite stopping place for tourists. They'd sample from the spigot, have their jugs filled, and watch as the Parducci label was pasted on the bottle.

Another major player in Mendocino County wine is Fetzer, just off U.S. Highway 101 in Hopland. In the 1950s Bernard Fetzer bought vineyards in the Redwood Valley that had been established a century earlier by gold miner Anson Seward. Some of the vines actually dated from Seward's earlier planting.

Today there are more than 35 other wineries in the Mendocino County area, producing an abundance of award-winning vintages. Of the county's 2.25 million total acres, just 14,000 acres are planted to vineyards—and 25 percent of that acreage is certified organic. Mendocino's wine regions are divided into six valley areas, each noted for the different varieties of grapes produced under slightly different climatic conditions.

PLANNING YOUR EXCURSION

Where to begin? To make your decision easier, I have listed only tasting rooms that are open to the public regularly, although some wineries require appointments for tours.

Tasting room hours at wineries generally range from 10:00 A.M. to 5:00 P.M. daily, but some have shorter hours. If there's a particular winery you absolutely must visit, call ahead to find out how early or late you can arrive.

Most—but not all—Napa Valley wineries charge a reasonable fee for tasting, as well as some Sonoma County and Mendocino County establishments. The fees can range from about $3.00 to $10.00—prices fluctuate depending on the wines being poured. (Reserve wines and library wines, if offered, run a bit higher.) The tasting fee can be applied toward the purchase of a bottle, and you usually get to keep the logo glass. Many wineries also have picnic areas for enjoying munchies you bring along or buy on-site, but please purchase a bottle of the winery's own product to go with your food. It's just good manners.

I wouldn't for a second discourage you from visiting individual wineries, but if your time is limited, there is another way to sample the fruits of many wineries. Several independent wine tasting rooms, most of which feature tastes of limited production wines, have recently opened in the region for the convenience of visitors seeking particular labels or those who prefer to do their tasting in one spot (see the close-up in this chapter for details).

Many wineries also operate their own clubs and publish newsletters so that you can continue to enjoy the experience—and savor their wines—after you return home. If you find a favorite label during your Wine Country travels, sign up in the tasting room to receive shipments of new releases and invitations to members-only events.

As done throughout the book, I arrange the winery listings in the geographical sequence explained in the How to Use This Book chapter. I begin with Napa County wineries, followed by those in Sonoma and Mendocino Counties. (See the Lake County chapter for information on its wineries.)

NAPA COUNTY WINERIES

Domaine Carneros
1240 Duhig Road, Carneros
(707) 257–0101
www.domainecarneros.com
This imposing winery was inspired by the Louis XV–style Château de la Marquetterie in Champagne, country estate of the Taittinger family, which founded Domaine Carneros in 1987. The atmosphere is très français, with a looming portrait of Madame de Pompadour in the main lobby.

You can enjoy your beverage (with complimentary hors d'oeuvres) in the salon or on the patio, which is swept by breezes off San Pablo Bay. Domaine Carneros offers three types of sparkling wine (Brut Cuvée, Blanc de Blancs, and Brut Rosé) and its Famous Gate Pinot Noir. Free winery tours are hourly from 11:00 A.M. to 4:00 P.M. every day.

Carneros Creek
1285 Dealy Lane, Carneros
(707) 253–WINE
www.carneros-creek.com
San Franciscan Francis Mahoney started a trend in 1972 when he established the first winery in Carneros after the repeal of Prohibition. Carneros was little more than lonely cattle land then, but its bay-cooled hills are now coveted by grape growers. Carneros Creek is a modest, homey facility, with arbor-covered picnic tables in back that offer a view to magnificent Artesa. The winery's reputation is steeped in Pinot Noir, which still makes up a majority of its production. (It also produces Chardonnay.)

Artesa Winery
1345 Henry Road, Carneros
(707) 224–1668
www.artesawinery.com
Dug into the top of a hill, with native grasses planted over its sloping walls, this winery looks like a half-unearthed Mayan ruin—until you get inside, where the breezy central atrium and reflecting pools are nothing but modern elegance. Artesa is owned by Codorniu, one of the world's biggest producers of champagne, or cava. The Raventos family has been making wine since the 16th century (a Codorniu married a Raventos in 1659) and making *méthode champenoise* sparkling wine since 1872. The Napa outpost bottles three varieties, including the limited Reserve Cuvée, and also offers Chardonnay, Cabernet Sauvignon, and Pinot Noir. There are two free tours daily, and reservations are recommended.

Monticello Vineyards
4242 Big Ranch Road, Napa
(707) 253-2802, (800) 743-6668
www.corleyfamilynapavalley.com
Proprietor Jay Corley is a big fan of
Thomas Jefferson. So big, he named his
winery Monticello and built a small-scale
"Jefferson House," patterned after the
founding father's Virginia mansion, to
serve as the company's offices and culinary center. It's a pretty setting on Big
Ranch Road, which heads north out of
Napa city about halfway between Highway 29 and the Silverado Trail. There is a
vivid rose garden and a shady picnic area
called the Grove. Monticello makes Cabernet, Chardonnay, Merlot, Pinot Noir, champagne, and, weather permitting, a
late-harvest Semillon.

Trefethen Vineyards
1160 Oak Knoll Avenue, Napa
(707) 255-7700
www.trefethen.com
When Capt. Hamden McIntyre built the
Eshcol winery in 1886, the three-story,
wooden, gravity-flow architectural design
was standard. Grapes were crushed on the
third floor, fermented on the second, and
stored at ground level. Today the old Eshcol building is the centerpiece of Trefethen
Vineyards, and it's the last gravity-flow
winery building in Napa Valley. Trefethen is
a throwback in another way too: Surrounding the winery are hundreds of acres of
Chardonnay, Cabernet Sauvignon, Riesling,
and Merlot plus gardens, walnut trees, and
oaks. It was Eugene Trefethen, an executive for Kaiser (the massive construction
firm responsible for Hoover Dam and the
San Francisco–Oakland Bay Bridge), who
bought the estate in 1968. His son, John,
and John's wife, Janet, started the winery
five years later.

The Hess Collection Winery
4411 Redwood Road, Napa
(707) 255-1144, (877) 707-HESS
www.hesscollection.com
The "collection" is a stunning assemblage
of modern art (see the Arts and Culture

chapter). The Hess is Donald Hess, the
Swiss millionaire whose holdings include
Valser St. Petersquelle, one of Switzerland's most popular mineral waters. Hess
keeps it simple as far as the wines go,
with Chardonnay and Cabernet Sauvignon, bottling both under the Hess Collection label and a second, lower-priced
label called Hess Select.

---

*For a fabulous view of the Carneros
region, it's worth the trip to Artesa Winery, an architectural wonder. Drink in the
expansive vista while sipping cava on
the tasting room patio.*

Clos Du Val
5330 Silverado Trail, Napa
(707) 259-2225, (800) 820-1972
www.closduval.com
Clos Du Val is French in more than name
only. Founder John Goelet is descended
from a distinguished Bordeaux wine merchant family, the Guestiers, and president/
winemaker Bernard Portet is a sixth-
generation vintner from the same French
region. They crushed their first Napa Valley
harvest together in 1972, and their ivy-
covered, stone tasting room opened in 1983.
Clos Du Val now produces several wines,
including its signature Reserve Cabernet
Sauvignon. Tours are given by appointment, and you can picnic on the grounds.

Chimney Rock Winery
5350 Silverado Trail, Napa
(707) 257-2641, (800) 257-2641
www.chimneyrock.com
At the foot of the hills east of the Silverado
Trail—including the outcrop from which it
draws its name—is Chimney Rock, a stately
white structure of Cape Dutch style,
cloaked (in the summer) or picketed (in the
winter) by a row of poplars. Ask if you can
see the wine cellar, where resides a faithful
reproduction of the Ganymede frieze
depicting the gods' cupbearer atop a fierce
eagle. The winery makes Fumé Blanc,
Cabernet Franc, and Cabernet Sauvignon.

WINERIES

Stag's Leap Wine Cellars
5766 Silverado Trail, Napa
(707) 944-2020, (866) 422-7523
www.cask23.com

Stag's Leap founder Warren Winiarski was a liberal arts lecturer at the University of Chicago, but his destiny should have been clear: In Polish, "winiarski" means "from wine" or "winemaker's son." Founded in 1972, Stag's Leap was a little-known family winery until 1976, when it outshone the best of French Bordeaux in the famous Bicentennial tasting in Paris. Since then it has been a Napa Valley landmark. The winery produces several types of wine, red and white. Its reputation, however, is staked upon Cabernet Sauvignon, especially the versions made from the Stag's Leap and Fay vineyards, including the world-renowned Cask 23. (*Note:* Stag's Leap Wine Cellars is not to be confused with Stags' Leap Winery or the Stags Leap District, all of which get their name from the rock outcropping that overlooks the scene.)

Pine Ridge Winery
5901 Silverado Trail, Napa
(707) 253-7500, (800) 575-9777
www.pineridgewinery.com

The pines aren't only high on the ridge. There is a grove of them surrounding the picnic area, making for a cool experience on a hot Napa Valley day. Pine Ridge currently produces Chardonnay, Chenin Blanc-Viognier, Cabernet Sauvignon, Cabernet Franc, Malbec, and Merlot. If you can't fit a tour into your schedule, investigate the Pine Ridge Demonstration Vineyard adjacent to the winery. It displays various combinations of rootstock, clone, and trellising apparatus.

Steltzner Vineyards
5998 Silverado Trail, Napa
(707) 252-7272, (800) 707-9463
www.steltzner.com

Dick and Christine Steltzner started making wines for bulk sale in 1977, and they opened their Silverado Trail winery in 1983. (The current structure was built in 1992.) Steltzner is noted for its reds, as are all labels within the Stags Leap appellation. Its wines include Cabernet Sauvignon, Claret, and a South African varietal called Pinotage.

Silverado Vineyards
6121 Silverado Trail, Napa
(707) 257-1770
www.silveradovineyards.com

This is no Mickey Mouse winery, despite ownership by Walt Disney's daughter, Diane Disney Miller, and Diane's husband, Ron Miller. The Millers are longtime Napa Valley denizens. Silverado offers great views above the trail and a winery crafted of native stone and redwood. It made its reputation with Chardonnay but probably is best known these days for its estate-grown Cabernet Sauvignon.

Robert Sinskey Vineyards
6320 Silverado Trail, Napa
(707) 944-9090, (800) 869-2030
www.robertsinskey.com

This is another multigenerational operation, with founder Robert Sinskey, M.D., having passed the reins to his son, Rob. Sinskey Vineyards, which has been crushing grapes since 1986, is known for tackling Merlot and the tricky Pinot Noir, grown in the winery's Carneros vineyards. ("Heathens in the land of Cabernet," as they describe themselves.) Winemaker Jeff Virnig also creates small quantities of a half-dozen other varieties, including a Stags Leap District Claret and a Pinot Blanc. The cathedral-like winery combines Napa Valley stone and California redwood.

Domaine Chandon
1 California Drive, Yountville
(707) 944-2280, (800) 736-2892
www.chandon.com

Domaine Chandon, child of world-renowned Moët-Hennessy, is a trendsetter. It was California's first French-owned winery (established in 1973), and the first to use the champagne varietal Pinot Eunier in sparkling wine. It welcomes visitors to Le Salon, an open, terraced, cafe-style tasting room where you get samples of their cuvées as well as complimentary hors d'oeuvres. On weekends Chandon's renowned tours run every hour (on the hour, except for opening and closing times), and they pretty much tell you everything you need to know about fermentation, aging, riddling, and disgorging. The scenic winery produces several types of sparkling wine plus brandy and pear liqueur. See the Restaurants chapter for information on Chandon's exclusive eatery, or call the phone number listed to inquire about upcoming musical events.

Goosecross Cellars
1119 State Lane, Yountville
(707) 944-1986, (800) 276-9210
www.goosecross.com
Goosecross Cellars likes to refer to itself as a microwinery, and the feeling is unquestionably intimate on this lonely lane off the Yountville Cross Road. The winery was established in 1985 by college buddies David Topper, the CEO, and Geoff Gorsuch, the winemaker. ("Goosecross" is an Old English derivation of Gorsuch.) They produce Chardonnay and Cabernet Sauvignon, in quantities that barely surpass 7,500 cases a year. If you have some free time Saturday (autumn only) from 11:00 A.M. until about 12:30 P.M., sign up for the acclaimed Goosecross Wine Basics class, a hands-on crash course designed to remove the "snobbery and mysticism" from grape appreciation. The free class includes a full tour of the vineyard and winery. This winery asks that you phone ahead before stopping by for tasting (even if it's from your cell phone a mile away) anytime between 10:00 A.M. and 4:00 P.M. daily.

Cosentino Winery
7415 St. Helena Highway S., Yountville
(707) 944-1220
www.cosentinowinery.com
Mitch Cosentino crafts a variety of wines and sells them in an affable, low-key setting right next door to Mustards Grill (see the Restaurants chapter). Cosentino's Meritage reds stand out, as do his Merlots

and Zinfandels. He also is no stranger to dessert wines. The winemaker prides himself on his "punched cap fermentation" process, a traditional, labor-intensive technique that involves continually dunking the floating grape skins (the cap) into the juice during fermentation.

Silver Oak Cellars
915 Oakville Crossroad, Oakville
(707) 944-8808, (800) 273-8809
www.silveroak.com
Wine & Spirits' 1996 poll of restaurants determined that Silver Oak produced the most popular Cabernet Sauvignon in America. The secret? Do one thing and do it well. Silver Oak is all Cabernet, all the time. Silver Oak was founded in 1972 by Ray Duncan and Justin Meyer, who had recently abandoned his post as the Christian Brothers' Napa Valley winemaker. His company has two winery sites: one in Napa Valley at the site of the Oakville Dairy, and another in Alexander Valley in the old Lyeth Winery. The Oakville facility has a tasting room in an impressive masonry structure. Tours are by appointment only, and because the tasting room can get swamped on summer Saturdays, the winery suggests arriving early or calling ahead on those days. The tasting room is closed on Sunday.

Robert Mondavi Winery
7801 St. Helena Highway S., Oakville
(707) 226-1395, (888) RMONDAVI
www.robertmondaviwinery.com
More than any other individual, Robert Mondavi is credited with educating the world about California wine. The winery in Oakville that bears his name has been a must-see stop along the Napa Valley wine road for decades. Wine-and-food programs have long been popular with visitors, as well as the many art exhibits and jazz and classical concerts. It's also known for its in-depth tasting tours that run three to four hours and include a picnic or sit-down dinner. (*Note:* In late 2004, the Robert Mondavi corporation was purchased by Constellation Brands, the

Wine Country Appellations

Wines labeled with a certain appellation name must be produced using a minimum of 75 to 85 percent of grapes (depending on the varietal) from that specific region. Below are the recognized appellations (American viticultural areas, or AVAs) of the four counties in Wine Country. Note that the North Coast AVA is a broad one, applying to wines from several different counties, including Napa, Sonoma, Mendocino, and Lake; Los Carneros is shared by Napa and Sonoma Counties.

Napa County
Atlas Peak, Chiles Valley, Diamond Mountain, Howell Mountain, Los Carneros, Mount Veeder, Napa Valley, North Coast, Oak Knoll District, Oakville, Rutherford, Spring Mountain District, St. Helena, Stags Leap District, Wild Horse Valley, Yountville

Sonoma County
Alexander Valley, Bennett Valley, Chalk Hill, Dry Creek Valley, Knights Valley, Los Carneros, North Coast, Northern Sonoma, Rockpile, Russian River Valley, Sonoma Coast, Sonoma County Green Valley, Sonoma Mountain, Sonoma Valley

Mendocino County
Anderson Valley, Cole Ranch, McDowell Valley, Mendocino, Mendocino Ridge, North Coast, Potter Valley, Redwood Valley, Yorkville Highlands

Lake County
Benmore Valley, Clear Lake, Guenoc Valley, High Valley (proposed), North Coast, Red Hills

Sources: Alcohol and Tobacco Tax and Trade Bureau; Mendocino Wine Growers Alliance; Lake County Visitor Information; the Wine Institute

---

world's largest owner of fine wine producers, in a deal that shook up the industry and ended a long family legacy. At the time this book went to press, the Oakville tasting room continued to welcome visitors, but its long-term future and a restructuring of Mondavi's wine production were still being determined. Call the number listed to learn more.)

Opus One
7900 St. Helena Highway S., Oakville
(707) 944-9442
www.opusonewinery.com
When Robert Mondavi and Baron Philippe de Rothschild announced this joint venture in 1979, it created quite a stir in the wine world. But it also added credence to what the French had recently discovered: California wines are among the best in the world. Though the baron died in 1988, the business went forward, and groundbreaking on this architectural masterpiece took place in 1989.

As you might expect from such a team of wine royalty, this is an elegant winery that produces one pricey product. Opus One is a big red wine—a blend that's predominantly Cabernet Sauvignon—that sells for $140 per bottle. You can try this hearty drink for $25 a taste in the winery's Partners' Room. A concierge greets you at the door and ushers you to the tasting room. Calling ahead is strongly recommended, as this showplace is frequently booked for private functions.

Turnbull Wine Cellars
8210 St. Helena Highway S., Oakville
(707) 963-5839, (800) 887-6285
www.turnbullwines.com
The winery is located just north of the Oakville Crossroad, and its vineyards are primarily contained within the Oakville viticultural area. Turnbull's production is about 10,000 cases per year, with most of it in Cabernet Sauvignon, along with Merlot, Syrah, Sauvignon Blanc, and Sangiovese.

St. Supéry Vineyards & Winery
8440 St. Helena Highway S., Rutherford
(707) 963-4507, (800) 942-0809
www.stsupery.com
More than its intriguing historical setting and its rich lineup of wines, St. Supéry is known for its Wine Discovery Center. You can wander through the display vineyard and the exhibit gallery (the SmellaVision display is a must-see) or sign up for a $10 guided tour. St. Supéry (named for a one-time owner of the property) has a lengthy list of wines, with all the standards plus surprises such as a dessert Moscato and a Zinfandel Rosé sold only at the winery. Skalli also produces kosher Chardonnay and Cabernet under the Mt. Maroma label.

Peju Province Winery
8466 St. Helena Highway S., Rutherford
(707) 963-3600, (800) 446-PEJU
www.peju.com
Everything may look familiar as you head into Peju Province, as Herta Peju's prolific flower beds have been photographed for numerous garden magazines. Husband Tony sticks to wine making, and his Cabernet Sauvignon has won many awards. (He also makes Chardonnay, Cabernet Franc, Colombard, Merlot, a dry rosé and, occasionally, a late-harvest Chardonnay.) The Pejus opened their French provincial-style facility in 1991 and produce about 15,000 cases a year.

Niebaum-Coppola Estate Winery
1991 St. Helena Highway S., Rutherford
(707) 968-1100, (800) RUBICON
www.niebaum-coppola.com
Yes, it's that Coppola, a winemaker almost as long as he has been a filmmaker. Francis and his wife, Eleanor, purchased a lavish Victorian and prime acreage in 1975, then discovered the story behind the locale. The house was built in 1881 by Gustave Niebaum, a Finnish sea captain who founded Inglenook, perhaps the most respected winery in California before corporate raiders used the name to sell jug wine. Enchanted by the history, Coppola used the substantial profits from his film *Bram Stoker's Dracula* to reunify Niebaum's original estate in 1995. The purchase included the original château, which the director renovated (check out the staircase made from exotic Belizean hardwoods). It now houses the tasting room and a museum of wine and film. Coppola's five Oscars stand at attention on the second floor, along with the Don's desk and chair from *The Godfather,* an authentic Tucker automobile, costumes from the aforementioned *Dracula,* and other memorabilia from his work in film. Niebaum-Coppola releases several wines under the Francis Coppola Family Wines label, but is best known for Rubicon, its Cabernet Sauvignon-Merlot-Cabernet Franc meritage that is made to last 100 years.

ZD Wines
8383 Silverado Trail, Rutherford
(707) 963-5188, (800) 487-7757
www.zdwines.com
ZD might be last on the alphabetical list, but it has been first elsewhere, such as the Los Angeles County Fair, where the 1996 Chardonnay was named Best of Class. And the label is clearly bipartisan—it has been served at the White House during three presidential administrations. ZD got its start in Sonoma County in 1969 then moved to Napa County a decade later. Today it makes primarily Chardonnay, Pinot Noir, and Cabernet Sauvignon.

Mumm Napa Valley
8445 Silverado Trail, Rutherford
(707) 967-7700, (800) 686-6272
www.mummcuveenapa.com
The setting in Mumm's tasting salon is one of the most soothing in the valley, with a long wall of glass that faces uncluttered vineyard. (It's definitely the place to bring a date.) The Pinot Noir and Chardonnay are available only at the winery for tasting. They offer tours of the winery on the hour; the last stop is the photo gallery, which is reason enough to make a pilgrimage (see the Arts and Culture chapter). Mumm Napa Valley was launched in 1979, a coventure between G. H. Mumm of France and Joseph E. Seagram and Sons of New York. The winery currently bottles three Bruts—Blanc de Blancs, Blanc de Noir, and Brut Prestige—and a vintage sparkler, DVX, its prestige cuvée.

The Napa Valley Grape Growers Association has launched a registry of historic vineyards with the goal of documenting all vineyards that existed there prior to Prohibition and the names of those who planted the vines.

Beaulieu Vineyard
1960 St. Helena Highway S., Rutherford
(707) 967-5230, (800) 264-6918
www.bvwines.com
The oldest continuously producing winery in Napa Valley isn't Charles Krug or Beringer. It's Beaulieu, which was founded by Georges de Latour in 1900 and survived Prohibition by turning out sacramental wines. By 1940 Beaulieu might have been the nation's most famous winery, a status no doubt aided by de Latour's recruitment of young, Russian-born enologist Andre Tchelistcheff, who was more or less the Luther Burbank of the wine industry. The winery's Napa Series is made up of Cabernet Sauvignon, Chardonnay, Pinot Noir, Sauvignon Blanc, Zinfandel, and Merlot; the Signet Collec-

tion includes everything from Viognier to Pinot Gris. (The Georges de Latour Private Reserve Cabernet, hunted by collectors, remains BV's benchmark product.)

Grgich Hills Cellar
1829 St. Helena Highway S., Rutherford
(707) 963-2784, (800) 532-3057
www.grgich.com
The Grgich is Miljenko Grgich. The Hills, you might be surprised to learn, is a reference not to the rugged terrain around Rutherford, but rather to Austin Hills of the Hills Brothers coffee family. Hills added his business acumen to Grgich's winemaking skills back in 1977, and they have been making tasty wines ever since. Grgich Hills is known for its buttery, creamy Chardonnay, though it also produces Sauvignon Blanc, Zinfandel, Cabernet Sauvignon, and a late-harvest dessert wine. Visitors may purchase library wines, which are available only at the winery.

Villa Mt. Eden Winery
Conn Creek Winery, 8711 Silverado Trail, St. Helena
(707) 963-9100, (800) 793-7960
www.conncreek.com
You can break two bottles of wine with one stone here. The Silverado Trail tasting room houses Villa Mt. Eden and Conn Creek, sister wineries owned by Stimson Lane Vineyards of Woodinville, Washington. Villa Mt. Eden is descended, however tenuously, from Mt. Eden Vineyards, established in 1881 as the 11th bonded winery in Napa Valley. It now produces seven basic varietals, including Cabernet Sauvignon, Chardonnay, Zinfandel, and Pinot Noir. Conn Creek bottles a tiny amount of reserve wines, primarily Cabernet and a meritage.

Franciscan Oakville Estate
1178 Galleron Road, Rutherford
(707) 967-3830, (800) 529-WINE
www.franciscan.com
Franciscan specializes in Cabernet Sauvignon, Merlot, and Cabernet Franc, with all the grapes for Magnificat (a meritage blend) coming from its 240-acre estate in

the heart of the Oakville appellation. It also sets itself apart through its experiments in "wild" yeast fermentation, using the native yeast of each vineyard to help ferment those particular grapes. The winery's Cuvée Sauvage Chardonnay is 100 percent wild yeast, barrel fermented. Outside the winery, which is right off Highway 29, you'll encounter the Rutherford Bench, a tongue-in-cheek reference to a local geologic feature.

Rutherford Hill Winery
200 Rutherford Hill Road, Rutherford
(707) 963-7194, (800) MERLOT-1
www.rutherfordhill.com
Rutherford Hill produces numerous varietals (including a Zinfandel Port), but the name has become nearly synonymous with Merlot. It's also known as one of the most pleasant places to visit, with picnic grounds amid shady oaks and olive trees, and stunning views of Napa Valley. (Because of its popularity, you might think about calling ahead to reserve a table.) Rutherford Hill's wine caves are said to be some of the most extensive in America, with nearly a mile of tunnels, galleries, and passageways.

Rutherford Hill hosts a regular "Blending in the Caves" class for small groups to learn the basic principles of making wine. You get to create your very own blend to take home in a bottle. It's offered by reservations only, so call ahead to inquire about dates.

Raymond Vineyard & Cellar
849 Zinfandel Lane, St. Helena
(707) 963-3141, (800) 525-2659
www.raymondwine.com
Raymond has a strong reputation for Chardonnay and Cabernet Sauvignon, though it also bottles Sauvignon Blanc, Merlot, and Pinot Noir. It produces under four distinct brands: Amberhill, Raymond Estates, Raymond Napa Valley Reserve, and Raymond Generations. The winery's Napa Valley vineyards are supplemented by a large Chardonnay plot in Monterey County, on the Central Coast.

Milat Vineyards
1091 St. Helena Highway S., St. Helena
(707) 963-0758, (800) 54-MILAT
www.milat.com
This is an intimate, family-run winery, 2 miles south of St. Helena. The Milats have been growing and selling grapes to Napa Valley wineries since 1949, and in 1986 they finally decided to affix their own label. Milat bottles Chardonnay, Chenin Blanc, Zinfandel, Cabernet Sauvignon, and a blush table wine called Zivio, selling the bulk of their production from the tasting room.

V. Sattui Winery
1111 White Lane, St. Helena
(707) 963-7774, (800) 799-2337
www.vsattui.com
If you have made a few trips to Napa Valley, you probably know V. Sattui as the place with all the picnickers. It's a favorite for itinerant eaters, primarily because of an ample, shady picnic area and well-stocked deli featuring homemade items. The current wine list is immense, with two Chardonnays, two Johannisberg Rieslings, two Zinfandels, four Cabernet Sauvignons, and many others—all of them sold exclusively at the winery.

Whitehall Lane Winery
1563 St. Helena Highway S., St. Helena
(707) 963-9454, (800) 963-9454
www.whitehalllane.com
As wineries go, this one is a youngster in Napa Valley. The Leonardini family of San Francisco purchased Whitehall Lane Winery from foreign investors in 1993 and brought in new equipment, a new barrel program, and plans for expanding production and acquiring vineyards. It now produces award-winning Sauvignon Blanc, Chardonnay, Merlot, and Cabernet Sauvignon. There's even an orange muscat dessert wine, Belmuscato.

Heitz Wine Cellar
436 St. Helena Highway S., St. Helena
(707) 963-3542
www.heitzcellar.com
The winery you visit is not the current

Heitz facility, but rather the original facility opened by Joe and Alice Heitz in 1961. The winery built its reputation on Chardonnay, though now it is known more for its Cabernet Sauvignon. Three special Cabs are vineyard designated: Martha's Vineyard (near Oakville), Bella Oaks Vineyard, and Trailside Vineyard (both near Rutherford). Heitz also makes Zinfandel and a Grignolino, a light red.

Prager Winery & Port Works
1281 Lewelling Lane, St. Helena
(707) 963–PORT, (800) 969–PORT
www.pragerport.com
Prager makes Chardonnay and Cabernet but is really known for its port, which accounts for about 85 percent of production. One of the top sellers is the Royal Escort Port, produced from Petite Sirah grapes. Prager's facilities are inside an old carriage house, part of the John Thomann Winery and Distillery, constructed in 1865. The intimate tasting room is plastered with money donated by visitors—everything from Indonesian rupiah to Toys "R" Us Geoffrey dollars.

Sutter Home Winery
277 St. Helena Highway S., St. Helena
(707) 963–3104
www.sutterhome.com
What was once a small, family-run winery is now a gigantic family-run winery, thanks to unqualified marketing genius. The facilities date from 1874, the name from 1906, when the new Swiss-American co-owner named it after her father, John A. Sutter. Sutter Home has been owned by the Trincheros since 1947, and the family gets credit (or blame, depending on your outlook) for inventing White Zinfandel—which it originally called Oeil de Pedrix, "Eye of the Partridge"—in the 1970s. Sutter Home has numerous vineyards in Napa and Lake Counties but grows the bulk of its grapes in the Sacramento Valley, Sacramento Delta, and Sierra foothill regions. The company produces nine varieties of wine beyond the Zinfandel plus Fre, the best-selling nonalcoholic wines in America.

Louis M. Martini Winery
254 St. Helena Highway S., St. Helena
(707) 963–2736, (800) 321–WINE
www.louismartini.com
Louis M. was an Italian immigrant, born near Genoa, who founded the L. M. Martini Grape Products Co. in Kingsburg, California, in 1922. The "Grand Old Man" built his Napa Valley winery 11 years later. The company's vineyards are far-flung, stretching from Sonoma Valley to the Russian River Valley to Lake County to Chiles Valley to Pope Valley (two areas in eastern Napa County). The winery makes a wide range of wines, from Cabernet Sauvignon to Barbera to Merlot. It also produces cream sherry and dry sherry.

Merryvale Vineyards
1000 Main Street, St. Helena
(707) 963–2225, (800) 326–6069
www.merryvale.com
Merryvale is hard to miss, as it sits in Sunny St. Helena. That's not a reference to the town, but to the old winery that dates from the 1930s. The stolid stone structure took new life when it was founded as Merryvale by four partners (the same four who started San Francisco's Pacific Union Realty) in 1983. And then Merryvale was purchased by the Swiss family Schlatter in 1996. The facility produces several varietals, including Chardonnay, Cabernet Sauvignon, Merlot, and a dessert wine called Antigua. There are no tours, but Merryvale does offer wine component tasting seminars every Saturday and Sunday at 10:30 A.M. The cost is $15, and reservations are recommended.

Beringer Vineyards
2000 Main Street, St. Helena
(707) 963–7115
www.beringer.com
Just as you pass through the row of elms that forms a canopy over Highway 29 just north of St. Helena, what you'll see to the west is Beringer, arguably the most majestic of all Napa Valley wineries. Beringer produces a half-dozen wines that vary from high quality to high volume. The

tours, which run every hour and last about 30 minutes, are extremely popular. They include an excursion into the wine caves tunneled into the hillside and a finale in the tasting room, where you receive mouthfuls of two different wines. The winery's Rhine House, the impressive structure that grabs your attention from the highway, is a preserved historical landmark built by Jacob and Frederick Beringer in 1876. The tasting room, with its pine floors and slate roof, was Frederick's mansion.

Charles Krug Winery
2800 Main Street, St. Helena
(707) 967-2200, (800) 682-KRUG
www.charleskrug.com
There is a lot of history working at this 19th-century structure. It was Napa Valley's first winery, founded in 1861 by the eponymous Prussian immigrant, political theorist, and editor of *Staats Zeitung,* the Pacific Coast's first German-language newspaper. Charles Krug, the winery, also shares the history of the Mondavi family, that dynasty of California wine making. Cesare Mondavi bought Krug in 1943; his wife, Rosa, took over upon Cesare's death in 1959, and their son, Peter, became general manager in 1966. Now Peter's sons, Marc and Peter Jr., oversee most of the winery's operations, including the wine making, marketing, and sales. Charles Krug bottles at least 10 varieties of wine, including the full-bodied Vintage Selection Cabernet Sauvignon and Generations, a traditional Bordeaux blend.

Markham Vineyards
2812 St. Helena Highway N., St. Helena
(707) 963-5292
www.markhamvineyards.com
The fortress north of St. Helena, with its fountains and eucalyptus trees, has seen a lot of change in its 120-plus years. It was built of stone quarried from nearby Glass Mountain by Bordeaux immigrant and failed prospector Jean Laurent in 1874, but it was used for bulk wines until 1977. The tasting room is not in the old structure but rather in a new addition on its north side. Markham's Merlot, Sauvignon Blanc, and Chardonnay all at various times have been rated No. 1 in the state by *Wine Spectator*. Their less expensive Glass Mountain Quarry wines have also received accolades.

St. Clement Vineyards
2867 St. Helena Highway N., St. Helena
(707) 967-3033, (800) 331-8266
www.stclement.com
The St. Clement winery is eye-catching anytime, but especially at night, when the pristine Victorian is bathed by floodlights. The house dates from 1878, when it became Johannaburg winery, the eighth in Napa Valley. It was a private residence for most of the 20th century, until Dr. Bill Casey started St. Clement in 1975. The winery bottles five varietals and is best known for its Carneros Chardonnay and Cabernet Sauvignon. If you are feeling flushed as you leave, use it as an excuse to sit on the porch swing on the veranda—you'll want to stay there all day.

Freemark Abbey Winery
3022 St. Helena Highway N., St. Helena
(707) 963-9694, (800) 963-9698
www.freemarkabbey.com
Freemark Abbey was never home to a group of monks. The name comes from a triumvirate that purchased the winery in 1939: Charles Freeman, Markquand Foster, and Albert (Abbey) Ahern. Long before that (starting in 1886, to be exact), the winery was known as Tychson Hill, named for California's first female vintner, Josephine Tychson. The winery concentrates on several varietals: Cabernet Sauvignon, Chardonnay, Merlot, Petite Sirah, Sangiovese, Viognier, and Johannisberg Riesling. Among those are three esteemed single-vineyard wines—Cabernet Bosche, Sycamore Vineyards Cabernet Sauvignon, and Carpy Ranch Chardonnay. You also should keep an eye out for the Edelwein Gold, a sauterne-like dessert wine made only when conditions are right.

CLOSE-UP

A Glass of Bourassa Viognier, Please...

Before you give up trying to find a store that sells a particular cult wine you've heard about, step into one of the wine tasting collectives that have popped up in recent years in Wine Country. Boutique and artisan wines are the primary products sold in these comfortable establishments, which for a fee offer tastes of the fruits of small-production wineries that may not have tasting rooms of their own. The wines poured are created by talented vintners who are passionate about crafting small amounts of great vino—and who also require an outlet for their products to be sampled and purchased. Fees can range from $2.00 to $20.00, depending on the number of pours you desire. (By the way, Bourassa Viognier can be sipped at Wineries of Napa Valley.)

Napa County
Backroom Wines
974 Franklin Street, Napa
(707) 226-1378
www.backroomwines.com

Bounty Hunter
975 First Street, Napa
(707) 255-0622
www.bountyhunterwine.com

Napa Wine Merchants
1146 First Street, Napa
(707) 257-6796
www.napawinemerchants.com

Vintner's Collective
1245 Main Street, Napa
(707) 255-7150
www.vintnerscollective.com

Folie à Deux Winery
3070 St. Helena Highway N., St. Helena
(707) 963-1160, (800) 473-4454
www.folieadeux.com
Give this one extra credit for a sense of humor. "Folie à deux" is a French term that means "shared madness." It's a psychiatric diagnosis that the original owners, two mental health professionals, found appropriate. They even requisitioned a logo that resembles a Rorschach inkblot. You don't have to be not-all-there to enjoy Folie à Deux's wines, however. The broad selection includes Sangiovese, Cabernet Sauvignon, Muscat, and a special Amador Zinfandel from the oldest Zin vines in California, those of the 1870s Grandpere Vineyard.

Rombauer Vineyards
3522 Silverado Trail, St. Helena
(707) 963-5170, (800) 622-2206
www.rombauervineyards.com
If the name rings a bell, think of food, not wine. Vintner Koerner Rombauer's great aunt, Irma Rombauer, has been in practically every kitchen in America: She's the author of *The Joy of Cooking*. Koerner makes six types of wine, including two—a Cabernet Franc and a Zinfandel—sold only from the tasting room. Rombauer is at the end of a long, steep driveway, and its views of the Napa Valley floor are hard to match—bring lunch and take advantage of the picnic tables.

Wineries of Napa Valley
1285 Napa Town Center, Napa
(707) 253-9450
www.napavintages.com

A Dozen Vintners
3000 St. Helena Highway N., St. Helena
(707) 967-0666
www.adozenvintners.com

Tasting on Main
1142 Main Street, St. Helena
(707) 967-1042
www.tastingonmain.com

Sonoma County
The Cellar Door
1395 Broadway, Sonoma
(707) 938-4466
www.sonomacellardoor.com

Family Wineries of Sonoma County
9200 Sonoma Highway, Kenwood
(707) 833-5504
www.familywineries.com

Locals
21023 Geyserville Avenue, Geyserville
(707) 857-4900
www.tastelocalwines.com

Sonoma-Enoteca
35 East Napa Street, Sonoma
(707) 935-1200
www.sonoma-enoteca.com

The Wine Room
9575 Sonoma Highway, Kenwood
(707) 833-6131
www.the-wine-room.com

Frank Family Vineyards
1091 Larkmead Lane, Calistoga
(707) 942-0859, (800) 574-9463
www.frankfamilyvineyards.com
This one isn't as gargantuan as some of Napa's other champagneries, but it's a treat for visitors: a sublime spot on one of the valley's less-traveled crossroads; a charming picnic area behind the 1906 stone building, on the National Registry of Historic Places; and sparkling and still wines sold only on the premises. The winery was known as Larkmead Cellars back in the old days, when it produced still wines, then was operated as Hans Kornell Champagne Cellars. The champagne line

includes Blanc de Blancs, Blanc de Noirs, Brut, and Rouge.

Dutch Henry
4300 Silverado Trail, Calistoga
(707) 942-5771, (888) 224-5879
www.dutchhenry.com
The two families that own Dutch Henry, Chafen and Phelps, run it like a mom-and-pop winery. (There is no relation to famous vintner Joseph Phelps—"unfortunately," says winemaker Scott Chafen.) They pour in the cellar, and a tour consists of looking in different directions while you get the lowdown. The winery, named for nearby Dutch Henry Canyon, produces

only about 4,800 cases a year, and its line includes Chardonnay, Merlot, Cabernet, and a meritage.

Sterling Vineyards
1111 Dunaweal Lane, Calistoga
(707) 942-3345, (800) 726-6136
www.sterlingvineyards.com
First-time visitors can be forgiven for unfailingly asking, "Is that a monastery up on the hill south of Calistoga?" Not exactly. It's Sterling Vineyards, with its white stucco, Ionic-style architecture and knoll-top regality. Wine tasting here literally has been elevated to an event. A gondola takes you to the top of the hill, where you are free to sip samples and wander on a self-guided tour. Wide-angle views of the valley are worth the trip up the hill. It's $15 for adults for the whole experience. Most of Sterling's production falls among four wines—Cabernet Sauvignon, Chardonnay, Sauvignon Blanc, and Merlot, including several vineyard-designated versions. It also bottles small lots of lesser-known wines that it sells only at the winery, such as Malvasia Bianca and Charbono. Sterling was founded by English paper broker Peter Newton, who left behind a Brit legacy—the old bells of St. Dunstan's Church, which chime on the half hour.

Clos Pegase Winery
1060 Dunaweal Lane, Calistoga
(707) 942-4981, (800) 366-8583
www.clospegase.com
Jan Shrem's winery is named for Pegasus, the winged horse whose hooves are said to have unleashed the Spring of the Muses, bringing both wine and art to the masses. Shrem, who built his fortune publishing reference and technical books in Japan, is preoccupied with both wine and art. His collection of sculpture and painting is profiled in the Arts and Culture chapter, and his wines—Cabernet Sauvignon, Chardonnay, Merlot, and Petite Sirah port—are some of the best in the valley. The winery itself, designed by renowned Princeton architect Michael Graves (who was commissioned to build a "temple to wine"), is a stark, modern landmark of earth tones, angles, and curves.

Cuvaison Winery
4550 Silverado Trail, Calistoga
(707) 942-6266, (800) 253-9463
www.cuvaison.com
When Silicon Valley engineers Thomas Cottrell and Thomas Parkhill started a small upvalley winery in 1969, they called it Cuvaison, a French term for the fermentation of wine on the grape skins. The winery is particularly known for Chardonnay. Cuvaison gets most of its grapes from its 400-acre vineyard in Carneros. The winery has a pleasant picnic area, shaded by centuries-old oak trees.

Graeser Winery
255 Petrified Forest Road, Calistoga
(707) 942-4437, (800) 898-4682
www.graeserwinery.com
Want to get a feeling for the Napa Valley wine industry circa 1890? Take a drive to Graeser, about 2 miles northwest of Calistoga. The tasting room is in an 1886 home. If no one answers, ring the doorbell, a rope attached to the bell tower over the house. It's a bucolic setting once known as La Perlita del Monte ("The Little Pearl of the Mountain"), and Richard Graeser can genuinely claim a unique mountainside microclimate for his grapes, which are the traditional Burgundian varietals: Cabernet Sauvignon, Cabernet Franc, and Merlot. Richard will even autograph your bottle of wine if you ask nicely.

Chateau Montelena
1429 Tubbs Lane, Calistoga
(707) 942-5105
www.montelena.com
Montelena was one of the two Napa Valley wineries—Stag's Leap being the other—that rocked the French establishment at a famous blind tasting in Paris in 1976. It was a Chardonnay that prevailed that day, and the winery still makes one of the valley's best, along with top-notch Cabernet Sauvignon and Johannisberg Riesling.

Chateau Montelena's name and origins go back much further than 1976. The winery was started by Alfred L. Tubbs in the late 1800s, but no wine had been produced for 50 years when new owner Jim Barrett filled the barrels again in 1972. The building, nothing short of a hilltop castle with walls 3 to 10 feet thick, dates from Tubbs's day, and a subsequent owner added Jade Lake and its Chinese gardens, a must-see if you're seeking an oasis of tranquillity.

SONOMA COUNTY WINERIES

Southern Sonoma

Bartholomew Park Winery
1000 Vineyard Lane, Sonoma
(707) 935-9511
www.bartpark.com
Formerly the Hacienda Winery, the winery and adjacent park were renamed for Frank Bartholomew, former foreign correspondent with United Press International (later its president). The winery's picnic sites, set among native oaks, are unequalled, with tables overlooking vistas of vineyards. A fascinating first-class museum next to the tasting room is dedicated to the property's colorful history. Look for a large display of Victorian-era photographs that document viticultural practices from that period. Wall murals, a display of soil samples, and a topographical map explain present-day vineyard practices.

Buena Vista Winery
18000 Old Winery Road, Sonoma
(707) 938-1266, (800) 926-1266
www.buenavistawinery.com
Huge shade trees surround Buena Vista, the oldest premium winery in California, established in 1857 by Count Agoston Haraszthy (see the close-up "The Father of California Viticulture," in the History chapter). The winery offers a guided historical presentation daily at 11:00 A.M. and 2:00 P.M. for $15. Two of the winery's stone buildings are registered as state historic landmarks. Chinese laborers dug long tunnels into the hillside for wine aging, and Buena Vista's buildings are made from the salvaged rock. The Press House, built in 1862, houses a gift shop, displays a fine collection of art, and offers complimentary tastings. Buena Vista has a second tasting room in downtown Sonoma, at the southeast corner of the plaza (494 First Street E.) in Pinelli's Corner Store (once the historic Pinelli Mission Hardware Store). Both the winery and the downtown Sonoma tasting room feature wines by Buena Vista, Robert Stemmler, and Haywood.

Cline Cellars
24737 Highway 121, Sonoma
(707) 935-4310, (800) 546-2070
www.clinecellars.com
After spending his childhood learning farming and wine making from his grandfather Avaleriano Jacuzzi (of spa fame), Fred Cline founded Cline Cellars in 1982 on the sandy soils of Contra Costa County. His brother Matt joined him in 1991 as winemaker, and they relocated to the Sonoma Valley. The tasting room is in an 1850s farmhouse with a large, old-fashioned porch. Picnic grounds surrounded by 1,100 rosebushes make for a pleasant lunch stop, with sweeping views of the Sonoma Valley on a site that was once a Miwok village. Complimentary tastings feature Rhône-style red wines—Syrah and Mouvedre—as well as several white wines. Facilities are available for special events and weddings.

Gloria Ferrer Champagne Caves
23555 Highway 121, Sonoma
(707) 996-7256
www.gloriaferrer.com
The vineyards stretch across the hills, and from the hillock above, the Spanish-style winery overlooks the estate vineyards and the rolling Carneros hills. This is one of seven wineries owned and operated by the Ferrer family of Barcelona, which has produced *méthode champenoise* sparkling wine for more than 100 years. You can tour the facility with its state-of-the-art caves

and learn the secrets of the *méthode champenoise* process. Others may choose to linger on the vista terrace, noshing gourmet appetizers and sipping sparkling wine. Picnic tables are available for those who buy a bottle of wine to go with the comestibles. There is often musical entertainment on weekends, and there's plenty of banquet and meeting space.

Gundlach Bundschu Winery
2000 Denmark Street, Sonoma
(707) 938–5277
www.gunbun.com

Jacob Gundlach and his brother-in-law, Charles Bundschu, established this winery in 1858 on land east of Sonoma that they called Rhinefarm. Today Gundlach Bundschu produces 50,000 cases of premium, award-winning wines a year, specializing in Merlot, Pinot Noir, Chardonnay, Cabernet, and Zinfandel. Picnic tables are in a grove of oak trees overlooking a lake.

This winery is known throughout the community for its sense of humor and the wacky posters it creates to market its products. In one, a woman behind the wheel of an old car is exchanging words with a motorcycle cop, who says, "If you can't say Gundlach Bundschu Gewürztraminer, you shouldn't be driving."

Ravenswood Winery
18701 Gehricke Road, Sonoma
(707) 933–2332, (888) 669–4679
www.ravenswood-wine.com

It's hard not to like a winery that lives by the motto "No Wimpy Wines!" Ravenswood excels at antisnobbery behavior, with a friendly and funny tasting room staff and a down-to-earth winemaker, Joel Peterson, who believes "wine belongs on the table, not on a pedestal or in an ivory tower." The decidedly unwimpy wines produced by Ravenswood are primarily Zinfandel (not to be confused with White Zinfandel), and they refer to their winery as "Zinfomania Central." Tours may include samples of wines directly out of the barrel. You can also participate in the bottling of a special blend just for you (for a $25

fee). And if your nose is up to the challenge, there's a daily (2:00 P.M.) "smelling" seminar to help you learn more about the bouquet of wine and enjoy a lot of laughs in the process. On weekends from May through September, barbecues are held in the picnic facilities.

Schug Carneros Estate Winery
602 Bonneau Road, Sonoma
(707) 939–9363, (800) 966–9365
www.schugwinery.com

This lifelong dream of owner-winemaster Walter Schug spans four decades and two continents. A native of Germany's Rhine River valley and a graduate of a prestigious German wine institute, Walter left for California determined to find success with his Pinot Noir, which has since been proclaimed no less than world class by critics in both the United States and Europe. The winery, built in 1990 of post-and-beam architecture, reflects the Schug family's German heritage. Schug still maintains close ties to Europe, and it's a likely possibility you'll meet European neighbors while you're in the tasting room to enjoy complimentary sips.

Robledo Family Winery
21901 Bonness Road, Sonoma
(707) 939–6903
www.robledofamilywinery.com

Here's a true American success story. The founder of this winery, Reynaldo Robledo, came to the United States from Mexico at the age of 16. He spent years toiling in the vineyards, first pruning the vines and then slowly working his way up to vineyard manager and later becoming a respected viticultural consultant. He dreamed of one day owning his own winery and growing his own grapes, and with hard work and persistence, his dream became reality. Founded in 1997, the Robledo Family Winery opened its tasting room in 2004. Reynaldo's wife and their seven sons and two daughters are all active in the business, which produces five wine varietals. Stop by the tasting room to sample their delicious Seven Brothers Sauvignon Blanc.

Viansa Winery and Italian Marketplace
25200 Arnold Drive, Sonoma
(707) 935-4700, (800) 995-4740
www.viansa.com
When Sam Sebastiani visited the homeland of his grandfather in Italy, he was astounded to see that Farneta, Italy, looked exactly like the Sonoma Valley. The winery that Sam and his wife, Vicki (Viansa combines "Sam" and "Vicki"), established is about as Italian in aura as you will find this side of the Atlantic. Olive trees were imported from Italy, the architecture is Italian, and the garden paths that wind between levels of the winery are in Tuscan style.

The wine tasting room (sips are complimentary) is also a tasting room for some stunning gourmet foods. Visitors can wander about, picking up samples of olive-anchovy pesto, hot sweet mustards, blood orange vinegar, and other aromatic foods. Plenty of tables are available at various patio levels overlooking Sonoma Valley and Sam's award-winning wildlife preserve. Sam Sebastiani adheres to his loyalty to Italian-style wines; his winery features Piccolo Toscano (a chianti type of grape), Sothena (a Dolcetto grape), and Nebbiolo (the name of the grape and the wine) plus 40 other varieties. The winery also offers specialty wine and food tasting programs.

Sebastiani Vineyards
389 Fourth Street E., Sonoma
(707) 933-3230, (800) 888-5532
www.sebastiani.com
One of the few original family wineries still remaining, Sebastiani is extremely proud of its wines and its Italian heritage. Founder Samuele Sebastiani learned wine making from the monks in Farneta, Italy, before he came to America in 1894 at the age of 19 and went to work hauling cobblestones. In 1904 he bought the old Sonoma Mission vineyard, where the padres had been making altar wines for 80 years.

The winery is 3 blocks east of Sonoma Plaza, set amid the vineyards from which Sebastiani produces its special Cherryblock Cabernet wines. A great convenience for visitors is the winery's trolley, which allows people to park at the winery and catch a shuttle back to the plaza. Tastings are also available at Sebastiani on the Square at 40 West Spain Street in Sonoma, on the northwest corner of the plaza.

If you have only one day to tour Sonoma County, you can't go wrong if you start in the Sonoma Valley. It's the closest of the premium wine-growing regions to San Francisco, only 45 minutes from the Golden Gate.

Benziger Family Winery
1883 London Ranch Road, Glen Ellen
(707) 935-3000, (888) 490-2739
www.benziger.com
You could easily spend an entire day at the Benziger Family Winery, which is perched on the side of Sonoma Mountain high above the Sonoma Valley floor and the town of Glen Ellen. Guests can picnic in the redwood grove, visit an experimental vineyard, enjoy complimentary wine tasting, and take in a one-of-a-kind educational vineyard tour aboard a motorized tram. The Benzigers emigrated from White Plains, New York, to their mountain ranch next to Jack London State Historic Park (see the Parks and Recreation chapter). They have since built a reputation for grape-growing innovation that produces award-winning wines in the Imagery series—Merlot, Chardonnay, and an unusual Bordeaux varietal, Cabernet Franc.

Wellington Vineyards
11600 Dunbar Road, Glen Ellen
(707) 939-0708, (800) 816-9463
www.wellingtonvineyards.com
Operating a small, family vineyard and winery producing just 6,000 cases a year, John and Peter Wellington nevertheless produce a wide range of wines, concentrating on reds like Zinfandel, Merlot, and Cabernet. They also produce a couple of unusual wines unique to the area, including a Rhône-style blend, Côtes de

Sonoma. The winery and tasting room are surrounded by vines, some more than a century old.

Kunde Estate Winery & Vineyards
10155 Sonoma Highway, Kenwood
(707) 833-5501
www.kunde.com
Louis Kunde arrived in California from Germany in 1884 and founded his ranch in 1904. Four generations of Kundes have worked the ranch, which stretches for 1.5 miles along Sonoma Highway and extends from the valley up into the mountains above. Today's tasting room is a replica of Louis Kunde's old barn, built on the site of the original. The Kunde family ages its wine in 32,000 square feet of caves dug into the hillside, providing an ideal environment for natural aging. Timbers from the old barn were used to handcraft tables and benches. Picnic grounds are surrounded by scenic vineyards. There's a nice gift shop inside, and tours are available Friday through Sunday. Chardonnay vineyards surround the tasting rooms, where samples are complimentary.

Kenwood Vineyards
9592 Sonoma Highway, Kenwood
(707) 833-5891
www.kenwoodvineyards.com
When the Pagani brothers founded this winery in 1906, Jack London lived on the estate next door. Both estate owners are gone now, and the winery was bought by three college chums, all wine lovers, in 1970. The grapes they use are still grown on the London ranch, and the label on a special bottling shows a picture of Jack London's signature and a wolf, Jack's nickname. The tasting room is rustic, the sips are complimentary, and the atmosphere is charmingly informal. Kenwood is known for its Sauvignon Blanc, Zinfandels, and Cabernets.

Chateau St. Jean
8555 Sonoma Highway, Kenwood
(707) 833-4134, (800) 543-7572
www.chateaustjean.com
Nestled against the tranquil slopes of

Sugarloaf Ridge, Chateau St. Jean (named for former owner Ken Sheffield's sister and pronounced "gene") was founded in 1973. An elegant château on the grounds of this 250-acre estate was built in 1920 and is now a showplace surrounded by beautiful gardens. It's a lovely spot for picnicking. Chateau St. Jean's Cabernet Sauvignon has been served at the White House, and Queen Elizabeth has sipped its Chardonnay.

Landmark Vineyards
101 Adobe Canyon Road, Kenwood
(707) 833-0053, (800) 452-6365
www.landmarkwine.com
Perhaps the most spectacular aspect of this Spanish mission–style winery is its expansive interior courtyard, facing onto dramatic, hulking Sugarloaf Mountain. The hospitality center at Landmark is a magnificent facility, featuring a granite tasting bar, a warm fireplace for chilly days, and a full-wall mural by noted Sonoma County artist Claudia Wagar. The pond-side picnic area is a picturesque location for lunch or for just lounging and watching the clouds drift by. A tower conference room offers a 360-degree view that must be distracting to those attending the meetings held there. Landmark's production focuses on Chardonnay, and three labels have won awards: Overlook, from Sonoma County vineyards; Damaris Reserve, from Alexander Valley appellation; and Two Williams Vineyard, from southern Sonoma Valley.

St. Francis Winery and Vineyards
100 Pythian Road, Santa Rosa
(707) 833-4666, (800) 543-7713
www.stfranciswinery.com
Joseph Martin, who left the corporate world in 1971 to become a vintner, named his winery after St. Francis of Assisi and San Francisco de Solano Mission in Sonoma. His first harvest came in 1979 with production of 4,000 cases. Today his benchmark varietals are Chardonnay and Merlot, rich with character and complexity, but the portfolio also includes Cabernet Sauvignon and Zinfandel. The visitor cen-

ter is a beauty, with terrific views and a huge gift shop and special reserve wine tasting bar.

Ledson Winery & Vineyards
7335 Sonoma Highway, Santa Rosa
(707) 537-3810
www.ledson.com

When this 16,000-square-foot French Normandy structure was first erected, it seemed ideally suited to be a fancy haunted castle, set far back from the highway and with rocky mountains as a mysterious backdrop. But that all changed when the castle opened and the warmth and beauty of the place became apparent. Owned by the Ledson family, longtime Sonoma Valley farmers, this hospitality center has three tasting rooms, a clothing and gift boutique, and a terrific gourmet market. But what really sets it apart are the picnic grounds, where on any given weekend in summer there might be a jazz combo or an art show to add to your wining and dining experience.

Construction on the building, which was originally intended as a private home, began in 1993. The Ledsons soon realized the emerging castle was getting too much attention for their liking, so they decided it would work better as a winery open to the public. Ledson wines are sold only at the winery and are served at the Ledson Hotel's restaurant in Sonoma (see the Hotels, Motels, and Inns chapter), and are on the wine lists at many other fine restaurants. The wines have garnered some great reviews in *Wine Spectator* while amassing a variety of awards. The winery is known for its Merlot and Chardonnay, but it also produces Sauvignon Blanc, Johannisberg Riesling, and Orange Muscat.

Matanzas Creek Winery
6097 Bennett Valley Road, Santa Rosa
(707) 528-6464, (800) 590-6464
www.matanzascreek.com

Matanzas Creek Winery is recognized as one of the country's best. Ensconced at the base of Bennett Mountain, the environ-mentally friendly wine-making facility boasts one of the most sophisticated research laboratories in California. There winemakers have conducted more than 100 experiments in progressive wine making. In the early 1990s, Matanzas released a new wine, Journey, made in a radically progressive wine-making program. Although its $70 price raised some controversy, the first 1990 Chardonnay sold out on release and was hailed by critics as the finest Chardonnay ever produced in America. Picnic facilities are available as well as a self-guided garden tour that includes one of the largest plantings of lavender in Northern California. Look for handmade lavender products in the gift shop.

Paradise Ridge Winery
4545 Thomas Lake Harris Drive, Santa Rosa
(707) 528-9463
www.prwinery.com

Welcome to Paradise! For Walter and Marijki Byck, Paradise came to be on the day in 1994 when they opened the doors to their new winery, a California-style structure with breathtaking views from the decks. In fact, the view is so exciting the winery stays open late on Wednesday evenings just so visitors can catch the sunset. After purchasing a 156-acre ranch adjoining the old Fountain Grove Winery, the Bycks planted 18 acres of Sauvignon Blanc and Chardonnay grapes, determined to produce the finest wines possible. In addition to their award-winning wines, they also feature a historical exhibit and world-class sculpture garden.

Northern Sonoma

Armida Winery
2201 Westside Road, Healdsburg
(707) 433-2222
www.armida.com

Tastings here are charmingly casual (and complimentary), and the setting is spectacular. Built on the side of a hill, the winery looks out on the Dry Creek and

WINERIES

Russian River Valleys, with Alexander Valley, Geyser Peak, and Mount St. Helena to the east and south. High on the hillside, three geodesic domes house the winery, lab, and administrative offices. If you've been looking forward to a game of Italian boccie ball (or if you'd like to learn what it is), visit the boccie court near the picnic grounds. Vineyards are south of the winery, producing Amida's five varietals: Merlot, Gewürztraminer, Chardonnay, Pinot Noir, and the recently added Zinfandel.

Roshambo Winery
3000 Westside Road, Healdsburg
(707) 431-2051, (888) 525-WINE
www.roshambowinery.com
Architecture along Westside Road was shaken up when this sleek structure opened its doors. Roshambo is operated by the third generation of the Johnson family, longtime grape growers in Sonoma County. It specializes in estate wines, and its 2001 Imago Chardonnay walked off with the sweepstakes prize for white wine in the 2002 Sonoma County Harvest Fair judging. Winemaker Paul Brasset also creates memorable Sauvignon Blanc, Syrah, Pinot Noir, Zinfandel, and Merlot. The tasting room has a beautiful view of Russian River Valley vineyards, and you can count on rotating art exhibits that lean toward the unusual.

Many winery tasting rooms do double-duty as art galleries. For example, Roshambo near Healdsburg offers exhibits of modern art that change frequently, and Paradise Ridge Winery in Santa Rosa maintains a sculpture garden.

Belvedere Winery
4035 Westside Road, Healdsburg
(707) 431-4442, (800) 433-8296
www.belvederewinery.com
This winery, in the coastal foothills of the Russian River Valley, takes its name from the Italian word for "beautiful view." A trip

to the winery reveals just that. Taste world-class wines while you enjoy a picnic on the sunny deck or under an oak tree in a beautiful garden setting. The picturesque vineyards of the Russian River Valley will spread out before you. Belvedere specialties are Zinfandel, Chardonnay, Merlot, and Cabernet Sauvignon from their premium vineyards in the Alexander, Dry Creek, and Russian River Valleys.

Foppiano Vineyards
12707 Old Redwood Highway,
Healdsburg
(707) 433-7272
www.foppiano.com
This is the oldest family-owned winery in Sonoma County, whose history reaches back to 1896. Founded by John Foppiano, a disenchanted gold miner who decided to get back to his farming roots, the winery is now being run by fourth-generation Foppianos, producing 200,000 cases a year of Cabernet Sauvignon, Petite Sirah, Zinfandel, Merlot, Pinot Noir, Chardonnay, and Sauvignon Blanc. Some of the producing vines are more than 100 years old.

Kendall-Jackson Tasting Room
337 Healdsburg Avenue, Healdsburg
(707) 433-7102, (800) 769-3649
www.kj.com
The hugely successful Kendall-Jackson operation encompasses several wineries. The largest of these is Kendall-Jackson itself. The company describes the others—Edmeades, Camelot, Calina (Chile), La Crema, and Robert Pepi—as "Artisans and Estates."

To learn more about each winery and the wide span of varietals Kendall-Jackson produces, the Healdsburg store is the place to visit. The friendly folks at the K-J store will be happy to direct you to their other location: Kendall-Jackson Wine Center, 5007 Fulton Road, Fulton, (707) 571-8100. The Wine Center on Fulton Road features a viticulture exhibit, where students from Santa Rosa Junior College—and visitors—can become acquainted with 26 varietals and 19 trellising systems.

Martinelli Winery
3360 River Road, northwest of
Santa Rosa
(707) 525-0570, (800) 346-1627
www.martinelliwinery.com
This family-run winery tends more than 350 acres of vines in the Russian River Valley, which it uses for its own wines and sells to other vintners. The winery specializes in Zinfandel—the Jackass Hill variety from the vineyard of the same name is considered by experts to be extraordinarily complex. They also produce a fine Sauvignon Blanc, Gewürztraminer, Chardonnay, and Pinot Noir. The winery is housed in an old hop kiln, just a short hop from US 101 off the River Road exit.

Mill Creek Vineyards
1401 Westside Road, Healdsburg
(707) 431-2121, (877) 349-2121
www.millcreekwinery.com
This beautifully landscaped winery is set on a rise above the vineyard, which has been operated since 1975 by the Kreck family. The tasting room, complete with working waterwheel and a mill pond, is in an air-conditioned two-story redwood building. The bar top, trusses, and beams are all made from one redwood tree from the Kreck ranch on Mill Creek Road. A 3,000-square-foot picnic deck overlooks the Dry Creek Valley, Fitch Mountain, and Mount St. Helena.

Rodney Strong Vineyards
11455 Old Redwood Highway,
Healdsburg
(707) 431-1533, (800) 678-4763
www.rodneystrong.com
In 1959, long before Sonoma County was "discovered" as a premium grape-growing region, Rodney Strong began an exhaustive search for the very best vineyards. Ultimately, he selected several vineyards in the Chalk Hill, Alexander Valley, and Russian River Valley appellations. The winery, a low-lying building with a roof spreading across it like the wings of a giant eagle, is situated among acres of prime vineyards. The winery's estate wines are named after the individual vineyards where the grapes grow—for example, the Charlotte's Home, a Sauvignon Blanc, and Alexander's Crown, a Cabernet. Picnic areas are available. For special occasions there's a garden area adjacent to the vineyards (contact the vineyard for details).

Windsor Vineyards Tasting Room
308-B Center Street, Healdsburg
(707) 433-2822, (800) 204-9463
www.windsorvineyards.com
Windsor offers a wide variety of wines that have brought home several awards. In 1959 Windsor was one of the first wineries to stake a claim to Sonoma County. Vineyards were set out in three valleys— Alexander, Dry Creek, and Russian River.

All wines are sold direct to the consumer through one of the three tasting rooms (Healdsburg, Tiburon, and Marlboro, New York).

Dry Creek Vineyards
3770 Lambert Bridge Road, Healdsburg
(707) 433-1000, (800) 864-9463
www.drycreekvineyard.com
Opened in 1972, this was the first new winery in Sonoma County's Dry Creek Valley since the days of Prohibition, and it led to a dramatic wave of change in this long-neglected grape-growing region.

Dry Creek Vineyards produces Fumé Blanc, Chenin Blanc, Cabernet Sauvignon, and other wines, including the estate-bottled meritage (a Bordeaux blend). The gray stone winery resembles a French country wine chateau. The tasting room, voted among the top 10 in Sonoma County by a local magazine, is casual and informal. When the weather turns cool in October, there's a warm fireplace. When the sun spreads warm yellow patches on the lawn, a picnic lunch in the gardens is a perfect idea.

Ferrari-Carano Vineyard & Winery
8761 Dry Creek Road, Healdsburg
(707) 433-6700, (800) 831-0381
www.ferrari-carano.com
The Wine Shop at Villa Fiore (the name of the château that houses the Ferrari-Carano

CLOSE-UP

Bored with Cabernet?
Weary of Chardonnay?

Wine Country is busy experimenting with many wine-grape varietals beyond Chardonnay and Cabernet that are changing the climate in the wine world and soon will be more noticeable at your favorite wine shop.

Leading the pack of white varietals taking the industry by storm is actually an old favorite: Sauvignon Blanc. "A lot of people had been predicting it, and now there's an interesting rebirth of Sauvignon Blanc and Fumé Blanc going on in Napa Valley," says Clay Gregory, former president of the board of directors of the Napa Valley Vintners Association and one-time general manager at Robert Mondavi Winery. "Frankly, consumers are getting a little tired of oaky Chardonnays."

To illustrate his point, Clay says many acres of Chardonnay grapes grown north of the Carneros region are being pulled out in favor of other varieties that grow more successfully in the warmer valley air. He adds that the cooler Carneros appellation, shared by both Napa County and Sonoma County, is better suited to Sauvignon Blanc grapes than Chardonnay, although Chardonnay will continue to be grown there. "But a lot of wine people now prefer Sauvignon Blanc," he says.

Nick Frey, executive director of the Sonoma County Grape Growers Association, agrees with Clay. "The movement now is toward Sauvignon Blanc rather than Chardonnay," says Nick. "Sauvignon Blanc is produced without oak, and it

operation) is one of California's friendliest and most enchanting Wine Country destinations. Visitors will discover magnificent gardens, critically acclaimed wines, and unique gifts. The spectacular underground barrel cellar where the wines of Don and Rhonda Carano age is also a favorite. Among the wines poured at the wine shop are Fumé Blanc, Chardonnay, Merlot, and a late harvest dessert wine called Eldorado Gold.

Lake Sonoma Winery
9990 Dry Creek Road, Geyserville
(707) 473-2999, (800) 750-9463
www.lakesonomawinery.net

Lake Sonoma Winery is notable for its breathtaking view of Dry Creek Valley and Warm Springs Dam. Gourmet picnic fare is available in the deli and can be enjoyed on the wooded picnic grounds with a bottle of Chardonnay, Cabernet, Zinfandel, or Cinsault. The winery is adjacent to Lake Sonoma Recreation Area.

Lambert Bridge Winery
4085 West Dry Creek Road, Healdsburg
(707) 431-9600, (800) 975-0555
www.lambertbridge.com
Established in 1975, the winery takes its name from a neighboring landmark bridge that spans Dry Creek. Many of the wines

bursts with clean, crisp fruit. It's a food-friendly wine and a good value."

Among other white varietals, Viognier (vee-own-YAY) has been receiving its share of attention in the last couple of years, says Clay. "Viognier is very floral and aromatic—it smells like it's going to be sweet but it's actually dry." Yet instead of being "the next big white wine," as had once been predicted, Nick believes Viognier will likely be used more for blending, especially with Sauvignon Blanc. Also flashing brightly on the wine industry radar are Pinot Gris, Marsanne, and Roussanne.

In red wines, Syrah (or *Shiraz,* as Australian vintners spell it) is generating the most excitement, says Clay. "Cabernet Sauvignon is king in Napa Valley for the foreseeable future, but Syrah is coming up fast as the next big variety to plant. It grows well in many climates, the wines have a lot of character, and it's not as 'intellectual' as Cabernet." Nick agrees: "Syrah is going to be a very important wine very soon."

Bordeaux varieties getting more buzz these days include Petit Verdot, Cabernet Franc, and Malbec, while another old favorite, Zinfandel (not *White* Zinfandel) is making a welcome comeback. "There are still many old Zin vines around here that produce terrific wines, and most were planted by Italian immigrants," says Clay. Another small-production grape, the Spanish varietal Tempranillo, is likely to be a "next generation" wine, he adds.

Clay reminds wine lovers that, as in other kinds of perennial agriculture, ramping up to produce new varietals can take time. "But one of the hallmarks of Californians is our constant experimentation and desire to try new things."

of this small, high-quality winery are available only in the charming tasting room, where the wine-stained tasting bar was made from oak casks. A crackling fireplace cheers on frosty days, and on sunny days the picnic grounds may be the most elegant in Dry Creek Valley. The tasting room also features gourmet mustards to complement the winery's wines, which include Viognier, Merlot, and Zinfandel.

Preston Vineyards
9282 West Dry Creek Road, Healdsburg
(707) 433-3372, (800) 305-9707
www.prestonvineyards.com
According to the folks at family-owned Preston Winery, "Having fun is no scandal." They take pride in being known as the alternative winery: the place to go when you want something different and delicious. Not only can you taste some unusual wines, but you can also enjoy some freshly baked bread and picnic among flowers, herbs, vegetable gardens, and olive trees. If that's not enough fun, you can play a game of boccie on the house courts.

Preston is slightly off the beaten path, but with so much going for it, the adventure is worth it. The 115 acres of grapes grow without insecticides and produce flavorful, eccentric wines such as Viognier,

Moscato Curioso, Barbera, Syrah, and Marsanne.

Those large structures with propellers you see rising high out of vineyards are wind machines, which help protect delicate vines against frost. The wind machines keep the air circulating so the coldest air does not settle on the vines.

Quivira Vineyards
4900 West Dry Creek Road, Healdsburg
(707) 431-8333, (800) 292-8339
www.quivirawine.com
For centuries, European explorers searched for the legendary New World land called Quivira. It was thought to be on the Pacific Coast in the region now known as Sonoma County. Three centuries ago European mapmakers placed it just about where the Quivira Winery is located now. Whatever else you find out here about the legends of Quivira, you will also encounter some excellent Sauvignon Blanc, Zinfandel, and a Rhône-style blend. This is a great place for a picnic, complete with terrific views.

Clos du Bois
19410 Geyserville Avenue, Geyserville
(707) 857-3100, (800) 222-3189
www.closdubois.com
Clos du Bois got its start in Sonoma County as a vineyard operation in the early 1970s, with 590 acres of vineyards in the Alexander Valley. Today, it is one of Sonoma County's most honored wineries, located on a 40-acre site in the heart of the beautiful Alexander Valley, and with approximately 1,000 prime acres of vineyard in Alexander and Dry Creek Valleys. The winery produces Sauvignon Blanc, Chardonnay, Gewürztraminer, Pinot Noir, Merlot, Zinfandel, and Cabernet Sauvignon. In addition, they produce an exceptional Winemaker's Reserve Cabernet Sauvignon, and their Reserve Chardonnay from the Flintwood vineyard is impressive.

Canyon Road Winery
19550 Geyserville Avenue, Geyserville
(707) 857-3417, (800) 793-9463
www.canyonroadwinery.com
A warm and friendly tasting room serves Canyon Road's Cabernet Sauvignon, Sauvignon Blanc, Merlot, Reisling, and Chardonnay, as well as wines of the Venezia and Nervo labels. A country deli and gift shop makes it easy to sit down for a picnic with a shared bottle of Canyon Road wine.

Canyon Road's wine club, known as the Roadies Club, uses a newsletter to announce opportunities to join in the autumn crush and do a little grape stomping. Other benefits of Roadie membership include a seminar on wines in the spring, a chance to visit with the winemaker, and an opportunity to receive shipments of select wines at discount prices.

Chateau Souverain
Independence Lane at US 101, Geyserville
(707) 433-8281, (888) 809-4637
www.chateausouverain.com
This architecturally striking winery is one of the few with a restaurant—the Alexander Valley Grille is open daily for lunch and Friday, Saturday, and Sunday for dinner. Chateau Souverain's "room with a view" tasting room features a host of award-winning wines, such as Cabernet Sauvignon, Merlot, Zinfandel, Viognier, and Sauvignon Blanc made from selected vineyards within the Alexander Valley, Dry Creek, and Carneros appellations.

Field Stone Winery
10075 Highway 128, east of Healdsburg
(707) 433-7266, (800) 544-7273
www.fieldstonewinery.com
Eleven miles east of Healdsburg in the Alexander Valley, Field Stone Winery was built of large native cobblestones and is partially dug into a small knoll, creating a wine cellar in the European style. Beautiful picnic grounds under spreading oaks are the setting for summer events, including concerts, Shakespearean plays, and dinners. The estate-bottled wines include Cabernet

Sauvignon, Merlot, and Petite Sirah, as well as three stylish whites—Sauvignon Blanc, Chardonnay, and Gewürztraminer.

Geyser Peak Winery
22281 Chianti Road, Geyserville
(707) 857-9400, (800) 255-9463
www.geyserpeakwinery.com
One of the fastest-growing wineries in Sonoma County, Geyser Peak now distributes wines throughout the United States, as well as Switzerland, Germany, and Hong Kong. Though particularly known for its Chardonnay, Geyser Peak produces a number of fine varieties, including Merlot, Cabernet Sauvignon, Zinfandel, Sauvignon Blanc, California Riesling, and Gewürztraminer.

A lovely picnic area overlooks the Alexander Valley, and the Panoramic Trail—winding up behind the winery—and the Margot Patterson Doss Trail—named for a well-known San Francisco walker and writer—will appeal to hikers.

Hanna Winery
9280 Highway 128, Healdsburg
(707) 431-4310, (888) 426-6288
www.hannawinery.com
Dr. Elias S. Hanna, a Marin County surgeon who was born and raised on a farm in Syria, founded Hanna Winery in 1985. His winery now produces about 34,000 cases of Sauvignon Blanc, Chardonnay, Cabernet Sauvignon, Merlot, and Pinot Noir annually. You can taste Hanna wines at two hospitality centers, one at 5353 Occidental Road in Santa Rosa and the other on Highway 128 in Alexander Valley. The patio of the visitor center in Healdsburg is a lovely place for a picnic, with panoramic views of the Alexander Valley and Hanna's magnificent hillside vineyard. It's also a grand setting for weddings or corporate events.

Johnson's Alexander Valley Wines
8333 Highway 128, Healdsburg
(707) 433-2319
www.johnsonavwines.com
From time to time, the tasting room resonates with the mighty sound of a 1924 theater pipe organ. Tom Johnson makes the wine; Jay Johnson repairs old organs. This is a small, family winery producing seven varietals (Zinfandel and Cabernet are two) from family vineyards, all exclusively sold at the winery or online. Picnic tables are available, and you may enjoy an informal tour hosted by a member of the Johnson family.

Pedroncelli Winery
1220 Canyon Road, Geyserville
(707) 857-3531, (800) 836-3894
www.pedroncelli.com
John Pedroncelli, a native of Lombardy, Italy, bought the vineyard property that was to bear his name in 1927—the vines planted there had been yielding grapes for more than 20 years. During Prohibition, the winery sold grapes to home winemakers; after the repeal, it sold wine in bulk to other wineries. Today the winery uses grapes harvested from the Dry Creek Valley to produce excellent Cabernet, Zinfandel, and Pinot Noir wines. Tucked 2 miles up Canyon Road from US 101, the charmingly rustic Pedroncelli Winery offers picnic tables for a pleasant lunch.

Simi Winery
16275 Healdsburg Avenue, Healdsburg
(707) 433-6981, (800) 746-4880
www.simiwinery.com
In 1881 two Italian immigrant brothers, Guiseppe and Pietro Simi, bought a winery near the grain depot in Healdsburg for $2,250 in gold coins. They built a magnificent, hand-hewn stone winery, and their business soon doubled. Then, in the midst of success, both brothers died, and Guiseppe's teenage daughter Isabelle took over. Prohibition was a blow for her, but when it ended, she had one of the winery's enormous redwood tanks rolled outside and created a retail tasting room. Isabelle could be found there until her late 80s, still selling Simi wines. The winery is now owned by the French company Moët-Hennessy, which has turned Simi's distinctive wines into part of a winemaking estate of worldwide recognition.

Trentadue Winery
19170 Geyserville Avenue, Geyserville
(707) 433-3104, (888) 332-3032
www.trentadue.com
Founded in 1969, the family-owned and -operated Trentadue has achieved an outstanding reputation not only for rare and unusual wines but also for highly regarded, better-known varieties. Visitors are offered complimentary tastings of the many varieties (including Petite Sirah, Cabernet, and Sangiovese) and can spend time browsing through a fine collection of wine-related gifts, fine crystal, and china personally selected by Evelyn Trentadue. A gourmet food shop supplies items to snack on in the picnic area.

West County/ Russian River

Davis Bynum Winery
8075 Westside Road, Healdsburg
(707) 433-2611, (800) 826-1073
www.davisbynum.com
Believing that there is "something of a spiritual union between the organic farmer and his soil and his vines," Davis Bynum cultivates vineyards in accordance with California organic farming standards. To increase the ecological diversity and health of his fields, Bynum has mixed in 130 olive trees, 120 mandarin trees, caper berries, sea berries, lavender, plums, kiwis, pomegranates, avocados, guavas, and figs with his vines. The cool, coastal Russian River Valley gives Bynum's wines an intense varietal character. They include Fumé Blanc, Zinfandel, Chardonnay, Pinot Noir, Merlot, and Cabernet Sauvignon. With the winery perched on a hillside, the picnic grounds offer a most pleasant view.

Hop Kiln Winery
6050 Westside Road, Healdsburg
(707) 433-6491
www.hopkilnwinery.com
Housed in an old stone building that was once a hop-drying kiln, the tasting room at Hop Kiln displays a fine collection of wine-making tools and a gallery of old photos showing the history of the hop industry, which bustled in Sonoma County during the early 1900s. The Hop Kiln was declared a state historic landmark in 1977 and has been the setting for several motion pictures. The tasting room is cool, rustic, and pleasant and serves complimentary samplings of Zinfandel, Chardonnay, and two popular blends, Marty Griffin's Big Red and Thousand Flowers. Owner and community activist Dr. Marty Griffin—a retired internist who founded the winery in the early 1970s—is less involved in Hop Kiln's wine making these days and more intent on saving the nearby Russian River from runoff degradation and mining. Hop Kiln's grounds are a great place to have a picnic and reflect Griffin's love of nature. A picturesque pond inhabited by local wildfowl sparkles next to the tasting room, and trees provide plenty of shade around the outdoor tables.

Topolos at Russian River Vineyards, Winery & Restaurant
5700 Gravenstein Highway, Forestville
(707) 887-1575 (winery), (800)
867-6567 (orders), (707) 887-1562
(restaurant)
www.topolos.net
Established in 1963, this winery has won awards not only for its exceptional wines but also for its unique, environmentally sound agricultural methods. In 1999 Topolos was named Environmental Business of the Year by the Sonoma County Conservation Council. Topolos's vineyard was the first in the nation certified as biodynamic—it is also certified according to California organic farm standards. (Biodynamics is a method of farming based on the philosophy of Rudolf Steiner and follows a chemical-free, spiritual approach.)

A Wine Tasting Primer

"Quaffable, but far from transcendent." That's how the character of Miles in the 2004 Academy Award–nominated and Golden Globe–winning film *Sideways* described a particular Chardonnay he was sampling in a winery tasting room. The hit movie about two buddies—one obsessed with Pinot Noir and the other clueless about wine but always thirsty—made for entertaining fiction about the tasting room experience. Lofty statements such as those uttered by Miles in the movie may be the reason some people shy away from wine. They believe, wrongly, that it's a drink only for snobs, and that tasting rooms are for characters with raised pinkies and attitude.

On the contrary, tasting rooms in Wine Country are fun, educational, and decidedly nonsnobby. You needn't feel silly or self-conscious about sipping wine among strangers—tasting room personnel are patient and friendly, and they enjoy chatting with visitors and answering questions. You may also meet interesting wine tasters from around the world and strike up conversations with like-minded folks you would not have had the chance to meet otherwise. For instance, the person pouring your Pinot could be the winemaker who created it.

During your enological experience, remember that the pleasure of wine comes from several senses—sight, smell, taste, and touch. Here are a couple of suggestions to keep you from feeling completely lost during your first winery adventures. (Rest assured that you will learn much more as you travel from one tasting room to another.)

Sight: Hold the glass to the light and enjoy the wine's color.

Smell: Swirl the wine gently in the glass to release its fragrances. Sniff sharply to carry the aroma to the nerve ends high in the nose.

Taste: Take a drink and roll it in your mouth to reach all the taste bud areas. Connoisseurs learn to draw in air over the wine still in their mouth. It looks silly, but it carries fumes to the nasal cavity, where most of the subtle olfactory differences emerge. Try to pick out tastes that are familiar to you, such as berry or pepper.

Touch: Chew the wine, just as if you were munching on some mashed potatoes. Note the amount of astringency present and get its "feel."

Aftertaste: Swallow the wine and note the taste sensations remaining, also known as "the length." The aftertaste should always be pleasant, though it's often quite different from your first impression upon sipping.

Visitors can sample complimentary sips of Zinfandel and Chardonnay and browse the gift shop.

Korbel Champagne Cellars
13250 River Road, Guerneville
(707) 824-7000, (800) 656-7235
www.korbel.com

When the three Czech Korbel brothers emigrated from Bohemia, they settled in a redwood forest along the Russian River, tried several different enterprises—including cigar-box manufacture—and finally resolved to become winemakers. They built their handsome brick winery in 1886, including a quaint turreted tower at the south end. The story behind this tower is a fascinating one. Before leaving Prague, the youngest Korbel inadvertently fired his pistola in the midst of the townfolk, who had gathered to hear the news called out by the town crier. He was jailed briefly, and upon his release the three brothers fled the country. The tower of the winery is a sentimental duplicate of the jail where young Joseph spent his last days in his home country.

Korbel has an excellent tour of both the champagne cellars and the antique rose garden that surrounds the old summer house. The champagne is produced in the *méthode champenoise,* the traditional French method in which the second fermentation takes place in the same bottle.

MENDOCINO COUNTY WINERIES

U.S. Highway 101

Fetzer Vineyards
13601 Old River Road, Hopland
(707) 744-7600, (800) 846-8637
www.fetzer.com
Bernard Fetzer, a lumber executive, purchased the winery's Redwood Valley Home Ranch in 1958 as a place to raise his large family and grow fine grapes for home winemakers. Ownership of the winery has changed over the years, but Fetzer wines have won critical praise and tons of gold medals, especially for its Chardonnay.

The tasting room and visitor center, located 1 mile east of Hopland, features intimate vineyard and garden tours and offers tastings of new releases as well as

---

In summer you may spot shimmering strips of Mylar streaming atop rows of vines. The reflective material is used to scare away birds that like to feed on the emerging grapes.

---

older wines. A full-service deli with a spacious picnic area is also open to the public. The 50-acre Valley Oaks Ranch is home to vineyards, dozens of old barns, a dining pavilion overlooking Lake Fume, and the 5-acre 100 percent organic Bantera Garden, which includes countless varieties of fruits, vegetables, herbs, and flowers, both edible and decorative. All grapes and plants are grown organically, without use of pesticides or synthetic fertilizers. Also on the property is a charming bed-and-breakfast (see the Bed-and-Breakfast Inns chapter).

Jepson Vineyards
10400 South US 101, Ukiah
(707) 468-8936, (800) 516-7342
www.jepsonwine.com
In addition to producing Chardonnay, Merlot, Sauvignon Blanc, and some sparkling and dessert wines, Bob and Alice Jepson, along with winemaker Alison Schneider, have created a special niche by producing Alambic Pot Still Brandy, estate grown and bottled.

Milano Family Winery
14594 South US 101, Hopland
(707) 744-1396, (800) 564-2582
www.milanowinery.com
In the early 1900s Vincenzo Milone came to Mendocino County with his father, discovered some agriculturally rich land near Hopland, and planted grapes. They also built a hop kiln at the foot of Duncan's Peak, near their home. Today that hop kiln is the tasting room for Milano Winery. The kiln is one of the few left from the days when the nearby village of Hopland was earning its name growing and curing hops.

Parducci Wine Cellars
501 Parducci Road, Ukiah
(707) 462-9463, (888) 362-9463
www.parducci.com
Since 1932 Parducci Wine Cellars has made wine according to a simple philosophy: Wine is an honest, natural product that should never be overprocessed, never be masked by too much oak, and never

have its essential flavor and aroma filtered away. Parducci is Mendocino's oldest operating winery, but it is dedicated to contemporary consumers, using modern wine-making techniques and evolving wine styles. Parducci's conviction is that whites should be fermented cold and bottled cold to retain the liveliness, crispness, and freshness of the varietals. Parducci white wines produce a slight spritz from carbon dioxide, a natural retainer of the varietal flavors for which Parducci wines are famous.

Redwood Valley Cellars
7051 North State Street, off US 101,
Redwood Valley
(707) 485-0322
www.redwoodvalleycellars.com
This is actually a tasting room for Braren-Pauli Winery in Petaluma. Redwood Valley Cellars also produces wine from grapes grown in Potter Valley. Located between Ukiah and Willits, at the West Road exit off US 101, Redwood Valley Cellars offers complimentary tastings.

Highway 128

Greenwood Ridge Vineyards
5501 Highway 128, Philo
(707) 895-2002
www.greenwoodridge.com
Allan Green, a graphic artist turned winemaker, has crafted a lovely Anderson Valley winery and tasting room with a wraparound deck and a view of the hilltop ridge where his vines grow. On one wall of the tasting room are the ribbons his wine received for its excellence—White Riesling, Late Harvest Riesling, Sauvignon Blanc, Chardonnay, Zinfandel, Pinot Noir, Merlot, and Cabernet Sauvignon. Three Greenwood wines have been included in the *Wine Spectator*'s annual list of the top-100 wines of the world. In another corner of the tasting room (samples are complimentary, by the way), you'll see Green's collection of 5,000 wine corks, arranged innovatively into a sculpture.

Handley Cellars
3151 Highway 128, Philo
(707) 895-3876, (800) 733-3151
www.handleycellars.com
Fermentation science is a natural interest for Milla Handley, the winemaker and owner who is also the great-great-granddaughter of brewing giant Henry Weinhard. After receiving her degree in enology and working six years in the wine industry, she and her husband, Rex, founded Handley Cellars in the basement of their home near Philo. Today's tasting room is a far cry from that basement winery. As visitors sip wine, they are surrounded by the Handley family's collection of folk art from around the world. Located 6 miles northwest of Philo, the tasting room offers samples of their unusual Pinot Menieur, as well as an excellent Pinot Noir. Complimentary hors d'oeuvres are presented along with the wines the first weekend of every month.

Winemakers in the United States exported approximately 96 million gallons of wine in 2003, a 29 percent increase over the previous year. The United Kingdom is the top importer of U.S. wines.

Husch Vineyards
4400 Highway 128, Philo
(707) 895-3216, (800) 554-8724
www.huschvineyards.com
Farming has been the occupation for three generations of the Oswald family, owners of Husch Vineyards. Theirs is the oldest winery in Anderson Valley and still contains some of its first varietal plantings. Originally planted in 1969 and bonded in 1971 by the Husches, it was purchased by the Oswalds in 1979. All Husch wines are made from grapes grown only on the family-owned vineyards, including the original 21-acre block of Pinot Noir, Gewürztraminer, and Chardonnay.

CLOSE-UP

A Key Ingredient in the Making of Your Wine: Farmworkers

As you glide past Wine Country's thousands of acres of vineyards, moving from tasting room to tasting room, take a moment to remember the people who are the backbone of the wine industry: the tireless farmworkers who pick the grapes, prune the vines, and maintain the fields year-round.

Farming by machinery is commonplace in California's hot interior valleys, where the wine grapes are less desirable and ultimately used in less flavorful wines. But the premium grapes grown in Wine Country are lovingly tended throughout their growing season by thousands of callused hands and strong backs, making our wines truly a hand-crafted commodity.

At harvest time, the most popular season for visitors, farmworkers dot the vineyards, quickly plucking the grape bunches off the vines. They bring in the crop when the berries are at their peak of flavor and ready for crushing, working long hours to get the job done.

So when sipping your next glass of Napa Valley Cabernet or Sonoma County Pinot Noir, say a toast to the many farmworkers who had a hand in making the wines great.

Navarro Vineyards
5601 Highway 128, Philo
(707) 895-3686, (800) 537-9463
www.navarrowine.com
Ted Bennett has been making Anderson Valley Gewürztraminer since 1973, and over the years he has developed a successful formula for this grape, which requires a long growing season. His wife, Deborah, serves guests in the tasting rooms. "We're not a big corporate winery," she says. "We're the '70s homesteaders who happened to like wine." Navarro Vineyards seeks to make a fine wine but doesn't forget about "the guy in a camper van with three kids who just wants to enjoy a bottle," says winemaker Jim Klein, whose efforts produce 30,000 cases a year.

Roederer Estate
4501 Highway 128, Philo
(707) 895-2288
www.roederer-estate.com
The wines created by the European firm headed by Madame Orly-Roederer have been world famous for 200 years. Now they are being produced in the Anderson Valley under the direction of her grandson, Jean-Claude Rouzard, who came here in 1981 in search of the perfect appellation. To create the perfect wine, Roederer uses only the first juice, pressed from the pulp with minimal skin contact. Subsequent pressings are not used, and even the first pressing is further critiqued, with 30 percent later discarded to be faithful to the Roederer style.

Yorkville Vineyards & Cellars
Highway 128 at Mile Marker 40.4,
Yorkville
(707) 894-9177
www.yorkville-cellars.com
The 30-acre vineyard owned by the Wallo family lies at 1,000 feet above sea level, where sun-filled days and cool nights combine to create premium-quality grapes. Since its establishment in 1982, the Yorkville Vineyards estate has been farmed organically. Instead of using pesticides and herbicides, the family counts on seasonal cover to serve as an alternative for insects to attack instead of the vine. Yorkville Vineyards has been certified organic by the state of California every year since 1986. Yorkville grows seven Bordeaux varietals and makes at least one unusual wine—Eleanor of Aquitaine, a half-and-half blend of Sauvignon Blanc and Semillon, aged in French oak barrels only.

WINE SHOPS

As you would expect, they don't just make 'em, pour 'em, and sell 'em in Wine Country—there is also a variety of stores dedicated to the display, presentation, storage, and properly outfitted enjoyment of wines. In addition, some shops offer amazing selections of wines from our region and beyond, along with all the decadent accouterments. So light up that fat, pricey cigar and take a look at a few favorite wine shops.

Napa County

J.V. Wine & Spirits
426 First Street, Napa
(707) 253-2624, (877) 4-MY-WINE
www.jvwarehouse.com
Great bargains in wine can be found here. Napa residents tend to shop at this store for their premium vino, and there is much to choose from. Most are at discount prices, and they will pack up assorted cases and ship them home for you too. It lives up to its reputation—and it's just across the river bridge from Copia.

The Vintage 1870 Wine Cellar
6525 Washington Street, Yountville
(707) 944-9070, (800) WINE-4-US
www.vintagewinecellar.com
Ironic that the stables of the old Groezinger Winery would end up as the one piece of the property expressly devoted to wine. Unlike most wine shops, this one is licensed for tastings—it pours about a dozen selections, all day long. On the shelves you'll find everything from $5.00 bottles to an imperial of Mondavi 1978 Reserve Cabernet Sauvignon that goes for $1,000. The shop also sells a few cigars.

St. Helena Wine Merchants
699 St. Helena Highway S., St. Helena
(707) 963-7888, (800) 729-9463
www.shwinemerchants.com
Across the road from V. Sattui Winery is this unpretentious purveyor of wines. Merchants aims to carry the sort of small-availability labels that out-of-state visitors read about but can't find at home—Harlan, Dominus, and Maya come to mind as examples. Don't be surprised if you bump into a local winemaker or two during your visit.

Dean & DeLuca
607 St. Helena Highway S., St. Helena
(707) 967-9980
www.deandeluca.com
When these classy New Yorkers set up shop in Wine Country (see the Shopping chapter), it changed the face of retail wine sales in Napa Valley. D&D has the most extensive collection of California wines you could ever hope to see: 1,200 labels, and that's just 750-milliliter bottles. The wines are arranged alphabetically within varietal categories. Forget about trying to note every wine; by the time you make it to the last Zinfandel, they probably will have added a few more bottles.

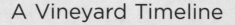
A Vineyard Timeline

Wine Country vineyards are buzzing with activity just about any time of the year. Here's a brief wrap-up of what happens and when.

March and April: Leaves begin to emerge during bud break in mid-March, followed in April by the full unfurling of leaves. Buds resembling miniature bunches of grapes begin to appear.

May and June: Vines continue to send out shoots or "canes" that will create the vine's leaf canopy. (Shoots become canes as they mature.) Most vines have completed their bloom by the end of May, though the floral show is rather bland. Good weather is essential during this time—not too much rain or heat—to allow the successful self-pollination of the grapes. Care is also taken to prevent threat of frost. This is achieved through the use of wind machines, smudge pots, and sprinklers.

July and August: Grapes grow to their full size by mid-July and begin to change color and soften in a process known as *veraison.* Red wine grapes begin to turn red, blue, or black, depending on the varietal; whites become translucent yellow. For most varieties, the proper sugar levels required to make great wine are still several weeks away. However, harvest begins in August of Chardonnay and Pinot Noir

grapes used for sparkling wines, as they reach their optimum sugar levels before other varieties.

September and October: Harvest (also referred to as the "crush") intensifies to a fever pitch. Following the picking of Chardonnay and Pinot Noir grapes, Sauvignon Blanc, Zinfandel, and Merlot are harvested. Usually the last to mature, Cabernet Sauvignon brings the harvest to an end by late October.

November and December: Following harvest, vines take on the colors of fall. White wine varietals turn yellow and gold, while red wine varieties turn crimson. Cooler weather and winter rains trigger the vines into dormancy. As the quiet time of year settles over the vineyards, experienced workers begin methodically pruning the vines to cut back wood that bore fruit the previous year. Winter rains of between 24 and 40 inches will be needed to replenish the groundwater that will carry the vine through the next growing season.

January and February: Expert pruning continues through the wet months, setting the stage for early spring and the new burst of growth to come.

Source: Sonoma County Grape Growers Association

Calistoga Wine Stop
1458 Lincoln Avenue, No. 2, Calistoga
(707) 942–5556, (800) 648–4521
Before you even get to the wine, there's a lot of history worth noting here. The Wine Stop is in the Depot, that big yellow wood building that was what it claims to be. Built in 1868, it's the second-oldest train station

left in California (though no trains have stopped here since 1963). The wine shop itself is jammed inside a 19th-century boxcar, which limits the elbow room but doesn't impair the Napa-Sonoma–concentrated selection. (Owner Tom Pelter estimates that 75 percent of his stock is made in those two counties.) Pelter is something of a port aficionado, which explains the high density of Portugal's fortified wine in his store.

Enoteca Wine Shop
1345 Lincoln Avenue, Calistoga
(707) 942-1117
www.enotecawineshop.com
Discreetly cached on the second floor of Calistoga's 111-year-old I.O.O.F. building is this classy wine shop. (*Enoteca* is an Italian word meaning "wine cellar" or "wine library.") They tend toward artisanal vintners who produce hundreds of cases rather than tens of thousands. And they draw from all over the world, as evidenced by their affection for the likes of Chateau Musar in Lebanon.

Sonoma County

The Wine Exchange of Sonoma
452 First Street E., Sonoma
(707) 938-1794, (800) 938-1794
www.winexsonoma.com
Looking for a more efficient way to sample local wines than driving from one place to another? Interested in a place that carries hard-to-find wines and will even ship them anywhere allowed by law? The Wine Exchange is the place for you, with some 800 premium wines and 280 beers in stock. It's opposite the Sonoma Plaza, with a tasting bar that features 18 wines and six draft beers.

Sonoma Wine Hardware
536 Broadway, Sonoma
(707) 939-1694, (866) 231-9463
www.winehardware.com

Napa Valley Wine Hardware
659 Main Street, St. Helena
(707) 967-5503, (866) 611-9463
www.winehardware.com

You just scored your first case of great Cabernet Sauvignon—now how can you store it properly back home? Your next stop should be at one of these shops. The stores do not sell wine (they leave that up to you); their main focus is wine storage systems. Under the same ownership, both stores have similar inventories, but the Sonoma store features a slightly larger showroom and a larger library of wine books. On display in both are a multitude of cabinets, racks, and other hardware for storing and enjoying wine, and lots of accessories too.

Taylor & Norton Wine Merchants
19210 Sonoma Highway, Sonoma
(707) 939-6611
www.taylorandnorton.com
You'll have no trouble finding every local and regional wine you've been looking for in this wine shop. More than that, Taylor & Norton carries wines from other U.S. areas as well as wines from Europe and other foreign wine-producing regions. While shopping for wine, you might want to browse through a handsome selection of antique wine decanters and glasses, some from the Victorian era. They're pricey but so beautiful you may not be able to resist taking home a souvenir.

The Wine Shop
331 Healdsburg Avenue, Healdsburg
(707) 433-0433

45050 Main Street, Mendocino
(707) 937-3397
It's all wine here; in fact, these are wine bars, meaning they are licensed by the state to serve and charge for full glasses of wine, not tastings. But the selection is enormous: The shops specialize in hard-to-find small production wines worldwide, with more than 600 wineries represented. They will ship your selections too.

ATTRACTIONS

So you've had a go at wine tasting, feasted on some fabulous food, and now you're ready for something completely different. This is your chapter. Sure, wineries, mud baths, and world-class restaurants are attractions in their own right, and all those selling points are detailed in other chapters. In this chapter, however, you'll find everything worth visiting that defies categorical lumping. That might be a culturally rich historical site (such as Fort Ross), a museum (such as the Sharpsteen Museum in Calistoga), a scenic jaunt (such as the Skunk Train), or even a good old-fashioned bit of fun (such as Infineon Raceway). Please note that some of the attractions are seasonal, so always call ahead before planning your itinerary.

PRICE CODE

The price code below reflects the admission price or fees for two adults in high season, not including gratuities, where appropriate.

$	Less than $15
$$	$15 to $50
$$$	$51 to $150
$$$$	More than $151

MAIN EVENTS

Napa County

Seguin Moreau Napa Cooperage   Free
151 Camino Dorado, Napa
(707) 252-3408
www.seguin-moreau.fr
You've seen how the wine is blended, now take a good look at how the barrels get toasted. The only U.S. outpost of the famed French wine barrel makers, Tonnellerie Seguin Moreau Cooperage, is located in Napa. Watch the crew of skilled coopers bend, shave, and roast the oak staves over open flames in the floor, then hammer them together using steel hoops. It's a craft that has changed little in hundreds of years of wine making. Tours are offered Monday through Friday at 9:00 and 11:00 A.M. and 1:30 P.M.

Copia: The American Center for Wine,
Food and the Arts $$
500 First Street, Napa
(707) 259-1600, (888) 51-COPIA
www.copia.org
Wine industry legend Robert Mondavi spent his golden years getting this megaproject off the ground (see the close-up about Copia in this chapter). At a construction cost of $55 million, the 80,000-squarefoot cultural museum and educational center features lively programs, classes, exhibitions, and demonstrations to bring together world-renowned chefs and home cooks, winemakers and wine lovers, and artists—from experts to amateurs.

Napa Firefighters Museum   Free
1201 Main Street, Napa
(707) 259-0609
This museum will give you a deeper appreciation of the folks who fight the flames. Inside you'll see a hand pumper and a steamer, hose carts, engines, ladder trucks, old fire equipment and uniforms, and photos from many eras of puttin' out fires. The museum is open 11:00 A.M. to 4:00 P.M. Wednesday through Sunday.

Veterans Home of California   Free
California Drive, Yountville
(707) 944-4916, (800) 404-VETS
The museum in the old chapel of the Veterans Home features rotating displays of documents, photographs, models, uniforms, and weapons from various eras of

U.S. military history. It's open only by appointment. However, just strolling around the manicured grounds of this Spanish revival complex, much of which dates from 1918, is a pleasure. Look for the signs on Highway 29 just south of Domaine Chandon.

Napa Valley Museum $
55 Presidents Circle, Yountville
(707) 944-0500
www.napavalleymuseum.org
A major capital project that was years in the planning, the nonprofit museum celebrates the artistic, historical, and cultural heritage of the valley, with a permanent exhibit called "The Land and People of the Napa Valley." Its central, permanent exhibition is "California Wine: The Science of an Art." Using music, the spoken word, and the power of technology (including 26 videodisc players and nine microcomputers), it effectively presents the winemaking process in near entirety. A huge hit in 2004 was a show of modern American art loaned to the museum by Napa Valley private collectors.

The Napa Valley Museum is open Wednesday through Monday 10:00 A.M. to 5:00 P.M. (until 8:00 P.M. on the first Thursday of the month). Admission is $4.50 for adults, $3.50 for students and seniors age 60 or older, and $2.50 for youth ages 7 to 17.

Silverado Museum $
1490 Library Lane, St. Helena
(707) 963-3757
www.silveradomuseum.org
A California museum devoted to a Scottish novelist might seem a bit strange, but, hey, Robert Louis Stevenson did help immortalize the area with his *The Silverado Squatters.* He also penned classics such as *Treasure Island, Dr. Jekyll and Mr. Hyde,* and others you'll read all about at the museum. It has first editions, artifacts from the Stevenson home, personal letters and photographs, and a few original manuscripts (though most of those reside at

Yale University). The museum is closed Monday but open the rest of the week from noon to 4:00 P.M.

Bale Grist Mill State Historic Park $
3369 Highway 29, St. Helena
(707) 963-2236
www.parks.ca.gov/default.asp?page_id=482
The friendly miller will tell you how this park is a working reminder of the days when "milling" involved more than driving to Safeway for a bag of all-purpose flour. Dr. Edward Bale built the wood-frame mill in 1846, and it has been painstakingly refurbished. The park is open 10:00 A.M. to 5:00 P.M. daily, but the best times to visit are weekend days at 11:30 A.M. and 1:00, 2:30, and 3:30 P.M. That's when the park cranks up the wooden, 36-foot waterwheel and gets those original quartz stones to grinding wheat or corn. Admission is $1.00 for adults; children under 16 free. From here you can hike to adjacent Bothe–Napa Valley State Park (see the Parks and Recreation chapter).

The Sharpsteen Museum Free
1311 Washington Street, Calistoga
(707) 942-5911
www.sharpsteen-museum.org
If every small town in America had a museum as lively and authentic as the Sharpsteen, maybe we wouldn't be so ignorant of history. The museum was founded in the 1970s by Ben Sharpsteen, who produced such films as *Fantasia* and *Snow White* for Walt Disney. (Sharpsteen's Academy Award Oscar statuette from his days with Disney gleams inside a special display case.) The crowning piece of his legacy is a 32-foot scale-model diorama that lays out the grounds of Sam Brannan's Calistoga spa, circa 1860 (see the History chapter for more on Brannan). One of the original cottages from that spa serves as a museum annex.

The museum is open 10:00 A.M. to 4:00 P.M. daily from April through September and noon to 4:00 P.M. daily from Octo-

Copia: The World's Only Wine, Food, Art (and Fun) Center

When Robert Mondavi puts his mind to making a project happen, it usually happens. His vision for this must-see attraction became reality in 2001 after 10 years of planning and more than two years of construction.

Copia: The American Center for Wine, Food and the Arts is described as "a cultural institution, museum, and educational center dedicated to the character of wine and food in close association with the arts and humanities, and to celebrating these as unique expressions of American life, culture, and heritage." That's the official Copia statement, but the place is really a fun house for foodies and wine enthusiasts, with fabulous art and exhibits to round out the experience. You can bet it's the only place like it in the world.

Built from private donations at a cost of about $55 million ($20 million from Mr. Mondavi alone), Copia is 80,000 square feet of stone, concrete, metal, and glass with gardens inspired by the 16th-century kitchen gardens at Villandry in France's Loire Valley. Rising along the banks of the Napa River, Copia, named for the goddess of abundance, is surrounded by three-and-a-half acres of organic culinary gardens ranging from olive and citrus orchards, to a collection of lavender shrubs from around the world, to groves of nut-bearing trees and beds of herbs and root vegetables.

Inside Copia are art exhibits and unique sculptures, an amphitheater for concerts and performances, an indoor theater for films and lectures, a rare books library, a demonstration kitchen, classrooms for learning about food and wine, a cafe featuring picnic-style fare, a gift shop, and gourmet dining and wine tasting.

A permanent exhibit, "Forks in the Road: Food, Wine and the American Table," takes a lighthearted look at the place of food and wine in American life today and features interactive exhibits that both kids and adults will find entertaining. There's more trivia than you can shake a ladle at: What sweet treat was named for a small Massachusetts town? The Fig Newton. What fizzy drink was

ber through March. Admission donations accepted.

Old Faithful Geyser of California $
1299 Tubbs Lane, Calistoga
(707) 942-6463
www.oldfaithfulgeyser.com

About every 40 minutes on the yearly average (depending on how much water is in the aquifer), the earth gurgles, puffs, and blows a stream of boiling water (350 degrees hot!) about 60 feet into the air off Tubbs Lane. Welcome to Calistoga's geyser, one of only three in world that originally called Lithiated Lemon? 7-Up! The Copia Kids Garden opened in April 2005, offering an imaginative and functional space designed specifically for the enjoyment and education of children. A chicken coop, rabbit hutch, and gardener's shed are among the fun diversions just for little ones. With the naming of a new executive director in 2005, the center also plans a few other changes and additions to its regular attractions, including a public gourmet marketplace.

Julia's Kitchen, the center's full-service dining room with an open kitchen, is named for the late Julia Child, the legendary food maven and an advisor in Copia's development for more than five years. (As an honorary trustee of Copia, she donated her personal collection of copper cookware, used for several decades in her own kitchen, to be put on display.) The restaurant's executive chef is Victor Scargle (see the Restaurants chapter). The open kitchen allows visitors to watch distinguished American chefs and cooking teachers at work. For extra fun, ask for seats at the counter (there are only four), where you can watch the culinary action up close.

Copia is located at 500 First Street at the eastern edge of downtown Napa. Admission is $12.50 for adults, $10.00 for

Copia: The American Center for Wine, Food and the Arts includes a permanent display dedicated to food consumption in America.
JEAN SAYLOR DOPPENBERG

teens and seniors, and $7.50 for children. To learn more about this one-of-a-kind attraction, call (707) 259-1600 or visit www.copia.org.

can call themselves Old Faithful without shame. There is a working seismograph in the entryway (the geyser is said to predict earthquakes), and outside near the erupting pond, for some reason, is a pen of Tennessee Fainting goats, a rare breed suffering from myatonia, which causes

them to lock up and topple when startled. The Old Faithful complex is open 9:00 A.M. to 6:00 P.M. daily in the warm months, 9:00 A.M. to 5:00 P.M. in the winter. Admission is $8.00 for adults, $7.00 for seniors, and $3.00 for kids ages 6 through 12.

Villa Ca'Toga $$
Off Tubbs Lane, Calistoga
(707) 942-3900
www.catoga.com

Italian artist Carlo Marchiori is one of the eminent trompe l'oeil artists in the world, and Villa Ca'Toga—a mansion and work in progress on the outskirts of Calistoga—is his vision come to life. Faux pillars, staircases, and hanging plants are painted in three-dimensional realism on two-dimensional walls. Alcoves end abruptly at painted backdrops, and surprises lie around every corner (even for the initiated—Marchiori is constantly adding new sculptures). The house is open Saturday from May to October for a one-hour tour that begins at 11:00 A.M. Reservations are necessary, and you pick up your tickets and a map to the property at the Ca'Toga Galleria D'Arte at 1206 Cedar Street in downtown Calistoga (see the Arts and Culture chapter). Tickets are $20 per person, and children over 12 are welcome.

Petrified Forest $
4100 Petrified Forest Road, Calistoga
(707) 942-6667
www.petrifiedforest.org

It's not as spooky as it sounds, unless you think too hard about the advancing wall of muddy volcanic ash that leveled these trees about three million years ago, following massive eruptions to the northeast. The trees lay unmolested until 1870, when a gent later known as "Petrified Charlie" Evans happened upon a rock-hard stump while tending his cows. The rest is tourist-industry history. A short loop takes you past all the highlights, including the Monarch, a petrified, 105-foot redwood with a diameter of 6 feet. Guided walks are offered on Sunday at 2:00 P.M. The museum and store are open daily 9:00 A.M. to 6:00 P.M. Admission is $6.00 for adults, $5.00 for youngsters ages 12 through 17 and seniors 60 and over, and $3.00 for kids under 12.

Sonoma County

SOUTHERN SONOMA

Depot Park Museum Free
270 First Street W., Sonoma
(707) 938-1762
www.vom.com/depot

This is more than a museum; it's an authentic piece of Sonoma city's history. Originally the depot was on the downtown plaza, much to the chagrin of Sonomans, who felt the plaza had been turned into a railroad yard, turntable and all. After some pressure, the depot was moved in 1890 to its present site. The museum now houses a terrific collection of historic memorabilia focusing on the 19th century. Several rooms are furnished in Victorian style, and a good deal of emphasis is placed on the life of Gen. Mariano Vallejo (see the History chapter). Pioneer artifacts and exhibits of Native American culture are nicely displayed. Temporary exhibits shed light on specific historical periods, crafts, and events. The museum is open 1:00 to 4:30 P.M. Wednesday through Sunday. Admission donations are welcome.

Train Town $
20264 Broadway, Sonoma
(707) 938-3912
www.traintown.com

Train Town is the most well-developed scale railroad in America—a joy for anyone of any age. You climb into a miniature train, one-fourth the normal size, and chug your way through 10 acres of planned landscaped park filled with thousands of native trees, animals, bridges over lakes, tunnels, waterfalls, and replicas of historic buildings. Two miniature engines and handcrafted railroad cars take passengers on the 20-minute ride to Lakeville, a pint-sized, western-flavored hamlet populated with geese and ducks. Along the way there's a stop to pet some llamas and goats. Trains operate daily in summer from 10:00 A.M. to 5:00 P.M. In winter it's a shorter, weekend schedule. The fare is $3.75 for adults and $3.25 for children 12 and younger and seniors.

Vintage Aircraft Co. $$$$
23982 Arnold Drive, Sonoma
(707) 938-2444
www.vintageaircraft.com
You step back into the 1940s when you step onto the tarmac and check out Christopher Prevost's fleet of authentic 1940 Boeing-built Stearman biplanes. One of the planes is a North American–built World War II Navy SNJ-4, designed to train pilot candidates for the air force and navy. Meticulously restored and maintained, the planes tempt thrill seekers to take one of several rides offered by Prevost. For the truly brave, Prevost offers a variety of aerobatic flights—the most intense is appropriately named Kamikaze. Weekday flights are by appointment.

Infineon Raceway $$
Highways 37 and 121, Sonoma
(707) 938-8448, (800) 870-7223
www.infineonraceway.com
Each year you'll see some of the top names in the racing world compete at Infineon (formerly known as Sears Point Raceway) on the grueling road course, the rugged motocross dirt track, and the drag strip. Legends such as Mario Andretti, Al Unser (Sr. and Jr.), and Jeff Gordon have all toured the track as well as Hollywood celebrities such as Paul Newman, Clint Eastwood, and James Garner. Annual events include NASCAR road races and sports car racing by the Sports Car Club of America with TRANS-AM, Formula Atlantic, and Pro Formula Ford entrants. Bike events include AMA motorcycle road races and several motocross races. Prices for events vary. (See the Spectator Sports chapter for more details.)

Historic Town of Sonoma $
Various sites
A national landmark and the largest square of its kind in California, the Sonoma Plaza evokes the feel of Old Europe. It is an ideal picnic spot, with numerous tables under nearly 200 trees, a playground, and a duck pond.

Surrounding the plaza are some of the buildings that marked the start of the village, then owned by Mexico and ruled by Gen. Mariano Vallejo. It makes a lovely walking tour, and one $2.00 ticket, available at any of the following sites, will give you access to the mission, the barracks, Vallejo's home, and the Petaluma Adobe.

Mission San Francisco Solano, founded in 1823 as the last of California's Franciscan missions, is diagonally opposite the plaza's northeast corner. Today's mission is a faithful re-creation of the original. Only the priests' quarters date from the founding. It's open 10:00 A.M. to 5:00 P.M. daily.

Sonoma Barracks, across from the mission, housed Vallejo's Mexican troops, sheltered the Bear Flag soldiers, and served as a U.S. military headquarters in the 1840s and 1850s. Today the barracks are restored to their Mexican-era appearance, with exhibits inside and an attractive gift shop with California items. Grizzly bears once battled bulls in the enclosed courtyard behind the barracks, while spectators gambled on the outcome. It's open 10:00 A.M. to 5:00 P.M. daily.

Salvador Vallejo Adobe (Swiss Hotel) has a bar and restaurant that have long been favorites of residents and visitors alike. The locally famous drink, "Bear's Hair" sherry, is served in the saloon. Originally the adobe was built for General Vallejo's brother, Salvador, in the 1840s. It has been known as the Swiss Hotel since the 1880s.

Salvador Vallejo Adobe (El Dorado Hotel), a Monterey colonial adobe, has had a checkered history as a government office, college, winery, and hotel. Salvador Vallejo built it between 1836 and 1846. Subsequently it was occupied by the Bear Flag party members and U.S. Gen. John C. Frémont during the opening days of the Mexican-American War. Presbyterian settlers operated Cumberland College at the adobe from 1858 until 1864.

El Paseo de Sonoma (Pinelli Building) is one of several plaza structures built of native stone. The building survived a 1911 fire when Augustino Pinelli let firefighters douse flames with his barrels of wine. Today several shops and restaurants can be found on the passageway behind First Street East and Spain Street. Blue Wing Inn, on East Spain Street across from the mission, was once a rowdy gold rush–era saloon visited by future President U. S. Grant, Lt. William Tecumseh Sherman, Kit Carson, and notorious bandit Joaquin Murietta.

General Vallejo's Home (Lachryma Montis) is not on the plaza but 3 blocks down West Spain Street. General Vallejo built this Gothic revival home at a cost of $50,000 in 1851 and named it Lachryma Montis ("tears of the mountain") because of a spring on the property. Abandoning Spanish-style architecture, he built a grand Victorian and furnished it with European imports. He had redwood lumber hauled in from the port at Vallejo, while bricks and marble mantels were shipped from Hawaii. Landscaping, a glass pavilion (now gone), and every convenience of the time were included. The Vallejos' 15th and 16th children were born at Lachryma Montis.

Vallejo's once-great holdings eventually were reduced to only the acreage around this home. Many of the original furnishings are still in place. The kitchen located in a separate building kept the heat of cooking away from the rest of the house. A charming little guesthouse remains on the property, and a short walk up the hill leads to the room of one of the Vallejo children. Picnic tables are set around a stream that runs through the property. Now a state historic park, Lachryma Montis is open 10:00 A.M. to 5:00 P.M. daily.

Jack London State Historic Park $
2400 London Ranch Road off Arnold
Drive, Glen Ellen
(707) 938–5216
www.jacklondonpark.com

Jack London called it his Beauty Ranch, but he wanted to achieve more than aesthetic satisfaction here. His goal was to achieve a scientifically operated ranch where new techniques could be developed. Many buildings remain from his experiment in ranching: stone stables where he kept his prize horses, the last vestiges of his famous scientific piggery, and the farmhouse where he lived for five years and wrote most of his stories. In the center of the 1,400 acres is the rubble of Wolf House, the lava-stone mansion he had hoped to live in, which burned to the ground in 1913. The half-mile trail to the Wolf House ruins passes through a forest of oak, madrone, and buckeye trees. Nearby is London's grave, marked only by a stone from the ruins of the house.

At the top of the hill, as you enter the state park, is the House of Happy Walls, built by London's wife, Charmian, after his death. It contains memorabilia of his life as a war correspondent, his abortive trip around the world with Charmian in a ship he designed himself, and a load of information about his writing life. Displayed are some of the 600 rejection slips he received, the first from the *Saturday Evening Post*. Seven miles of hiking, mountain biking, and equestrian trails are available. The museum is open daily except for major holidays from 10:00 A.M. to 5:00 P.M., and admission is $3.00 per car ($2.00 when seniors are riding).

Petaluma Historical Museum Free
20 Fourth Street, Petaluma
(707) 778–4398
www.petalumamuseum.com
A large, freestanding, stained-glass dome accents the beauty of this 1906 Carnegie Free Library—one of the hundreds that philanthropist Andrew Carnegie built and donated in the early 20th century. You'll find a 19th-century horse-drawn fire wagon here, along with Native American artifacts, pioneer relics, and displays describing Petaluma's dairy and poultry beginnings. An exhibit about the Petaluma River illustrates how the town became an

important manufacturing and trading hub when Petaluma was one of California's largest cities.

The museum offers brochures for self-guided walking tours of the city, featuring the famous Iron Front buildings and beautiful Victorian homes. In addition, docents costumed in Victorian attire lead guided tours of historic downtown on weekends. It's free, but donations are accepted. Hours are 10:00 A.M. to 4:00 P.M. Wednesday through Saturday.

Petaluma Adobe State Historic Park $
3325 Adobe Road at Casa Grande Road, Petaluma
(707) 762-4871
www.parks.sonoma.net/adobe.html
Once the headquarters of Gen. Mariano Vallejo's 100-square-mile Rancho Petaluma, this enormous two-story adobe overlooking Petaluma stands as a monument to California's early history. A self-guided tour of the structure offers views of the period-furnished kitchen, the living quarters where the Vallejo family stayed when they spent their summer holiday at the rancho, and the guest rooms. The rustic chairs and candle sconces are of Spanish motif. Outside you will find replicas of the beehive ovens where cooks baked bread for rancho residents. Occasionally the ranger in charge may put in a loaf or two, using the same recipe the Vallejo servants used. The ranch is open daily (except Thanksgiving, Christmas, and New Year's Day) from 10:00 A.M. to 5:00 P.M. The $3.00 admission fee, $2.00 for children ages 6 to 12, entitles you to visit any of the sites on historic Sonoma Plaza (see previous listing).

Luther Burbank Home and Gardens $
Santa Rosa and Sonoma Avenues, Santa Rosa
(707) 524-5445
www.lutherburbank.org
During his 53 years in Santa Rosa, horticulturist Luther Burbank changed the plant world, improving and hybridizing more than 800 varieties (see the close-up "Genius in the Garden" in this chapter).

This National Historic Landmark features Burbank's home, a carriage house, and the greenhouse where he performed his experiments. Outside you'll find a lovely garden filled with the plants Burbank introduced to the world. Docent-led house tours are offered on the half hour Tuesday through Sunday from April through October. House tours, which are $4.00 for adults and free for children 12 and younger, run 10:00 A.M. to 3:30 P.M. The gardens are open daily at no charge or $3.00 for an audio self-tour.

Jesse Peter Native American
Art Museum   Free
Santa Rosa Junior College, 1501 Mendocino Avenue, Santa Rosa
(707) 527-4479
www.santarosa.edu/museum
Dedicated to arts and crafts created by Native Americans from the 19th century up to the present day, this museum contains an extensive assortment of baskets, including the extraordinarily beautiful baskets of the Pomo tribe. Most items displayed represent the work of California tribes, although beadwork of the Plains and Plateau tribes is on hand as well as some Eskimo art. There are replicas of a southwestern pueblo, a Pomo roundhouse, and a Klamath River *xonta* (a family shelter). The museum is open Monday through Friday (except for school holidays) from mid-August through May.

Sonoma County Museum $
425 Seventh Street, Santa Rosa
(707) 579-1500
www.sonomacountymuseum.com
Housed in the old post office built after the 1906 earthquake, the museum was moved and restored as a part of local grassroots activities. The lower floor is devoted to an extensive collection of art exhibits, exhibits on the history and heritage of the county, and photographs of the local landscape and people. The second floor is given over to exciting temporary exhibits. Past ones have included displays of cartoon art and a woodwork-

Genius in the Garden

Luther Burbank (1849–1926) knew plants not just for what they were but for what they could become. The nation's most renowned and prolific horticulturist, he dedicated his life to the propagation of new plant varieties, many of which are still valued today for their extraordinary beauty and utility.

Born in Lancaster, Massachusetts, Luther began his career at the age of 21, when he accidentally discovered a potato that had sprouted a seed ball on his farm. At the time, the European potato blight had recently spread to the United States, and farmers were in danger of losing their crops. From the 23 seeds he found in the seed ball, Luther developed a hardy, high-yielding variety of potato, the "Burbank potato," which eventually became the predominant type grown in the United States—today's russet potato is a descendant of the Burbank variety.

But this was only the beginning for a man whose name would become associated with nearly a thousand other new plants. Perhaps sensing his destiny, Luther quickly sold the rights to his new potato for $150 to a local seed dealer and used the proceeds to finance a trip to Santa Rosa, where his brother had been living.

Inspired by his brother's letters describing a gardener's paradise, Luther had dreamt of California for years. When he finally set foot in Santa Rosa in 1875, he found it beyond even his expectations. Yet, like most people who believe they have stumbled upon the promised land, Luther wanted to keep it a secret. Fearing that should the news leak out "all scuffs would come out here, get drunk, and curse the whole country," he warned his family back east to avoid speaking favorably about California.

It wasn't long before Luther acquired some land near "downtown" Santa Rosa—then a jumble of 726 houses, 6 hotels, 7 churches, and 22 saloons—and began his work. Though he had achieved some notoriety through early efforts, it wasn't until 1893, when he published his catalog *New Creations in Fruits and Flowers,* that he achieved widespread fame. At the time the propagation of new plant varieties was a slow, tedious process, and such a large offering—more than a hundred varieties—by a single individual was a surprise, if not downright shocking. Among individuals and groups who believed that God alone could "create" a new plant, Luther was considered an infidel.

But the results quickly trumped the skeptics. Gardeners from coast to coast and abroad bought Luther's plants, which were exceptionally hardy and high yielding. The catalog turned Luther into a popular hero, and his stature ranked with such greats as Thomas Edison and Henry Ford—Edison and Ford both personally admired Luther and visited him at his home in Santa Rosa.

Luther's plant varieties are legion, and it is difficult to do justice to the

The Luther Burbank Home and Gardens in Santa Rosa stand as a testament to the nation's greatest horticulturist. JOHN NAGIECKI

breadth and inventiveness of his creations. Varieties such as elephant garlic, plumcot (a cross between a plum and apricot), and the ubiquitous Shasta daisy are still popular today.

Luther had a genius for detecting desirable qualities in young plants and nurturing them into new strains. Having had no formal training, he relied more on intuition than rigorous scientific methodology and employed his unique gifts on a large scale in thousands of simultaneous experiments. At the time of his death in 1926, he had more than 3,000 experiments under way and was growing more than 5,000 species.

Throughout his long career Luther sought to produce high-quality plant varieties that would help increase the world's food supply. But more importantly, his work was inspired by a deep love of beauty. "The urge to beauty," he wrote, "and the need for beautiful and gracious and lovely things in life is as vital as the need for bread."

I firmly believe, from what I have seen, that this is the chosen spot of all this earth as far as Nature is concerned.

—Luther Burbank

ing exhibit of bowls, boxes, and furniture. The Wild Oat Gift Shop has a particularly intriguing assortment of books and items with Sonoma County themes. The museum and gift shop are open 11:00 A.M. to 4:00 P.M. Wednesday through Sunday year-round. Admission is $5.00 for adults, $2.00 for seniors and students.

Redwood Empire Ice Arena $
1667 West Steele Lane, Santa Rosa
(707) 546-7147
www.snoopyshomeice.com

Outside of Charlie Brown, who will always be universally loved, the Redwood Empire Ice Arena may be the most appreciated gift cartoonist Charles Schulz (1922-2000) gave Sonoma County. His career started in Minnesota and ballooned to fame, with his work appearing in more than 1,800 newspapers in 65 countries worldwide. Schulz was a resident of Santa Rosa, where he created many of his cartoons.

The arena offers a full range of skating, and many world champions have glided across the ice here. Open daily, but hours vary, with mornings reserved for special programs and classes. The cost is $7.00 for adults and teens and $5.50 for children younger than 12. Aside from the arena, visitors will delight in the gift shop with hundreds of items from the lives of the Peanuts gang.

Charles M. Schulz Museum and Research Center $$
2301 Hardies Lane, Santa Rosa
(707) 579-4452
www.schulzmuseum.org

Peanuts creator Charles Schulz didn't live long enough to see this museum dedicated to his legacy come to life (he died in early 2000), but he would be humbled by the result. Adjacent to Schulz's Redwood Empire Ice Arena (see previous listing), the $8 million museum opened in 2002. Within its 27,000 square feet are permanent and temporary displays of the cartoonist's 50-year body of work; a research library and archives for students, cartoonists, and scholars; and classrooms. Worth seeing is the 17-by-22-foot mural crafted from more than 3,500 individual Peanuts comic strips printed on ceramic tiles. Also on display is the wooden drawing board where Schulz drew his one-dimensional characters, in a re-creation of his art studio. Admission is $8.00 for adults, $5.00 for seniors and children under 18, and free for toddlers. Closed Tuesday.

Safari West $$$
3115 Porter Creek Road, Santa Rosa
(707) 579-2551, (800) 616-2695
www.safariwest.com

This is a little different from those drive-through safari parks where tourists outnumber perplexed animals by about 100 to 1. Safari West is a private preserve and working ranch dedicated to conservation and propagation of endangered species—the 400 acres of Safari West are home to 400 exotic mammals and birds. You can gaze at herds of zebra or watch a giraffe crane its mammoth neck to eat out of your hand.

Guests spend an unparalleled two-and-a-half hours on a unique educational trek through the rolling hills of the preserve. Accompanied by a naturalist, groups get the rarest of opportunities to photograph herds of antelope, eland, gazelle, zebra, and many more types of animals. Because the critters live in vast acreage, they are comfortable with vehicles and can be seen up close. (One group was even treated to the birth of an antelope.) Wear comfortable clothing and bring sunscreen and a hat. Oh, and the proprietors can customize tours if you have a particular interest in, say, springboks. Cost of a basic tour is $58 for adults, $28 for children three to nine, and free for toddlers. Safari West also includes overnight accommodations. The South African–made "tents" feature hardwood floors, bathrooms, and king-size beds. Visits are by appointment only. Leave your pets at home.

Pacific Coast Air Museum $
2330 Airport Boulevard, Santa Rosa
(707) 575-7900
www.pacificcoastairmuseum.org
Located next to Sonoma County's Charles
M. Schulz Airport, the Pacific Coast Air
Museum was formed by local aviators
interested in restoring and preserving
retired military aircraft. The collection
ranges from a Korean War-era RF-86
Sabre and Huey helicopter—which saw
combat in Vietnam—to an F-16 Viper
flown by the commander of the navy's
Top Gun flight school and an F-14A Tom-
cat that saw duty on several U.S. carriers.
The museum is open every Tuesday and
Thursday 10:00 A.M. to 2:00 P.M., and every
Saturday and Sunday 10:00 A.M. to 4:00
P.M. On the third weekend of each month,
museum staff unlatch the canopy of a featured aircraft and let visitors climb aboard
to get a feel of what it's like behind the
wheel of a war bird. The museum also
sponsors a weekend air show—Wings over
Wine Country—each August (see the Festivals and Annual Events chapter).

NORTHERN SONOMA

Windsor Waterworks and Slides $$
8225 Conde Lane, Windsor
(707) 838-7760, (707) 838-7360
This recreational park offers welcome
relief from hot summer days. Among the
attractions are an inner-tube slide, speed
slide, body slide, splash fountain with
squirt guns, swimming pool and wading
pool, large picnic area with barbecue pits,
and an arcade. Kids can play table tennis,
horseshoes, and volleyball. A snack bar is
available. The park is open every day from
May through September from 11:00 A.M. to
7:00 P.M. The entrance fee is $13.25 for
those 13 and older and $12.25 for kids
ages 4 to 12. There's a special rate of
$9.75 after 4:00 P.M. for the "afternoon
splash." (See the Kidstuff chapter for more
on this attraction.)

*Inside the Charles M. Schulz Museum is
a wall from a Colorado house where the
cartoonist briefly lived, on which he
painted some of his early cartoon char-
acters in 1951. The artwork was later dis-
covered under layers of paint, and the
wall was carefully removed and shipped
to Santa Rosa for display in the
museum.*

Healdsburg Museum Free
221 Matheson Street, Healdsburg
(707) 431-3325
www.healdsburgmuseum.org
This museum is in a refurbished Carnegie
library building and features both perma-
nent and changing exhibits. The county's
history is depicted from prehistoric times
to the present, and displays include
antique firearms, 19th-century clothing,
tools, and an outstanding collection of
Pomo basketry and crafts. The archives
contain more than 5,000 historical photo-
graphs and newspapers dating to 1865.
Healdsburg Museum is open Tuesday
through Sunday 11:00 A.M. to 4:00 P.M.

WEST COUNTY/RUSSIAN RIVER

**Luther Burbank Gold Ridge
Experiment Farm** Free
7781 Bodega Avenue, Sebastopol
(707) 829-6711
www.wschs-grf.pon.net/bef.htm
On this 18-acre experimental farm, horti-
culturist Luther Burbank built a cottage
and worked to perfect Gravenstein apples,
plums, cherries, grapes, and lilies.
Although he lived and worked in Santa
Rosa, this is where he conducted his horti-
cultural research between 1895 and 1926.
Free guided tours, available by appoint-
ment from April through mid-October,
explore Burbank's gardens and visit his
restored cottage. The gardens are open
for free self-guided tours year-round.

West County Museum   **Free**
261 South Main Street, Sebastopol
(707) 829-6711
www.wschs-grf.pon.net
A restored railroad depot houses the collections of the Western Sonoma County Historical Society. The Triggs Reference Room contains books, photographs, magazines, newspapers, audiotapes, and videotapes on local history. West County Museum is open 1:00 to 4:00 P.M. Thursday through Sunday. There is no admission fee, but donations are welcomed.

Children's Bell Tower   **Free**
2255 Highway 1, Bodega Bay
(707) 875-3422
www.nicholasgreen.org
In 1994 Nicholas Green, a seven-year-old boy from Bodega Bay, was tragically shot and killed by robbers during a vacation with his family in Italy. Nicholas's parents bravely chose to donate his organs to seven sick Italians, who were given a new chance to live a full life. The heartbreaking yet life-affirming tale received worldwide media attention and was turned into a movie. It also gave birth to this moving monument dedicated to the memory of Nicholas and the positive aftermath of his death. Families, schools, and churches around Italy donated all of the 140 bells that ring the 18-foot-high tower. The large bell in the center, blessed by Pope John Paul II, is inscribed with the names of the seven recipients of Nicholas's organs. The memorial is behind the Bodega Bay Community Center, at the north edge of town on the ocean side of the highway. Park in the small lot behind the center and stroll down to the tower. (Nicholas is buried in Bodega, a short distance inland. His grave is also an inspirational sight.)

Fort Ross State Historic Park   **$**
19005 Highway 1, north of Jenner
(707) 847-3286
www.parks.ca.gov/default.asp?page_id=449
On a grassy, windswept bluff north of Jenner stands a ruddy, wooden stockade, its

main gate facing the Pacific Ocean. The 14-foot walls are made of weather-beaten redwood. Inside is a small chapel dedicated to St. Nicholas and topped with an orthodox cross. In another building, seal and otter pelts hang on walls above casks marked in Cyrillic characters.

Now part of a state historic park, Fort Ross provides a fascinating glimpse into the history of the settlement founded with the aim of supplying food for the fledgling Russian colony in Alaska, where Russia's eastward push ended in the early 1800s (see the History chapter). The museum in the visitor center exhibits Russian and Native American artifacts, and the gift shop offers crafts made by the local Pomo tribe as well as goods imported from Russia.

Join more than 100 costumed participants for the annual Living History Day—held on the third or last Saturday of July—to get a taste of what life was like for the Russians 200 years ago (see the Festivals and Annual Events chapter). The park is open daily 10:00 A.M. to 4:30 P.M. There is no entrance fee for cyclists or hikers. Vehicles pay $2.00 for parking.

Berry's Saw Mill   **Free**
Highway 116 and Cazadero Highway, Cazadero
(707) 865-2365
www.berrysmill.com
This authentic sawmill offers visitors an opportunity to see trees sawed, split, and planed into usable lumber. Visitors can explore the mill on an informal basis—guided tours are not offered. It's open at no charge Monday through Friday 7:45 A.M. to 4:30 P.M.

Mendocino County

Real Goods Solar Living Center   **Free**
13771 U.S. Highway 101, Hopland
(707) 744-2100
www.realgoods.com
This shop is a giant demonstration project for residential energy efficiency and alter-

native earth-friendly designs. The large main building at the center is built of straw bales, and it's powered entirely by solar panels and wind turbines. You can shop from a wide selection of environmentally conscious products such as solar panels, hemp goods, and water filtration systems and enjoy a tour of the 12 acres of beautiful permaculture organic gardens and ponds. For the kids, there's a special area for playing and learning, including a unique solar calendar: They call it a 21st-century Stonehenge. The Solar Living Center is open daily 10:00 A.M. to 6:00 P.M. Each August the center sponsors a solar festival that features environmental activists (see the Festivals and Annual Events chapter).

Grace Hudson Museum and Sun House $
431 South Main Street, Ukiah
(707) 467-2836
www.gracehudsonmuseum.org
Grace Hudson Museum is an art, history, and anthropology museum focusing on the life works of Grace Hudson, who painted more than 650 oils, primarily of the local Pomo people. She was already a talented painter when she married ethnologist Dr. John Hudson and focused her art on Native American subjects. The museum displays Hudson's portraits of Pomos, exhibits of Native American arts and crafts, and changing shows by local artists. Sun House, which shares the site, is a charming Craftsman bungalow that was the Hudson residence. The museum is open Wednesday through Saturday 10:00 A.M. to 4:30 P.M. and noon to 4:30 P.M. on Sunday. Tours of the Sun House are offered on the hour, noon to 3:00 P.M.

Held-Poage Memorial Home and Library Free
Mendocino County Historical Society,
603 West Perkins Street, Ukiah
(707) 462-6969
www.pacificsites.com
A treasure trove of historical information, the library holds 4,500 books on county,

state, and national history. Along with 13,500 historical photographic negatives and microfilms pertaining to Northern California history, the library offers documents, maps, scrapbooks, genealogies, and more. Researchers from all over the United States contact the society for assistance. All this information is housed in the historic Queen Anne–style Victorian home built in 1903 for William D. Held and Ethel Poage Held, who were dedicated to the collection of archival materials about California. The home is open Monday through Friday 1:00 to 4:00 P.M. Closed holidays. Donations are welcome.

Pomo Cultural Center Free
1003 Marina Drive, Lake Mendocino, Ukiah
(707) 485-8285, (707) 485-8685 (gift shop)
This small museum was built by the Army Corps of Engineers and is operated by the local Coyote Tribal Council. The round shape of the center is modeled on the Pomo ceremonial dance house, where cultural knowledge was passed down through the generations. On display are examples of Pomo basketry, a demonstration of clamshell moneymaking, and a hands-on exhibit of different animal skins. The museum is open 9:00 A.M. to 5:00 P.M. Wednesday through Sunday, April through mid-November, and is closed in winter.

Mendocino County Museum Free
400 East Commercial Street, Willits
(707) 459-2736
www.co.mendocino.ca.us/museum
This large, modern museum displays artifacts and interpretations of the cultural history of the county, with a particular focus on local Pomo and Yuki tribes. A fascinating aspect is the collection of oral history interviews from Mendocino citizens. There's also an exhibit about Seabiscuit, the famed racehorse that spent his twilight years at Ridgewood Ranch nearby. It's open Wednesday through Sunday 10.00 A.M. to 4:30 P.M. Donations are gladly accepted.

**Anderson Valley Historical
Society Museum**   **Free**
Highway 128, 1 mile north of Boonville
(707) 895-3207
www.andersonvalleychamber.com
In a century-old schoolhouse on the side
of the road, this museum showcases
Anderson Valley pioneer life. Displays
include a sheepshearing shed, a black-
smith shop, Pomo Indian basketry and
tools, and antique agricultural and lumber
industry equipment. There is also an
exhibit devoted to "Boontling," the valley's
unique folk dialect. Open Friday through
Sunday 1:00 to 4:00 P.M. When the flag is
flying, the museum is open.

**Point Arena Lighthouse
and Museum**   **$**
45500 Lighthouse Road, Point Arena
(707) 882-2777, (877) 725-4448
www.pointarenalighthouse.com
The lighthouse, originally built in 1870 and
rebuilt after the 1906 earthquake, still
shines a warning to keep ships off the dangerous rocks and shoals. At 115 feet, it's the
tallest lighthouse in California. The light is
now automated, but plans call for the
ancient Fresnel lens to be restored. The
Coast Guard facilities have been turned into
a maritime museum, with several guest cottages run by a local nonprofit organization.
Visitors may climb the light tower and view
the broad terraces that run down to the
sea or admire the lens that remains in place
in the light room at the top. Offshore,
scuba divers enjoy the Arena Rock Underwater Preserve, an area of abundant marine
flora and fauna, as well as the sunken wreck
of a freighter. The lighthouse museum is
open daily 10:00 A.M. to 4:30 P.M. in summer
and 10:00 A.M. to 3:30 P.M. in winter. Admission is $5.00 for adults and teens and $1.00
for kids younger than 12.

**Greenwood State Park
Visitors Center**   **Free**
5980 South Highway 1, Elk
(707) 937-5804
www.parks.ca.gov/default.asp?page_id+
447

This small history center tells the story of
the tiny coastal town of Elk, from its founding by the Greenwood brothers in the late
1800s through its history as a logging and
lumber town. Housed in the former L. E.
White Lumber Company office—which was
in operation from 1884 to 1916—the center
includes a large mural depicting how lumber was transported down the steep cliffs
to waiting ships. The visitor center is open
Saturday and Sunday, March through October, 11:00 A.M. to 1:00 P.M.

**Ford House Museum and
Visitor Center**   **Free**
735 Main Street, Mendocino
(707) 937-5397
The Ford House, built in 1854, was originally the residence of Mendocino lumber
mill owner Jerome Bursley Ford. Today it
serves as a museum and visitor center for
Mendocino Headlands State Park. This is
where to find out everything you need to
know for your visit to the charming village
of Mendocino and the wild shores off the
headlands. During the whale migrations
from January through March, there are
docent-led whale-watching walks on Saturday. At the height of the wildflower season in late spring, knowledgeable docents
lead walks through a riot of color and tell
about the flowers. Ford House is open
daily 11:00 A.M. to 4:00 P.M. The docent
walks are free, though small donations are
encouraged.

Kelley House Museum   **$**
45007 Albion Street, Mendocino
(707) 937-5791
www.mendocinohistory.org
The house looks like a home transplanted
from a Maine coastal town, a reflection of
the fact that many New Englanders came
to Mendocino in earlier times. Its walls display a collection of historic photographs
of days when redwood logs were loaded
onto waiting ships via chutes and long
piers. Displays tell the story of the logging
and shipping industries that turned a wild,
lonely coast into a thriving, driving city.
The museum is open daily in summer

11:00 A.M. to 3:00 P.M.; closed Wednesday in the off-season. There is a $2.00 (suggested) admission fee.

Anchor Charters $$$
Noyo Harbor, North Harbor Drive, Fort Bragg
(707) 964-3854
www.anchorcharterboats.com
Once on the endangered species list, the gray whale has made a comeback and can be seen traveling between the Bering Sea and Baja California from late November through late April. Although whales can be seen from shore, it is exciting to board a charter boat and see them directly in the waters they inhabit. Dress for any weather because it can change quickly from sunny and warm to cloudy and cool. Bring along a camera with a telephoto lens, a telescope (just like the old mariners), or a pair of binoculars. Other whale-watching excursions leave from Noyo Harbor as well (see the On the Water chapter). Anchor Charters cruises last approximately two hours. They also offer fishing excursions for salmon, rockfish, and albacore tuna.

Mendocino Coast Botanical Gardens $
18220 North Highway 1, Fort Bragg
(707) 964-4352
www.gardenbythesea.org
This 47-acre delight is one of only three botanical gardens in the United States situated oceanside. Founded in 1961, the gardens were purchased by grants from the California Coastal Conservancy and have been operated as a nonprofit public trust since 1992. The collections here are divided into garden rooms of perennials, rhododendrons (which grow wild in abundance in this county), heathers, succulents, ivies, fuchsias, dwarf conifers, and other native species. Two creeks flow through the gardens, and more than 3 miles of trails provide easy access to the coast and opportunities for visitors to enjoy and learn about plants and nature.

A favorite haunt of local painters, the grounds include picnic tables tucked in quiet spaces for those who have had the foresight to bring lunch. Two miles south of Fort Bragg, the gardens are open daily 9:00 A.M. to 5:00 P.M. from March to October and 9:00 A.M. to 4:00 P.M. from November to February. Admission is $7.50 for adults, $6.00 for seniors, $3.00 for children 13 to 17, and $1.00 for kids 6 to 12.

Footlighters Little Theater $$
245 East Laurel Street, Fort Bragg
(707) 964-3806
A Gay Nineties night of family theater since 1943, Footlighter plays are written by the cast and performed by most of the same people year after year. There's a little light cancan, a chance to hiss the villain, and plenty of laughs. The audience sits around tables drinking coffee, beer, or soft drinks and munching on pretzels. The cast makes its own costumes, and nobody is paid. In fact, they pay dues to belong! Performances are every Wednesday and Saturday at 8:00 P.M., Memorial Day to Labor Day.

Triangle Tattoo Museum Free
356-B North Main Street, Fort Bragg
(707) 964-8814
www.triangletattoo.com
It's one of only a dozen places in the world dedicated to the documentation and preservation of tattoo history. The museum displays thousands of images of skin art, including those from several different nations and different periods in history. Several color prints of New Zealand's Maori people show both men and women with the cultural markings called Moko. Other tattoo portraits highlight designs from Borneo, Samoa, Japan, India, Burma, Zaire, and Native American tribes. The museum is open noon to 6:00 P.M. Sunday through Thursday, noon to 8:00 P.M. Friday and Saturday. Admission is free. Five tattoo artists are on hand, and international guests have been known to stop by.

Guest House Museum $
343 North Main Street, Fort Bragg
(707) 961–2840
Much of Fort Bragg's history is displayed here. Built entirely of redwood for the Fort Bragg Redwood Company in the 19th century, the building later became the guesthouse for friends and customers of C. R. Johnson, founder of Union Lumber Company. Along with a wonderful collection of photographs and artifacts, the museum displays historic equipment such as steam donkeys, rigging blocks, locomotives, and high wheels once used in log harvesting. The museum is open 11:00 A.M. to 4:00 P.M. Wednesday through Sunday; during the summer it's open 10:00 A.M. to 4:00 P.M. Tuesday through Sunday.

Sierra Railroad Skunk Train $$$
Laurel Street Depot, Fort Bragg
(707) 964–6371, (800) 866–1690
www.skunktrain.com
Named the Skunk Train in the 1920s by locals who did not appreciate the aroma emitted by the former gas locomotive engines, this pioneering logging railroad now transports visitors from Fort Bragg to the Northspur station using diesel engines. Along the serpentine route you will cross numerous bridges and trestles, all the while gliding deep through forests of majestic redwood trees, including one tree estimated to be a thousand years old. Snacks and light refreshments are available on the trains, as well as restrooms. The Train Singer entertains with railroad songs and lots of humor. Tickets run $35 to $45 for adults and $20 for children ages 3 to 11. Toddlers ride free.

BALLOONS, PLANES, AND GONDOLAS

It's hard to find a Wine Country brochure that doesn't include a photo of a multicolored hot-air balloon drifting over vine-scored hills. Somewhere along the way, ballooning became part of the everyday scenery. It is a natural fit. Hot-air balloons are splashy, even extravagant, but in a way that celebrates the physical environment rather than tramples it.

The flying machines are quite safe, and most pilots are FAA certified; feel free to ask about their qualifications when you phone. It is true that balloon pilots have limited control over the direction of their rigs, except on a vertical scale. This means there is always a chance you'll make an unscheduled stop in an open field, but it will likely be a gentle one, and the company's chase team will be right on your heels.

As for capacity, the balloon gondolas accommodate anywhere from 4 to 16 passengers. Those of average size hold 6 to 8 people. Dress in layers when riding in a balloon—the shifts in altitude, the breezes, and the heat from the fire make it hard to predict what level of clothing will be comfortable. And if you are a tall person, be sure to bring a cap—radiant heat from the burner can be unpleasant after an hour or so.

Napa County

Wine Country Helicopters $$$$
2030 Airport Road, Napa Valley Airport, Napa
(707) 226–8470
www.winecountryhelicopters.com
Here's a chance to get above the traffic and see Napa Valley and Sonoma County the way birds do. This service offers a wide range of tours and will also arrange custom tours. Certified pilots steer a four-passenger Bell Jet Ranger or a six-passenger Bell Long Ranger to just about any place in Wine Country. Most flights begin and end at Napa Valley Airport; other arrangements can be made to your specifications. A basic 45-minute tour over Napa Valley is $800; a more extensive flight over Napa Valley and Sonoma Valley, lasting approximately 65 minutes, is $1,000. Other options include a trek to the Russian River for a picnic, flying to and from the Rockpile appellation in Sonoma County for wine

tasting, or a six-hour chopper tour to a working cattle ranch with horseback riding thrown in. They will even whiz you to Lake Tahoe if you so desire. The sky's the limit, weather permitting.

Balloons Above the Valley $$$$
5091 Solano Avenue, Napa
(707) 253-2222, (800) GO-HOT-AIR
www.balloonrides.com
Launching from a variety of sites near Yountville, this company will take you on a drifting, one-hour flight and throw in a champagne brunch for $210 per person.

Napa River Adventures $$
10 Peninsula Court, Napa
(707) 224-9080
www.napariveradventures.com
Ready to watch some wildlife along the Napa River? Adventures await during regularly scheduled two-hour cruises for up to 11 people aboard an electric boat. Bring along a bottle of wine, if you'd like, and explore nature in comfort, spotting herons, river otters, and egrets as you float gently on tidal waters (no rapids on this river). This is a great adventure for the kids too, who ride for half price if they are 12 and younger. Several package deals are available, including a golf-and-cruise combo and a wine tasting/cruise package. Reservations for all cruises are a must. Canoe and kayak rentals are also available.

Gondola Servizio $$$
Main Street, Napa
(510) 663-6603, (866) 737-8494
www.gondolaservizio.com
With the addition of more tourist attractions in downtown Napa and the beautification project along the Napa River, it was a natural to include—gondolas! Come aboard for a gentle float on the river and experience the art of *voga alla Veneziana* (Venetian rowing). Your host, Angelino Sandri, will sing songs (in Italian) for special occasions or love songs for lovers. Prices and duration of trips vary; the least expensive ride is $55 for two—or add

extra time, wine, and a picnic meal for about $125. The service docks at Hatt Market near the Napa River Inn.

Adventures Aloft $$$$
6525 Washington Street, Yountville
(707) 944-4408, (800) 944-4408
www.napavalleyaloft.com
These experienced balloon pilots charge $205 for adults, $170 for youth ages 6 to 16. They will shuttle you to the launch site from anywhere in Napa Valley for no extra charge, with coffee and pastries served upon arrival and a sparkling wine breakfast afterward. You have the option of helping to blow up the balloons (no, your cheeks won't get tired) before your one-hour flight. Reservations are required.

Napa Valley Balloons, Inc. $$$$
6795 Washington Street, Yountville
(707) 944-0228, (800) 253-2224
www.napavalleyballoons.com
This is a scenic ride before you ever leave the ground. The company launches from Domaine Chandon at dawn, after a continental breakfast. Postflight you get a champagne brunch at Napa Valley Grille and a color photo of the occasion. In between you'll spend an hour in the air (three to five hours for the entire experience). Meet the van at the southwest corner of Washington Square. It costs $185 per person. Reservations are required.

Bonaventura Balloon Company $$$$
Rancho Caymus Inn, 1145 Rutherford
Cross Road, Rutherford
(707) 944-2822, (800) FLY-NAPA
www.bonaventuraballoons.com
Bonaventura works "the heart of the valley," from Oakville to St. Helena. The balloons take off at sunrise and stay aloft for 60 to 90 minutes. The company never rushes a flight (only one per balloon each day) and never puts more than six people in the basket. The price, $189 to $198 per person, includes breakfast at either Rancho Caymus or Meadowood Resort.

Sonoma County

Aerostat Adventures $$$$
5091 Solano Avenue, Napa
(707) 433–3777, (800) 579–0183
www.aerostat-adventures.com
The address says Napa, but this is the branch of a ballooning empire that drifts over Sonoma County. Aerostat enjoys an exclusive launch site out of the Rodney Strong vineyards near Healdsburg. The location affords spectacular views of the Dry Creek Valley, Alexander Valley, and Russian River wine regions. Upon touchdown, passengers can look forward to a big champagne brunch. Cost of the flight and brunch is $195.

Scenic Aerial Tours $$$
P.O. Box 12186, Santa Rosa 95406
(707) 542–8687, (877) 542–8687
www.northcoastair.com
Pick your pleasure—coast, vineyards, or San Francisco? Sweeping over our beautiful scenery from the air in a small plane is a wonderful way to drink in the sights, especially if your time is limited. This service flies seven days a week, as long as the weather cooperates. Rates begin at $89 per person for a 45-minute tour over the coastal waters or above numerous wine-growing valleys. The Grand Tour lasts about 100 minutes and costs $149 per person.

TOURS

Napa County

Napa Valley Bike Tours $$$
68 Coombs Street, Napa
(707) 251–TOUR, (800) 707–BIKE
www.napavalleybiketours.com
You feel the breeze, you burn the calories, but someone else wrestles with the logistics. Sound all right? These winery tours begin at 9:30 A.M., end about 3:00 P.M., and cost $115 per person. Along with a bicycle and helmet, you'll get a fully catered picnic, a friendly guide, and a support van to lug bottles of wine (and bodies of worn-out riders). Napa Valley Bike Tours also rents cycles by the hour ($10) and day ($30)—tandems run $20 and $70.

Wine & Dine Tours $$$$
2021 Olive Avenue, St. Helena
(707) 963–8930, (800) WINE–TOUR
www.wineanddinetour.com
A full-service company? Wine & Dine does everything but brush your teeth for you. In addition to organizing guided tours, they handles restaurant reservations, accommodations, ground and air transportation, corporate meetings and event planning, balloon flights, spa treatments, and golf—for any number from 2 to 2,000. A typical day tour might include transportation, tours, and tastings at three wineries and an elegant lunch at one of the wineries. Rates vary, but figure on $400 total for a car (one to six people) plus $45 per person for lunch.

Destination: Napa Valley Tours $$$
523 Westgate Drive, Angwin
(707) 256–3307
www.tournapavalley.com
If your tastes are more highbrow than hedonistic, this might be the package for you. Destination: Napa Valley Tours offers chauffeur-driven private tours of wineries, but it goes far beyond that to incorporate local lore and wine industry history. Prices for a full-day experience range from $65 to $100 per person, depending upon location of pickup and return. (They'll go all the way to San Francisco to get you.)

Getaway Adventures
& Bike Shop $$$$
1311 Washington Street, Calistoga
(707) 342–0332, (800) 499–BIKE
www.getawayadventures.com
The folks at Getaway will rent you a bicycle anytime you drop in, but they can do a lot more than that upon request. They do winery tours: six varied wineries, a champagne cellar visit, and a shady picnic lunch for $115 (which includes basic tast-

ing fees). They even arrange kayak trips: Lake Berryessa, Lake Hennessy, or the Russian River for $135.

Sonoma County

Goodtime Touring $$$$
18503 Sonoma Highway, Sonoma
(707) 938-0453, (888) 525-0453
www.goodtimetouring.com
Goodtime Touring offers daily guided Wine Country bicycle tours for beginning and intermediate cyclists, with stops at several outstanding wineries in the Sonoma and Kenwood areas. Every rider is supplied with a new 21-speed mountain bike and helmet, and a van shuttle is on hand to carry winery booty or to give weary cyclists a lift. Rates (including an elegant catered lunch) are $89 per person. Tours run from 10:30 A.M. to 3:30 P.M., Monday through Saturday.

In Mendocino in May? Rhododendron tours take place that month, the peak flowering season, at Mendocino Coast Botanical Gardens south of Fort Bragg. The docent-led walks are included in the admission price. Call (707) 964-4352 for details.

Carriage Occasions $$$$
530 Irwin Lane, Santa Rosa
(707) 546-2568
www.thebridalpath.com
Limousines and antique cars simply not ostentatious enough for you? How about a horse-drawn carriage? This company will meet you in Napa, Sonoma, or Alexander Valley and customize a two- to three-hour winery tour. Prices vary from town to town. You must book in advance.

FESTIVALS AND ANNUAL EVENTS

I n Wine Country every season brings its share of gala events. From January to December there's always some kind of music, food, or farm celebration going on. In autumn we have the "crush" and a slew of harvest fairs, and when spring blossoms begin to appear—whether apple, pear, or the venerated mustard blossom— they are saluted in grand style.

Wineries play a major role in this celebratory milieu, sponsoring concerts and other major cultural events. Their lovely courtyards, grand estate lawns, and unique wine caves are some of the best places to listen to music, whether it's a symphony, chamber music, or jazz.

I couldn't possibly list all the festivals and events that occur throughout the year, but I've selected some popular favorites to get you started. For more information, check with the local chambers of commerce listed in the Area Overview chapter.

JANUARY

Sonoma County

Sonoma Valley Olive Festival
Various locations, Sonoma
(707) 996-1090
www.olivefestival.com
In case you didn't know, we grow lots of olives in Wine Country. So holding a shindig to salute the mighty olive seemed like a natural thing to do. The first annual Sonoma Valley Olive Festival took place during winter 2001–02, with oil tastings, special dinners, demonstrations of olives being turned into oil, a visual arts contest with olives as the theme, and more. The Feast of the Olive and Founders Dinner is the most expensive event, at $150 per person; the remaining festivities vary in price. The whole affair begins in early December and ends in late February.

Old-Time Fiddle Contest
Cloverdale Fairgrounds, 1 Citrus Fair Drive, Cloverdale
(707) 894-2067
www.cloverdale.net/visit/fiddleco.htm
Sixty or more contestants, novice to pro, gather at the fairgrounds on Citrus Fair Drive for an old-fashioned fiddling contest. But some of the best action is not on the stage; it's in a side room where curious visitors can look in on some wild, free-form jamming. This free event is sponsored by the Cloverdale Historical Society on the fourth Saturday of January. The indoor event usually draws a festive crowd of about 1,200. The 2005 contest was the 30th annual.

Mendocino County

Mendocino Crab & Wine Days
Various locations, Mendocino County
(800) 726-2780, (800) 466-3636
www.mendocinocoast.com,
www.gomendo.com
This is a 10-day festival in late January dedicated to two favorite delicacies: premium wine and Dungeness crab. You can count on a series of winemaker dinners, cooking classes, and various crab-and-wine tastings up and down the Mendocino coastline. There's also crab Louie lunches, Dungeness crab specials nightly at most area restaurants, commercial crabbing demonstrations, and a crabcake cook-off in the village of Mendocino. Bibs optional.

FEBRUARY

Napa County

Mustard Magic
The Culinary Institute of America at
Greystone, 2555 Main Street, St. Helena
(707) 259-9020
www.mustardfestival.org
This grand fete officially launches the
annual Napa Valley Mustard Festival on a
Saturday in late January or early February.
The focus is on the arts, including an exhibition and silent auction of entries in the
Mustard Festival Fine Art Contest. Other
pleasantries include hors d'oeuvres and
desserts created by prominent local chefs,
ultrapremium wine tastings, and music
(live opera, for instance). Admission to
Mustard Magic is $125 in advance, $150 at
the door.

Blessing of the Balloons
Domaine Chandon, 1 California Drive,
Yountville
(707) 944-8793
Only seven or eight balloons usually
ascend to mark the first weekend of the
Mustard Festival, but the blessing draws
anywhere from 200 to 400 people. You
must convince yourself to leave your
warm and cozy B&B pretty darn early to
catch the action, which begins at 6:45
A.M., but it's worth it.

Chocolate Cabernet Fantasy
Sterling Vineyards, 1111 Dunaweal Lane,
Calistoga
(707) 942-3345, (800) 726-6136
www.sterlingvineyards.com
Looking for a little decadence? Nero
might have been attracted to this three-
hour get-together off Dunaweal Lane,
about 2 miles south of Calistoga. The
Soroptimists fix the desserts (mostly
chocolate), Sterling donates its renowned
Cabs, and you take care of the rest. There
is dance music too. The fantasy is held on
a Friday or Saturday night around Valentine's Day. Tickets are $20, with all pro-
ceeds going to charity.

Sonoma County

Citrus Fair
Cloverdale Fairgrounds, 1 Citrus Fair
Drive, Cloverdale
(707) 894-3992
www.cloverdalecitrusfair.org
Here's how to brighten up winter. On the
weekend nearest President's Day, the citizens of Cloverdale come together in a jolly
event organized by the Citrus Fair Association. It starts off with a downtown parade
then moves out to the fairgrounds, with
square dancing, country-western dancing,
line dancing, and regular dancing. There is
a carnival for young people and beer tasting and wine tasting for grownups. On
Sunday you can attend a concert by a
popular western music group such as
Smokin' Armadillo. Admission is $6.00 for
adults, $5.00 for seniors and kids ages 6 to
13, and $3.00 for kids 5 and under.

Mendocino County

St. Mary's Mardi Gras
Redwood Empire Fairgrounds, 1055
State Street, Ukiah
(707) 462-3888
www.redwoodempirefair.com
For Ukiah, it's the biggest money-raising
event of the year, a two-day celebration
on a weekend in mid-February that raises
money for St. Mary's Elementary School.
On Saturday night there's a dinner and
dance held at Carl Purdy Hall at the fair-

*Grapevine pruning competitions are held
every February in Sonoma and Napa
Counties to honor North Coast farmworkers and bestow upon two of them
the "best pruner" championship title.*

grounds, with live music by one of the local bands. But Sunday is given over to family fun, with carnival rides and game booths for children. For adults, a wine auction gives bidders a chance to vie for bottles of the vintners' best or for weekend getaways contributed by hotels or resorts. Entrance to the event is free; carnival tickets cost varying amounts.

MARCH

Napa County

Mustard on the Silverado Trail
Various locations
(707) 259-9020
www.mustardfestival.org
The wine producers that line Napa Valley's "other" north-south artery, the Silverado Trail, demand overdue attention on a weekend in early March. About 15 wineries—including Mumm Napa Valley, Rutherford Hill, Sterling, and ZD (see the Wineries chapter)—go above and beyond the call of duty, offering special tours, wine-and-food pairings, entertainment, barrel tastings, and so forth. It's a great way to familiarize yourself with the "quiet side" of the valley, and it's free of charge. The two-day open house series is part of the Mustard Festival.

Napa Valley Classic Irish Festival
Kolbe Academy, 1600 F Street, Napa
(707) 255-6412
www.kolbe.org
Nobody dyes the Napa River green for St. Patrick's Day, but the folks at Kolbe Academy do a fine job of celebrating from 2:00 to 5:00 on an afternoon near the holiday. Food, including wine and ale, is inside the school. The entertainment is in the yard (weather permitting), and includes bagpipes, singing, and traditional Irish dancing. Figure on $25 for adults, $15 for children ages 4 to 12. This is the academy's one major fund-raiser each year.

The Awards
Copia: The American Center for Wine, Food and the Arts, Napa
(707) 259-9020
www.mustardfestival.org
Lest your springtime excursions begin to convince you that mustard is merely a treat for the eyes, here is an evening that pits Napa Valley's best chefs in a spread-off. Guests get to taste the entries, along with food and wine. There is live music as well. The event costs $100 and is held the night before the Marketplace (see next listing).

The Marketplace
Copia: The American Center for Wine, Food and the Arts, Napa
(707) 259-9020
www.mustardfestival.org
This is the Mustard Festival's signature event. Copia's halls and open spaces come alive with cooking demonstrations by celebrity chefs, wine and mustard tastings, gourmet food products, microbrews, fine art, local crafts, horse-drawn carriage rides, eclectic musical offerings on three stages, historical displays, and barrel-making demonstrations. It's a two-day event (11:00 A.M. to 5:00 P.M. both days) on a weekend in mid-March. Admission is $30.00 for adults, $10.00 for students, and $5.00 for children under five. Net proceeds benefit a wide range of nonprofit groups.

A Taste of Yountville
Washington Street, Yountville
(707) 944-0904
www.mustardfestival.org
Yountville likes to boast that it has more gourmet restaurants and premium wineries than any other town of comparable size. So on the third weekend in March, the hamlet sets up a solid-mile gauntlet of food, olive oil, vinegar, mustard, wine, and beer for the sampling public to prove it. Local merchants get into the act with fashion shows, tours, furniture restoration displays, and even tips on table setting.

Most demonstrations are free, and tasting tickets are reasonable (around $1.00). Even if you are beyond temptation, it might be worth your time to stroll the 6 blocks through downtown just to hear the live music and watch the entertainment. This is a Mustard Festival event.

The Photo Finish
Mumm Napa Valley, 8445 Silverado Trail, Rutherford
(707) 259-9020
www.mustardfestival.org
With this grand finale, the Mustard Festival usually leaves 'em longing for more as it heads into hibernation for a year. Mumm's hallways and visitor center are filled with lovers of photography, food, wine, and music (doesn't leave many of us out, does it?) on the last Saturday in March or the first in April. The food is by Napa Valley chefs, the wine is primarily from Silverado Trail labels, and the camera work is by the contestants in the annual Napa Valley Mustard Festival Photography Contest. Awards are presented in the tasting room at about 9:00 P.M. Tickets to the Photo Finish cost $75 per person in advance, $95 at the door.

Sonoma County

Russian River Barrel Tasting
Alexander, Dry Creek, and Russian River Valleys
(800) 723-6336
www.wineroad.com
This annual event sponsored by the Russian River Wine Road Association is a weekend festival of tasting, entertainment, and viticulture education. The tasting focuses on unreleased wines from wineries located in the Alexander, Dry Creek, and Russian River Valleys, offering participants the opportunity to taste wines straight from the barrel and to purchase "futures." You pay $5.00 for a special logo glass at the first winery you visit, then take the glass with you for free tastes at many more participating wineries.

Mendocino County

Whale Festivals
Mendocino and Fort Bragg
(707) 961-6300, (800) 726-2780
www.mendocinocoast.com
One of the best reasons to visit the Mendocino coast in winter is to watch the gray whales cut through the choppy seas during their annual migration, a 12,000-mile round-trip from the arctic circle to Baja California. It's a cause for celebration, and there are festivals in two cities—in Mendocino the first weekend in March and in Fort Bragg on the third weekend—to welcome the migrating mammals. Whale-watching cruises set out from Noyo Harbor (various prices). There's music; marine art exhibits; discussions about whales at state parks; samplings of wine, beer, and chowder all over the towns (pay as you taste); and more.

APRIL

Napa County

April in Carneros
Various locations
(707) 938-5906, (800) 825-9475
www.carneroswineries.org
The Carneros area, in the bay-cooled hills between Sonoma and Napa, has emerged as Wine Country's next great appellation. You can judge for yourself over one weekend in mid-April, when 20 or more wineries open their doors and stage special events. About a quarter of the participating producers are normally open by appointment only, and others don't even have proper wineries there—guests are welcomed instead to production facilities. New vintages are released, accompanied by barrel tastings, food pairings, music, and even cigar-smoking demonstrations (inhaling optional). Maps are distributed at the open houses, and there is no charge for attending. The circuit tends to be less crowded on Sunday.

The men-only Bohemian Grove encampment of some of the world's most powerful leaders and household names, held annually in west Sonoma County near Monte Rio, was lampooned in a 2002 film called Teddy Bear's Picnic—the creation of actor/comedy writer Harry Shearer.

Kitchens in the Vineyards Tour
Various locations
(707) 258-5559
www.napavalleymusic.com

The emphasis is on food during this all-day affair in late April or early May that gives you a peek into one-of-a-kind kitchens, dining rooms, and gardens from Napa to St. Helena. The event benefits Music in the Vineyards' Chamber Music Festival held in August. Tickets are $40 in advance, $45 the day of the tour.

Sonoma County

Sheepshearing at the Adobe
Petaluma Adobe State Park, 3325
Adobe Road, Petaluma
(707) 762-4871, (866) 240-4655
www.petaluma.org,
www.visitpetaluma.com

On a Saturday in mid-April, 4-H'ers and docents gather at the adobe building that was once the ranch home of Gen. Mariano Vallejo (see the History chapter) to demonstrate the arts of wool cleaning, weaving, and sheepshearing. It's all done to pay homage to an age-old craft. Looms are available for those who want to try their hand at the craft. Bring along a picnic and make a day of it. There's no charge for the event, but park admission is $3.00 per adult ($2.00 for ages 6 to 12).

Butter and Egg Days
Various locations, Petaluma
(707) 762-2785
www.petaluma.org,
www.visitpetaluma.com

Petaluma celebrates its storied past through this popular event. Once known as the world's egg basket, Petaluma is now largely dairy country, thus the hometown Butter and Egg Days parade. This includes an egg toss in downtown and a parade of marching bands and (best of all) residents dressed as chickens and pats of butter. The Cutest Little Chick in Town contest adds to the fun. It all happens the last complete weekend in April, and there are food booths, other entertainment, and an antiques fair.

Apple Blossom Festival
Various locations, Sebastopol
(877) 828-4748
www.sebastopol.net

It's a weekend in April, and it's a salute to the apple and its snow-white blooms. Festivities include the crowning of the Apple Blossom Queen, a mile-long parade down Main Street, and two days of good-time partying with plenty of blues, country, and gospel music. There's an art show, crafts made by local artisans, and plenty of products made from apples. The festival is sponsored by the local chamber of commerce, and events are held in Ives Park (282 High Street) and at the Veterans Memorial Building next door. Admission is $5.00 for adults, $2.00 for seniors and children ages 11 to 17.

Bodega Bay Fishermen's Festival
Westside Park, Bodega Bay
(707) 875-3422
www.bodegabay.com

This annual event takes place at Westside Park during a weekend in April. It features foot races, the Blessing of the Fleet, a boat parade, and a bathtub race that includes tubs crafted out of anything that floats—from Styrofoam to milk cartons. Directions to the park are well posted. A $3.00 donation is requested.

MAY

Napa County

MaiFest
Napa County Fairgrounds, 1435 North
Oak Street, Calistoga
(707) 942-5356
www.napacountyfairgrounds.com
Upvalley's wurst festival is one of its best.
Watch traditional German folk dancing.
Sway to the soothing oompah-pah of
Ottmar Stubler and His Pretzel Benders.
More to the point, eat and drink in the
robust style of Bavaria. Spaten is the most-
requested brew at this all-day Saturday
event in late April or early May, though
Napa Valley Brewing Company offers its
competent lineup of microbrews along
with three or four wineries. Tickets are $10
in advance, $12 at the gate. Food and bev-
erages are extra (though reasonable), as
are raffle tickets. First prize is two round-
trip airline tickets from San Francisco to
Munich. MaiFest bankrolls a scholarship
fund for Calistoga High School.

Hidden Gardens Tour
Various locations
(707) 255-1836, (888) 255-1836
www.napacountylandmarks.org
This is an organized, go-at-your-own-pace
afternoon walking tour of pocket gardens
and historic homes on a weekend in May
or June. Explorers hit about 10 gardens
and then enjoy an outdoor reception. It
costs $20.00 on tour day. If you buy tick-
ets in advance, it's $8.00 for members of
Napa County Landmarks and $15.00 for
nonmembers. Landmarks also offers self-
guided walking tours on 10 Saturdays
between May and September. Call for
details.

Merlot in May—International Merlot
Conference
Sterling Vineyards, 1111 Dunaweal Lane,
Calistoga
(707) 942-3345, (800) 726-6136
www.sterlingvineyards.com
This conference featuring Merlot producers from around the world is now open to
the public (over 21 only, please). If Merlot
is your drink, you'll be in heaven. Sample a
huge array of the red stuff from as many
as 130 producers during a four-hour afternoon consumer tasting. Tickets are $35
and sold in advance only.

Picnic Day
Fuller Park, Napa
(707) 253-0376
On the Friday before Memorial Day, normally serene Fuller Park becomes a
squirming, squealing square full of toddlers and preschoolers. Community
Resources for Children sponsors this free
event. There is ice cream and oodles of
activities and games, from face painting
to bubble blowing to lamb petting. To get
to Fuller Park from Highway 29, take the
Downtown Napa exit (Second Street),
turn right at Jefferson Street, and proceed
2 blocks.

Sonoma County

Luther Burbank Rose Festival and Parade
Various locations, Santa Rosa
(707) 545-1414
www.lutherburbank.org
Find a spot along Santa Rosa's streets on
a mid-May weekend to watch a parade
that dates from 1894 and now draws more
than 20,000 people. Floats created with
thousands of roses are the highlight of the
parade, which begins in front of Burbank's
home on Santa Rosa Avenue and winds
its way through town to the Veterans
Memorial Building. The event honors the
world-famous horticulturist who improved
800 plant varieties, including the Santa
Rosa rose, while living in Santa Rosa (see
the Attractions chapter). Other festival
events take place at various sites in the
downtown area and include street fair
exhibits, food booths, performances by
singing groups, carnival rides, folk dancing, an antiques fair, a firefighter's compe-

tition, and displays of firefighting equipment. There's an awards ceremony to honor the best of the parade floats.

Sonoma Country Fair and Twilight Parade
Various locations, Healdsburg
(707) 431-7644
www.sonomacountyfair.com
Scheduled for the last weekend in May, this is the longest-running event in Healdsburg and the only fair in California that's nonprofit. The Future Farmers of America sponsor this event, in which everything's free except the food. There's a parade on Thursday, a livestock show and auction on Friday, and kids' activities on Saturday. Food and game booths are run by local youth organizations.

Mendocino County

Boonville Beer Festival
Mendocino County Fairgrounds, 14400
Highway 128, Boonville
(707) 895-3011
www.avbc.com
Sure, they make great wine in Mendocino County, but they also craft awesome brews. When the weather turns warm, this one-day festival on a Saturday in early May is a great place to beat the heat. Sip cold beer made by local breweries and by others from around the world—about 50 breweries participated in the 2004 event. Where else can you sample a beer made from watermelon and a raisin beer in the same place? Expect good food and live music to enhance the experience. Tickets are $25.00 in advance, or $30.00 at the door—cash only, please. (Designated drivers can enter for $5.00.)

Great Rubber Ducky Race
Wages Creek, Westport
(707) 964-2872
www.mendocinocoast.com
Westport is the northernmost town on the Mendocino coast. It's isolated, and the residents like it that way. But the locals have

a sense of humor, proven by their annual Great Rubber Ducky Race. It takes place on Mother's Day and is held on the wide, white sand beaches of Wages Creek just north of the town. Anyone who wants to enter can simply bring a rubber ducky from home (some people fancy them up a bit), launch it in the creek, and wait to see how long it takes to float downstream to meet the ocean. Meanwhile, the barbecue coals are lighted (the menu is beef, not duck). Everyone is cool and laid back, watching the clouds float across the blue sky and keeping an eye on the fleet of ducks bobbing downstream.

The event is organized by the Westport Village Society to preserve the headlands as open space. The sunshine is free; race entry combined with the beef dinner is $10.

JUNE
Napa County

Auction Napa Valley
Meadowood Napa Valley,
900 Meadowood Lane, St. Helena
(707) 942-9775, (800) 982-1371
www.napavintners.org
The 2005 event was this charity auction's 25th year. Since it began, the auction has raised more than $50 million for local agencies and nonprofits in health care, youth services, and housing. The auction weekend (the first Thursday-through-Sunday block in June) draws high rollers from around the world, who have the means to bid on limited-production cult wines and wine/dinner/travel packages. (Three bottles of Screaming Eagle Cabernet Sauvignon, for instance, once sold for $220,000.) There are always a few show-biz celebrities milling about too. In 2005 the auction underwent an extensive restructuring to scale back the number of lots in order to shorten the length of the live auction, to focus more on dinners with vintners and other intimate events, and to

create affordable activities so that local residents and tourists can also participate. The auction weekend raised more than $10 million for charity, fueled in part by a hilarious 30-minute routine by Jay Leno, who warmed up the crowd before the serious bidding got under way. (See the close-up in this chapter for more about wine auctions.)

Vintage 1870 Father's Day Invitational Auto Show
Vintage 1870, 6525 Washington Street, Yountville
(707) 944-2451
www.vintage1870.com

When Dad begins to rebel against loud ties and cheap cologne, take him to a car show for Father's Day. The north parking lot of Vintage 1870 will be double-parked with 85 to 90 cars—from Vipers to DeSoto Coupes and from a 1939 Packard limousine to a boss old Woody. While you examine the cars, you can eat, drink (everything from Calistoga water to margaritas), and listen to music. The show runs from 11:00 A.M. to 4:00 P.M. and is free to the public, excluding food.

Wine Country Kennel Club
Napa Valley Exposition, 575 Third Street, Napa
(707) 253-4900
www.napavalleyexpo.com

The dog days of summer start a little early in Napa—on a weekend in late June, to be exact. That's when some 2,000 well-groomed pooches strut around the halls and grounds of the Exposition. There are separate shows on Saturday and Sunday, each from 8:00 A.M. until about 6:00 P.M. There are eight age-and-experience classes (including two puppy classes) and seven dog groups: sporting, hound/working, terrier, toy, nonsporting, herding, and miscellaneous breeds. The animals vie for points, ribbons, trophies, and the ever-popular pat on the head. There is no charge to spectators. The Lions Club provides food, including a pancake breakfast.

Sonoma County

Ox Roast
Sonoma Plaza, Sonoma
(707) 938-4626
www.sonomavalley.com

For more than 30 years, the first Sunday in June has been marked by aromatic smoke rising from the town's central plaza. The annual Ox Roast is one giant picnic with barbecued beef, corn on the cob, and plenty of beer and wine. You'll pay $3.00 to $9.00 for the meal (beer and wine are extra, and there's also a vegetarian plate), and it all goes to benefit the local community center.

Health and Harmony Music and Arts Festival
Sonoma County Fairgrounds, Santa Rosa
(707) 861-2035
www.harmonyfestival.com

For more than two decades, loyal throngs of locals have been buying hemp clothing, eyeing belly dancers, and pounding the drums of world-beat music at this Sonoma County institution. For some, the annual affair in mid-June is like returning to the hippie days of 1967—but the hippies all sport gray ponytails these days. There's always plenty of free music on several stages (Jefferson Starship one year, for example) and a huge number of vendors selling everything from holistic health products to Indian cottons. Admission is about $20 in advance, $25 at the door.

Cloverdale Heritage Days
124 South Cloverdale Boulevard, Cloverdale
(707) 894-4470
www.cloverdale.net

The citizens of Cloverdale close off the main boulevard of town once each year to celebrate the memory of days past. Events include wine tasting, cow-chip tossing (the local Boys and Girls Club collects the cow chips), a gold rush foot race, and a barbecue from 5:00 to 7:00 P.M.

There's also country music and dancing outdoors on the plaza. It's all free except the food.

Stumptown Daze
Main Street and Rodeo Grounds,
Guerneville
(877) 644-9001
www.russianriver.com
This is a great treat for Dad on Father's Day weekend. A parade, with school bands and preschool kids on bikes, starts at 11:00 A.M. Saturday and follows a route that's subject to local politics, so you might want to call in advance to find out where to park your folding chair. After the parade everyone heads over to the town of Duncans Mills, about 6 miles west of Guerneville on Highway 116. At 2:00 P.M. the rodeo starts, with all those events you expect—calf roping, bull riding, and barrel racing. On Sunday there's more free rodeo, and some horseback games. Where'd the name originate? Guerneville gained the moniker "Stumptown" in its early days when redwood trees were mercilessly chopped down, leaving only a forest of stumps.

Mendocino County

Spring Carnival
Redwood Empire Fairgrounds, 1055
North State Street, Ukiah
(707) 462-3884
www.redwoodempirefair.com
It's free to enter the gates to the spring fair, held the first weekend in June each year. Entrance to the carnival field is also free, with varying prices for individual thrill rides. Grandstand shows are held Friday and Saturday from 2:00 P.M. on and feature motor sports events such as stock car races. Admission to the grandstand is $10.00 to $12.00, and kids ages 10 and younger pay $8.00 to $10.00.

Mendocino Wine Affair
Various locations, Hopland
(707) 468-9886
www.mendowine.com
Once a year Mendocino's wineries kick out the jams at this two-day event held at Brutocao Cellars and Fetzer Vineyards in Hopland. On a Saturday in mid-June, the fun begins at 10:00 A.M. with cooking demonstrations (featuring celebrated chef John Ash in 2004) and then a luncheon. Wines by 40 producers are sampled all afternoon, followed by a live auction (an all-day silent auction also takes place). Admission to the Saturday affair is $125 ($175 if you dine with the chef).

JULY
Napa County

Napa County Fair
Napa County Fairgrounds, 1435 North
Oak Street, Calistoga
(707) 942-5111
www.napacountyfairgrounds.com
This celebration (during Fourth of July weekend) features plenty of wine to taste, but there's also the usual assortment of carnival rides, livestock exhibits, arts and crafts, and cavity-creating snacks. The fair includes one or two nights of sprint-car racing and two nights of concerts, with recent headliners such as country heavyweights LeAnn Rimes, Toby Keith, and Faith Hill. Admission is $5.00 for adults; $2.00 for kids ages 6 to 12. Two separate events—the Miss Napa County Fair Pageant and the Champagne Art Preview—are held on the eve of the fair.

Fourth of July Celebrations
Napa (707) 257-9529
Calistoga (707) 942-6333
Veterans Park is the gathering place for a slew of activity in Napa, including food,

carnival games, and wine tasting. Since 1995 the patriotism has expanded to include eight hours of music at the park by a lineup of five or six bands.

Serving as interlude to the Napa County Fair is a sublime slice of Americana. People come from miles around for Calistoga's annual Silverado Parade, placing lawn chairs along the route hours in advance. Past parades have featured the sparkling rigs of the volunteer fire department, horsemen, bikers, clowns, a kazoo corps, and floats ranging from sweet to absurd. The procession starts at 11:00 A.M. You do not want to miss it.

Napa Valley Shakespeare Festival
Riverbend Performance Plaza, Hatt Mill,
500 Main Street, Napa
(707) 251-WILL
www.napashakespeare.org
To be or not to be . . . the question is, "Which night shall we attend?" The Bard's most popular works (and the creations of other notable playwrights) are performed over four weekends, beginning the weekend after the Fourth of July, on Friday through Sunday nights at 7:00. Tickets run about $18 to $24 for adults and $14 to $18 for seniors, students, and children under 12.

Meadowood Croquet Classic
Meadowood Napa Valley,
900 Meadowood Lane, St. Helena
(707) 963-3646, (800) 458-8080
www.meadowood.com
This is no carefree backyard play day. Members of the U.S. Croquet Association flock to Meadowood in late July for a week of serious mallet wielding. Guests at the resort may watch the preliminary competition for no charge during the week. On Saturday comes the finale: the championship round plus an auction (for charity) and an early-evening gourmet dinner. It's an elegant affair, with some 200 diners attired in natty whites and seated adjacent to the croquet courts. The finale package costs upward of $100 per person. During the rest of the year, Meadowood croquet pro Jerry Stark gives

lessons in this rarefied sport of kings—ranging from $25 to $35 an hour.

Sonoma County

Old-Fashioned Fourth of July Celebration
Sonoma Plaza
(707) 938-4626
www.sonomavalley.com
You'd think someone rolled back the clock a few decades to see how Sonoma celebrates Independence Day. In fact, some locals say the Fourth of July is their favorite holiday. Arrive early for a good place to watch the 10:00 A.M. parade that circles Sonoma Plaza. After the parade, townsfolk assemble in the plaza for more band music, the singing of the national anthem, a patriotic speech, and the presentation of awards for parade entrants. Locals laze around the rest of the day, then reassemble at nightfall for the big finale—a fireworks display put on by the city fire department (partially funded by an appreciative public) in a large field next to the Vallejo Home.

World Pillow Fighting Championships
Plaza Park, Warm Springs Road,
Kenwood
(707) 833-2440
www.kenwoodpillowfights.com
Like to get wet and muddy in front of hundreds of cheering onlookers? Approaching its fourth decade, this annual event brings out a special breed of human—brave men and women who face each other one-on-one while straddling a slippery metal pole suspended over a mud pit. The opponents then vigorously swing pillows at one another. The one left on the pole is the winner. The men generally outnumber the women, but you can count on about 100 contestants. It's good, clean (well, sort of) fun on the Fourth of July that also includes a hometown parade, live bands such as local favorites Rat Pack or 5 A.M., kids' activities, and plenty of food and drink. Admission is $5.00 for adults; free for children ages 12 and under.

CLOSE-UP

Wine Auctions for Charity:
From Ultrachic to Down-home

Napa Valley and Sonoma Valley are only a few miles apart, yet the two regions are worlds apart when comparing their annual wine auctions for charity. Auction Napa Valley is the big kahuna of charity wine auctions, the largest of its kind in the world. On the quieter side of the Mayacmas range, the smaller Sonoma Valley Harvest Wine Auction shares the same noble goal as its neighbor: to raise gobs of money for local charities.

In general, both auctions are several-day events in summer, with two or three days set aside for a whirlwind romp of winery dinners, open houses, and special wine and food tastings. Both events are capped off with their main attraction, the live auction, set on the grounds of their respective destination resorts: Meadowood in Napa Valley and the Fairmont Sonoma Mission Inn in Sonoma.

The number of lots (or packages) up for bid at auction vary significantly; some are wine only, from one bottle to many, perhaps in custom-designed boxes. Bids such as the $650,000 paid for eight double magnums—that's 24 liters—of Screaming Eagle Cabernet Sauvignon really add up: In 2005 this auction raised more than $10 million for charity in one weekend.

While the Napa Valley auction weekend has always had "chic" written all over it, the Sonoma Valley affair by comparison is "down-home." The Sonoma Valley is no less refined when it comes to wine affairs and wine-making talent, but the Sonoma vintners long ago decided that their auction wouldn't be as big or as high falutin' as Napa's. Each year they set out to raise a serious pile of cash, just like Napa, but they have a lot of laughs doing it.

The Sonoma live auction is less stuffy, and the vintners provide the goofy entertainment and the stand-up comedy. Tommy Smothers, owner of Remick Ridge Winery in Sonoma Valley

Salute to the Arts
Sonoma Plaza
(707) 938–1133
www.salutetothearts.com
On the third or fourth weekend in July, the entire Sonoma Plaza in the heart of town is transformed into an elegant, lively outdoor setting, featuring five stages filled with theater troupe performances and a variety of music and dance. Fine art by Sonoma Valley artists, children's activities, and the best in local cuisine, wine, and handcrafted beers are available. Admission to the festival is free. Cheap tickets for food and wine may be purchased, or you can employ various package prices that include a souvenir wine glass and plate.

and half of the legendary Smothers Brothers, takes the stage frequently during the bidding to energize the audience and keep the fun and games moving along. As in Napa, dress is "Wine Country casual," but in Sonoma that means just about anything goes, from Hawaiian shirts and shorts for the men to sundresses for the ladies.

Yes, the big bucks really do go to local charities. The beneficiaries in Napa Valley include 27 health care, youth, and housing nonprofit agencies. In Sonoma Valley the good causes range from community health centers to vineyard workers' services to the regional Boys and Girls Club.

If you decide to attend one of these events, you may walk away not only with some killer wine but also with the knowledge that you contributed significantly to improving the quality of life for the less fortunate, and you had a good time doing it.

You can learn more about these auctions—and request an invitation—by visiting their respective Web sites: www.napavintners.org and www.sonoma valleywine.com.

Silliness is celebrated at the Sonoma Valley Harvest Wine Auction. JEAN SAYLOR DOPPENBERG

Fort Ross Living History Days
Fort Ross State Park, north of Jenner
(707) 847-3286
www.parks.sonoma.net/fortross.html
On the last Saturday in July, some 100 volunteers and staff participants don period attire and reenact a typical day at Fort Ross in the mid-1800s, during the days of Russian settlement when the commandant and his wife lived elegantly in the wilderness surroundings (see the History chapter). Bring a picnic! Coastal weather is unpredictable, so pack a sun hat and warm clothes. Admission is $3.00 per vehicle.

Sonoma County Fair
Sonoma County Fairgrounds,
1350 Bennett Valley Road, Santa Rosa
(707) 545-4203
www.sonomacountyfair.com
This two-week event begins the last week in July and features carnival rides, a flower show, horse racing, livestock competitions, lots of live music, and a wide array of food and other vendors. This fair is a long-standing Sonoma County institution, and it is not to be missed. General admission is $7.00.

Mendocino County

Willits Frontier Days
Various locations, Willits
(707) 459-6330
www.willits.org
A three-day event during the Fourth of July weekend, it's claimed to be the longest continuous rodeo in California. Besides roping and steer riding, there is a Fourth of July parade, horseshoe pitching, dances, a carnival, cowboy breakfast, talent show, barbecue, and crafts show. Most of it happens in midtown or on the rodeo grounds.

AUGUST

Napa County

Napa Town and Country Fair
Napa Valley Exposition, 575 Third
Street, Napa
(707) 253-4900
www.napavalleyexpo.com
You can join the 65,000-odd people who come to the Exposition over five days in early to mid-August—just don't call it a county fair. Napa's one and only official county fair is in Calistoga in July (see previous listing), but this is a more-than-reasonable facsimile. There are homemade jams and oversize zucchini, 4-H livestock, crowd-pleasers such as a lumberjack competition, a high-diving exhibition, wine tasting, and a kiddie carnival. Headliners

at this event have spanned the range from Chubby Checker to Chinese acrobats.

Admission is $7.00 for adults and teens and $4.00 for seniors and children ages 6 to 12. There is an additional charge for events in the grandstand, specifically a rodeo and a demolition derby.

Mostly Mozart
Various locations
(707) 252-8671
On a Sunday afternoon in mid-August, the Napa Valley Music Associates occupy a local winery or landmark to offer tribute to that impish Austrian composer. This musical event usually begins with a "legacy," a series of dramatic vignettes and musical samplers from the life of Wolfgang Amadeus M., and possibly Schubert or some other classical giant. Tickets are about $30, and they include the legacy, the concert, a reception, and often a tour of the venue. All proceeds benefit NVMA's ongoing music programs.

Day for the Queen at Silverado
Silverado Country Club & Resort,
1600 Atlas Peak Road, Napa
(707) 257-4044, (707) 251-1882
www.qvhf.org
For one day in August, Silverado Country Club becomes a large, lush hat passed for Queen of the Valley Hospital. The full bill includes a fashion show, tennis tournament and golf tournament, lunch, an evening barbecue, dancing, and a silent auction. The cost depends on how many events you mix and match. The fashion show and lunch are $45; golf and lunch are $130; golf, tennis, and the barbecue are $255; you get the idea.

Sonoma County

Wings over Wine Country Air Show
Charles M. Schulz–Sonoma County
Airport, 2330 Airport Boulevard,
Santa Rosa
(707) 575-7900
www.pacificcoastairmuseum.org

This two-day air show sponsored by the Pacific Coast Air Museum (see the Attractions chapter) showcases a variety of daredevil performances that will have you craning and squinting in disbelief. In addition to the aerial demonstrations by a variety of WW II aircraft and other vintage fighters, the event features an outstanding demonstration of an F-16 fighter jet in action, courtesy of the air force demo team. Bring your earplugs. Admission is $12.00 per day—children 12 and under are free, and seniors are $5.00.

Sonoma County Folk Festival
Cinnabar Performing Arts Theater,
3333 Petaluma Boulevard N., Petaluma
(707) 838-4857
www.socofoso.org,
www.cinnabartheater.org
Renowned throughout the United States since 1986, this is a wonderful indoor music festival. It's a one-day event held in August, with a varied lineup of musicians. You'll hear everything from traditional and original acoustic music to blues, Caribbean grooves, country and '40s music. Instrumental workshops offer a chance to learn to play folk instruments from dulcimer to banjo, and there is a kids-for-kids concert.

Dixie Jazz Festival
DoubleTree Hotel, 1 DoubleTree Drive,
Rohnert Park
(707) 539-3494
www.doubletree.com
A late August weekend of solid jazz brings traditional purveyors of the genre from across the country. They play Dixieland and ragtime from 2:00 P.M. to midnight on Friday, 10:00 A.M. to midnight Saturday, and 9:00 A.M. to 6:00 P.M. Sunday. Don't miss the gospel services Sunday morning. There are five venues at the DoubleTree Hotel at 1 DoubleTree Drive in Rohnert Park. For admission prices, which come in a variety of packages, call the above number.

Cotati Accordion Festival
La Plaza Park, West Silva Avenue and
Redwood Highway, Cotati
(707) 664-0444
www.cotatifest.com
On the weekend before Labor Day, accordion players from around the world descend on La Plaza Park. For them, this is a world classic—a two-day extravaganza with professionals playing tangos, Irish clogging music, and all else in between. The event's appeal is largely to a mature crowd, but on the morning of the second day, kid players show what they can do. Admission is $10 for one day, $18 for both. Kids 15 and under are admitted free.

Old Adobe Fiesta
Petaluma Adobe State Park, 3325 Adobe
Road, Petaluma
(707) 762-4871
www.petaluma.org,
www.visitpetaluma.com
Costumed volunteers display craft demonstrations, food preparation, blacksmithing, and other period activities from 10:00 A.M. to 4:00 P.M. on this historic rancho (see the History chapter). There is also Hispanic music, Native American dancing, and a whisker contest. Enjoy food, kid games, farm animals, and more. Park admission is $3.00 for adults, $2.00 for kids ages 6 to 12.

Gravenstein Apple Fair
Ragle Road, 1 mile north of Bodega
Highway, Sebastopol
(707) 571-8288
www.farmtrails.org/gravfair.htm
Traditionally scheduled for a mid-August weekend at Ragle Park in Sebastopol, the Apple Fair features local cuisine and food demonstrations, an animal petting zoo, arts and crafts, and of course lots of Gravenstein apples and plenty of pie. Music and kids' activities fill the day. Admission is $6.00 for adults, $4.00 for seniors and kids ages 6 to 16, and $1.00 for kids younger than 5. Pets not allowed.

Mendocino County

SolFest
Real Goods Solar Living Center, 13771
U.S. Highway 101, Hopland
(707) 744-2017
www.solfest.org
Real Goods, a renewable energy retail store, hosts this annual environmental gala, where you can take a ride in an electric car, tour solar energy exhibits, attend an alternative energy workshop, or simply nosh on organic food and drink and enjoy the music. Cost for adults is $6.00 per day or $10.00 for both days.

> **i** *One of the oldest wine harvest celebrations in the nation, the Valley of the Moon Vintage Festival, is held every September around the plaza in Sonoma.*

Redwood Empire Fair
Redwood Empire Fairgrounds, 1055
North State Street, Ukiah
(707) 462-3884
www.redwoodempirefair.com
Held the second weekend in August at the fairgrounds on North State Street, it's a bang-up event (literally, if you consider the Destruction Derby) with a big carnival, country-western concerts, lots of livestock events, and plenty of family fun. Admission is $6.00 for adults and teens, $3.00 for kids ages 6 to 12, and free for those under 5.

Art in the Redwoods
Various locations, Gualala
(707) 884-1138
www.gualalaarts.org
Held the third weekend in August, Art in the Redwoods includes fine art, crafts, food and beverage booths, games for children, and daylong musical and theatrical entertainment. The event is sponsored by Gualala Art Center, and the fun takes

place at the center and Bower Park. There is a $5.00 admission charge.

SEPTEMBER

Napa County

Symphony on the River
Third Street Bridge, Napa
(707) 254-8520
www.napavalleysymphony.org
The Napa Valley Symphony brings its music to the masses for one night a year—the Sunday before Labor Day. The action centers around Third Street Bridge in downtown Napa, where the symphony performs between 7:00 and about 9:15 P.M. The show is followed by fireworks and preceded by a mixer at Veterans Park, where vendors sell food, wine, and crafts starting at about 3:00 P.M. It's all organized by Friends of the Napa River.

Music Festival for Mental Health
Staglin Family Vineyard, 1570 Bella Oaks
Lane, Rutherford
(707) 944-0477
www.staglinfamily.com
It's not a very sexy title, but the event itself is rather divine. On a Saturday or Sunday in mid-September, a reception and dinner are staged in a big, open-sided tent overlooking the winery and Napa Valley. Past entertainment has included the Ramsey Lewis Trio and classical music performed under the baton of a celebrity guest conductor. Proceeds from this event go to much-needed research into brain disorders and mental illness. Some 60 to 70 ultrapremium Napa Valley wineries pour their goods throughout. The base price is $250 per person for the reception, $2,500 if you stay for dinner, and the best tables are reserved for $10,000 to $50,000. Nobel Prize winner John Nash, subject of the book and movie *A Beautiful Mind,* attended the 2002 event, which raised $2.4 million.

Sonoma County

Women's Weekend
Various locations, Guerneville
(877) 644-9001
www.womensweekend.com
This annual event is a big party that features a golf tournament, author readings, a great pool party, exotic and unusual crafts and other wares, and music and entertainment. There's a serious side too, with proceeds from various events donated to West County health centers to fight breast cancer.

Sonoma Valley Harvest Wine Auction
Various locations, Sonoma
(707) 935-0803
www.sonomavalleywine.com
Events during the Labor Day weekend occur at various wineries and vineyards and include a wine auction and dinner dance, celebrity-chef dinners, barbecue picnics, entertainment, and wine tasting panels. It's four days of irreverent fun and frivolity to raise money for various charities. Sunday's auctions culminate with an extravagant dinner buffet and live dance band. (See the close-up in this chapter.)

Prices and package deals vary widely year to year as do the charities that benefit. Get information on tickets from Sonoma Vintners and Growers Alliance at the listed number.

Heirloom Tomato Festival
Kendall-Jackson Wine Center,
5007 Fulton Road, Santa Rosa
(800) 769-3649
www.kj.com
The lowly tomato is elevated to superstar status at this festival dedicated to the enjoyment of the juicy fruit that comes in many shapes and colors. In early September, at the height of the tomato harvest in local backyards, as many as 175 different varieties can be sampled in some fashion. For five hours, nearly 40 restaurants and purveyors of gourmet food offer tomato-inspired goodies in bite-size portions, along with cooking demonstrations, wine tasting, food and wine seminars, and even an art show. Amateur gardeners can enter their own tomato crop in a "beauty" contest with categories such as Ugliest Tomato. Tickets are sold in advance only for $40 per person.

Russian River Jazz Festival
Johnson's Beach, Guerneville
(707) 869-3940
www.rrfestivals.com
At least eight internationally recognized jazz artists get together the first week in September for two all-day concerts on the Russian River. Food and drinks are available. Prices for jazz under the redwoods range from $33 to $75 for two days.

Valley of the Moon Vintage Festival
Sonoma Plaza
(707) 996-2109
www.sonomavinfest.org
At 106 years and counting, Valley of the Moon Vintage Festival, held annually on the last weekend in September on the plaza in Sonoma, is among the oldest wine harvest celebrations in the nation. It features a traditional Friday-evening wine tasting party and a full weekend of historical pageants, the blessing of the grapes, parades, concerts, and wine and food tastings. The festival is easy to find—just drive to Sonoma, and it'll be smack in the center of town. If you want to attend the Friday-night wine tasting event, however, you'll need to order tickets at least a month in advance—it's a sellout every year.

Mendocino County

Roots of Motive Power Festival
Mendocino County Museum, 400 East
Commercial Street, Willits
(707) 459-2736
www.rootsofmotivepower.com
This is a way to relive the excitement and dangers of everyday lumberjack work in the redwoods. In mid-September the Men

docino County Museum brings out some of the tools of the trade—antique locomotives and yarders and old steam donkeys (a steam-powered machine that replaced the donkey for pulling large logs). What really draws a crowd is the two-day lumberjack handcar race event, held in front of the Skunk Train railroad depot. Other than the race entry fee, the entire event is free.

Fiesta Patrias
Redwood Empire Fairgrounds, 1055 North State Street, Ukiah
(707) 463-8181
www.redwoodempirefair.com
To celebrate Mexican Independence Day on September 16, the Latino Club of Ukiah stages a Fiesta Patrias event to select a Latina queen. Actually the object is not so much a beauty contest as a way to raise money for a scholarship fund. The contenders spend a lot of time and energy before the event in soliciting money from merchants, selling tamales and tickets, and other fund-raising endeavors. Each year some $10,000 is made available to help local students of Latin descent go to college. The festivities include fireworks and folk dancing.

Mendocino County Fair and Apple Show
14400 Highway 128, Boonville
(707) 895-3011
www.mendocountyfair.com
This is a traditional three-day family event held on a mid-September weekend and highlighted by a rodeo, sheepdog trials, rides for kids of all ages, and country-western dancing in the town of Boonville, located in the Anderson Valley. Admission is $6.00 for adults and $3.00 for children younger than 12.

Paul Bunyan Days
Various locations, Fort Bragg
(707) 964-8687, (707) 964-3356
www.paulbunyandays.com
Held each year on Labor Day weekend, this community celebration is a tribute to Paul Bunyan, the legendary giant lumberjack and folk hero. Numerous events keep

things hopping for four days. A Sunday logging show gives visitors a look at what professional loggers do in the way of strenuous activity. Most events are free, and the location changes, so call for the current site.

Winesong
Mendocino Coast Botanical Gardens,
18220 Highway 1, Fort Bragg
(707) 961-4688
www.winesong.org
More than 60 wineries and 50 restaurants participate in this wine tasting and auction, held at the delightful 47-acre botanical gardens in mid-September (see also the Attractions chapter). Winesong benefits the Mendocino Coast Hospital Foundation. The site is filled with native plants—rhododendron, heather, fuchsia, and dwarf conifers. It's a perfect site to sample Mendocino's famous wines. There's no entrance fee, but there is a charge for the wine.

OCTOBER
Napa County

Southwest Art in the Wine Country
Lee Youngman Galleries, 1316 Lincoln Avenue, Calistoga
(707) 942-0585
www.leeyoungmangalleries.com
If your idea of art is Native American spirit guides, dusty cowboys, fiery desert sunsets, and howling coyotes, don't miss this annual show at an upvalley winery. About 35 artists usually display varied works in late September or early October. Saturday is by RSVP only; Sunday is open to the general public at no charge. A silent auction benefits the Boy Scouts of America.

Calistoga Beer and Sausage Festival
Napa County Fairgrounds, 1435 North Oak Street, Calistoga
(707) 942-6333
www.calistogafun.com/beer
You might think you have to speak in

hushed tones when you discuss beer in Wine Country, but this festival is well regarded and has been going on for more than two decades The sudsfest features a chili cook-off, music, and samples from about 30 microbreweries (see the close-up in the Nightlife chapter), not to mention sausage companies and mustard makers. Twenty dollars gets you in the door and entitles you to a bottomless souvenir cup and borderless plate. It's a one-day affair in late September or early October.

Ghost Wineries Tour
(707) 252-3270
www.napalandtrust.org

Just as September in Wine Country brings on the crush, October hustles in the annual one-day Ghost Wineries Tour. Typically, five or six "ghost" wineries (some of the oldest forced to close during Prohibition) are revisited on a self-guided tour. Additional staff are on hand to greet visitors, and picnics are encouraged. Participants drive their own vehicles between the wineries at their own leisure.

Old Mill Days
Bale Grist Mill State Historic Park, 3369 North St. Helena Highway, St. Helena
(707) 942-4575
www.parks.ca.gov/default.asp?page_id= 482

The folks at the Bale Grist Mill celebrate the end of harvest by partying like it's 1869. Coopers, weavers, storytellers, and old-time fiddlers don period costumes to lend a touch of authenticity to the 19th-century goings-on. The kids can make cornhusk dolls or dye wheat. And the park rangers offer nonstop tours of the mill, which will be busy grinding whole wheat flour and cornmeal. It's a two-day event in mid-October. The cost is $4.00 for adults and $2.00 for children.

Napa Valley Open Studios Tour
Various locations
(707) 257-2117
www.artscouncilnapavalley.org

Come see real live artists in their natural habitats! On successive weekends in mid to late October, Napa Valley creative types throw open the doors to their studios and welcome the self-guided with refreshments. The format tends to be upvalley one weekend and downvalley the next. The Napa Valley Arts Council distributes maps prior to the free event; all you do is drive and gawk. At least 80 artists usually participate.

Hometown Harvest Festival
Adams Street, St. Helena
(707) 963-5706
www.sthelena.com

This festival, a one-day event on a Saturday in October, includes arts and crafts, a fun run, a carnival, wine tasting, and a canine Frisbee-catching contest. The highlight is the pet parade, an advancing column of dogs, cats, horses, llamas, roosters, and lizards. Most of the action swirls around St. Helena Elementary School, on Adams Street between Oak and Stockton Streets. There is no admission fee, and most of the proceeds from vendor sales go toward building St. Helena a new community center.

Sonoma County

Sonoma County Harvest Fair
Sonoma County Fairgrounds, 1350 Bennett Valley Road, Santa Rosa
(707) 545-4203
www.harvestfair.org

This harvest festival on the first full weekend in October features a world-championship grape stomp, wine tasting, produce exhibits, food, arts, crafts, amateur beer and wine booths, music, and kids' exhibits. It's a bustling fair that brings in droves of wine lovers from the Bay Area and beyond. Wine and food tasting tickets are extra, but you get a souvenir glass, and you will sip the top award winners in their specific categories—perhaps the only chance you'll get, because the wines are sometimes very limited production vintages. General admission is $5.00, but it's

$2.00 for seniors on Friday and $2.00 for kids ages 7 to 12.

Mendocino County

**Chainsaw Sculpture Championship
Fort Bragg
(707) 964-4251
www.fortbragg.org**
Where else can manly men bearing chainsaws demonstrate their sensitive side? Professional and novice chainsaw sculptors from around the nation gather every year in October to reduce a block of redwood or pine into a thing of beauty, based on certain themes (such as nautical, wine, and timber). In the process, they generate truckloads of sawdust over four days to complete their mission. Three winners are chosen from the pro, intermediate, and novice categories, and cash prizes are awarded. Later, the stately sculptures are auctioned off to benefit the Fort Bragg–Mendocino Coast Historical Society.

NOVEMBER

Napa County

**Napa Valley Wine Festival
Napa Valley Exposition, 575 Third Street, Napa
(707) 253-3563
www.napavalleyexpo.com**
Encouraging kids to drink is not good, but encouraging kids through a drinking festival is another matter altogether. This gig on the first Saturday in November raises about $50,000 a year for the Napa Valley Unified School District. The fun includes a live auction, with about 50 valley wineries pouring and 1,000 guests sipping; student-provided music as a backdrop; and a pasta dinner for sustenance. Tickets are $30 in advance, $35 at the door.

**Festival of Lights
Vintage 1870, 6525 Washington Street, Yountville
(707) 944-2451
www.vintage1870.com**
This isn't so much the lighting of a tree as the lighting of a town. At about 6:00 P.M. the day after Thanksgiving, all of Yountville flicks its switches and is bathed in fairy lights. Christmas is beckoned with singers, street performers, hayrides, and roasted chestnuts from 2:00 to 9:00 P.M. There is no admission fee, though you must buy tickets for food and wine. The extravaganza sets off a month of special dinners, musical performances, and the like around Yountville.

Sonoma County

**Santa's Arrival
Petaluma Riverfront, Petaluma
(707) 769-0429
www.petaluma.org,
www.visitpetaluma.com**
On the last Saturday in November, Santa makes his way into Petaluma by boat. While awaiting his arrival, the children stay busy with a variety of entertainment options. As might be expected, Santa's first move is to start handing out candy canes. Then he steps into an antique wagon chosen from the collection at the county museum (considered the largest collection in North America) and leads a parade of beautiful wagons in a circular route around town. It ends in historic Petaluma, where merchants hold a Share the Spirit event with an array of treats for all.

Mendocino County

**Thanksgiving Festival
Mendocino Art Center, 45200 Little Lake Road, Mendocino
(707) 937-5818
www.mendocinoartcenter.org**

A jolly festival at the Mendocino Art Center to survey the newest in professional arts and crafts occurs the weekend after Thanksgiving. Every inch of the center (and outside it, if the weather is cooperative) is filled with booths displaying crafters' works, from tie-dye to watercolors. A separate room has been reserved for kids to play, and there is always a visit from Santa.

DECEMBER

Napa County

Carols in the Caves
Various Napa and Sonoma wineries
(925) 866-9559
www.carolsinthecaves.com
Local musician David Auerbach is a multi-instrumentalist likely to play two dozen musical devices including dulcimers, pan pipes, and psalteries. As you might guess, he specializes in unusual folk instruments, and he brings out the best of each in the flawless acoustic environment of wine caves. The Carols in the Caves series consists of a minimum of eight simple, informal concerts, two or three per weekend between Thanksgiving and Christmas— and sometimes running into January for a Twelfth Night celebration. Locations vary from year to year and week to week. Cost for each show is about $30 per person.

Holiday Candlelight Tour
Various locations, Napa
(707) 255-1836
On the second Saturday in December, Napa County Landmarks (a local preservation society) organizes a 3:00 to 8:00 P.M. walking tour in a selected historic neighborhood. The stroll and open houses are usually in Napa but can turn up anywhere in the county. Many of the hosts put out cookies or cider, and there is a sweets-and-wine reception from 4:00 to 10:00 P.M. at a particularly fabulous building. Expect eight or nine stops, with strolling carolers and glowing luminaries along the way. The cost is $15 for Napa County Landmarks members, $18 for everyone else signing up in advance. It's $25 if you pay at the door.

Pioneer Christmas
Bale Grist Mill State Historic Park, 3369 North St. Helena Highway, St. Helena
(707) 942-4575
www.parks.ca.gov/default.asp?page_id= 482
Ever wonder how Americans celebrated Christmas in the 1850s? What you can expect are Christmas carols sung to the accompaniment of mandolin and fiddle. You can string popcorn and cranberries, drink apple cider, and, for a nominal charge, decorate gingerbread cookies. The miller will probably be there giving tours, and he may be grinding out fresh flour and cornmeal too. Adults pay $4.00; it's $2.00 for the kids.

Sonoma County

Sonoma Valley Olive Festival
Various locations, Sonoma
(707) 996-1090
www.olivefestival.com
December is the official kickoff month for this several-weeks-long annual event (see more details under the January listing).

Russian River Christmas Extravaganza
Various locations, Guerneville
(707) 869-9000
www.russianriver.com
Guerneville celebrates the holidays with a series of events guaranteed to raise everyone's spirits. The first is an evening open house with hors d'oeuvres and refreshments available free at many downtown businesses. The highlight of the evening is the lighting of the Christmas tree in Guerneville Plaza, plus carolers and carriage rides throughout downtown. Next is the World Dance Celebration held at the Veterans Hall. This cultural music and

dance exhibition features African, Irish, Scottish, Mexican, Caribbean, and other ethnic dance. The crowning event is the parade of lights, featuring trucks, horses, marching bands, antique cars, floats, and more, all decorated with Christmas lights. Check the Web site or phone number for exact dates and times.

Holiday Crafts Fair and Open House
Various locations, Cloverdale
(707) 894-4470
www.cloverdale.net
The first Saturday in December, Cloverdale shop owners host an open house with hors d'oeuvres and refreshments. The afternoon features the Parkside Chapel Singers performing in the downtown

plaza. And there's Christmas cheer to be had at the Wine and Visitor Center.

Mendocino County

A Smalltown Christmas
Various locations, Ukiah
(707) 462-4705
www.ukiahchamber.com
Santa flies into the local airport, and from there he rides a fire truck around town to visit all the shopping centers. A music program is held in the downtown area and is followed by the Truckers Light Parade. Kick off the Christmas spirit with this event, held the first weekend in December.

SHOPPING 🎁

A trip to Wine Country isn't complete without at least a day or two of serious shopping. But I don't mean hitting the malls. Instead, this chapter features one-of-a-kind shops and stores around small town squares, in sight of the Pacific Ocean, or housed in fascinating old structures. The picturesque plazas of Healdsburg and Sonoma, together with the charming main drags in St. Helena and Calistoga, are some of the best places to find just the right gift for someone back home or a special remembrance of Wine Country to keep for yourself. This chapter also includes some of the many antiques stores and bookstores around the region.

Don't forget to peruse the possibilities in countless winery gifts shops. Many stock their own private-label olive oils and vinegars, as well as logo apparel, kitchen accessories, wine-oriented cookbooks, and a plethora of other items.

These stores keep reasonably regular hours daily, and some may be open shorter hours on Sunday. It's best to call ahead if you're in doubt.

UNIQUE SHOPS

Napa County

Shackford's
1350 Main Street, Napa
(707) 226-2132
World-class restaurants necessitate a lot of chefs, and most Napa Valley kitchen whizzes do their shopping at Shackford's. So do the common cooks, and one step into the store will show you why. This is the nirvana of pots and pans. You'll find whole aisles of knives (Wusthof Trident, Sebatier, Forschner, and many more), pans (Calphalon, All-Clad, Look, etc., etc.), and cutting boards (wood, acrylic, poly, yada yada yada). The KitchenAid mixers are lined up like a panzer division, and the pot racks hang like chandeliers. It's all priced competitively.

The Beaded Nomad
1238 First Street, Napa
(707) 258-8004
There aren't many stores where prices start at three cents. The Nomad stocks more types of beads than you thought existed on the seven continents of this world—beads of metal, thread, plastic, glass, wood, fimo (a polymer clay), ceramic, and even hemp. You can assemble your beads right there in the store (mixing is encouraged), and staff will provide design assistance and repair. The shop even offers classes in basic and advanced stringing. It also carries masks and jewelry from exotic locales.

JHM Stamps & Collectibles
The Book Merchant and Sirius Bindery,
1330 Second Street, Napa
(707) 226-7511 (JHM),
(707) 259-1326 (Book Merchant)
Double your highbrow pleasure at one address housing two businesses. JHM, the only stamp shop within a 40-mile radius, has been on Second Street for more than 20 years. It has stamps from all over the world and a wide range of philatelic supplies—albums, refill pages, catalogs, and more. JHM also has boxes of blank postcards from every state in the union. The Book Merchant deals in antique and collectible books, especially those concerning local history. You might find a five-part library of Freemasonry, old pulp paperbacks, a 24-volume Dumas collection, signed first editions, or the complete work of Dickens in 20 volumes.

Inti
1139 First Street, Napa
(707) 258-8034
That this store was named for the Incan sun god tells you all you need to know about the business. It's a hodgepodge of imported multiethnic crafts popular with children of the '60s and their children—and anyone else looking for interesting decorations that won't devastate their checkbooks. Inti has jewelry, wood carvings, furniture, musical instruments, purses, candles, incense, batiks from Bali, and rugs from Peru. Oversize tapestries hang on the walls, and clothing from India and Indonesia hangs on racks.

Napa Valley Pianos
1141 First Street, Napa
(707) 224-5397
When a local winery or resort needs a grand piano for a one-night fete, it goes to Napa Valley Pianos. That's partly because this is the only piano store in Napa County, but also because of the shop's sterling reputation. It has both new and old pianos of varying sizes and new electronic keyboards too. All pianos are tuned twice—once in the store and again after delivery. One drawback: Few of them fit in the trunk of a rental car.

Overland Sheepskin Company
6505 Washington Street, Yountville
(707) 944-0778
www.overland.com
If it once bleated, you'll find it here. Overland's Jim Leahy began making sheepskin coats by hand in Taos, New Mexico, in 1973. Now the family-owned company sells its woolly wear at 11 locations around the nation, including this locale in Yountville. Try on the sheepskin slippers, or sit on a stack of amazingly plush rugs. Almost everything is 100 percent sheepskin, from the car seat covers to the coats (even the lining). Overland sells leather goods made by other manufacturers, including Australian outback dusters, hats, footwear, and water buffalo bags from India.

Mosswood
6550 Washington Street, Yountville
(707) 944-8151
www.yountville.com/shopping
When you have fully decorated your house and it's time to turn to the garden, Mosswood is here for you. This place has fountains, bird feeders, statuary, weather vanes, wind chimes, and more. The line of birdhouses is particularly impressive, with copper-domed, thatched-roof, and pebbled models. Mosswood also carries decorative interior accessories, including the Gracey Knight collection of bright, hand-painted furniture, featuring dozens of different knobs and pulls.

Napa Valley Grapevine Wreath Company
8901 Conn Creek Road (Rutherford Cross Road), Rutherford
(707) 963-8893
www.grapevinewreath.com
While most grape growers are pruning, stacking, and burning vines in the winter, this company is building its inventory. The Wood family (a partner in the original Freemark Abbey investment group) trims its 80 acres of Cabernet Sauvignon plants, strips the leaves, and fashions the vines into decorative wreaths—and a whole lot more. They make dozens of styles of baskets, plus cornucopias, hearts, crosses, stars, wine carriers, even reindeer and magic wands. All of it is handmade, distinct, and highly durable.

Dean & DeLuca
607 St. Helena Highway S., St. Helena
(707) 967-9980
www.deandeluca.com
Twenty years after the first Dean & DeLuca opened in SoHo in 1977, the ultra-premium food purveyors brought their act to Napa Valley. And while the massive wine section (see the Wineries chapter) is what sets this one apart from the other four branches, there is plenty more to woo your senses. Such as jam and marmalade jars by the dozen and an ocean of olive oil compartmentalized into 16-ounce

bottles. You can find dried beans and rice, dried fruit, tins of dried herbs, teas and coffees, cigars, chocolates, and sweetly packaged edibles you never knew existed. And you can complete the experience with a high-quality cooking utensil, a cookbook, or a basket. Dean & DeLuca has a sandwich-and-salad bar called Market Cafe, an espresso bar and bakery, fresh produce, and a central deli with no end of meats, cheeses, and olives. But most of all it has its reputation for service, a commodity delivered by a squadron of friendly attendants in white chef's coats. This is a great place for assembling a delicious feast to enjoy at your favorite winery's picnic area.

St. Helena Olive Oil Co.
Highways 29 and 128, Rutherford
(707) 967–1003
www.sholiveoil.com

Olive oil is as ancient a pursuit as wine, and it gets the same reverent treatment at St. Helena Olive Oil Co. This is one place where you can sample some of the best. Most of the fruit comes from the Central Valley, but the company contracted with a Napa Valley olive grower to produce the high-end Cask 85 line. St. Helena Olive Oil also imports balsamic vinegar from Italy and makes a few types of its own, including five flavored balsamics (with fresh berries) and a Cabernet vinegar. Everything is natural—no sugars or preservatives—and available in 60-, 250-, or 375-milliliter vessels.

Napa Valley Olive Oil Co.
835 Charter Oak Avenue, St. Helena
(707) 963–4173

For more than 50 years, this white clapboard barn has been distributing premier olive oil to Napa Valley and the world. The old mill and hydraulic presses are still here, but the olives are pressed in the Sacramento Valley now. Still, the Particelli family bottles and packages all of its oils in St. Helena (except for the extra virgin). That's a lot of bottling—about 100,000 cases per

year. The oil is available in sizes ranging from pints to gallons.

Napa Style
801 Main Street, St. Helena
(707) 967–0405, (866) 776–6272
www.napastyle.com

Here are two words that gourmet chefs know all about: gray salt. It's the best type of salt for cooking, so says Michael Chiarello, and he should know. He founded Tra Vigne restaurant in St. Helena, among other achievements in the food world. Add this new business venture into the mix and he's a bit like the Martha Stewart of the West Coast (he has a TV show too). His retail store in St. Helena and mail-order catalog are devoted to entertaining with style—*Napa style*—and both feature glassware, table linens, and small appliances, along with staples such as gray salt (harvested from France's Normandy coast), olive oils and vinegars, pasta, and preserves. The store is at the corner of Charter Oak Avenue and Main Street.

Vanderbilt and Company
1429 Main Street, St. Helena
(707) 963–1010

"Barn" would be too pedestrian a word for this upmarket emporium of home furnishings. But the effect created by the room's high open beams and skylights is not far removed. Inside are semienclosed alcoves devoted to, say, boldly painted Vietri tableware or the ornately muraled Wright Collection of furniture. Vanderbilt has glassware from Salas and Schott, a brimming Crabtree & Evelyn cupboard, linens and tablecloths, pillows and pillowcases, candles, baskets, and woven or twisted wine racks.

Calla Lily Fine Linens
1222 Main Street, St. Helena
(707) 963–8188

None of this "we sell a little bit of everything" here. Calla Lily inhabits a well-defined realm of linens, towels, rugs, and bathrobes, and only the best of each. The colors tend to be soft and muted, the prices steep, but the owners explain that some of the linens will last decades. Calla Lily also handles custom orders and offers select personal care products for the discriminating visitor.

Murray N' Gibbs
1220 Adams Street, St. Helena
(707) 963–3115

This store, founded by an interior designer, features the functional artwork of many valley locals, including drapery rods shaped like olive branches, colorful tissue boxes, and hand-painted tables. You'll also find jewelry, festive bowls, cups and plates, upholstered furniture by Lee and Shabby Chic, wall art and candles, plus enough picture frames to surround every head in Wine Country.

Tapioca Tiger
1234 Adams Street, St. Helena
(707) 967–0608

Not all kid stores are alike, as this one adeptly proves. Tapioca Tiger finds some items made just down the road and others manufactured overseas. The shop specializes in clothing (boys and girls, newborn to size 7) and toys. The clothes are highly original designs, everything from sweetly sophisticated European items to funky domestic lines. Many of the toys are handmade by small producers—items like wooden dinosaurs and dressable plush cats. Tapioca Tiger also features children's bedding and furniture.

Fideaux
1312 Main Street, St. Helena
(707) 967–9935

43 North Street, Healdsburg
(707) 433–9935

Greeting customers on a recent visit to this shop was a shirt that read, "I Kiss My Dog on the Lips." If that sentiment warms your heart rather than turns your stomach, this is the store for you. Dogs and cats are shaggy royalty here. Fideaux (pronounced "Fido"—get it?) offers numerous squeeze-

and-squeak toys, a wide selection of pet collars, collapsible dog dishes for hiking, pet futon beds (made for the Fideaux label), and even wine-barrel doghouses. They also stock the basics: shampoo, food, kitty litter, etc.

WilkesSport
1219 Main Street, St. Helena
(707) 963–4323
www.wilkessport.com

The well-heeled crowd that buys its tailored suits from the Wilkes Bashford Company of San Francisco probably looks here for its weekend activewear. The shop has a small but flawless selection of pants, sport coats, shirts, shoes, and accessories, featuring fine Italian fabrics. Examples of the manufacturers are Zegna for men and Piazza and Sempione for women.

Amelia Claire
1230 Main Street, St. Helena
(707) 963–8502

Rene Sculatti's boutique specializes in sun hats, shoes, and accessories for those see-and-be-seen summer months. Name a color and a decorative twist for your head, and you'll probably find both here—and you may even find it at impulse-buying prices.

IMG Home
3431 St. Helena Highway N., St. Helena
(707) 963–4595
www.shopimg.com

One of several Bay Area furniture showrooms of IMG Home, this Wine Country outpost offers globally inspired furniture and home accessories. It's all contained in an old white house alongside Highway 29 north of St. Helena. Look for the sign of the wine-sipping pig above the door—it's easy to spot.

Hurd Beeswax Candles
1255 Lincoln Avenue, Calistoga
(707) 942–7410, (800) 977–7211
www.hurdbeeswaxcandles.com

Get your candles and wine here: This store combines the art of beeswax candle crafting with a tasting bar that pours wines produced by the same family that owns the candle business. There are all-beeswax candles by the score, in an endless combination of sizes and styles. A demonstration beehive adds special interest, with the bees busy at work generating some of the raw material from which the two-legged artisans create their masterpieces. For an upclose look at the making of these fine candles, tours of the factory in St. Helena are offered; inquire at the numbers above.

Calistoga Pottery
1001 Foothill Boulevard, Calistoga
(707) 942–0216
www.calistogapottery.com
Sally and Jeff Manfredi run this pottery studio from the back of their home, and while popularity has surged, in some ways it's all very similar to how it was in 1980. Everything is fired on-site. They have remained loyal to a handful of rugged-looking glazes because their customers, in turn, have remained loyal to Calistoga Pottery. The company aims for utilitarian stoneware—platters, plates, pitchers, bowls, mugs, kettles, etc.—that complements food. (Sally used to be a painter, Jeff a chef.) Much of the work is made to order, but you can always find some pots for sale on the shelves.

The Candy Cellar
1367 Lincoln Avenue, Calistoga
(707) 942–6990
If you have not just one sweet tooth but a whole mouthful of them, abandon all hope when you enter this place. You'll see barrels filled with saltwater taffy, jawbreakers, swirls, crunches, bubble gum, lollipops, and all the Jelly Bellies of the rainbow. Most of it is sold by weight, so you can mix and match. But you'll probably head straight for the award-winning fudge—10 to 15 flavors mixed right on the spot, including the likes of chewy praline, maple nut, rocky road, and caffe latte.

Sonoma County

SOUTHERN SONOMA

Along the dozens of buildings from yesteryear that rim the plaza in the town of Sonoma, visitors come to search out galleries, specialty shops, and fine boutiques to find the unusual, the elegant, the unexpected. Beyond the main streets are more shops tucked into El Paseo de Sonoma, a charming enclave behind the corner of East Spain and First Streets. The path down the Mercato leads to more wonderful shopping. The plaza is Sonoma's main shopping scene. Here are just some of the many retail establishments you can explore.

Spirits in Stone
452 First Street E., Sonoma
(707) 938–2200

401 Healdsburg Avenue, Healdsburg
(707) 723–1723
www.spiritsinstone.com
Laura and Tony Ponter are on a mission: to import the best in elegant, simple sculpture from the Shona ("people of the mist") tribe in Zimbabwe and to demonstrate that "the spirit in stone" has much to teach us all about dignity, compassion, and peace. There is something almost magnetic about these profound sculptures—a feeling that you must reach out and touch them, and you are encouraged to do so. Large pieces are pricey, but the smaller sculptures are affordable and tempting for any lover of fine things. (See the gallery listings in the Arts and Culture chapter for more information.)

Flag Emporium
20089 Broadway, Sonoma
(707) 996–8140
www.flagemporium.com
How often do you run into a store totally devoted to flags of the world? You'll find every flag here, including some in the category of "discontinued country." The flags come in every size and every price. At

press time, this store had changed its hours of operation to Monday through Friday only.

One of the best ways to spend a Friday evening from late May to late September is at the downtown Napa Chef's Market. It's where you will find fresh produce, wine and beer, activities for kids, and lots of cooking demonstrations by Napa chefs.

Bear Moon Clothing
117 East Napa Street, Sonoma
(707) 935-3392

This is the place to go to find products that keep the environment in mind. Brand names include S.F. City Lights, Royal Robbins, Mishi, and Woolrich Outdoor Wear. You'll find clothing and soft linens, cottons, tencel, and down-to-earth blends for life's simple pleasures. It's all natural. The store's motto, "quality clothing in natural fabrics with fashion and the environment in mind," pretty much sums up what Bear Moon is all about.

Sonoma Cheese Factory
2 West Spain Street, Sonoma
(707) 996-1000
www.sonomajack.com

This may be the most popular shop on the plaza. People see cheese makers produce this extraordinary local cheese and sample or buy one of the dozens of varieties of Jack or cheddar cheese. There's an array of gourmet items to go with the cheese. You can take it all home or turn it into a picnic on the green plaza lawn. If you like, they'll make you a sandwich to eat at the sidewalk tables.

Vella Cheese Company
315 Second Street E., Sonoma
(707) 938-3232, (800) 848-0505
www.vellacheese.com

Some of the best cheese in the world is made on East Second Street, around the corner from the main drag, by Thomas Vella and his son, Ignazio. The family has operated out of the same 1905 rough-cut stone building since 1931; it's an architectural wonder in shaky, earthquakey California. The shop doesn't have the same exposure as the main street shops, but Vella Dry Jack has won international prizes, and the cheddar is so sharp it makes your mouth pucker.

Milagros
414 First Street E., Sonoma
(707) 939-0834
www.milagrosgallery.com

Following the covered passageway called El Paseo, which winds between East Spain and East First Streets, you'll suddenly believe you've wandered into another country and another time. There before you is Milagros, a fabulous store of affordable fine Mexican folk art, featuring whimsical Oaxacan wood carvings, Spanish colonial sconces, handcrafted jewelry from all over Latin America, Talavera bowls, and wonderful masks. This shop also displays a rare collection of religious Mexican folk art. Milagros, which means "miracles" in Spanish, is named after the figures sold in front of churches in Mexico.

Sonoma Rock & Mineral
414 First Street E., Sonoma
(707) 996-7200

El Paseo courtyard has another shop worthy of a visit, particularly if you're interested in things lapidary. It's hard to believe the earth holds such wondrous rocks and stones. The display is professionally arranged in a spacious setting, with beautiful polished stones to buy.

Baksheesh Handcrafted Gifts
423 First Street W., Sonoma
(707) 939-2847

106-B Matheson Street, Healdsburg
(707) 473-0880
www.vom.com/baksheesh

Fair trade for artists in developing nations is the business of these stores. There's a little bit of everything here, and at reasonable prices—home decor, jewelry, toys and games, garden accessories and planters, even musical instruments. The owners work with trade organizations that guarantee living wages to the artists for their crafts, which are magnificent.

La Villeta de Sonoma
27 Fremont Drive, Sonoma
(707) 939-9392
www.lavilleta.com
The beautiful handcrafted terra-cotta designer accessories in this unusual shop were created by some of Mexico's best sculptors and ceramic artists. But what you see here won't remind you of Mexico; it will remind you of Portugal or Italy, Greece or Spain, even North Africa. The shop opened in mid-1997 and is a branch of a larger store in Guadalajara, where artisans respected in their fields turn out urns, plates, paintings, and furniture that are styled from the beautiful museum pieces of the Mediterranean. The shop is at the junction of Highways 116 and 121.

OTHER SOUTHERN SONOMA SHOPS

The Olive Press
14301 Arnold Drive, Glen Ellen
(707) 939-8900, (800) 965-4839
www.theolivepress.com
Inspired by the cooperatives of northern Italy, the Olive Press was created by a group of olive aficionados. Its purpose? To press olives for commercial producers, small-harvest growers, and hobbyists eager to make oil from homegrown olives. Visitors can sample a premium selection of olive oils, and during harvest season (October through March) they can view the pressing process. A bounty of olive-related specialty foods and gifts is available for purchase.

Snoopy's Gallery and Gift Shop
1666 West Steele Lane, Santa Rosa
(707) 546-3385
www.snoopygift.com
Snoopy's Gallery features a museum containing awards, drawings, and personal memorabilia from Peanuts creator Charles M. Schulz. The gift shop has the largest selection of Snoopy products in the world. The Redwood Empire Ice Arena is one block away on the right, and the Charles M. Schulz Museum and Research Center is nearby (see the Attractions chapter).

Gado Gado International
Railroad Square, 129 Fourth Street, Santa Rosa
(707) 525-8244
www.gadogadointl.com
When you pass through the doors of Gado Gado, you slip into another world. Browse among exotic Asian furniture, much of it crafted from recycled teak taken from ancient dismantled dwellings. Hand-carved puppets are everywhere in every size, as are tribal artworks and sculptures, architectural elements, beaded boxes, hats, baskets, and countless other decorative accessories.

Sonoma Outfitters
145 Third Street, Santa Rosa
(707) 528-1920, (800) 290-1920
www.sonomaoutfitters.com
For sports enthusiasts, this is the place to go. It's immense (more than 11,000 square feet), and the inventory is sure to cover everything you need for just about any sport. There's an enormous amount of boating and camping equipment—tents and sleeping bags, hiking boots and climbing shoes, canoes, rubber and plastic kayaks, ski clothing, in-line skates, you name it. It's sports equipment from wall to wall.

NORTHERN SONOMA

The pretty plaza that makes Healdsburg so charming was built in 1852 by Harmon Heald, who sold lots for $15. Today, $15 will barely cover lunch, and the stores that sold harnesses and hardware in Heald's day are now occupied by charming shops filled with jewelry, books, fine art, clothing, and home furnishings. These shops are open every day.

Robinson & Co.
108 Matheson Street, Healdsburg
(707) 433-7116
Billed as "purveyors of fine coffees and cookwares," the store lives up to the claim. You encounter the aroma of coffee beans when you walk in, and there is a varied inventory of kitchenware. The shop is contemporary and glossy, filled with all the accoutrements you need to become a world-class chef, including the cookbooks that tell you how to go about it. David Robinson, the store's personable and welcoming owner, will be happy to acquaint you with his other products, including Italian porcelain, European and Australian pottery, French hand soaps, spices, and Williamsburg candles.

Seeing blue? You may notice while wine tasting and dining in Sonoma Valley that your vino is served in blue-stemmed glasses. The glasses distinguish your wine as being produced in the Sonoma Valley appellation. You can buy your own set of glasses at the Sonoma Valley Visitors Bureau.

Oakville Grocery Co.
124 Matheson Street, Healdsburg
(707) 433-3200

7856 St. Helena Highway, Oakville
(707) 944-8802, (800) 736-6602
www.oakvillegrocery.com
The Healdsburg location is a branch of the same wonderful gourmet grocery store whose jam-packed shelves in the Napa Valley have attracted passersby for decades. At this location it has metamorphosed into a gentrified, glossy emporium of most everything gourmet and delicious. Here you can stock your kitchen pantry with exotic mustards, duck pâté, caviar, Greek olives, and more. You can eat lunch

here too, selecting salads, sandwiches, and yummy desserts to be eaten under umbrellas on the sun-drenched patio. Be sure to pick up a copy of the latest catalog—your mouth will water—that features custom gift packages for ordering by mail for yourself and others.

Working Gardener
330 Healdsburg Avenue, Healdsburg
(707) 473-9045
www.workinggardener.com
Owner Merede Graham has fashioned an inviting store for gardeners, stocked with everything from practical tools to luxurious gifts, including Tuscan-inspired planters and pots, lavender goodies, and a wide assortment of outdoor decor. She has so much to offer, it takes two floors to show it all off.

Seasons of the Vineyard
113 Plaza Street, Healdsburg
(707) 431-2222
www.seasonsofthevineyard.com
Here's a store that embodies all the gifts and decorative objects that can turn a house into a home. Owned by Rhonda Carano, of Ferrari-Carano Vineyards, it's a cornucopia of fabulous table settings, wreaths, furniture, linens, and other home accents. Rhonda also carries the locally produced Hare Hollow line of seasoned vinegars and olive oils. And don't forget to look up—the ornate tin ceiling dates from 1883.

Art and All That Jazz
119 Plaza Street, Healdsburg
(707) 433-7900
www.artandallthatjazz.com
Jessica Felix, whose works have been shown at the Smithsonian Institution as well as prominent galleries across the country, has been designing spirited jewelry since 1970. Her shop serves as a gallery that includes the work of others in art glass, ceramics, photography, and collage, and it offers an eclectic selection of jazz and Brazilian music.

WEST COUNTY/RUSSIAN RIVER

Incredible Records & CDs
112 North Main Street, Sebastopol
(707) 824-8099
www.incrediblerecordsandcds.com
Forget the Rock and Roll Hall of Fame in Cleveland. Sonoma County has its own "museum" masquerading as a record/CD store in Sebastopol. Owner Jonathon Lipsin had a similar store in Toronto for many years, with much of the same priceless rock memorabilia on display. It's not exhibited in fancy museum style; it's mostly a jumble of taped and pushpinned treasures, creating a mosaic of the weird and the wonderful, with no wall space left unused. There are vintage rock posters aplenty; a rare collection of early Beatles photos (including the proof sheets) taken by photographer Dezo Hoffmann, who accompanied the moptops around the world; the Who's contract to perform at Woodstock in 1969 (they earned $12,500, by the way); a fringed vest worn by Steve Miller in the '60s; a guitar used by Randy Bachman in the '70s; and an assortment of odd pencil drawings made by Jim Morrison at the tender age of 14, which foretold his future legacy as the Lizard King. And that's just for starters.

Don't be surprised to find Carlos Santana or Tom Waits standing next to you at the racks—they pop in from time to time to do their music shopping.

California Carnivores
2833 Old Gravenstein Highway, Sebastopol
(707) 824-0433
www.californiacarnivores.com
It's been called "Little Shop of Horrors," but it's one of the most fascinating spots you'll see in a month of Sundays. About 550 carnivorous plants grow here, with about 120 varieties for sale. These are the meat eaters of the plant world and are endless fun to watch. An unsuspecting fly circles above the Venus flytrap and makes what will be its final landing. Other plants, like the pitcher plant or the blad-

derwort, are even more unkind to insects. The plants are easy to care for and inexpensive—you could get a dandy one for between $4.00 and $10.00 and perhaps be fly free forever. If you'd like to send one to a friend, a mail-order service is provided.

Hand Goods
3627 Main Street, Occidental
(707) 874-2161
www.handgoods.com
Proclaiming a "distinctive mall-free experience," Hand Goods is located in the tiny hillside hamlet of Occidental. Since 1971 the shop has offered a wide variety of fine, locally made handcrafts, featuring the work of more than 100 artists. The ceramics encompass everything from functional tableware to ornamental sculpture, from painted oil lamps to ikebana vases. You'll also find Shaker boxes and fine furniture, embroidered Thai jackets, and batik baby clothing. If it's jewelry you're looking for, Hand Goods offers local and imported earrings, necklaces, pins, and bracelets in every price range. Handwoven Zapotec rugs from Oaxaca are a perennial favorite and come in all sizes and colors.

R. S. Basso Home
186 North Main Street, Sebastopol
(707) 829-1426

115 Plaza Street, Healdsburg
(707) 431-1925
Ron and Mary Basso began making custom sofas and chairs in the early 1980s in Sebastopol, and their presence has spread to one additional Wine Country location, plus others in Palo Alto and Danville. They also operate a fabric store. The Sebastopol store has been significantly expanded, with 28,000 square feet of retail space on two floors. The Bassos still manufacture the frames to specification in Sebastopol, and you can choose from thousands of fabrics to cover yours. They ship all over the nation, or farther— Ecuador on at least one occasion. R. S. Basso has fine art, floor and table lamps,

Wine Country's Fabulous Farm Trails

Wandering from one winery to another, Wine Country visitors are likely to come across green and white signs posted in some farmyards announcing "Farm Trails." Wine isn't the only thing this countryside turns out. Produce is our other forte.

Farm Trails was organized in 1973 by a group of farmers dedicated to the promotion and preservation of the agricultural heritage of the region. During the ensuing decades it has guided consumers through the spectacular countryside to "experience a farm," sample local fresh foods and wines, or select a rare plant from a specialty nursery. Maps and a guide have been printed to lead you to 100 farms open to the public, all eager to sell their goods directly to drop-in consumers. You can pick one up at a number of Wine Country visitor bureaus, hotels, fruit stands, and grocery stores.

The maps outline in fine detail the tranquil backroads and old-time farms that lie slumbering off the main thoroughfares. You'll never forget your first tangy bite of a Gravenstein apple picked right off the tree or the juicy you-pick-it strawberry you pop in your mouth. The product index includes other intriguing headings—hayrides, goats (pygmy), llamas and emus and pigs (Vietnamese), quails (and quail eggs), bees, wax, and pollen.

The produce of the Farm Trails group is as diverse as California's terrain and climate. From the fog-chilled valleys near the coast to the sunbaked fields inland, you'll find everything from smoked salmon to cacti and, best of all, have a chance to chat with the people who make their living from agriculture. Here you can learn the pleasures and pitfalls of an industry that's seldom showcased.

figurines, wrought-iron chandeliers, and framed sketches and photos from eras past. And check out the magnificent mirrors, framed with embossed tin, inlaid stone tiger stripes, or hand-painted Devonshire roses.

Studio Nouveau
25195 B Street, Duncans Mills
(707) 865–2461
www.studionouveau.com
Tucked behind the Cape Fear Cafe in a Hobbit-size cottage sits Studio Nouveau, which owner Andrea Record describes as carrying "objects of beauty." She has so

much it spills out of the tiny store and onto a deck. Much of it she created herself, especially the pottery. There are also classic wooden wall hangings, candles, jewelry, scarves, and unique garden planters.

Mendocino County

U.S. HIGHWAY 101

Real Goods Store
13771 South US 101, Hopland
(707) 744–2100, (800) 994–4243
www.realgoods.com

Locals always stick their necks out for visitors along the Farm Trails. JOHN NAGIECKI

Built as part of the Real Goods Solar Living Center (see the Attractions chapter), Real Goods Store is both a retail store and educational center. A thousand items are available, including a vast number of high-tech devices—from a laptop briefcase that doubles as a solar collector (yes, it will power your PC wherever you go) to a better mouse trap (it does not crush or kill its victims). Stop in (or order a catalog), buy some hemp socks or a solar-powered fountain, and learn to spurn bugs without noxious repellents. The array of innovative products offered is mind-boggling, and it makes you wonder why we keep burning fossil fuels.

Hoyman-Browe Studio
323 North Main Street, Ukiah
(707) 468-8835
www.earthenware.com
Trained in the European school of pottery making, Douglas Browe and his wife, Jan Hoyman, have established a studio in the traditional, old-time format—training apprentices and displaying their work. Much of the output from the studio is sold to restaurants across the country, but the

showroom at the studio doesn't just have pots. There are tea sets, huge presentation platters, jardinieres, and 10-gallon flower pots, as well as tableware with bright designs of fruits, flowers, and vegetables.

Mendocino Bounty
200 South School Street, Ukiah
(707) 463-6711
This small shop is filled with food and wine made in Mendocino County and stuff for the kitchen. You'll find colorful bowls, linens, and gift baskets filled with products. If you wish, the basket can be custom designed—let's say a pasta basket filled with grapeseed oil, organic herbs, and unusual pastas that are hard to find anywhere else. There's a breakfast basket with honey, local syrup, breakfast cakes, and a special waffle mix prepared by Mendocino's famous Cafe Beaujolais (see the Restaurants chapter).

Grace Hudson Museum
431 South Main Street, Ukiah
(707) 467-2836
www.gracehudsonmuseum.org
Grace Hudson's portraiture of Native Americans—particularly the Pomo tribe—brought her national recognition. The museum's gift shop collection of Native American crafts, books, and jewelry reflects that same fascination. A fine sampling of books explores all facets of Native American culture, and there's a nice selection of items for children. The gift shop is open Wednesday through Sunday. A jaunt through the museum is free, but donations are appreciated (see the Attractions chapter).

MENDOCINO COAST

Velvet Rabbit
38140 Highway 1, Gualala
(707) 884-1501
Shop to operatic music while you browse through the works of selected artisans in a variety of fields, from stained glass, bronze sculptures, carved stone, and wooden boxes from England, to china, crystal, hand-blown glass, and shells from all over the world.

The Courtyard
Kasten and Main Streets, Mendocino
(707) 937-0917
Here you'll discover all those kitchen gadgets that will make you wonder how you ever got along without them. The display of imported English teapots is large enough to convince you you're back in Sussex. Maybe you'll go home with a matching set of table linens and crockery. If you don't know how to cook, the shop will take care of that too—there is a large library of cookbooks.

Lark in the Morning Musique
10460 Kasten Street, Mendocino
(707) 937-5275
www.larkinam.com
If you have a passion for musical instruments, you shouldn't pass up this shop. From alpenhorns to zithers, they fill every corner and hang from the ceiling—dulcimers, mandolins, banjos (with four or five strings), hurdy-gurdies, ukuleles, concertinas and accordions, harps, bagpipes, and drums of every size. There's barely enough room to turn around inside, but it's chock-full of fascinating instruments you've probably never seen before.

The Golden Goose
45094 Main Street, Mendocino
(707) 937-4655
Don't even think of saving this shop for the end of your shopping tour. It has beds covered with down quilts and down pillows so fluffy you'll be overcome by the need to plop into bed and forget the rest of your stops. If you'd like to take home a bed full of luxurious sheets and down, it will probably run up a bill of about $1,500.

Panache
45110 Main Street, Mendocino
(707) 937-0947

10400 Kasten Street, Mendocino
(707) 937-1234
www.thepanachegallery.com
You'll find art galleries all over town because Mendocino is artists' heaven. But it's worth stopping in to see the metal

sculpture of Don Quixote that's on exhibit front and center in the Kasten Street location. It's like none other. Panache is also the place to buy the fruit and vegetable paintings of Gerald Stinski, who moved to Mendocino in 1991 to pursue his art dreams.

Deja-Vu Hat Co.
10470 Lansing Street, Mendocino
(707) 937-4120, (800) 489-8123
www.dejavuhats.com
Who wouldn't want to see the largest selection of hats in Northern California? There's something for everyone who owns a head—felts, fine fur, straws, Stetsons, Akubras, Borsalinos, panamas, and Deja-Vu's own dress hats.

Mendocino Coast Botanical Gardens
18220 North Highway 1, Fort Bragg
(707) 964-4352
www.gardenbythesea.org
This 47-acre showcase garden displays wondrous collections of rhododendrons, azaleas, heathers, and succulents. Some of these species can be purchased in the retail nursery that helps support the nonprofit effort. Travelers might consider one of the sempervivum ("live forever") succulents, as a memento of Northern California. They're inexpensive and travel well. There's also a gift shop with cards, vases, and so forth, as well as a shop for outdoor garden supplies. Admission prices are $7.50 general, $6.00 for seniors, $3.00 for juniors ages 13 to 17, and $1.00 for kids ages 6 to 12. (For more on the Mendocino Coast Botanical Gardens, see the Attractions chapter.)

Harvest Market
171 Boatyard Drive, Fort Bragg
(707) 964-7000
www.harvestmarket.com
Well, yes, it's a grocery store. But this is the one you wish was just around the corner from your kitchen. Homegrown produce, fresh local seafood, and fresh-baked bread are imaginatively displayed. The folks at Harvest Market will make you a

picnic basket to go or fill your ice chest with the best foods in town.

Hot Pepper Jelly Company
330 North Main Street, Fort Bragg
(707) 961-1899, (800) 892-4823
www.hotpepperjelly.com
With 30 varieties of jelly to sample, you'll be licking your lips and fingers for hours. Don't neglect the old-time favorites, ginger pepper, Chardonnay conserve, or very cherry marmalade. For kicks, try the jalapeno pepper jam. All of Carol Hall jellies are handmade in small batches. They're sold nationwide, and the lineup also includes chutneys, dessert toppings, fruit syrups, mustards, vinegars, and salsa.

For the Shell of It
344 North Main Street, Fort Bragg
(707) 961-0461
Here you'll find pieces of the ocean, without the water. Long aisles hold everything from scallop shells for serving seafood to tiny shells made into earrings. But these are not local shells—remember that the state parks system discourages you from carrying any part of the beach away.

Fiddles & Cameras
400 North Main Street, Fort Bragg
(707) 964-7370
As befits a small community, sometimes retailers double up on their specialties. Fiddles and cameras are precisely what you can buy at this store. The stock runs to mostly stringed instruments of all types, instructional tapes, and sheet music and music books. But there's also a huge selection of cameras, and you can pick up binoculars for spotting whales too.

ANTIQUES

Napa County

The Neighborhood
1400 First Street, Napa
(707) 259-1900
Yes, it is almost big enough to be its own

CLOSE-UP

Our Other Nectar

Color, bouquet, and taste—the words traditionally associated with wine tasting. But there's another nectar grown and bottled in Wine Country that is judged by foodies in much the same way: olive oil.

Color refers to the tinged green from the chlorophyll found in green olives or the yellow of mature olives. As the oil becomes oxidized, a red tint may appear.

Bouquet is determined by the volatile compounds in the oil, such as alcohols, ketones, and esters.

Taste involves the bouquet in combination with the four gustatory senses: salty, acid, bitter, and sweet.

Today's emphasis on improved health and better eating has brought a new appreciation for olive oil—not only the one- and three-liter bulk offerings found in most supermarkets but the hand-harvested, finely milled, flavorful, creatively bottled, and limited-availability artisan varieties found in places such as Wine Country.

Indeed, countless wineries now bottle their own brands and feature them prominently in their gift shops. The oils may be infused with many flavors, ranging from lemon to hot chili. Other creative combinations may blend orange and thyme, basil and chili, and mixed herbs and sun-dried tomato. And a meaty porcini mushroom–flavored oil is reputedly an aphrodisiac.

Olive trees are grown for oil production in all Wine Country counties, and the olives are generally harvested following the autumn wine-grape crush.

Transforming olives into oil is not complicated. High-quality fruit is crushed in either stone grinders or metal hammer mills. The paste is then mixed until oil droplets begin to form, and then pressed in either single-batch hydraulic presses or continuous-flow spinning presses. The olive juice—containing both water and oil—is then separated in centrifuge separators similar to those used to separate cream from milk. From that, the "liquid gold" is revealed.

Newly pressed olive oils, which have the strongest flavors, are sometimes known as one- or two-cough oils. When the oil hits the back of your throat, the bitterness may produce an involuntary cough . . . or two—much like gulping down a shot of whiskey. But with olive oil, bitter is often considered a desirable trait.

neighborhood. This showroom takes up half a block in downtown Napa, and inside it displays on two levels. Poke around and find everything from mission benches to barber chairs, framed photos of American Indians to ice sleds, and rough willow chairs to green bottles from the old Vichy Hot Springs in Sonoma.

There is no shortage of oil in Wine Country; distinctive home-grown olive oils dominate the shelves in most upscale groceries. LOREN DOPPENBERG

Several Wine Country companies offer a peek into the production of olive oil. In Sonoma County, the Olive Press in Glen Ellen (707-939-8900; www.theolive press.com) operates as a co-op for a handful of small-harvest producers to press at a common facility. Learn about the hammermill pressing technique and purchase an olive cutting to take home. The store is located at 14301 Arnold Drive.

In Napa Valley, St. Helena Olive Oil Company (800-939-9880; www.sholive oil.com), located at Rutherford Cross-roads (the corner of Highways 29 and 128), has a retail showroom selling oodles of olive oil labels, wine vinegars, and other goodies. The store also features a demonstration press. Napa Valley Olive Oil Company (707-963-4173) now bottles its oils elsewhere but keeps the original press on display for visitors. The store is located at 835 Charter Oak Avenue, east of Tra Vigne restaurant, in St. Helena—look for the big white barn.

Red Hen Antiques
5091 St. Helena Highway, Napa
(707) 257-0822
This is something of a local landmark

about halfway between Napa and Yountville. It has been Red Hen since 1983, and it was the Napa Valley Garden Shop for many years before that. Look for the

Not every state will allow interstate wine shipments into its territory, so ask your wine merchant in advance.

big chicken facing the highway. Inside you'll find a collective of 80 dealers peddling a wide range of goods.

Antique Fair
6512 Washington Street, Yountville
(707) 944-8440
www.antiquefair.com
This shop has been around for a long time (since 1971), but not as long as its merchandise. Antique Fair specializes in high-quality French antiquities from about 1890, *la crème* of Lyon and Paris estates. The proprietors have jewelry, statuettes, silverware, armoires, and bookcases. They're known for old beds they have converted to queen size.

Erika Hills Antiques
115 Main Street, St. Helena
(707) 963-0919
Just south of St. Helena you will spy a line of statuary along Highway 29 and, behind it, a former church that has been painted ocher and converted into an antiques store. This is Erika Hills, the namesake house of ancient delights. Inside you will find Limoges plates, Venetian glass, brightly accented Mexican chairs, baroque angels from Austria, and sturdy oak chairs salvaged right off the farm. Most but not all of the furniture is painted, and everything leans toward the high end.

St. Helena St. Helena Antiques
1231 Main Street, St. Helena
(707) 963-5878
This ultrahigh-end locale feels like a turn-of-the-20th-century shop in London or New England. Customers are met at the door by two life-size, cartoonish "greeters"—a chef and a winemaker—carved from single trunks. (They're menu boards from the 1860s.)

If there is a specialty, it's wine-related items: corkscrews, bottles, racks, and practically anything that might have been salvaged from an old winery.

Lone Dog Fine Art & Antiques
1345 Lincoln Avenue, Suite A, Calistoga
(707) 942-1115
Proprietor Frederick Schrader has a wealth of experience in gathering artifacts. Lone Dog shares space with Enoteca Wine Shop (see the Wineries chapter) in the wonderfully restored I.O.O.F. building (also known as the Odd Fellows building). It's the perfect setting for Schrader's collection, which includes framed lithographs of 19th-century local scenes and wine-related tools and paraphernalia.

Sonoma County

SOUTHERN SONOMA

Sonoma Country Antiques
23999 Arnold Drive, Sonoma
(707) 938-8315
www.sonomacountryantiques.com
Looking for English and Victorian or Georgian pine designs and furnishings from the period 1820 to 1900? This dealer either has it or can obtain it for you. This is a one-of-a-kind showplace of unique pine antiques that would fit perfectly in the modern home.

Margaret's Antiques of Sonoma
472 Second Street W., Sonoma
(707) 938-8036
Tucked away in a cozy white cottage that dates to the 1870s and is now a historic landmark, Margaret's Antiques replaced the family that lived in the house for 100 years. The shop's specialties are art glass, china, furniture, dolls, pottery, and linens from the 1800s, although it does have a few collectibles that are more recent.

Chelsea Antiques
148 Petaluma Boulevard N., Petaluma
(707) 763-7686

This is a collective that features a wonderful selection of decorative antiques, collectibles, and architectural and garden items in three buildings. Chelsea represents just about every field of antiques collecting.

Vintage Bank Antiques
101 Petaluma Boulevard N., Petaluma
(707) 769-3097
It's one of those wonderful old banks that has ceilings two stories high and a small window on the second level overlooking the bank floor—so the manager could monitor his tellers and cashiers. Today it's a collective for 48 dealers, giving you three floors to explore. What you'll find is jewelry, furniture, vintage clothing, porcelain, gentlemen's collectibles, dinnerware, and lots more.

Antique Marketplace & Annex
248 Petaluma Boulevard N., Petaluma
(707) 765-1155
It claims to have the finest and largest selection of antique furniture in Petaluma. Included is a large selection of pine and country furniture.

Kentucky Street Antiques
127 Kentucky Street, Petaluma
(707) 765-1698
Nine dealers display their collections here, showing everything from country to classic—furniture, china, glassware, toys, tools, old advertising, paper, and jewelry.

Whistle Stop Antiques
130 Fourth Street, Santa Rosa
(707) 542-9474
www.railroadsquare.net
This is where it all began—Sonoma County's original collective, now more than 25 years old. With 10,000 square feet of space and more than 35 dealers, it's a collector's paradise with thousands of items from dishes to doorknobs. You'll find clock repair, refinishing supplies, antique books, and a wonderful assortment of glassware, jewelry, furniture, and collectibles.

Railroad Square Basement Antiques
100 Fourth Street, Santa Rosa
(707) 569-9646
www.railroadsquare.net
You enter this shop on Wilson Street. It features a fine collection of vintage furniture, glassware, pottery, kitchenware, china, and cookbooks. Closed Tuesday.

NORTHERN SONOMA
Mill Street Antiques
44 Mill Street, Healdsburg
(707) 433-8409
Inside a big orange building, more than 40 dealers showcase their wares in 20,000 square feet of space. You'll find furniture—classic to country—glass, china, silver, fine oil paintings by listed artists, plus some eccentric goodies that need a home, such as gas station collectibles, metal signs, and 1950s memorabilia.

Healdsburg Classics
226 Healdsburg Avenue, Healdsburg
(707) 433-4315
This is an enormous warehouse with a roster of some 20 dealers. It would be difficult to name something that isn't here, rather than what is. However, anyone looking for indoor-outdoor furniture or yard pieces will not be disappointed.

Antique Harvest
225 Healdsburg Avenue, Healdsburg
(707) 433-0223
Items range from country pine to Victorian, with lamps, brass, art deco furnishings, and Maxfield Parrish prints to boot. Meander through and check out the wares of more than 12 dealers.

Jimtown Store
6706 Highway 128, Healdsburg
(707) 433-1212
www.jimtown.com
Not only can you find American antiques, folk art, and primitives here, you can also have some "real food" (as they advertise) and a truly good cup of coffee.

SONOMA COAST

Wooden Duck Antique Shop
132 Bodega Lane, Bodega
(707) 876–3176
You'll spot the big yellow house (once a Druids hall) from the highway as you head toward the ocean. The store is open only Saturday and Sunday, but you'll find some fine 18th- and 19th-century furniture, plus a lot of Americana—pewter, glass, silver, whale oil lamps, and some English Staffordshire china. There's also a fine collection of antique guns.

WEST COUNTY/RUSSIAN RIVER

Llano House Antiques
4353 Gravenstein Highway S., Sebastopol
(707) 829–9322
Housed in the oldest wooden building in Sonoma County, Llano House Antiques deals mainly in American oak furniture, Depression glass, and kitchen collectibles.

Antique Society
2661 Gravenstein Highway S., Sebastopol
(707) 829–1733
www.antiquesociety.com
Antique Society is right when it claims "there's no place quite like" its collective. With more than 100 dealers, it is simply immense. You'll find just about anything you're looking for here, and the dealers claim to have "country prices."

School Bell Antiques
3555 Gravenstein Highway S., Sebastopol
(707) 823–2878
Housed in a charming old schoolhouse is a 24-dealer collective. The schoolhouse alone is worth the visit.

Sebastopol Antique Mall
755 Petaluma Avenue, Sebastopol
(707) 823–1936
www.sebastopolantiquemall.com
Want to take home a star? You'll find fabulous studio portraits and scene stills of yesterday's film stars—say, John Wayne or Elvis—with autographs guaranteed authentic, all from the private collection of Laurel Proeme. A signed photo might be had for $75, with Elvis priced a little higher. You'll find a lot more, and since this is a mall, you can also stop for coffee, wine, or lunch at a gourmet cafe.

Mendocino County

Hopland Antiques
13456 US 101, Hopland
(707) 744–1023
Much of the merchandise in this large building came from buying complete estates, so you'll find a lot of furniture, home accessories, and excellent estate jewelry.

Li'l Stinker Antiques
20029 North US 101, Willits
(707) 459–2486
It's all furniture here—no small stuff. Some of it dates from the 1830s. The store has been in business under the same owner since 1967.

Whistlestop Antiques
350 North Franklin Street, Fort Bragg
(707) 961–0902
www.the-whistlestop.com
Here they call about half the stock "temporary collectibles" and the other half antiques, on the assumption half the collecting community are "only temporary custodians." The extensive selection of elegant glassware includes Fostoria, Heisey, Cambridge, and many others, as well as Depression glass and carnival glass. They also carry a fine line of American furniture.

BOOKSTORES

Napa County

Bookends Book Store
1014 Coombs Street, Napa
(707) 224-1077
www.bookends.booksense.com
Bookends counts a couple of big-chain bookstores as neighbors in downtown Napa but manages to hold its own. How? With substantial sections on subjects such as computers, business, biography, self-help, crafts, children's books, and family (things like birth, child rearing, and weddings).

Bookends has plenty of magazines and fiction and a large collection of travel guides and maps, including a comprehensive set of Wine Country maps.

Copperfield's Books
Bel Aire Plaza Shopping Center, Trancas Street and Highway 29, Napa
(707) 252-8002

1330 Lincoln Avenue, Calistoga
(707) 942-1616
www.copperfields.com
Wine Country literati have been relying on Copperfield's for years. The Napa Valley stores (there are also three locations in Sonoma County; see next section) are well stocked and well staffed. Expect new, used, and rare books as well as excellent children's sections.

Main Street Books
1315 Main Street, St. Helena
(707) 963-1338
This business has been around since 1983 but recently reinvented itself. Main Street Books is now an extremely small shop that emphasizes used items. (It's the only upvalley used-book store.) The cramped quarters and carefully selected titles are bound to remind you of a classic London bookstall.

The Calistoga Bookstore
1343 Lincoln Avenue, Calistoga
(707) 942-4123
This bookstore, nicely set in the 19th-century Odd Fellows building, knows its audience. Catering largely to tourists, it has a large collection of oversize coffee-table books and Northern California travel guides. And because this is a spa town, Calistoga Bookstore gets into the act with material on massage, Reiki, reflexology, nutrition, yoga, and other healthful pursuits. It even goes one step further—into Celtic and Arthurian, new age and Eastern religion, feng shui, and sexuality.

Sonoma County

SOUTHERN SONOMA

Sonoma Bookends Bookstore
201 West Napa Street, No. 15, Sonoma
(707) 938-5926
www.sonomabookends.com
It's a general interest bookstore with an eye toward tourists in the wide selection of Wine Country books. The store's travel section focuses on California, but there's a fine selection of U.S. Geological Survey maps.

Readers' Books
130 East Napa Street, Sonoma
(707) 939-1779
www.readersbook.com
Described by *Travel & Leisure* as a "honey pot" ("You can't help but get stuck there"), Readers' is a bookstore with many rooms, one of which is strictly for children's books and serves as a gathering room for youngsters. The store has gained some fame for its authors' readings.

Jack London Bookstore
14300 Arnold Drive, Glen Ellen
(707) 996-2888
Used and new books are sold here, with a special concentration of books dealing with the life of author Jack London. Closed Tuesday.

Book Warehouse
2200 Petaluma Boulevard N., Petaluma
(707) 778-6981

This is a clearance bookstore tucked in the southwest corner of the Petaluma Village Premium Outlet. It sells the same range of books as any general bookstore, but all have been purchased from stock that has not been sold in other stores.

Copperfield's Books
140 Kentucky Street, Petaluma
(707) 762-0563

2316 Montgomery Drive, Santa Rosa
(707) 578-8938

138 North Main Street, Sebastopol
(707) 823-2618
www.copperfields.com

Copperfield's has built its business on customer service and is highly respected in Sonoma County. The shelves are filled with general-interest publications, and there's a great children's section with occasional special events for children (see the Kidstuff chapter). The Petaluma store deals in new and used books.

NORTHERN SONOMA

Toyon Books
104 Matheson Street, Healdsburg
(707) 433-9270
www.toyonbooks.com

Travelers looking for more information about Sonoma County's wineries will find a fine selection of wine-related books at the front of the store. The selection at Toyon Books is geared toward general reading, but a group of books specializes in spiritual and self-awareness subjects.

Levin & Company
306 Center Street, Healdsburg
(707) 433-1118

It would be hard to find a more appealing bookstore—a large, airy room displays books on three large islands in the center of the store. Beyond that there's a cozy

room with a comfortable couch in the mystery novel section, and then another cozy room with books on women's studies. A WPA-style mural spans one wall. There's also a children's room.

Levin & Company offers primarily new books—quality fiction, interior design, and garden titles. Upstairs in the loft you'll find an art gallery displaying the works of some 15 local artists.

SONOMA COAST

Fort Ross Book & Gift Shop
19005 Highway 1, north of Jenner
(707) 847-3437
www.parks.ca.gov/default.asp?page_id=449

Located 11 miles north of the town of Jenner, the state park shop has a unique selection of books highlighting the Russian settlers and Native Americans, plus the natural history of the Fort Ross area (see the History chapter).

Mendocino County

U.S. HIGHWAY 101

The Mendocino Book Company
102 South School Street, Ukiah
(707) 468-5940

It's billed as the largest bookstore between Santa Rosa and Portland, with special orders and mail orders welcome. It's a true family bookstore, featuring a young readers' room. In addition to books, there's an excellent selection of magazines and newspapers.

Leaves of Grass Bookstore
15 South Main Street, Willits
(707) 459-3744

Besides the books, this store has an excellent selection of U.S. Geological Survey topographical maps. Also available are educational games and toys for kids, plus books on tape for travelers.

MENDOCINO COAST

**Gallery Bookshop & Bookwinkle's
Children's Books
Main and Kasten Streets, Mendocino
(707) 937-2665
www.gallerybookshop.com**
Here's a world-class bookstore stocking
more than 25,000 titles, plus cards, magazines, and newspapers. The section on
local history is comprehensive. Bookwinkle's is a perfect place to shop for children's books.

**Ford House Museum and Visitor Center
735 Main Street, Mendocino
(707) 937-5397**
This is one of Mendocino's earliest resi-
dences as well as the headquarters of

Mendocino Headlands State Park (see the
Attractions chapter). Here you can find
out about beach walks and whale
watches. The selection of books covers
everything that ever happened to Mendocino and the people who have lived here.
There are even books about the movies
that have been filmed in Mendocino.

**Cheshire Bookshop
363 North Franklin Street, Fort Bragg
(707) 964-5918**
This full-service bookstore has been operated by the same owner in Fort Bragg
since 1973. The shop is spacious,
uncrowded, and well organized.

ARTS AND CULTURE 📱

Writer Jack London, who arrived in the Sonoma Valley in the early 1900s, found a powerful muse here, writing most of the works in his oeuvre, including *The Call of the Wild*. London was neither the first—nor the last—to be inspired by this land. Robert Louis Stevenson was perhaps the earliest wordsmith to arrive, making St. Helena his temporary home in the 1880s and penning *The Silverado Squatters*.

The natural tranquillity and abundant beauty of the place has stirred the soul and inspired the imagination of numerous writers, artists, musicians, and thespians. Today, all sorts of creative types call this home. Don't be surprised to bump into blues guitarist and singer Boz Scaggs in Glen Ellen or see actor/director Robert Redford biking along Highway 29. You might encounter the gravelly voiced entertainer Tom Waits while shopping in Sebastopol, see comedy legend Tom Smothers while dining in the Valley of the Moon, or come face-to-face with former Grateful Dead percussionist Mickey Hart as you stroll through Occidental—all are local residents.

Winery tasting rooms frequently double as art galleries, and the winery courtyards and surrounding grounds often serve as theaters and concert halls. Several examples are spotlighted in this chapter.

Here is a rundown of some of the Wine Country's best arts and culture, presented in three categories: theater, music and dance, and visual arts.

ℹ️ *Every first Tuesday of the month, from 7:30 to 9:00 P.M., free open-mike poetry readings take place at Cafe Society Napa at 1000 Main Street in Napa.*

THEATER COMPANIES AND VENUES

Napa County

Dreamweavers Theatre
1637 Imola Avenue, Napa
(707) 255-5483
www.dreamweaverstheatre.org
This is Napa's only nonprofit live theater, supported by memberships, donations, and ticket sales—and completely staffed by volunteers. The troupe incorporated in 1987, and in 2000 it renovated a former nightclub in the River Park Shopping Center. There is a main theater for big productions and a "black box" area for smaller shows. Dreamweavers has traditionally staged five shows a year for four weekends each, with smaller projects filling the gaps. Recent shows have included *Bus Stop, Underneath the Lintel,* and *Biloxi Blues*. Tickets typically run $12 to $15. Dreamweavers also sponsors a young actors' theater, with performances by the kids.

Napa Valley Opera House
1030 Main Street, Napa
(707) 226-7372
www.nvoh.org
Thanks to the deep pockets of Robert Mondavi and his wife, Margrit Biever, this landmark building was completely renovated and reopened in 2002. Built in 1879 in the Italianate style, the opera house had been dark for 88 years, the victim of earthquake damage and the decline of vaudeville. There are two venues here—a 183-seat theater and a 500-seat theater. Musicals, jazz, cabaret, family shows, world music and dance, and comedy are just some of the entertainment offered. Recent shows have included stagings of the *Vagina Monologues, Love & Taxes,*

Pirates of Penzance, and the brilliance of Lily Tomlin. Tickets are reasonable—from $15 to $45. Allow yourself extra time for parking; two city garages are close by.

Napa Valley College Theater
2277 Napa-Vallejo Highway, Napa
(707) 253-3200
www.napavalley.edu
The drama students of Napa Valley College stage several events at their campus theater during the academic year, August through May. Some examples of recent undertakings are *Amadeus, The Snow Queen, Oklahoma, De Donde, Noises Off,* and *Equus.*

Prices range from $5.00 to $12.00; ask about student and senior discounts. See the Music and Dance section for more NVC productions.

Tucker Farm Center
1201 Tucker Road, Calistoga
(707) 942-9695
Nobody is trying to be facetious here. It really is a theater, but for most of its existence it has served as a working support center for local farmers. The stage company, mostly Calistogans, performs original works in the summer, fun musicals and comedies in the spring and fall. The theater building, which doubles as a meeting hall or whatever else the growers need it for, holds about 120 patrons for most performances. Admission is $10 to $20. The center is off Highway 29, just north of Bothe-Napa Valley State Park.

Sonoma County

Andrews Hall
276 East Napa Street, Sonoma
(707) 938-4626
A classic brick structure, Andrews Hall is a leftover from 1916, when it was the Sonoma Grammar School. More recently it achieved modest national exposure when it was selected as one of the settings for the hit movie *Scream.* It's a small theater that's now part of the Sonoma Community Center and will seat up to 299—it takes on no airs for being grand. There's a friendly hometown atmosphere about it, and it offers a surprisingly diverse assortment of talent, with five major performances staged each winter season using mainly local actors.

The stage is small, so plays generally run to those requiring few actors and uncomplicated sets such as *Mame, A Child's Christmas in Wales,* and murder mysteries. December usually brings a Christmas-themed production. Occasional musical evenings bring the internationally recognized Brass Works of San Francisco or a performance by the Baguette Quartet. The intimate, 50-seat Black Box Theater behind Andrews Hall stages one-act plays, sometimes written by local authors. Admission is set at $10 to $12 per event at Andrews Hall, or a season of five performances is $60.

Avalon Players
Various locations
(707) 996-3264
www.sonomashakespeare.com
This group has been performing Shakespeare's plays since 1980 and has become something of a tradition among theater lovers. A lighthearted spirit of fun prevails, and people come from Los Angeles and San Francisco—there are even some regulars from as far away as Texas—to watch the Avalon group perform. Whole families attend, kids and grandparents included. This is "Shakespeare with a twist"—the audience can expect an occasional actor to leave the stage and carry on the performance amidst the viewers. In 2004 the group performed *Twelfth Night* at Gundlach-Bundschu Winery and *The Taming of the Shrew* at Bartholomew Park Winery.

Seating is at picnic tables and is on a first-come, first-served basis. It has become the custom among those who come often to bring some fanciful picnic fare and elaborate table settings. Tickets are priced $5.00 to $20.00, depending on the show and the venue.

Now Starring in a Theater Near You: Wine Country

Ever since Alfred Hitchcock put sleepy Santa Rosa on the map in 1942, when he came to town to make his classic thriller *Shadow of a Doubt,* Hollywood moviemakers have returned again and again to Wine Country to capture its rural charms and natural beauty on film.

The list of movies partially or entirely filmed here over the past 50 years is lengthy and impressive. From simple love stories to megaprojects that lean to computer-generated imagery, nearly every genre of motion picture has fea-tured Northern California locations in a starring role.

Here's a brief list of some better-known theatrical movies of the last four-plus decades—and more recent blockbusters—in which our three-county region served as a backdrop in one way or another:
American Graffiti
The Animal
Apocalypse Now
Bandits
Basic Instinct

Sonoma State University
1801 East Cotati Avenue, Rohnert Park
(707) 644-2353
www.sonoma.edu/Depts/PerformingArts/
This university is one of 20 campuses in the California state university system (see the Relocation chapter). Performing arts get top billing at Sonoma State, with works from the pens of local playwrights and international favorites performed year-round, along with dance recitals and musi-cal concerts. The school's Everett B. Person Theatre seats 475, and it has featured such Broadway plays as *You're a Good Man Charlie Brown* and *Scapino.* A smaller the-ater seating 175 presents plays in the round, mostly student productions suitable for the more intimate stage. *Waiting for Godot* is a good example. There is also Warren Audi-torium, which is devoted to music events throughout the year, from jazz to chamber music. Meanwhile, construction on the $60 million Green Music Center was scheduled to get under way in spring 2005. Prices of tickets vary but generally run in the range of $5.00 to $25.00.

Spreckels Performing Arts Center
5409 Snyder Lane, Rohnert Park
(707) 588-3400
www.spreckelsonline.com
This is one Sonoma County building designed specifically for the arts. When the city of Rohnert Park was developed in the late 1970s, an $8 million performing arts complex of 35,000 square feet was included in the master plan.

The center houses two theaters designed and built exclusively for dance, music, and theatrical performances. The Nellie W. Codding Theatre seats 511 patrons and offers performances from

Beverly Hillbillies
The Birds
Black Rain
The Candidate
Cheaper by the Dozen (2003 version)
Cujo
Die Hard 2
Flatliners
The Goonies
Grand Avenue (HBO)
The Horse Whisperer
I Know What You Did Last Summer
Inventing the Abbotts
It's a Mad Mad Mad Mad World
Lolita
Mumford
Peggy Sue Got Married

Phenomenon
Pollyanna
The Russians Are Coming, the
   Russians Are Coming
Scream
True Crime
Tucker: The Man and His Dream
A Walk in the Clouds

In addition to full-length feature films, many made-for-TV movies and TV commercials are shot here. Particularly popular is the Sonoma County coastline—its ultragreen hills, rocky cliffs, and switchbacked highway make a snazzy setting for car commercials.

nationally known arts groups. The innovative Bette Condiotti Experimental Theatre seats 175 and presents more unusual and creative programming. Main Stage ticket prices usually run $11 to $22.

6th Street Playhouse
52 West Sixth Street, Railroad Square, Santa Rosa
(707) 523–4185
www.6thstreetplayhouse.com
Take two theater companies, add a million dollars and an old building, and you get the newest theatrical venue in Sonoma County—the 6th Street Playhouse. After moving from venue to venue for more than 20 years, two longtime acting troupes now have a permanent home to showcase their talents. The Santa Rosa Players and Actors Theatre teamed up in 2004 to renovate a former cannery building more than 100

years old in Santa Rosa's historic Railroad Square, where they will collaborate and present semiprofessional and community theater productions. One month it might be the Actors Theatre mounting a staging of Stones in His Pockets or other experimental shows; the next month it could be a rousing production of such classic musicals as Mame or Guys and Dolls. Ticket prices were still being determined as this book went to press.

Luther Burbank Center for the Arts
50 Mark West Springs Road, Santa Rosa
(707) 546–3600
www.lbc.net
This elegant center became a reality in 1981 when the Christian Life Center, a religious organization, was forced to sell the property as part of its bankruptcy proceedings. The Luther Burbank Foundation

moved in and reopened it as a regional arts hub. It's still going strong, with concerts and cultural events of all kinds.

Multilayered chandeliers light up the expansive 6,000-square-foot lobby, which is matched by the huge 1,500-seat main theater. Expect the finest in ballets, choral performances, symphonies, films, operas, and concerts of all kinds in this inviting setting. Tickets run from $15 to $100, depending on the event.

Santa Rosa Junior College Summer Repertory Theatre
1501 Mendocino Avenue, Santa Rosa
(707) 527-4343
www.santarosa.edu/srt
With more than 30 seasons under its belt, the SRT is a longtime local favorite. Running from mid-June into early August, plays rotate throughout the season and include musicals, dramas, and comedies. The lineup for the 2005 season included *Agnes of God, The Full Monty,* and *The Man Who Came to Dinner.* Performances are held variously at the college, Luther Burbank Center for the Arts (see previous listing), or local high schools. This is a professional training program geared to actors in graduate school, all of whom come on scholarships for summer work. Paid directors are well known and usually work on a rotating basis—six work each season. Ticket prices range from $8.00 to $20.00.

Sonoma County Repertory Theatre
104 North Main Street, Sebastopol
(707) 823-0177
www.the-rep.com
Once voted Sonoma County's best theater troupe, Main Street Theatre was formed in 1991, then in 1996 teamed up with a sister company to form Sonoma County Repertory Theatre. The group offers an intriguing selection of fare—the 2005 season featured *The Night of the Iguana, American Buffalo,* and *Shakespeare Abridged.*

In addition, the theater offers year-round multidisciplinary training for both children and adults, plus children's theater

and a summer Shakespeare festival. Admission prices are generally $15 to $20.

Mendocino County

Ukiah Players Theatre
1041 Low Gap Road, Ukiah
(707) 462-9226
www.ukiahplayerstheatre.org
Offering an eclectic mix, Ukiah Players Theatre stages five plays each season (October to June). In addition, the theater offers readings for original, unproduced scripts, one of them eventually selected for production. These can be tricky presentations, as the audience must become accustomed to the fact that there is no action on stage.

Ukiah Players Theatre has been producing plays since 1977, sometimes performing in rented spaces, such as an abandoned 7-Eleven. It was reborn and revitalized in the mid-1980s when members of the company set out to build their own theater. The whole community came together, with everyone donating materials to the cause, landscaping included. The present structure seats 138 but will be enlarged to seat 198. Tickets for play productions are priced at $10 to $12—season passes are $50. The staged readings are $4.00 or $5.00.

Mendocino Theatre Company
45200 Little Lake Street, Mendocino
(707) 937-4477
www.1mtc.org
The Mendocino Theatre Company has been offering high-quality theater productions for more than 25 years. The cozy 83-seat Helen Schoeni Theatre offers an intimate setting for a mix of comedies (*Picasso at the Lapin Agile*), drama (Eugene O'Neill's *A Moon for the Misbegotten*), and mainstream presentations. The 2005 season included *Diary of Anne Frank* and *One Shoe Off.* The theater adjoins the historic Mendocino Art Center (see listing under Visual Arts Organiza-

tions, Venues, and Galleries in this chapter). The company produces six plays a year with shows Thursday through Sunday nights. Tickets are $10 to $15.

Gloriana Opera Company
210 North Corry Street, Fort Bragg
(707) 964-7469
www.gloriana.org
Here's musical theater in grand style, featuring a full cast with lavish costumes, sets, and choreography. This group has been creating melodious magic since 1977, performing musical theater from *The Mikado* to *Fiddler on the Roof* to *Annie Get Your Gun.* The company's new theater seats 150. The season is year-round, with performances Thursday through Sunday at 8:00 P.M. Tickets are priced at $18 to $20.

Looking at theater from a different angle, Gloriana also has experimented with a series called Showcase Performances, designed to combine the highest values of musical theater with an elegant simplicity of production style, minimal sets, and simple costuming. Children's programs and workshops offer kids opportunities to express themselves in a creative environment through the skills and techniques of musical theater. For kids fourth grade and up, there are workshops in acting, singing, dancing, and makeup.

MUSIC AND DANCE ORGANIZATIONS AND VENUES

Napa County

Jarvis Conservatory
1711 Main Street, Napa
(707) 255-5445
www.jarvisconservatory.com
The Jarvis Conservatory was founded in 1973 as a nonprofit generator of scholarships for students of the performing arts. The corporation took a great leap in 1994 when it acquired its own educational facilities. And what facilities they are, centered around the Lisbon Winery, a registered historic landmark built in 1882. Performances are in a 221-seat theater in the acoustically superb, expensively equipped, stone winery building. The conservatory's offerings feature a mix of students and visiting professionals. The first Saturday of each month is opera night, and the specialty of the house is zarzuela, a splendidly costumed, melodramatic form of Spanish opera. Admission for shows can range from $10 and $30.

Napa Valley Symphony
2407 California Boulevard, Napa
(707) 22-MUSIC
www.napavalleysymphony.org
The symphony, conducted by Asher Raboy, plays with an assurance and aptitude you might not expect to find in a city of 76,000. Its primary venue is the newly refurbished Lincoln Theater at the Veterans Home of California. The Napa Valley Symphony has tackled Beethoven, Tchaikovsky, and Mahler; Baroque chamber music; and jazzy compositions by Artie Shaw. It has welcomed guests such as pianist Ursula Oppens, clarinetist Todd Palmer, and violinist Amy Oshiro. Tickets are generally from $20 to $50; series prices range from $115 to $250 for adults.

Napa Valley College Theater
2277 Napa-Vallejo Highway, Napa
(707) 253-3200
www.napavalley.edu
The college's esteemed music program puts on a variety of performances, such as orchestra and vocal recitals, even cabaret nights, during the August-through-May academic year. The theater also has lured independent groups, such as the North Bay Philharmonic Orchestra, the North Bay Wind Ensemble, and the Billy Browning Jazz Orchestra. Occasionally events are staged off campus, usually at wineries. Prices range from $5.00 to $10.00. Ask about senior and student discounts.

Chamber Music in Napa Valley
Napa Valley Opera House, 1030 Main
Street, Napa
(707) 963-1391
www.chambermusicnapa.org
This group brings the soothing sounds of
chamber music to Wine Country. Artists
performing in 2005 included the Tokyo
String Quartet, Prazak String Quartet,
pianist Garrick Ohlsson, and baritone Russell Braun. Tickets are sold by subscription
only (six concerts cost $120), but some
tickets are available for $10 on a first-
come, first-served basis the night of the
performance.

Paulin Hall Auditorium
Pacific Union College, Angwin
(707) 965-6201, (800) 862-7080
www.puc.edu
The forested heights of Howell Mountain
might be an unlikely spot for the sweet
melodies of classical music, but Pacific
Union College (PUC) is able to attract
frontline talent to Paulin Hall. Recent performers have included soprano Marnie
Breckenridge, Romanian-born pianist
Eduard Stan, and Troika Balalaikas, an
American trio that dresses in traditional
costume and plays the folk songs of
czarist Russia. The Fine Arts series usually
runs from October to April. The cost is
$5.00 for adults and $3.00 for children
per show, or pay $20.00 and $9.00,
respectively, for five programs.

Sonoma County

Sonoma Valley Chorale
Veterans Memorial Building, 126 First
Street W., Sonoma
(707) 935-1576
www.sonomavalleychorale.org
This professional-level, 140-member chorus
has been singing together since the early
1970s. Its annual concert series brings
audiences to their feet with music that
might be classical, sacred, or Broadway.
The chorale has sung with the Napa Valley
and Santa Rosa Symphonies (see listings

in this section) and even for the opening
ceremony at a Giants baseball game.
They've made two European tours, singing
their way through France, Italy, and Great
Britain—they toured Germany in 2001.
Their regular venue is the Veterans Memorial Building auditorium, which has tiered
theater seating for 400. Tickets are $18 for
adults and $14 for seniors and children.

Cinnabar Performing Arts Theater
3333 Petaluma Boulevard N., Petaluma
(707) 763-8920
www.cinnabartheater.org
In the summer of 1970, Marvin Klebe
abandoned his career singing baritone
with the San Francisco Opera Company,
bought a 60-year-old, two-room schoolhouse surrounded by dairy cows and
chickens on the outskirts of Petaluma, and
began transforming the structure into a
theater. Disenchanted with the usual regi-
mentation of grand opera, Marvin's goal
was to provide a stage for experimental
works that would involve the local community.

Today Cinnabar Theater features an
outstanding array of entertainers, performing everything from Bach to rock.
Candlelight concerts give a rare and
romantic opportunity to hear chamber
music the way some of our ancestors did.
Concerts are held not only at Cinnabar
Theater, but also in some of Petaluma's
loveliest gardens and mansions, intimate
art galleries, and in the downtown Polly
Klaas Theater (a school for young acting
hopefuls). The Summer Music Festival
presents the best in classical music, ethnic
music, musical comedy, opera, and children's music. Performance tickets are
$9.00 to $22.00.

Santa Rosa Symphony
50 Santa Rosa Avenue, Suite 410,
Santa Rosa
(707) 546-8742
www.santarosasymphony.com
The Santa Rosa Symphony was founded by
George Trombley in 1927. Thirty-two eager
(and some talented) amateur musicians

played for the first time at the local Elks Club. It is said that Mr. T (as his players called him) was fond of spirited selections. Under his direction the orchestra played Dvorak's *Slavonic Dance* at most concerts. These performances were enlivened by the gusto of Mr. T, who stomped his foot on the podium until the dust flew. Trombley's tenure lasted 30 years, when Maestro Corrick Brown took over the baton and held it for another 37 years.

The orchestra has long since left the Elks Club and now makes its home at the Luther Burbank Center for the Arts (see listing under Theater Companies and Venues in this chapter). The concert season consists of seven three-day events plus a pops concert and picnic in June (table seating and lawn seating are available), a Redwoods Music Festival in August, and other special events in August and September. There is also a Symphony Youth Orchestra, providing two free concerts for children (particularly popular with kindergarten through third-grade students). Adult ticket prices range between $17 and $30.

Mendocino County

Mendocino Ballet
209 South State Street, Ukiah
(707) 463-2290
www.mendocinoballet.org
This regional dance company offers students the opportunity to demonstrate their talents in local dance productions. The ballet has been offering classical and contemporary works by local and guest choreographers, and it features regular performances of *Peter and the Wolf, The Dream of Sleeping Beauty, Sweet Coppelia*, and the *Nutcracker.* The company also presents lecture demonstrations in schools throughout Lake and Mendocino Counties, offering an educational arts experience to thousands of children.

In Napa Valley, you're never too young to begin an appreciation of classical music. Every year, the Napa Valley Symphony performs concerts for first-, third-, and fifth-grade students in Napa Valley, free of charge to the schools.

VISUAL ARTS ORGANIZATIONS, VENUES, AND GALLERIES

To make it easier for you to skip from one gallery to the next one you will encounter, listings in this section are presented in the intracounty geographical sequence outlined in the How to Use This Book chapter.

Napa County

di Rosa Preserve
5200 Highway 121/12, Napa
(707) 226-5991
www.dirosapreserve.org
The subtitle of this collection is Art & Nature, and indeed many of the pieces are blended into the scenery of Carneros, that cool-climate grape-growing region on the north side of San Pablo Bay (see the Wineries chapter). Rene and Veronica di Rosa have been gathering artwork for more than 30 years, and their current display tends to the whimsical, even outrageous. All of it was produced in the Bay Area in the latter part of the 20th century. The indoor space includes a circa-1886 winery the di Rosas converted into their home plus some contemporary galleries full of works of various media. Ticket prices range from $12 to $15. The preserve offers two tours a day—9:25 A.M. and 12:55 P.M.—Tuesday through Friday from October through May, and Monday through Thursday from June through September. There are also Saturday morning tours at 9:25 and 10:25.

Jessel Miller Gallery
1019 Atlas Peak Road, Napa
(707) 257-2350, (888) 702-6323
www.jesselgallery.com

On the road to Silverado Country Club, in a stately, vine-covered, white-brick building, is the studio of esteemed watercolorist Jessel Miller. The gallery shows the work of both emerging and established artists, in media from oil to collage to jewelry. It also offers public tours, lectures, and demonstrations. The gallery is open 10:00 A.M. to 5:00 P.M. daily.

Henry Joseph Gallery
2475 Solano Avenue, Napa
(707) 224-4356

This gallery is devoted to the California style—that spontaneous, impressionistic form spawned by a group of Californians in the 1930s. Painters such as Charles Surrendorf, Jade Fon, and Justin Faivre made the California style easily distinguishable from traditional English watercolor. The gallery also represents prominent Napa Valley artists like Roger Blum, Bill King, and Jay Golik. If you pop for an original, you can have it framed at the affiliated Napa Frame Studio. Hours of operation are 10:00 A.M. to 5:30 P.M. Tuesday through Friday and 10:00 A.M. to 3:00 P.M. Saturday.

Napa Valley Art Association
1520 Behrens Street, Napa
(707) 255-9616

The Napa Valley Art Association was formed as a nonprofit corporation in 1953 to provide local artists with satisfactory facilities. At the association's once-a-month meetings (usually on the fourth Monday), guest artists demonstrate their skills and ideas. Those demonstrations are often videotaped for future observation. You can pay a $24.00 annual fee for membership or surrender a nominal $2.00 charge to attend a single meeting. The association hosts occasional shows of its members' work—everything from still lifes to portraits and landscapes to abstracts, in all sorts of media. Call the association for more information.

The Hess Collection Winery
4411 Redwood Road, Napa
(707) 255-1144, (877) 707-HESS
www.hesscollection.com

Donald Hess, the Swiss businessman who made his millions bottling water before he turned to wine, is a passionate art collector, and some of the best of his collection is here in Napa Valley. His three-story, 13,000-square-foot gallery is part of the winery and just as much of a draw to visitors. Hess collects only works by contemporary artists, and the list is impressive: Francis Bacon, Frank Stella, Henri Machaux, and Theodoros Stamos, to name a few. Some of the outstanding conceptual pieces include a group of oversize headless figures fashioned by Polish artist Magdalena Abakanowicz and a vintage Underwood typewriter going up in flames, a work by Argentinian Leopoldo Maler. There is no charge to enter the museum, which is open 10:00 A.M. to 4:00 P.M. daily.

Images Fine Art
North: 6540 Washington Street, Yountville
(707) 944-0404

South: 6505 Washington Street, Yountville
(707) 944-0606
www.imagesnapavalley.com

North and south have never been closer than at these twin galleries in downtown Yountville. The northern room came first; the southern was added in 1996. Neither has a specialty, just best-selling artists represented in a dramatic, two-story space with vaulted ceilings. Contributors include David Dodsworth, Guy Buffet, Roy Fairchild, and Pradzynski. Both galleries are open daily 10:00 A.M. to 5:00 P.M.

RAKU Ceramics Collection
Beard Plaza, 6540 Washington Street, Yountville
(707) 944-9424

Raku, the process originally used to make bowls for tea ceremony in medieval Japan, involves using tongs to remove red-hot pots from the kiln, then cooling the ceramics quickly in the air or in water. Most of what you see here gets an additional copper-flashing technique. The pots, sprayed with copper, are covered with a pail after firing. When the pot is removed, the copper oxidizes and flashes in a rainbow of colors. RAKU has work by more than 75 ceramists, including Greg Milne, Ed Risak, and Tom and Nancy Giusti. Open daily 10:00 A.M. to 5:00 P.M.

Mumm Napa Valley
8445 Silverado Trail, Rutherford
(707) 967-7700, (800) 686-6272
www.mummnapavalley.com

This winery is probably the Napa Valley's premier venue for photography. Luminaries such as Imogen Cunningham, Galen Rowell, Sebastio Salgado, and William Neill have been represented on the walls. But the rotating exhibitions have a hard time diverting attention from the winery's one permanent collection: "The Story of a Winery" by Ansel Adams. The legendary Californian was hired in 1959 to document construction of new wine cellars, care of the vineyards, and the process of wine making from vine to bottle. There is no admission charge to the galleries, which are open from 10:00 A.M. to 5:00 P.M. daily.

I. Wolk Gallery
180 Rutherford Hill Road, Rutherford
(707) 963-9922

1354 Main Street, St. Helena
(707) 963-8800
www.iwolkgallery.com

These galleries are known for their tasteful art presented in lovely, immaculate spaces. Expect everything from paintings and works on paper to photography and sculpture. The galleries are open 10:00 A.M. to 5:30 P.M. Wednesday through Monday.

Art on Main
1359 Main Street, St. Helena
(707) 963-3350
www.imagesnapavalley.com

As one of St. Helena's most prominent and centrally located spaces, Art on Main focuses on, but is not limited to, images of

vineyards and wine. It's primarily a venue for Northern California artists and traditional styles. An example is Gail Packer's extensive series of multiplate etchings, with frames designed by artist Hildy Henry. Other contributors include Garberville's Josh Adam and Hopland's Ray Voisard. Open daily 10:00 A.M. to 5:00 P.M.

Artists of the Valley
3111 St. Helena Highway N., St. Helena
(707) 967-0229

Located in the St. Helena Premium Outlets, this new gallery spotlights the work of more than 40 local artists. The multimedia on display includes etched glass, acrylic on canvas, watercolor, sculpture, jewelry, photography, stained glass, murals, and even the written word. The gallery is open 10:00 A.M. to 6:00 P.M. Thursday through Monday.

Rasmussen Art Gallery
Pacific Union College, Angwin
(707) 965-6311, (800) 862-7080
www.puc.edu

Pacific Union College's stylish art gallery is largely a showplace for its own students, faculty, and alumni. It isn't limited to these groups, though. Other recent exhibitions have included the drawings of Samuel Fleming Lewis and the experimental photography of Cliff Rusch. Admission is free, and the gallery is open 1:00 to 5:00 P.M. on Tuesday, Thursday, Saturday, and Sunday.

Clos Pegase Winery
1060 Dunaweal Lane, Calistoga
(707) 942-4981, (800) 366-8583
www.clospegase.com

Art is everywhere at Clos Pegase, from the winery itself—something of a huge modern sculpture—to French and Italian carvings of Bacchus tucked into the wine caves. The variety is impressive too, from granite sculptures to watercolors and collages. Clos Pegase offers a self-guided walking tour of the premises, as well as guided tours of the facility and wine caves at 11:00 A.M. and 2:00 P.M. (no reservation required). Among the pieces are a giant bronze thumb by Cesar Baldachini (designer of the "Cesar," the French equivalent of the Oscar); Michael Scranton's *Wrecking Ball,* an enervating installation in the Reserve Room; and a Henry Moore sculpture (*Mother Earth*) in the portico. In addition, a wine-in-art slide presentation, created by proprietor Jan Shrem, is given inside the caves at 2:00 P.M. on the third Saturday of each month (December and January excluded). The show is free.

The first Friday of every month, Fort Bragg's downtown galleries and businesses open their doors with public receptions for visiting artists.

Ca'Toga Galleria D'Arte
1206 Cedar Street, Calistoga
(707) 942–3900
www.catoga.com
Escape into a world of Renaissance, baroque, and neoclassic styles of painting in Carlo Marchiori's fabulous gallery off Lincoln Avenue. You may recognize his work—he has been commissioned to produce murals found in the world's finest hotels and attractions, including San Francisco's Westin St. Francis and Tokyo's DisneySea. He also lives in Calistoga, and his Villa Ca'-Toga outside of town is open for weekly tours in summer (see the Attractions chapter). The gallery is open 11:00 A.M. to 6:00 P.M. Thursday through Monday.

Lee Youngman Galleries
1316 Lincoln Avenue, Calistoga
(707) 942–0585, (800) 551–0585
www.leeyoungmangalleries.com
Owner Lee Love Youngman has long been surrounded by creative men. Her father, Ralph Love, was a painter from the early California school who has work hung in major museums. And her husband, Paul Youngman, is noted for his contemporary landscapes, architectural renderings, and marines. Lee's gallery has a decidedly

Southwest bent. It represents more than 60 full-time artists, including big shots such as Neil Boyle and Mark Geller. The gallery is open 10:00 A.M. to 5:00 P.M. Monday through Saturday and 11:00 A.M. to 4:00 P.M. Sunday.

Sonoma County

Cornerstone Festival of Gardens
23570 Arnold Drive (Highway 121), Sonoma
(707) 933–3010
www.cornerstonegardens.com
Art goes outdoors at this unique marriage of sculpture and landscaped gardens. The nearly 10-acre site mixes contemporary artwork with nature, such as *The Blue Tree* by Claude Cormier—a real tree completely covered in blue plastic balls. There's also a maze of screen doors surrounded by hay bales, and the Daisy Border, a field of more than 300 common garden pinwheel daisies creating a blur of color on windy days. You've got to see it all to believe it. The outdoor gallery is located across the highway from Gloria Ferrer Champagne Caves. Admission is $9.00 for adults, $7.50 for seniors, $6.50 for students, and $4.00 for children. Open daily 10:00 A.M. to 5:00 P.M. (on Monday hours are noon to 4:00 P.M.).

Sonoma Valley Museum of Art
551 Broadway, Sonoma
(707) 939–7862
www.svma.org
A town that should have had an art museum years ago finally has one. Located in a former furniture store, the museum has already staged more than 30 exhibits in its short life. The first major show was an exhibition of 90 Latin American drawings and paintings by 30 renowned artists. There has also been a display of pottery, textiles, wood, and toys on loan from the Mexican Museum of Art in San Francisco. The museum is open 11:00 A.M. to 5:00 P.M. Wednesday through

Sunday. Admission is $5.00 per person or $8.00 for families; come on Sunday and it's free for everyone.

Spirits in Stone
452 First Street E., Sonoma
(707) 938-2200

401 Healdsburg Avenue, Healdsburg
(707) 723-1723
www.spiritsinstone.com
"Must touch to appreciate" is the byword when visiting this collection of Zimbabwe Shona sculpture. The form's sleek surface is beyond description. *Newsweek* has called Shona sculpture "the most important new art form to emerge from Africa this century." You can also find African photographs, paintings, and music at these museum-quality galleries, which are open daily 10:00 A.M. to 6:00 P.M.

Sonoma State University Art Gallery
1801 East Cotati Avenue, Rohnert Park
(707) 664-2295
www.sonoma.edu/ArtGallery
Changing exhibits of contemporary art are combined with works by artists known regionally, nationally, and internationally. The gallery is open Tuesday through Friday 11:00 A.M. to 4:00 P.M. and noon to 4:00 P.M. on weekends. Admission is free.

Cultural Arts Council of Sonoma County
529 Fifth Street, Santa Rosa
(707) 579-2787
www.cacsc.org
Curating new exhibits every eight weeks, the council serves as a resource center for artists and provides a gallery for their work. A typical art competition commissioned by the Sonoma Land Trust challenged artists to portray imagery inspired by Sonoma County's agricultural environment. It's not just two-dimensional art. For several years the council has sponsored a gospel music concert, sharing a unique American art form in performances at Santa Rosa High School.

Museum of Contemporary Art
Luther Burbank Center for the Arts,
50 Mark West Springs Road, Santa Rosa
(707) 527-0297
www.lbc.net
The only fine arts museum serving the Northern California coast and northern San Francisco Bay Area, MOCA features local artists whose work transcends conventional painting, sculpture, photography, and architecture. An interactive salon is held on occasional Friday evenings throughout the year. These feature guest speakers from all walks of the artistic community. In summer months visitors can enjoy the outdoor Film Cafe, which pairs short experimental films with excellent local food and wine. Museum hours are Monday through Friday 10:00 A.M. to 4:00 P.M. (to 8:00 P.M. on Thursday), and Saturday and Sunday 11:00 A.M. to 4:00 P.M.

The Ren Brown Collection
1781 Highway 1, Bodega Bay
(707) 875-2922, (800) 585-2921
www.renbrown.com
Housed in a building with shoji screens and a small Japanese garden, this gallery is dedicated to showing contemporary art from both sides of the Pacific. The major focus is on modern Japanese prints by artists such as Shigeki Kuroda, Toko Shinoda, and Ryohei Tanaka, whose works often appear in prominent museums. The items shown at Ren Brown represent the largest selections of contemporary Japanese prints in California. Also featured are the works of several regional California artists. You'll see watercolor; sculpture in stone and bronze; acrylic paintings; as well as woodcut, silk screen, mezzotint, and lithograph art. All in all, some 75 artists are represented on two floors of the gallery, which is open 10:00 A.M. to 5:00 P.M. Wednesday through Sunday.

Christopher Queen Galleries
John Orr's Garden, No. 4, Duncans Mills
(707) 865-1318
www.christopherqueen.com

From January through May, on the third Saturday of the month, professional stand-up comics perform live at the Ukiah Valley Conference Center at 200 South School Street in Ukiah. Doors open at 7:00 P.M. Call (707) 463-6729 for details.

On Highway 116 in historic Duncans Mills, this gallery features nationally known wildlife artists, including Thomas Brenders, John Bateman, and Thomas Quinn. Serigraphs by John Powell and Don Hatfield also are on display. The Upstairs Salon features an extensive display of important early California artists. The galleries are open every day but Tuesday from 11:00 A.M. to 5:00 P.M., and by appointment.

Sea Ranch Lodge
60 Sea Walk Drive, Sea Ranch
(707) 785-2371
www.searanchlodge.com
Various artists and photographers display their work in the Sea Ranch Lodge's Fireside Room overlooking the ocean. New exhibits are posted each month, introduced with a reception of wine and hors d'oeuvres. Call for a list of upcoming exhibits.

Mendocino County

Gualala Arts Center
46501 Gualala Road, Gualala
(707) 884-1138
www.gualalaarts.org
In the early 1900s Gualala was a lumbermill center, abandoned when sawmills closed down. But in the 1960s the beauty of the area attracted artists and other creative people. They painted, photographed, wrote, acted, and watched whales. They attracted other talented people, and for more than three decades Gualala has

become recognized as a center for the arts, drawing people from miles around to soak up the cultural atmosphere.

The focal point of all this art activity is a 15,000-square-foot arts center, established in 1997 and set in the forest. The scope of the center's activities is quite varied. You'll find popular and classical music concerts, lectures, exhibits, youth and adult art classes, theater productions, and meeting space for artists, photographers, quilters, poets, weavers, and book groups.

The mid-August Art in the Redwoods extravaganza (see the Festivals and Annual Events chapter) attracts more than 350 artistic entries, and approximately 5,000 people attend each year.

Alinder Gallery
39150 South Highway 1, Gualala
(707) 884-4884
www.alindergallery.com
Internationally respected authorities Mary and Jim Alinder manage this gallery. While specializing in original Ansel Adams images, the gallery maintains an excellent inventory of work by many other great photographers. Alinder Gallery is open 10:00 A.M. to 6:00 P.M. Tuesday through Sunday.

Mendocino Art Center
45200 Little Lake Street, Mendocino
(707) 937-5818, (800) 653-3328
www.mendocinoartcenter.org
This is an educational organization that features classes in everything from furniture making to bead artistry. Year-round courses in fine arts, ceramics, and children's art, conducted by paid artists-in-residence, draw students from around the country. A spacious gallery at the center features the work of established and emerging artists of local, regional, and national reputation. An additional showcase gallery is at 560 Main Street, open daily 10:00 A.M. to 5:00 P.M. in spring and summer, 10:00 A.M. to 4:00 P.M. in winter.

Northcoast Artists Gallery
362 North Main Street, Fort Bragg
(707) 964-8266
www.northcoastartists.org
This is a cooperative gallery with 22 artists showing their work. Started in 1986 with nine artists, it's now like a family, with several members of the original group still involved. Others come and go. Artists in oil paintings, ceramics, woodwork, and producers of silk screens and fine paper products are featured. The gallery is open daily 10:00 A.M. to 6:00 P.M.

PARKS AND RECREATION

As if world-class restaurants and a galaxy of wineries were not enough to lure visitors, Wine Country also offers a phenomenal outdoor environment. From majestic inland mountains to the crashing waves of an unspoiled and awe-inspiring coastline, you won't find a better place to breathe in fresh air while getting a little exercise. If you're itching to hike, bike, or otherwise become one with nature, this chapter will point you in the right direction.

Featured first are the primary parks and recreation areas in the region, followed by separate sections on golf, bicycling, bowling, horseback riding, swimming, and tennis. There is no individual section on hiking, as almost all of the parks offer trails. While campgrounds and primitive camping sites are mentioned in these listings, more specific information may be found in the Camping chapter. If you break out in a rash at the sight of Winnebagos, don't fret. There is plenty of recreational activity that goes beyond hiking and camping in the parks. If you run out of things to do, turn to the On the Water chapter and read about a whole different order of activities.

PARKS

Like the statewide system as a whole, the California state parks within the Wine Country offer an almost inconceivable diversity of ecosystems. While visitors to Mackerricher State Park are turning up their collars and waiting for the dense coastal fog to lift on a summer morning, folks are already in the water at Clear Lake State Park. See the grasslands of Austin Creek one day and the redwood canopy of Admiral William Standley the next, and try to convince yourself you're on the same planet. And that doesn't even address the historic parks, which are listed in the Attractions chapter.

Included in this section, along with the state lands, are major regional parks and recreation areas that offer more than a lawn and a playground. You're never far from one of them. (You're probably even closer to a municipal park—consult a local map or ask around.) Deciding where to go might depend on when you'll be there. Only the inland, northern entries, such as Mendocino National Forest, are likely to be affected by winter snow. But all the parks have a chance of being wet and dreary between November and February, while spring and autumn are always safe bets. Summer takes more thought. The coastal parks and state beaches are wonderful retreats from the heat, but some of the valley parks will put you right into the oven.

Unless otherwise stated, parks are open year-round and 24 hours a day. Most regional parks have no admission charge. Pets are welcome in campgrounds and picnic areas but usually not on trails or beaches.

With millions of jittery city folks visiting California's parks each year, the campgrounds are often filled to the brim, especially between Memorial Day and Labor Day. You can make reservations up to seven months in advance by phoning ReserveAmerica (see the number listed in the box in this chapter). All major credit cards are accepted.

In Sonoma County, several regional parks with camping facilities take reservations. Because the nearly 200 campsites at the county's four coastal campgrounds are occupied by more than 100,000 people each year, reservations are a must. You can call (707) 565–CAMP (2267) to reserve a camping spot at these Sonoma County regional parks: Gualala Point, Stillwater Cove, Doran, and Spring Lake. (All are profiled in this chapter and in the Camping chapter.)

Napa County

Bothe–Napa Valley State Park
Highway 29, 4 miles south of Calistoga
(707) 942–4575
www.parks.ca.gov/default.asp?page_id= 477
A trail of cars crawls along Highway 29, but you can leave it behind by exploring this 1,900-acre retreat. Follow shady Ritchey Creek with its redwoods and maples, then venture deeper into terrain covered by oak, hazel, laurel, and madrone. From Coyote Peak you can gaze east into a rugged canyon—not a vineyard in sight. And in summer you can enjoy the cool, spring-fed swimming pool in the picnic area. There is a campground (see the Camping chapter) and a horse concession with guided rides. Bothe is just off Highway 29, between Calistoga and St. Helena. Parallel to the highway runs a 1.02-mile trail that connects Bothe with the Bale Grist Mill State Historic Park.

Robert Louis Stevenson State Park
Highway 29 between Calistoga and Middletown
(707) 942–4575
www.parks.ca.gov/default.asp?page_id= 472
Between Calistoga and Middletown, at the crest of Highway 29, is Stevenson State Park. Less than a mile from the trailhead rests a memorial to the noted author, who in 1880 spent his honeymoon squatting here and weathering a long illness. (His experience wound up as the basis for *The Silverado Squatters;* see the History chapter.) A steep 100 yards from the memorial, you will encounter a fire road/trail that

winds 5 miles to the top of Mount St. Helena, offering brilliant views throughout. If you spin in a circle at the 4,343-foot summit, you'll probably be able to see the snowcapped Sierra Nevada Mountains to the east, the shining Pacific Ocean to the west, Mount Diablo to the south, and, on good days, Mount Shasta 192 miles to the north. The trail is highly exposed, so bring plenty of water and sunblock. The picnic area near the highway is lovely, although a bit noisy. Be advised there are no restrooms and parking is limited, but the vistas at the top are usually worth the trouble.

Sonoma County

SOUTHERN SONOMA

Sonoma Valley Regional Park
13630 Highway 12, Glen Ellen
(707) 565–2041
www.sonoma-county.org
A 162-acre spread just outside Glen Ellen, Sonoma Valley has a paved, 2-mile bicycle trail and about 5 miles of hiking trails through meadows and oak-dense terrain, plus a picnic area. Just across the highway is Bouverie Wildflower Preserve. Open daily from sunup to sundown. Dogs must be leashed. Parking is $4.00.

Sugarloaf Ridge State Park
Adobe Canyon Road, 11 miles north of Sonoma on Highway 12
(707) 833–5712
www.parks.sonoma.net/sugarlf.html, www.parks.ca.gov/default.asp?page_id= 481
Standing at the summit of Bald Mountain, you don't have to choose between Sonoma and Napa Valleys—you can see them both at the same time. It's a startling view that is aided by identifying signs. And speaking of distant vistas, Sugarloaf recently added an observatory with the most powerful publicly accessible telescope in the state. The park as a whole is rugged and steep, an adventurous contrast to the gentle valleys below. Look for

deer, gray fox, and even bobcat and mountain lion. The chaparral can get hot in the summer, but you'll be shaded (sometimes by redwoods) if you stay next to Sonoma Creek.

Because day parking is limited, the road entering Sugarloaf Ridge tends to congest with spillover traffic, so try to arrive early on weekends. The 7-mile Bald Mountain loop is the highlight of the park's numerous and well-marked trails. The park is on Adobe Canyon Road, 9 miles east of Santa Rosa or 11 miles north of Sonoma on Highway 12.

Helen Putnam Regional Park
411 Chileno Valley Road, 1 mile southwest of Petaluma
(707) 565-2041
www.sonoma-county.org
Just outside downtown Petaluma, 216-acre Helen Putnam Park has hiking, biking, and horse trails that lead to exceptional views of town and farmland. There is a playground and a picnic area with a gazebo. The park is open sunrise to sunset. From Petaluma Boulevard, go west on Western Avenue and turn left on Chileno Valley Road. Parking is $4.00. Dogs must be leashed.

Fairfield Osborn Preserve
6543 Lichau Road, east of Cotati
(707) 795-5069
www.sonoma.edu/Org/preserve
Formerly operated by the Nature Conservancy and now owned and managed by Sonoma State University, Fairfield Osborn is a jewel of a preserve that butts up against the western slope of 2,465-foot Sonoma Mountain, east of Cotati. The 210-acre holding has 6 miles of trails through oak woodlands, meadows, and riparian forest. The preserve is not open to the public on a daily basis. However, on Saturday and Sunday in the spring and fall, naturalists lead hikes at 10:00 A.M. and 1:00 P.M. No reservations are required.

The cost is $3.00 for adults; children 12 and under are free. Call for directions and exact dates.

Crane Creek Regional Park
6107 Pressley Road, east of Rohnert Park
(707) 565-2041
www.sonoma-county.org
No, Rohnert Park isn't made up entirely of Home Depots and Wal-Marts. This pleasant, 128-acre park is just east of Sonoma State University, in the foothills of Sonoma Mountain. It has a picnic area and 3 miles of trails open to people on foot, bicycles, and horses. Follow the creek past buckeye, oak, and maple. Crane Creek is on Pressley Road; take Roberts Road east from Petaluma Hill Road. The park is open sunrise to sunset. Parking is $4.00. Dogs must be leashed. Drinking water is not available in the park.

Annadel State Park
Channel Drive, southeast of Santa Rosa
(707) 539-3911
www.parks.sonoma.net/Annadel.html,
www.parks.ca.gov/default.asp?page_id=480
One minute you're in Santa Rosa—the largest city in Wine Country—and the next you're hiking in the solitude of a 5,000-acre parcel of undulating meadow and oak woodland. Within Annadel, you'll find one large natural marsh and one man-made lake, Ilsanjo, stocked with black bass and bluegill. One of the best hikes is the Warren Richardson–Ledson Marsh Loop, a 7.5-mile outing that takes you to Ledson with its bulrushes, cattails, and bird life. Primary trail junctions are marked, but you should think about carrying a park map to help you sort out the details. There are several picnic sites in the park, which is open 9:00 A.M. to sunset daily. Get there by taking Montgomery Drive to Channel Drive on the east side of Santa Rosa.

Spring Lake Regional Park
Summerfield Road, Santa Rosa
(707) 539-8092
www.sonoma-county.org
Most of this 320-acre park is consumed by the central lake, popular with boaters and swimmers in the summer and with a reputation for harboring huge bass.

Around the lake are a 2-mile bike path and a parcourse plus about 15 miles of hiking and equestrian trails. Spring Lake also has a developed campground, scads of picnic tables, and a visitor center that's open on weekends. The park is attached to the north end of Annadel State Park. The west entrance is on Newanga Avenue, off Summerfield Road in Santa Rosa; the east entrance is on Violetti Drive, off Montgomery Road.

NORTHERN SONOMA

Lake Sonoma
Stewarts Point–Skaggs Springs Road, off Dry Creek Road, west of Geyserville
(707) 433-9483
www.parks.sonoma.net/laktrls.html
Lake Sonoma's primary recreational offerings are detailed in the On the Water chapter. However, the 18,000-acre park that surrounds the lake is filled with possibilities of its own, including more than 40 miles of trails with views of the lake. The visitor center has Pomo Indian artifacts, and the California Department of Fish and Game operates a nearby fish hatchery (see the Kidstuff chapter). A self-guided nature trail begins at the center. Lake Sonoma also has a large developed campground and 15 primitive campgrounds around the lake. From Geyserville, go west on Canyon Road, turn right on Dry Creek Road, and after about 3 miles bend left onto Stewarts Point–Skaggs Springs Road.

SONOMA COAST

Doran Regional Park and Westside Regional Park
Highway 1, south and west of Bodega Bay
(707) 875-3540
www.sonoma-county.org
These two recreation areas are on the south and northwest sides, respectively, of ultraprotected Bodega Bay. The bay's water-based attractions are profiled in the On the Water chapter. But the parks feature wavy sand dunes and, at Doran, a 2-mile stretch of beach. Each park has a campground, with 47 sites at Westside and 133 at Doran (see the Camping chapter). Each is reached from Highway 1. For Doran Park, turn west at Doran Park Road; for Westside Park, turn west at Bay Flat Road. Parking is $5.00 in summer, $4.00 the rest of the year. Dogs must be leashed.

Sonoma Coast State Beach
Off Highway 1
(707) 875-3483
www.parks.sonoma.net/coast.html, www.parks.ca.gov/default.asp?page_id=451
The 100-foot bluffs, the ruinous offshore rocks and arches, the coastal scrub plateaus, the black-sand coves—it all adds up to a dramatic oceanside landscape. The park stretches 16.6 miles along the jagged coastline and offers three trails. The main attraction is Goat Rock, a large, wave-battered massif near the main parking lot. In spring the bluffs are decorated with lupine, sea pinks, and Indian paintbrush. There is whale watching from Bodega Head and a seal colony at the mouth of the Russian River. Numerous marked and unmarked roads provide access to the beaches, some of them ending in parking lots, some not. All are found off Highway 1 between Bodega Bay and the high bluffs 4.8 miles north of Jenner—the town with the visitor center. There are two campgrounds, at Bodega Dunes and Wrights Beach. There also are two environmental camps; ask for a map at the visitor center. A final word: To get in this water, you'd have to be a lunatic, a harbor seal, or a surfer in a wetsuit.

Stillwater Cove Regional Park
22455 Highway 1, approx. 15 miles north of Jenner
(707) 847-3245
www.sonoma-county.org
Even if you're not an abalone diver or a surf fisher, Stillwater Cove is a worthwhile stop. It has a picnic area and 5 miles of hiking trails amid the redwoods. It also has one developed campground with showers and flush toilets. In the park is a preserved one-room schoolhouse from the 19th cen-

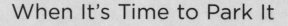

When It's Time to Park It

Here are some helpful numbers and Web sites to keep in mind when considering a visit to one of the state parks.

California State Park Information
(916) 653–6995, (800) 777–0369
www.parks.ca.gov

ReserveAmerica Camping Reservations
(800) 444–7275
www.reserveamerica.com

ReserveAmerica Customer Service/
  Cancellations
(800) 695–2269

Special Services for the Handicapped
(916) 653–8148

Caltrans Road/Weather Information
(800) 427–7623

---

tury. Day use parking is $4.00. Dogs must be leashed.

Salt Point State Park
Off Highway 1
(707) 847–3221
www.parks.sonoma.net/coast.html,
www.parks.ca.gov/default.asp?page_id=
453
Salt Point and neighboring Kruse Rhododendron State Reserve (see the following listing) have a little bit of something for everyone. Salt Point has about 10 miles of rocky coastline featuring sea stacks, arches, and tafoni—those eerily sculpted knobs, ribs, and honeycombs that look like they were crafted for horror movies. The inland portion of the 6,000-acre park has hiking trails through coastal brush, Bishop pine, and Douglas fir, not to mention a ridgetop pygmy forest with half-pint cypress, pine, and redwood. Salt Point also boasts one of California's first underwater parks, Gerstle Cove Marine Reserve, a favorite for scuba divers (and for fish, which are fully protected there). The park has two campgrounds plus walk-in campsites; see the Camping chapter. It straddles Highway 1, about 16 miles north of Jenner or 18 miles south of Gualala.

Kruse Rhododendron State Reserve
Off Highway 1 on Kruse Ranch Road
(707) 847–3221
www.parks.sonoma.net/coast.html,
www.parks.ca.gov/default.asp?page_id=
448
This 317-acre reserve near Salt Point State Park was donated in 1933 by Edward P. E. Kruse, whose family raised sheep, logged, and harvested tanbark there. From April through June the pink and violet rhododendron blossoms brighten the shady forest of fir and second-growth redwood. Five miles of hiking trails offer great opportunities to view the blooms. The reserve is off Highway 1, toward the north end of Salt Point, and is open sunup to sunset.

Gualala Point Regional Park
Off Highway 1, 1 mile south of Gualala
(707) 785–2377
www.sonoma-county.org
Located just south of the town of Gualala, the park offers both seaside and riverside environments. Anglers show up for saltwater and freshwater fishing. Hikers enjoy 6 miles of trails. Picnickers have several site options, some with barbecue pits. And campers are greeted by a developed area in the redwoods. The visitor center is

open 10:30 A.M. to 3:00 P.M. Friday through Monday. Day-use parking is $4.00. Dogs must be leashed and have proof of rabies vaccination.

WEST COUNTY/RUSSIAN RIVER

Ragle Ranch Regional Park
500 Ragle Road, 1 mile north of Bodega Highway, Sebastopol
(707) 565-2041, (707) 823-7262
www.sonoma-county.org

This 157-acre park offers the usual family-oriented facilities—baseball diamonds, playgrounds, a soccer field, a volleyball court, and picnic sites—but also claims hiking and equestrian trails through rugged oak woodlands and marshes. There is a parcourse too. Each August the park hosts the annual Gravenstein Apple Fair (see the Festivals and Annual Events chapter). The park is off Ragle Road, 1 mile north of Bodega Highway on the western perimeter of Sebastopol, and is open sunup to sunset.

Armstrong Redwoods State Reserve
Armstrong Woods Road, near Guerneville
(707) 869-2015
www.parks.sonoma.net/Armstrng.html, www.parks.ca.gov/default.asp?page_id= 450

In the 1870s lumberman Col. James Armstrong saw the errors of his clear-cutting ways and preserved a large chunk of old-growth redwood forest for posterity. Today it forms the core of 805-acre Armstrong Redwoods Reserve. Don't forget to say hello to two of the most impressive specimens in the park: the 1,400-year-old Colonel Armstrong Tree and the tallest tree in the area, the 310-foot Parson Jones Tree (named for the colonel's son-in-law). Next to the Jones Tree is a gigantic log cross section, whose growth rings chart the course of history back to the first millennium—unfortunately, the tree had been cut by vandals in the 1970s. To get to Armstrong from Guerneville, turn north off River Road onto Armstrong Woods Road

and proceed 2.2 miles. The reserve is open daily 8:00 A.M. to one hour after sunset.

Austin Creek State Recreation Area
Armstrong Woods Road, near Guerneville
(707) 869-2015
www.parks.sonoma.net/austin.html, www.parks.ca.gov/default.asp?page_id= 452

Directly adjacent to Armstrong Redwoods Reserve is 5,683-acre Austin Creek State Recreation Area. Austin Creek has 22 miles of trails that hikers must share with horses, which often come in large groups. (Mountain bikes are allowed only on paved roads and on a 5-mile dirt road called the East Austin Creek Trail.) Keep an eye open for deer, wild turkeys, raccoons, and possibly even world-famous ceramic artists. One of the latter, Marguerite Wildenhain, lived here, and her home and workshop—Pond Farm—are within the park, though off-limits since Wildenhain's death. There is a drive-in campground and four backcountry campsites within the recreation area. To get to Austin Creek, follow the directions for Armstrong Woods and, after reaching the entrance, continue another 3.6 miles to Bullfrog Pond Campground.

Mendocino County

U.S. HIGHWAY 101

Lake Mendocino Recreation Area
Lake Mendocino Drive, off US 101
(707) 462-7581
www.spn.usace.army.mil/mendocino

About as pretty as man-made lakes come, Lake Mendocino is surrounded by 1,800 acres of hills, vineyards, and pear orchards. There are 18 miles of riding trails and nearly as many of hiking trails. You can also take advantage of five day-use picnic areas and three developed campgrounds. (You can reach another 20 primitive campsites with a boat.) To get there, head east on Lake Mendocino Drive from ℹ️ *The secret is out: Now officially open to the public is a once-secret trail along the Sonoma coast. Shorttail Gulch Trail begins on Osprey Drive and winds down a shaded path to a staircase descent of approximately 200 steps.*

U.S. Highway 101, just north of Ukiah, or go south on Marina Drive from Highway 20 near Calpella. (See the On the Water chapter for more details.)

Montgomery Woods State Reserve
Orr Springs Road, north of Ukiah
(707) 937-5804
www.parks.ca.gov/default.asp?page_id=434

Montgomery Woods is an isolated sanctuary northwest of Ukiah. The 2-mile nature trail not only guides you alongside giant trees but also takes you right through them, with steps and passageways carved into toppled specimens. You'll visit five redwood groves along Montgomery Creek, including the splendid Grubbs' Memorial Grove. You can pick up a printed guide at the beginning of the trail. Montgomery Woods has one creekside picnic site and no water. It is open sunrise to sunset. From downtown Ukiah, take Orr Springs Road northwest for about 12 miles.

Admiral William Standley State Recreation Area
Branscomb Road, off US 101, 14 miles west of Laytonville
(707) 247-3318
www.parks.ca.gov/default.asp?page_id=424

Admiral Standley's namesake is small (45 acres), hard to get to, and rarely crowded. It's a beautiful piece of forest, with virgin redwoods interspersed among Douglas firs, madrone, rhododendron, and mushrooms. It is also a popular salmon and steelhead fishing spot. There are no trails, however, so don't wander far from the parking area. From US 101 in Laytonville,

turn left on Branscomb Road and drive 12 miles. The recreation area is set on either side of the road, and signs can be difficult to spot. It is open sunup to sundown.

Standish-Hickey State Recreation Area
US 101, 1 mile north of Leggett
(707) 925-6482
www.parks.ca.gov/default.asp?page_id=423

This sizable park presents your basic gigantic redwoods plus access to the south fork of the Eel River. The Big Tree Loop starts at Redwood Campground and ends near Miles Standish Tree, a 225-foot, 1,200-year-old giant that towers over its second-growth neighbors. Still visible on its side are the ax marks delivered—as the legend goes—by a 1930s evangelist who vowed to chop down the biggest tree he could find. Miles Standish lives on, while the evangelist has gone to that great lumber mill in the sky. In summer it's swimming that lures most visitors. The Eel is punctuated with deep pools formed by rock outcrops. The best is at the tail end of a wide bend, where the Big Tree Loop crosses the river. The pool is nearly 20 feet deep, with a sandy floor. There is no shade, so bring sunscreen and a hat.

Standish-Hickey has three campgrounds and a picnic area.

Smith Redwoods State Reserve
US 101, 4 miles north of Leggett
(707) 247-3318
www.parks.ca.gov/default.asp?page_id=427

Little more than a roadside attraction, this 665-acre park has no trails or picnic facilities. It does, however, give you an up-close encounter with some of the largest trees in the world. Don't be shy, big fella, give that tree a hug. You can walk through two stumps. And if you're in need of a dunk, both a 60-foot waterfall (across the highway) and the South Fork of the Eel River are close at hand. It is open sunup to sundown.

HIGHWAY 128

Mailliard Redwoods State Reserve
Fish Rock Road, off Highway 128
(707) 937-5804
www.parks.ca.gov/default.asp?page_id=
439

There isn't much here for hikers or bikers, but if you're in the area, your eyes will appreciate the detour. Mailliard has 242 acres of virgin and second-growth redwoods along the headwaters of Garcia River. You can reach the park from Highway 128, 7.3 miles east of Boonville. Turn south on Fish Rock Road and proceed about 3 miles. There is one picnic area nearly a mile into the park. Open sunrise to sunset.

Hendy Woods State Park
Philo-Greenwood Road, off Highway 128
(707) 895-3141
www.parks.ca.gov/default.asp?page_id=
438

There are campsites, a picnic area, and trails for hikers, mountain bikers, and equestrians. The Gentle Giants All-Access Trail is a surfaced path that accesses Big Hendy, Anderson Valley's last extensive grove of old-growth coastal redwoods. Another short trail leads to the hermit hut, a partially collapsed, thatched-roof lean-to that the Boonville Hermit used as his abode from the end of World War II (when he jumped his Russian ship) until he died in 1981. To get to Hendy Woods, take Highway 128 2.8 miles west of Philo and turn south on Philo–Greenwood Road.

Navarro River Redwoods
Highway 128, between Navarro and
Highway 1
(707) 937-5804
www.parks.ca.gov/default.asp?page_id=
435

Because this is America, you get to enjoy the beauty of Navarro River without leaving your rental car. The park straddles Highway 128 between Navarro and the coast, and the highway basically shadows the river. It's a shady corridor of second-growth redwoods, alders, and tan oak. There are plenty of turnouts if you want a breath of fresh air or a short stroll. In the fall you'll likely see people fishing for steelhead. The river also has one overnight campground.

MENDOCINO COAST

Schooner Gulch
Off Highway 1, 3.5 miles south of Point
Arena
(707) 937-5804
www.parks.ca.gov/default.asp?page_id=
446

This park contains two beaches, separated by a bulging headland. The north lobe is Bowling Ball Beach, named for the perfectly spherical boulders revealed at low tide. (It might be worth it to consult a tide chart before visiting.) The cliffs abutting this mile-long strand of hard-packed sand are misshapen and interesting. The south lobe is Schooner Gulch, which is rockier and preferred by fishermen. The actual gulch feeds into the sea amidst a jumble of logs. There is no drinking water in the park, so bring your own. It's open sunrise to sunset.

Manchester State Beach
Kinney Road, off Highway 1
(707) 937-5804
www.parks.ca.gov/default.asp?page_id=
437

Manchester's diverse topography encompasses rocky shore, dunes (both grassy and bald), marshes, a lagoon, and a coastal plain. It's a place where anglers, birdwatchers, and rowdy kids can find common ground. The avian wealth includes northern harriers, tundra swans, ducks, herons, and pelicans. The drift-log shelters along the 5 miles of beach attest to the relentless winds that buffet the area. There is a primitive campground and hiking trails, including the 5-mile Beach–Inland Loop. To reach Manchester from Highway 1, turn west onto Kinney Road and drive a little more than a half mile.

Greenwood Creek State Beach
Highway 1, near Elk
(707) 937-5804
www.parks.ca.gov/default.asp?page_id=
447
This park is quite small on the horizontal scale but impressive on the vertical—it encompasses both the gravelly beach and the overlooking bluff, some 150 feet above. Most of the picnic sites are up top. From the shore you can see the three rock islands that punctuate the cove and watch for the bobbing heads of harbor seals. Greenwood Creek is west of Highway 1, adjacent to the town of Elk. The visitor center is Elk's original mill office. Greenwood Creek State Beach is open sunrise to sunset.

September and October are generally the finest months for coastal activities. During this time, the cool winds usually disappear and the fog stays out to sea.

Van Damme State Park
Highway 1, 2.5 miles south of Mendocino
(707) 937-5804
www.parks.ca.gov/default.asp?page_id=
443
Don't worry, you aren't likely to be bothered by aggressive action-adventure heroes in this fascinating park. What you will get is a smorgasbord of redwoods, beach, underwater bounty, swamp, and pygmy trees. The Fern Canyon Trail is a 4.9-mile meander through a dark, cool fern forest. Separate minitrails take you to the pygmy forest, with its 4-foot pines and cypresses, and a bog. Hikers and bikers share some trails, but not all. If you get claustrophobic in the woods, take a kayak tour of the small cove accessible at the Van Damme beach parking lot.

Van Damme has both developed campgrounds and hike-in tent sites, as discussed in the Camping chapter. It has a picnic area on the beach and an undersea preserve. And don't miss the re-created surge channel at the visitor center. The park is 2.5 miles south of Mendocino on

Highway 1—turn east for the main park, west for the beach.

Mendocino Headlands State Park
Main Street, Mendocino
(707) 937-5804
www.parks.ca.gov/default.asp?page_id=
442
This is the town of Mendocino's wrap-around park on the bluffs, offering spectacular views of the sea on all sides. Spring brings wildflowers, winter ushers migrating gray whales, and summer draws sunbathers and hardy swimmers to Big River Beach, just south of the headlands. The miles of blowholes, arches, and craggy stacks are there year-round. There is a picnic area along Heeser Drive at the north end of town; in town is the Ford House Museum and Visitor Center with its fine historical displays. The Headlands Trail, 6 miles round-trip, skirts the edges of the bluffs. The park is open sunrise to sunset.

Russian Gulch State Park
Off Highway 1, 2 miles north of Mendocino
(707) 937-5804
www.parks.ca.gov/default.asp?page_id=
432
Here you have the option of walking along the coast, where waves crash like giant cymbals, or wandering through the serenity of the forest. The Headland Trail offers two sideshow oddities: a blowhole fed by a sea cave and an inland punchbowl, connected to the sea by another hidden cave. The Fern Canyon Trail, meanwhile, takes you alongside Russian Gulch to a delicate, 36-foot waterfall. It's a 6-mile round-trip stroll through alder, California laurel, redwood, and of course ferns. The park has campsites and a picnic area.

Caspar Headlands State Beach and Reserve
Point Cabrillo Drive, off Highway 1, Caspar
(707) 937-5804
www.parks.ca.gov/default.asp?page_id=
444
These twin holdings are small (less than five acres between them) and highly regu-

lated. You can visit the bluff-top reserve—with its far-reaching views—only with a permit, obtainable at the Mendocino District Office, 2 miles north of Mendocino. Get a map there too, as the reserve interlocks with a private housing development and it's easy to trespass. The beach, about a quarter mile long, opens onto a square bay. It's popular with swimmers, divers, and anglers. This is no place for the meek. Caspar Headlands has no toilets, no picnic tables, and no water. Undeterred? From Highway 1 in Caspar, turn west on Point Cabrillo Drive. The park is open sunrise to sunset.

Jug Handle State Reserve
Off Highway 1, just north of Caspar
(707) 937-5804
www.parks.ca.gov/default.asp?page_id=441
This is another coastal park that gives you surf-and-turf options. One trail roams the soaring headlands, with views of Jug Handle Bay to the north and a similar inlet to the south. Look for sea stacks and an arch. The Ecological Staircase Trail is a 5-mile, round-trip tour of three marine terraces—a geologic showcase that displays about 250,000 years of elemental activity. The first terrace is meadow-transition habitat, the second is a mixed conifer forest, and the third is a redwood–Douglas fir complex. At the end of the line, for no extra charge, is a pygmy forest. The trails are for hikers only, and visitors should bring their own water. Jug Handle is open sunup to sundown.

Jackson Demonstration State Forest
State Department of Forestry, 802 North Main Street, Fort Bragg
(707) 964-5674
www.fire.ca.gov
Sprawling between Willits and the coast in the vicinity of Highway 20, this state holding has 50,000 acres of oak, pine, and redwood, not to mention a pygmy forest. There are 25 miles of fire road and two other trails suitable as footpaths. It's a mixed bag—as state forests often are—

with some pristine areas and others that have been logged or mined.

Mackerricher State Park
West of Highway 1, 3 miles north of Fort Bragg
(707) 937-5804
www.parks.ca.gov/default.asp?page_id=436
Mackerricher is a prime slice of Northern California coast, with 8 miles of beach, large dunes, grassy headlands, and even freshwater Lake Cleone. Gray whales migrate offshore between December and March, and humans migrate to the headlands to watch them. If you're into cetacean anatomy, a 30-foot gray whale skeleton lies near the ranger station, just beyond the main entrance. The footpaths are varied. The Laguna Trail circles the lake and its marshy border. The Seal Point Trail leads to a harbor seal watching station. And the Haul Road Bicycle Route is a one-time logging road that runs the length of the park, about 7 miles. It's closed to motorized vehicles and so is popular with cyclists and runners. Of course, you can simply walk down the beach for miles if you prefer. Mackerricher has two campgrounds and several picnic areas. The main entrance is 3 miles north of Fort Bragg, just west of Highway 1. The Pudding Creek Day Area is only a half mile north of Fort Bragg.

Westport–Union Landing State Beach
Off Highway 1, just north of Westport
(707) 937-5804
www.parks.ca.gov/default.asp?page_id=440
North of the town of Westport is a series of four oceanside bluffs separated by creek canyons and interspersed with beaches. Together they form this skinny park, with its 50-foot cliffs and craggy shoreline. It's a favorite haunt for storm watchers, who can practically feel the spray from the angry waves.

Anglers come for spawning surf smelt in spring and summer. Pete's Beach and the sand below Abalone Point are fun to explore, but they don't offer much wiggle room, so watch out for sleeper waves— large, forceful waves that appear without warning. Westport–Union Landing has several access points off Highway 1, between a quarter mile and 4 miles north of Westport. It offers open, grassy camp-sites but no water.

Sinkyone Wilderness State Park
County Road 431, west of Leggett
(707) 986–7711
www.parks.ca.gov/default.asp?page_id= 429
Wonder what the Mendocino coast looked like before a certain bipedal mammal clogged up the scenery? Here's your answer. The Sinkyone Wilderness is part of the Lost Coast, a once-busy stretch of shoreline that has been isolated by its lack of contact with major roads.

There are two entrances to the park, one at the south end and another at the north. Between them lies a long expanse of unadulterated nature: forested ridges, rugged coast, black-sand beaches, and riparian ecosystem.

The Needle Rock Visitor Center is in a restored, turn-of-the-20th-century ranch house; nearby is a short trail to Needle Rock Beach. There is a drive-in camp-ground at Usal Creek (the south entrance) and walk-in sites near Bear Harbor in the north. To get to Usal Creek, follow Highway 1 west from Leggett and, 14 miles later, turn right on County Road 431 and proceed 5.5 miles. To get to Needle Rock, make your way to Redway, 2.5 miles west of Gar-berville and US 101. Turn south on Briceland Road and continue past Whitethorn; the road turns to gravel after 17 miles. Then it's 7.2 miles to the visitor center.

Mendocino National Forest
(707) 983–6118, (530) 934–3316
www.fs.fed.us/r5/mendocino
If I tried to present a detailed account of the options here, the book would be called "Insiders' Guide to Mendocino

National Forest." This is an immense, million-acre tract of mountainous terrain in the Coast Range that encompasses almost all of the upper half of Lake County and the northeast tip of Mendo-cino County, not to mention parts of Glenn, Tehama, and Trinity Counties. The forest boasts two wilderness areas (closed to motorized vehicles), 2,000-acre Lake Pillsbury, several smaller lakes, and various tributaries of the Eel River. Trails? Yes, more than 160 miles, including off-highway vehicle paths near Upper Lake and Stoneyford. Campgrounds? Ten developed sites (see the Camping chapter) and numerous primitive camps. There are many routes into the forest. Perhaps the most prominent is Elk Mountain Road, which heads north from the town of Upper Lake. About a mile north of Upper Lake is a ranger station dispensing maps and advice. Another station is on Highway 162, where the route name changes from Covelo Road to Mendocino Pass Road (about 2 miles north of Covelo in Mendo-cino County). There is no charge for day use of the forest.

GOLF

Wine Country isn't a hacker's mecca in the way of a Scottsdale or a Myrtle Beach. On the other hand, the mild climate and the stunning terrain do lend themselves to the links, especially for those who consider walking from fairway to green a form of exercise.

The facilities in our coverage area range from nine-hole pitch-and-putts to manicured, PGA-caliber courses. Most have some sort of refreshment option— either a snack bar or a full-service restau-rant. And practically all of them have pro shops where you can buy anything you forgot to pack. Following are some basic descriptions of the public courses. Like airfares, greens fees are always fluctuat-ing, but I give you some general figures in the listings.

Napa County

Napa Golf Course at Kennedy Park
2295 Streblow Drive, Napa
(707) 255-4333
www.playnapa.com
With John F. Kennedy Memorial Regional Park and the Napa River to the west and the open spaces of Napa Valley College to the north, this is a nicely placed 18-hole, par 72 course that runs about 6730 yards. Fees range from $31 to $42. A cart is an additional $13 per person. Ask about the reduced senior rates. Napa Golf Course is easy to walk but quite difficult to shoot. This is a challenging course.

Vintners Golf Club
7901 Solano Avenue, Yountville
(707) 944-1992
www.vintnersgolfclub.com
Napa County's newest golfing attraction is a nine-hole course with true, fast greens and a backdrop of the historic Veterans Home of California buildings. Total yardage is 2700; par is 34. Vintners is full of amenities, including a clubhouse that serves breakfast, lunch, and appetizers (including alcohol), and a full pro shop. A lighted, covered, 36-stall driving range has been joined by a smaller grass range. Here are your greens fees: $18 for 9 holes and $24 for 18 holes during the week; $28 for 9 holes and $36 for 18 holes on Saturday and Sunday. Rent an electric cart for 9 holes ($16) or 18 ($24).

Mount St. Helena Golf Course
Napa County Fairgrounds,
1435 North Oak Street, Calistoga
(707) 942-9966
www.napacountyfairgrounds.com
The course itself is modest—nothing special, one might go so far as to say—but Calistoga's scenic situation, within a horse shoe toss of rugged hills, makes this a fine place to spend a few hours. Play all day for $12 during the week, $18 on weekends. After 4:00 P.M. the price dips to $7.00 during the week and $10.00 on weekends. The nine-hole course is 2748 yards and par 34 for men, 2647 yards and par 35 for "ladies," as they say in the golf world.

Sonoma County

Los Arroyos Golf Course
5000 Stage Gulch Road, Sonoma
(707) 938-8835
This nine-hole course is just southwest of Sonoma, adjacent to Highway 116. Weekend greens fees are $12 for 9 holes and $17 for 18. Play during the week for $10 or $15. Pull carts are $2.00. Los Arroyos has a snack bar.

Adobe Creek Golf & Country Club
1901 Frates Road, Petaluma
(707) 765-3000
www.adobecreek.com
Adobe Creek, designed by Robert Trent Jones Jr., is an 18-hole, par 72, 6986-yard course on the southeast edge of Petaluma (just south of Petaluma Adobe State Historic Park). It has a grass driving range, and greens fees range from $32 to $75 depending on time of the week and day. Carts are $13 to $26. Collared shirts and soft spikes are mandatory.

Rooster Run Golf Club
2301 East Washington Street, Petaluma
(707) 778-1211
www.roosterrun.com
Rooster Run opened in 1998 and has since become Wine Country's supreme public-golf bargain. Situated across the street from Petaluma Airport, the course is subject to the same afternoon winds that bedevil its neighbor, Adobe Creek Golf Course. The front nine includes an island green on the par 3 number 6. You'll need an oasis after number 5—rated the course's most difficult. Rooster Run management likes to boast that the course includes "the toughest four finishing holes in Northern California golf." Believe it. Regular rates are $33 Monday through Thursday, $38 Friday and $53 on weekends; the corresponding rates for certified Petaluma residents are $26, $30, and $42.

Seniors play for $22 Monday through Wednesday. Juniors pay $10 after 2:30 P.M. Monday through Thursday.

ℹ️ *A great place to watch surfers—or catch a wave for yourself—is Salmon Creek Beach on the Sonoma coast.*

Foxtail Golf Club
100 Golf Course Drive, Rohnert Park
(707) 584-7766
www.playfoxtail.com
Extensive renovations on the two courses at this establishment now make for a more satisfying game. The South Course is a par 71, 6500-yard layout with new tees, contoured fairways, and 14 new bunkers. The North Course now has new drainage and 45 new bunkers. The lush redwood trees are still there among newly recontoured greens. Weekday fees range from $28 to $32; weekend fees are from $36. The cart fee is $11 per person.

Bennett Valley Golf Course
3330 Yulupa Avenue, Santa Rosa
(707) 528-3673
www.bvgolf.org
Bennett Valley is the perfect place for a golf course, with the peaks of Annadel State Park forming a backdrop to the east. It's an 18-hole, par 72 course that runs 6600 yards. You'll pay $34 on weekends, $23 during the week if you're an out of towner; residents pay $26 and $17. A cart costs an additional $22. Major construction began in spring 2005 on a new clubhouse, restaurant, and pro shop.

The Oakmont Golf Club
7025 Oakmont Drive, Santa Rosa
(707) 539-0415 (West Course),
(707) 538-2454 (East Course)
www.oakmontgc.com
With two 18-hole courses—the championship, par 72 West Course and the executive, par 63 East Course—this is one of the Santa Rosa area's premier facilities.

Oakmont is just southeast of town, off Highway 12 where it starts to wind down toward the Valley of the Moon. Prices range from $32 to $50. Carts are $26 each. You can choose between a snack bar and a sit-down restaurant.

Wikiup Golf Course
5001 Carriage Lane, Wikiup
(707) 546-8787
www.golfwikiup.com
Wikiup is a cul-de-sac neighborhood just north of Santa Rosa, and the community pretty much revolves around the nine-hole, par 29 executive golf course. Weekday greens fees are $11 for 9 holes, $16 for 18; on Saturday and Sunday it's $14 for 9 and $21 for 18.

Windsor Golf Club
1340 Nineteenth Hole Drive, Windsor
(707) 838-7888
www.windsorgolf.com
This is a challenging and well-maintained facility—a par 72, 6169-yard championship course—that has hosted the Nike Tour on several occasions. Nontournament greens fees are $33 to $53. Twilight (after 2:00 P.M.) rates are several bucks less. A full cart will cost you $26, $18 after 2:00 P.M. Windsor has a restaurant and a snack bar, and golf lessons are available. Because of the frequency of tournaments, call in advance for reservations.

Tayman Park Golf Course
927 South Fitch Mountain Road, Healdsburg
(707) 433-4275
www.taymanparkgolf.com
Sonoma County's oldest golf course (dating to 1923) has been significantly renovated over the past few years. New is a three-tiered driving range and a clubhouse with some of the best views in the county. At the eastern edge of central Healdsburg, about a quarter mile from one stretch of the Russian River and a half mile from another, the course is a par 70 nine-holer. It's also one of the best golf bargains you'll find in the area: weekdays

it's $12 for 9 holes, $18 for 18; weekends it's $15 and $21.

Bodega Harbour Golf Links
21301 Heron Drive, Bodega Bay
(707) 875–3538, (800) 503–8158
www.bodegaharbourgolf.com
This seaside course offers wonderful salty breezes and ocean sparkle. Designed by Robert Trent Jones Jr., Bodega Harbour has rolling fairways, cavernous pot bunkers, native coastal rough, and marsh-lands. (Remember, players are prohibited from entering the marsh on holes 16, 17, and 18.) The 18th has been voted the best finishing hole in Northern California. The par is 70, and the yardage measures 5711 from the white tees. Greens fees are $60 Monday through Thursday, $90 on Friday and Saturday, and $70 on Sunday (all rates include cart rental). The clubhouse restaurant serves lunch daily, dinner on Friday and Saturday nights, and breakfast on weekend mornings. Bodega Harbour Golf Links has golf-and-lodging packages in conjunction with several hotels in Bodega Bay and with vacation rental agencies that offer private homes border-ing the course.

Sebastopol Golf Course
2881 Scott's Right-of-Way, Sebastopol
(707) 823–9852
This is your one and only option in Sebastopol. It's a 9-hole, par 66 for 18 holes course. Weekdays you'll pay $10 for 9 holes, $18 for 18 holes. Carts are $10 for 9 holes; $15 for 18.

Northwood Golf Course
19400 Highway 116, Monte Rio
(707) 865–1116
www.northwoodgolf.com
Set in an elbow of the Russian River and surrounded by redwood trees, this is one of the more beautiful Wine Country courses. The wind is almost always gentle and the temperatures are moderated by the tall trees. Northwood is a par 36, nine-hole course designed by Alister Macken-

zie. Fees range from $16 to $38; carts are $12 to $24.

Mendocino County

Ukiah Municipal Golf Course
599 Park Boulevard, Ukiah
(707) 467–2832
Mendocino County's biggest city has its only 18-hole golf course, par 70 Ukiah Municipal. The 5850-yard course is known to be fairly forgiving. Greens fees vary but generally work out to $23 on weekdays, $27 on weekends. Add $20 if you want a cart. Ukiah Municipal has a snack bar.

Little River Inn
7901 North Highway 1, Little River
(707) 937–5667, (888) 466–5683
www.littleriverinn.com
The inn, a popular vacation retreat (see the Spas and Resorts chapter), also has a 9-hole, par 35 golf course. Actually, it has an 11-hole course, so if you play 18 holes (par 71, 5458 yards) you can experience two new greens. There is a driving range (off mats, not grass) and a putting green. The rates for 9 holes are $20 on weekdays, $30 on weekends. For 18 holes you pay $30 during the week, $35 on weekends. Carts are $16 for 9 holes, $24 for 18 holes.

BICYCLE RENTALS

You may not be Greg LeMond, a three-time winner of the Tour de France, but you may still want to traverse the scenic roads of Wine Country on two wheels. One of LeMond's five favorite places to ride his bicycle is Sonoma County, and from the seat of a rented bike, you'll see for yourself why he's right. In general, Wine Country roads are conducive to bik-ing, with ample shoulders along some of the more scenic and popular roads, and light car traffic on others. Rentals are easy to find, and many establishments offer maps and sound advice. The listings below will get you started planning your two-wheeled adventure.

Napa County

Bicycle Trax
796 Soscol Avenue, Napa
(707) 258-TRAX

St. Helena Cyclery
1156 Main Street, St. Helena
(707) 963-7736
www.sthelenacyclery.com

Calistoga Bike Shop
1318 Lincoln Avenue, Calistoga
(707) 942-9687
www.calistogabikeshop.com

Getaway Bike Shop
1522 Lincoln Avenue, Calistoga
(707) 942-0332, (800) 859-2453
www.getawayadventures.com

Sonoma County

Sonoma Valley Cyclery
20093 Broadway, Sonoma
(707) 935-3377
www.sonomavalleycyclery.com

The Goodtime Bicycle Company
18503 Highway 12, Sonoma
(707) 938-0453, (888) 525-0453
www.goodtimetouring.com

The Bicycle Factory
110 Kentucky Street, Petaluma
(707) 763-7515;
195 North Main Street, Sebastopol
(707) 829-1880

Rincon Cyclery
4927 Sonoma Highway, Suite H, Santa Rosa
(707) 538-0868, (800) 965-BIKE
www.rinconcyclery.com

Spoke Folk Cyclery
201 Center Street, Healdsburg
(707) 433-7171
www.spokefolk.com

Mendocino County

Catch a Canoe & Bicycles Too
Highway 1 and Comptche-Ukiah Road, Mendocino
(707) 937-0273, (800) 320-BIKE

Fort Bragg Cyclery
221 North Main Street, Fort Bragg
(707) 964-3509

BOWLING

You remembered to pack your bowling ball, yes? If not, the lanes below rent all the gear you need for knocking down pins and tallying up strikes.

Napa County

Napa Bowl
494 Soscol Avenue, Napa
(707) 224-8331

Sonoma County

AMF Boulevard Lanes
1100 Petaluma Boulevard S., Petaluma
(707) 762-4581

Double Decker Lanes
300 Golf Course Drive, Rohnert Park
(707) 585-0226

Continental Lanes
765 Sebastopol Road, Santa Rosa
(707) 523-2695

Windsor Bowl
8801 Conde Lane, Windsor
(707) 837-9889

Mendocino County

Yokayo Bowl
1401 North State Street, Ukiah
(707) 462-8686

Noyo Bowl
900 North Main Street, Fort Bragg
(707) 964-4051

HORSEBACK RIDING

Many of the trails in the state parks, state forests, and recreation areas of Wine Country are open to horses. You did bring yours, didn't you? If it wouldn't fit in your overnight bag, there are a few outfits that will rent you a steed. Prices begin at approximately $40 per person for a one-hour ride. You provide the cowboy hat and the harmonica.

Triple Creek Horse Outfit
Sonoma/Napa locations
(707) 933-1600
www.triplecreekhorseoutfit.com
A new owner took over this longtime business in 2003 but kept the horses and the popular routes through three state parks (the name of the business refers to three creeks in the three parks): Bothe–Napa Valley, Jack London, and Sugarloaf Ridge (see previous listings and the Attractions chapter). The Jack London rides—offered April through November—skirt vineyards owned by the author's descendants. The Bothe ride also is available for reservation April through November, offering the shade of Ritchey Creek and the peace of the Mayacmas Mountains. The company operates year-round in Sugarloaf Ridge, weather and trails permitting, and the views from the saddle are fabulous.

Reservations are a must. Riders must be at least eight years old. Open-toed shoes are not permitted, and the weight limit is 240 pounds.

Chanslor Guest Ranch and Stables
2660 Highway 1, Bodega Bay
(707) 875-3333
www.chanslor.com
You can lead a horse to the water, but you can't make him surf. Chanslor offers four daily beach rides from its inland property—over the dunes to Bodega Bay and back. There are other options too: the one-and-a-half-hour Salmon Creek Trail, which winds into a canyon and around much of the company's 730 acres; the one-hour Eagle View ride, where you are likely to spot a couple of resident bald eagles; and a half-hour, trek through the Wetlands Preservation Habitat.

SWIMMING

If you are not fortunate enough to be staying (or living) next to any Wine Country lakes during those summer hot spells, you might feel the need to jump into a different body of water—specifically, the rectangular, chlorinated kind. Below is a partial list of public swimming facilities. Call for more information on lessons, admission fees, and no-kids or kids-only periods.

Also, some spas permit walk-in (dive-in?) swimmers who pay for day use of their mineral pools. Search out the Spas and Resorts chapter for relevant information.

Napa County

St. Helena Community Pool
1401 Grayson Avenue, St. Helena
(707) 963-7946

Sonoma County

Petaluma Swim Center
900 East Washington Street, Petaluma
(707) 778-4410

Alicia Pool
300 Arlen Drive, Rohnert Park
(707) 795-7265

Benicia Pool
7469 Bernice Avenue, Rohnert Park
(707) 795-7582

Ladybug Pool
8517 Liman Way, Rohnert Park
(707) 664-1070

Honeybee Pool
1170 Golf Course Drive, Rohnert Park
(707) 586-1413

When visiting coastal parks, be prepared for sudden changes in the weather. It's best to dress in "California layers," as it may be sunny and warm, then foggy, then chilly and windy—sometimes all within a few minutes.

Magnolia Pool
1501 Middlebrook Way, Rohnert Park
(707) 795-8619

Finley Aquatic Complex
2060 West College Avenue, Santa Rosa
(707) 543-3760

Ridgeway Swim Center
455 Ridgeway Avenue, Santa Rosa
(707) 543-3421

Healdsburg Municipal Swimming Pool
360 Monte Vista Avenue, Healdsburg
(707) 433-1109

Cloverdale Memorial Pool
105 West First Street, Cloverdale
(707) 894-3236

Ives Pool
7400 Willow Street, Sebastopol
(707) 823-8693
www.ivespool.org

Mendocino County

Ukiah Municipal Swimming Pool
511 Park Boulevard, Ukiah
(707) 467-2831

Willits Municipal Swimming Pool
429 North Main Street, Willits
(707) 459-5778

TENNIS

If you think tennis is just the sort of vigorous-yet-natty sport that would flourish in Wine Country, you're right on target. Because of the geographic enormity of the area, however, a complete list of available courts would be harder to handle than an Anna Kournikova first serve. So here's a list of city recreation departments throughout the region. The folks on the other end of the line will tell you where the courts are—many of them are after-hours high school facilities—whether you need reservations, what it costs to play there, and whether the courts are lighted.

Napa County

City of American Canyon Recreation
(707) 647-4566

City of Napa Parks and Recreation
(707) 257-9529

Town of Yountville Recreation
(707) 944-8712

City of St. Helena Recreation
Department
(707) 963-5706

City of Calistoga Parks and Recreation
(707) 942-2838

Sonoma County

Sonoma City Hall
(707) 938-3681

City of Petaluma Parks & Recreation
(707) 778-4380

City of Cotati
(707) 792-4600

City of Rohnert Park
Recreation Department
(707) 588-3456

City of Santa Rosa
Recreation & Parks Offices
(707) 543-3282

Town of Windsor Parks and Recreation
(707) 838-1260

City of Healdsburg
(707) 431-3300

City of Cloverdale
(707) 894-2521

City of Sebastopol Recreation
Information
(707) 823-1511

Mendocino County

City of Ukiah Recreation
(707) 463-6237

City of Willits
(707) 459-4601

City of Point Arena
(707) 882-2122

Fort Bragg Recreation Center
(707) 964-2231

LAKE COUNTY

Lake County is sometimes overlooked by Wine Country visitors because of its remoteness in relation to the concentrated wine valleys found in Napa and Sonoma Counties. But if you are passionate about water sports, love live entertainment performed by household names, or embrace an appreciation for award-winning wine, Lake County is worth a side trip during your visit to the region.

Clear Lake, with its scenic shores and many water-related activities, brings tourists by the thousands. Likewise, Konocti Harbor Resort is a huge draw for Bay Area music lovers. For vinophiles there are several tasting rooms to visit, including the historic Guenoc Winery. Read on for more about these attractions.

AREA OVERVIEW

Lake County's economy is ruled mostly by agriculture. Its 803,840 acres burst forth with walnuts, kiwi fruit, wild rice, apples, wheat, barley, and Sudan grass—just to name a few. Other commodities include wool, milk, cheese, honey, beeswax, timber, and livestock. But pears are royalty here—and the Bartlett is king. Wine grapes also figure prominently in the overall agricultural picture, with the number of vineyards increasing, new tasting rooms opening, and an annual wine-grape crop valued at approximately $33 million.

The first town you encounter in Lake County as you drive north on Highway 29 is Middletown, an old-fashioned country burg with a couple of hearty cafes along its truncated Main Street, as well as a thriving microbrewery. The Cobb Mountain resort area, north of Middletown via Highway 175, supports a series of tiny communities, with Cobb the foremost representative. The town sits at 2,500 feet,

providing welcome breezes and pinebough cover when the mercury rises during the summer.

Moving north you come to the many towns that ring Clear Lake like chairs arranged around a popular swimming pool. Lower Lake is the southernmost locality, with a quaint old downtown. Above that is Clearlake, the county's largest city (a whopping 13,950 people!). It's largely a collection of small motels and old-style resorts that cater to anglers, boaters, and overheated families.

North of Clearlake, on Highway 20 and around a bend of the lake, is Clearlake Oaks. On the southwestern shore of Clear Lake is Kelseyville, a tidy community with a rural economy at the base of Mount Konocti. It's one of the few towns in the area that doesn't actually cozy up to the lake, though it's only about 3 miles away.

Lakeport is a pleasant town of about 5,125 on the westernmost bulge of the lake. It has been the county seat since 1861, and today it is known as something of a retirement haven. Lucerne and Nice (pronounced like the French city, or your sibling's daughter, not the adjective) occupy the quieter, greener northern section of Clear Lake. Locals call Lucerne "Little Switzerland," and they have been known to don alpine garb to prove the point. Finally comes Upper Lake, which is not on Clear Lake at all but about 3 miles due north of its uppermost shore.

Lake County's median household income ($27,295, according to the 2000 census) and its population (64,446) is the lowest among the counties that encompass Wine Country. Its cost of housing is about half that of the other three counties, and it is more remote and isolated. But the locals—many of them part-time residents with vacation homes—like it that way. Nonetheless, the California Employment Development Department forecasts that Lake County's population will nearly double during the next two decades.

HISTORY

For centuries Pomo tribes lived around Clear Lake, bathing in the hot springs and playing games on the small islands that dot the lake. Volcanic Mount Konocti, with its eerie caves, was considered sacred ground.

The first white men at Clear Lake were probably Russian fur trappers from Fort Ross. Next came French-Canadian fur trappers and American mountain men. Then in 1836 Gen. Mariano Vallejo's brother, Salvador, brought cattle and horses onto a newly acquired land grant. For the most part, Salvador ran the ranch from Sonoma headquarters, and the Pomo lifestyle was not interrupted.

But in 1847 Salvador sold out to two Americans, Andrew Kelsey and Charles Stone. They enslaved the natives, oppressed them, and starved them. In desperation, two of the Pomos were hired to steal a steer, but they bungled the job. Fearing a cruel reprisal, they decided to kill Stone and Kelsey. Stone died from an arrow, Kelsey at the hands of a Pomo woman whose son had been tortured. Frightened settlers called in the military from Benicia. A battle ensued, and the Pomos, holed up on a Clear Lake island, were massacred, giving the name Bloody Island to the site. The island is no more, as farmers reclaimed the marshes around it. But the name of Andrew Kelsey lives on in Kelseyville.

In the early 1850s wagon trains began arriving and settlers started raising cattle and planting fields. By 1857 a county government had been set up in a tiny wooden courthouse, and Lakeport was on its way to being the county seat. A number of vineyards and wineries appeared, most of them clinging to the valleys around Clear Lake, as the rest of the county was quite rugged.

But wine would not be the real attraction in the area. That would turn out to be the hot springs that bubbled up everywhere. By 1880, 100,000 people had traveled to Lake County to partake of the beneficial waters and luxuriate in the elegant hotels adjacent to the mineral springs. Posh casinos, music halls redolent with gold leaf, and formal dining rooms gleaming with silver and crystal were just some of the luxuries offered during leisure hours, while the more energetic indulged in bowling, croquet, lawn tennis, and riding.

For generations many faithfully vacationed at these spas, not only for health benefits but also as a gathering place for the social elite. The undoing of this salubrious way of life was the invention of the combustion engine. With the advent of the automobile, people no longer lingered for weeks. Instead, they came for a few days and moved on to another spot. The fine old hotels degenerated, and most of them burned. It was the end of a gracious era that had lasted a half century.

Of all the rich and famous who made their way to Lake County, none was more illustrious than the vibrant, graceful Lillie Langtry—famed actress and vivacious mistress of Britain's Prince of Wales, later crowned King Edward VII. She came to Guenoc Valley in 1887, weary of the acting circuit and trying to get a divorce from her English husband. She bought a 4,000-acre ranch and intended to raise grapes and thoroughbred horses. With her was her celebrated lover, Freddie Gebhart, a wealthy horseman who had bought an adjoining 3,200 acres.

Langtry was enchanted with Lake County from the moment she arrived via jostling stagecoach from St. Helena at the end of the railroad line. In addition to raising cattle and horses, Langtry wanted to produce wine from her own grapes and winery. She decided that no one but a Frenchman could cope with this challenge, and she engaged a capable man from Bordeaux.

If you're in Lake County in the spring, try something truly off the beaten path: a one-hour narrated wagon trip through the wildflowers of Bear Valley, followed by an authentic chuckwagon barbecue. Call the Eleven Roses Ranch at (707) 998-4471 to learn more.

The vintage that resulted never reached market. "A new law putting liquor into bond for a period spoiled the sale of those bottles with a picture of myself on the label," she complained. Langtry stayed at the ranch a fortnight and eagerly looked to return after completing her committed engagements. However, she never saw the ranch again, though she owned it 18 years.

When Prohibition dealt its death blow to wine making, Lake County turned its land over to pears, walnuts, and grazing pasture. Not until the 1960s did the vineyards reappear. Now there are several top-rated wineries in operation.

ON THE WATER

They don't call it Lake County for nothing. It has several significant wet spots, but Clear Lake takes the prize. Three things about Clear Lake are clear: It is big, it is shallow, and it is old. With 43,785 acres of surface area, it's the largest natural freshwater lake within California. And yet the volume of water contained therein is not staggering. That's because the average depth of the lake is less than 30 feet.

Scientists are convinced that lakes of some sort have existed at this site for some 2.5 million years, possibly making Clear Lake the oldest lake in North America. They figure the upper arm, between Lakeport and Lucerne, has been underwater continuously for 450,000 years.

In terms of its importance to the identity of the county, Clear Lake is the undeniable hub. Almost all the towns in Lake County are clustered around the shoreline,

and access for all is faithfully preserved. There are 11 public ramps around the lake, providing an array of launch points. (Permission is required for use of beaches and ramps not posted as public.)

Clear Lake is known as the Bass Capital of the West. Two-thirds of the fish caught here are largemouth bass, and spring is the season to reel 'em in, especially from docks or in pockets formed in the beds of tule reeds. Bass might be the most plentiful, but also swimming in these waters are channel catfish, bluegill, and crappie.

WINERIES

Guenoc and Langtry Estate Vineyards
21000 Butts Canyon Road, Middletown
(707) 987-2385
www.guenoc.com
That charming countenance you see gracing bottles of Guenoc wine is Lillie Langtry—the "Jersey Lily," beloved stage actress of the late 19th century. Langtry ran the business from 1888 to 1906, and her palatial home is still the centerpiece of the property. The vineyards sit on the border of Napa and Lake Counties in Guenoc Valley, the only federally approved appellation under single proprietorship. The winery produces a wide range of vino, from Chardonnay and Cabernet Sauvignon to Petite Sirah, and even the occasional port.

Ployez Winery
11171 South Highway 29, Lower Lake
(707) 994-2106
www.ployezwinery.com
You probably thought the only thing French in Lake County was the fries at Burger King, but along comes Gerald Ployez, a fourth-generation winemaker from Champagne whose east-of-the-Atlantic family still bottles under the Ployez-Jacquemari label. Gerald opened this winery in 1997, and he concentrates mostly on Chardonnay and Sauvignon Blanc, though he produces three types of red too.

Wildhurst Vineyards
3855 Main Street, Kelseyville
(707) 279-4302, (800) 595-9463
www.wildhurst.com

When Myron and Marilyn Holdenried started this winery in 1991, it was just a case of diversification: Myron is a fifth-generation Kelseyville farmer. In fact he had already been growing grapes and pears for 25 years. Wildhurst started at the site of the old Steurmer Winery in Lower Lake, then moved to Kelseyville in 1996; a year later it unveiled its tasting room in a refurbished Odd Fellows Hall. (The winery is 2 miles away and not open to the public.) Wildhurst is primarily noted for its Merlot but makes three other reds and a couple of whites, all under the Clear Lake appellation.

Steele Wines
4350 Thomas Drive, Kelseyville
(707) 279-9475
www.steelewines.com

Kendall-Jackson was the pride of Lake County until it "went Sonoma" a few years ago. But Lake still can brag of its hold on one of the men who nurtured that winery to prominence: Jed Steele. He dabbles in a number of varietals, but generally sticks to Chardonnay, Pinot Noir, and Zinfandel, with grapes from as far south as Santa Barbara County and as far north as Mendocino. You also might stumble upon a farmers' market if you arrive Saturday morning, or the Harvest Festival if you get there on the second weekend of October.

Ceago Del Lago Vinegardens
5115 East Highway 20, Lucerne
(707) 274-1462
www.ceago.com

Founded by Jim Fetzer of the renowned Fetzer wine-making dynasty, this winery opened in late 2004 on the north shore of Clear Lake, between Nice and Lucerne. The winemakers employ both back-to-the-earth organic and biodynamic grape-growing methods, which can be complex but basically involve using no chemicals, fertilizing with compost, and rotating crops. They use a flock of sheep in their vineyards to control weeds. In the tasting room (for a $5.00 fee) you can sample several wines from their collection, including a Sauvignon Blanc and a Cabernet Sauvignon. A pier is right outside on the lake for boaters who wish to motor on up for a bit of bottled refreshment. Future plans for this site include a hotel and spa.

Take a deep breath: For more than a decade, Lake County has met or exceeded standards for air quality set by the California Air Resources Board. It's the only area in the state with such a record.

Tulip Hill Winery
4900 Bartlett Springs Road, Nice
(707) 274-9373
www.tuliphillwinery.com

A small winery producing 8,000 cases annually, Tulip Hill is named for the 30,000 tulip bulbs planted by owner Budge Brown in the winery's Pope Valley vineyards in Napa County. Other grapes used in its wines come from vineyards in the Mount Oso appellation and Lake County. In fact, its Zinfandel is made from 100 percent Lake County grapes, grown in a small vineyard at the base of Mount Konocti. Tulip Hill also produces Chardonnay, Cabernet Sauvignon, and a white meritage (a 50-50 blend of Merlot and Syrah). The $5.00 tasting fee is waived if you buy a bottle.

BREWPUBS

Mount St. Helena Brewing & Restaurant
21167 Calistoga Street, Middletown
(707) 987-2106
www.mtsthelenabrew.com

As microbreweries go, this one has lots of gold and silver medals to show for its trouble. The beer menu includes Honey Wheat Ale, Palisades Pale Ale, Imperial

Phone Numbers for Lake County

Lake County Visitor Information Center
6110 East Highway 20, Lucerne
(707) 274-5652, (800) 525-3743
www.lakecounty.com

Clear Lake Chamber of Commerce
4700 Golf Avenue, Clearlake
(707) 994-3600
www.clearlakechamber.com

Lakeport Regional Chamber of
Commerce
875 Lakeport Boulevard, Lakeport
(707) 263-5092
www.lakeportchamber.com

Stout, an English-style Brown Ale, India Pale Ale, and Belgian Wit. The food menu is extensive, with everything from pasta to house specialties of the red meat variety to a wide selection of pizzas. There's even a black bean burger or Thai noodles for vegetarians.

ATTRACTIONS

PRICE CODE

The price code below reflects the admission price or fees for two adults in high season, not including gratuities where appropriate.

$	Less than $15
$$	$15 to $50
$$$	$51 to $150

Konocti Harbor Resort & Spa $$$
8727 Soda Bay Road, Kelseyville
(707) 279-4281, (800) 660-LAKE
www.konoctiharbor.com
In a few short years, Konocti Harbor has managed to place itself among the top music venues in Northern California. In fact, the resort's Joe Mazzola Classic Concert Showroom was named by *Performance* magazine as America's No. 1 small concert venue.

The resort actually has several different sites for performance. The Konocti Field Amphitheater, which operates between May and October, puts you under the stars for major concerts. This lakeside amphitheater seats 5,000, all within 200 feet of the stage, and with magnificent views as a backdrop to the performers. It pulls big acts, some contemporary, some revived. The lineup has included the likes of Wynonna, Vince Gill, Styx, Doobie Brothers, Cheap Trick, Don Henley, Journey, Jonny Lang, Merle Haggard, and Tim McGraw. Tickets usually range from $29 to $49.

Predating the amphitheater was the Classic Concert Showroom, a 1,000-occupancy dinner theater with two VIP balconies and tiered seating. The showroom tends to showcase stars more appropriate to an intimate setting, such as Ray Charles, B. B. King, Eddie Money, Ringo Starr, the Pretenders, and Bill Cosby. These tickets are in the $35 to $60 range, more if you include buffet dinner. Meanwhile, the Full Moon Saloon, right next to Clear Lake, has live entertainment Friday and Saturday year-round, seven days a week from June through Labor Day. The saloon has indoor and outdoor seating and a sizable dance floor. From time to time musicians from the big shows drop in to the saloon after their own performance and hop up onstage to jam with the house bands.

Most people know Konocti Harbor as a premier concert venue for post-40 rockers, but there's a lot going on here even after the last drumbeat. The resort has 100 acres of lakefront property and 250 guest accommodations that range from basic rooms to apartment suites to beach cottages to fully equipped VIP suites. Many, but not all, of the rooms have views of Clear Lake. Basic rooms are $69 in off-season; $89 on weekends and concert nights. Deluxe lodgings are $99/$129; Jacuzzi suites with fireplaces run $169/$259. The price spectrum is wide, so call for more information.

Konocti Harbor bustles with activity. There is a tennis complex, gym, two swimming pools, two wading pools, shuffle board courts, horseshoe pits, sand volleyball courts, and a softball field. And because the lake is primary among attractions, the resort has a 100-slip marina, launch ramp, and certified boat repair shop. It also offers a rental fleet (ski boats, Waverunners, etc.) and, believe it or not, a bass fishing pro. Konocti's Dancing Springs Spa features massage, herbal wraps, loofa treatments, facials, manicures, and more. If you must mix business and pleasure, the meeting facilities can handle groups from 10 to 700.

Calpine Geothermal Plant Tour   Free
15500 Central Park Road, Middletown
(707) 987-4270, (866) GEYSERS
www.calpine.com, www.geysers.com
Perhaps you've already indulged in a mud bath and had a soak in a hot mineral pool. Can you stand just a little more hot water? Steam, to be exact, as it comes out of the ground to generate electricity at the Geysers. Technically they aren't geysers but "fumaroles," and they can usually be seen boiling up out of a distant hillside on the Sonoma County/Lake County line. The steam comes from subterranean cauldrons and it's being corralled by Calpine

Corporation to make electricity. There are 19 power units at the remote site, with a total net generating capacity of 850 megawatts, or enough to turn on the lights in 850,000 homes.

I don't know of another geothermal power plant tour anywhere in the world, and you can't beat the price: It's all free. Buses depart from the visitor center in Middletown at 10:00 A.M., noon, and 2:00 P.M., Thursday through Monday. (Reservations are encouraged.) Each tour from beginning to end takes approximately 75 to 90 minutes, and you'll learn all about the colorful history of the site. The visitor center has a gift shop and picnic area, along with interactive displays about geothermal energy.

Mount Konocti, the peak that rises 4,300 feet on the west shore of Clear Lake, is a dormant volcano that last erupted 100,000 years ago.

Clear Lake Queen $$
Library Park, Lakeport
(707) 994-5432
www.paddlewheel.com
This attraction was made to feel old. It's a 110-foot, triple-deck, paddlewheel boat that would look more at home in the Mississippi Delta. (Sorry, the wheel is just for show—the *Queen* is powered by two massive diesel engines.) You can watch the shoreline activity while you eat lunch or dinner. High-season prices run from $16 to $18 for sightseeing only, to $28 for a two-hour lunch or brunch cruise, to $35 for a three-hour dinner. (The dining floors are warm and enclosed.) The *Queen* runs Wednesday through Sunday during the summer, Friday and Saturday during the winter—but it will

Middletown's nickname "Steam City" comes from the Geysers steamfields in the hills above the town.

run any day there's enough people to make a trip, so call to inquire.

Outrageous Waters $
Highway 53 & Old State Highway 53,
Clearlake
(707) 995–1402
www.outrageouswaters.com
Beat the heat in Lake County by taking a long slide into a pool at this water park. Next to the slides is a fun center with volleyball courts and a video arcade. A grand prix racetrack features 15 cars with nine-horsepower engines maneuvering a pro-fessionally banked concrete track. Hardball and softball batting cages round out the energy-burning attractions. Outrageous Waters also has a food concession, storage lockers, and a kiddie pool. The water park is closed after summer, but the fun center is open all year. The park is open 11:00 A.M. to 7:00 P.M. daily in summer. Admission is $13.95 for adults, $9.95 for children shorter than 48 inches (children 3 and under are free), and $3.95 for seniors 55 and older. ID-bearing Lake County residents get a discount, and the whole world gets one after 4:30 P.M.

ON THE WATER ☀

Great rivers, fine lakes, and a spectacular ocean—take your pick. From all-day deep-sea fishing excursions to an afternoon swim in a lake, the aquatic activities and adventures available in Wine Country are plentiful.

The best place to begin is along the 150 miles or so of coastline that borders the Pacific in Sonoma and Mendocino Counties. If you're thinking of palm-studded sandy beaches, you'll be surprised by what you find here. This section of California's coast bears little resemblance to its southern counterpart—that relatively mild stretch of oceanfront lined with sunbathers from Santa Barbara to San Diego. North of San Francisco the continent drops precipitously to the sea, with narrow crescents of beach occasionally flanking the rocky bluffs—you will not see a single high-rise hotel along this coast. And the ocean is rarely even-tempered here, alternating between violent fits of rage and quiet moods of calm. Its best times are during the summer months, when the sun burns through the morning fog and the wind is low.

Wine Country rivers generally flow lazily through forests, meadows, and marshes, rarely achieving enough momentum to produce whitewater. A short section of the Russian River above Cloverdale and the portion of the Eel River in Mendocino County are two exceptions. When water volume is high, these stretches can get quite rough, reaching Class IV and V whitewater status. And of course, during the rainy winter months many Wine Country creeks—which are dry in summer—flow with gusto, some serving as spawning grounds for salmon and steelhead.

As for the lake situation, well, generally speaking this is no Minnesota. Only in Lake County will you find natural lakes in Wine Country (see the previous chapter). There are a handful there, including Clear Lake and the Blue Lakes. All are teeming with fish and great for swimming and water sports.

So here's a rundown of the places and the ways to get wet.

THE PACIFIC

Sonoma County

SONOMA COAST

The Sonoma coast feels wild and remote. It is hilly, almost mountainous at times, with coastal ranches stretching for miles along the bluffs. Bodega Bay, the county's largest coastal town, is home to approximately 300 commercial fishing boats. Its protected harbor is also an attractive spot for sporting activities. The shoreline on the west side of the harbor is great for windsurfing or launching a kayak. There's hardly a day when you don't see the fluorescent sails of a sailboard darting about or the rhythmic movements of a kayaker plying the waters.

Surfers looking for the perfect wave will not be disappointed. Two of the most popular spots are Salmon Creek, just north of Bodega Bay, and Goat Rock State Beach, farther up the coast near Jenner. But it's always a good idea to contact a local surf shop for advice—it's a long coastline, and you can spend a lot of time looking.

Sportfishing is big at Bodega Bay. Charter boats sail every day and, depending on the season, come back with a mix of rock cod, lingcod, halibut, salmon, albacore tuna, and crab.

North from Bodega Bay is a series of state beaches accessible from clearly marked parking areas. These are a part of the Sonoma Coast State Beach, and they are ideal spots for fishing, beachcombing, picnicking, and parties—unfortunately the chilly waters are unsafe for swimming, and there are no lifeguards. A ranger station, just north of Bodega Bay at Salmon Creek, is where you can get maps and information. Park rangers also offer whale-watching walks.

See the Parks and Recreation and Attractions chapters for more information on the Sonoma Coast State Beach and other coastal-area recreation sites, including Doran and Westside Regional Parks, Stillwater Cove Regional Park, Fort Ross State Park, Salt Point State Park, Kruse Rhododendron State Reserve, and Gualala Point Regional Park.

Mendocino County

MENDOCINO COAST

For sheer drama, nothing compares with the splendor of the view from the town of Mendocino, built on a rocky peninsula, where the sound of waves crashing against the cliffs is always in the air. The shoreline here is a labyrinth of rugged offshore spires and sea stacks, churning coves, and wave-sculpted arches and sea tunnels. This is one of the most soul-stirring settings in the state, with ocean views often mesmerizing visitors for hours. A popular activity here—aside from shopping—is to find a comfortable spot on the bluffs and simply watch wave after wave roll in.

Another favorite attraction along this scenic seashore is at Russian Gulch State Park, where a unique "punch bowl" was formed when a large sea cave collapsed. Waves enter through a tunnel in one side and crash around the interior of the bowl, letting go a distinctive array of throaty echoes. Russian Gulch State Park is just 2 miles north of Mendocino (see the Parks and Recreation chapter).

Fishing is a popular sport along the Mendocino coast. Greenwood Creek State Beach, a day-use state beach near the town of Elk (at the intersection of Highways 1 and 128), is popular with picnickers

and ocean anglers who want easy access to the beaches. Additional angling spots along the Mendocino coast include Schooner Gulch State Park and Manchester State Beach, on Kinney Road off Highway 1, where there's a bonus of two creeks that run with salmon and steelhead during winter. (See the Parks and Recreation chapter for more on Manchester State Beach and Schooner Gulch.)

Abalone diving is a popular sport around these parts for the adventuresome, experienced diver. The abalone is a giant marine snail with a powerful foot that can lock a strong grip on rock surfaces. One of these mollusks can yield more than a pound of delicious white meat. Unfortunately, abalone is becoming an endangered species. Rules for abalone diving (including size limits) are strict. The mollusks can be harvested from April to December, excluding July, but check with the state Department of Parks and Recreation at any state beach for the latest regulations—all abalone divers must have a valid fishing license bearing an abalone stamp. And above all, consult with park rangers and locals about the dangers of abalone diving. Every year brings a few tragic drownings—even among veteran divers—along this shoreline.

For more information on other popular recreational spots on or near the Mendocino coast—including Van Damme State Park, Mendocino Headlands State Park, Jug Handle State Reserve, Jackson State Forest, Mackerricher State Park, Westport–Union Landing State Beach, and Sinkyone Wilderness State Park—see the Parks and Recreation chapter.

THE RIVERS

Napa County

NAPA RIVER

Though most of the Napa River's length snakes from Mount St. Helena to the town of Napa, the big-time angling is mostly confined to extreme points south, especially as the river broadens between the Butler Bridge (the airborne stretch of Highway 12/29) and Carquinez Strait. Summer fishing isn't great in these tidal waters, but autumn brings hungry striped bass and sturgeon. Try live bait, such as mudsuckers or bullheads for the stripers, live bass shrimp or mud shrimp for the sturgeon.

The many sloughs that feed into Napa River in this marshy area are also good bets for striped bass. If you're looking for a full-service resort, try the Napa Valley Marina, (707) 252-8011, or Napa Sea Ranch, (707) 252-2799, both on or near Cuttings Wharf Road.

Sonoma County

RUSSIAN RIVER

Called Slavyanka (Slavic girl) by Russian settlers in the 19th century, the Russian River begins in Mendocino County just above Ukiah. The East Branch of the Russian receives water diverted from the Eel River, which flows through an aqueduct cut through a hill. The diversion, which has been going on since 1908, has recently become controversial because of its impact on the Eel River's fisheries. Water from the Eel is used to feed the PG&E Potter Valley hydroelectric plant; it also helps to keep the Russian from being reduced to a trickle through the dry summer months.

Below Hopland, the Russian falls precipitously through a narrow canyon—alongside U.S. Highway 101—and then slows to a more languid pace for the rest of the trip through Sonoma County. It rolls past small wineries, campgrounds, and several towns before reaching the sea at Jenner. During the summer months canoeists, kayakers, rafters, and inner-tubists converge on the river. The more ambitious paddle the entire 70-mile stretch of relatively flat water below Cloverdale to Jenner, while most visitors

The ocean along the Northern California coast is unsafe for swimming. It's cold, about 50 degrees, and the strong currents will whisk you off toward Japan before you can say sayonara. Large and powerful waves—called sleeper waves—also occur without warning, occasionally sweeping beachcombers off coastal rocks and sand shores. Take my advice: Enjoy the view and stay clear of the breakers.

opt for a one-day trip of about 10 miles—often between Forestville and Guerneville. April through September is the best time to canoe the Russian. It's a beautiful run through quiet waters among redwoods, past summer resorts, quaint old homes, and the occasional nude beach. (See the Provisioners listings in this chapter for information on area river outfitters.)

For more on Russian River area wineries, see the Wineries chapter. To find out about camping options, see the Camping chapter.

Mendocino County

EEL RIVER

This river is a sight to behold, sparkling in emerald greens, turquoise blues, and foamy white as it tumbles over boulders, through narrow gorges, and past tall redwood and fir forests. The Eel begins in a cauldron formed by an ancient volcano in Mendocino National Forest, and then it winds north for nearly 150 miles before spilling into the Pacific near Ferndale in Humboldt County. The third-largest river in the state (following the Sacramento and the Klamath), the Eel and its tributaries are home to chinook and coho salmon and steelhead, which migrate from the ocean to the river's spawning grounds each year. Though several dams, a hydroelectric plant, and the massive Russian River diversion—about 52 billion gallons ℹ *Be advised that when water levels in streams and tributaries are running low, particularly in the fall, many are off-limits to fishing. To find out if angling is permitted in certain streams, call the Department of Fish and Game at (707) 944-5533 or (707) 442-4502 for a recorded update.*

annually—have all had an impact on the fish population, the river still boasts one of the most abundant fisheries in the state and has a reputation for producing large, hard-fighting lunkers.

The Russian River water diversion has kept the Eel in near drought condition every summer and fall for 100 years. While it is hardly a boatable river during these times, it is great for swimming, particularly in the deeper holes. At other times of year, however, this is not a swimmer's river. During high water flows, the Eel becomes a roaring torrent, running hell-for-leather to the sea. The Mendocino County section offers some of the best whitewater in the state. It's a heart-thumping ride, featuring mile after mile of Class III and IV rapids. A word of advice and caution: This is a difficult whitewater river navigable by expert guides or highly experienced kayakers only—anyone else will certainly be ground to a fine pulp by the sharp rocks and churning waters. Inner-tubists, neophyte river rafters, or any other novice boater should head for the more placid waters of the Russian River.

GUALALA RIVER

Although the portion of the Gualala River most people see is the wide swath that spreads out where the river joins the Pacific (and where kayakers set out to sea), the Gualala does wind far into the interior of the county, through forests of redwoods and groves of ferns. In a good wet year, when winter rains have drenched the land and the river is full, it is possible to kayak almost 10 miles inland. That would be a rare

year, but even paddling only a mile or so upriver is rewarding, giving a different view of the natural splendors of Northern California. With some luck, you'll witness soaring ospreys, great blue herons, and brown pelicans; catch a glimpse of the playful river otters; and watch the variety of birds that call the forest home.

Motorboats are not permitted on the river, but anglers in rowboats sometimes make their way upstream to cast a line in search of trout. During the winter rainy season, the river swells and roars out to sea, washing out beach sands that had accumulated near its mouth during the summer.

NAVARRO RIVER

Motoring along the rolling hills of Highway 128 and into Anderson Valley, drivers suddenly encounter "a redwood tunnel to the sea" and their first look at the Navarro River. For first-time visitors and longtime residents alike, the redwoods along the Navarro River are a magnificent sight to behold. Second-growth redwood groves stretch along the river, making a home for riverbank denizens such as the belted kingfisher, along with families of raccoons and black-tailed deer. This is a great river for kayaking, and some of the kayak companies operating out of Sonoma County bring groups here (see the Provisioners listings for more information).

THE LAKES
Napa County

LAKE HENNESSEY

About 5 miles east of St. Helena is an 850-acre reservoir owned by the city of Napa and surrounded by rolling hills covered with grass and dappled with oak trees. Lake Hennessey was formed by the construction of Conn Dam. The Department of Fish and Game stocks Lake Hennessey with trout in the fall, winter, and spring, and you'll find a few bass, bluegill, and catfish as well. Motorized boats are allowed on the water if they don't exceed 14 feet and 10 horsepower; sailboats are permitted if they are 16 feet or shorter. Swimming and kayaking are prohibited. There is a $4.00 access fee for visiting the lake, and an additional $1.00 special fishing permit is also required. There is no particular place to pay for the fishing permit, so just be ready to fork over the buck if you see the Lake Hennessey caretaker.

LAKE BERRYESSA

It was more than 40 years ago that Putah Creek was dammed, creating Lake Berryessa between two legs of California's Coast Range (and drowning the town of Monticello). The ragged perimeter gives Berryessa 165 miles of shoreline, more than surrounds massive Lake Tahoe. The north end of the lake is shallow, with gentle, grassy hills sloping down to the water. Contrast that with the south end and its steep, rocky terrain dotted with manzanita and oak. The eastern shore of the lake, meanwhile, is off-limits to the public.

The Federal Bureau of Reclamation owns the shoreline of Lake Berryessa, and major redevelopment plans for the lake were being discussed at press time. Within the next few years, the bureau intends to complete a redesign and refurbishing of the lake's recreational areas and a restoration of the natural environment.

The trout and salmon fishing are great here in the spring; in the fall the trout feed on shad near the surface early in the day. Cast between the dam and the Narrows, or troll in Markley Cove or Skiers Cove. Look for largemouth bass in the coves, smallmouth and spotted bass on the big island in the middle of the lake or at steep, jagged points in up to 40 feet of water. Bluegill usually hang out in the backs of shallow coves all around the lake, and catfish are plentiful at Capell Cove, Pope Creek, and Putah Creek.

There are several marinas along Knoxville Road and Highway 128. Keep in mind that this lake is heavily trafficked,

especially in the summer. Berryessa welcomes more than 1.5 million visitors each year.

Sonoma County

LAKE SONOMA

Designed to control Russian River flooding, the Warm Springs Dam has created some 3,600 surface acres of scenic recreational waters. Located 11 miles north of Healdsburg on Dry Creek Road, this is primarily a boating lake, although waterskiers and Jet Skiers are allowed in designated areas. Skiing is not always considered desirable because of the many large trees that have been partially submerged. Kayakers, however, have no trouble paddling their way through the treetops.

Fishing is the main recreational sport. Generally speaking, boat fishing is more successful than shore fishing, and the upper reaches of the lake usually produce the best results. Fish include smallmouth bass, red ear sunfish, green sunfish, and rainbow trout. A public boat ramp is available, as well as the full-service Lake Sonoma Marina. The fish hatchery is always great fun (see the Kidstuff chapter), and there's an interesting visitor center. Swimming is a possibility, but much of the shoreline is rocky.

Mendocino County

LAKE MENDOCINO

Ten miles north of Ukiah off Highway 20, Lake Mendocino offers waterskiing, pleasure boating, sailing, windsurfing, and swimming. It's an aesthetically pleasing body of water and is popular in the Ukiah Valley, where summer temperatures can be sweltering.

Everything you could want for fun in the water can be rented here—Sea-Doos, Jet Skis, fishing boats, and pontoon boats.

> *February and March are typically the best months to spot large numbers of whales off the coastlines of Sonoma and Mendocino Counties. Watch long enough and you may see a whale "breach," or leap out of the water.*

All you need is a swimsuit. The visitor center offers information about the lake, Pomo Indian culture, and the Coyote Valley. The Interpretive Cultural Center has exhibits of Pomo Indian crafts, pottery, jewelry, and decorative arts. This area is a great place for a summer picnic.

PROVISIONERS: CHARTERS, WATERCRAFT, LESSONS

Here's a sampling of Wine Country businesses that cater to the aqua-nut. You'll find information on renting everything from a Jet Ski to kayaks, and lots of these folks will either guide you along or teach you what you need to know to have a safe and enjoyable experience.

Napa County

A Wet Pleasure Jet Ski & Boat Rentals
5800 Knoxville Road, Lake Berryessa
(707) 966-4204
A Wet Pleasure has a full lineup of aluminum fishing boats (14- or 16-footers), ski boats, pedal boats, 24-foot patio boats, and Yamaha Jet Skis. Boat rentals cost $60 for eight hours.

Sonoma County

W. C. "Bob" Trowbridge Canoe Trips
13840 Old Redwood Highway,
Healdsburg
(707) 433-7247, (800) 640-1386 (information and reservation line)
www.trowbridgecanoe.com

The company, named for the man who started it in 1953 (and whose granddaughter still helps run the shop), offers a wide range of canoe and kayak outings on the Russian River from April to October. You can choose from afternoon, half-day paddles for two to three hours; full days from four to six hours; or even a five-day canoe excursion.

Burke's Russian River Canoe Trips
8600 River Road, Forestville
(707) 887-1222
www.burkescanoetrips.com
Burke's provides your canoe, paddles, and life jackets starting at just $50 per canoe. Your trip begins at Burke's base near Forestville and ends 10 miles downstream at Guerneville. Burke's then shuttles you back to your car at Forestville. It's a leisurely four- to five-hour downstream paddle, with the opportunity for many stops on warm sunny beaches.

Bodega Bay Sportfishing Center
1410-B Bay Flat Road, Bodega Bay
(707) 875-3344
www.usa.fishing.com
These folks operate charter boats out of Bodega Bay for either full-day or half-day fishing trips for bay or ocean fishing. You'll be going after rock cod, lingcod, salmon (April through November), halibut, and Dungeness crab. Fishing tackle is available. Whale-watching trips run from November to February. The center specializes in evening cruises.

The cost of excursions begins at $75 if you're going for the fish listed above, and you can fish for them in combinations. Going out 60 to 80 miles for salmon or halibut would require a negotiated cost.

The company also operates from another location, the Boathouse, at 1445 Highway 1. It's the culinary extension of the business, with a sit-down restaurant that serves fish-and-chips, calamari, scallops, prawns, oysters, hot dogs, burgers, beer, and wine. Food is available for takeout, and box lunches may be ordered.

Bodega Bay Surf Shack
1400 Highway 1, Pelican Plaza, Bodega Bay
(707) 875-3944
www.bodegabaysurf.com

Bodega Bay Kayak
1580 East Shore Drive, Blue Whale Shopping Center, Bodega Bay
(707) 875-8899
www.bodegabaykayak.com

These two shops are a must-stop for any visitor eager to glean the optimum amount of local surfing or kayaking knowledge. Bob Miller, the Surf Shack's friendly and welcoming owner, has been surfing nearby Salmon Creek Beach and other primo wave spots since 1984. His shop offers surfboards, wetsuit rentals, and surfing lessons. Bike rentals also are available, along with a great selection of men's and women's beachwear and casual clothing. The nearby kayak shop offers single and tandem kayaks for half-day and all-day rental on sheltered Bodega Bay. More adventurous paddlers may want to consider signing up for the shop's guided tour of the coast.

High Tide Surf Shop
9 Fourth Street, Petaluma
(707) 763-3860
www.waveslave.com

Located in the McNear Building, part of Petaluma's historic downtown, High Tide is a relative newcomer, having arrived in 1992. If you should pass through "the crossroads to the beach," as proprietor Len Crain likes to call the neighborhood, don't expect his shop to be open before noon. Then again, you might want to avail yourself of a High Tide public service, a continuous broadcast of the coastal weather report and surf conditions emanating from a not-so-loud speaker above the recessed doorway.

High Tide stocks a complete line of custom surfboards, body boards, skim boards, and accessories, plus a large selection of wetsuits for men, women, and children of all sizes and shapes. Even if

the surf isn't calling your name, there's a rack full of Hawaiian shirts and a good selection of swimwear.

You may wonder about our coastal waters and the likelihood of encountering "jaws" during your visit. Yes, sharks happen. Though attacks are rare, great white sharks along the Sonoma coast have been known to attack anything that resembles prey, including kayaks and surfboards. If you go into the water, stay alert.

Windwalker Board Sports and School of Windsurfing
4347 Harrison Grade Road, Occidental
(707) 874-2331
www.wind-walker.com

Windwalker offers windsurfing lessons in Bodega Bay, where conditions are particularly favorable for learning the sport—a mile of 3-foot-deep water with consistent winds. The shop also rents wetsuits, boards, and sails.

Windwalker is unique in another respect: It offers bed-and-breakfast packages in a variety of accommodations and a wide price range.

King's Sport and Tackle Shop
16258 Main Street, Guerneville
(707) 869-2156

You can buy just about anything you need for the outdoor life here. Whether you're a camping, fishing, or archery enthusiast, or you don't know a striped bass from a catfish, King's friendly and knowledgeable staff can provide you with sportswear, footwear, camping gear and accessories,

---

Dogs on leashes are allowed at many beaches along the Sonoma coast. However, dogs are prohibited at Salmon Creek's north and south beaches, at Miwok Beach, and Coleman Beach.

---

fresh- and saltwater bait and tackle, and guns and ammo. Or select custom, hand-tied flies, dry bags for river activities, and equipment for abalone diving.

King's also provides guide service for fishing on the Russian River during steel-head, salmon, and bass season. A local hunting guide is available to help you stalk wild boar, deer, and turkey. King's rents kayaks ($25 a day for one-person kayaks, $40 for two) and gives guided river tours at any time of year, weather permitting.

Mendocino County

All Aboard Adventures
Noyo Harbor, Fort Bragg
(707) 964-1881
www.allaboardadventures.com
Hop aboard Captain Tim's *Sea Hawk* for salmon, rock cod, and lingcod fishing. Tim has been working charter boats for more than 20 years out of Fort Bragg, and the *Sea Hawk* is his newest purchase. Trips are at 7:00 A.M. and 1:00 P.M. daily. Deep-sea fishing trips are between $45 and $55

(tackle kits are extra, rod and bait are included). During January through April, All Aboard features two-hour whale-watching excursions for $25.

Rubicon Adventures
9743 Highway 116, Forestville
(707) 887-2452
www.rubiconadventures.com
Owner Bill Mashek has been leading whitewater tours since 1971. One example: a two-day excursion on the Eel River for $185 per person, including meals. Wetsuits are encouraged, but not provided (they can be easily rented), and Rubicon takes care of the shuttle arrangements.

Tributary Whitewater Tours
20480 Woodbury Drive, Grass Valley
(800) 672-3846
www.whitewatertours.com
Tributary has been guiding whitewater tours on all the major California rivers for more than two decades. Its two-day Eel River trip in Mendocino County runs during the months of April and May and costs approximately $200 per person (wetsuits and camping gear are extra). The company provides the boats—deluxe seven-person whitewater rafts—guides, and all meals. Though their headquarters is located near the Sierra Nevada Mountains, Tributary will rendezvous with clients for the Eel River trip at the takeout point at Dos Rios off Highway 162.

SPECTATOR SPORTS

The Wine Country approach to spectator sports varies from the occasional upscale PGA golf event to the more populist sprint-car racing. And professional-level happenings are always available in the Bay Area and Sacramento. No fewer than eight pro sports franchises take the field (or diamond, or court, or rink) within two hours of Wine Country—each is covered in this chapter. Though the list goes on and on, I had to draw the line somewhere. Other Bay Area sporting events—from boxing matches to major golf and tennis tournaments—are not listed here.

Also note that some sports outings seemed more appropriately included in the Festivals and Annual Events chapter—the annual rodeo at the Sonoma County Fair is an example. And if the activity is more participatory than vicarious in nature, look for it in the Parks and Recreation or On the Water chapters.

The radio stations listed below every franchise name are the teams' English-language flagship stations, and the phone numbers are ticket sources. For major events you also can try TicketMaster at (415) 421–8497.

BASEBALL

San Francisco Giants
SBC Park, China Basin
(415) 972-2000
www.sfgiants.com
KNBR 680 AM
One of two franchises—the Los Angeles Dodgers being the other—to open major-league baseball to westward expansion in 1958, the Giants have been a team of individual standouts but little collective success. The team has won several National League West championships and two pennants in its 40-or-so years in San Francisco, losing the World Series to the Yankees in 1962, to the Oakland A's in 1989, and to the Anaheim Angels in 2002.

Yet in this city, style points are almost as valuable as titles, and the Giants have had plenty of style. The 1960s squads had big clout from legendary center fielder Willie Mays, first basemen Willie McCovey and Orlando Cepeda, and the brilliant pitcher Juan Marichal.

Today, Barry Bonds continues to be a one-man draw. In 2001 Bonds went down in the history books for hitting 73 home runs during regular season play. He also set records for slugging percentage (.863) and walks (177). He hit his 600th career home run in 2002, joining an exclusive club of only three other players in the history of the game: Babe Ruth, Willie Mays, and Hank Aaron. But Bonds's image was tarnished in 2004 as allegations swirled around him that he used performance-enhancing steroids.

The Giants do their thing at SBC Park. Designed by the renowned architectural group of HOK Sports Facilities, it's a nostalgic wonder along the lines of Baltimore's Oriole Park at Camden Yards and Cleveland's Jacobs Field. The ballpark hugs San Francisco Bay—so close, in fact, that prodigious drives to right field end up in salt water, retrieved by a canine employee. The stadium includes a brewpub, a bayside promenade that allows fans to peek through the fence for no charge, and, unlike Monster Park, ample public transportation options. Current Giants ticket prices range from $9 to $45.

Oakland Athletics
Network Associates Coliseum, off
Interstate 880, about 5 miles south of
Interstate 980
(510) 638–4900
www.oaklandathletics.com,
www.coliseum.com
KFRC 610 AM

The Athletics' history in Oakland has been the steepest of roller-coaster rides. The A's had been unqualifiedly dreadful in Kansas City, but they immediately posted their first winning record in 16 years after moving to the Bay Area in 1968. Reggie Jackson hit the home runs and made the headlines, but the strength of the team was pitching, led by starters Jim "Catfish" Hunter and Vida Blue, and handlebar-mustachioed reliever Rollie Fingers. But Finley soon sold off his stars, and the Athletics sank into ineptitude. They played games in the late 1970s that drew fewer than 1,000 fans.

The A's became Major League Baseball's best team from 1988 to 1990. Dave Stewart won 20 or more games four straight years, Dennis Eckersley was reborn as baseball's eminent closer, Rickey Henderson returned to his hometown to steal bases and runs, and hitting giants such as Jose Canseco and Mark McGwire drove opposing pitchers into deep depression. Oakland was upset by the Dodgers in '88 and the Reds in '90 but flattened the Giants in 1989's "Bay Bridge Series," which was interrupted by the 7.1-magnitude Loma Prieta earthquake.

If you're going to the Oakland Coliseum or the Arena for a game, consider taking BART, the Bay Area Rapid Transit system. You can park in Richmond, at the northwest tip of what is commonly called the East Bay, and take a train to the coliseum's doorstep. Call (510) 236–2278 for schedules and directions.

The renovated Network Associates Coliseum lies south of downtown Oakland, right off Interstate 880. The cheapest A's ticket is $3.00; the most expensive is $30.00, and all of them are half price if you are younger than 15 or older than 60.

FOOTBALL

San Francisco 49ers
Monster Park at Candlestick Point, off
U.S. Highway 101, about 1.5 miles south
of Interstate 280
(415) 656–4900, (415) 467–1994
www.49ers.com
KGO 810 AM

The caps, the T-shirts, the bumper stickers, and the bar decorations are there to make sure you don't forget, not even for a minute, that Wine Country is Niners country. It wasn't always this way, of course. The team had its core following for decades, but it wasn't until the harmonic convergence of Bill Walsh and Joe Montana that the serious adulation began.

The 49ers were in the Super Bowl by January 1982, and they'd be back four times in the next 13 seasons. Along the way, Montana was replaced by scrambling Steve Young, now retired from the game. Wide receiver Dwight Clark was replaced by Jerry Rice, maybe the best player ever to wear an NFL uniform. Even Walsh was replaced with protégé George Seifert, who was in turn supplanted by Steve Mariucci in 1997. Through it all, the team hardly missed a beat—until 1999, when it sank to the bottom of the NFL. They took another hit in 2001, when Jerry Rice defected to the Oakland Raiders.

A few end notes: 49ers tickets are about $50, but good luck purchasing one. The games have been sold out since 1981. Allow at least 90 minutes to Candlestick Point from either Napa or Santa Rosa, progressively longer from points farther north. And for heaven's sake, bring a jacket and a thermos of something hot.

Oakland Raiders
Network Associates Coliseum, off I-880,
about 5 miles south of I-980
(800) 949-2626
www.raiders.com, www.coliseum.com
The Ticket, 1050 AM/KVON 1440 AM

That wasn't a tremor you felt in June 1995, it was the earth shifting back onto its proper axis upon the Raiders' return to Oakland—the first time a pro sports franchise had come back to a city it once fled.

The team's pinnacle was 1972 to 1976, when the blustery John Madden coached at least seven Pro Football Hall of Fame players: center Jim Otto, guard Gene Upshaw, tackle Art Shell, wide receiver Fred Biletnikoff, kicker George Blanda, linebacker Ted Hendricks, and cornerback Willie Brown (not to be confused with San Francisco's iconoclastic former mayor of the same name).

Stars of the 1980s included soft-spoken quarterback Jim Plunkett, relentless defensive end Howie Long, and incomparable running back Marcus Allen. Davis's never-ending search for the right head coach continued in 1998, when he brought in young Jon Gruden, an offensive whiz kid from the Philadelphia Eagles.

The Raiders' rich on-field history notwithstanding, the best reason to come to Oakland on an autumn Sunday always has been the spontaneous circus that erupts in the parking lot and the cheap seats. It's a freak show of the highest order. Expect to see Darth Vaders, Grim Reapers, dangling bronco effigies, and more Harley-Davidsons and pirate tattoos than you can shake a cutlass at. Tickets are $41, $51, and $61.

Finally, take note that the Raiders moved their summer training camp to Napa in 1996. They practice on a field behind the Napa Valley Marriott Hotel at 3425 Solano Avenue, which runs parallel to Highway 29. Those sessions are closed to the public, but the team has an annual fan day in July—and perhaps a couple of open workouts—at Memorial Stadium, which is near the intersection of Jefferson Street and Pueblo Avenue.

Legendary quarterback Joe Montana owns a ranch in Knights Valley, which is sort of a southern extension of Alexander Valley. Don't be surprised to see him shopping at the Palisades Market in Calistoga.

BASKETBALL

Golden State Warriors
The Arena in Oakland, off I-880, about
5 miles south of I-980
(510) 569-2121, (888) 479-4667
www.warriors.com
KNBR 680 AM

Born in Philadelphia in the 1940s, the Warriors moved west, becoming the San Francisco Warriors from 1962 to 1971, before floating across the bay to Oakland to become Golden State.

The team that brought Wilt Chamberlain from Philadelphia in 1962 has won only one NBA title on the West Coast. That came in 1975, when superstar Rick Barry and a gang of overachievers shocked the Washington Bullets in a four-game sweep. Big-time performers such as Nate Thurmond and Cazzie Russell came before 1974–75, Bernard King and World B. Free after, but no other Warriors team has gone all the way.

Things seemed to be looking up under coach Don Nelson in the early 1990s, but the situation blew up when Nelson feuded with star forward Chris Webber in 1994–95. Warriors tickets range from $10 to $113.

Sacramento Kings
ARCO Arena, near the northeast corner
of I-5 and I-80
(916) 928-6900
www.kings.com
KHTK 1140 AM

Game after game, ARCO Arena is filled to the rafters with screaming, maniacal Kings fans. Finally, they've got something to shout about. In their first 13 seasons in Sacramento the Kings never had a winning season. But the love of hoops was unconditional here. Sellouts are practically a Sacramento city ordinance.

Existing franchises in various sports, including the Raiders and the A's, certainly have taken notice, making overtures to Sacramento in the recent past regarding possible moves. (Sacramento has been the Kings' home since 1985, but they've moved before—from Rochester, Cincinnati, and Kansas City.)

ARCO Arena is just north of Sacramento. From the Wine Country, take Interstate 80 to Sacramento and turn off on Interstate 5 north. Take the Del Paso Road exit and follow the signs. Tickets range from $10 to $155 per game, though all but the cheapest seats are snapped up by season-ticket holders.

HOCKEY

San Jose Sharks
H-P Pavilion, off I-880
(408) 287-4275
www.sjsharks.com
KUFX 98.5 FM

The Sharks made a reputation as giant killers as they knocked off high-ranked opponents, Detroit and then Calgary, in the opening rounds of the 1994 and 1995 NHL playoffs. But the problem for San Jose has been getting to the playoffs. The Sharks have been known as the bottom feeders of the Western Conference, though coach Darryl Sutter's 1999–2000 squad was eminently respectable.

H-P Pavilion is a tidy venue smack-dab in the middle of a tidy city, and professional hockey has been an incongruous hit in Silicon Valley. To get to the arena, exit I-880 at Coleman Avenue, turn left on Coleman, right on Julian, and follow the parking signs.

Be advised that San Jose is about 40 miles south of San Francisco or Oakland, so getting there and back from Wine Country takes an investment of a full day

or a long evening. Sharks tickets range from $18 for the most distant upper-reserved seats to $102 for sideline club seats. Many others are in the $35 to $72 range.

SOCCER

San Jose Earthquakes
Spartan Stadium, off I-280
(408) 985-GOAL
www.sjearthquakes.com
KLIV 1590 AM

When Major League Soccer officially set up shop in spring of 1996, the fledgling league chose San Jose as the site of its inaugural game. The city had everything MLS was looking for: an established soccer tradition, a first-rate stadium, and a well-run organization headed by transplanted Englishman Peter Bridgwater. More than 31,000 fans crammed into Spartan Stadium on April 6, 1996, and the Clash (as they were then known) did not disappoint, leaving with a 1-0 victory over D.C. United.

Midfielder Eddie Lewis was named to the U.S. National Team for 1999 while gifted forward Ronald Cerritos played for El Salvador. In 2000 they meshed under the tutelage of Bay Area favorite Lother Osiander. The Earthquakes won the MLS Cup in 2001 over the L.A. Galaxy, on the winning goal of Cerritos. In 2003, with the phenomenal Landon Donovan, they earned the cup in a victory over the Chicago Fire.

Spartan Stadium is on the San Jose State University campus, accessible by I-280 in the heart of San Jose. Exit at Seventh Street, turn right on Seventh, and proceed about 1.5 miles to the stadium. (And please note the distance caveat stated at the end of the Sharks' summary.) Adult tickets range from $13 for behind-the-goal seats to $45 for the "premier" category. The Major League Soccer schedule runs from March through October.

GOLF

**Charles Schwab Cup Championship
Sonoma Golf Club, Sonoma
(707) 996-0300
www.sonomagolfclub.com**
This is the final event on the Champions
Tour (what used to be called the PGA
Seniors Tour), a four-day party in late
October at the Sonoma Golf Club, a private par 72, 7093-yard course built in
1928. Tour players 50 and older have
included Hale Irwin, Tom Watson, Jim
Thorpe (who won the 2003 event), and
Gil Morgan. In 2004 a relative youngster
to the tour, Mark McNulty, shot a final-
round 66 to win the $2.5 million champi-
onship by a stroke over Tom Kite. Ticket
prices vary depending on what you want
to see: $30 gets you in for two days of
practice rounds; a grounds pass is $30 for
the tournament weekend. Add access to
the wine festival and it goes up to $45 per
day. Taking part in the whole enchilada
costs between $100 and $150.

MOTOR SPORTS

Don't be surprised if the still air of your
summer evening is suddenly torn apart by
the growl of a 750-horsepower engine,
the scent of ripening grapes replaced by a
whiff of high-octane fuel. Love 'em or hate
'em, racing machines are here to stay in
Wine Country.

**Calistoga Speedway
Napa County Fairgrounds, 1435 North
Oak Street, Calistoga
(707) 942-5111
www.napacountyfairgrounds.com**
Calistoga is a gathering point for devotees
of sprint cars, those miniature, winged
beasts that evolved from old Indy 500
roadsters. Pound for pound, sprint cars
pack as much power as modern-day Indy
cars, and they seem to be as loud. They
produce downward force, which helps
the car grip the track; the larger one also

happens to provide handy space for
advertising.
Calistoga Speedway's half-mile dirt
track hosts approximately seven sprint-car
nights a year: in early May, Memorial Day
weekend, in mid-June, and Labor Day
weekend. A typical program might include
four 10-lap heat races, a feature-inversion
dash, a 12-lap semi-main event, and a 25-
lap feature event. Tickets run about $20
for a single race to $110 for a three-day
package.

**Infineon Raceway
Highways 37 and 121, south of Sonoma
(800) 870-RACE
www.infineonraceway.com**
If it's nitro-burning, rubber-ripping, and
asphalt-grabbing, chances are you'll find it
here. This might be the world's busiest
raceway, with an average of 340 days a
year of activity including 50 of 52 weekends. Much of that is devoted to the resident Russell Racing School, but there is
plenty of competition among a variety of
internally combusting machines. Annual
events at this raceway include the
NASCAR Nextel Cup and the LeMans
Series Grand Prix.
Besides the twisting, 12-turn, 2.52-mile
road course and the quarter-mile drag
strip, Infineon offers 700,000 square feet
of coexisting shop space and posh, tower
VIP seats. The facility is in a beautiful corner of lush rolling hills at the southern tip
of Sonoma County. If you just want a look,
it's open to the public free of charge on
weekdays. If you want to get truly revved,
race tickets range from $15 to $100, with
many in the $15 to $25 range.
A $50 million facelift over the last few
years added more comfort for spectators:
a new seven-story-high grandstand at the
start/finish line with seating for 12,000,
luxury boxes, and improved restrooms and
concession stands, as well as two underground pedestrian walkways. The track
and pit areas also underwent major renovations, and a new drag strip was built.

> *Vrrrooooom! There's always something going on (or round and round) at Infineon Raceway. If you love big engines and fast cars, you will find them here—many different competitions take place throughout the year, particularly in summer.*

Petaluma Speedway
Petaluma Fairgrounds, 100 Fairgrounds Drive
(707) 762-7223
www.petalumaspeedway.com
Check the notes about sprint cars listed in the Calistoga Speedway section and apply them here. NARC stages two events on Petaluma's three-eighths-mile, semi-banked track over the July Fourth weekend and in early October. The fairgrounds are just west of U.S. Highway 101 on East Washington Street.

MARATHONS AND RUNNING EVENTS

Vineman Marathon
Northern Sonoma County
(707) 528-1630
www.vineman.com
This popular event—in its 14th year—attracts more than 2,000 participants from throughout the world. It is set mostly on the backroads of northern Sonoma County, with the swimming portion held in the Russian River at Guerneville. The full course includes a 112-mile cycle, 26.2-mile run, and 2.4-mile swim. A Half Vineman is also featured.

Napa Valley Marathon
Calistoga to Napa
(707) 255-2609
www.napa-marathon.com
If you're gonna torture yourself, you might as well do it in Eden. This is an unbeatable course: 26.2 miles due south along the Sil-

verado Trail, hills hugging the left side of the road, and a yellow sea of blooming mustard to the right. Only the last half mile, the approach to the finish line at Vintage High School, is within any city limits. And after three moderate hills in the first 6 miles, the course offers a gently rolling descent. *Runner's World* magazine named this one of the top-20 marathons in America in 2002.

The Napa Valley Marathon usually takes place the first Sunday in March. The 2005 edition was the 27th annual. You can park at Vintage High and take a shuttle bus to the start line (just south of Calistoga on the Silverado Trail) but be punctual—the last bus leaves at 5:30 A.M. Weather can vary, of course, but bet on lifting fog and temperatures in the mid-40s at start time (7:00 A.M.), progressing to warm sunshine later in the morning. Early entry costs $60, and it jumps to $75 on prerace Saturday.

The Relay
Calistoga to Santa Cruz
(650) 508-9700
www.TheRelay.com
The marathon doesn't present enough of a challenge for you? Try the Relay, a 199-mile trek that winds through 7 counties and 36 cities from Calistoga to Santa Cruz, past cow pastures and redwoods and across the Golden Gate Bridge.

Everything about this race is unique, except for sore feet and sweaty bodies. Start times are staggered, and teams of 12 competitors split up 36 3-to-7-mile legs, with vans leapfrogging runners to their next start position. The race heads south from Calistoga on the Silverado Trail, with competitors running through the night and the first finishers reaching the Pacific Ocean early the next morning. Several Silicon Valley companies have been involved, presenting more peculiarities. This was the first race in which runners wore bar codes and got scanned at checkpoints.

The Relay is run under a full moon in September or October. The entry fee is $40 per runner, climbing to $50 in August. Individuals looking for a team have two options: Find one yourself at the Web site, or mark the appropriate box on your application and organizers will place you.

BICYCLE ROAD RACES

Cherry Pie Criterium
Napa Valley Corporate Park, Napa
(707) 224-2369

The carbo-loading comes after the race at this event. Besides the $1,500 or so in prize money—including $600 for the Pro I–II division—the top three finishers in each class are awarded fresh cherry pies. The 2005 Cherry Pie is the 30th annual. The 1-mile course, which includes one modest hill, is bounded by Napa Valley Corporate Drive, Napa Valley Corporate Way, and Trefethen Way. The simplest way to find the start/finish line is to look for the famous Grape Crusher statue south of Napa. Between 300 and 350 racers split up into 11 divisions, including a recumbent category. It is run the second or third Sunday in February.

Napa Grand Prix
First and Main Streets, Napa
(707) 963-7736

This criterium (a timed road race, with the winner determined by number of laps completed) got its start just a decade ago, but its following is on the upswing. Hoping for a breeze off the Napa River in early August, the restaurants of downtown Napa put extra tables on the sidewalk so their customers can sip cool drinks and watch the colors go blurring by. The master's race is a U.S. Cycling Federation district championship, and there are several other divisions, including

a 90-minute pro race that draws about 80 riders. The 0.7-mile course is bounded by First, School, Second, and Main Streets.

Petaluma Criterium
Downtown Petaluma
(707) 766-7501
www.eastsidecycles.com,
www.ncnca.com

Eastside Cycles in Petaluma is the promoter of this popular cycling race, which takes place in downtown Petaluma on a Sunday in August. (The event returns in 2005 after a one-year hiatus.) The entry fee is $20, and cash prizes are awarded.

Wine Country Cycling Classic
Graton and Santa Rosa
(707) 544-4803
www.srcc.com

What started as the Santa Rosa Criterium in 1984 has become a two-day road event, the largest of its kind in Northern California. The Wine Country Cycling Classic takes place in late March or early April and includes a total field of nearly 1,500 riders. The first day features the Graton Road Race, staged on an 11-mile course that presents four short, rolling climbs and one certified calf burner. The pro division race is 88 miles long and pays about $4,000. Graton is 3.5 miles north of Sebastopol, just west of Highway 116.

As many as 5,000 spokeheads turn out to watch the action on the second day on a flat, fast 0.7-mile course in downtown Santa Rosa. The racing is only part of a day of festivities that often includes a live band. The Senior I/Pro division competes for 90 minutes and splits about $3,500. The starting/finish line is on Sonoma Avenue. Take the Downtown Santa Rosa exit from US 101 and head east on Third Street to Santa Rosa Avenue. Turn right and proceed two blocks.

HORSE RACING

Sonoma County Fairgrounds
Highway 12, east of US 101,
Santa Rosa
(707) 545-4200
www.sonomacountyfair.com
If the hoofbeat of the thoroughbreds should happen to draw your attention in midsummer, heed the call to the colors. What you'll find at the Sonoma County Fair from late July through early August is one of the country's most entertaining 12-day horse-racing meets. Top jockeys such as Russell Baze, Dennis Carr, and Rafael Meza guide the trainees of Jerry Hollendorfer, Brent Sumja, Lloyd Mason, and others as thousands cheer home the world's greatest four-legged athletes. Wagering on the competition is optional. First post is 1:15 P.M.

The Jockey Club
1350 Bennett Valley Road, Santa Rosa
(707) 524-6340
www.sonomacountyfair.com/jockey.asp
This is where Wine Country's wise guys and other hip handicappers amuse themselves when the shed rows across the street aren't booked with blood stock. It's a year-round off-track concession offering races live via satellite TV from major courses in California (e.g., Golden Gate Fields, Bay Meadows, Santa Anita, Hollywood Park, Del Mar), New York, and Florida.

A small cover charge gets you through the door and into a well-kept room stocked with 8 projection big-screen TVs, 70 monitors, a full bar, and complete food and beverage services. Friendly clerks will take your wagers, or you may purchase a voucher and have at the auto-tote self-serve screens yourself. Either way, remember: There's a winner in each race.

COLLEGE SPORTS

With only three four-year colleges inside its borders, expansive Wine Country isn't exactly a hotbed of collegiate sports. Again, the Bay Area might be the place to turn if you really feel like waving a pom-pom and belting out fight songs. Here is a brief look at your options.

Sonoma State University
1801 East Cotati Avenue, Rohnert Park
(707) 664-2701
www.sonoma.edu/athletics
With a couple of players going on to the NFL, including Pro Bowl guard Larry Allen of the Dallas Cowboys, the NCAA Division II Seawolves reached a respected place among small football programs. That came to an end in 1997, when the university dropped football in the face of formidable travel expenses.

Sonoma State still has plenty of athletics. Soccer is king and queen there: The women, who made it to the Division II championship game in 1998, enjoyed great success in the '90s, winning six straight Northern California Athletic Conference titles from 1990 to 1995 and a national championship in 1990. The men won five of seven NCAC titles between 1990 and 1996, and went on in 2002 to win the NCAA Division II national championship—the first ever for any SSU men's team.

Pacific Union College
1 Angwin Avenue, Angwin
(707) 965-6344
www.puc.edu
Tiny PUC has to scramble to come up with funding for sports, but the NAIA Division II school does what it can. It fields men's and/or women's teams in soccer, volleyball, tennis, cross-country, basketball, golf, and softball, with all but tennis staged on campus. The Pioneers have produced recent California Pacific Conference champions in women's basketball and men's golf.

University of California
2223 Fulton Street, Berkeley
(800) 462-3277
www.calbears.com
Known primarily for its academics and tradition of radical politics, Cal also has a rich sports heritage, with Rose Bowl victories

dating to 1921 (28–0 over Ohio State). The Golden Bear's football program, which produced such stars as Craig Morton, Steve Bartkowski, Wesley Walker, and Chuck Muncie, has seen better days. Coach Bruce Snyder took the Bears to strong conference finishes and a Citrus Bowl victory in the early 1990s, but since then the program has floundered.

Bears basketball experienced a recent renaissance, begun by phenomenal point guard Jason Kidd (now an NBA star) in the early '90s. In 1996–97, first-year coach Ben Braun took over a team in disarray (and headed for NCAA probation, thanks to the misdeeds of his predecessor Todd Bozeman), lost leading scorer Ed Gray at the end of the Pac-10 schedule, and still managed to invade the NCAA tourney's Sweet Sixteen.

KIDSTUFF 👫

You've just exited your tenth tasting room of the day and have an impressive collection of souvenir glasses, coasters, and corkscrews from an assortment of winery gift shops. The kids are bored, but they have energy left to burn. If you don't find a suitable diversion for them soon, you'll have a full-blown mutiny on your hands.

No need to worry—you don't have to change your plans and head to Orlando. There are plenty of opportunities for pleasing the little ones while entertaining the big kids too. Many of the attractions in this chapter are reliable kid pleasers, guaranteed to put a smile on small faces.

In addition, check out the Attractions chapter, which features information on many other family-oriented fun stuff, such as Safari West and the Pacific Coast Air Museum. And read about great outdoor destinations for all ages in the Parks and Recreation and On the Water chapters.

NAPA COUNTY

Napa Skate Park
Vajome and Clinton Streets, Napa
(707) 257-9529
If they're bouncing off the walls, just put a skateboard or a scooter under their feet and give 'em a gentle nudge. The skate park is just about what you'd expect: a cemented city block with an assortment of hills, dips, ramps, and pathways. This is a free, do-it-yourself attraction. Bring your own gear, supervise your own children, bandage your own knees. Roller skates and roller blades are welcome too.

John F. Kennedy Memorial Regional Park
Streblow Drive off Highway 121, Napa
(707) 257-9529
The largest of Napa's municipal parks at 340 acres, Kennedy has four group picnic areas, hiking and jogging trails, volleyball courts, a lighted baseball diamond, and a multiuse ball field. It also has a duck pond and playground for the really young ones, plus a boat ramp for family outings. It's a tranquil, breezy setting adjacent to the Napa River.

Paradise Miniature Golf
640 Third Street, Napa
(707) 258-1695
What would a family road trip be without a few rounds of miniature golf? Paradise is in the heart of Napa (which some would say is in the heart of paradise). It has a 19-hole course and a snack bar with candy and soft drinks. A couple of favorites: the 5th hole, with its grand loop-the-loop and, best of all, the 17th—the Valley Fog Hole—which tests your bad-weather vision as well as your hand-eye coordination. The cost is $3.50 for adults, $2.00 for kids 12 and younger, and $3.00 for members of the "senior tour." Paradise is open 3:00 to 7:00 P.M. Monday through Friday and 11:00 A.M. to 7:00 P.M. Saturday and Sunday during the summer.

Playground Fantástico
Old Sonoma Road at Freeway Drive, Napa
(707) 257-9529
When a city the size of Napa can pull together more than 1,500 volunteers for an intensive six-day community project, you know the result will be something special. In this case the result is a world-class, 15,000-square-foot playground with an estimated worth of $2 million, built in 2002 entirely with donated materials and labor. There are two themed sandboxes, two castles, one area for tots and another for older children, a tree house, a train station, and much more. No shortcuts were taken in the quality of the materials and creativity—nearly everything is tastefully

constructed from wood. At the entrance is a 22-foot-tall work of art described as "part Fred Flintstone meets the Michelin Man meets pick-up sticks" by one of the creative minds behind the project. It's fun, and it's free.

Carolyn Parr Nature Museum
3107 Browns Valley Road, Napa
(707) 255-6465

This modest facility a mile west of Highway 29 is sponsored by the Napa Valley Naturalists. People come here to see the museum's dioramas, which show five habitats: grassland, chaparral, marshland, riparian, and woodland/forest. Inside each diorama are examples of native plants and animal specimens, from raccoons and wood ducks to king snakes and badgers. There is an extensive raptor display and a special kids' section with such hands-on items as pelts and skulls. Adults enjoy the Carolyn Parr museum too, but the small scale seems ideally suited to children. Admission is free. The museum is open 1:00 to 4:00 P.M. Saturday and Sunday and for group tours by appointment (50 cents per head). It is at the entrance to Westwood Hills Park, a 111-acre green space with picnic facilities and a self-guided nature trail.

Learning Faire
964 Pearl Street, Napa
(707) 253-1024
www.learningfaire.com

This Napa toy store, under the same ownership for more than 20 years, prides itself on selectivity. All products are pre-screened for safety, and they sell nothing that promotes violence. Learning Faire stocks Brio, Thomas wooden trains, Legos, plenty of other toys, and lots of games, puzzles, crafts, books, cassettes, and CDs. There are hands-on stations and the occasional market-research play day—when manufacturer reps bring new toys for kids to sample.

The Toy Cellar
Vintage 1870, 6525 Washington Street, Yountville
(707) 944-2144

Sprawling Vintage 1870 tends to be a lot more popular with moms than juniors. The antidote? Let the kids roam around the Toy Cellar with its books and Brio trains, its Beanie Babies and Playmobil, its Steiff bears and model rockets, its LGB German trains and old-fashioned metal jack-in-the-boxes. Meanwhile, Dad can pop down to the wine cellar (see the Wineries chapter).

Crane Park
Highway 29 and Grayson Avenue, St. Helena
(707) 963-5706

St. Helena families and kids of every stripe gather at this well-kept sanctuary. The 10-acre park has two baseball diamonds, horseshoe pits, lighted boccie courts and tennis courts, substantial picnic setups, a playground, and volleyball pits. On summer Fridays the farmers' market is here.

Smith's Mount St. Helena Trout Farm and Hatchery
18401 Ida Clayton Road, Calistoga
(707) 987-3651

Smith's has been raising trout for private ponds for six decades. On weekends the staff open up the three-quarter-acre lake to the public, and locals have learned that it's one of the best diversions in the area for children. The proprietors provide poles and bait, and they even clean and bag the trout for you afterward. All you do is bait, cast, and reel. You pay only for the fish you take—$3.00 to $5.00, depending on size. From Highway 128 in Knights Valley, just north of Calistoga, go 7 miles north at the big sign for Smith's. On Saturday and Sunday from February through October, the fun lasts 10:00 A.M. to 5:00 P.M.

Petrified Forest
4100 Petrified Forest Road, Calistoga
(707) 942-6667
www.petrifiedforest.org
The trees died a few million years ago, but they remain alive forever as stone sculptures of what they used to be. Paths wind in and out through the fossilized forest (see the Attractions chapter). Visitors can take a quarter-mile loop that requires about 20 minutes to stroll. Almost as interesting as the forest is the museum and gift shop, where you can buy all kinds of good stuff—stones you've never seen before and pieces of wood turned to stone. There's also a good selection of books. Guided walks are offered on Sunday at 2:00 P.M. The museum and store are open daily 9:00 A.M. to 6:00 P.M. Admission is $6.00 for adults; $5.00 for youngsters ages 12 through 17 and seniors 60 and over; and $3.00 for kids under 12.

SONOMA COUNTY

Southern Sonoma

The Clubhouse Family Fun Center
19171 Sonoma Highway, Sonoma
(707) 996-3616
When's the last time you paid less than 10 bucks for 18 holes of golf? The course is laid out to look like historic Sonoma, with ponds, fountains, and a lifelike city hall. Not just for kids, it's a great place for teens. The Clubhouse also features the latest video games as well as sports games like air hockey, basketball, and football video games. To put an extra spin on a great family day, have a hot dog at the pondside picnic area. The course and game room are open noon to 8:00 P.M. Monday through Thursday, noon to 10:00 P.M. Friday and Saturday, and 10:00 A.M. to 9:00 P.M. Sunday. Special packages are available for family groups and birthday parties.

Train Town
20264 Broadway, Sonoma
(707) 938-3912
www.traintown.com
It's difficult to say who gets the most fun out of this train ride, kids or adults. The whole layout is so cleverly crafted that it's a marvel of dedication to the art of the train buff. The miniature train travels through scenic landscapes of trees, lakes, bridges, a 140-foot-long tunnel, and a small-scale replica of a turn-of-the-20th-century Sonoma Valley town called Lakeville. Midway along, the best part for many kids is the petting zoo. For five minutes the train stops and everyone hauls out to pet llamas, horses, and miniature goats and to feed the ducks and geese. Back at the station there's a carousel ride ($1.00) and some interesting mechanical exhibits. Trains operate 10:00 A.M. to 5:00 P.M. every day in summer. Winter hours are 10:00 A.M. to 5:00 P.M. Friday through Sunday. Trains leave every 30 minutes. Adult fare is $3.75; kids and seniors go for $3.25.

Morton's Warm Springs Resort
1651 Warm Springs Road, Kenwood
(707) 833-5511, (800) 551-2177
www.mortonswarmsprings.com
One of the last of the natural mineral-water swimming holes, Morton's has three beautiful pools—for toddlers, for kids, and for the family. More fun can be had at the volleyball and basketball courts, horseshoe pits, baseball field, boccie ball court, and game room with all the latest video games. There are 11 naturally landscaped picnic areas (one by a stream) with barbecue pits and shaded tables. Morton's is well known locally as a family gathering place and for hosting family and corporate picnics of up to 2,400 people. Parking is available at no extra charge. The snack bar is conveniently close to the pools with ice-cold drinks and a wide selection of hot dogs, hamburgers, chips,

and all those picnic eats that make a family day so much fun. Morton's is open from the first weekend in May through most of September. Call or visit the Web site for updated information on days, hours of operation, and admission fees.

Early Work Toy Station
601 Petaluma Boulevard North, Petaluma
(707) 765-1993
www.earlywork.com
Early Work was formerly a shop for teachers looking for educational materials, but it is now open to the public. It's a great favorite with children because of its selection of creative toys and learning materials. There's something for everyone here, from age 1 to 100. Toys and books cover art, science, math, and language. There's an event schedule that changes from month to month—call the store for times or check its Web site.

Jungle Vibes
136 Kentucky Street, Petaluma
(707) 762-6583, (800) 804-0007
www.junglevibes.com
They call it a nature and science store, but it's really an adventure where nature and science meet world culture. At this unique Petaluma store, walking in the door is like entering another country. A taste of adventure and multicultural exploration goes a long way in our busy lives, and Jungle Vibes is set to help the community explore the world, using nature and science toys and books to complement an authentic collection of ethnic arts and sounds. This is the place to expand your child's world.

Victoria's Fashion Stables
4193 Old Adobe Road, Petaluma
(707) 665-0600
www.fashionstables.com
No, it's not related to that tantalizing fashion catalog. This place is pure, clean barnyard fun, featuring good stuff for good kids—small, medium, or large.

You can't beat Sonoma's Train Town for family fun. In addition to miniature trains, there's a petting zoo, Ferris wheel, and merry-go-round.

For the little ones, there's a petting zoo along with pony rides. This isn't your average petting zoo, though. You'll start by seeing clucking chickens and waddling ducks; proceed to greeting pygmy goats, potbellied pigs, and baby horses; and then go on to a lesson in how to milk a cow. Pony rides are suitable for even very small children—the staff will walk beside the horse and hold junior steady if necessary. The stables are open every day except Tuesday. Appointments are preferred though drop-ins can usually be accommodated. Every October there's a pumpkin patch here. Victoria's also operates a day-use and overnight campground, with fishing nearby. Wait, there's more: a horse and carriage service for weddings.

Cal Skate
6100 Commerce Boulevard,
Rohnert Park
(707) 585-0500
www.calskate.com
Kids of all ages love to roller-skate here. The arena is open from 9:30 A.M. to 8:00 P.M., and it offers special sessions—such as the tiny tots session for kids eight and under. There is also plenty of open skating. Adult prices are $3.50 to $4.75.

Scandia Family Fun Center
5301 Redwood Drive, Rohnert Park
(707) 584-1398
www.scandiafunland.com
There's fun for everyone here: miniature golf, batting cages, go-karts, a video arcade, an Indy raceway, Tidal Wave bumper boats, and a snack bar. It opens every day at 10:00 A.M. and stays open until 11:00 P.M. on weekdays and midnight on weekends. Prices vary by attraction.

Toobtown—Q-Zar Family Center
6591 Commerce Boulevard, Rohnert Park
(707) 588-8100
Toobtown is for children ages 2 to 12 and younger, offering unlimited play in a four-story tube structure, plus a dinosaur bounce, fun in the gym, three bumper-boat rides in a pond, and lots of rides on horses and tortoises and spaceships. Socks are required by the dress code. (Q-Zar laser tag is for children seven and older.) Hours are 10:00 A.M. to 8:00 P.M. Sunday through Thursday, 10:00 A.M. to 9:00 P.M. Friday and Saturday. Weekday prices are $4.95; it's $6.95 on the weekend.

Copperfield's Books
2316 Montgomery Drive, Santa Rosa
(707) 578-8938
www.copperfields.com
Voted best kids' bookstore by an independent Sonoma County readers' poll, Copperfield's keeps up a steady stream of events to get kids interested in reading. Book promotions are creatively staged. For the Cat in the Hat program, kids had a chance to get their picture taken with the Cat himself. Family Fun Night brought out Curious George and provided an opportunity to help the man in the yellow hat find his curious companion. Occasional get-togethers with balloons and storytelling give book reading a party atmosphere. (See the Bookstores section of the Shopping chapter for more on Copperfield's.)

Environmental Discovery Center
Spring Lake Regional Park, Violetti Road, Santa Rosa
(707) 539-2865
www.sonomacounty.org/parks/foundation
Here's a treat for the kids and the parents too. The former visitor center on the eastern edge of this park was creatively converted recently into a terrific facility for children to learn about the environment around them. Exhibits are always changing, but one of the most popular is a tide pool populated with interesting sea creatures that can be picked up and examined. Expect interactive games, an aquarium, puzzles, and many other activities geared to youngsters. The center is open 10:00 A.M. to 5:00 P.M. Wednesday through Friday and noon to 5:00 P.M. weekends. Admission is free; parking at Spring Lake is $4.00.

Howarth Park
630 Summerfield Road, Santa Rosa
(707) 543-3425
www.santarosarec.com
One of 27 parks in Santa Rosa, Howarth is the big one, a 152-acre retreat into the world of nature. There's a 25-acre lake where families can rent canoes, rowboats, paddleboats, and sailboats and even take sailing lessons. Kids and parents also can fish for trout, bluegill, and bass throughout the year. In another part of the park, a simulated steam train follows a quarter-mile track over a bridge and through a tunnel. The latest addition to the park is the Land of Imagination, with an elaborate climbing structure, a frontier town, a Mexican rancho facade, and life-size animal sculptures. Bring a picnic and have a great day! The park is open 6:00 A.M. to 9:00 P.M. in summer and 6:00 A.M. to 6:00 P.M. in winter. Boat rentals (fishing is optional and subject to state regulations) and amusement rides are in operation 11:00 A.M. to 5:00 P.M. Tuesday through Sunday during summer and on weekends in spring and fall.

Redwood Empire Ice Arena
1667 West Steele Lane, Santa Rosa
(707) 546-7147
www.snoopyshomeice.com
Charles Schulz, famous for his *Peanuts* cartoons, grew up in Minnesota and never lost his love for ice-skating. The rink he built in Santa Rosa is a beautiful venue compared to the outdoor rinks he knew in his youth. A full range of skating is offered, with mornings reserved for pro-

grams and classes (many world champions have trained here). The arena is open daily, but hours vary. The cost is $7.00 for adults and teens and $5.50 for children younger than 12. Aside from the ice arena, there's a wonderful Snoopy's Gallery gift shop that's appealing to all ages (see the Shopping chapter). You can also buy skates here, both ice and roller. (For more information on the arena and the Charles M. Schulz Museum next door, see the Attractions chapter.)

Riley Street Art Supplies
103 Maxwell Court, Santa Rosa
(707) 526-2416

500 West Napa Street, Sonoma
(707) 935-3199
www.rileystreet.com
These are great places to pick up childrens' craft supplies, including face-painting kits, tempera paints, tattoo books, how-to-draw books, and build-your-own foam dinosaur kits. For one week each July (exact dates vary), a kids' art camp is held at the Santa Rosa store from 9:00 A.M. to 1:00 P.M. at a cost of $120 per child. Youngsters get professional instruction in whatever medium is suitable for their age. This is a premier shopping spot for professional artists and craftspeople.

Santa Rosa Junior College Planetarium
2001 Lark Hall, 1501 Mendocino Avenue,
Santa Rosa
(707) 527-4371
www.santarosa.edu
Star-studded shows feature various astronomical phenomena, with the night sky projected (with special effects) onto the dome by state-of-the-art equipment. Offered only during the school year, shows are scheduled at 7:00 and 8:30 P.M. on Friday and Saturday and at 1:30 and 3:00 P.M. on Sunday. Cost is $4.00 for adult general admission and $2.00 for students and seniors, all on a first-come, first-served basis. Children younger than five are not admitted.

Northern Sonoma

Windsor Waterworks & Slides
8225 Conde Lane, Windsor
(707) 838-7360, (707) 838-7760
The excitement begins 42 feet up, where you can pair up with a friend or go it alone on the big double-tube river ride. Or maybe you'd rather plunge down the speed slide for the thrill of a lifetime. Want more? Try King Richard's run, a giant of a slide, with double tubes that propel you through a tunnel of fun. The height requirement for those thrill rides is 45 inches. But the little ones (at least 36 inches tall) haven't been forgotten. There's a special body flume just for them. Between rides, there's time to swim, play volleyball, pitch horseshoes, or take a whack at Ping-Pong. Windsor Waterworks is open 11:00 A.M. to 7:00 P.M. from May through September (weekends only until June 15). Adults and teens pay $13.25 for full use of the park, kids ages 4 to 12 are $12.25, and those younger than 4 are free. There is another option: An afternoon splash special running from 4:00 to 7:00 P.M. is only $9.75 per person.

The Toyworks
2759 Fourth Street, Santa Rosa
(707) 526-2099

6940 Sebastopol Avenue, Sebastopol
(707) 829-2003
www.sonomatoyworks.com
A store of educational toys, Toyworks claims 13,000 different items, from European toys, Lego blocks, and science and nature items to educational books and Lionel trains. Store hours are 10:00 A.M. to 6:00 P.M. Monday through Saturday and 11:00 A.M. to 5:00 P.M. Sunday.

Lake Sonoma Fish Hatchery
3333 Skaggs Springs Road, Geyserville
(707) 433-9483
www.parks.sonoma.net
Here's a chance to peek in on all phases of fish life, depending on the season. In sum-

mer you'll see the small, young fish; later in the season, from late October through March, you'll be able to watch the coho salmon and steelheads returning to spawn and climbing the fish ladder. The coho salmon will die after spawning, but the steelheads will live to return to the sea. Once the eggs have been laid and fertilized, the fish hatchery starts collecting the eggs once a week—each Thursday at 10:30 A.M. Summer hours here are 9:00 A.M. to 5:00 P.M. daily; winter hours are 9:00 A.M. to 4:00 P.M. Wednesday through Sunday. There is no charge. Visitors also will enjoy a display of Native American artifacts, plus information on local geology.

West County/ Russian River

Pet-a-Llama Ranch
**5505 Lone Pine Road, Sebastopol
(707) 823-9395
www.pet-a-llama.com**
You only need to look into a llama's soulful, gentle eyes and stroke its long, softly curving banana ears to fall in love. The llama's long eyelashes are to be envied; their arched necks give them dignity. The place to get acquainted with these exotic animals is at Pet-a-Llama Ranch, where two dozen of them live and entertain visitors. School groups come during the week to learn about the animals' habits, get up close and personal with them, and give them a snack. Saturday and Sunday, though, is open house from 10:00 A.M. to 4:00 P.M. from April to December. Kids will get a kick out of feeding them (it's 50 cents) and listening to the manager of the ranch tell what llama life is all about— where they come from, what they eat, and how they're used as pack animals in their native South America.

MENDOCINO COUNTY

Pomo Cultural Center
**1003 Marine Drive, Lake Mendocino, Ukiah
(707) 485-8285, (707) 485-8685 (gift shop)**
The round shape of the center is modeled on the Pomo tribe's ceremonial dance house, where cultural knowledge was passed down through the generations. Kids will be intrigued with the games the Pomo played, will learn how clamshells were used as money, and will have the chance to hold animal skins in the wild animal exhibit. The gift shop, operated by the Pomo, has a fascinating collection of items made by local Native Americans. Admission is free. The museum is open 9:00 A.M. to 5:00 P.M. Wednesday through Sunday from April through mid-November and is closed in winter (see the Attractions chapter).

Mendocino Coast Recreation and Park District
**213 East Laurel Street, Fort Bragg
(707) 964-9446
www.mcrpd.us**
This county recreation program provides fun for kids the whole summer long. An indoor swimming pool is available for recreational swimming and for swim classes. Day use of the pool is $2.00 for kids, $3.00 for adults, and $2.50 for seniors. A multiuse gymnasium provides other athletic activities including roller-skating, available at $2.00 (75 cents for skates). Schedules vary by week and month, so it is necessary to call or drop by for activity information. A complete schedule is available by mail.

Sierra Railroad Skunk Train
**Laurel Street Depot, Fort Bragg
(707) 964-6371, (800) 866-1690
www.skunktrain.com**
This "Skunk" got its name from the odor of earlier gas engines, but today the train

is moved by steam (or sometimes diesel fuel). And what child doesn't love a train ride? Gather the family and hop aboard for an adventure through redwood forests and over bridges and trestles. If the kids get hungry, there are snacks and light refreshments on board, and restrooms too. The little ones will get a kick out of the Train Singer, who entertains with railroad songs. Tickets run $35 to $45 for adults and $20 for children ages 3 to 11. Toddlers ride free. (For more on the Skunk Train, see the Attractions chapter.)

Triangle Tattoo Museum
356-B North Main Street, Fort Bragg
(707) 964–8814
www.triangletattoo.com
Here are some amazing examples of skin art among various peoples of the world and an opportunity to see the tools used and learn how tattooing is done. (See the Attractions chapter for more information.) The museum is open noon to 6:00 P.M. Sunday through Thursday, noon to 8:00 P.M. Friday and Saturday. Admission is free, and tours are given upon request.

OUTSIDE THE WINE COUNTRY

Six Flags Marine World
Marine World Parkway, Vallejo, California
(707) 643–6722
www.sixflags.com/marineworld

Yes, it falls outside this book's "official" boundaries, but rare is the Wine Country parent who hasn't succumbed to the splashy fun of Marine World. Run by the Six Flags Corporation, the park has occupied its present 160-acre spot since 1986. It's one of those places that is impossible to conquer in a day, though you can certainly try. The long bill of shows includes performances by whales and dolphins, sea lions, tigers, lions, and humans on water skis. The ongoing attractions are too numerous to list—among them are Shark Experience, Walrus Experience, Ocean Discovery, Butterfly World, Elephant Encounter, the Primate Play Area, and the Animal Nursery. And don't miss two recent additions: a 10-story roller coaster called Roar and the V-2 Vertical Velocity Spiral Coaster, one of only three like it in the world. One-day tickets are $47.99 for persons over 48 inches tall, $25.99 for those under 48 inches, and $35.99 for seniors 55 or older (children 2 and under get in free). Two-day passes are available at significant discounts. Parking is $10 per vehicle. From Napa, go south on Highway 29, then east on Highway 37 for just more than a mile. Days and hours of operation vary by season, so call ahead.

DAY TRIPS 🚗

Northern California is brimming with intriguing destinations, so it's understandable that Wine Country visitors might want to veer off the wine trail long enough to experience another taste of the Golden State. That's fine with me—I respect your wanderlust and encourage you to broaden your travel horizons. Fortunately, several exceptional locations are within a few hours' drive of Napa or Santa Rosa.

To the south, the Marin Headlands, part of the Golden Gate National Recreation Area, offer scenic drives and hikes and the best views (usually above the fog) of the Golden Gate Bridge and San Francisco. Nearby Sausalito and Tiburon are charming burgs with bayside dining and lodging, phenomenal views, interesting shops, and convenient ferries across the bay to San Francisco. Berkeley is still funky, and farther east the Gold Country towns of the Sierra foothills are rich in history. All of these are suitable excursions, and so are the three areas outlined in this chapter.

Depending on where you start, the spots I'm recommending may be enjoyed as long day trips. But if you have the time, plan for an overnight or weekend getaway.

POINT REYES NATIONAL SEASHORE

Just southwest of Wine Country, Point Reyes offers miles of windswept beaches and magnificent palisades. Walk along cliffside trails (not too close to the edge, please), roll down lofty dunes, explore tidal marshes, and wander through a foggy forest. You're equally likely to bump into a tule elk, a sea lion, or a cow.

Dividing Point Reyes from the bulk of Marin County is the long, skinny arm of Tomales Bay and the infamous San Andreas Fault—the active demarcation line between the Pacific and North American tectonic plates. Point Reyes is moving away from the rest of the mainland, heading toward Alaska at the rate of 2 inches a year.

To get to the park, take Petaluma–Point Reyes Road southwest from Petaluma for about 20 miles. A good place to start your excursion in the 71,000-acre park is the Bear Valley Visitor Center, a big barn of a building just off Highway 1 near Olema. Close to the center you'll encounter Morgan Horse Ranch, Kule Loklo, and several hiking trails. Morgan Ranch is the only working horse-breeding farm in the national park system. Kule Loklo is a re-creation of a Miwok village, with traditional domed shelters. If you visit in July, you might get to witness the annual Native American Celebration, during which Miwok-descended basket makers, stone carvers, singers, and dancers bring the exhibit to life.

While some visitors simply want to flop down on the pearly sand for a good read or nap, others come to explore the diversity of fascinating natural attractions. Limantour Estero is an estuary where most of the bird-watchers flock; McClures Beach has excellent tide pools; the windy Great Beach, one of the longest in the state, gets high marks from beachcombers; and Drakes Beach (which, like Drakes Bay and Drakes Estero, is named for Sir Francis Drake, the English privateer who supposedly landed here in 1579) is a Northern California rarity: a safe swimming beach. Of course, hiking routes abound, including 70 miles of trails in a big chunk of park set aside as wilderness area.

Probably foremost among attractions is Point Reyes Lighthouse, built about 1870 to help prevent the many shipwrecks that had plagued the treacherous, rocky shoreline for centuries. It is also one of California's best spots for whale watching.

In the fall gray whales migrate from Alaska to their breeding grounds in Baja California. In spring they return north with their young. The peak watching season is Christmas through the end of January, when it's not uncommon to see 100 or more spouts rise in a day.

In the southern end of the park, near the time-warp town of Bolinas, is the Point Reyes Bird Observatory—the first of its kind when founded in 1965. A rest stop on the western migratory superhighway, the aviary plays host to an incredible diversity of bird species, one of the largest in the continental United States. Nearly 350 varieties regularly show up in the Audubon Society's annual Christmas bird count. The observatory offers classes, interpretive exhibits, and a nature trail.

Even the villages are pretty here. Point Reyes Station and Inverness, in particular, have remained undisturbed by the masses of visitors. Note that the local microclimate is highly unpredictable—except at the actual point, which is the foggiest place on the West Coast. For more up-to-date information, look for a copy of *Coastal Traveler,* a free quarterly published by the *Point Reyes Light,* the area's Pulitzer Prize–winning newspaper, or call the Point Reyes National Seashore at (415) 663-1092.

THE BIG TREES

California's legendary redwood forests have inspired poetry and major awe (and more than a little avarice) during the last 200 years. Though they are often confused with their inland cousin, the giant sequoia, the redwood—or coast redwood as it is called—is a variety unto itself, with a coastal range that extends from Monterey to southwest Oregon. Santa Rosa considers itself the capital of the Redwood Empire, and several Wine Country parks are home to these noble giants (see the Parks and Recreation chapter). But if you really want to behold these extraordinary trees in all their grandeur, you have

Built 307 steps below the visitor center at the southern tip of the peninsula, the Point Reyes Lighthouse invites you to walk down for a closer look. But beware! The return climb up the narrow stairs is an aerobic challenge not intended for the meek. Pace yourself on the return and use the rest platforms along the staircase.

to drive north to Humboldt County. There you will find the last large stands of California's coast redwoods.

Sequoia sempervirens covered some two million acres when Archibald Menzies first gave them botanical classification in 1794. The state government created several parks around individual groves in the 1920s, but by 1965 logging had reduced the redwood ecosystem to about 300,000 acres. This prompted the U.S. government to consolidate various state, federal, and private holdings into Redwood National Park in 1968.

More land was added to the park in 1978, after bitter wrangling between environmental and proindustry groups and deterioration of virgin growth due to upstream logging along Redwood Creek. The 110,000-acre national park is the destination of many visitors, along with three remaining state parks: Jedediah Smith Redwoods, Del Norte Coast Redwoods, and Prairie Creek Redwoods. All four parks are adjacent and, in fact, comanaged by the National Park Service and the California Department of Parks and Recreation. The national park is a World Heritage Site, the only one on the Pacific coast of the United States. Prairie Creek, meanwhile, is home to the last herds of Roosevelt elk in California.

The 7,500-acre Headwaters Forest Reserve is the most recent entry in the list of protected ancient groves. The reserve, made famous by the tree-sitting, old-growth activist Julia Butterfly, came into being as part of a $480 million controver-

i *Look up in wonder: Three of the tallest trees in the world can be found in Redwood National Forest in Humboldt County.*

sial deal struck between the U.S. government and the Pacific Lumber Company.

Farther south, between Garberville and Ferndale, is the famed Avenue of the Giants, a 33-mile stretch of roadway that parallels U.S. Highway 101 and offers up the most majestic succession of trees on the planet. The avenue follows the Eel River and cuts through 51,000-acre Humboldt Redwoods State Park, the largest state park in Northern California. Along the road you'll encounter a hollow redwood (the Chimney Tree), a redwood trunk made into a domicile (One-Log House), and a redwood you can bisect without leaving the car (Shrine Drive-Thru Tree, one of the state's oldest surviving tourist attractions).

What are the big groves like? It's like walking into one of Europe's grandest old cathedrals, only with better ventilation. The huge trunks absorb every trace of sound, with the exception of the occasional notes of a Swainson's thrush or Wilson's warbler that float down from the branches above. The forest bed, soft with many layers of needles, crunches under your feet, and the lush fern understory lends a primordial feel to the place that goes to the bone.

The trees are indeed ancient, with the oldest dated at approximately 2,200 years. And big? Three of the six tallest trees in the world, including the grand-champion, 368-foot Howard Libby Redwood, are in the national park. What is the secret to their great size? Moisture, and lots of it. The 50 to 80 inches of annual rainfall that drenches coastal California quenches most of the redwood's tremendous thirst, while fog, almost a daily occurrence, keeps the trees damp and cool when the rains subside.

All the attractions mentioned here are accessed via US 101 between Garberville and Crescent City, just south of the Oregon border. From Wine Country, simply continue north on US 101 through Mendocino County; Garberville is about 10 miles past the county line. Admission to the state parks is $6.00, which will get you into all of them. There is no charge to enter the national park. Camping and hiking options abound. For more information, call the northern parks at (707) 464-6101 or Humboldt Redwoods State Park at (707) 946-2409.

LAKE TAHOE

Nature has lavished on Lake Tahoe the bluest waters, the most majestic pines, the most handsome mountains, and the most brilliant cloud-studded skies you'll find anywhere—all that and keno too! Mark Twain was the first travel writer to tour the Lake of the Sky. His awestruck descriptions have since been quoted by a thousand equally dumbfounded travel writers who can scarcely describe the indescribable. Photos simply don't capture this cobalt-blue beauty, nor do paintings. The colors are right, but oddly, they seem too perfect, too vivid.

Tahoe lies half in California and half in Nevada (the south shore is a two-hour drive from Sacramento, on U.S. Highway 50), which gives impetus for pilgrimages by a swarm of weekend gamblers. They head for our neighbor state and hope Lady Luck will smooch the slot machine or gaming table they've selected.

But Tahoe's best bet is the lake itself. At 12 miles wide and 22 miles long, it offers all the water-oriented fun one would expect from the largest alpine lake in North America (in the Western Hemisphere, only Lake Titicaca is larger). At 97 percent pure—the same as distilled water—Lake Tahoe is as clean as it is beautiful. Fortunately, the Sierra Club and other environmental groups are fighting to keep it that way.

Lake Tahoe is North America's second-deepest lake (maximum depth 1,645 feet). If all the water were somehow released from the lake—and if water behaved very differently than it does in real life—it would cover the entire state of California to a depth of 8 inches.

Look out across the waters, and you'll see colorful hot-air balloons rising from a barge in the middle of the lake just as the sun makes its appearance over the edge of the Sierra Nevada Mountains. Two-masted sailboats cut a leisurely path across the waves, while yachts hurry on their way. Couples in canoes or kayaks paddle through the shallow waters. Anglers, waiting patiently for the trout to find them, sit in their fishing boats, unimpressed by the brave soul hovering above them, dangling from a rainbow-hued parasail.

In addition, the M.S. *Dixie II* takes passengers on two, sometimes three, cruises a day—an afternoon run that crosses the lake to Emerald Bay (with its turquoise waters), and a morning cruise that features a big breakfast while following the shoreline.

For a look at the lake as a whole, nothing beats the spectacular 72-mile perimeter drive. It takes about five hours (with scenic stops) on a good weather day. Plan to begin your drive early. In summer, pack or buy a picnic lunch for a brief sojourn in an adjacent park. In winter, include a midday pit stop at a ski area.

Options exist for numerous side trips while traveling around the lake.

Heading clockwise from South Lake Tahoe, you'll soon climb a steep grade to a point overlooking the breathtaking vistas of Emerald Bay State Park. Below is the 39-room Vikingsholm Castle, a 19th-century mansion built by Laura Knight, who fell in love with Norway and sent craftsmen there to copy museum pieces for her home. Tours are available to those who walk the half mile down the hill, which is the only visitor access except by boat. Vistas along the entire west shore are so stunning, you'll be maxing out the megapixels on your digital camera before you know it. Heading northeast, you'll pass what has essentially always been the residential zone of Tahoe. San Francisco's early social elite spent their summers here, and millionaires put up huge estates. Hollywood has come calling more than once, and one of these homes figured prominently in the filming of *The Godfather II*.

Tahoe's oldest permanent settlement is Tahoe City, on the northwest shores of the lake. Three shopping complexes and several condominium projects give this town a year-round population of 2,000. Near the site of the bridge over the Truckee River (called Fanny Bridge because of the people hanging over its floodgates), there's a wonderful collection of Indian lore at the Gatekeeper's Museum. Tahoe City is also the take-off point for three-hour rafting trips down the Truckee River, and it is a favored location for fishermen who head out to deep water with a guide in search of mackinaw and cutthroat trout.

The lake's north shore abounds with interesting geological formations—immense boulders and tiny carnelian stones. Along the north shore you'll cross the state line into Nevada, where gambling is legal. One of its more famous casinos, the Cal-Neva, once belonged to Frank Sinatra. Those were the days when Hollywood luminaries filled the lobby. At the northeast corner of the lake, you'll find Incline Village, with its shopping center, fine art galleries, craft shops, restaurants, and, for culture vultures, drama, opera, Shakespeare, and mime, courtesy of the North Tahoe Fine Arts Council.

South of Incline Village lies one of Tahoe's best beaches—Sand Harbor State Beach, strewn with giant boulders, the refuse of Tahoe's ice age. Paths climb to the top of one of the granite outcroppings, allowing a view down into turquoise waters so clear that submerged boulders as high as a house can be seen in full detail. Facilities for picnicking and barbecuing in a wooded setting are unusually pleasant.

Most of Tahoe's east shore is privately owned, but there is a small area (recognizable by a proliferation of parked cars) where sun worshippers thread their way down a footpath through the forest and spread out nude on the massive rocks to achieve that all-over tan. Zephyr Cove, meanwhile, is where you set sail on the M.S. *Dixie*. It's near the state line.

And there are other options for side trips. At Incline Village, for example, there's a junction with Highway 27 that will take you to Reno or to Virginia City, the latter a lively ghost town recalling days when silver taken from its mines built San Francisco and made millionaires whose names are still familiar. Its wooden plank streets and weathered buildings are surprisingly authentic, though the usual tourist shops line the street as well. (Look to the buildings' upper stories for a true feeling of the Old West.) Reno, calling

itself the "biggest little city in the world," is rife with sleek, splashy gambling casinos. The city has achieved a modest fame among nearby California cities for its inexpensive hotel rooms. It is also home to the National Bowling Association, which is quartered in a massive complex of bowling lanes and offices.

In winter some of the best skiing in the world can be had at South Lake Tahoe—specifically at Heavenly Valley. If you're not on hand during the winter months, take advantage of the tram anyway; ride to the top of the mountain and take a stroll along the path that skirts the rim. It's a breathtaking view, and you can sip wine and have lunch at the summit's inviting patio. Be sure to bring along a panoramic camera to freeze-frame the magnificent scenery for later enjoyment.

RELOCATION

The first 22 chapters of this book may have given you plenty of reasons to make your home in Wine Country. Reading about our green and gold mountains, the Mediterranean climate, the wild coastline of the Pacific Ocean, miles and miles of lush vineyards, great wine, fabulous food, art galleries, and San Francisco only a short drive away—well, who wouldn't want to live here year-round? But let's be practical. It's one thing to be a visitor on vacation—it's quite another to become a resident.

Used to the razzle-dazzle of big city life? The slower pace of Wine Country might make you yawn. Turned off by day after day of winter fog and drizzle? You probably should settle elsewhere. Skeptical about living in a state governed by an action movie star? I understand. As you know, there are many factors to consider when choosing a new city or state to call home. No one place is ideal for everybody, so be certain Wine Country is right for you before putting down roots.

If you do decide to relocate, welcome! I hope you will thoroughly enjoy all that Wine Country has to offer. This chapter gives you a taste of what's available in real estate, retirement resources, educational opportunities, child care options, and health care. But be aware that you will need a good job or a very comfortable retirement income to afford the cost of housing, which can eat up a considerable chunk of your wages. Read on for more about the real estate market in our region.

REAL ESTATE

"California Fixer-Upper—Yours for Only $999,995!" declares the goofy picture postcard found in many gift shops in Wine Country. The photo shows a crumbling pile of ancient wood that once resembled a home, with a collapsed roof and a Sold sign on the one wall still standing. It's an exaggeration, of course, but closer to the truth than I like to admit to anyone unfamiliar with California real estate. Million-dollar home sales are now commonplace in many areas of California—including Wine Country—and record numbers of seven-figure properties were sold across the state in 2004. And believe it or not, some of these houses do need a little fixing up.

When will the bubble finally burst? Experts on California real estate continue to debate this subject, even as home prices leap higher. But it's generally agreed that if and when the market stabilizes, home prices are not likely to drop from their current levels.

Napa County

Make no mistake about it: You pay dearly for quality of life here. In early 2005 the median sales price of a single-family detached home in Napa County was approximately $520,000. (Median price means that half of the sales were at a higher price and half were lower.)

Bargain prices (if you can call them that) may still be found in American Canyon, just south of Napa. But as you head north on Highway 29, the meter on home costs begins to spin faster. As a general rule, Yountville is more expensive than Napa, the Oakville-Rutherford area is more expensive than Yountville, and St. Helena is the most expensive town in the valley. The price tags drop again in Calistoga, down to about the Yountville level. Along the way, you will find every sort of residence imaginable: new tract homes, spectacular Victorians, modest 1940s bungalows, mountaintop castles, Tuscan-inspired villas, and prefab structures.

But what you will see most as you travel Highway 29 is vineyards. That's because the whole of Napa County is a designated agricultural preserve, a decision ratified by the county Board of Supervisors in 1968. The designation put development decisions in the hands of the board and set a 20-acre minimum for any new subdivision of land—a dimension that has increased in increments over the years.

In Napa, most of the Victorian splendor is in Old Town—located among the letter streets south of Lincoln Avenue between California Boulevard and Jefferson Street—and the Napa Abajo/Fuller Park area. Fuller Park, in fact, is a historical preservation district. The boundaries of the preservation district are ragged, but it is bordered more or less by Jefferson, Third, Brown, and Pine Streets.

Home prices in the city of Napa skyrocketed over the past couple of years, with the median price going up approximately 25 percent between 2003 and 2004. Houses with asking prices in the $500,000 to $600,000 range are the norm. Townhouses and condominiums, when you can find them, can go as high as $400,000 or more, depending on the location.

St. Helena is the burg that best typifies the Wine Country dream: charming early-century stone-front buildings, modest scale, vineyard views, and well-kept flower gardens. Accordingly, the prices tend to be sky-high here, especially on the west side. In fact, approximately 42 homes were sold for $1 million-plus in and around this small town in 2004, which puts "sky-high" into perspective. Calistoga offers more of a mixed bag, but it does have some wonder-fully restored old houses, especially on Cedar and Myrtle Streets just northwest of Lincoln Avenue. But country estates are considered the true gems, especially if they have significant acreage.

Which brings us to the price of vineyard land. If you've fantasized about owning a hobby vineyard, investing in a few acres of grapes and living the life of a gentleman farmer, be prepared for sticker shock. Your name may not be Gallo or Gates, but you will still need a sizable bankroll to enter into the grape-growing business here. Vineyards in this region represent some of the most valuable agricultural land in America.

If you're willing to settle for a lower-quality parcel (less fruit density, old trellises, and no developable homesites), expect to pay at least $50,000 per acre. More modern and higher-density vineyards top out around $100,000 per acre. If your fantasy includes building a modest winery on that property, be prepared to wait about two years for approval of the use permits, at a cost of nearly $1 million. And that's all before you begin construction. Want a tasting room too? Good luck. Napa County officials are saying no to many new winery proposals, especially those with big plans for tasting rooms and event centers.

RENTALS

What a difference a couple of years can make. Apartment rents stabilized in Napa as a surplus of new apartment units and complexes were built, so move-in specials offering discounts and lower security deposits are being used to entice renters. A one-bedroom apartment will cost $800 or more; a two-bedroom unit runs about $1,000. The typical two-bedroom house in Napa can set you back about $1,300 per month; the price goes up to $1,600 and beyond for a three-bedroom, two-bath domicile, depending on location. A similar home in St. Helena starts at about $1,600, while some with more amenities rent for well over $2,000 per month.

In Calistoga a studio apartment, if you can find one, might be around $800; a two-bedroom apartment is just shy of $1,000. Two-bedroom homes may be had for $1,110 to $1,250 per month.

REAL ESTATE COMPANIES

Prudential California Realty
2015 Redwood Road, Napa
(707) 259-4900
www.prudentialnapa.com

Century 21 Alpha Realty
1290 Jefferson Street, Napa
(707) 255-8711
www.century21alpharealty.com

Coldwell Banker Brokers of the Valley
1775 Lincoln Avenue, Napa
(707) 258-5200

1289 Main Street, St. Helena
(707) 963-1152

6505 Washington Street, Yountville
(707) 944-0421
www.cbnapavalley.com

Continental Real Estate
743 First Street, Napa
(707) 257-1177
www.napavalleyrealty.com

RE/MAX Napa Valley
780 Trancas Street, Napa
(707) 255-0845
www.remax-napavalley-ca.com
www.nvplatinum.com

Silverado Associates
24 Greenbriar Circle, Napa
(707) 257-7575
www.silveradorealtyinc.com

Morgan Lane
944 Main Street, Napa
(707) 252-2177, (800) 511-1030

1109 Jefferson Street, Napa
(707) 252-5528

6795 Washington Street, Yountville
(707) 944-8500

The Viewshed Ordinance was passed by Napa County's Board of Supervisors in 2001 to camouflage new homes and buildings that go up on the valley's scenic hillsides. All new structures must now blend better into their natural environment.

1350 Oak Street, St. Helena
(707) 963-5226
Relocation services: (800) 511-1030
www.morganlane.com

Arroyo Real Estate
1540 Railroad Avenue, St. Helena
(707) 963-1342
www.arroyorealestate.com

Frank Howard Allen Realtors
1316 Main Street, St. Helena
(707) 963-5266

802 Vallejo Street, Napa
(707) 265-1600
www.winecountrygroup.com

Up Valley Associates
1126 Adams Street, St. Helena
(707) 963-1222, (800) 326-6073
www.napavalleyrealestate.com

Pacific Union
1508 Main Street, St. Helena
(707) 967-1340, (707) 251-8805
www.pacunion.com

California Properties
13 Angwin Plaza, Angwin
(707) 965-2485, (800) 788-0410
www.napavalleyrealestate.net

Beck & Taylor
1406 Lincoln Avenue, Calistoga
(707) 942-5500
www.naparealty.com

Calistoga Realty Co.
1473-C Lincoln Avenue, Calistoga
(707) 942-9422
www.calistoga-realty.com

Department of Motor Vehicles

Modern man's least favorite chore is most likely a trip to the DMV. The scarcity of DMV offices in Wine Country only adds to the frustration level. That's why appointments are strongly encouraged (a driver's test will not be given without one, in fact) and will usually make the experience less painful. In California every new resident who plans to operate a motorized vehicle is required to take up his or her business in person with the DMV almost as soon as the moving van is unloaded.

In general, cars and trucks brought into California from other states or countries must be registered within 20 days of establishing your residency or accepting employment. (These vehicles may also be subject to additional fees at the time of registration.) Drivers should arrange to get their new California licenses within 10 days of putting down roots. Make it easy on yourself and schedule an appointment to wrap up all of your new DMV business at once.

Statewide, the DMV information and appointment line is (800) 777-0133/TTY (800) 368-4327. The DMV Web site (www.dmv.ca.gov) is well designed and easy to navigate, and most of your questions can be answered there.

Napa County
2550 Napa Valley Corporate Drive, Napa

Sonoma County
715 Southpoint Boulevard, Petaluma
2570 Corby Avenue, Santa Rosa

Mendocino County
410 South Franklin Street, Fort Bragg
543 South Orchard Avenue, Ukiah

Sonoma County

Like the rest of the Bay Area, housing prices broke records in Sonoma County over the past couple of years. By mid-2005 high demand and low interest rates pushed the median price of a home here to approximately $600,000.

Much of the county's growth is centered around the city of Santa Rosa. With a current population of about 154,400, it is the county's largest city. Here, as in most cities, home seekers will find neighborhoods of high-priced, handsome Victorian homes, a score of new modern housing developments (some still in progress), and a wide variety of medium- and lower-priced homes.

In summer 2005 median prices in the northwest sector of Santa Rosa were about $505,000; in the southeast, $580,000; in the southwest, $536,000; and $695,000 in the northeast.

Prices vary in towns to the north along the U.S. Highway 101 corridor. Median prices are $805,000 in Healdsburg and $495,000 in Cloverdale.

An interesting real estate situation exists in the town of Windsor. Until the late 1980s, it was a sleepy village, but then it was discovered by housing developers. They just kept building and building. As a result, almost everything in the town is of recent origin. Now incorporated, Windsor is a fast-growing city—second only to nearby Cloverdale—with median home prices at about $590,000.

The area around the town of Sebastopol on the edge of Apple Country is, in a way, an anomaly in the county—a place where many homes are set on large acreage. People who live here like the idea of country living with amenities such as extra guesthouses and plenty of room for dogs to run and horses to graze. Because of the superlarge lot sizes, Sebastopol has among the highest housing prices in the county. Estate-size lots, rambling homes, and miniranches will often top the $1 million mark. The median home price is $765,000.

Though San Francisco-bound commuters live in all parts of the county, most live in the southernmost reaches—a fact that has influenced average home prices there. Median home prices in the border towns of Petaluma and Sonoma in mid-2005 ranged between $625,000 and $667,000.

There is little residential property along the Sonoma coast, which is one reason median home prices are about $750,000. The large, modern Sea Ranch development at the northeastern edge of the county offers homes on sites that range from a quarter acre to three or more acres. For people who love the ocean, life along the Sonoma coast is indeed soul satisfying.

To help in your search for a home, local chambers of commerce are clearinghouses of information. Also, the North Coast Builders Exchange in Santa Rosa, (707) 542-9502, can help with information for individuals hiring contractors or building custom homes.

RENTALS

A glut of new apartment projects, primarily in and around Santa Rosa, forced landlords to make deals to fill their units. Rental rates have stayed about the same as a result—expect to pay from $750 for a studio apartment and up to $1,500 for a three-bedroom unit. You can generally find lower rents in outlying areas of the county.

REAL ESTATE COMPANIES

Prudential California Real Estate
326 Healdsburg Avenue, Healdsburg
(707) 433-4150

16315 Main Street, Guerneville
(707) 869-9011
www.pruweb.com

Frank Howard Allen Realtors
470 First Street East, Sonoma
(707) 939-2000

9200 Sonoma Highway, Kenwood
(707) 833-2881

905 East Washington Street, Petaluma
(707) 762-7766

340 Center Street, Healdsburg
(707) 431-9440

6876 Sebastopol Avenue, Sebastopol
(707) 824-5400
www.fhallen.com

Coldwell Banker
333 South McDowell Boulevard, Petaluma
(707) 762-6611

790 Sonoma Avenue, Santa Rosa
(707) 527-8567
www.cbnorcal.com

If you love Victorian-era homes, Wine Country has many historic areas to choose from. In Sonoma County, check out Petaluma's west side, Sonoma's east side, and most of the streets that radiate off the central plaza in Healdsburg.

RE/MAX Central
320 College Avenue, Santa Rosa
(707) 524-3500

371 Windsor River Road, Windsor
(707) 837-7800
www.santarosa-homes.com

Century 21
616 Petaluma Boulevard S., Petaluma
(707) 769-9000

1057 College Avenue, Santa Rosa
(707) 577-7777

Voter Registration

Whenever you move, you must reregister to vote. The Registrar of Voters offices in Wine Country, listed here, can supply information and forms to get you signed up to vote. You may also call the toll-free number for the California Secretary of State to learn more: (800) 345-8683. The state's Web site for voting and election information is at www.ss.ca.gov/elections.

Napa County
900 Coombs Street, Room 256, Napa
(707) 253-4321

Sonoma County
435 Fiscal Drive, Santa Rosa
(707) 565-6800

Mendocino County
501 Low Gap Road, Ukiah
(707) 463-4371

107 North Street, Healdsburg
(707) 433-4404

114 Lake Street, Cloverdale
(707) 894-5232
www.century21.com

Griewe Real Estate
141 East Napa Street, Sonoma
(707) 938-0916
www.griewerealestate.com

Morgan Lane
500 Broadway, Sonoma
(707) 935-5777
www.morganlane.com

Coralee Barkela & Company
1815 Fourth Street, Santa Rosa
(707) 542-9200
www.coraleebarkela.com

Pacific Union Residential Brokerage
640 Broadway, Sonoma
(707) 939-9500
www.pacunion.com

Mid-Towne Realty, Inc.
709 Healdsburg Avenue, Healdsburg
(707) 433-6555
www.midtownerealty.com

North County Properties
21069 Geyserville Avenue, Geyserville
(707) 857-1728

Sea Ranch Realty
Sea Ranch Lodge, Sea Ranch
(707) 785-2494
www.888searanch.com

Mendocino County

The rugged Mendocino coast stretches 120 miles along the Pacific from its southern point at Gualala to the King Mountain range on the north. Each of the small towns and hamlets that dot the coastline has its own unique identity and charm. And each has a different set of real estate values.

If you long for a view of the sea, it will cost you. But what it costs depends on where you want to settle. Fort Bragg, with a population of about 7,000, is basically a lumbering and fishing community, though tourism is on the rise. Most of Fort Bragg's homes are long established, but there is some new construction. Average price of single-family dwellings in the area is $400,000, though ocean views can go as high as $550,000.

Eight miles south in tiny Mendocino (population 1,000), the cost of housing rises steeply. A two-bedroom home in the village, without a view of the water, will likely be priced at $550,000. Add an ocean view, and the price jumps dramatically— these addresses top out in the millions.

In the inland valleys, a few modest-sized towns and hamlets cling to US 101— Hopland, Ukiah, and Willits. The landscape is agricultural, and it is prime grape-growing territory. Nestled in the valley below the spectacular Coast Range is Ukiah, county seat and Mendocino's largest city (population 15,900). It's a blend of businesses, recreational opportunities, affordable housing, verdant vineyards and orchards, and untamed wilderness. The city's west side includes hundreds of historic homes and buildings shaded by a lush canopy of mature trees. Average price for a three-bedroom home is $350,000, average home rental runs $1,300 a month, and apartments rent for $750 on average.

Known mainly as a railroad hub and lumber community, the town of Willits, 25 miles north of Ukiah, is at the western edge of the Little Lake Valley, 1,350 feet above sea level. The chaparral and oak glades characteristic of the southern part of the county give way here to thick red-wood and fir forests that stretch to the Oregon border.

With a population of 5,000, the town itself is not very large; however, the sur-rounding area includes a surprising num-ber of homes, bringing the greater Willits population to nearly 15,000. Home prices are more modest here, running between $250,000 to $450,000 for a three-bedroom home.

You'll find other information about the Mendocino market in the real estate pages of the *Fort Bragg Advocate-News*. Chambers of commerce often prove to be valuable resources as well. The Greater Ukiah Chamber of Commerce is at 200 South School Street. Call (707) 462-4705 for assistance.

REAL ESTATE COMPANIES

Wally Johnson Realty
3810 Eastside Calpella Road, Ukiah
(707) 485-8700, (800) 289-8542
www.wallyjohnsonrealty.com

E. S. Wolf & Company
514 South School Street, Ukiah
(707) 463-2719
www.eswolf.com

Pacific Properties
36 South Street, Willits
(707) 459-6175, (800) 767-9546

Mendo Realty
690 South Main Street, Fort Bragg
(707) 964-3610

1061 Main Street, Mendocino
(707) 937-5822
www.mendorealty.com

Sea Cottage Real Estate
45120 Main Street, Mendocino
(707) 937-0423, (800) 707-0423
www.seacottage.com

RETIREMENT HOUSING OPTIONS

In the past few years, Wine Country has attracted many new retirees and seniors. To meet the demands for shelter, new senior housing projects are springing up across the region.

This is particularly true in the area of independent-living apartment complexes that provide housekeeping, meals, and laundry services, while allowing for complete freedom of movement and individuality. Following are examples of this type of retirement-living option (with a couple of other independent-living choices thrown in) within our area.

Napa County

The Meadows of Napa Valley
1800 Atrium Parkway, Napa
(707) 257-7885
www.meadowsofnapavalley.org
Three levels of personalized care are offered at this 20-acre residential retirement community. The apartments are available in one- and two-bedroom floorplans, augmented by the assisted-living program and a skilled nursing center with rehabilitation services in a homelike setting. There's also a gift shop and beauty/barber shop on-site.

Aegis of Napa
2100 Redwood Road, Napa
(707) 251-1409
www.aegisal.com
Studio apartments, one-bedroom flats, and shared suites are offered at this community, along with Life's Neighborhood, an Alzheimer's program. This facility's Small Indulgences program helps family caregivers by keeping track of each resident's favorite foods, flowers, and special treats.

Silverado Orchards
601 Pope Street, St. Helena
(707) 963-3688
www.silveradoorchards.com
In a quiet, green setting between St. Helena proper and the Silverado Trail is this popular retirement community. Silverado Orchards has 80 units all together—small studios, deluxe studios, one-bedroom apartments, and a couple of two-bedroom units. It's an active population that takes advantage of the immediate area's pleasant walking routes, plus twice-a-week exercise classes.

Woodbridge Village
727 Hunt Avenue, St. Helena
(707) 963-3231
Several years ago this HUD-supported retirement complex won an award for best landscaping in St. Helena, and the parklike grounds have only improved since then, the managers say, thanks in part to some resident green thumbs. Woodbridge is a series of tidy one-bedroom, one-bath apartments, most of them grouped into fourplexes. HUD defines a senior as anyone age 62 or older.

Rancho de Calistoga
2412 Foothill Boulevard, Calistoga
(707) 942-6971
Yes, it's a mobile-home park, but if all of them looked like this, they would have a very different reputation. Centuries-old oak trees tower over the big lawn area out front, and the whole community is full of flowering plants. Rancho de Calistoga has a total of 184 lots. It also has a clubhouse, recreation building, pool, and spa. Activities include bingo twice a month, bridge, poker, exercise classes, quilting, potlucks, and Wednesday-morning brunch. The park is meant for seniors 55 and older.

Sonoma County

Westlake Wine Country House
800 Oregon Street, Sonoma
(707) 996-7101
www.westlakecompany.com
Billed as a "luxury congregate retirement facility," Westlake Wine Country offers one- and two-bedroom suites, fully carpeted (bring your own furniture), with a small kitchen, private deck, or balcony and three meals a day in a rather elegant dining room. The Westlake van takes residents to shopping or medical appointments, or you can use a parking space for your own car.

Westlake House Springs
4855 Snyder Lane, Rohnert Park
(707) 585-7878
www.westlakecompany.com
Although the Springs enjoys country views of rolling green farmlands, the property is near shopping, 1 block from a large med-

ical complex, and a short putt to the nearest golf course. This complex is owned by the same company as Sonoma's Westlake Wine Country House (see previous listing), with accommodations slightly upgraded in price and style. The complex consists of 176 apartments and 190 residents.

Valley Orchards Retirement Community
2100 East Washington Street, Petaluma
(707) 778-6030
www.petalumachamber.com
No medical or nursing service is provided here, the manager says, "but from time to time the resident may contract for outside assistance for bathing or personal care, which makes it a good bit cheaper than assisted living." Valley Orchards provides three meals a day, utilities, cable TV, transportation three days a week, housekeeping once a week, bathroom and bedroom laundry, 24-hour emergency assistance, and yard maintenance. Valley Orchard's 104 units are split between large studios and one- and two-bedroom apartments.

Friends House
684 Benicia Drive, Santa Rosa
(707) 538-0152
www.friendshouse.org
A Quaker institution, Friends House is composed of four interrelated programs for the older person: independent-living apartments and houses, an adult day-care center, an assisted-living facility, and a skilled-nursing facility. A large part of the six-acre Friends House site contains 60 garden apartments. People live in their own homes with their own belongings and garden space. One- and two-bedroom apartments are available, and recently some three-bedroom, two-bath homes were added to accommodate couples who want more space within the Friends House community.

Renaissance at the Lodge at Paulin Creek
2375 Range Avenue, Santa Rosa
(707) 575-3722, (800) 900-HOME
www.renaissancesl.com

The Lodge is set in parklike grounds with inviting courtyards. Apartments are sunny and bright, with the charm of designer fabrics, art reproductions, and handmade quilts. They range from studios to three-bedroom, two-bath units. Some dining options are offered—you can either be served graciously in the dining room or serve yourself casually from the salad and hot entree buffet. Amenities include a pool, fitness trail, billiards room, an opportunity to garden, and a calendar of day trips.

Mendocino County

Redwood Meadows
1475 Baechtel Road, Willits
(707) 459-1616
In a lovely setting with walkways and green belts, Redwood Meadows is a senior apartment community open to active, independent seniors older than 55. The community center houses a game room, craft room, and community lounge. Because it is right next door to the Willits Senior Center (see listing in that section), the amenities of that group are easily accessible. Meals are not served, but the dining room is a center for potlucks, parties, movies, lectures, and other social events. Small pets are allowed.

The Woods
43300 Little River Airport Road,
Little River
(707) 937-6132, (800) GO-WOODS
www.ncphs.org
Quality manufactured homes nestled among redwoods, pines, and rhododendrons make up this residential community for seniors. The Woods is on 37 sunbelt acres connected by winding roads that lead walkers to a heated indoor pool and spa, the clubhouse, library, and art room. State park beaches and golf courses are minutes away. Assisted-living facilities are also available.

Redwood Coast Seniors
490 North Harold Street, Fort Bragg
(707) 964-0443
This organization maintains a list of Fort Bragg senior housing. Entries are all clean, well-maintained apartments or detached houses, with rents on a sliding scale according to income.

SENIOR SERVICES

Most senior citizens who choose to live in Wine Country are spending their retirement years actively pursuing good health and happiness. Everyone, however, needs a little help and guidance from time to time to lead a satisfying life. Here are a few connections to make it easier for seniors to find their way around in new territory.

Napa County

The Volunteer Center of Napa County
1820 Jefferson Street, Napa
(707) 252-6222, (707) 963-3922
www.volunteernapa.org
The Volunteer Center does all sorts of good work in the county, and its Senior Services Program, funded by the Napa-Solano Area Agency on Aging (see listing in this section) and the United Way, is foremost on the list. Especially valuable is the *Senior Guide* it publishes each year. It's a well-organized catalog of write-ups and phone numbers, with suggestions on topics ranging from health services and home care to housing and transportation.

Comprehensive Services for Older Adults
900 Coombs Street, Suite 257, Napa
(707) 253-4625, (800) 498-9455
www.napachamber.org

This program, administered by the Napa County Health and Human Services Agency, offers in-home care to the aged, blind, and disabled who can't afford to fend for themselves. The manifold services include household tasks and shopping, nonmedical personal care when needed to ensure safety, alcohol and drug counseling, adult protective services, and psychiatric case management for seniors 62 or older who suffer from mental illness or Alzheimer's disease. Comprehensive Services also assists with procurement of food stamps and Medi-Cal (state-subsidized medical insurance) benefits.

Senior Class
Queen of the Valley Hospital,
1000 Trancas Street, Napa
(707) 253-9000
www.thequeen.org
Queen of the Valley has targeted older adults for health promotion and education with this membership program since 1986. Members are offered classes, lectures, and health screenings, conducted by the hospital's able team of health care professionals. It's $15 to join and $10 a year thereafter, though nobody is turned away.

Napa Valley Dining Club
1500 Jefferson Street, Napa
(707) 253-6112, (800) 788-0124
This service cooks up hot, nutritious meals for people 60 years or older on a donation basis. When needed, the club will transport guests to one of six Napa County sites or deliver food to homes. Call one day in advance for reservations.

Adult Day Services of Napa Valley
3295 Claremont Way, Suite 3, Napa
(707) 258-9087
The frail elderly and younger functionally impaired adults are the focus of this organization. Daily hot lunches, caregiver respites, social activities, and transportation assistance are all provided.

Garden Haven Adult Day Center
2447 Old Sonoma Road, Napa
(707) 253-3425
Even the most devoted caregiver needs an occasional break, and here is a day center you can trust to watch over your elderly relative or friend, especially if he or she is afflicted with Alzheimer's or dementia. Activities include music, exercise regimens, crafts, cooking, and gardening. Wheelchairs are welcome. The center is open Monday, Tuesday, Thursday, and Friday 10:00 A.M. to 3:00 P.M. The cost is $12.50 per day.

Napa-Solano Area Agency on Aging
1443 Main Street, Napa
(707) 664-6612, (800) 510-2020
www.aans.org
People 55 and older who are mentally and physically fit, and who are looking for a little extra cash, are encouraged to get in touch with this agency. They'll help you find part-time employment.

Sonoma County

Council on Aging
730 Bennett Valley Road, Santa Rosa
(707) 525-0143
www.councilonaging.com
This is the overall program that provides many of the benefits that are incorporated in member organizations such as the senior centers listed subsequently. Council on Aging provides dining rooms with a hot, healthy noontime meal at many locations in Sonoma County. The Meals on Wheels program delivers hot meals seven days a week to the homes of temporarily or chronically homebound seniors. Legal consultation services are provided, as well as money management programs, health insurance counseling, and door-to-door transportation for seniors with doctor visits. The council offers an excellent *Senior Resource Guide* available at senior centers or by calling the listed number.

AARP Senior Community Service Employment Program
2050 West Steele Lane, Suite E-2, Santa Rosa
(707) 525-9190
www.aarp/scsep
Partially government sponsored, this is an American Association of Retired Persons (AARP) program to help low-income seniors get back into the workforce through on-the-job training with organizations such as the American Red Cross and Goodwill Industries. It is also an employment office that can find jobs in the private sector after training.

North Bay HI-CAP
3262 Airway Drive, Suite C, Santa Rosa
(800) 303-4477
The North Bay Health Insurance Counseling and Advocacy Program (HI-CAP) covers six counties north of the Golden Gate Bridge (including all in Wine Country). The center offers one-on-one counseling by trained volunteers registered by the California Department of Aging. They provide independent, unbiased information on health insurance, including Medicare and supplemental programs. They also help clients sort out their medical finances and make sure they are being billed appropriately for Medicare. There is no charge for this service.

Petaluma Ecumenical Project
1400 Caulfield Lane, Petaluma
(707) 762-2336
In 1977 three local ministers came together to find a way to provide low-cost housing for seniors. With community backing, the Petaluma Ecumenical Project sought out suitable building sites and developed architectural plans. The group has built and manages nine projects and is now supported by 11 churches and AARP contributions.

Jewish Seniors Program
3855 Montgomery Drive, Santa Rosa
(707) 528-4222
www.jcagency.org
The wide spectrum of entertainment and educational opportunities offered through this program includes musical events, folk dancing, autobiographical writing, book discussion, parties, and trips. Want to learn Yiddish? That's an option too! The group welcomes participants from all denominations.

Mendocino County

Multipurpose Senior Services Program
301 South State Street, Ukiah
(707) 468-9347

205 South Main Street, Fort Bragg
(707) 964-4027
www.communitycare707.com
The Multipurpose Senior Services Program is a nonprofit community agency that strives to meet the needs of people with disabilities so that they can remain in their own homes and live an independent life of dignity. Some of the home-care services that MSSP helps obtain include personal care, home repairs, housecleaning, shopping, transportation, and home-delivered meals. The agency serves Ukiah, Willits, Hopland, Potter Valley, and the Fort Bragg/Mendocino area, plus Lake County.

SENIOR CENTERS

They're social centers, educational resources, service sources, and just plain fun places for seniors with leisure time. Most of the centers publish newsletters so everyone can find out what's in store. All have an extensive, varied program of activities, and all offer services such as blood pressure and hearing testing, legal counsel, and tax assistance on a regular basis.

Napa County

Senior Citizens Center
1500 Jefferson Street, Napa
(707) 255-1800
www.cityofnapa.org
Older residents get one-stop shopping at this office. Nearly 60 organizations—including the Senior Friendship Club and Napa Grange—use the center as a meeting place. It's open Monday through Friday 8:00 A.M. to 4:00 P.M. Activities range from dances, bingo, and potluck dinners to arts and crafts and pancake breakfasts. Friday mornings welcome guest speakers for Senior Seminars. Call for a monthly schedule of events.

Berryessa Senior Citizens
4380 Spanish Flat Loop Road, Berryessa
(707) 966-0206
The highlands surrounding Lake Berryessa sound like a nice place for retired folks—and, well, they are. This center has a strong lineup of health, educational, social, and recreational programs. If you call for a monthly schedule, you'll discover potluck meals, bingo, crafts, Adventure College classes, trips, dances, and more.

Sonoma County

SOUTHERN SONOMA

Vintage House
264 First Street E., Sonoma
(707) 996-0311
www.sonomachamber.com
Staffed largely by senior volunteers, Vintage House is open Monday through Friday, serving more than 1,000 individuals each month with up to 70 classes and activities, most of them free or low cost. The choices include art classes, line dancing, tap dancing, international folk dance instruction, canasta, bridge in several forms, exercise classes, and French, Italian, and Spanish at

levels for beginner, intermediate, and advanced speakers. The Vintage House Singers, a choral group, is coached by a professional music director and performs twice a year. The Department of Motor Vehicles has a representative visit each month to administer driving tests, and the tax man cometh during his season. Lunch is served Tuesday, Thursday, and Friday in the dining room for a small fee.

Lucchesi Park Senior Center
(Petaluma Community Center)
211 Novak Drive, Petaluma
(707) 778-4399
www.cityofpetaluma.net

This facility largely houses the recreational part of Petaluma's senior program—the local meal program is now administered by the adjacent Petaluma People Services Center. Line dancing events draw 25 to 40 participants each week, and ballroom dancing attracts 100 or more. Group exercise goes over big, along with the computer classes, eclectic discussion groups, art instruction, and creative writing classes. Many day trips and extended trips are sponsored. The center also sponsors flu shots and blood-pressure testing.

Rohnert Park Senior Center
6800 Hunter Drive, Suite A, Rohnert Park
(707) 585-6780

Active seniors as well as disabled persons who can manage on their own are welcome here to chat, play cards, and watch the once-a-month movie. General activities include line dancing, bridge, basketry, Spanish classes, a craft shop, and a billiards table. Every other month an early-evening dance (held the second Tuesday of each month from 1:00 to 4:00 P.M.) brings out a lively crowd. In fact, it has grown so popular that the center had to move it to a larger facility—the Community Center on 5401 Snyder Lane. According to the director, seniors often claim this is the best center around, and it draws older folks from as far away as Ukiah. A noon meal is served daily.

Santa Rosa Senior Center
704 Bennett Valley Road, Santa Rosa
(707) 545-8608
www.santarosarec.com

Dancing is big here—afternoon ballroom dancing once a week, line dancing, and tap dancing. Bingo, bridge, whist, chess, and pinochle games are lively, and there are three billiards tables. Watercolor painting classes are a big draw, and there's creative writing, a poetry group, and Spanish instruction. The drama group puts on shows, and a choral group attracts those who like to belt out a tune. There are also clinics for blood pressure, allergy screening, chiropractic evaluations, and even toenail clipping. Once a month the Friendship Club organizes a potluck lunch. Meals are served Monday to Friday at 4:00 P.M. The Council on Aging also uses the center kitchen to prepare meals for delivery to the homebound.

The Senior Center in Santa Rosa offers a multitude of free services to golden-agers, including allergy, hearing, and blood pressure screenings; chiropractic consultations; and legal aid.

NORTHERN SONOMA

Windsor Senior Center
9231 Foxwood Drive, Windsor
(707) 838-1250

This center is surrounded by roses—45 varieties, in fact, in a lovely garden. In the artistic category, classes are available in oil and pastel painting and sculpture. Card players have a choice of pinochle or bridge, and seniors can learn to play the guitar, study genealogy, or join in a quilting bee.

For the athletic, the boccie ball court is an attraction, as is the horseshoe pit. But most popular of all is the swimming pool: Windsor tends to be hot in summer, and the pool is a terrific place to cool off. It is outfitted for the disabled, who can be lowered from wheelchair to water by a special lift device.

Healdsburg Senior Center
133 Matheson Street, Healdsburg
(707) 431-3324
www.healdsburg.org

Lunch is served here Monday through Friday, and a bus service is available to bring seniors to the center as well as to take them to shopping areas and other destinations around town. Crafts are popular here, with a group meeting once a week to work on handcrafts including the art of flower arranging. An unusually talented group of woodworkers has been awarded several honors for items created at the center. Bingo brings the lucky and unlucky to play each Thursday. Department of Motor Vehicles testing also is provided.

Cloverdale Senior Multi-Purpose Center
311 North Main Street, Cloverdale
(707) 894-4826

Weekly blood-pressure screenings, visits by an optometrist, and hearing-aid maintenance are among the services offered in Cloverdale. Line dancing is offered one day each week, and an instructor comes in to help seniors create an autobiographical record of their lives. A newsletter keeps seniors apprised of coming attractions at the center, where lunch is served every weekday.

WEST COUNTY/RUSSIAN RIVER

Sebastopol Burbank Senior Center
167 North High Street, Sebastopol
(707) 829-2440
www.sebastopolseniorcenter.org

This center receives laudable backing from the community, and several stores and bakeries bring in day-old products to distribute among the members. Lunch is served in the dining room each weekday, and home-delivered meals are dispatched to those who cannot come in. Card games and bingo are regular sources of entertainment, and every once in a while, there's a special program by a harp and flute duo.

Russian River Community Senior Center
15010 Armstrong Woods Road, Guerneville
(707) 869-0618
www.russianriver.com

Both on-site lunch and Meals on Wheels are provided from this center, and because this is a rural area, limited transportation is provided. Afternoon field trips and picnics are ideally suited to this vacation spot with its many scenic locales. Writing autobiographies and exercise classes are among indoor activities.

Mendocino County

U.S. HIGHWAY 101

Ukiah Senior Center
499 Leslie Street, Ukiah
(707) 462-4343
www.ukiahchamber.com

A lot happens here, and it would be hard not to have fun. There's line dancing, ballroom dancing, and dancing classes, plus a Saturday night dance to practice your lessons. You can play bingo, pinochle, bridge, Scrabble, or chess; learn to knit or crochet; or practice tai chi. The exercise class is on Tuesday, Wednesday, and Thursday. Legal help, tax assistance, and health screenings are available. Lunch is served in the dining room each weekday.

Willits Senior Center
1501 Baechtel Road, Willits
(707) 459-6826
www.willits.org

A noon meal is served at the center and delivered to shut-ins. Seniors enjoy movies and bingo twice a week and a dance once a month. Breakfast is served once a month, and special weekend dinners are staged monthly. A worthy program at Willits is Extra Hands—a plan to hire people to do chores like gardening, cleaning house, and shopping for seniors who find these activities difficult. Drivers are provided to take people to medical appointments. The center is fortunate: there are approximately 100 volunteers to help. Some funds are created by a thrift shop run by the seniors themselves.

MENDOCINO COAST

South Coast Senior Citizens
140 Main Street, Point Arena
(707) 882-2137
Arts and crafts occupy part of the daily schedule in Point Arena. An abalone breakfast is served on the second Sunday each month, and a spaghetti dinner is served on the fourth Friday. Monthly bus trips are scheduled to visit various spots and happenings. The dining room serves a noon meal twice a week and provides transportation so seniors can get to the center. Delivered meals also are offered on the same days.

Fort Bragg Senior Center
490 North Harold Street, Fort Bragg
(707) 964-0443
Seniors enjoy bingo twice a week and can take a course in writing provided by the College of the Redwoods staff. From time to time a four-week improvisation class gives seniors a chance to practice acting, and occasionally a professional writer comes to tell seniors how they can learn to write and sell their output. A hot meal is served each weekday from 11:30 A.M. to 12:30 P.M., with transportation provided.

RETIREMENT ACTIVITIES

Educational

Several agencies and area schools offer opportunities for inquisitive, mature men and women to prove there is no age limit to new intellectual experiences. In addition to the resources listed, many senior centers throughout Wine Country offer classes in writing, foreign languages, computer skills, and other subjects. In addition, retirees can look to courses offered by Wine Country colleges (see that section).

The Lifelong Learning Institute at Sonoma State University was established for students 50 years and older who want to learn new skills or pursue subjects that stir their fancy. The classes are intended for pure enjoyment, with no homework, no tests, and no grades. To learn more, please call (707) 664-2691.

NAPA COUNTY

Napa Valley College Community Education
2277 Napa-Vallejo Highway, Napa
(707) 253-3070, (707) 967-2900
www.napacommunityed.org

North Bay Driving School
1878 El Centro Avenue, Napa
(707) 252-2066
www.cal-driver-ed.com

Pacific Union College Extension, Angwin
(707) 965-6311, (800) 862-7080
www.puc.edu

SONOMA COUNTY

Petaluma Adult Education Center
200 Douglas Street, Petaluma
(707) 778-4633
www.petalumachamber.org

Sonoma State University Gerontology Program
1801 East Cotati Avenue, Rohnert Park
(707) 664-2411
www.sonoma.edu

Lewis Adult Education Center
2230 Lomitas Avenue, Santa Rosa
(707) 522-3280
www.lewisadult.com

Santa Rosa Junior College
1501 Mendocino Avenue, Santa Rosa
(707) 527-4011
www.santarosa.edu

New Vista Adult Education School
6980 Analy Avenue, Sebastopol
(707) 824-6455
www.sebastopol.org

Volunteer

A number of programs are available that put to use the skills, talents, and personalities of older individuals who choose to work full- or part-time for little or no remuneration. Here are some places to start your search.

Volunteer Center of Napa Valley
1820 Jefferson Street, Napa
(707) 252-6222, (707) 963-3922
www.volunteernapa.org

Volunteer Center of Sonoma County
153 Stony Circle, Santa Rosa
(707) 573-3399
www.volunteernow.org

Volunteer Network of Mendocino County
413 North State Street, Ukiah
(707) 462-2596
www.volunteercentersca.org

Retired and Senior Volunteer Program (RSVP)
264 First Street E., Sonoma
(707) 996-4644

17A Fourth Street, Petaluma
(707) 762-0111

1041 Fourth Street, Santa Rosa
(707) 573-3399
www.volunteernow.org

Service Corps of Retired Executives (SCORE)
777 Sonoma Avenue, Suite 115-B,
Santa Rosa
(707) 571-8342
www.score.org

Foster Grandparent Program
15000 Arnold Drive, Eldridge
(707) 938-6201

413 North State Street, Ukiah
(707) 462-1954
www.seniorcorps.org

PUBLIC SCHOOLS

Napa County

Anyone who questions Napa County's commitment to education would do well to look at the many charitable events devoted to private or public schools, some of them featuring ultrapremium wines generously donated by the biggest names in the valley for live and silent auctions. A recent fund-raiser for Trinity Grammar and Prep School in Napa raised $60,000 in one afternoon. Among the big names donating items for auction were—in addition to scores of Napa Valley wineries—the Oakland Raiders, the Petrified Forest, and the Winchester Mystery House in San Jose. A baseball bat signed by Barry Bonds also went up for bid.

In 2004, there were 20,000 pupils enrolled in Napa County public schools, dispersed among five districts: Calistoga Joint Union, Napa Valley Unified, St. Helena Unified, Howell Mountain, and Pope Valley.

Bilingual education is one of the many hot-button issues facing California schools. As with many areas of the state, a large immigrant population—in this case, almost wholly from Mexico—mingles with those who migrated earlier. Figures from a recent report about the Napa Valley Unified School District revealed that more than 24 percent of students are learning English as a second language and the percentage of Hispanic students has almost doubled in the past decade, to 32.6 percent.

On the academic side, Napa County's chartered performance remains relatively strong. SAT I scores are always well above the state average, and participation is usually high. In other testing, Napa County's students traditionally rank high on their Academic Performance Index (API) scores, with pupils in all grades showing improvement on the Stanford 9 tests that surpassed goals set for them by the State of California.

Other success stories abound: Ten school campuses in Napa County have received California Distinguished School Awards based on evaluations of their curricula, test scores, school environments, parental participation, and special programs.

Progress has also been achieved through the New Technology High School, a Napa facility where students spend most of their time online or in-lab, with minimal teacher supervision. New Tech (www.techhigh.napanet.net), named a U.S. Department of Education Demonstration School for its technological advances, graduated its first senior class of future Silicon Valley moguls in 1998.

Sonoma County

Sonoma County's schools have consistently ranked in the top half of the state, although they're funded at less than the state average. Thirty-eight of the county's schools have been named California Distinguished Schools, and four have been recognized as National Blue Ribbon schools. Within Sonoma County's 40 school districts, 154 schools serve students from kindergarten through 12th grade. There are 92 elementary schools, 20 junior high schools, 15 high schools, 29 special alternative schools, and 25 charter schools. Total enrollment in 2004 was approximately 73,000.

The growth in diversity among Sonoma County students is significant. Today local schools are educating the most culturally, socially, academically, and linguistically diverse student population in the county's history. More than 7 percent of the county's students are limited in their ability to speak English, 8 percent are enrolled in programs for gifted students, and nearly 4 percent attend alternative programs such as independent study, home study, or continuation school.

Schools recognize an obligation to offer opportunities for success for all kids. Secondary school students receive the majority of efforts in this direction, because of larger student populations at the higher grade levels. For example, for those who can't keep up, schools allow a home-study arrangement. This demands that at least one parent be a stay-at-home presence. Students meet with teachers at specified intervals to review their progress.

The public school system also is working to address the needs of teens who have problems with alcohol or other drugs. Through programs such as Clean and Sober, the dropout rate for Sonoma County, at 2.8 percent, is considerably lower than the state average of 4.4 percent, and it continues to go down.

While attending to the needs of students with special needs, Sonoma County schools also consistently score in the top third of the state for every grade level and subject tested through the California Assessment Program. Average SAT scores for the county are usually higher than state and national averages.

Mendocino County

The size of this county is so immense and the geography so diverse—with its communities separated by forests, mountains, and winding roads—that schools within the system operate almost independently of each other, relying on guidelines from the central offices of the county superintendent of schools. There are 12 districts that include 28 elementary schools, 15 middle schools, and 21 high schools (including continuation high schools). Enrollment for the 2004–05 school year countywide was approximately 14,693; roughly 700 students attend charter schools.

Academic standards are high, with most schools posting average SAT scores at or slightly above national levels. About 35 percent of students go on to college, generally of the two-year community type. Special emphasis is put on vocational job training, with programs specifically aimed at jobs like firefighting (Mendocino County is heavily forested) and agriculture (since the area is mostly rural). This sort of training starts as early as grade nine for those who have no plans to go on to college and can benefit from learning a vocation.

There are other special programs. Preschool classes are offered, as well as classes for those for whom English is a second language. The high school in Ukiah, the county seat, has classes at Juvenile Hall for young people who have run afoul of the law, as well as a Clean and Sober program for students with alcohol or drug problems.

Athletic programs are available, usually including basketball, baseball, softball, soccer, track, volleyball, and cheerleading and in some districts swimming, golf, and tennis. Fort Bragg High School is proud of its exemplary drama program that has given students an opportunity to work with acting and stage management. It has been extremely popular. Mendocino High School has an outstanding program called Windows to the Future, initiated in 1991, that links traditional studies in arts and sciences with computer technology. And here's a major advantage to having a widely scattered county population: Class sizes in Mendocino County schools are generally small, often having fewer than 20 students per teacher.

PRIVATE SCHOOLS

Napa County

Justin-Siena High School
4026 Maher Street, Napa
(707) 255-0950
www.justin-siena.com

Kolbe Academy
1600 F Street, Napa
(707) 256-4306
www.kolbe.org

The Oxbow School
530 Third Street, Napa
(707) 255-6000
www.oxbowschool.org

Napa Adventist Junior Academy
2201 Pine Street, Napa
(707) 255-5233
www.najasda.com

St. John's Lutheran School
3521 Linda Vista Avenue, Napa
(707) 226-7970

St. Apollinaris Elementary School
3700 Lassen Street, Napa
(707) 224-6525

Foothills Adventist Elementary School
711 Sunnyside Road, St. Helena
(707) 963-3546
www.napanet.net/~foothilo

St. Helena Montessori School
1328 Spring Street, St. Helena
(707) 963-1527

St. Helena Catholic School
1255 Oak Avenue, St. Helena
(707) 963-4677
www.sthelenacatholicchurch.org/school

Sonoma County

Old Adobe School
252 West Spain Street, Sonoma
(707) 938-4510

St. Francis Solano School
342 West Napa Street, Sonoma
(707) 996-4994
www.saintfrancissolano.org

The Presentation School
276 East Napa Street, Sonoma
(707) 996-2496
www.presentationschool.com

St. Vincent de Paul High School
849 Keokuk Street (at Magnolia),
Petaluma
(707) 763-1032
www.svhs-pet.org

Adobe Christian Preschool/Daycare
2875 Adobe Road, Petaluma
(707) 763-2012

Ursuline High School
90 Ursuline Road, Santa Rosa
(707) 524-1130
www.ursulinehs.org

Cardinal Newman High School
50 Ursuline Road, Santa Rosa
(707) 546-6470
www.cardinalnewman.org

St. Luke Lutheran School
905 Mendocino Avenue, Santa Rosa
(707) 545-0526
www.stluke-lcms.org

Stuart School
431 Humboldt Street, Santa Rosa
(707) 528-0721
www.stuartprep.8k.com

Merryhill Country School
4044 Mayette Avenue (Infants through
junior kindergarten), Santa Rosa
(707) 575-7660

4580 Bennett View Drive (K-8),
Santa Rosa
(707) 575-0910
www.merryhill-school.com

The Bridge School
1625 Franklin Avenue, Santa Rosa
(707) 575-7959

Little Angels Children's Center
4305 Hoen Avenue, Santa Rosa
(707) 579-4305

1363 Fulton Road, Santa Rosa
(707) 528-2933

California was the first state in the nation to approve charter schools—the first ones opened their doors here in 1993. Though they remain public institutions, these schools are free of many of the regulations governing regular schools. In 2004-05, Sonoma County had 25 charter schools.

Mendocino County

Mariposa Institute
3800 Low Gap Road, Ukiah
(707) 462-1016

Cozy Corner Children's Center
530 South Main Street, Ukiah
(707) 462-1251

Melville Montessori School
4015 Second Gate Road, Willits
(707) 459-3100

Deep Valley Christian School
8555 Uva Drive, Redwood Valley
(707) 485-8778
www.deepvalleychristianschool.org

TWO-YEAR COLLEGES

Napa County

Napa Valley College
2277 Napa-Vallejo Highway (Highway 221), Napa
(707) 253-3000, (800) 826-1077
www.napavalley.edu
Napa Valley College dates from 1942 and has occupied its current site—180 tree-lined acres near the Napa River—since 1965. It's a two-year community college with about 9,000 students and associate degree programs in a spectrum of fields, including business administration, health care, and, not surprisingly, viticulture and wine technology. On-campus facilities include a Child and Family Studies and Services complex and an Olympic-size swimming pool. The school has an Upper Valley Campus on the outskirts of St. Helena and a Small Business Development Center in Napa. It also shares a guaranteed transfer agreement with the University of California at Davis, Sacramento State University, and Sonoma State University.

Sonoma County

Santa Rosa Junior College
1501 Mendocino Avenue, Santa Rosa
(707) 527-4011
www.santarosa.edu
The scholarship program at Santa Rosa Junior College is unique in all of America because of an association with the county-based Exchange Bank. In 1948 the bank's president, Frank P. Doyle, set up a trust that in the 1950-51 school year paid out $19,475 in scholarships to 95 students. In 2003-04, dividends from the trust awarded more than $7.5 million in scholarships to approximately 5,731 students. Located on more than 100 acres, the college has a full-time enrollment of almost 7,000. Emphasis centers on general education, transfer education for students headed to four-year institutions, and

occupational education in the fields of dental hygiene, radiologic technology, respiratory therapy, and many other areas.

A recent addition to Santa Rosa Junior College is an 87-seat planetarium. It has a dome 40 feet in diameter and 27 feet high. An additional 40-acre campus in east Petaluma offers occupational training, national park ranger training, police and fire technology, and public safety.

Empire College
3035 Cleveland Avenue, Santa Rosa
(707) 546-4000
www.empcol.com
Empire College offers four specialized associate degrees—in accounting, office technology, legal office administration, and medical assistance. Its School of Law awards juris doctor degrees in a four-year evening program. It also offers certificates to those studying to become legal secretaries, medical administrative/clinical assistants, medical transcriptionists, bookkeepers, and travel and tourism agents. A state-accredited college, Empire has operated since 1961 and now has some 500 students.

Mendocino County

Mendocino College
1000 Hensley Creek Road, Ukiah
(707) 463-3073
www.mendocino.cc.ca.us
The campus of Mendocino College occupies 126 acres and serves a rural area that encompasses 3,200 square miles. The school has additional educational centers at Willits and at Lakeport in Lake County. Founded in 1972 as a junior college, Mendocino provides the first two years of study for a four-year degree or confers an associate degree with vocational training in a wide variety of fields. There are programs in horticulture, agriculture, administration of justice, business administration, computer and information sciences, and premed and prenursing, to name a few.

Both the Willits and Lake County centers provide administrative services and classrooms, plus counseling and financial aid assistance. Mendocino College has an additional facility at Point Arena, 50 miles southwest of Ukiah, which serves as a field laboratory for science classes in marine biology, geology, and meteorology.

College of the Redwoods
1211 Del Mar Drive, Fort Bragg
(707) 962-2600
www.redwoods.cc.ca.us

The main campus of College of the Redwoods is at Eureka in Humboldt County. This is a two-year community college offering associate degrees, career training, and enrichment classes to residents of the North Coast. Students receive top academic instruction in science, mathematics, and humanities courses, which transfer to Humboldt State University and other four-year colleges and universities across the nation.

The Fort Bragg campus is well known for courses in fine woodworking. It has a one-year program (though many sign up for a second year); its fame is such that students come to Fort Bragg from all over the world to study cabinetry and furniture making. The college also offers a program that links art with computer technology to provide for study in phototransfer work and graphics communication. College of the Redwoods has no athletic program.

FOUR-YEAR COLLEGES AND UNIVERSITIES

Napa County

Pacific Union College
100 Howell Mountain Road N., Angwin
(707) 965-6311, (800) 862-7080
www.puc.edu

PUC is a small (just more than 1,600 students), private, Seventh-day Adventist college surrounded by 1,800 acres of crops and forest on top of Howell Mountain, where it has been since 1906. The views

Napa Valley College and Santa Rosa Junior College both offer several courses—semester-long and shorter—in viticulture and wine making. SRJC also offers classes such as Wine Industry Event Planning, Wine Marketing Fundamentals, and Media in the Wine and Vineyard Industry.

are fabulous, and the education is highly regarded. *U.S. News & World Report* ranked the school the top liberal-arts college in California in 1998, and the *Right College* places it in the top 10 in the nation for the percentage of male graduates who enter medical school. The student-faculty ratio is an appealing 12-to-1.

Pacific Union is most definitely a unique experience. The student body is ethnically diverse, the cafeteria is vegetarian (in line with Seventh-day Adventist practice), and the Abroad Program offers overseas study, including full-year programs in Argentina, Austria, France, Kenya, and Spain. Service is a big part of a PUC student's commitment. Many strike out on yearlong missions, and even more are actively involved with local homeless shelters, prison ministries, and the like. The college offers associate, bachelor's, and master's degrees in 19 academic departments.

Sonoma County

University of Northern California
1304 Southpoint Boulevard, Suite 220, Petaluma
(707) 765-6400
www.uncm.edu

This new university, established in 1993, welcomes students from around the world. It aspires to become a premier engineering and scientific university with substantial programs in the liberal arts. Students enjoy small classes with ample individual attention from professors dedicated to quality teaching. Interdisciplinary

Public Libraries

Napa County

3421 Broadway, American Canyon;
(707) 644-1136

580 Coombs Street, Napa;
(707) 253-4241

6548 Yountville Avenue, Yountville;
(707) 944-1888

1108 Myrtle, Calistoga; (707) 942-4833

Sonoma County

755 West Napa Street, Sonoma;
(707) 996-5217

100 Fairgrounds Drive, Petaluma;
(707) 763-9801

6250 Lynne Conde Way, Rohnert
Park-Cotati; (707) 584-9121

Third and E Streets, Santa Rosa (main
branch); (707) 545-0831

150 Coddingtown Center, Santa Rosa;
(707) 546-2265

6959 Montecito Boulevard, Santa Rosa;
(707) 537-0162

9291 Old Redwood Highway, Windsor;
(707) 838-1020

Piper and Center Streets, Healdsburg;
(707) 433-3772

401 North Cloverdale Boulevard,
Cloverdale; (707) 894-5271

7050 Covey Road, Forestville;
(707) 887-7654

14107 Armstrong Woods Road,
Guerneville; (707) 869-9004

73 Main Street, Occidental;
(707) 874-3080

7140 Bodega Avenue, Sebastopol;
(707) 823-7691

Mendocino County

309 East Commercial Street, Willits;
(707) 459-5908

105 North Main Street, Ukiah;
(707) 463-4491

76301 Main Street, Covelo;
(707) 983-6736

225 Main Street, Point Arena;
(707) 882-3114

499 East Laurel Street, Fort Bragg;
(707) 964-2020

studies are encouraged, and all academic programs emphasize the importance of effective communication for success in the modern world. The university focuses on programs in biological technology, and its degree programs include the B.E., M.S., and Ph.D. in biomedical engineering, the B.A. and M.B.A. in applied linguistics, and the B.A. in Chinese.

Sonoma State University
1801 East Cotati Avenue, Rohnert Park
(707) 664-2880
www.sonoma.edu

This university was established on 270 acres of farmland in 1960. Today it offers undergraduate liberal arts and science curricula and 13 master's degree programs to a student population of about 7,000. Its computer engineering graduates walk directly into high-paying jobs, and similar results are expected for those completing the new wine business program. The school's Sonoma Plan is considered a model nursing program throughout America. In 2000 the university unveiled a new three-story, 215,000-square-foot Jean and Charles Schulz Information Center. This elegant structure—named in honor of the renowned Peanuts cartoonist and his wife—is home to both the university library and the campus information technology department. In 2004 a $15 million recreation center opened, equipped with a rock climbing wall and indoor soccer, volleyball, and basketball courts.

Performing arts get top billing at the campus, with plays from the pens of local writers and international favorites performed year-round, along with dance recitals and musical concerts (see the Arts and Culture chapter).

OTHER INSTITUTES OF HIGHER LEARNING

Napa County

The Culinary Institute of America at Greystone
2555 Main Street, St. Helena
(707) 967-1100
www.ciachef.edu
This learning institution devoted to the gustatory arts is one of the perks of living in Wine Country. It is the only center in the world dedicated exclusively to continuing education for professionals in the food, wine, health, and hospitality fields—and it's a beauty.

It all began some years ago, when executives of the Culinary Institute of America, that factory of chefs in Hyde Park, New York, looked at some 50 potential sites to establish a West Coast center for continuing education. Their logical choice was Greystone, the majestic winery built in 1888 and used by the Christian Brothers to make sparkling wine from 1950 to 1989. After a massive gift from the Heublein Corporation (then owners of the property) and a $14 million renovation, the CIA opened for business in Napa Valley in 1995.

Inside, the facilities are almost as impressive as the 22-inch-thick tufa stone walls that frame Greystone's exterior. The third story is an immense teaching kitchen

More than 50 Napa Valley wineries take part every year in an event called Taste for Knowledge, a wine tasting and wine auction usually held in November. Sponsored by the Napa Valley Unified Education Foundation, the event has raised more than a million dollars to date for direct classroom enrichment in local schools.

with 15,000 square feet of undivided floor space, 35-foot ceilings, and clusters of exquisite Bonnet stoves. In the middle of the space is a dining area where students sample the various assignments they and their cohorts have handed in.

The building also houses a 125-seat amphitheater used for cooking demonstrations and lectures; the Wine Spectator Greystone Restaurant (see the Restaurants chapter for more on that); and the Spice Islands Marketplace with its preponderance of cooking equipment, books, and uniforms. Outside the old winery are garlic and onion beds, seven terraces of herbs, an edible flower and herbal tea garden, and, off-site, 15 acres of Merlot grapes and an organic fruit and vegetable garden.

Courses vary in length from three days to the 30-week, two-semester Baking and Pastry Arts Certification Program. (The average class duration is one week.) The faculty is drawn from three sources: the small but talented core of resident instructors, visiting teachers from Hyde Park, and guest instructors.

Sonoma County

Western Institute of Science and Health
130 Avram Avenue, Rohnert Park
(707) 664-9267, (800) 437-9474
www.westerni.org
The Western Institute of Science and Health offers an Associate of Science program for physical therapist assistants and helps its students find employment in hos-

pitals, outpatient clinics, public schools, and home-health agencies. The institute teaches students, through academic courses and clinical internship experiences, how to effectively treat patients who suffer from physical impairment. Graduates must pass a state examination given by the Physical Therapy Examination Committee before they may practice in California.

New College of California
99 Sixth Street, Santa Rosa
(707) 568-0122, (888) 437-3460
www.newcollege.edu/northbay/campus
.htm
This alternative college's main campus is in San Francisco, where students can earn undergraduate and graduate degrees in subjects that range from women's spirituality to poetics. The north bay campus—located in a quaint brick building off Railroad Square—offers both B.A. and M.A. degrees in the subjects of culture, ecology, and sustainable community. The B.A. degree is a one-year weekend completion program designed for students who are working and unable to attend traditionally scheduled classes. Applicants must have already acquired at least 45 units from another institution to enter the program.

Mendocino County

Dharma Realm Buddhist University
City of Ten Thousand Buddhas, 5251
Kindness Avenue, Ukiah
(707) 468-9112
www.drba.org
State-approved Dharma Realm University offers year-round education to qualified students, with programs leading to bachelor's, master's, and doctoral certificates. The emphasis is on Buddhist study and practice, including loyalty, felicity, humanness, and righteousness. Students are given the opportunity to develop their innate wholesome wisdom. At the same time, high standards of academic excellence are maintained. Degrees are cur-

rently offered in Buddhist studies and practice, translation, and Buddhist education. Full scholarships are available to qualified students.

CHILD CARE

Whether you're visiting for a few days or putting down roots for a several years, finding qualified child care can be a daunting task.

Each county has at least one organization that will help you sort out all the factors, free of charge. These agencies are able to quote prices, describe individual providers, and refer you to ones in which you might be interested.

Napa County

Community Resources for Children
5 Financial Plaza, Suite 224, Napa
(707) 253-0376 (general information),
(707) 253-0366 (referrals),
(800) 696-4CRC
www.crcnapa.org

Sonoma County

Community Child Care Council
396 Tesconi Court, Santa Rosa
(707) 544-3077
www.sonoma4cs.org

River Child Care Services
16315 First Street, Guerneville
(707) 869-3613
www.sonic.net/~rccs

Mendocino and Lake Counties

North Coast Opportunities, Inc.
413 North State Street, Ukiah
(707) 462-1954

156 Humboldt Street S., Willits
(707) 459-2019

155 Cypress Street, Fort Bragg
(707) 964-3080

14893 Lakeshore Drive, Clearlake
(707) 995-0495

850 Lakeport Boulevard, Lakeport
(707) 263-4688

WALK-IN/PROMPT-CARE CENTERS

Napa County

ExpressCare
Queen of the Valley Hospital
1000 Trancas Street, Napa
(707) 257-4008
www.thequeen.org
This walk-in center, an adjunct of Queen of the Valley's emergency room, is open 10:00 A.M. to 10:00 P.M. daily and can address a variety of nonlethal illnesses, allergies, and injuries. Board-certified physicians are on hand to treat you, and they will make referrals or deliver follow-up care if needed.

Sonoma County

St. Joseph Urgent Care Centers
Rohnert Park Healthcare Center
1450 Medical Center Drive, Rohnert Park
(707) 584-0672

1287 Fulton Road, Santa Rosa
(707) 543-2000
www.stjosephhealth.org
Both of these convenient clinics, operated by St. Joseph Health System–Sonoma County, are for people who need to see a medical professional but whose injuries or illnesses are not emergencies. The doctors and nurses can patch up your minor medical problems quickly and efficiently and provide diagnostic and lab services too. The Rohnert Park location is open daily

8:00 A.M. to 9:00 P.M.; the Santa Rosa clinic is open daily 10:00 A.M. to 8:00 P.M.

HOSPITALS

Napa County

Queen of the Valley Hospital
1000 Trancas Street, Napa
(707) 252-4411
www.thequeen.org
With 179 beds, QVH has a community cancer center, a high-end imaging department, home-care services, maternity services (including an intensive-care nursery), occupational health services, a regional heart center where open-heart surgeries are performed, and a respiratory-care department. It also features an upgraded vascular and interventional radiology lab, an expanded maternity unit, and improved MRI technology.

Queen of the Valley is the designated trauma center for Napa County, with a 24-hour emergency room.

The Acute Rehabilitation Center offers comprehensive physical, occupational, and speech therapies for people who have experienced trauma (such as a stroke or spinal cord injury). Queen of the Valley is part of the St. Joseph Health System, which emphasizes dignity, service, justice, and excellence.

If you are a Kaiser Permanente member staying in Wine Country, note that the hospital group operates a medical center in Vallejo, only 15 miles from Napa, and another in Santa Rosa.

St. Helena Hospital
650 Sanitarium Road, Deer Park
(707) 963-3611,
TTY/TDD: (707) 963-6527
www.sthelenahospital.org
This full-service community hospital, off the Silverado Trail about 3 miles northeast

Health Care in Wine Country

Considering that most of Wine Country is rural, the population relatively sparse, and the towns small to midsize, health care is amazingly accessible and the quality is excellent. Hospital staffs (from the doctors on down to the volunteer helpers) are "small-town friendly" and more easy-going than their big-city counterparts. But their dedication to medicine is just as serious.

However, the nationwide nursing shortage and other health care industry crises have also affected medical facilities locally, with scaled-back services and shorter hours of operation at many places. The smaller community hospitals in particular have been hard hit by financial constraints and in response have reduced their services and trimmed staffs. Yet the larger facilities are expanding services, building new wings, and acquiring new and better equipment. Along the way, they are receiving accolades for their skills and expertise.

of St. Helena, dates from the 1800s, when a sanitarium was a health resort—hence the street name.

St. Helena Hospital, with 181 beds, has a wide range of specialties, including cardiac surgery, cardiovascular rehabilitation, pulmonary rehabilitation, mental health services, oncology, obstetrics, pain rehabilitation, and preventive medicine.

A member of the Adventist Health network of facilities, St. Helena is known for its cardiovascular lab—a major heart center for Northern California.

St. Helena has a Women's Center in downtown St. Helena, providing mammography, bone-density testing, a health resource library, and a wide range of health education classes and support groups. The Women's Center is at 1299 Pine Street; call (707) 963–1912.

Sonoma County

Sonoma Valley Hospital
347 Andrieux Street, Sonoma
(707) 935–5000
www.svh.com
When Sonoma Valley Hospital was created in 1944, the vision was to combine

the best of medicine with a warm and caring staff. Since then, tremendous advances in research and diagnosis have changed the face of medicine. But the hospital remains a warm, caring, family-oriented hospital with the same small-town spirit that permeates the community from which it draws its patients.

Today's 83-bed facility serves 40,000 people in Sonoma Valley. The credentialed medical staff numbers appproximately 136 active, consulting, and courtesy physicians involved in 25 different disciplines. A full range of cardiopulmonary testing equipment is available, along with cardiac rehab programs. A birth center provides a comfortable, homey place where labor, delivery, recovery, and postpartum phases all take place in one room with the family at hand.

Petaluma Valley Hospital
400 North McDowell Boulevard, Petaluma
(707) 778–1111
www.stjosephhealth.org
With 82 beds and 30 medical specialties from cardiology to urology, this facility, operated by the St. Joseph Health System–Sonoma County, is a busy place. The attractive two-story, 24-year-old hospital

is also a genuine community resource. There's a full-service emergency department with a physician on duty 24 hours a day and a helipad for emergency helicopter air transport.

Santa Rosa Memorial Hospital
1165 Montgomery Drive, Santa Rosa
(707) 546-3210
www.stjosephhealth.org
Memorial Hospital opened its doors in 1950 under the guidance of the Sisters of St. Joseph, founders of eight other hospitals on the West Coast since 1920. All services and programs are guided by the healing mission of the Sisters—service, excellence, justice, and dignity for all members of the community. The hospital is the flagship facility for St. Joseph Health System–Sonoma County, which operates several clinics and acute-care facilities throughout the region.

In 2000 Memorial Hospital was named the designated trauma center for Sonoma, Lake, and Mendocino Counties, making it the busiest and best-equipped hospital of its kind north of the Golden Gate.

In addition to cutting-edge surgical facilities and medical equipment, the 359-bed Memorial Hospital has some unique services including the mobile medical and dental clinics, which serve children ages 16 and younger from low-income families that have difficulty locating affordable health care. Care is provided by medical professionals who speak English and Spanish.

To give new parents extra peace of mind, the hospital partners with University of California–San Francisco Medical Center to operate an intensive-care nursery for ill newborns on-site.

In 2000 the St. Joseph Health System added another dimension to its services: A palliative care unit, across the street from Santa Rosa Memorial Hospital. One of only two units of its kind in California, this acute-care service focuses on end-of-life pain management and improving the quality of life for those with life-threatening illness. In 2003 the hospital opened a $20 million ambulatory surgery center across the street from its main campus, where outpatient surgeries of all types are performed.

Sutter Warrack Hospital
2449 Summerfield Road, Santa Rosa
(707) 542-9030
www.suttersantarosa.org
Built in 1960, Warrack is a 69-bed hospital with four operating rooms. Its primary services cover intensive and coronary care, pediatric surgery, and diagnostic imaging. Emergency care is available 24 hours a day, with a physician always on duty.

Sutter Medical Center of Santa Rosa
3325 Chanate Road, Santa Rosa
(707) 576-4000
www.suttersantarosa.org
This hospital was established in 1866 and has provided advanced health care services for Sonoma County and the adjoining communities for nearly 140 years.

As a teaching institution affiliated with the University of California at San Francisco School of Medicine, Sutter is regionally recognized for its wide range of specialty services, including a high-risk maternity department and an emergency trauma care program. It offers other special services too. The 175-bed facility's major expansion in 2001 was to its cardiovascular services. The Heart Center provides a complete range of cardiac services, from open-heart surgery to cardiac rehabilitation.

Healdsburg District Hospital
1375 University Avenue, Healdsburg
(707) 431-6500
www.h-g-h.org
Today the hospital is a far cry from the World War I–era, wood-frame building that burned to the ground in the 1930s. It's now a modern facility with 15 beds. Services include 24-hour emergency care, physical therapy and occupational medicine services, same-day surgery center, and a new respite care service.

When Finding Help Is Urgent

Call 911 during any medical emergency. If an ambulance is not what you need, consider one of the following numbers. In the first group are phone numbers that apply throughout the Wine Country. They are followed by county-specific numbers.

Throughout Wine Country
Poison Control Center
(800) 222-1222

California HIV/AIDS Hotline
(800) 367-2437

Crisis Line for the Handicapped
(800) 426-4263

California Smokers Helpline
(800) 662-8887

California Department of Drug and Alcohol Problems
(800) 879-2772

Centers for Disease Control and Prevention (Sexually Transmitted Disease Hotline)
(800) 227-8922

Medical Board of California (Central Complaint Unit)
(800) 633-2322

Dental Referral
(800) DENTIST

Napa County
Suicide Prevention
(707) 963-2555, (800) 784-2433

Palm Drive Hospital
501 Petaluma Avenue, Sebastopol
(707) 823-8511
www.palmdrivehospital.com
Palm Drive's future as a small community hospital has been tested during the past few years. Currently it has 49 beds and one operating room, and its emergency room is staffed 24 hours a day.

Mendocino County

Ukiah Valley Medical Center
275 Hospital Drive, Ukiah
(707) 462-3111
www.uvmc.org
A member of the Adventist Health Corporation, this 116-bed hospital has offered a full spectrum of outpatient treatment and surgery since its inception in 1956, when it was known as Hillside Hospital. In 1979 it joined the Adventist Health group. This affiliation provides the advantage of being connected to a network of locations so that patients can be transferred quickly, by helicopter if necessary, to whichever Adventist Health hospital specializes in treating the particular problem.

Frank R. Howard Memorial Hospital
Madrone and Manzanita Streets, Willits
(707) 459-6801
www.howardhospital.com
Affiliated with the Adventist Health group since 1986, Frank R. Howard Memorial Hospital serves a population in a wide area of wilderness and ranch and forest land as far north as the Oregon border. There is 24-hour emergency service. While the hospital is small (just 28 beds), its connection with the Adventist group gives it wide latitude in serving patients through larger hospitals in the group.

Napa County Health and Human
Services Department
(707) 253-4279

Napa Valley AIDS Project
(707) 258-2437

Napa County Alcohol and Drug Services
(707) 253-4412

Napa Emergency Women's Services
(707) 255-6397

Sonoma County

Sonoma County Department of Health
Services and Center for HIV Prevention
and Care
(707) 565-4620

Suicide Prevention
(800) 784-2433

Crisis Line for the Handicapped
(800) 426-4263

Department of Alcohol and Drug
Programs
(800) 879-2772

Mendocino County

Mendocino County Health Department
(800) 734-7793, (707) 472-2600

Mendocino County Suicide Prevention
(800) 575-4357

Community Care AIDS Project of
Mendocino and Lake Counties
(707) 462-3041

Department of Alcohol and
Drug Problems
(707) 961-2522 (Fort Bragg)
(707) 472-2637 (Ukiah)

Redwood Coast Medical Services
46900 Ocean Drive, Gualala
(707) 884-4005
www.rcms-healthcare.org
In a town too small to accommodate a
hospital, this federally qualified medical-
service facility fills a gap with medical spe-
cialists that include an ophthalmologist,
cardiologist, oncologist, and orthopedist.
The office is open 8:00 A.M. to 6:00 P.M.
Monday through Friday and 9:00 A.M. to
1:00 P.M. Saturday. However, doctors are on
duty 24 hours a day to treat injuries and
medical emergencies for visitors and residents alike and can be reached for services after Redwood Coast closes.

Mendocino Coast District Hospital
700 River Drive, Fort Bragg
(707) 961-1234
www.mcdh.org
Its garden setting makes this lone hospital

on the Mendocino coast very attractive.
Created by the cities of the coastal community in 1971, it still maintains an attitude
that locals call "neighbors taking care of
neighbors." Patients from large cities often
remark on this small-town support and
warmth and on how amazingly caring the
hospital personnel can be. With 52 beds,
two operating rooms, and an outpatient
surgery area, services offered include criti-
cal-care facilities, 24-hour emergency
service, laboratory services, radiology, and
cardiopulmonary care.

HOSPICE CARE

Napa County

Hospice of Napa Valley
414 South Jefferson Street, Napa
(707) 258-9080, (800) 451-4664

Local practitioners of holistic health swear by the Share Guide, which covers everything from psychic workshops to natural food products. It is available free throughout Wine Country at many newsstands, in coffeehouses, and at most alternative lifestyle outlets. Visit its Web site (www.shareguide.com) to get the lowdown on new age goings-on in the region.

If the time comes to end the aggressive search for a cure and to focus instead on comfort and symptom alleviation as death approaches, hospice care is the appropriate choice. Hospice of Napa Valley, a nonprofit organization and a joint community service of St. Helena Hospital and Queen of the Valley Hospital, has been serving the county since 1979.

Sonoma County

Hospice of Petaluma
416 Payran Street, Petaluma
(707) 778-6242

Memorial Hospice
821 Mendocino Avenue, Santa Rosa
(707) 568-1094
www.stjosephhealth.org
Working in tandem as part of the St. Joseph Health System–Sonoma County, these agencies provide support and care

for persons facing life-threatening illnesses so that they may live as fully and comfortably as possible. Hospice of Petaluma (working with Memorial Hospice of Santa Rosa) benefits the community served by Petaluma Valley and Santa Rosa Memorial Hospitals. A counseling and social work staff offer emotional support, counseling, and information about community resources. A hospice chaplain provides spiritual support.

ALTERNATIVE HEALTH CARE

Alternative forms of treatment and prevention proliferate and thrive in this region. Why? First of all, this is Wine Country, where health and quality of life are paramount. And second, this is California, where people tend to be open-minded in their decision making.

So if you're in search of a less traditional cure for what ails you, you're in luck. Within a short drive you can find homeopaths and naturopaths, ayurvedics and herbalists, acupuncturists and acupressurists, chiropractors and yoga gurus, reflexologists and hypnotists—and practitioners of Reiki, rolfing, and biofeedback. You can even find a few shaman healers if you try hard enough. If you want to verify a license, call the Medical Board of California at (916) 263-2382.

MEDIA

When you visit Wine Country, you're probably here to forget about the outside world for a few days, to escape from the 24/7 onslaught of the media. But when you do feel like plugging back into reality—or if you're a new or soon-to-be resident—the local media stands ready to enlighten you. In addition to daily and weekly newspapers and niche publications, this chapter lists radio stations and cable TV providers. *Note:* Anyone needing their daily fix of the *New York Times, Wall Street Journal,* or the nearby *San Francisco Chronicle* can find racks for these newspapers in most Wine Country communities.

DAILY NEWSPAPERS

Napa County

The Napa Valley Register
1615 Second Street, Napa
(707) 226-3711, (800) 504-6397
www.napanews.com
Napa County's only daily dates from 1863, though it has gone through a few changes of ownership since Abe Lincoln's administration. The paper is now owned by Lee Enterprises.

The *Register* ably handles the entire county, nodding to St. Helena and Calistoga in its upvalley section. The paper uses wire-service reports but does a lot of local reporting, such as a multifaceted 1997 series about the valley's farmworkers that garnered much acclaim.

The *Register* is an afternoon paper during the week, switching to morning delivery on Saturday and Sunday. It prints its community calendar on Thursday and Sunday. The calendar lists upcoming musical performances, lectures, and fundraisers. Also worth noting here is its monthly news-rack supplement: *Inside Napa Valley*, a tourist-aimed tabloid with features on art, food, wine, and coming events. The supplement is free.

Sonoma County

The Press Democrat
427 Mendocino Avenue, Santa Rosa
(707) 546-2020
www.pressdemocrat.com
For many Sonoma County residents as well as readers in adjoining counties, the morning *Press Democrat* is the paper for local, national, and international daily news, with a circulation of about 93,000 (104,000 on Sunday).

The *P.D.,* as locals call it, is owned by the *New York Times* now but has been serving the Sonoma County area since 1857. Although the paper's name includes the word *democrat,* the editorial stance is more middle-of-the-road.

A strong sports section features popular columnists such as Bob Padecky and

Truffles, anyone? The Press Democrat's *Wednesday edition carries a "tidbits" calendar that gives suggestions for food and wine fun for the current week. These may include hors d'oeuvres tastings, wine barrel tastings, or short cooking classes at such places as Ramekins Sonoma Valley Culinary School in Sonoma (whose chocolate truffles workshop costs just $65).*

Lowell Cohn. On the entertainment scene, local residents keep abreast of what's going on about town through a lively entertainment section called "Q." Columns by Chris Coursey, Chris Smith, and Gaye LeBaron also offer colorful, behind-the-scenes coverage of Sonoma County people, places, and history.

Mendocino County

Ukiah Daily Journal
590 South School Street, Ukiah
(707) 468-0123
www.ukiahdailyjournal.com
This newspaper's roots go back to 1860, when it was called the *Redwood Journal*. With a circulation of 8,500, the *Daily Journal* covers local and county news that the metropolitan dailies don't. Coverage includes sports, society news, club activities, high school events, and news from Mendocino College, located in the Ukiah foothills.

OTHER NEWSPAPERS

Napa County

American Canyon Eagle
3429 Broadway, Suite C-1, American Canyon
(707) 256-2210
www.americancanyoneagle.com
Published every Tuesday, the *Eagle* documents what's happening in the predominantly residential community of American Canyon, south of Napa. This paper is owned by Lee Enterprises.

St. Helena Star
1328 Main Street, St. Helena
(707) 963-2731
www.sthelenastar.com
St. Helena's well-preserved Victorian charm even extends to its newspaper, the *Star*, owned by Lee Enterprises. The paper

attempts to stay within the city limits, plus Angwin and its Howell Mountain environs.

The paper astutely covers the important local issues—growth, tourism, elections—and its wine coverage is getting more comprehensive. (There is a special wine edition every October.) But even the editors will admit that the feature best known for reeling in readers is the precious police log. You don't really know St. Helena until you have studied this compendium of barking dogs, double-parked cars, and nosy neighbors.

The Weekly Calistogan
1424 Lincoln Avenue, Calistoga
(707) 942-4035
www.weeklycalistogan.com
This might be the only newspaper in the nation whose motto is longer than some of its features. And I quote: "Published at the Head of the Napa Valley, a Beautiful and Fertile Section of Country, Possessing a Climate that for Health and Comfort is Not Surpassed on Earth." Amen.

The *Calistogan* is owned by Lee Enterprises, and like its sister paper, the *St. Helena Star,* comes out each Thursday.

Sonoma County

The Sonoma Index-Tribune
117 West Napa Street, Sonoma
(707) 938-2111
www.sonomanews.com
Established in 1879, the twice-weekly *Sonoma Index-Tribune* has been in the same family since 1884.

Serving the Sonoma Valley—a region approximately 18 miles long that extends from San Pablo Bay north to Kenwood— the paper publishes every Tuesday and Friday, with a paid circulation of 12,500. The *Index-Tribune* is an award-winning community newspaper, covering all aspects of local news—schools, city government, the fire and water boards, the wine business, prep and youth sports, adult recreational sports leagues, even bake sales and spaghetti dinners.

In 1997 the *Index-Tribune* received five awards for excellence in the annual California Newspaper Publishers Association Better Newspapers Contest, including a coveted honor in the general excellence category.

Argus Courier
830 Petaluma Boulevard N., Petaluma
(707) 762-4541
www.arguscourier.com
Published each Wednesday, this publication (now owned by the *New York Times*) has been in business since 1855, making it the oldest paper in Sonoma County. It focuses on Petaluma community news and information on arts and entertainment. Circulation is 8,500.

The Community Voice
5625 State Farm Drive, Rohnert Park
(707) 584-2222
www.thecommunityvoice.com
The *Community Voice,* published every Wednesday, is the local newspaper for residents of Rohnert Park and Cotati. It tells them what is going on in their schools and neighborhoods. Columnists write up the news about anniversaries, birthdays, and other small-town happenings. The paper's well-designed sports section covers local recreational activities—especially youth sports—with the intensity that city papers use to cover the major leagues.

The newspaper works closely with the Rohnert Park and Cotati chambers of commerce, is involved in promoting local business, and beats the drum for many local events and institutions. There is also a reporter covering Sonoma State University.

North Bay Bohemian
216 E Street, Santa Rosa
(707) 527-1200
www.bohemian.com
Before becoming the *Bohemian* in 2000, this free weekly tabloid was known as the *Sonoma County Independent*—and before

that it was the *West Sonoma County Paper.* In 1994 the paper joined a Bay Area group of alternative weeklies, Metro Newspapers. Formerly serving only Sonoma County, the *Bohemian* now covers Marin and Napa Counties, featuring news stories relating to civic issues—from an indy perspective—as well as a reliable culture and entertainment department. This weekly comes out each Thursday, with numerous distribution points in the three counties.

Sonoma County Herald-Recorder
1818 Fourth Street, Santa Rosa
(707) 545-1166
Published twice a week with a readership of 5,000, the *Herald-Recorder* covers real estate, business, and legal news, with statistical information from the *Recorder*'s office and county clerk plus news affecting local attorneys and real estate interests.

Sonoma-Marin Farm News
870 Piner Road, Santa Rosa
(707) 544-5575
www.sonomacountyfarmbureau.com
The Farm Bureau has been distributing its monthly agricultural newspaper to the ranchers of Sonoma County and adjoining Marin County for 25 years. The publication covers different laws and regulations that affect farmlands and disseminates information on wetlands and tree ordinances that apply to vineyards and dairy and cattle ranches. There is also general farming and viticulture news. Circulation is 3,200.

North Bay Business Journal
5464 Skylane Boulevard, Suite B,
Santa Rosa
(707) 579-2900
www.busjrnl.com
The *Business Journal* publishes strictly business news, focusing on new startups, expansions of existing firms, and information on relocations. Circulation is more than 10,000. Usually the 40-page-plus journal, recently purchased by the *New York Times,* will include a profile of a top-level executive describing the company,

its history, and anticipation of future progress. Published weekly, the *Business Journal* covers Sonoma, Marin, and Napa Counties. It also prints a monthly wine industry *Business Journal* and a year-end *Book of Lists*.

Healdsburg Tribune and Windsor Times
5 Mitchell Lane, Healdsburg
(707) 433-4451
www.sonomawest.com/healdsburg,
www.sonomawest.com/windsor

The *Tribune* has had different owners since its inception more than 130 years ago, but it is now part of the Sonoma West Publishers newspaper group, which also publishes the *Sonoma West Times & News* (see listing). This is a well-rounded weekly, covering all the news of Healdsburg and Geyersville: community affairs and events, legal matters, and local personalities. The paper also prints occasional special sections. The *Windsor Times* too is strictly locally oriented—and owned by the Sonoma West Publishers. Both the *Healdsburg Tribune* and *Windsor Times* print on Wednesday. Together, the newspapers' circulation is approximately 9,000.

Cloverdale Reveille
207 North Cloverdale Boulevard,
Cloverdale
(707) 894-3339
www.cloverdale.net

This community newspaper is published on Wednesday and covers community and school news. Records stacked away in old files indicate the *Reveille* was first published in 1879. Present circulation of the *Cloverdale Reveille* is 2,400.

Bodega Bay Navigator
1580 Eastshore Road, Bodega Bay
(707) 875-3574

A weekly newspaper established in 1986, with a circulation of 1,400, the *Bodega Bay Navigator* comes out on Thursday and is distributed through most of West County. It focuses on both community news and global issues and has printed some controversial or unusual stories that other small papers often shy away from. For example, the *Navigator* has published stories on teen pregnancy services, violence, and the plight of the Navajo nation.

Sonoma West Times & News
130 South Main Street, Suite 114,
Sebastopol
(707) 823-7845
www.sonomawest.com

Locally owned and intimately focused, this paper covers Sebastopol and the Russian River area. The publisher says the *Times & News* is "about our families, our towns, about the guy next door." Those towns are primarily Sebastopol, Bodega Bay, and Guerneville. Look for the paper each Wednesday.

Mendocino County

Fort Bragg Advocate-News
450 North Franklin Street, Fort Bragg
(707) 964-5642
www.advocate-news.com

Mendocino Beacon
(707) 937-5874
www.mendocinobeacon.com

Both of these weeklies trace their roots to the heydays of the lumber industry that gave birth to the towns. The *Mendocino Beacon-News* came first in 1877, followed by the *Advocate News* in 1889. Early news coverage focused on forests and shipping and sawmills. Today the slant is local with a strong appeal to tourists. The *Advocate* and *Beacon* are based in Fort Bragg; the *Beacon* serves the village of Mendocino. Each covers news of the community, the arts, school affairs, and local personalities. One of the most popular features in both papers is the calendar of events.

Independent Coast Observer
38500 South Highway 1, Gualala
(707) 884-3501
www.mendonoma.com
This weekly paper covers the coastal area from Jenner to Elk. Strictly a visitors' publication, it offers news of upcoming events, art exhibits (with a rundown on some of the artists), and reviews of musical groups performing in Mendocino and elsewhere in the area. There are 3,000 copies printed each week and distributed to restaurants along the coast. A free supplement, *Destination Mendonoma,* is published once a year in May.

Anderson Valley Advertiser
12451 Anderson Valley Road, Boonville
(707) 895-3016
www.theava.com
Published weekly, the *AVA* comes out on Wednesday and covers news of Anderson Valley, an area largely devoted to farming and vineyards. With a motto of "The Country Weekly That Tells It Like It Is," the paper gives in-depth coverage to political matters in the valley, particularly to the activities of the board of supervisors, and often challenges political policies.

MAGAZINES

North Bay Biz
3565 Airway Drive, Santa Rosa
(707) 575-8282
www.northbaybiz.com
Norman Rosinski publishes and edits this glossy monthly magazine, impressive with its well-designed cover and artistic inside pages. It has provided nearly 30 years of business intelligence in Sonoma County. It covers technology, real estate, and wine and other industries. An annual issue identifies the top-500 industries in the county, ranked by gross revenues. The magazine's annual wine issue also doubles as the official program of the Sonoma County Harvest Fair. Circulation is more than 7,000.

RADIO STATIONS

Station List

ADULT CONTEMPORARY
KSAY-98.5 FM
KTDE-100.5 FM
KVYN-99.3 FM
KWNE-94.5 FM
KXBX-98.3 FM
KZST-100.1 FM

CHRISTIAN
KLVR-91.9 FM
KNDL-89.9 FM

COUNTRY
KFGY-92.9 FM
KQPM-105.9
KRPQ-104.9 FM
KUKI-103.3 FM

JAZZ
KJZY-93.7 FM

NEWS, TALK, SPORTS
KPMO-1300 AM
KSRO-1350 AM
KVON-1440 AM
KZYZ-91.5 FM

OLDIES, STANDARDS
KMFB-92.7 FM
KXBX-1270 AM

PUBLIC RADIO
KRCB-90.9 and 91.1 FM
KZYX-90.7 FM

ROCK
KMHX-104.1 FM (Alternative)
KOZT-95.3 (Classic rock)
KRSH-95.5 and 95.9 FM (Classic rock and blues)
KSXY-98.7
KVRV-97.7 FM (Rock oldies)
KXFX-101.7 FM, 1250 AM

SPANISH

KBBF-89.1 FM
KDAC-1230 AM
KGRP-100.9 FM
KLLK-1250 AM
KRRS-1460 AM
KTOB-1490 AM
KUKI-1400 AM

TELEVISION

Station List

ABC: KGO Channel 7 (Napa, Sonoma, Mendocino, Lake)
  CBS: KPIX Channel 5 (Napa, Sonoma, Mendocino, Lake); KOVR Channel 14 (Lake)
  NBC: KNTV Channel 11 (Napa, Sonoma, Mendocino, Lake)
  FOX: KTVU Channel 2 (Napa, Sonoma, Mendocino, Lake)
  PBS: KQED Channel 9 (Napa, Sonoma, Mendocino, Lake); KRCB Channel 22 (Sonoma)
  UPN: KBHK Channel 44 (Napa, Sonoma, Mendocino) and Channel 12 (Lake)
  Independents: KFTY Channel 50 (Sonoma, Mendocino)

Local Broadcast Channels

KFTY Channel 50 (Independent)
533 Mendocino Avenue, Santa Rosa
(707) 526-5050
www.newschannel50.com
Started in 1981 by Wichard Brown, then owner of the *Marin Independent Journal,* this station is now owned by Clear Channel Communications. KFTY serves the six counties just north of San Francisco. General programming includes news, movies, sitcoms, and public interest programs,

with a special 30-minute North Bay news program Monday through Friday at 7:00 P.M. and a one-hour news program at 10:00 P.M.

KRCB Channel 22 (Public TV)
5850 Labath Avenue, Rohnert Park
(707) 585-8522
www.krcb.org
This public television station was started in 1984 and now reaches the counties of Sonoma, Napa, Mendocino, and Lake, plus portions of Alameda, Marin, Solano, and Contra Costa Counties. It even broadcasts to San Francisco.
  Programming is typical public television fare: *Sesame Street, Nova, This Old House,* news programs, a *North Bay Journal* featuring regional business news, and *Expressions,* which features local artists.

CABLE TV

Napa County
Sonoma County

Comcast Corp.
(800) 266-2278
www.comcast.com
If you live in one of these two counties, this is your cable TV provider. Comcast has the monopoly in Wine Country, and reviews of its service are mixed. But there's no sign it will change anytime soon. Comcast offers standard cable and digital services in several packages.

Mendocino County

Adelphia Communications
1060 North State Street, Ukiah
(707) 462-8737

1260 North Main Street, Fort Bragg
(800) 626-6299
www.adelphia.com
Adelphia provides two levels of basic
cable TV service with slightly varied channel lineups to customers in Ukiah, Willits,
and Fort Bragg.

Central Valley Cable
38951 South Highway 1, Gualala
(707) 884-4111
This cable TV provider services the
coastal region of Mendocino County,
including Gualala, Point Arena, and Manchester, with some service to Sea Ranch
residents in northern Sonoma County.

WORSHIP 🙏

Here in Wine Country, where a certain sense of spontaneity dominates the culture, an amazingly eclectic assortment of houses of worship has taken root and prospered. In Sonoma County alone, with a thinly spread population of about 472,700 (no larger than a good-size American city), the Yellow Pages list nearly 60 different faiths.

That would be in line with figures gathered at the turn of the 20th century, when it was revealed that Sonoma County had more churches than any other county in the state except San Francisco. The zeal of the early religious organizers and preachers sustained the pioneers and laid a firm foundation for church building of the future.

Although the earliest religious activity had been the domain of the Spanish missionaries—particularly under the direction of Father Jose Altimira, who established the mission in Sonoma—that system broke down when the young republic of Mexico secularized the missions in the 1830s, leaving a religious vacuum (see the History chapter). But when the first American families started to move into the Sonoma and Napa Valleys early in the 1860s to establish farms and businesses, organized religion moved apace. Some of the churches built in those times remain. Many have been designated historic landmarks, their congregations dedicated to keeping the coffers filled and the clapboard freshly painted.

NAPA COUNTY

The story of spirituality in Napa County—or, more accurately, of European-rooted religion—is sprinkled with visionaries, hard knocks, and roustabouts. Fittingly, the tale more or less begins with the gold rush. Among the starry-eyed prospectors who

gravitated to California in 1849 was James Milton Small, an ordained minister of the Cumberland Presbyterian Church. In the fall of 1850, Small gave up on gold and moved to Napa to save souls, preaching to early settlers in the dining room of a boardinghouse.

Three years later the national Presbyterian Board of Missionaries sent the Rev. J. C. Herron from Philadelphia to the Napa Valley. He sermonized in the old courthouse, a trying experience according to church records.

It was in reaction to the poor conditions in the courthouse that the Presbyterians built the first church in Napa city in 1855, at a time when white settlers were true pioneers. After the congregation moved its facilities a couple of years later, the old edifice was reduced to service as a paint shop. In 1858 it was purchased by a group of black Methodists, who splintered from their white congregation, moved the structure to Washington Street, and called it the African Methodist Church. That church is gone, but a bell purchased for $600 by the main Presbyterian congregation in 1868 announces the hour of prayer even today at the First Presbyterian Church at 1333 Third Street in Napa.

Rev. S. D. Simonds is said to have been the first Methodist Episcopal preacher to reside in Napa Valley. That was about 1851. A year later Rev. Asa White delivered a sermon in a grove of redwood trees known as Paradise Park. The grove was part of the Tucker farm, about halfway between St. Helena and Calistoga, and it became the site of the first church in Napa Valley in 1853.

The Methodists built a separate church in Napa in 1856. The Methodists also laid the foundation for a church in Calistoga in 1868, but construction didn't go much further. The railroad wanted the land, and there wasn't much the railroad didn't get.

In 1917 a new Methodist church opened in Napa. During the dedication service, it was reported that $31,000 had been raised for building the church—$5,000 short of the total cost. Addressing the congregation, Bishop Adna Leonard said, "A collection is now in order. This is a courteous congregation. I am going to ask you to remain until the benediction is reached." Leonard's lock-the-doors-until-we're-solvent strategy worked. He marked pledges on a blackboard and eventually reached the $36,000 goal. That building stands today, a registered landmark of English Gothic architecture.

The Christian Church appeared in the valley in 1853, when J. P. McCorkle preached under a madrone tree in Yountville.

The Roman Catholics held occasional services in Margaret McEnerny's boarding-house on Main Street in Napa in the mid-1850s. (The priest would ride over from the Sonoma mission.) Napa merchant George Cornwell, a non-Catholic, donated land on Main Street, and St. John the Baptist Church was erected in 1858.

The first Catholic church in St. Helena was built in 1866; actually, it was the remodeled home of a Mrs. Sheehan at Oak Avenue and Tainter Street. When the local parishioners got a new church in 1878, they paid $72 for the old bell from the Napa courthouse.

The Seventh-day Adventist Church held its first meetings in 1873, in tents at the site of what is today known as Fuller Park in Napa, and a church was dedicated in the winter of 1873–74.

The history of Calistoga, meanwhile, is inexorably entwined with the Church of Jesus Christ of Latter-day Saints, for Sam Brannan, that iconoclastic founding father and California's first millionaire, was a Mormon. After sailing around Cape Horn with a church group in the 1840s, Brannan hung onto the collected tithings. He wanted San Francisco to be the center of Mormon culture, not Salt Lake City. Brigham Young saw otherwise, and he eventually excommunicated Brannan for

Twice each year, on Memorial Day and the Fourth of July, the Russian Orthodox Church conducts services at the chapel at Fort Ross. The events generally feature the extraordinary voices of a Russian choir from San Francisco and a colorful procession to the nearby cemetery to consecrate the graves of the old Russian settlers.

absconding with those funds.

The first Latter-day Saints church in the valley was in St. Helena, adjacent to where that town's current Mormon church stands on Spring Street.

By 1963, Napa County counted some 37 separate churches, representing 20 denominations. Today it's more like 70 churches and 40 denominations, not to mention the many spiritual individualists who defy traditional classification.

SONOMA COUNTY

A zealous young Spanish priest, Father Jose Altimira, was the first to bring Christianity to these parts. He came to what is now Sonoma County in 1823 to establish the Mission San Francisco de Solano, northernmost in a chain of missions spaced along California's coast. Despite the overthrow of the Spanish rulers in Mexico, Altimira was nothing if not enthusiastic, and he convinced his colleagues in the church that the area would be a better climate than San Francisco for the Native American converts.

A small Russian Orthodox chapel was built on the coast in western Sonoma County about the time the Spanish secularized their missions. The wooden chapel was a part of the Russian American Company's settlement at Fort Ross (see the History chapter). The Russians abandoned the fort in 1841, taking all the icons from the chapel with them, leaving behind only a large bell, candelabra, candlestand, and a lectern.

The Russians had come and gone by

the time other church activity began to stir in the established city of Sonoma. In approximately 1859, Congregationalists founded Cumberland Presbyterian College, a learning center where services were also sometimes held. But some distance from the village there lived a rancher named Edwin Sutherland, who decided he would start his own church under the protecting branches of a large live oak tree on his property. He had five children, his sister across the road had six, and with the children of a few neighbors he established the Big Tree Sunday School in his own backyard.

Within three years, Sutherland began forming a church in the village. It would be called the First Congregational Church of Sonoma. That church still stands today, though in a different location, at 252 West Spain Street.

For years, one of the lesser-known secrets about First Baptist Church in Santa Rosa was that it had been built out of a single 3,000-year-old redwood tree. The tree, 275 feet high and 18 feet in diameter, came from a ranch near Guerneville. The congregation had been unaware of the church's unique status until 1900, when a member, attorney Thomas Butts, told his story. He had been employed by a Guernevillle mill at the time the tree was felled. The mill's owner, knowing the intended purpose of the tree, personally monitored every step of the milling process to ensure the wood wasn't mingled with other lumber.

In 1939 Robert Ripley, a church member, featured the church in his "Believe It or Not" column and gave it instant fame. For many years, the Church of One Tree, at 492 Sonoma Avenue in Santa Rosa, housed the Robert Ripley Museum. Although it started as a Baptist church, One Tree became a church for many faiths, and on any given Sunday as many as 5,000 people worshipped there—as many as 10 services were offered there each week.

The 1870s and 1880s saw tremendous expansion of church activity in Sonoma County. Denominations sprang up like dogs to the dinner bell, including Methodists, Baptists, Presbyterians, Episcopalians, and a sizable number of fundamentalist groups.

One of the most renowned preachers of Sonoma County was the Rev. James Woods, who established a Presbyterian church in Healdsburg in 1858. His first congregation included Cyrus Alexander, who owned the entire valley north of Healdsburg and was himself a minister. In fact, it was Alexander who proposed that if the church could raise $1,000, he would put up $800 to secure the Methodist property on the plaza, which was up for sale. The lot was eventually purchased and the church was renovated and occupied.

The church remained there until 1932, when the Presbyterians and Methodists decided to join forces; one church had the building, the other had a large congregation. At about the same time, the Church of Christ established a congregation in Healdsburg, followed by the Seventh-day Adventists and the Episcopalians.

In Santa Rosa, the first semblance of a Catholic church (a wooden building with eight pews) was erected in 1860 on a lot donated by one of General Vallejo's relatives, Julio Carrillo. For the next 15 years, a priest came up from Marin County once a month to offer Mass at St. Rose. Finally, in 1876, a new parish formed that included Sebastopol, Healdsburg, Cloverdale, and Guerneville.

Today, St. Rose parish serves as the mother church in Santa Rosa, with a seating capacity of 500. The church that was built in 1900 still stands as a historic monument, but it is empty and unused, declared unsafe in earthquake conditions. Still grand, it is now surrounded by a new church that wraps around it like a boomerang. The new building at 398 10th Street is stunning, with walls of colored glass.

Churches that once fell neatly into a half-dozen denominations—mainly Methodist, Baptist, Catholic—have now splintered into dozens of churches. It started during the Civil War when Southern Methodists and Southern Baptists started their own congregations to denote their sympathies with the South. Today there are Independent Baptists, Fundamental Baptists, and GARBC Baptists. We have various branches of Presbyterians including Korean Western. We have Buddhist and Soto Zen centers, and we have Pentecostal, Orthodox Eastern, new age churches, and a group called Metropolitan Community, plus a Church of God of Prophecy and the Foursquare Gospel.

MENDOCINO COUNTY

A rough bunch of citizens populated the Mendocino Coast in 1854. The gold rush had waned and lumber was the new booming industry in need of many strong backs. Single men by the hundreds poured in from everywhere to work in the mills.

By 1859 eight determined members from the village of Mendocino had applied to the Presbyterian denomination for status as an established congregation, and a mere nine years later they built a church. It was a lovely little white church, in the Gothic style, designed by the same architect who designed the state capitol in Sacramento. Today, the Mendocino Presbyterian Church is one of the first structures to catch your eye as you enter the village of Mendocino.

Now a California Historical Landmark, the church also is listed in the federal Registry of Historic Places. From its original eight charter members, it has grown to a membership of more than 200—this oldest of California's still-active Presbyterian churches is still vigorous and young.

Perhaps the first church to be established in Fort Bragg was the First Baptist at the corner of East Pine and North Franklin Streets. Like most early churches, the congregation first met at a home in nearby Caspar, beginning in 1878. By 1887 a formal church with a handsome, tall steeple was under construction on land donated by the Fort Bragg Lumber Company.

One of the grand features of this early church was a beautiful, 1,200-pound bell,

purchased in England and shipped around Cape Horn. It was said the bell rang so clearly you could hear it all the way to Caspar—several miles to the south—on a windy day. But by 1932 the clapper had worn out and had to be replaced—unfortunately by a clapper so heavy it cracked the bell. Another clapper, furnished by the fire department, would fit only upside down. At last the bell came down and was set behind the church, where weeds soon overgrew it. Rescued by a church member, it is now proudly displayed in front of the church with a plaque on it.

The First Methodist Church at 270 North Pine Street in Ukiah originally served two congregations—one dating to 1850, the other to 1857. In 1926 they united and built a new church. When fire ravaged that building, they put another right on top of it—a brick building with grounds that spread out over a full city block. (They're still finding rubble from the old church under the sanctuary.) Its steeple stands out as you come into town on U.S. Highway 101.

Perhaps the most beautiful of Mendocino's spiritual centers is the Sagely City of Ten Thousand Buddhas, set among 488 acres of groves and meadows in Ukiah's lovely Valley at Talmage. The campus consists of 70 buildings, including the Dharma Realm Buddhist University (see the listing in the Relocation chapter), on approximately 80 landscaped acres. An atmosphere of quiet peace pervades the City of Ten Thousand Buddhas. Everyone shares a common goal: the sincere pursuit of spiritual truth and value, along with a desire to become wiser and more compassionate.

Incorporated in the United States in 1959, the Dharma Realm Buddhist Association seeks to spread the teachings of the Buddha in America. In 1966 the Most Venerable Master Hsuan Hua set up a center for Buddhist study in San Francisco. It has been moved to the Ukiah Valley to become one of California's foremost Buddhist centers.

INDEX

ABOUT THE AUTHOR

JEAN SAYLOR DOPPENBERG

A 17-year resident of Wine Country, Jean grew up on the outskirts of Des Moines, Iowa, surrounded by cornfields, not grapevines. She worked in the newsroom of the *Des Moines Register* for more than a decade, writing everything from obituaries to restaurant reviews. After visiting San Francisco and Wine Country in the early 1980s, Jean returned in 1988 and settled in Santa Rosa. She has completed courses in winery public relations and wine marketing and has written for a publication that covers the business end of the wine industry. In addition, she has co-authored another guide to Wine Country and has written freelance articles for the local hospitality and wine industries.

Jean Saylor Doppenberg
WWW.STORYPHOTO.COM

HELP US KEEP THIS GUIDE UP TO DATE

Every effort has been made by the author and editors to make this guide as accurate and useful as possible. However, many things can change after a guide is published—phone numbers change, facilities come under new management, etc.

We would love to hear from you concerning your experiences with this guide and how you feel it could be improved and be kept up to date. While we may not be able to respond to all comments and suggestions, we'll take them to heart and we'll also make certain to share them with the authors. Please send your comments and suggestions to the following address:

The Globe Pequot Press
Reader Response/Editorial Department
P.O. Box 480
Guilford, CT 06437

Or you may e-mail us at:

editorial@GlobePequot.com

Thanks for your input, and happy travels!

THE INSIDER'S SOURCE

With more than 540 West-related titles, we have the area covered. Whether you're looking for the path less traveled, a favorite place to eat, family-friendly fun, a breathtaking hike, or enchanting local attractions, our pages are filled with ideas to get you from one state to the next.

For a complete listing of all our titles, please visit our Web site at www.GlobePequot.com. The Globe Pequot Press is the largest publisher of local travel books in the United States and is a leading source for outdoor recreation guides.

FOR BOOKS TO THE WEST